APPROVED LAW SCHOOLS:

Statistical Information on American Bar Association Approved Law Schools

1998 Edition

Compiled by the
Office of the Consultant on Legal Education
for the American Bar Association

Editors:
Rick L. Morgan
Kurt Snyder, Esq.

MACMILLAN • USA

Opinions expressed in this publication are not to be deemed to represent the views of the ABA or the Section unless and until adopted pursuant to their Bylaws.

Macmillan General Reference
A Simon & Schuster Macmillan Company
1633 Broadway
New York, NY 10019-6785

ISBN: 0-02-861757-6

Manufactured in the United States of America

10 9 8 7 6 5 4 3 2 1

Table of Contents

Please read.

The information made available through this publication was collected from questionnaires completed during the Fall 1996 academic semester and submitted by American Bar Association ("ABA") approved law schools to the ABA's Consultant on Legal Education as part of the accreditation process. The completed questionnaires provided to the Consultant's Office are certified by the Dean of each law school. Each certification is submitted to the Consultant's Office as an assurance that the information provided accurately reflects prevailing conditions at the law school for which the certification is given. However, the Consultant's Office conducts no audit to verify the accuracy of the information submitted by the respective institutions.

In addition to the information submitted by the respective law schools, this publication also includes material provided by various organizations with an interest in legal education. The views expressed in this book are not necessarily those of the ABA, the Section of Legal Education and Admissions to the Bar, or the Consultant's Office. Opinions expressed in this publication are not to be deemed to represent the views of the ABA or the Section unless and until adopted pursuant to their Bylaws.

Thank You!!!

James P. White, Consultant on Legal Education to the American Bar Association, and the Consultant's Staff would like to thank the various organizations, law schools, authors, bar examiners, and volunteers without whose assistance this book would not have become a reality. In particular, we owe much gratitude to the following individuals for volunteering their many hours of work: Associate Dean Paul Ciraulo, St. John's University School of Law; Dean Rudolph C. Hasl, St. John's University School of Law; Dean Steven R. Smith, California Western School of Law; and Associate Dean Peter A. Winograd, University of New Mexico School of Law. Furthermore, we would like to thank the following people and organizations: Linda Bernbach, Editorial Director and Charles A. Wall, Vice President, Editor-in-Chief at the Macmillan Consumer Information Group; Christopher A. Brown, Esq. associate at Woodard, Emhardt, Naughton, Moriarty & McNett; Jeffrey E. Hanson, Director, Debt Management Services at the Access Group℠; Thomas Hutchinson, Esq., associate at Krieg, DeVault, Alexander & Capehart; Bill Kennish, Micron Systems; Professor Wayne McCormack, University of Utah College of Law; David Milne, Esq., associate at Scopelitis, Garvin, Light & Hanson; Erica Moeser, Esq., President of the National Conference of Bar Examiners; Paula A. Patton, Esq., Executive Director of the National Association for Law Placement; David Prominski, student at the Indiana University School of Law - Indianapolis; Dean Frank T. Read, South Texas College of Law; Philip D. Shelton, Esq., Executive Director and President of the Law School Admissions Council; Professor Claude R. Sowle, University of Miami School of Law; Robert A. Stein, Executive Director of the American Bar Association; David R. Stewart, Esq. of Sidley & Austin; Terra Tarrents, Writer's Ink; and Richard J. Vittenson, Esq., Manager, Publication Policies & Contracting, for the American Bar Association. And finally, the editors of the book, Rick L. Morgan and Kurt Snyder, Esq., would like to thank their spouses, Terrie Morgan and Debbie Snyder, for supporting them in this endeavor.

Office of the Consultant on Legal Education
550 West North Street, Suite 349
Indianapolis, Indiana 46202
http://www.abanet.org/legaled

James P. White, Consultant
Arthur R. Gaudio, Deputy Consultant
Kurt Snyder, Assistant Consultant
Marilyn S. Shannon, Executive Administrator
Cathy A. Schrage, Executive Assistant
Rick L. Morgan, Data Specialist
Mary D. Barron, Senior Administrative Secretary
Claudia S. Fisher, Administrative Secretary
Kimberly S. Massie, Administrative Secretary
Mary L. Kronoshek, Administrative Secretary
DeeAndria V. Hampton, Administrative Secretary

Section of Legal Education and
Admissions to the Bar
750 North Lake Shore Drive
Chicago, Illinois 60611
http://www.abanet.org/legaled

Carol A. Weiss, Staff Director
Suzanne Rose, Assistant Staff Director
Michelle Deanne Ekanemesang, Administrative Assistant

OFFICERS AND COUNCIL OF THE SECTION OF LEGAL EDUCATION AND ADMISSIONS TO THE BAR, 1996-97

Officers

RUDOLPH C. HASL
Chairperson
Dean, St. John's University School of Law
Jamaica, New York

BEVERLY TARPLEY
Chairperson-elect
Scarborough, Tarpley & Fouts
Abilene, Texas

RANDALL T. SHEPARD
Vice-Chairperson
Chief Justice, Indiana Supreme Court
Indianapolis, Indiana

HENRY RAMSEY, JR.
Secretary
Berkeley, California

ERICA MOESER
Last Retiring Chairperson
President, National Conference of Bar Examiners
Madison, Wisconsin

JOSE GARCIA-PEDROSA
Section Delegate to the House of Delegates
City Manager, City of Miami Beach
Miami Beach, Florida

NORMAN REDLICH
Section Delegate to the House of Delegates
Wachtell, Lipton, Rosen & Katz
New York, New York

GORDON D. SCHABER
Secretary Emeritus
University Counsel and former Dean, McGeorge School of Law
Sacramento, California

Members of the Council

MARTHA W. BARNETT
Holland & Knight
Tallahassee, Florida

JULIUS L. CHAMBERS
Chancellor, North Carolina Central University
Durham, North Carolina

LAURA N. GASAWAY
Professor, University of North Carolina School of Law
Chapel Hill, North Carolina

HERMA HILL KAY
Dean, U. of California School of Law - Berkeley
Berkeley, California

JOHN R. KRAMER
Professor and former Dean, Tulane University School of Law
New Orleans, Louisiana

ELIZABETH B. LACY
Justice, Virginia Supreme Court
Richmond, Virginia

GARY H. PALM
Professor, University of Chicago School of Law
Chicago, Illinois

WILLIAM R. RAKES
Gentry, Locke, Rakes & Moore
Roanoke, Virginia

E. THOMAS SULLIVAN
Dean, University of Minnesota School of Law
Minneapolis, Minnesota

GERALD W. VANDEWALLE
Chief Justice, North Dakota Supreme Court
Bismarck, North Dakota

ROBERT K. WALSH
Dean, Wake Forest University School of Law
Winston-Salem, North Carolina

DIANE C. YU
General Counsel, State Bar of California
San Francisco, California

J. SCOTT DICKMAN
Young Lawyers Division Liaison
Tulsa, Oklahoma

DANIEL G. PEZOLD
Law Student Division Liaison
Student, Whittier Law School
Arcadia, California

MARIANNA S. SMITH
Board of Governors Liaison
Bethesda, Maryland

ACCREDITATION COMMITTEE OF THE SECTION OF LEGAL EDUCATION AND ADMISSIONS TO THE BAR, 1996-97

Officers

JEFFREY E. LEWIS
Chairperson
Professor and former Dean, University of Florida College of Law
Gainesville, Florida

LIZABETH A. MOODY
Vice-Chairperson
Dean, Stetson University College of Law
St. Petersburg, Florida

Members of the Accreditation Committee

BERNARD F. ASHE
Private Practice, retired
Delmar, New York

J. MARTIN BURKE
Visiting Professor, New York University School of Law
New York, New York

MICHAEL J. DAVIS
Professor, University of Kansas School of Law
Lawrence, Kansas
Stinson, Mag, & Fizzell
Kansas City, Missouri

STEVEN P. FRANKINO
Dean, Villanova University School of Law
Villanova, Pennsylvania

DAN J. FREEHLING
Professor, Associate Dean, & Director of Law Library
Boston University School of Law
Boston, Massachusetts

HARRY E. GROVES
Professor Emeritus, University of North Carolina School of Law
Chapel Hill, North Carolina

JOHN L. LAHEY
President, Quinnipiac College
Hamden, Connecticut
(public member)

SOLOMON OLIVER, JR.
Judge, United States District Court
Cleveland, Ohio

MARÍA RAMÍREZ
Executive Director, International P.A.C.E.
Clifton Park, New York
(public member)

SHARREN B. ROSE
Nelson & Schmeling
Green Bay, Wisconsin

LEONARD P. STRICKMAN
Dean, University of Arkansas School of Law - Fayetteville
Fayetteville, Arkansas

BEVERLY TARPLEY
Scarborough, Tarpley, & Fouts
Abilene, Texas

DAVID G. TRAGER
Judge, United States District Court, Eastern District of New York
Brooklyn, New York

DIANE C. YU
General Counsel, State Bar of California
San Francisco, California

Chapter One
Introduction

The American Bar Association's Section of Legal Education and Admissions to the Bar, as part of the information process relating to the accreditation of American law schools, is pleased to present the first edition of *ABA Approved Law Schools: Statistical Information on American Bar Association Approved Law Schools.* In 1893 the ABA created its first section, the Section of Legal Education and Admissions to the Bar. The mission of the Section of Legal Education and Admissions to the Bar is: to be a creative national force in providing leadership and services to those responsible for and those who benefit from a sound program of legal education and bar admissions; and to provide a fair, effective, and efficient accrediting system for American law schools that promotes quality legal education and to continue to serve, through its Council, as the nationally recognized accrediting body for American law schools.

The highest courts and bar admission authorities in the various states began in the early 1920s to look to the ABA's Accreditation Standards in establishing bar admission criteria. Over the past seventy years, the accreditation process in law schools has developed under certain fundamental principles. First, the profession itself is best equipped to be the ultimate judge of quality. Second, participation by different components of the profession, the bench, bar and professorate, is the best way to form that professional judgment. Third, a thorough understanding of the operation and legitimacy of the accreditation process is required for it to be effective.

Today, graduation from an ABA-approved law school provides a student with an education that complies with a minimum set of standards promulgated by the legal profession. Moreover, the education obtained at these approved institutions meets the legal education requirements for bar admission in every state in the United States.

The purpose of accreditation is not only to review a law school's compliance with the Standards, but also to provide a vehicle for sharing information relating to ongoing developments in legal education. Professional review of law schools ensures a confidence by individual state admitting authorities that the public is served by lawyers who have received a legal education meeting standards of the profession.

Since the 1950s the Council of the Section of Legal Education and Admissions to the Bar has served as the national accrediting agency for professional schools of law, as recognized by the United States Department of Education. The administration of the accreditation of law schools project is undertaken by the Office of the Consultant on Legal Education to the ABA under the leadership of James P. White.

Please note that this book contains information concerning those law schools that were approved by the ABA as of October 1, 1996. The approval status of an individual law school could change, however. Therefore, if you would like to confirm whether an individual law school is approved by the ABA at a specific time after October 1, you should contact the ABA directly. The purpose of this book is to provide consumers with basic information about approved schools in a similar format. However, it should be noted that applicants should not use this book as the sole source of information regarding application and admission. Rather, this book should supplement other avenues of evaluating respective schools including making direct contact with admission offices, professors, students, alumni or a prelaw advisor. In addition to statistics on all ABA approved law schools, this book contains information intended to help individuals prepare for the rigors and costs associated with attending law school.

American Bar Association Approval

Approval is triggered when a school files an application and will only be granted after a finding that the school offers a sound program of legal education which complies with the Standards for Approval of Law Schools of the ABA. The accreditation process involves regularly scheduled on-site evaluations, careful analysis of self-study data, and emphasis on the steady improvement of the quality of the law school's educational program. Approval is granted or continued based upon the school's compliance with the ABA Standards for Approval of Law Schools. A law school is approved by action of the House of Delegates of the ABA. Responsibility for administering the ABA's program of accreditation has been placed with the Council of the Section of Legal Education and Admissions to the Bar.

Since the adoption of the first law school accreditation Standards by the ABA in 1921, state supreme courts and other bar admitting authorities have encouraged the ABA's accreditation efforts, and the vast majority of states rely upon ABA accreditation to determine whether an applicant meets the educational requirements for admission to the bar. Graduation from a state-approved law school which is not ABA approved may qualify a person to take the bar examination in the state in which the school is located, but may not qualify the person for the examination in other states.

One facet of the accreditation process is a detailed Annual Questionnaire completed by each approved school. This document serves several important functions. The data from the questionnaire are utilized to prepare comparative statistics on all phases of law school operation, which are used by the Accreditation Committee and Council in their accreditation review process. The comparative data are compiled and distributed to approved law schools that subscribe to the law school statistical service. Additionally, careful analysis of these data serves to identify problems a school may be experiencing which call for a special visit or some other form of assistance. They also identify trends in legal education. Moreover, the information collected from the questionnaire is used to satisfy Department of Education requirements by providing consumers with basic information. Standard 509 of the Standards for Approval of

Law Schools and Interpretations, as adopted the ABA House of Delegates in August, 1996, states:

Standard 509. BASIC CONSUMER INFORMATION.

A law school shall publish basic consumer information. The information shall be published in a fair and accurate manner reflective of actual practice.

Interpretation 509-1:
The following categories of consumer information are considered basic:

(1) admission data;
(2) tuition, fees, living costs, financial aid, and refunds;
(3) enrollment data and graduation rates;
(4) composition and number of faculty and administrators;
(5) curricular offerings;
(6) library resources;
(7) physical facilities; and
(8) placement rates and bar passage data. (August 1996)

Interpretation 509-2:
To comply with its obligation to publish basic consumer information under the first sentence of this Standard, a law school may either provide the information to a publication designated by the Council or publish the information in its own publication. If the school chooses to meet this obligation through its own publication, the basic consumer information shall be published in a manner comparable to that used in the Council-designated publication, and the school shall provide the publication to all of its applicants. (August 1996)

A total of 180 institutions are approved by the American Bar Association: 179 confer the first degree in law (the J.D. degree); the other ABA-approved school is the U.S. Army Judge Advocate General's School, which offers an officer's residence graduate course, a specialized program beyond the first degree in law. One of the 179 ABA-approved law schools (Widener) also has a branch campus. As of October 1, 1996, four of the 179 law schools are provisionally approved: Roger Williams University, Texas Wesleyan University, Thomas Jefferson, and the District of Columbia School of Law. Hence, since October 1, 1995, the Regent University School of Law and the Seattle University School of Law became fully approved; and, the Thomas Jefferson School of Law became provisionally approved.

A law school is granted provisional approval when it establishes substantial compliance with each of the Standards and gives assurances that it will be in full compliance with all of the Standards within three years after receiving provisional approval. A law school that has been provisionally approved for two years will be considered for full approval by the House of Delegates of the ABA upon a finding by the Council that the school fully meets the Standards for Approval of Law Schools of the ABA, as interpreted by the Council, on a basis that assures continued compliance with the letter and the spirit of the Standards, with particular emphasis on a steady improvement in the quality of its educational program.

The students at provisionally approved law schools and persons who graduate while a school is provisionally approved are entitled to the same recognition accorded under the ABA Standards to students and graduates of fully approved law schools.

About the ABA

The American Bar Association is the national organization of the legal profession. While encouraging professional development among its members and providing leadership in the improvement of the law, the ABA focuses a significant portion of its efforts and resources on a wide range of activities to improve the administration of justice and the delivery of legal services to the public.

Public service activities take place in such varied areas as environmental and energy law; election reform; housing and urban growth; juvenile justice; judicial reform; protection of legal rights of prisoners, the mentally disabled, and the elderly; and delivery of legal services to the poor.

Founded on August 21, 1878, the American Bar Association is the largest voluntary professional organization in the world, with a current membership of more than 350,000 -- representing about half the lawyers in the United States. In addition, the Law Student Division has more than 35,000 members.

ABA membership is open to lawyers admitted to practice and in good standing before the bar of any state or territory of the United States. Members include judges, professors, government officials, court administrators, business executives, and lawyers working in other fields. Eligible to affiliate with the ABA as associates are nonlawyer judges, administrators, federal court and bar association executives, criminal justice professionals, and others in law related areas. Members of the legal profession in other nations can become international associates.

The ABA is committed to keeping its members and the general public informed of the latest developments in the law and law-related fields. To accomplish this goal, it publishes numerous books and pamphlets and, on a regular basis, a variety of magazines, journals, and newsletters. To order an ABA publication call the ABA Service Center at (800) 285-2221.

American Bar Association Headquarters
750 North Lake Shore Drive
Chicago, Illinois 60611
(312) 988-5000
http://www.abanet.org

Ensuring High-Quality Education

Written by Robert A. Stein, Executive Director of the American Bar Association

A core function of the ABA for more than 70 years has been our program of accreditation of law schools. I would like to describe this important program, which serves the public, law students, the legal profession and the justice system.

In 1952 the Council of the Section of Legal Education and Admissions to the Bar was formally recognized by the predecessor of the U.S. Department of Education as the national accrediting agency for law schools. However, as early as 1923, the Section Council first listed 39 law schools that conformed to the ABA Standards and Interpretations for legal education.

Today, there are 180 ABA-approved law schools. The Council's Accreditation Committee, composed of practicing attorneys, judges, law professors and public members, carries out the accreditation process under the direction of ABA Consultant on Legal Education Dean James P. White.

Teams of Evaluators

Overseeing about 30 site visits to law schools each year, the committee ensures the quality of these site evaluations by carefully screening and training its evaluators. Annually, nearly 250 volunteers join site teams—teams carefully chosen to include diversity in practice backgrounds, gender and ethnicity. The five- to seven-member teams receive extensive materials for the visit. Law schools complete an annual questionnaire, as well as a self-study, identifying where the school is, where it wants to go and what goals will take it there. Each team member is assigned an area of the school's program to review, on which he or she gathers voluminous information.

Any law school completing at least one full year of successful operation may apply for ABA-approved status, with approval granted based upon the school's compliance with ABA Standards. Provisionally approved schools undergo site evaluations yearly; fully approved schools are reviewed every seven years.

Site evaluation takes about three days. Teams evaluate the quality of the faculty, the administration, the library, and the effectiveness of the course of study and the skills training program. They review the admissions program, placement and bar exam passage experience, opportunities for racial minorities in all aspects of institutional life, and the school's physical plant. Team members meet with administrators, faculty, students, adjunct professors, legal writing teachers, library staff, alumni and other bar members. They visit several classes during the visit. Following the site visit, the team prepares a report for the Accreditation Committee, which makes a recommendation of approval or nonapproval to the Section Council, which, in turn, makes its recommendation of provisional or full approval to the ABA House of Delegates.

The process is constantly reviewed to ensure the validity and reliability of the ABA Standards, the opportunity for law schools to develop unique and diverse programs and missions, compliance with Education Department requirements, and acceptance by the highest courts of the 50 states.

The ABA Standards have continued to evolve into a comprehensive set of criteria by which legal education programs are evaluated. Their latest recodification was approved by the House on August 6, 1996 at the annual meeting. A product of extensive public hearings and comment, they reflect the vast developments in American legal education over the past 20 years, including new teaching methods, new technologies, integration of skills training into the curriculum, the growth of foreign programs, and post-J.D. programs of instruction.

Standard Procedures

As accreditor of law schools, the ABA provides a centralized, national process that avoids a fragmented approach to accreditation. The process recognizes the profession as the ultimate judge of quality of legal education in America. It is unique in the world in this respect. Through the ABA accreditation program, all segments of the profession -- practitioners, judges, law professors, corporate and government lawyers, and bar examiners -- can participate in the accreditation process as members of the Accreditation Committee and as site evaluators.

Recent court challenges have caused the ABA to thoroughly review its accreditation procedures and criteria. The process has benefited from this close examination. We can all be proud of the beneficial effect the ABA accreditation process has had on American legal education. The high quality of legal education available in the United States is in great measure a direct result of the ABA Standards and accreditation process.

Rating of Law Schools

No rating of law schools beyond the simple statement of their accreditation status is attempted or advocated by the American Bar Association. Qualities that make one kind of school good for one student may not be as important to another. The American Bar Association and its Section of Legal Education and Admissions to the Bar have issued disclaimers of any law school rating system. Prospective law students should consider a variety of factors in making their choice among approved schools.

Chapter Two

Pre-Law Preparation

Written by The Pre-Law Committee of the ABA Section of Legal Education and Admissions to the Bar

(What follows is a statement on preparation for legal education drafted by the Prelaw Committee of the ABA Section of Legal Education and Admissions to the Bar. It addresses the course of study and skills necessary to obtain admission into law school and to be a successful lawyer.)

Students who are successful in law school, and who become accomplished attorneys or use their legal education successfully in other areas of professional life, come to their legal education from widely differing educational and experiential backgrounds. As undergraduate students, some have majored in subjects that are traditionally considered paths to law school, such as history, English, philosophy, political science, economics or business. Other successful law students, however, have focused their undergraduate studies in areas as diverse as art, music theory, computer science, engineering, nursing or education. Many law students enter law school directly from their undergraduate studies and without having had any substantial work experience. Others begin their legal education significantly later in life, and they bring to their law school education the insights and perspectives gained from those life experiences.

Thus the ABA does **not** recommend any particular group of undergraduate majors, or courses, that should be taken by those wishing to prepare for legal education; developing such a list is neither possible nor desirable. The law is too multifaceted, and the human mind too adaptable, to permit such a linear approach to preparing for law school or the practice of law. Nonetheless, there are important skills and values, and significant bodies of knowledge, that can be acquired prior to law school and that will provide a sound foundation for a sophisticated legal education. This Statement presents the recommendations of the American Bar Association Section of Legal Education and Admissions to the Bar concerning preparation for a good law school experience.

Prospective law students should also consult closely with the prelaw advisor at their undergraduate institution. That individual may be able to assist current students in selecting courses or professors that will particularly assist in developing the skills and knowledge foundation that is emphasized in this statement. Taking difficult courses from demanding instructors is the best generic preparation for legal education. The prelaw advisor can also assist current and former students in choosing law schools to which to apply that are appropriate in light of a prospective student's interests and credentials. Finally, prospective law students should also consult the publications and admissions personnel of the schools to which they are considering applying for any specific recommendations that individual schools may have concerning preparation for law school.

There are numerous skills and values that are essential to success in law school and to competent lawyering. There also is a large body of information that law students, and attorneys, should possess. The three or four years that a student spends in obtaining a quality legal education can and do provide much of the information that a lawyer needs. Good legal education also aids in developing the many skills and values essential to competent lawyering. Sound legal education, however, must build upon and further refine skills, values and knowledge that the student already possesses. Even though a student may well be able to acquire in law school some specific fundamental skills and knowledge that the student's prelaw school experience has not provided, the student who comes to law school lacking a broad range of basic skills and knowledge will face an extremely difficult task.

Skills and Values

The core skills and values that are essential for competent lawyering include analytic and problem solving skills, critical reading abilities, writing skills, oral communication and listening abilities, general research skills, task organization and management skills, and the values of serving faithfully the interests of others while also promoting justice.[1] Thus, individuals who wish to prepare adequately for legal education, and for a career in law or for other professional service that involves the use of lawyering skills, should seek educational, extracurricular and life experiences that will assist them in developing those attributes.[2] Some brief comments about each of the listed skills and values follow.

Analytic and Problem Solving Skills

Students should seek courses and other experiences that will engage them in critical thinking about important issues, that will engender in them tolerance for uncertainty, and that will give them experience in structuring and evaluating arguments for and against propositions that are susceptible to reasoned debate. Students also should seek courses and other experiences that require them to apply previously developed principles or theories to new situations, and that demand that they develop solutions to new problems. Good legal education teaches students to "think like a lawyer," but the analytic and problem-solving skills required of attorneys are not fundamentally different from those employed by other professionals. The law school experience will develop and refine those crucial skills, but one must enter law school with a reasonably well developed set of analytic and problem solving abilities.

Critical Reading Abilities

Preparation for legal education should include substantial experience at close reading and critical analysis of complex textual material, for much of what law students and attorneys do involves careful reading and sophisticated comprehension of judicial opinions, statutes, documents, and other written materials. As with the

other skills discussed in this Statement, the requisite critical reading abilities may be acquired in a wide range of experiences, including the close reading of complex material in literature, political or economic theory, philosophy, or history. The particular nature of the materials examined is not crucial; what is important is that law school not be the first time that a student has been rigorously engaged in the enterprise of carefully reading and understanding, and critically analyzing, complex written material of substantial length. Potential law students should also be aware that the study and practice of law require the ability to read and assimilate large amounts of material, often in a short period of time.

Writing Skills

Those seeking to prepare for legal education should develop a high degree of skill at written communication. Language is the most important tool of a lawyer, and lawyers must learn to express themselves clearly and concisely. Legal education provides good training in writing, and particularly in the specific techniques and forms of written expression that are common in the law. Fundamental writing skills, however, should be acquired and refined before one enters law school. Those preparing for legal education should seek as many experiences as possible that will require rigorous and analytical writing, including preparing original pieces of substantial length and revising written work in response to constructive criticism.

Oral Communication and Listening Abilities

The ability to speak clearly and persuasively is another skill that is essential to success in law school and the practice of law. Lawyers also must have excellent listening skills if they are to understand their clients and others with whom they must interact daily. As with writing skills, legal education provides excellent opportunities for refining oral communication skills, and particularly for practicing the forms and techniques of oral expression that are most common in the practice of law. Before coming to law school, however, individuals should seek to develop their basic speaking and listening skills, such as by engaging in debate, making formal presentations in class, or speaking before groups in school, the community, or the workplace.

General Research Skills

Although there are many research sources and techniques that are specific to the law, an individual need not have developed any familiarity with these specific skills or materials before entering law school. However, the individual who comes to law school without ever having undertaken a project that requires significant library research and the analysis of large amounts of information obtained from that research will be at a severe disadvantage. Those wishing to prepare for legal education should select courses and seek experiences that will require them to plan a research strategy, to undertake substantial library research, and to analyze, organize and present a reasonably large amount of material. A basic ability to use a personal computer is also increasingly important for law students, both for word processing and for computerized legal research.

Task Organization and Management Skills

The study and practice of law require the ability to organize large amounts of information, to identify objectives, and to create a structure for applying that information in an efficient way in order to achieve desired results. Many law school courses, for example, are graded primarily on the basis of one examination at the end of the course, and many projects in the practice of law require the compilation of large amounts of information from a wide variety of sources, frequently over relatively brief periods of time. Thus those entering law school must be prepared to organize and assimilate large amounts of information in a manner that facilitates the recall and application of that information in an effective and efficient manner. Some of the requisite experience can be obtained through undertaking school projects that require substantial research and writing, or through the preparation of major reports for an employer, a school, or a civic organization.

Serving Others and Promoting Justice

Each member of the legal profession should be dedicated both to the objectives of serving others honestly, competently, and responsibly, and to the goals of improving fairness and the quality of justice in the legal system. Those thinking of entering this profession would be well served by having some significant experience, before coming to law school, in which they devoted substantial effort toward assisting others. Participation in public service projects or similar efforts at achieving objectives established for common purposes can be particularly helpful.

Knowledge

In addition to these fundamental skills and values, there are some basic areas of knowledge that are important to a sophisticated legal education and to the development of a competent attorney. As law becomes more pervasive in our society, an increasingly broad range of knowledge and information from other disciplines become relevant to lawyering and to any full understanding of the legal system. Some of that knowledge, particularly that most directly relevant to particular areas of the law, can be acquired in law school or when necessary for a particular project.

There are, however, generic types of knowledge that one should possess in order to have a full appreciation of the legal system in general, to understand how disputes might be resolved, to understand and apply various legal principles and standards, and to appreciate the context in which a legal problem or dispute arises. Some of the types of knowledge that are most useful, and that would most pervasively affect one's ability to derive the maximum benefit from legal education, include the following:

> A broad understanding of history, particularly American history, and the various factors (social, political,

economic, and cultural) that have influenced the development of the pluralistic society that presently exists in the United States;

A fundamental understanding of political thought and theory, and of the contemporary American political system;

A basic understanding of ethical theory and theories of justice;

A grounding in economics, particularly elementary micro-economic theory, and an understanding of the interaction between economic theory and public policy;

Some basic mathematical and financial skills, such as an understanding of basic precalculus mathematics and an ability to analyze financial data;

A basic understanding of human behavior and social interaction; and

An understanding of diverse cultures within and beyond the United States, of international institutions and issues, and of the increasing interdependence of the nations and communities within our world.

As law has become more woven into the fabric of our society, and as that society is increasingly influenced by disparate national and global forces, a broad knowledge base is essential for success in law school and for competence in the legal profession. Knowledge of specific areas of law can and will be acquired during a good legal education, but students must come to law school with much fundamental knowledge upon which legal education can build. Thus, those considering law school should focus their substantive preparation on acquiring the broad knowledge and perspectives outlined above.

Conclusion

The skills, values and knowledge discussed in this Statement may be acquired in a wide variety of ways. One may take undergraduate, graduate, or even high school courses that can assist an individual in acquiring much of the requisite information, skills and perspectives. One may also gain much of this essential background through self-learning (another essential lawyering skill), by reading, in the workplace, or through various other life experiences. Moreover, it is not essential that everyone come to law school having fully developed all of the skills, values and knowledge suggested in this Statement. Some of that foundation can be acquired during the initial years of law school. However, one who begins law school having already acquired most of the skills, values and knowledge listed in this Statement will have a significant advantage and will be well prepared to benefit fully from a sophisticated and challenging legal education.

---

[1] These core skill and value areas are drawn, in substantial part, from the Statement of Skills and Values contained in the 1992 Report of the American Bar Association Task Force on Law Schools and the Profession, *Legal Education and Professional Development — An Educational Continuum.*

[2] People with various disabilities, such as visual or hearing limitations, have been successful in law school and in the practice of law. Persons with such disabilities, however, should be cognizant of the particular challenges that they may face in law school and in the profession.

Chapter Three
Admissions Process

Written by Philip D. Shelton, Executive Director and President of the Law School Admission Council (LSAC)

Law school applicants can expect the admission process to be quite competitive. Most law schools receive more than enough applications from highly qualified candidates, many of whom would be perfectly capable of completing a law school education. The dilemma for admission committees is that limited space and resources mandate the denial of admission to many of these candidates.

Your Credentials

No concrete principles exist for predicting who will perform well in school. In order to be fair, schools rely heavily upon selection criteria that bear on expected performance in law school and can be applied objectively to all candidates. Law schools consider a variety of factors in admitting their students, and no single qualification will independently guarantee acceptance or rejection. However, the two factors that usually outweigh the rest are prior academic performance and the Law School Admission Test score.

Undergraduate performance is generally an important indicator of how someone is likely to perform in law school. Hence, many law schools look closely at college grades when considering individual applications. Course selection also can make a difference in admission evaluations. Applicants who have taken difficult or advanced courses in their undergraduate study often are evaluated in a more favorable light than students who have concentrated on easier or less advanced subjects.

Many law schools consider undergraduate-performance trends along with a student's numerical average. Thus, they may discount a slow start in a student's undergraduate career if he or she performs exceptionally well in the later school years. Similarly, admission committees may see an undergraduate's strong start followed by a mediocre finish as an indication of lesser potential to do well in law school. Candidates are advised to comment on irregular grade trends in the personal statement section of the application.

Choosing Schools

When selecting law schools to which you will apply, the general philosophy is that you should have a threefold plan: dream a little, be realistic, and be safe. Most applicants have no trouble selecting dream schools--those that are almost, but not quite, beyond their grasp--or safe schools--those for which admission is virtually certain. Applicants often have difficulty being realistic about their qualifications and their chances of being accepted at particular law schools.

Unquestionably, the number one strategic error in law school admission is a candidate's failure to evaluate realistically his or her own credentials.

Check your qualifications against the admission profile of the law schools to which you aspire with the information contained in this publication. Most schools publish statistics in this book on the GPA and LSAT 75th percentile and 25th percentile of the most recent entering class. You may use these data to help you determine where you should apply. Apply to those law schools whose student body profiles most closely match your personal profile. Those schools will be as anxious to accept you as you are to be admitted.

Other Sources of Information

The school's admission office. This is a good source for general information about your chances for admission. Do not hesitate to request admission counseling. Be sure to obtain current catalogs from each law school you are considering.

Your college or university prelaw advisor. Your prelaw advisor can often provide you with reliable information about which law schools fit your personal profile. He or she may also be able to tell you which law schools have accepted students from your school in the past and provide you with an overview of the admitted students' credentials. However, you should not necessarily narrow your focus to only those law schools where others from your undergraduate school have been admitted.

School representatives and alumni. Take advantage of opportunities to talk with law school representatives and alumni. When you talk with alumni, remember that law schools sometimes change fairly quickly. Try to talk to a recent graduate or to one who is active in alumni affairs and therefore knowledgeable about the school as it is today.

School visits. You can learn a surprising amount about a school from talks with students and faculty members. Many law schools have formal programs in which a currently enrolled student will take you on a tour of the campus and answer your questions. Such a first-hand experience can be quite valuable in assessing how you would fit into the school.

Admission Mechanics

Many law schools operate what is known as a rolling admission process: the school evaluates applications and informs candidates of admission decisions on a continuous basis over several months, usually beginning in late fall and extending to midsummer for waiting-list admissions.

At such schools, it is especially important for you to apply at the earliest possible date. The earlier you apply, the more places the school will have available. Most schools try to make comparable decisions throughout the admission season, even those that practice rolling admission. Still, it is disadvantageous to be one of the last applicants to complete a file. Furthermore, the more decisions you receive from law schools early in the process, the better able you will be to make your own decisions, such as whether to apply to more law schools or whether to accept a particular school's offer.

The average applicant applies to four or five law schools. You should be sure to place your applications at schools representing a range of admission standards. Even if you have top qualifications, you should apply to at least one safety school where you are almost certain of being admitted. This is your insurance policy. If you apply to a safety school in November, and are accepted in January or February, you may be disappointed but not panicked if you are later rejected by your top choices.

If you have strong qualifications, but you do not quite meet the competition of those currently being admitted at a particular law school, you may be placed on a waiting list for possible admission at a later date. The law school will send you a letter notifying you of its decision as early as April or as late as July.

It is up to you whether you wish to wait for a decision from a school that has put you on a waiting list or accept an offer from a school that has already accepted you.

Many law schools use seat deposits to help keep track of their new classes. For example, a school may require an initial acceptance fee of $200, which is credited to your first-term tuition if you actually register at the school; if you do not register, the deposit may be forfeited or partially refunded. A school may require a larger deposit around July 1, which is also credited to tuition. If you decline the offer of admission after you have paid your deposit, a portion of the money may be refunded, depending on the date you actually decline the offer. At some schools none of the deposit may be refunded.

Where to Attend

For some people, the choice of which law school to attend is an easy one. The most outstanding students will probably be able to go anywhere, and they will select the schools they perceive to be the most prestigious or which offer a program of particular interest. Others who need to stay in a particular area, perhaps because they have a family or a job they do not want to leave, will choose nearby schools or schools with part-time programs.

However, the majority of applicants will have to weigh a variety of personal and academic factors to come up with a list of potential schools. Then, once they have a list and more than one acceptance letter, they will have to choose a school. Applicants should consider carefully the offerings of each law school before making a decision. The quality of a law school is certainly a major consideration; however, estimations of quality are very subjective. Factors such as the campus atmosphere, the school's devotion to teaching and learning, and the applicant's enthusiasm for the school are very important. Remember that the law school is going to be your home for three years. Adjusting to law school and the general attitudes of a professional school is difficult enough without the additional distraction of culture shock.

All ABA approved law schools and many non ABA approved law schools require that you take the LSAT. The test consists of five 35-minute sections of multiple-choice questions, in three different areas. A 30-minute unscored writing sample is administered at the end of the test. The LSAT is designed to measure skills considered essential for success in law school: the reading and comprehension of complex texts with accuracy and insight; the organization and management of information and the ability to draw reasonable inferences from it; the ability to reason critically; and, the analysis and evaluation of the reasoning and argument of others.

Most law school applicants familiarize themselves with test mechanics and question types, practice on sample tests, and study the information available on test-taking techniques and strategies. Though it is difficult to say when examinees are sufficiently prepared, very few people achieve their full potential without some preparation.

The most difficult admission decisions are those regarding candidates who are neither so well qualified nor so deficient as to present a clear-cut case for acceptance or rejection. These applicants constitute the majority of the applicant pool at many law schools and are the candidates that most law schools spend the bulk of their time reviewing.

Law School admission committees also consider other criteria: undergraduate course of study; graduate work, if any; college attended; improvement in grades and grade distribution; college curricular and extracurricular activities; ethnic/racial background; individual character and personality; letters of recommendation; personal statement or essay; work experience or other post undergraduate experiences; community activities; motivation to study and reasons for deciding to study law; state of residency; difficulties overcome; pre-college preparation; and anything else that would distinguish you as a candidate.

(Excerpted, with permission, from The Official Guide to U.S. Law Schools, Law School Admission Council, Inc. (1997).)

See Chapter Seventeen for more information about the LSAT, Law Services, or LSDAS -- or contact Law Services directly.

Law Services
Box 2400
661 Penn Street
Newtown, PA 18940-0977
(215) 968-1314
http://www.lsac.org

Chapter Four

Finance & Debt Management*

Written by Jeffrey E. Hanson, Director, Debt Management Services, The Access Group, Box 7430, Wilmington, Delaware 19803-0430, (800) 282-1550 http://www.accessgrp.org

Introduction: Your Educational Investment

Your education probably is the biggest investment you'll ever make. It is an investment of both time and money. *An investment is the expenditure of scarce resources now in the hope of some benefit(s) that will yield a net positive return in the future.* A good investment is one where the benefits exceed the expenditure (costs) involved. You must consider the time and money you will invest in your education versus the personal and professional goals you have set for yourself. Then, make the best investment you can. Your goal should be to acquire the best possible training in a cost effective manner. This will maximize the probability that you will succeed in accomplishing both your professional and personal goals as well as experience the career you want.

How you pay for your legal training is an important decision that will influence the overall return on your educational investment. Unless you currently have enough money in the bank to pay all the costs of law school and this money is from your own earnings, you will need to finance your educational investment. In other words, you will be dependent on others to help you pay for your legal education. Just as you investigate which law schools have the best programs for you, so too you must gather information about how best to finance your education. This important decision should involve you, your family, and, unless your family can finance the full cost of your legal training, the school you want to attend.

You need to prepare now for the financial aspects of law school just as you are preparing for admission and enrollment in the school of your choice. Although your parents may be willing to handle your finances while you are in law school, it is best that you understand and become at least an equal participant with your parents in this process. If you don't, you may find that financing your legal education can become overly complicated and confusing. Remember, you will be the one signing the promissory notes for any loans you receive to finance your education. Understanding the terms and conditions of those loans will help you avoid problems during repayment. No matter how much your parents may want to assist, you — not your parents — will be legally responsible for your loans.

Will you be able to obtain sufficient funds to finance your educational costs?

You should be able to obtain financial assistance up to the estimated cost of attendance if you need it so long as:

- **you do not have credit problems,** and
- **you are a U.S. citizen or permanent resident.**

Conversely, sufficient financing may be difficult to obtain if you have credit problems and/or are an international student. Therefore, it is important to become well informed about your financing options as soon as possible.

How can you finance your education in a responsible manner?

Identify your goals. You need to identify your long-term personal, professional, and financial goals. You should attempt to answer the following questions as you go about setting your goals.

- How do I want to use what I have learned once I graduate?
- What do I want to accomplish in my career?
- Where do I want to work?
- How much do I hope to earn each year once I graduate?
- Where do I want to live?
- What kind of lifestyle do I want once I graduate?
- What are my hopes for a family?
- When do I want to retire?
- What kind of lifestyle do I want once I retire?

The worksheet in Figure 1 is an example of one way you can decide upon your goals. There also are books and software products available on the subject of personal finance that include sections on goal setting. Whatever approach works best for you, setting goals is an important step in financing your education in a responsible manner.

Make well-informed choices. The cost of law school really is up to you. How much you "spend" getting your degree is a function of the choices or decisions you make. In other words, the cost of your degree is a matter of ***CHOICE***. Careful budget planning is required in order to make choices that will maximize the long-term net return on your educational investment. For example:

- cost of tuition depends on the school you **CHOOSE**;
- cost of housing depends on where you **CHOOSE** to live;
- cost of food depends on how/where/what you **CHOOSE** to eat;
- cost of entertainment depends on what you **CHOOSE** to do for fun;
- cost of transportation depends on what mode of transportation you **CHOOSE** to use.

Once you make a choice, you must pay the required "cost." **As such, YOU are responsible for the choices you make.** No one else can claim that responsibility—not your parents, not your friends, not your siblings, not your financial aid officer, etc. You need to make the most well-informed choices you can through sound financial planning and careful budgeting of your scarce resources.

You will have financed your education in a responsible manner if you accomplish the following:

- You borrow the minimum amount necessary to achieve your educational goal.
- You repay your student loans according to the repayment schedule.
- You learn how to manage your financial affairs in a timely and efficient manner.
- You have no regrets once you graduate about spending the resources that are required to obtain your degree.
- You maximize the net return on your educational investment.
- You succeed in achieving your career objectives once you graduate.
- You are able to afford the lifestyle you want once you graduate.

The purpose of the information provided here is to help you plan the financing of your degree so that you can maximize the return on your educational investment and finance your education in a responsible manner. Answers are provided to ten important questions about financing a legal education.

Ten Important Questions About Financing A Legal Education

You should answer the ten questions listed below as you plan the financing of your legal education. Some of the questions are general and apply to any school you might attend; others are more specific to the programs and procedures of each school you are considering. You should evaluate these issues as you explore your financial options regardless of where you plan to attend law school. Remember, financing your legal education will involve a collaboration among you, your family, the school you attend, and your lender(s).

1. What should I be doing now to prepare for the cost of law school?

2. What can I do once I arrive on campus to minimize the cost of law school?

3. What financing options do I have if I cannot pay the full cost of law school from my own resources and those of my family?

4. What is the purpose of financial aid?

5. What is the basic philosophy of the financial aid system?

6. What is the financial aid process and how do I apply for financial assistance?

7. What is done with the information I provide?

8. What should I know about the loans I am offered?

9. What impact will these loans have on me after I complete law school?

10. Where can I get more information?

QUESTION #1: What should I be doing now to prepare for the cost of law school?

There are five steps you can take now to prepare for the cost of law school. These are steps that should be taken even before you have applied to and/or been admitted by a law school. They involve conversations with your family, the financial aid staff at the schools you are considering attending, and specific actions you should take.

You should determine what resources you will be able to contribute toward your educational expenses. Your resources include contributions from your family (and spouse, if married), the funds you will have saved by the time you enroll, and any scholarship funds you are awarded by private foundations, associations, or other organizations. This will require that you discuss the cost of law school with your family (and spouse, if married), and determine the extent to which they plan to assist you financially. You also will need to save as much money as you can before entering law school, and explore opportunities for scholarships/fellowships from private foundations, organizations, associations, as well as federal, state, and local government agencies.

The next step is to contact the law schools you are interested in attending to find out the expected cost of attendance so that you can determine if you will have sufficient funds to pay for your education or if you will need to seek additional assistance through the financial aid program offered by the school(s). If you think you will need additional financial assistance from the school, you will need to determine what financial assistance is offered, the required application procedures, and any applicable deadlines. You should find out how to obtain the necessary application forms and take the necessary steps to get them once they are available.

The third step is to make certain you don't have credit problems. You should contact one of the three national credit reporting agencies—TRW, CSC Credit Services, or Trans Union Corporation—to obtain a copy of your credit report. If you think you may have credit problems, you should review your credit history with the financial aid staff at the law school you want to attend before you

apply for loans. You can obtain a copy of your credit report by following the procedure described in Figure 2, "Obtaining Your Credit Report."

The fourth step is to be careful how you use your credit cards. Consumer credit is not an investment; it's simply a means of improving your standard of living on a temporary basis. Credit card debt is bad debt. Get your credit card and other consumer debts paid off as quickly as possible. You will not be able to borrow additional student loan funds to pay your credit card bills.

Finally, plan now and prepare yourself for the financial future you want when you complete law school by getting into some good financial habits. For most people, bad habits are hard to break and it is difficult to get into good habits, particularly when it comes to money. The following "Top 10 List" is a listing of ten good financial habits that will help you achieve your goals and guide you in financing of your legal education in a responsible manner. It is not too early to get into these habits if you have not already done so. The longer you wait, the more difficult it will be for you to form these habits.

Ten Good Habits For A Sound Financial Future

1. Always pay your credit card bill(s) in full each month.

You are using a credit card for convenience if you pay the bill in **FULL** each and every month. Conversely, if you don't pay the bill in full each month, you're using your credit card for credit and that means you're living beyond your means. In other words, you are living a lifestyle you currently cannot afford. Although this allows you to enjoy the immediate gratification from consuming whatever you have purchased, you are paying a very high price for it. Doing so is not responsible behavior and in the long run, it likely will prevent you from achieving your financial goals. It is much better to limit your use of credit cards; save them for emergencies.

2. Have only one credit card account.

You only need one credit card (e.g., VISA, MasterCard). These cards all work the same and are universally accepted. There is no need to have multiple accounts. Doing so merely increases the chance you'll charge more than you can afford to repay each month. Keep the one with the lowest limit ($1,000 should be sufficient in most cases). It has been found that people who maintain a balance in excess of $1,000 on a credit card account have considerable difficulty getting it paid off. Thus, it's probably a good idea to have a credit limit no higher than $1,000 to ensure that you do not get over-extended if you have a month or two when you cannot pay the full balance due.

3. Get in the habit of saving, even if you can save only $5 per month.

There are five important strategies to saving:

i. Set a savings **GOAL**—decide what you are saving for and how much you need to save, e.g., perhaps you want to save for the cost of a Bar Exam preparation course;

ii. Pay yourself first—put money into your savings at the start of the term, first of the month, or on payday; don't wait until the end of the term/month thinking that you will save whatever is leftover; if you do, you'll find that nothing is left;

iii. Have your savings account in a different bank or credit union from where you have your checking account;

iv. Make certain that the bank or credit union where you have your savings account is as far away as possible and very inconvenient to reach; and

v. Do NOT get an ATM card or checks for your savings account—make certain that the only way you can withdraw funds from your savings account is to go where you have your account and withdraw the funds personally.

These strategies should maximize your success in getting into the savings habit.

You might think that saving money is a counter-productive financial strategy if you are borrowing student loans to finance your education. Remember, however, that the purpose here is to establish the habit of saving and to save for a specific expense you will be incurring as you begin your career but for which you cannot obtain low-cost student loans (e.g., post-enrollment expenses such as the cost of Bar Exam preparation courses, Bar Exam application fees, job interview expenses). You probably should not be saving more than $25 per month, but in saving this amount, you should have enough set aside to pay for at least one of these post-enrollment expenses without having to rely upon your credit card(s) or other higher-cost loans.

4. Budget your money just as carefully as you budget your time. Put yourself on a monthly budget and stick to it.

There are many books available in bookstores on personal finance that include worksheets you can use to help you establish your monthly budget. There also are several software products available (e.g., Access Advisor) that you can use if you prefer a computerized approach to budgeting.

5. Keep accurate, well-organized records of your financial activities.

Your record keeping should include the amount of your accumulated debt, an estimate of your minimum monthly payments, and the name(s)/address(es) of your lender(s). You also should keep copies of all important financial documents (e.g., promissory notes, correspondence from your lender(s), financial aid announcements, application materials). There are many books and software products available in bookstores on personal finance that you can use.

6. Be realistic about how much money you will earn and the amount of your other financial resources once you graduate.

You may not be offered as much money as you expect when you graduate, so plan accordingly by estimating now what your discretionary (after-tax) income will be after you complete your training. See the worksheet in Figure 1: Planning For Your Future, to analyze how much you'll have each month. Some additional information about a few particular sections of Figure 1 will help you in completing the worksheet.

• Step 1: *"What I have to pay for"* versus *"What I want to pay for"*

There are things that you have to pay for and there are things you want to pay for. You have to pay for those things that are required by law (such as taxes), those that are required of professionals (such as malpractice insurance), and those that result from legally-binding contracts such as student loan promissory notes. The consequences for not paying these items are more than just personal discomfort or embarrassment; they can include imprisonment, financial ruin, legal action, and destruction of one's credit.

Many people mistake discretionary expenses such as rent, food, etc., as "have to" payments. The difference is that you can live without paying rent or you can limit how much you pay for housing and your other costs. For example, you can live with your parents, or you can live with a roommate, or in a less expensive location. The consequences of not paying "top dollar" for housing and your other living expenses typically is just discomfort and/or embarrassment. In essence, you perceive these items to be your short-term needs. It is important that you recognize the difference between these discretionary items and the "required" payments. Hopefully it will lead you to borrow/spend less.

You should estimate how much disposable (after-tax) income you expect to be earning per month once you begin working. You can expect your gross monthly income to be reduced by one-third (1/3) for taxes. Also, don't forget to subtract the cost of required professional expenses, your monthly student loan and credit card payments before you start looking at discretionary living expenses. You may find that the money you have left over for discretionary expenses such as housing, food, transportation, entertainment, etc., is considerably less than you expected.

• Step 2: *"Income"*

You should estimate how much you expect to earn per year. (Use current dollars so as to avoid the complication of inflation). This amount should be added to expected income from your spouse (if married) and any other income you expect (e.g., interest/dividend income). The total amount should be divided by 12 to arrive at the monthly income figure. **The monthly income figure is the important aspect of income to consider because that is what you have each month to pay your bills.** Looking only at annual income doesn't allow you to get a realistic perception of your financial strength.

7. Be a well informed borrower. Not all loans are alike; know the differences and borrow wisely.

Educate yourself about the loans you borrow. Read the promissory note for each loan you borrow before you sign the note. Know the terms and conditions of each loan you borrow and beware of the "fine print." Understand your rights and responsibilities as a borrower.

8. Don't live the lifestyle you are seeking until you've completed your degree.

Get in the habit of being thrifty. Borrow only what you need at the lowest possible cost. Remember, "If you live like a lawyer while in school, you may have to live like a student once you've graduated!"

9. Maintain a strong credit record.

Obtain a copy of your credit report on an annual basis and review it for errors. Your credit report is your financial transcript. It's comparable to your academic transcript and much more important in the world of credit and personal finance. Just as you are concerned about the quality and accuracy of your academic transcript, you should be concerned about the quality and accuracy of your financial transcript—i.e., your credit report. You can obtain a copy of your credit report by following the directions provided in Figure 2.

10. Borrow the minimum amount you need to achieve your goals.

• *Establish your goals.*

Refer to the worksheet in Figure 1 entitled, Planning For Your Future—Step 1, to help you identify both your short-term needs and long-term goals.

• *Learn about the principles of credit and personal finance, and how they impact your financial well-being.*

A number of useful references are at your local library or book store. In addition, a variety of computer software products also are available wherever software is sold.

- *Borrow the minimum amount you need.*

Every time you borrow money, whether by borrowing an education loan or by using your credit card(s), you are influencing your financial future. It is tempting to view the funds you are borrowing as "your money." It is not your money, however; it belongs to your lender. In essence, it is not your money until you have paid it back from your own earnings and your other resources. It is at that point that you feel the sacrifice because you have given up control of your own resources—resources that could have been used for some other purpose. In repaying the money you have borrowed, you will reduce your discretionary income. Therefore, you should ask yourself, "Do I really need this now?" every time you make a discretionary purchase with borrowed funds or with a credit card.

QUESTION #2: What can I do once I arrive on campus to minimize the cost of law school?

Be thrifty. Live as cheaply as you can. Remember, you are a student. You'll enjoy a more comfortable lifestyle once you've graduated if you minimize your borrowing while in school. Pay the **FULL** amount due for any credit card bill(s) you receive. Pay any interest that accrues on loans you are offered while in school if you can afford to do so, rather than let the interest accrue and capitalize. This will reduce the total cost of the loans you are borrowing and save you money once you enter repayment. Follow the budget you establish for yourself. If possible, work five to ten hours a week to help reduce the amount you need to borrow. Five hours per week should net you at least $1,000 for the year, which means you can reduce your borrowing by $1,000. Many schools offer part-time employment that also may provide an opportunity for you to study or get valuable professional experience. Continue working on the good financial habits listed previously.

QUESTION #3: What financing options do I have if I cannot pay the full cost of law school from my own resources and those of my family?

Important Disclosure: *As of the printing of this material, information regarding all aid programs is correct. Please note, however, that the specific details of these programs may change at any time due to changes in government legislation/regulation.*

There are three general financing options available if you cannot pay the full cost of law school from your own resources and those of your family: (1) grants/scholarships, (2) loans, and (3) work-study. The sources of these funding options include federal and state governments; the school you attend; banks and other lending organizations; and private foundations, civic organizations, and other associations. Note that education loans are the most common and abundant source of funding available to law students.

Grants/Scholarships

Grants and scholarships are funds you do not have to repay. Availability of these funds is limited. In some instances, a service commitment is required in order to receive funding. There are three principal sources for grant and scholarship funding: (1) government, (2) institutional, and (3) private/civic sources.

Grant and scholarship assistance from government sources (federal/state) is dependent on the availability of funding and, in the case of state programs, the state in which you reside/attend law school. Not all states offer grant/scholarship assistance to law students. You should contact the financial aid office at the school you plan to attend to inquire about the availability of federal and state grant assistance. Be advised that some of these programs require a service commitment in order to receive the funding. Service typically requires that you practice law (often times in the public interest) in a particular location for a specific period of time (usually one year of service for each year of funding support).

The institution you attend may award scholarship and/or grant assistance to students who meet their eligibility requirements. These scholarships/grants typically are funded from endowments and gifts given to the school as well as from general institutional revenues. Recipients usually have to meet specific requirements such as a strong undergraduate academic record (referred to as merit-based aid), demonstrated financial need (referred to as need-based aid), special career objectives, or a combination of these and/or other factors. In some cases, all students are considered for funding; in other cases, you may need to submit a specific application by a particular date. You should contact the school you plan to attend to determine if there are special application procedures and/or deadlines to be considered for an institutional grant/scholarship.

There are a number of civic organizations and other groups that provide scholarship funding to qualified law students. Many law schools have compiled a listing of such programs that have funded students attending their institution. You should contact the financial aid office at the school you plan to attend to obtain information about these private sources of grant/scholarship funding. You also can check the Internet and local bookstore for other sources of information on scholarships and grants.

Loan Programs

There are four general types of education loan programs: (1) federally-insured loans, (2) state-sponsored loans, (3) institutionally-funded loans, and (4) supplemental loans offered by private lenders. Federally-insured loans include the Federal Stafford Loan and the Federal Perkins Loan.

All law schools participate in the federal student loan programs sponsored by the U.S. Department of Education. U.S. citizens and eligible noncitizens pursuing a degree or certificate can participate in these programs, provided they are not currently in default nor owe a refund to any federal student aid program from which they previously received assistance. These federally-insured programs are summarized below.

Federal Loan Programs

Federal Stafford Loan (Subsidized/Unsubsidized)

Federal Stafford Loans are low-cost education loans that are insured by the federal government. They are available through the William D. Ford Federal Direct Loan (FDL) Program and the Federal Family Education Loan (FFEL) Program. The terms and conditions for the FDL and FFEL programs are similar. The source of loan funds, portions of the application process, and the repayment plans available to borrowers are the major differences between the two programs. The FDL Program is funded directly by the U.S. Government whereas the FFEL Program is funded by and the loans borrowed from commercial lenders such as banks, credit unions, and organizations such as The Access Group. The school you attend determines whether you borrow from the FDL or FFEL programs. If your school does not participate in the FDL Program, you will borrow your Federal Stafford Loans through the FFEL Program. The financial aid staff at the school you attend will explain the application process and differences in repayment options.

The Federal Stafford Loan is available in two forms: subsidized and unsubsidized. Both forms are low-cost loans that are insured by the federal government. In other words, the federal government guarantees to repay your lender if you fail to do so. It is through this federal guarantee that lenders are willing and able to offer these loans to you at such affordable rates.

- The *subsidized* Federal Stafford Loan is a need-based loan in which interest is paid by the federal government (i.e., subsidized) until you begin repayment and during approved deferment periods.

- The *unsubsidized* Federal Stafford Loan is not based on financial need. Interest on the *unsubsidized* Federal Stafford Loan is **NOT** paid by the federal government, and thus, must be paid by you—the borrower. You can pay the interest when billed or allow it to accrue and capitalize (i.e., be added to the principal) while in school. You can use the *unsubsidized* Federal Stafford Loan to meet financial need not covered by other sources and/or to replace an expected family contribution.

The maximum *subsidized* Federal Stafford Loan per year currently is $8,500 or the amount of your unmet financial need, whichever is less. The current combined annual maximum for *subsidized* and *unsubsidized* Federal Stafford Loans is $18,500 or your cost of attendance minus any other financial aid, whichever is less. Therefore, the maximum *unsubsidized* Federal Stafford Loan you can borrow in a given year is the difference between the combined annual maximum (typically, $18,500) and your *subsidized* Federal Stafford Loan eligibility. The cumulative maximum is $138,500, of which no more than $65,500 can be *subsidized* funds.

The interest rate for all Federal Stafford Loans (both *subsidized* and *unsubsidized*) disbursed on or after July 1, 1994, is variable, with a cap of 8.25%. This variable rate applies both to new borrowers (i.e., those with no outstanding Federal Stafford Loans) and to those who have outstanding loans with a fixed interest rate. In other words, **all** Federal Stafford Loans made after June 30, 1994, have a variable interest rate. The rate is adjusted annually on July 1. For loans made on or after July 1, 1995, the rate is equal to the 91-day Treasury Bill rate determined at the final auction in May plus 2.5% during in-school, grace, and eligible periods of deferment. During repayment it is equal to the 91-day Treasury Bill rate determined at the final auction in May plus 3.1%.

- The Federal Stafford Loan in-school interest rate for the period July 1, 1996, to June 30, 1997, is **7.66%**. The rate in repayment is **8.26%**.

You are charged two fees when borrowing a Federal Stafford Loan: (1) an origination fee, and (2) a guarantee fee. The origination fee is paid to the federal government and currently is three percent (3%) of the total amount borrowed. The guarantee fee is paid to the guarantee agency if borrowing from the FFEL Program and to the federal government if borrowing from the FDL Program. The amount of this fee varies depending upon the guarantor/lender, but cannot exceed one percent (1%) of the total amount borrowed. Both fees are deducted from each disbursement of your loan.

Repayment of principal is deferred on both the *subsidized* and *unsubsidized* Federal Stafford Loans so long as you are enrolled at least halftime as a student pursuing a degree or certificate. Repayment of principal (and interest on the *subsidized* loan) begins six months after you cease to be enrolled at least halftime (remember that interest on *unsubsidized* loans begins accruing as soon as funds are disbursed by your lender). This six-month period is called the "grace period." You should receive repayment information from your lender prior to or during the grace period. The repayment period extends from 5 to 10 years. There is no penalty for prepayment.

A deferment or forbearance may be available under certain conditions once repayment begins if you need to postpone repayment of your loan(s). A deferment is a temporary suspension of payment on your loan. Interest is subsidized during a deferment on *subsidized* Federal Stafford Loans. It is not subsidized on *unsubsidized* loans during a deferment, and thus, continues to accrue. A forbearance is a temporary suspension or reduction of payment of your loan that is granted by your lender due to economic hardship. Interest continues to accrue during a forbearance regardless of loan type. See the Federal Stafford Loan promissory note for more information.

Federal Perkins Loan

The Federal Perkins Loan is both a federally insured and federally subsidized loan program administered by the school you are attending. Funds for this program are provided by the federal government, with your school acting as the lender. The Federal Perkins Loan Program is designed to provide need-based, low interest financial assistance to students demonstrating high financial need. The exact loan amount offered to a student depends upon the availability of funds and the amount of his or her financial need, but cannot

exceed $5,000 per year. The cumulative maximum for this program is $30,000 and includes both undergraduate and graduate borrowing. Principal and interest are deferred during the in-school years. Repayment begins following a grace period of either six or nine months depending on when you received your first Federal Perkins Loan.

- The Federal Perkins Loan interest rate currently is fixed at 5.0%.

The repayment period can last up to 10 years. Deferments and forbearances are available under certain situations once you enter repayment (refer to the Federal Perkins Loan promissory note for details) if you need to postpone repayment of your loan(s).

State-Funded Loan Programs

Some states offer education loan programs. Eligibility for these loans may or may not be based on financial need. Information about the availability, terms, and application procedures for these loans can be obtained from the financial aid office at the school you plan to attend.

Institutional Loans

Many law schools have limited institutional loan funds available for qualified students. These loans may be used in limited amounts to cover financial need not met by federal loans. In other cases, they may be used as "loans of last resort" to assist those students who have difficulty obtaining assistance from other sources. Whatever the case, it is up to the financial aid staff to determine who is eligible to apply for these loans. Contact the financial aid staff at the school you plan to attend if you are interested in obtaining information about the availability and likelihood of being awarded an institutional loan.

Supplemental Private Loans

There are a number of private loan programs (e.g., Law Access® Loan Program, LawLoans, GradExcel, Professional Education Plan (PEP), GradAssist Loan). These loan programs are not based on financial need and tend to have higher fees/interest rates. They are intended to supplement the other financial assistance you are receiving. The financial aid staff at the school you plan to attend can provide more detailed information about the various supplemental loan programs available to law students. It is important to remember that you should borrow the minimum amount necessary, and that you cannot receive financial assistance in excess of the cost of attendance determined by the financial aid office.

Federal Work-Study

The Federal Work-Study (FWS) Program provides employment for law students who have demonstrated financial need. It allows you to earn money to help pay for your educational expenses. Community service work and work related to your course of study are encouraged. Eligibility for FWS funding depends on the availability of work-study funds at the school you are attending, the policies of the school, when you apply for financial assistance, and your level of financial need. These funds may be paid on an hourly basis or you may receive a salary from the institution you are attending. You can earn only up to the amount of your total FWS award. Be advised that not all law schools have work-study funding. Contact the financial aid office at the school you plan to attend to inquire about the availability of this program at that institution.

QUESTION #4: What is the purpose of financial aid?

Financial aid programs are designed to assist you and your family in financing your law school investment. You are permitted by current federal regulations to receive assistance up to the estimated cost of attendance for your degree program, as established by the financial aid office at the school you attend.

Following are questions you should ask about the financial aid program at each school you are interested in attending:

1. What is the philosophy of financial aid at the institution?
2. What grant and loan resources are available to meet my financial need?
3. Can I meet my full financial need using those resources?
4. Will my parents be expected to provide financial information and/or contribute to my educational expenses? (Will I be considered financially dependent or independent in terms of receiving institutional funding?) What options will I have if my parents refuse?
5. What is the financial aid process?
6. How do I apply for assistance?
7. What are the application deadlines?
8. What is done with all the information I provide?
9. Will my credit history affect my ability to get financial assistance?
10. What should I know about the loans I am offered?

General answers to some of these questions are provided in the following sections.

QUESTION #5: What is the basic philosophy of the financial aid system?

The basic philosophy of the system is to provide you with an opportunity to attend the school of your choice without regard to your financial circumstances. Some schools, however, may not have the means to meet your full financial need. Many schools also have criteria that require your parents to contribute to the extent possible before institutional resources will be offered to meet a portion of your financial need. You will want to ask the financial aid staff at each school you are considering attending about their policy on financial independence.

Although you will be considered by the federal government to be financially independent for the purposes of receiving federal funds, you may be considered financially *dependent* on your parents by the law school you are attending for the purposes of receiving institutional funds such as grants and scholarships. The institutional policy regarding financial independence typically is more stringent than the corresponding federal regulations. It may be based on one or more factors, including your age, your prior work experience, or your parents' tax filing status. The institutional policy is needed because there generally are insufficient school resources to adequately fund all students with grant and/or scholarship assistance. Thus, institutional dependency policies are designed to guarantee that the distribution of these scarce institutional dollars is fair and equitable.

QUESTION #6: What is the financial aid process and how do I apply for financial assistance?

The financial aid process is necessarily bureaucratic. It is a cooperative effort including you, your family, the financial aid staff at the school you are attending, and the lender(s) from which you borrow education loan funds. Financing your education with financial aid involves multiple steps and requires that you submit various application documents. There are three general steps to the overall process.

1. Apply for assistance
2. Receive the funds
3. Repay the loans you borrow

The first step in the financial aid process is to complete the required applications. The specific procedures can vary from one school to another based on the availability of institutional resources and the financial aid operation at the school you attend. The basic procedure, however, typically includes the following steps.

1. Contact the school(s) you are considering, to obtain information about their application procedures, deadlines, and any application materials they supply directly to you. *This should be done around the time you are applying for admission.*

2. Obtain the financial aid applications that are required by the law school you wish to attend.

- You will need to complete the *Free Application for Federal Student Aid* (*FAFSA*) if you are applying for federal student aid.

You can apply either by completing and mailing the paper version of the *FAFSA*, by applying electronically (through your school), or by using the U.S. Department of Education's new *FAFSA Express* software. You can obtain a *FAFSA* from any financial aid office or from the Federal Student Aid Information Center at P.O. Box 84, Washington, D.C. 20044. You also can call the Federal Student Aid Information Center at 1-800-4-FED-AID (1-800-433-3243).

Note that if you applied for federal student aid in the current academic year, you probably will receive a *Renewal Free Application for Federal Student Aid (Renewal FAFSA)* for the next academic year. That form can be used in place of the options described above.

You will receive a *Student Aid Report (SAR)* from the federal processor once your *FAFSA/Renewal FAFSA* has been processed. You should review the information carefully that is provided on the *SAR* and follow any instructions contained on it. The financial aid office at the school(s) you listed on your *FAFSA/Renewal FAFSA* also should receive the information electronically. They will use it to determine your eligibility for federal student aid funding.

- You also may need to complete a supplemental application, if required by the school you are attending.

The supplemental application typically requests information not contained on the *FAFSA/Renewal FAFSA* and is used for the purpose of awarding institutional funds. Some schools use fee-based supplemental applications such as the Need Access Application Diskette or the College Scholarship Service (CSS) Profile . Others use an institutional application and/or a combination of both a fee-based application and an institutional form. Whatever procedure is used, it is important to contact the financial aid office at the schools you're considering attending to obtain the necessary application material(s)/instructions.

- You also may be required to submit a copy of your most recent federal income tax return.

It is very important to complete your federal income tax return as soon as possible for the calendar year preceding the academic year for which you are applying for financial aid so that you will have the necessary information to complete the *FAFSA/Renewal FAFSA* and other application materials.

3. Complete all applications and submit them as directed by the deadline date.

- Make certain to obtain information about any application deadline dates from the financial aid staff at the school(s) you want to attend. You should apply as soon as possible even if there are no application deadlines, however, to avoid delays in receiving your financial aid award packet.

4. Your eligibility for assistance will be determined by the financial aid staff once all the application information has been received and reviewed. Then you will be sent a financial aid award notice/packet informing you of the assistance you are eligible to receive.

- It may take a number of weeks from the time you submit your application documents until you receive a financial aid award announcement/packet. Processing of your application materials (and those of all other students) can be a very time-consuming process.

5. Respond to your financial aid award announcement and return it to the financial aid office, as instructed.

- Typically you must indicate which portions of the award you accept and which portions you reject. Then you must return a copy of your award announcement to the financial aid office. Be certain to follow any deadline dates. Be aware that the financial aid staff has offered the most affordable financial aid package they can, based upon your financial situation, available resources, federal/state regulations, and institutional policies. If you feel you need additional assistance, contact the financial aid office.

6. Apply for any loans you need to borrow that you have been offered by the financial aid office.

- You will need to complete and submit the appropriate application(s), as instructed, for any loans you wish to borrow. Note that in some cases, you may be able to apply for your loan(s) electronically. You should be provided with specific instructions by the financial aid office on how to complete the loan application process. Adhere to any deadline dates and borrow the minimum amount you need. Remember, every dollar you borrow must be repaid with interest. This will have an impact on your financial future once you graduate.

7. Sign the promissory note(s) for your loan(s) if not part of the original loan application, and submit them to your lender(s).

- The promissory note(s) for your loan(s) may not be part of the loan application. If so, you will need to sign the promissory note(s) once the loan(s) has(have) been processed and approved. Loan funds cannot be disbursed to you until you have signed the promissory note for the loan. The promissory note is the legally binding contract between you and your lender.

Important reminders in applying for assistance:

- Complete all required forms—neatly!
- Be consistent when completing all forms.
- Answer all questions completely. Do not leave questions blank.
- Apply as early as possible.
- Adhere to all published deadlines.
- Keep copies of all forms.

QUESTION #7: What is done with all the information I provide?

Your "family contribution" is determined by the financial aid staff based on the financial information provided by you and your family using guidelines established by Congress and the law school.

Your "financial need" is calculated as the difference between the estimated "cost of attendance" for your degree program and the "family contribution" determined by the financial aid staff.

Your financial aid information is considered confidential and will be treated as such by the financial aid staff and your lender(s). Only those individuals responsible for processing your application materials will have access to the documents you and your family submit.

QUESTION #8: What should I know about the loans I am offered?

You should know the following information about each of the loans you are offered before you actually apply for the funds.

- Loan amount offered and maximum loan eligibility

You should get answers to the following questions about the loan amount you've been offered and your maximum annual and cumulative loan eligibility in the program. Have you been offered the maximum amount from the loan program or can you apply for more funds from the program if you need additional assistance later in the academic year? In borrowing the offered amount, how close will you be to your cumulative maximum in this loan program if such a maximum exists? Will you exhaust your loan eligibility in this program before you complete your degree?

- Co-signer requirements, if any

Although no federal loan programs currently require you to have a co-signer or co-borrower, some state, institutional, and private loan programs do require that you obtain a creditworthy co-signer in order to apply for the loan. In other cases, applying with a co-signer can reduce the cost of the loan. Whatever the situation, you should determine what co-signer requirements exist, if any, and the credit approval criteria for the loan. If you do not have someone who is willing or able to serve as your co-signer, you will need to find an alternative to the loan that is offered.

- Interest rate

The interest rate is the percentage rate you are charged to borrow the loan. You should know when interest starts accruing. You also should know whether the loan has a fixed or variable rate. If the rate is variable, you should know how it is calculated, how frequently it is adjusted, if it has a cap (in other words, an upper limit) and when the rate changes. Remember, the lower the rate, the less your loan will cost.

- Impact of my credit history on loan approval

Federal loans currently do not require a credit check. Institutional and supplemental loans from private lenders typically do require that your credit record be analyzed before your loan application can be approved. You should obtain a copy of your credit report using the steps given in Figure 2 so that you can check on the current status of your credit. If you have credit problems, you may have trouble obtaining the loan financing you need to attend law school. The financial aid staff at the school(s) you're considering may be able to counsel you about alternative financing options if you have credit problems. Having a copy of your credit report will help them advise you on your options.

- Availability of alternatives

Are there alternative loan options if you cannot meet the application and/or approval requirements of the loans you've been offered? It is important to answer this question early in the application process so that you can plan carefully for the financing of your education costs. The financial aid staff at the school(s) you're considering should be able to advise you about any financing alternatives.

- Repayment terms/grace period

It is very important that you understand the terms and conditions of each loan you borrow. This will allow you to make well-informed borrowing decisions. You should borrow the minimum amount you need at the lowest possible cost with the best possible repayment terms in order to maximize the investment in your education. The loan application and promissory note should provide the information you need. Remember to keep copies of these materials for future reference.

Cost of Attendance

minus

Family Contribution

equals

Financial Need

- Deferment and forbearance options

You may need to temporarily postpone repayment of your loans once you graduate. Therefore, it is important to know the deferment and forbearance options for each loan you borrow. This information should be contained in the application materials and the promissory note.

- Reputation of lender

An important aspect of borrowing an education loan is the relationship you hope to have with your lender. As such, there are a number of questions you should answer regarding the reputation of your lender before you make a final decision on which lender you will use. What is the reputation of the lender offering the loan you need to borrow? How easy is it to solve problems with the lender? How accessible is customer assistance? Does the lender provide a toll-free number you can call to get help? Does the lender specialize in making loans to law students? The financial aid staff at the school(s) you're considering may be able to help you answer these questions. You also should contact each potential lender you are considering for answers to these questions. Another source of information may be currently enrolled students who are borrowing from the lender in question.

QUESTION #9: What impact will these loans have on me after I complete law school?

Your education loans must be repaid. This will limit your disposable income during repayment.

What happens if I do not repay my loans?

Your lender will follow the collection procedures required by the government. If your account is not brought current, your delinquency will be reported to all national credit bureaus. Defaulted loans will affect your credit rating and jeopardize your future ability to borrow funds for any purpose. You also will be liable for any collection expenses that are incurred.

How can I effectively manage my loan portfolio?

1. Make a file folder for all your financial records. You should keep all documents in one place for easy reference. Some students keep a separate file folder for each loan type, and in some cases, a separate file for each lender if more than one lender is used for a particular loan. The types of materials to keep are: your copies of the loan applications, promissory notes, disclosure statements, and copies of all correspondence with the lender.

2. Keep a cumulative record of your education loans. This type of record keeping also enables you to estimate your projected debt level and monthly payments. It is important to keep this record up to date.

3. Keep lenders informed of any changes in your name, address and/or registration status. This must be done in writing.

4. Confirm all of your telephone conversations with your lenders with a follow-up letter. This is a sound practice in any business transaction.

What should I do if I experience difficulty repaying my loan?

The most important action to take is to contact your lender quickly before you go into default. Your lender may be willing to offer you a forbearance period under certain conditions. To qualify, you must demonstrate that you are willing to make the loan payments, but you are unable to do so because of extraordinary circumstances.

What if my monthly loan payments are not manageable? Is there a way to reduce the burden?

Yes. You should contact your lender regarding a Federal Consolidation Loan. A Federal Consolidation Loan will stretch your payments over a longer period of time and reduce your monthly installments into one manageable monthly repayment. It also fixes the interest rate on the loans you consolidate. The rate is equal to the weighted average of all rates consolidated rounded up to the nearest whole percent.

You gain more disposable income by refinancing your federal loans into a Federal Consolidation Loan. Doing so will reduce your monthly loan payments, thereby making the repayment of your education loan debt less difficult. The total amount you will repay increases, however, because of the extended repayment period and the potentially higher fixed interest rate. To consolidate your loans, you must be in repayment or the grace period, and you cannot be more than 90 days delinquent on the loans you are consolidating. You can consolidate any portion of your Federal Stafford, Federal SLS, Federal Perkins and other federal student loan portfolio. It is best, however, not to consolidate your Federal Perkins loans, if possible, as the increase in interest rate greatly adds to the overall cost of these loans.

Refinancing of supplemental loans borrowed from private lenders also may be available. Information on consolidating these loans should be available from the lenders and usually is described in the application materials for the loan. It is important to note, however, that these privately-funded loans cannot be consolidated with your federal loans.

QUESTION #10: Where can I get more information?

The best place to start when looking for more information is the financial aid office at the school you plan to attend. The financial aid staff are professionals who are trained to serve your educational financing needs. Several additional sources of useful information are listed below.

For general information about the federal student aid process/programs, refer to the following free U.S. Department of Education publication.:

- The Student Guide: Financial Aid from the U.S. Department of Education.

This publication and other general information can be obtained by contacting:

Federal Student Aid Information Center
P.O. Box 84
Washington, D.C. 20044
1-800-4-FED-AID
(1-800-433-3243)

The toll-free TDD number is: **1-800-730-8913**

To inquire about the processing status of your *Free Application for Federal Student Aid (FAFSA)/Renewal FAFSA*, contact:

- Federal Student Aid Information Center
1-319-337-5665

This is a toll call. Collect calls will not be accepted and you cannot inquire about the status of your *FAFSA/Renewal FAFSA* using the toll-free number. Also be aware that the financial aid staff will not be able to determine the status of your *FAFSA/Renewal FAFSA* before your application has been processed and the results have been forwarded to the school by the federal processing center.

There is a website on the Internet that provides useful, up-to-date information about the financial aid process. It includes additional references and resources. The name of the website is *FINAID: The Financial Aid Information Page.* You can access it at:

- **http://www.finaid.org**

There are several websites that offer information about individual spending and consumption behavior that may help you learn more about how to develop good financial habits. The name of each website and address are as follows:

- "Spending Personality Assessment"
http://www.ns.net/cash/selftest/selftest.html

- "The Seven Spending Personalities"
http://www.ns.net/cash/selftest7sp_info.html#fanatical

- "What is Your Financial Personality"
http://www.minnesotamutual.com/personal/perstest.html

- "Consumer World Links to Over 1,200 Sites"
http://www.consumerworld.org

Summary

Remember, your legal education is an INVESTMENT in your future. It can be a professionally rewarding and financially enriching experience if you:

- devise your long-term financial plan and manage your resources in a responsible manner while in school;
- make good, cost-effective, and well-informed CHOICES;
- develop a budget and live within that budget while in school;
- borrow the minimum amount needed to maximize the net return on your educational investment;
- avoid using credit cards except in emergencies;
- work with the advisers in your financial aid office to obtain the financial assistance you need and follow the directions they provide to you regarding your education loans.

Your education is an important key to your financial future and to your success. The questions answered here provide a guide on how to make the financing of your legal education more manageable. Knowing these answers should allow you to make responsible, well-informed financial decisions.

FIGURE 1: PLANNING FOR YOUR FUTURE

Step 1:

What are my short-term needs and long-term goals?

(These are the things I WANT to pay for.)

Short-Term Needs *(e.g., housing, food, transportation, clothing, entertainment)*	Estimated Monthly Cost
1.	$
2.	$
3.	$
4.	$
5.	$
6.	$
Total Cost of Short-Term Needs	$ **(1)**

Long-Term Goals *(e.g.,housing, investments, retirement planning)*	Estimated Monthly Cost
1.	$
2.	$
3.	$
4.	$
5.	$
6.	$
Total Cost of Long-Term Goals	$ **(2)**

TOTAL cost of all the things I want to pay for: *[(1) + (2)]* **$______________ (3)**

Step 2:

How far will my paycheck go?

INCOME

My annual salary/wages: $__________

My spouse's salary/wages: $__________

Other income: ____________________ $__________

Total annual income: *(sum of above)* $__________

Monthly Income: *(Total annual income ÷ 12)* $__________ (4)

WHAT I HAVE TO PAY FOR

Taxes: *(assume 1/3 of Total monthly income)* $__________

Malpractice insurance and/or other professional expense(s): $__________

My monthly student loan payment: $__________ ☞
(assume a monthly payment of $125 for every $10,000 you owe)

My spouse's monthly student loan payment: $__________

My total monthly credit card payment: $__________ ☞
(assume monthly payment is 2% of total credit card balance and include all other personal debt payments)

My spouse's total monthly credit card payment: $__________

Total of What I Have to Pay Each Month: *(sum of above)* $__________ (5)

DISCRETIONARY MONTHLY INCOME

Total monthly income: $__________ (4)

Total monthly required payments: $__________ (5)

Total Discretionary Income Available to Satisfy My Needs & Goals: *[(4) - (5)]* $__________ (6)

Step 3:

My financial balance sheet

Item	Amount
Total Discretionary Income Available to Satisfy Needs & Goals:	$ (6)
Total Cost of All Things I Want to Pay for:	$ (3)
Total Amount of Money Left Over Each Month: *[(6) - (3)]*	$ (7)

- What happens if the amount of money left over each month [i.e., amount (7)] is NEGATIVE? What should you do?

- What happens if the amount of money left over each month [i.e., amount (7)] is POSITIVE? What should you do?

FIGURE 2: OBTAINING YOUR CREDIT REPORT

You can request a copy of your credit report by sending a written request (*typed or printed*) to one of the three national credit reporting agencies at the addresses listed below.

- Your request should include the following information, and it must be **SIGNED**.
  - full name, including generation (e.g., Jr., Sr., I, II, III)
  - spouse's first name (if married)
  - current address (including zipcode)
  - any previous addresses for the past five years (including zipcodes)
  - social security number
  - date of birth
  - current employer (if unemployed, note that)
  - daytime telephone number
- You also should include a photocopy of documentation showing proof of your **CURRENT ADDRESS**, e.g., a recent billing statement from a major credit card company, a recent utility bill, your valid driver's license.

Most credit reporting agencies charge a fee to obtain a credit report. The current fees for the companies listed below are provided. You may want to call each company, however, to verify that the fee has not changed. You must pay the fee by check or money order made payable to the company from which you're obtaining the credit report. *Note that you are entitled to a free copy of your credit report if you have been denied credit within the past 60 days. In addition, TRW currently provides a complimentary credit report once every 12 months.*

MAJOR NATIONAL CREDIT REPORTING AGENCIES

TRW	TRW P.O. Box 8030 Layton, UT 84041-8030 (800) 682-7654	*(no fee)*
CSC Credit Services	CSC Credit Services P.O. Box 674402 Houston, TX 77267-4402 (800) 759-5979	*($8.00 fee unless denied credit in last 60 days)*
Trans Union Corporation	Trans Union Corporation P.O. Box 390 Springfield, PA 19064-0390 (215) 690-4900	*($8.00 fee unless denied credit in last 60 days)*

Be advised that credit criteria used to review/approve student loans can include the following: (1) absence of negative credit; (2) no bankruptcies, foreclosures, repossessions, charge-offs, or open judgments; (3) no prior education loan defaults unless paid in full or making satisfactory progress in repayment; and (4) absence of numerous past due accounts, i.e., no 30-, 60-, or 90-day delinquencies on consumer loans or revolving charge accounts within the past two years.

Chapter Five
Career Outlook

Written by The National Association for Law Placement (NALP)*

Just as every law school is unique in its curricular offerings and campus culture, they also differ in the range of services provided for career planning and employment. However, each career services office and the professionals who administer them have at least one thing in common -- law students and graduates are their most important constituents.

Career services administrators and staff know the search for employment in today's competitive legal marketplace requires a great deal of forethought, a significant investment of time, use of a variety of communication and technological tools, and development of critical job-search related skills. It is through the law school career services program that students and new professionals can acquire the tools they need to prepare for and obtain satisfying, rewarding careers as lawyers.

Programs and Activities of Career Services Offices

Law school career services offices are very important resource partners for students who take responsibility for their own careers and take the lead in their career planning and job search effort. Career services offices cannot and do not "broker" students into jobs, nor can they offer a guarantee of a job upon graduation. Instead, they provide specialized career counseling, collect and distribute vital information and resources, and offer critical skills training, while leading the efforts of the law school to establish relationships with employers. In performing these tasks, the career services office becomes a major marketing and outreach program for its law school, as well as an invaluable resource for both law students and graduates as they chart their career paths.

Career Planning, Advising and Counseling Services

Career planning and counseling services are valuable resources law students can use to enhance their job search activities. Career planning and counseling can be of great assistance if tailored to the needs of groups of students (first-years, third-years, part-time, etc.), as well as individual students. These services typically include an exploration of the many career options available to lawyers and a self-inventory experience to gain insight about career aspirations. Career counseling may also provide assistance in managing educational or consumer debt.

Job Search Assistance

The development of a successful job search and career plan requires law students and graduates to assume personal responsibility for charting their search and implementing a plan to undertake it. However, the law school career services office offers great significance to students in that effort: training in job prospecting, networking, resume writing, and interviewing; use of informational and technological resources to learn about employers and job opportunities; job postings and resume forwarding to assist students in connecting with employers who may not recruit locally; administration of on-campus interview programs; and management of mentoring programs between law students and alumni.

Alumni Career Resources

Some law schools have the resources to offer continuing support to law school graduates -- most of whom, if true to statistical data, will change jobs at least seven times during their professional careers. Law school alumni turn to their career planning offices for advice on resumes, referrals and resources, information on the hiring needs of specific employers, and access to career-related publications. Some career services programs publish newsletters especially for alumni, offer counseling services, and organize special networking or other activities.

Past Employment Experiences, Law Student and Lawyer Employment

Prior work experience may help define interest in a future career as a lawyer. Successful work experiences demonstrating capacity for learning, business acumen and ability to interact with clients are especially relevant to that future. However, no matter what someone did prior to law school, they are still "new lawyers" and thus, their compensation as a lawyer will generally be similar to others who accept jobs of the same type. Your background can be advantageous by attracting the interest of employers looking for a particular type of student or a special skill, however.

Summer Jobs During Law School

Summers offer an opportunity for many law students to gain real world experience as a paid or unpaid clerk in a law firm, government agency, public interest organization or law related business. Internships, externships, and clerkships with law firms are ways to acquire work experience, as is serving as a research assistant for a member of the law faculty. Law students who hope to work for a large law firm after graduation should be aware those firms hire entry-level lawyers primarily from their summer clerk programs. Moreover, summer jobs are important opportunities for law students to establish contacts and to receive evaluation of their work product.

School Term Employment

Students may choose to work during the school term -- perhaps to gain experience or financial support. In accordance with ABA Standards, full-time law students may not be employed for more than 20 hours per week by a legal employer; however, evening division students often continue the employment they had before they entered law school. These students will need to consider the relationship of their current career with law and may need to acquire legal work experience prior to graduation. This is particularly true if evening division students anticipate making a transition into law practice.

Graduates Acquire Jobs at Various Times

The search for a full-time job is a process dictated not only by the effort and commitment of the candidate but also by the unique recruiting practices of various types of employers.

Summer Clerkship May Lead to First-Year Associate Offer

Some law firms (typically large firms which can predict their needs well in advance) interview on campus in the fall to hire students for the following summer. If a student's performance is acceptable and the hiring needs of the firm have remained consistent with the size of the summer class, the student may receive an offer for a full-time job following graduation. Students receiving such offers make a decision on whether to accept such an offer during the fall of their third year of law school. Some government agencies (typically the Department of Justice and other large agencies) have Honors programs which work in a similar manner, although few of those agencies actually conduct on-campus interviews.

Employers Hire in Spring From Third Year Class

Smaller private practice employers and a significant number of public interest and government agencies interview and hire third-year law students during the spring of the student's third year. This timetable enables them to predict more accurately their hiring needs and offers both employers and students an additional semester of law school for hiring/career decisions.

Judicial Clerkships are a Source of Post-graduation Employment

Jobs as clerks for judges at the local, state or federal level provide postgraduate employment for about 12 percent of law graduates. These job offers typically encompass one or two years and provide invaluable experience in the court system. Judicial clerks balance the advantages of the clerkship experience with the delay of entering full-time practice.

Many Offers of Employment Occur After Graduation or Bar Passage

Many private practice employers, public interest agencies, and most government employers extend offers of employment after graduation from law school and bar passage. Thus, graduates may not acquire their first job until six to nine months after graduation. Understanding hiring practices of the broad range of legal employers enables job seekers to interpret a law school's data on employment more accurately. Law schools whose graduates are employed by a significant number of government or small firm employers will naturally have statistical data showing fewer graduates employed at graduation while schools whose graduates are employed primarily in large law firms will have statistical data that shows more graduates employed at graduation.

Principles and Standards Guide Job Offers and Responses

Both employers and students are guided in the employment process by NALP's *Principles and Standards for Law Placement and Recruitment Activities*. These guidelines are promulgated to ensure that students have an adequate opportunity to make decisions about offers of employment without undue pressure and that employers will receive responses from students in a timely manner. Copies of the *Principles and Standards* are available through each law school or by contacting NALP.

Graduates Choose Jobs According to Interests

Members of each graduating class acquire full and part-time jobs with an array of public and private, legal and nonlegal organizations. By definition, a "legal" job is a position requiring a juris doctor and requiring substantial use of legal skills and training. In contrast, "nonlegal" jobs are positions that do not require a juris doctor and may or may not make specific use of legal skills and background. Law graduates have in the past obtained legal, nonlegal, full and part-time jobs from these five general types of employers:

Private Practice -- includes all positions within a law firm, including solo practitioner, associate, law clerk, paralegal and administrative or support staff.

Public Interest -- includes positions funded by the Legal Services Corporation and others providing civil legal and indigent services as well as positions with nonprofit advocacy or cause-related organizations.

Government -- includes all levels and branches of government including public defender and prosecutor positions, positions with the military, and all other agencies such as the Small Business Administration, state and local transit authorities, congressional committees, law enforcement, and social services.

Judicial clerkship -- a one- or two-year appointment clerking for a judge on the federal, state, or local level.

Business and industry -- includes positions in accounting firms, insurance companies, banking and financial institutions, corporations, companies and organizations of all sizes such as private hospitals, retail establishments, consulting and public relations firms, political campaigns, trade associations, and labor unions.

Academic -- includes work as a law professor, law librarian,

administrator, or faculty member in higher education or other academic settings, including elementary and secondary schools.

Employment Outlook for New Lawyers

Making an informed choice to pursue a career in the law must include an examination of law school curricula, student services and admission requirements. Of equal importance is undertaking a comprehensive self-inventory on career aspirations and realistically and candidly assessing the options and prospects for employment after graduation.

The latter requires a basic understanding of how the legal profession has evolved during recent years, including the changes in the ways in which law is practiced, and how the growth of the profession will affect the employment prospects and experiences of future lawyers.

The legal profession has experienced significant changes in its demographic composition during the past two decades.

Since the early 1970s the composition of what was once known as "the gentlemanly profession" has been transformed by the entry of a substantial number of women and, to a lesser degree, minorities into the nation's law schools and ultimately into the practicing bar. In 1995, 43 percent of law graduates were women, a substantial increase over the 15 percent graduating in 1975. Minorities comprised 17 percent of the 1995 graduating class, compared to 5.4 graduating in 1975.

Since 1991, the percentage of graduates accepting legal positions as their first jobs has diminished from more than 80% to 76% in 1995. Private practice employment decreased from 62% in 1990 to the current rate of 56%.

The increased frequency with which graduates initially acquire nonlegal jobs after law school has been documented by NALP data -- and anecdotal information also suggests that attorneys leaving the practice of law to pursue nonlegal entrepreneurial or business careers has increased dramatically in recent years.

Law firm structure and strategies for hiring and growth have changed in response to the market economy.

In 1995 approximately 350 law firms employed more than 100 lawyers, a sharp contrast to the less than a dozen firms employing 100 lawyers in 1960 or the 47 firms doing so in 1978. Some analysts project that the number of large firms will continue to increase as a result of mergers and the competitive advantage offered by a national or international presence.

Today, legal employers carefully plan for growth and hire entry level, lateral, and summer clerks accordingly. Some law firms only

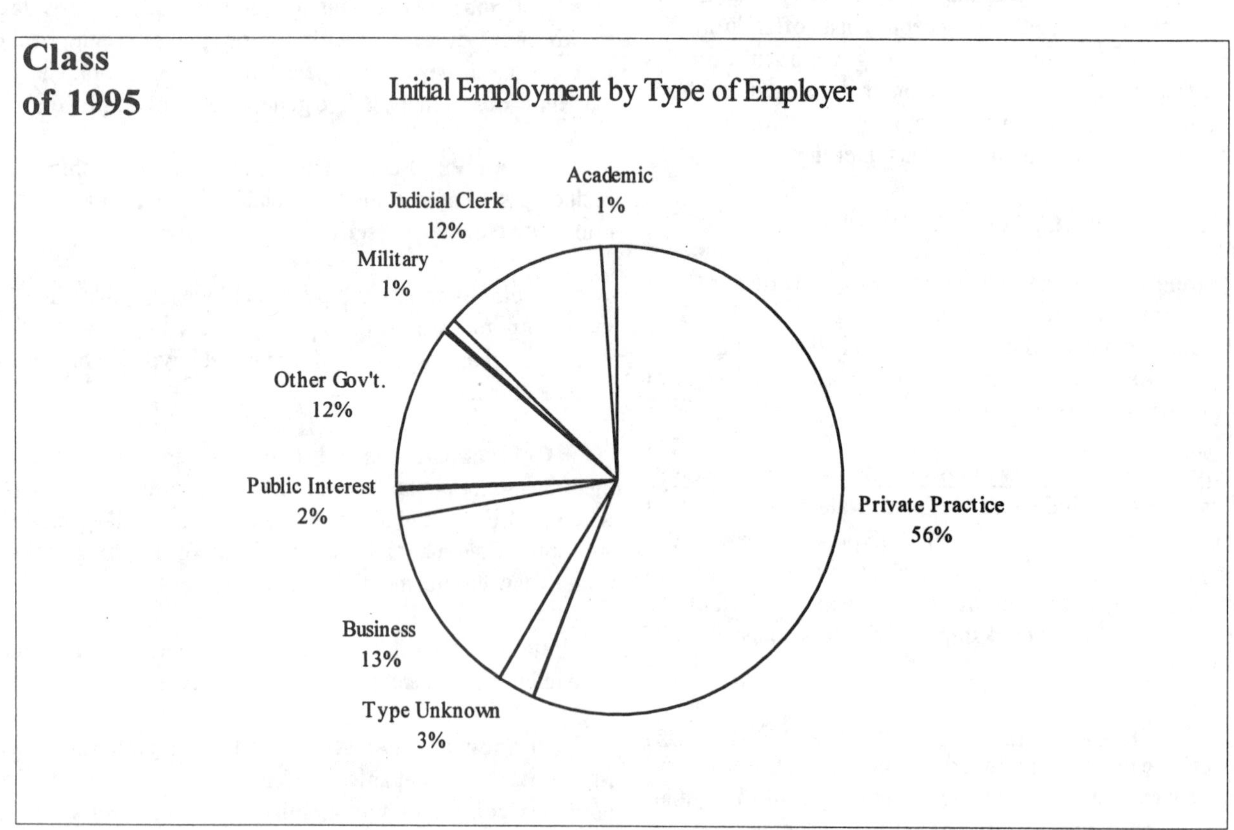

grow "internally" -- meaning they hire only entry level attorneys, monitoring and grooming them for partnership in their seventh or eighth year. This strategy precipitates the outplacement of a predictable percentage of associates each year -- those who are judged not to be partnership caliber.

Some firms grow through expansion or creation of practice groups -- a strategy that may predicate aggressive recruitment or "cherry picking" of lateral associates and experienced partners. Associates in today's legal market frequently make several lateral moves before settling into a partnership track at a firm and partners with a substantial book of business now move from firm to firm, an occurrence rare before the 1980s.

The business operations of law firms have changed in response to client demand and the need to be profitable.

In many respects, the law profession has been forced to conduct itself as a business. Managing partners must sustain "profitability" in order to retain partners who could, ostensibly, take their talent and clientele to other firms. Recruitment and accounting practices, like attorney overhead and billables, are carefully scrutinized for cost effectiveness. Thus, an attorney's success is tied, to a certain extent, to his profitability and his ability to cultivate clients for his firm.

Government and public interest hiring has declined during recent years due to budget restraints and calls for a smaller and more efficient government at the federal, state and local levels.

Law graduates who are dedicated to public service employment have generally been successful in obtaining jobs -- but sometimes only because they acted in an entrepreneurial manner and utilized special grant programs to fund their jobs. Graduates of the future are likely to find the opportunities in public service remain somewhat limited and median compensation is less likely to equal or exceed other employment.

Employment Experiences of Distinctive Graduates

Women and Minorities

Data on the Class of 1995 shows that fewer women entered private practice than in the past whereas more obtained government, clerkship, and public interest positions. The same was true for minorities compared to non-minorities, although the proportion of minorities obtaining clerkship positions was somewhat lower. About 48% of employed minority women obtained jobs in private practice compared with 54.6% of non-minority women. Among minority men,

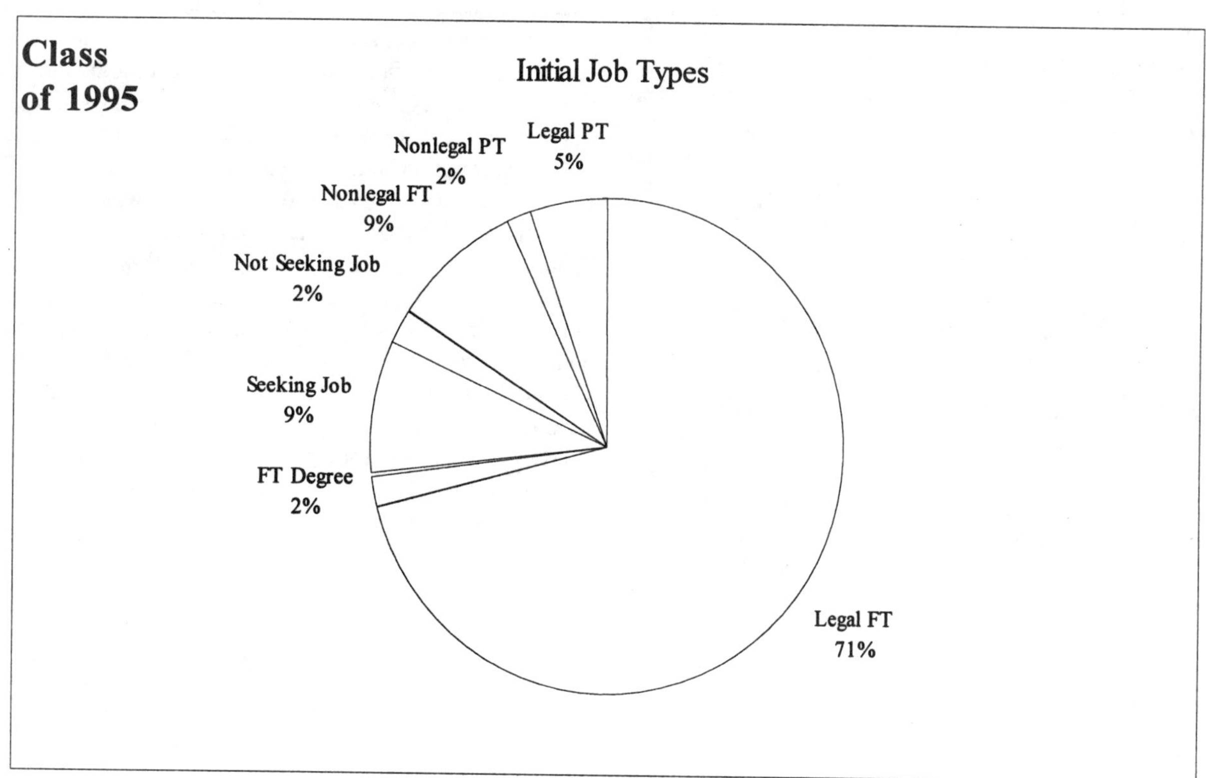

53.5% obtained private practice jobs compared with 60% of non-minority men. Viewed from another perspective, minorities -- who as a group constituted about 16% of the Class of 1995 -- obtained 14.2% of all law firm jobs obtained by the Class of 1995.

Graduates with Disabilities

NALP data on the Class of 1995 included a total of 273 graduates with disabilities. Compared to non-disabled graduates, disabled graduates were more likely to be unemployed six months after graduation and those who were employed were less likely to be employed in full-time legal positions. About half of the employed disabled graduates obtained jobs in private practice, while 18% obtained government jobs and 5.6% obtained public interest positions. Business and clerkships accounted for 13.6% and 10.5% of jobs, respectively. The median salary for disabled graduates was $36,000 compared to the national median for all graduates of $40,000.

Older Graduates

The median age of the Class of 1995 was 26. Compared to their counterparts age 30 or younger, those 31 or older were far less likely to be employed in a full-time legal job and far more likely to be employed in a nonlegal position. Unemployment rates were somewhat higher among graduates age 41 or older, but a larger portion of those who were unemployed reported that they were not seeking employment.

Jobs in business and academic settings were considerably more common among older employed graduates. While only 8.9% of employed graduates in the 20-25 age bracket acquired jobs in business and industry, about one-fifth of those age 36 or older did so.

Women age 31-35 reported median salaries of $41,600 and men age 31-35 reported median salaries of $46,000. Similarly, women age 41-45 reported median salaries of $40,000 while men in that same age bracket reported salaries of $48,000.

Geography Impacts Employment and Compensation of New Graduates

Two regions, the Mid-Atlantic and South Atlantic (US Census Bureau Regions) dominated the job market for new graduates, accounting for a plurality (40.7%) of the jobs obtained by the Class of 1995 for which a location was reported. The East North Central and Pacific states each accounted for an additional 13-14% of jobs. The East South Central and Mountain states accounted for the fewest jobs.

Median starting salaries were generally higher and more dispersed in regions supporting more jobs. Among these large regions, the median starting salary was the highest in the Pacific states and at $48,000 it was considerably above the $43,000 average starting salary in the Mid-Atlantic region -- the one that accounted for the most jobs.

Five Year Overview

During the past few years, the legal profession has weathered an economic recession which affected the employment of recent law school graduates. Since 1990, the number of law school graduates has increased while the percentage of graduates acquiring jobs in private practice has declined. Compensation levels have plateaued. The 1992 figure of $40,000 compared to $36,000 for 1991 is a result of increased percentage of jobs acquired in smaller and medium-sized firms -- firms which typically compensate at somewhat lower levels than larger private practice organizations. The chart to the bottom right illustrates the nature of the recent job market:

---

*The National Association for Law Placement is a nonprofit educational organization dedicated to meeting the needs of all participants in the legal employment process -- law schools, legal employers, and law students and graduates. Contributors to the preceding information included: Susan Benson, Director of Career Services, University of San Diego School of Law; Kathleen Brady, Assistant Dean of Career Planning and Placement, Fordham University School of Law; Deborah Hirsch, Assistant Dean for Career Services, University of Houston Law Center; Beth Kirch, Director of Career Services, University of Georgia School of Law; Nancy Krieger, formerly Director of Career Services, now Director of Alumni Services, University of Michigan Law School; Pam Malone, Assistant Dean for Career Services, Vanderbilt University School of Law; Cynthia L. Rold, Assistant Dean for Admissions and Financial Aid, Duke University School of Law; and Ellen Wayne, Assistant Dean and Director of Career Services, Columbia University Law School.

National Association for Law Placement (NALP) Charts

1995

	Number of Jobs Reported in Region	Median Salary for All Jobs
New England	1,627	$38,000
Mid Atlantic	5,480	$43,000
East North Central	3,819	$38,000
West North Central	1,864	$34,000
South Atlantic	5,230	$37,000
East South Atlantic	1,064	$35,000
West South Atlantic	2,392	$40,000
Mountain	1,183	$35,500
Pacific	3,506	$48,800

1995

	Number of Jobs Acquired	Median Salary
Academic	132	$35,000
Business/Industry	1,855	$43,000
Judical Clerkships	2,561	$34,000
Government	2,313	$33,000
Public Interest	274	$30,000
Private Practice All Sizes	9,774	$50,000
Private Practice 2-10 Attorneys	3,038	$32,500
Private Practice 11-25 Attorneys	1,185	$40,000
Private Practice 26-50 Attorneys	825	$48,000
Private Practice 51-100 Attorneys	879	$55,000
Private Practice 101-250	1,414	$62,000
Private Practice 250+ Attorneys	1,738	$72,000

	Class of 1990	Class of 1991	Class of 1992	Class of 1993	Class of 1994	Class of 1995
Number of Graduates	36,385	38,800	39,405	39,914	39,305	39,199
Percent employed six months post graduation	90%	85.9%	83.5%	83.4%	84.7%	86.7%
Percent employed in Private Practice Jobs	62.9%	60.8%	59.0%	57.1%	55.0%	56.1%
Compensation medians (all jobs)	$40,000	$40,000	$36,000	$36,000	$37,000	$40,000
Most frequently reported salaries	NA	NA	NA	NA	$30,000 (6.6%) $35,000 (5.4%)	$30,000 (7.4%) $35,000 (5.1%)

Chapter Six

Bar Admissions

Written by Erica Moeser, President of the National Conference of Bar Examiners

General Information

In order to obtain a license to practice law, almost all law school graduates must apply for bar admission through a state board of bar examiners. Most often this board is an agency of the highest state court in the jurisdiction, but occasionally the board is connected more closely to the state's bar association. The criteria for eligibility to take the bar examination or to otherwise qualify for bar admission are set by each state.

Licensing involves a demonstration of worthiness in two distinct areas. The first is competence. For initial licensure, competence is ordinarily established by a showing that the applicant holds an acceptable educational credential (with rare exception, a J.D. degree) from a law school that meets acceptable or established educational standards, and by achieving a passing score on the bar examination.

The most common testing configuration consists of a two-day bar examination, one day of which is devoted to the Multistate Bar Examination, a standardized 200-item test covering six areas (Constitutional Law, Contracts, Criminal Law, Evidence, Real Property, and Torts). The second day of testing is typically comprised of locally-crafted essays and multiple choice questions from a broader range of subject matters, although in some states, nationally developed tests such as the Multistate Essay Examination and the Multistate Performance Test are used to round out the test.

In addition, almost all jurisdictions require that the applicant present an acceptable score on the Multistate Professional Responsibility Examination, which is separately administered three times each year.

The second area of inquiry by bar examiners involves the character and fitness of applicants for a law license. In this regard, bar examiners seek background information concerning each applicant that is relevant to the appropriateness of granting a professional credential. Because law is a public profession, and because the degree of harm a lawyer, once licensed, can inflict is substantial, decisions about who should be admitted to practice law are made carefully by bar examining boards.

Boards of bar examiners in most jurisdictions expect to hear from prospective candidates during the final year of law school. Bar examinations are ordinarily offered at the end of February and July, with considerably more applicants taking the summer test because it falls after graduation from law school.

Some boards offer or require law student registration at an earlier point in law school. This preliminary processing, where available, permits the board to review character and fitness issues in advance.

As state-specific information is so important (and so variable) in the lawyer licensing process, law students are well-advised to contact the board in the jurisdiction(s) in which they are most likely to practice law.

Using the Charts in this Book

The charts provided in this book permit prospective law school applicants to learn something about the basic requirements for bar admission in each jurisdiction and to compare the performance of recent graduates from each school on the bar examination in those jurisdictions in which 30% or more of the law schools' graduates took the test. Note that the information provided relates to persons who took the bar examination in the state for the first time.

This information allows the reader to consider the following questions:

— Did graduates of one law school perform as well as the graduates of other law schools? For example, if 90% of one law school's graduates who took the test as first-time-takers passed the test compared to 60% from another law school, the prospective applicant may be validly concerned about whether the admissions policies of the second school are sufficiently selective, or whether the second school offers an education that will reasonably assure success on a licensing examination after three years of study.

— How does the passing percentage for first-time-takers at a law school compare with the overall pass rate for first-time-takers in the state? For example, while a law school with a passing percentage of 75% may be doing relatively well in a jurisdiction with an overall pass rate of 60%, a 75% pass rate may be of some concern in a jurisdiction in which the overall pass rate is 93%.

Of course, there are many reasons why one law school may outperform another in the long- or the short-run, and bar performance alone should not be used as the sole measure of assessing law school quality. Because each state's bar examining board sets its own passing score on the bar examination, comparisons of the passing percentages for law schools across state lines may not be as useful to prospective applicants.

In any event, the material appearing with regard to bar admissions offers needed insight into the performance of each law school's graduates. As it is necessary to obtain a license in order to practice law, applicants are better equipped to make application and attendance decisions when armed with bar passage information.

BAR ADMISSIONS

	Generally, is graduation from an ABA approved law school required? *	Registration of law students required?	May students take the bar exam prior to graduation?	Certain law school courses required for admission?	Require Multistate Bar Exam?	Require Multistate Professional Responsibility Exam?	Summer - 1995		Summer - 1996	
							% of First Time Takers Passing	% of First Time Takers Passing from ABA Approved Law Schools	% of First Time Takers Passing	% of First Time Takers Passing from ABA Approved Law Schools
Alabama	NO[1]	YES	NO	NO	YES	YES	83.1%	89.8%	84.5%	96.0%
Alaska	YES	NO	NO	NO	YES	YES	84%	84%	83%	83%
Arizona	YES	NO	NO	NO	YES	YES	83.9%	83.5%	82.8%	82.8%
Arkansas	YES	NO	NO	NO	YES	YES	84%	84%	84.2%	84.2%
California	NO	YES	NO	NO	YES	YES	73.4%	83.1%	68.8%	77.4%
Colorado	YES	NO	NO	NO	YES	YES	88%	NA	87%	NA
Connecticut	NO[2]	NO	NO	NO	YES	YES	83%	83%	84%	84%
Delaware	YES	YES	NO	NO	YES	NO	NA	NA	NA	NA
D.C.	NO	NO	NO	NO	YES	YES	74%	74%	77.5%	NA
Florida	YES	YES	NO	NO	YES	YES	84.35%	84.39%	76.4%	76.43%
Georgia	NO[3]	NO	NO	NO	YES	YES	80.8%	84.3%	88%	90%
Hawaii	YES	NO	NO	NO	YES	YES	78%	78%	NA	NA
Idaho	YES	NO	NO	NO	YES	YES	75%	75%	NA	NA
Illinois	YES	YES	NO	NO	YES	YES	87%	87%	86%	86%
Indiana	YES	NO	YES	YES	NO	YES	86%	86%	78%	78%
Iowa	YES	YES	YES	NO	YES	YES	87%	87%	75.1%	75.1%
Kansas	YES	NO	YES	NO	YES	YES	81.9%	81.9%	83.3%	83.3%
Kentucky	YES	NO	NO	YES	YES	YES	88%	88%	83.6%	83.6%
Louisiana	YES	NO	NO	NO	NO	YES	55%	55%	68.6%	68.6%
Maine	NO	NO	NO	NO	YES	YES	74%	74%	NA	76%
Maryland	YES	YES	NO	NO	YES	NO	75%	75%	76%	76%
Massachusetts	YES	NO	NO	NO	YES	YES	82.5%	84.77%	81.1%	82.3%
Michigan	YES	NO	NO	NO	YES	YES	70%	70%	84%	84%
Minnesota	YES	NO	NO	NO	YES	YES	89.9%	89.9%	89.3%	89.3%
Mississippi	YES	YES	YES	NO	YES	YES	86.6%	86.6%	93.8%	93.8%
Missouri	YES	YES	NO	NO	YES	YES	92%	92%	82.8%	82.8%
Montana	YES	NO	NO	NO	YES	YES	90%	90%	94%	94%
Nebraska	YES	NO	YES	NO	YES	YES	94%	94%	96.6%	96.6%
Nevada	YES	NO	YES	NO	YES	YES	69%	69%	69%	69%

* Graduation from a state-approved law school which is not ABA approved may qualify a person to take the bar examination in the state in which the school is located, but may not qualify the person for the examination in other states. You may wish to contact the bar admission authorities in the state(s) in which you intend to practice for more information on whether graduation from a law school that is not approved will qualify you to take the bar examination in that state. Please note that many jurisdictions have exceptions to the general rule. For example, many jurisdictions will allow individuals who did not graduate from an ABA approved law school to sit for the bar exam if they have been admitted to practice law in another state for a set amount of years.

1 The state of Alabama allows graduates of non-ABA approved schools to sit for the bar exam if the schools are located in the state of Alabama.

2 Connecticut will allow graduates of law schools approved by the Connecticut Bar Examiner Committee to sit for the bar exam.

3 Effective January 1, 1998 an applicant must be a graduate of an ABA approved law school in order to be eligible for admission in Georgia.

BAR ADMISSIONS

	Generally, is graduation from an ABA approved law school required?*	Registration of law students required?	May students take the bar exam prior to graduation?	Certain law school courses required for admission?	Require Multistate Bar Exam?	Require Multistate Professional Responsibility Exam?	Summer - 1995		Summer - 1996	
							% of First Time Takers Passing	% of First Time Takers Passing from ABA Approved Law Schools	% of First Time Takers Passing	% of First Time Takers Passing from ABA Approved Law Schools
New Hampshire	YES	YES	NO	NO	YES	YES	79.2%	79.2%	NA	NA
New Jersey	YES	NO	NO	NO	YES	YES	78%	78%	78%	78%
New Mexico	YES	NO	NO	NO	YES	YES	92%	NA	89%	NA
New York	YES	NO	NO	NO	YES	YES	78%	NA	78%	81%
North Carolina	YES	NO	YES	NO	YES	YES	85%	85%	81%	81%
North Dakota	YES	YES	NO	NO	YES	YES	85%	85%	90%	90%
Ohio	YES	YES	NO	YES	YES	YES	93%	93%	90%	90%
Oklahoma	YES	YES	NO	NO	YES	YES	75%	75%	81%	81%
Oregon	YES	NO	NO	NO	YES	YES	85%	85%	77%	77%
Pennsylvania	YES	NO	NO	NO	YES	NO	72.5%	72.5%	71.3%[4]	71.3%[4]
Rhode Island	YES	NO	NO	NO	YES	YES	71%	71%	67%	67%
South Carolina	YES	NO	NO	NO	YES	YES	92%	92%	90%	90%
South Dakota	YES	NO	NO	NO	YES	YES	91%	91%	86%	86%
Tennessee	YES	NO	NO	NO	YES	YES	79%	91.3%%	81%	86.8%
Texas	YES	YES	YES	NO	YES	YES	82.3%	82.3%	84.4%	84.4%
Utah	YES	NO	NO	NO	YES	YES	92%	92%	88.1%	88.1%
Vermont	YES	NO	NO	NO	YES	YES	78%	77%	90%	90%
Virginia	YES	NO	YES	NO	YES	NO	76.4%	76.7%	79.6%	79.9%
Washington	YES	NO	NO	NO	NO	NO	83%	83%	75.7%	75.7%
West Virginia	YES	NO	NO	NO	YES	YES	89%	89%	80%	80%
Wisconsin	YES	NO	YES	NO	YES	NO	83%	83%	92%	92%
Wyoming	YES	YES	NO	NO	YES	YES	59%	59%	55%	55%
Guam	YES	NO	NO	NO	YES	YES	82%	82%	NA	NA
N. Mariana Isl.	YES	NO	NO	NO	YES	YES	40%	40%	NA	NA
Puerto Rico	YES	NO	NO	NO	NO	NO	68%	69%	71%	71%
Virgin Islands	YES		NO	NO	YES	NO	72%	72%	NA	NA

* Graduation from a state-approved law school which is not ABA approved may qualify a person to take the bar examination in the state in which the school is located, but may not qualify the person for the examination in other states. You may wish to contact the bar admission authorities in the state(s) in which you intend to practice for more information on whether graduation from a law school that is not approved will qualify you to take the bar examination in that state. Please note that many jurisdictions have exceptions to the general rule. For example, many jurisdictions will allow individuals who did not graduate from an ABA approved law school to sit for the bar exam if they have been admitted to practice law in another state for a set amount of years.

4 This represents the over-all pass rate for Pennsylvania -- not the pass rate for first time takers.

DIRECTORY OF STATE BAR ADMISSION OFFICES

ALABAMA
Board of Bar Examiners
Alabama State Bar
P.O. Box 671
Montgomery, AL 36101
TEL: 205/269-1515

ALASKA
Committee of Law Examiners
Alaska Bar Association
P.O. Box 100279
Anchorage, AK 99510
TEL: 907/272-7469

ARIZONA
Committee on Examinations
and Character and Fitness
111 W. Monroe
Phoenix, AZ 85003-1742
TEL: 602/340-7295

ARKANSAS
State Board of Law Examiners
2400 Justice Building
625 Marshall
Little Rock, AR 72201
TEL: 501/374-1855

CALIFORNIA
The State Bar of California
Office of Admissions
555 Franklin Street
San Francisco, CA 94102
TEL: 415/561-8303

COLORADO
Supreme Court
Board of Law Examiners
600 17th St., Ste. 520-S
Denver, CO 80202
TEL: 303/893-8096

CONNECTICUT
Connecticut Bar Examining
Committee
287 Main Street
East Hartford, CT 06118-1885
TEL: 203/568-3450

DELAWARE
Board of Bar Examiners for
the State of Delaware
200 W. Ninth St., Ste. 300-B
Wilmington, DE 19801
TEL: 302/658-7309

DIST. OF COLUMBIA
Director of Admissions
D.C. Court of Appeals
Room 4200
500 Indiana Avenue, N.W.
Washington, DC 20001
TEL: 202/879-2710

FLORIDA
Florida Board of Bar Examiners
1891 Eider Court
Tallahassee, FL 32399-1750
TEL: 904/487-1292

GEORGIA
Supreme Court of Georgia
Office of Bar Admissions
P.O. Box 38466
Atlanta, GA 30334-0466
TEL: 404/656-3490

GUAM
Superior Court of Guam
Guam Judicial Center
120 West O'Brien Drive
Agana, GU 96910
TEL: 671/475-3199

HAWAII
Bar Admission Attorney
Supreme Court of Hawai'i
Ali'i lani Hale
417 South King Street
Honolulu, HI 96813-2912
TEL: 808/539-4977

IDAHO
Admissions Administrator
Idaho State Bar
PO Box 895
525 West Jefferson
Boise, ID 83701
TEL: 208/334-4500

ILLINOIS
Illinois Board of Admissions
to the Bar
430 First of America Center
Springfield, IL 62701
TEL: 217/522-5917

INDIANA
Indiana State Board of
Law Examiners
Suite 1070, South. Tower
115 W. Washington St., #1070
Indianapolis, IN 46204-3417
TEL: 317/232-2552

IOWA
Clerk
Supreme Court of Iowa
State Capitol Building
Des Moines, IA 50319
TEL: 515/281-5911

KANSAS
Kansas Board of Law
Examiners
Kansas Judicial Center
301 S. West 10th Ave., Rm.374
Topeka, KS 66612
TEL: 913/296-8410

KENTUCKY
Kentucky Board of Bar
Examiners
1510 Newtown Pike, Suite X
Lexington, KY 40511
TEL: 606/246-2381

LOUISIANA
Louisiana Committee on
Bar Admissions
601 St. Charles Avenue
New Orleans, LA 70130
TEL: 504/566-1600

MAINE
Maine Board of Bar Examiners
P.O. Box 30
Augusta, ME 04332-0030
TEL: 207/623-2464

MARYLAND
State Board of Law Examiners
People's Resource Center
100 Community Pl., Rm. 1.210
Crownsville, MD 21032-2026
TEL: 410/514-7044

MASSACHUSETTS
Massachusetts Board of Bar
Examiners
77 Franklin Street
Boston, MA 02110-1593
TEL: 617/482-4466, 4467

MICHIGAN
Michigan Board of Law
Examiners
200 Washington Square North
P.O. Box 30104
Lansing, MI 48909
TEL: 517/334-6992

MINNESOTA
Minnesota State Board of
Law Examiners
Minnesota Judicial Center
25 Constitution Avenue
Suite 110
St. Paul, MN 55155
TEL: 612/297-1800

MISSISSIPPI
Mississippi Board of
Bar Admissions
P.O. Box 1449
Jackson, MS 39215-1449
TEL: 601/354-6055

MISSOURI
Missouri State Board of
Law Examiners
P.O. Box 150
Jefferson City, MO 65102
TEL: 573/751-4144

MONTANA
Board of Bar Examiners
Room 315, Justice Building
215 North Sanders
Helena, MT 59620
TEL: 406/444-2621

NEBRASKA
Nebraska State Bar Commission
635 South 14th Street
P.O. Box 81809
Lincoln, NE 68501
TEL: 402/475-7091

NEVADA
State Bar of Nevada
201 Las Vegas Blvd. South
Suite 200
Las Vegas, NV 89101
TEL: 702/382-2200

NEW HAMPSHIRE
Clerk of the Supreme Court
Supreme Court Building
Noble Drive
Concord, NH 03301
TEL: 603/271-2646

NEW JERSEY
New Jersey Board of Bar
Examiners, CN 973
Trenton, NJ 08625
TEL: 609/984-7785

NEW MEXICO
New Mexico State Board of
Bar Examiners
9420 Indian School Rd. NE
Albuquerque, NM 87112
TEL: 505/271-9706

NEW YORK
New York State Board of
Law Examiners
7 Executive Centre Drive
Albany, NY 12203
TEL: 518/452-8700

NORTH CAROLINA
Board of Bar Examiners
P.O. Box 2946
208 Fayetteville Street
Raleigh, NC 27602
TEL: 919/828-4886

NORTH DAKOTA
State Bar Board
1st Floor, Judicial Wing
600 East Boulevard Avenue
Bismarck, ND 58505-0530
TEL: 701/328-4201
TDD: 701/328-2884

NORTHERN MARIANA ISLANDS
Supreme Court of the
Commonwealth of the
Northern Mariana Islands
P.O. Box 2165 CK
Saipan, MP 96950
TEL: 670/234-5175

OHIO
Ohio Board of Bar Examiners
Rhodes State Office Tower
30 East Broad Street, 2nd Floor
Columbus, OH 43215-3414
TEL: 614/466-1541

OKLAHOMA
Oklahoma Board of
Bar Examiners
P.O. Box 53036
Oklahoma City, OK 73152
TEL: 405/524-2365

OREGON
Admissions Director
5200 SW Meadows Road
P.O. Box 1689
Lake Oswego, OR 97035-0889
TEL: 503/620-0222 ext. 410

PENNSYLVANIA
Pennsylvania Board of
Law Examiners
5035 Ritter Road
Mechanicsburg, PA 17055
TEL: 717/795-7270

PUERTO RICO
Commonwealth of Puerto Rico
Supreme Court
P.O. Box 2392
San Juan, PR 00902-2392
TEL: 809/725-5030

RHODE ISLAND
Chief Deputy Clerk/Bar
Providence County Court Hse.
250 Benefit Street
Providence, RI 02903
TEL: 401/277-3272

SOUTH CAROLINA
South Carolina State Board of
Law Examiners
P.O. Box 11330
Columbia, SC 29211
TEL: 803/734-1080

SOUTH DAKOTA
South Dakota Board of
Bar Examiners
500 East Capitol
Pierre, SD 57501
TEL: 605/773-4898

TENNESSEE
Nashville City Center
511 Union Street, Suite 1420
Nashville, TN 37243-0740
TEL: 615/741-3234

TEXAS
Texas Board of Law Examiners
P.O. Box 13486
Austin, TX 78711-3486
TEL: 512/463-1621

UTAH
Utah State Bar
645 South 200 East
Salt Lake City, UT 84111-3834
TEL: 801/531-9077

VERMONT
Board of Bar Examiners
109 State Street
Montpelier, VT 05609-0702
TEL: 802/828-3281

VIRGIN ISLANDS
Committee of Bar Examiners
US District Court
P.O. Box 720
Charlotte Amalie,
St. Thomas, VI 00801
TEL: 809/774-5480

VIRGINIA
Virginia Board of
Bar Examiners
Shockoe Center, Suite 225
11 South 12th Street
Richmond, VA 23219
TEL: 804/786-7490

WASHINGTON
Washington Board of Bar
Examiners
500 Westin Building
2001 Sixth Avenue
Seattle, WA 98121-2599
TEL: 206/727-8209

WEST VIRGINIA
West Virginia Board of
Law Examiners
Building 1, E-400
1900 Kanawha Blvd., E.
Charleston, WV 25305-0837
TEL: 304/558-7815

WISCONSIN
Board of Bar Examiners
119 Martin Luther King, Jr.
Boulevard, Room 405
Madison, WI 53703-3355
TEL: 608/266-9760

WYOMING
State Board of Law Examiners
of Wyoming
P.O. Box 109
Cheyenne, WY 82003-0109
TEL: 307/632-9061

Chapter Seven

Other Organizations

Association of American Law Schools (AALS)

Founded in 1900, the nonprofit AALS has grown to 160 member law schools. The purpose of the Association is "the improvement of the legal profession through legal education." To carry out this mission, the AALS serves as the learned society for law teachers. It facilitates excellence in legal education through workshops, conferences, a quarterly newsletter and other publications, including the *AALS Directory of Law Teachers*, provided to law teachers and law schools. In addition, the AALS is legal education's principal representative to the federal government and to other national higher education organizations and learned societies.

Association of American Law Schools
1201 Connecticut Avenue, NW
Suite 800
Washington, DC 20036-2605
(202) 296-8851
http://www.aals.org

Law School Admission Council (LSAC)

LSAC is a nonprofit corporation whose members are 194 U.S. and Canadian law schools. It is best known as the sponsor of the Law School Admission Test (LSAT). Its other services include the Law School Data Assembly Service, which summarizes applicants' prior academic work and distributes that information to the law schools to which each candidate applies; Law School Forums--recruitment fairs, free-of-charge to applicants, held in seven American cities each year; and a host of outreach programs targeted to minorities underrepresented in the legal profession.

Law School Admission Council
Box 2000
Newtown, PA 18940-0998
(215) 968-1001
http://www.lsac.org

National Association for Law Placement (NALP)

Since its founding in 1971, the National Association for Law Placement (NALP) has served the legal community as a nonprofit organization dedicated to meeting the needs of the participants in the legal employment process. NALP provides information, coordination and standards that pertain to the hiring of law students and attorneys, and fosters fair and informed decision-making in legal career planning, recruiting and employment.

Virtually all of the ABA-accredited law schools and approximately 850 legal employers, including most of the largest law firms, corporations, public interest and government agencies are NALP members.

NALP is widely respected for its ability to provide essential research data on legal recruiting and employment. NALP's research spans more than two decades and is extensively referenced throughout the legal community. Additionally, NALP publishes definitive print and electronic resources designed to support clear and accurate communication between and education of all participants in the legal hiring process.

National Association for Law Placement
1666 Connecticut Avenue, Suite 325
Washington, DC 20009-1039
(202) 667-1666
http://www.nalp.org

National Conference of Bar Examiners (NCBE)

The nonprofit NCBE was formed in 1931. Its mission is to "work with other institutions to develop, maintain, and apply reasonable and uniform standards of education and character for eligibility for admission to the practice of law." The NCBE assists bar authorities in the various jurisdictions by providing uniform, high quality standardized examinations for testing applicants for admission to the practice of law, disseminating information concerning admission standards and practices and conducting educational programs for members and staffs of bar authorities. The NCBE also provides character and fitness services to the various bar authorities. NCBE tests include the Multistate Bar Exam and the Multistate Professional Responsibility Examination. In conjunction with the ABA, the NCBE publishes the *Comprehensive Guide to Bar Admission Requirements* containing bar admission requirements in all U.S. jurisdictions.

National Conference of Bar Examiners
333 North Michigan Avenue
Suite 1025
Chicago, Illinois 60601
(312) 641-0963

Chapter Eight

Values of the Profession

(What follows is Part II, without comments, of the Statement of Fundamental Lawyering Skills and Professional Values, written by the ABA's Section of Legal Education and Admissions to the Bar's Task Force on Law Schools and the Profession: Narrowing the Gap, chaired by Robert MacCrate. The purpose of the group was to study and improve the process by which new members of the profession are prepared for the practice of law. The Task Force was a diverse group, reflecting the various segments of the profession. It included members of the federal and state judiciary, deans and faculty members of law schools, and members of the practicing bar.)

1. *Provision of Competent Representation*

As a member of a profession dedicated to the service of clients, a lawyer should be committed to the values of:

1.1 *Attaining a Level of Competence in One's Own Field of Practice, including:*

(a) With regard to lawyering skills, developing a degree of proficiency that is sufficient to enable the lawyer to represent the client competently or to acquire whatever additional degree of proficiency is needed within the time available for doing so and without inappropriately burdening the client's resources;

(b) With regard to substantive knowledge (including both knowledge of the law and familiarity with the fields and disciplines other than law), acquiring sufficient knowledge to enable the lawyer to represent clients competently or to acquire whatever additional knowledge is needed within the time available for doing so and without inappropriately burdening the client's resources;

(c) Developing a realistic sense of the limits of the lawyer's own skills and knowledge;

(d) Developing practices that will enable the lawyer to represent clients consistently with the ethical rules of the profession, including the rules that require a lawyer:

(i) Work diligently and zealously on a client's behalf;

(ii) Avoid conflicts of interest that undermine or appear to undermine the lawyer's loyalty to a client;

(iii) Preserve a client's confidences and secrets;

(iv) Refrain from handling matters that are beyond the lawyer's range of competence (*see* Value §§ 1.3(a)(ii), 1.3(b)(ii) *infra*);

1.2 *Maintaining a Level of Competence in One's Own Field of Practice*, including:

(a) With regard to lawyering skills, engaging in whatever forms of study and learning are necessary to attain the degree of expertise that may be expected of any competent practitioner at the lawyer's level of experience;

(b) With regard to substantive knowledge, attending to new developments in the law or other relevant fields or disciplines, and engaging in whatever forms of study and learning are necessary to attain the degree of expertise that may be expected of any competent practitioner at the lawyer's level of experience;

(c) As the lawyer improves his or her skills and expands his or her knowledge of the field, maintaining a realistic sense of the new limits of his or her skills and knowledge;

(d) Maintaining the conditions of physical and mental alertness necessary for competence, including:

(i) Remaining constantly alert to the existence of problems that may impede or impair the lawyer's ability to provide competent representation (such as alcohol abuse, drug abuse, psychological or emotional problems, senility, or other types of health problems);

(ii) To the extent that the lawyer's ability to provide competent representation is impeded or impaired, taking whatever steps are necessary to ensure competent representation of his or her clients, including, when appropriate:

(A) Seeking treatment to remedy the problems that have resulted in the impairment of the lawyer's abilities;

(B) Until the lawyer has regained competence, enlisting whatever aid is necessary (including aid from other lawyers) to allow the lawyer to competently represent his or her clients;

(C) If the lawyer is unable to competently represent a client even with assistance, withdrawing from the representation and referring the client to another lawyer;

1.3 *Representing Clients in a Competent Manner, including,*

(a) With regard to lawyering skills:

(i) Applying his or her skills in a competent manner;

(ii) If the representation of a particular client requires types of skills or a degree of proficiency that the lawyer does not presently possess:

(A) Assessing whether the client would be best served by the lawyer's acquisition of the requisite skills (assuming it is possible to do so within the time available and without inappropriately burdening the client's resources), or by the lawyer's enlisting the aid of other lawyers or other individuals, or by referring the client to another lawyer;

(B) Advising the client of the limits of the lawyer's skills and the steps the lawyer intends to take to overcome or compensate for his or her limitations;

(b) With regard to substantive knowledge of the law or of other fields or disciplines:

(i) Applying his or her knowledge in a competent manner;

(ii) If the representation of a particular client requires knowledge that the lawyer does not presently possess:

(A) Assessing whether the client would best be served by the lawyer's acquisition of the requisite knowledge (assuming it is possible to do so with the time available and without inappropriately burdening the client's resources), or by the lawyer's enlisting the aid of other lawyers or experts from other fields, or by referring the client to another lawyer;

(B) Advising the client of the limits of the lawyer's knowledge and the steps the lawyer intends to take to overcome or compensate for his or her limitations;

(c) Devoting the time, effort, and resources necessary to competently represent the client;

(d) Representing the client in a manner that is consistent with the ethical rules of the profession.

2. *Striving to Promote Justice, Fairness, and Morality*

2.1 *Promoting Justice, Fairness, and Morality in One's Own Daily Practice, including:*

(a) To the extent required or permitted by the ethical rules of the profession, acting in conformance with considerations of justice, fairness, or morality when making decisions or acting on behalf of a client;

(b) To the extent required or permitted by the ethical rules of the profession, counseling clients to take considerations of justice, fairness, and morality in account when the client makes decisions or engages in conduct that may have an adverse effect on other individuals or on society;

(c) Treating other people (including clients, other attorneys, and support personnel) with dignity and respect;

2.2 *Contributing to the Profession's Fulfillment of its Responsibility to Ensure that Adequate Legal Services Are Provided to Those Who Cannot Afford to Pay for Them;*

2.3 *Contributing to the Profession's Fulfillment of its Responsibility to Enhance the Capacity of Law and Legal Institutions to Do Justice.*

3. *Striving to Improve the Profession*

As a member of a "self-governing" profession (AMERICAN BAR ASSOCIATION, MODEL RULES OF PROFESSIONAL CONDUCT, Preamble (1983)), a lawyer should be committed to the values of:

3.1 *Participating in Activities Designed to Improve the Profession;*

3.2 *Assist in the Training and Preparation of New Lawyers and the Continuing Education of the Bar;*

3.3 *Striving to Rid the Profession of Bias Based on Race, Religion, Ethnic Origin, Gender, Sexual Orientation, Age, or Disability, and to Rectify the Effects of These Biases.*

4. *Professional Self-Development*

As a member of a "learned profession" (AMERICAN BAR ASSOCIATION, MODEL RULES OF PROFESSIONAL CONDUCT, Preamble (1983)), a lawyer should be committed to the values of:

4.1 *Seeking Out and Taking Advantage of Opportunities to Increase One's Own Knowledge and Improve One's Own Skills,* including:

(a) Making use of the process of reflecting upon and learning from experience, which entails:

(i) Critically assessing one's own performance so as to evaluate:

(A) The quality of the preparation for the performance, including:

(I) An assessment of the appropriateness of the goals set for the performance and an analysis of whether it would have been possible and desirable to define the goals differently;

(II) An assessment of the appropriateness of the means chosen to pursue the goals and an analysis of whether it would have been possible and desirable to employ different means;

(III) The extent to which the planning process correctly anticipated the contingencies that arose and effectively prepared for these contingencies;

(IV) The accuracy of one's assessments of the likely perspectives, concerns, and reactions of any individuals with whom one interacted (such as, for example, clients, other lawyers, judges, mediators, legislators, and government officials);

(B) The quality of the performance itself, including:

(I) The effectiveness of any applications of the lawyering skills;

(II) The quality of the execution of the plans for the performance;

(III) The appropriateness and effectiveness of one's reactions to any unexpected events;

(C) The extent to which ethical issues were properly identified and resolved;

(ii) Identifying practices that will make it possible to replicate effective aspects of the performance in the future and/or guard against repetition of ineffective ones, including:

(A) Methods of thinking or analysis that will make it possible to plan more effectively for performances;

(B) Methods of improving future performances, including one's applications of lawyering skills;

(C) Methods of improving one's own abilities to perceive or resolve ethical issues;

(b) Taking advantage of courses of study for increasing one's knowledge of one's own field of practice, other fields of legal practice, and other relevant disciplines;

(c) Employing a consistent practice of reading about new developments in the law or other relevant fields or disciplines;

(d) Periodically meeting with other lawyers in one's own field of practice or other fields for the purpose of discussing substantive law, techniques, or topical issues;

4.2 *Selecting and Maintaining Employment That Will Allow the Lawyer to Develop As A Professional and To Pursue His or Her Professional and Personal Goals.*

Chapter Nine

Geographic Location

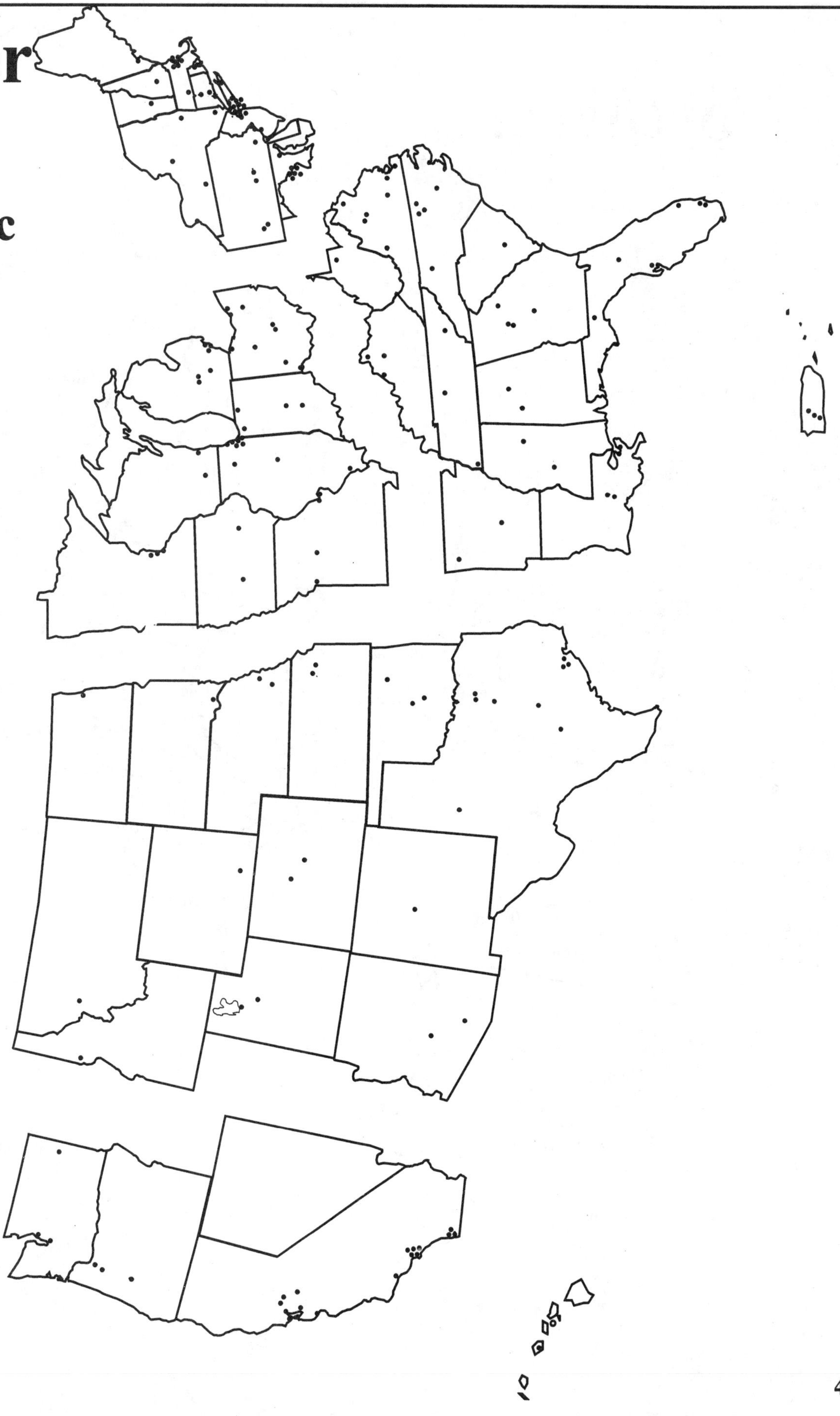

Northeast

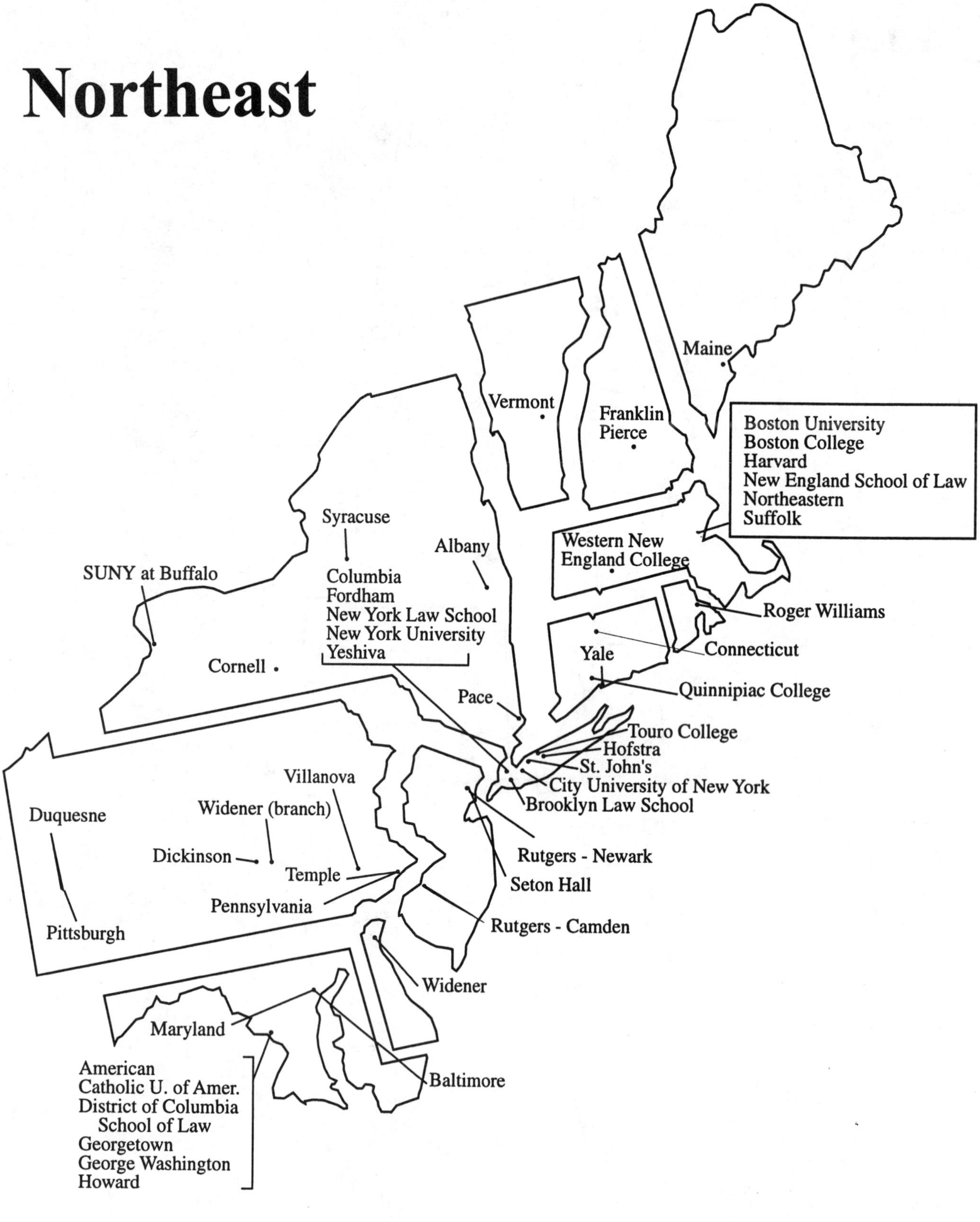

Maine

Vermont

Franklin Pierce

Boston University
Boston College
Harvard
New England School of Law
Northeastern
Suffolk

Western New England College

Roger Williams

Connecticut

Yale

Quinnipiac College

Syracuse

Albany

SUNY at Buffalo

Columbia
Fordham
New York Law School
New York University
Yeshiva

Cornell

Pace

Touro College

Hofstra

St. John's

City University of New York

Brooklyn Law School

Rutgers - Newark

Seton Hall

Rutgers - Camden

Villanova

Widener (branch)

Duquesne

Dickinson

Temple

Pennsylvania

Pittsburgh

Widener

Maryland

Baltimore

American
Catholic U. of Amer.
District of Columbia School of Law
Georgetown
George Washington
Howard

Midwest

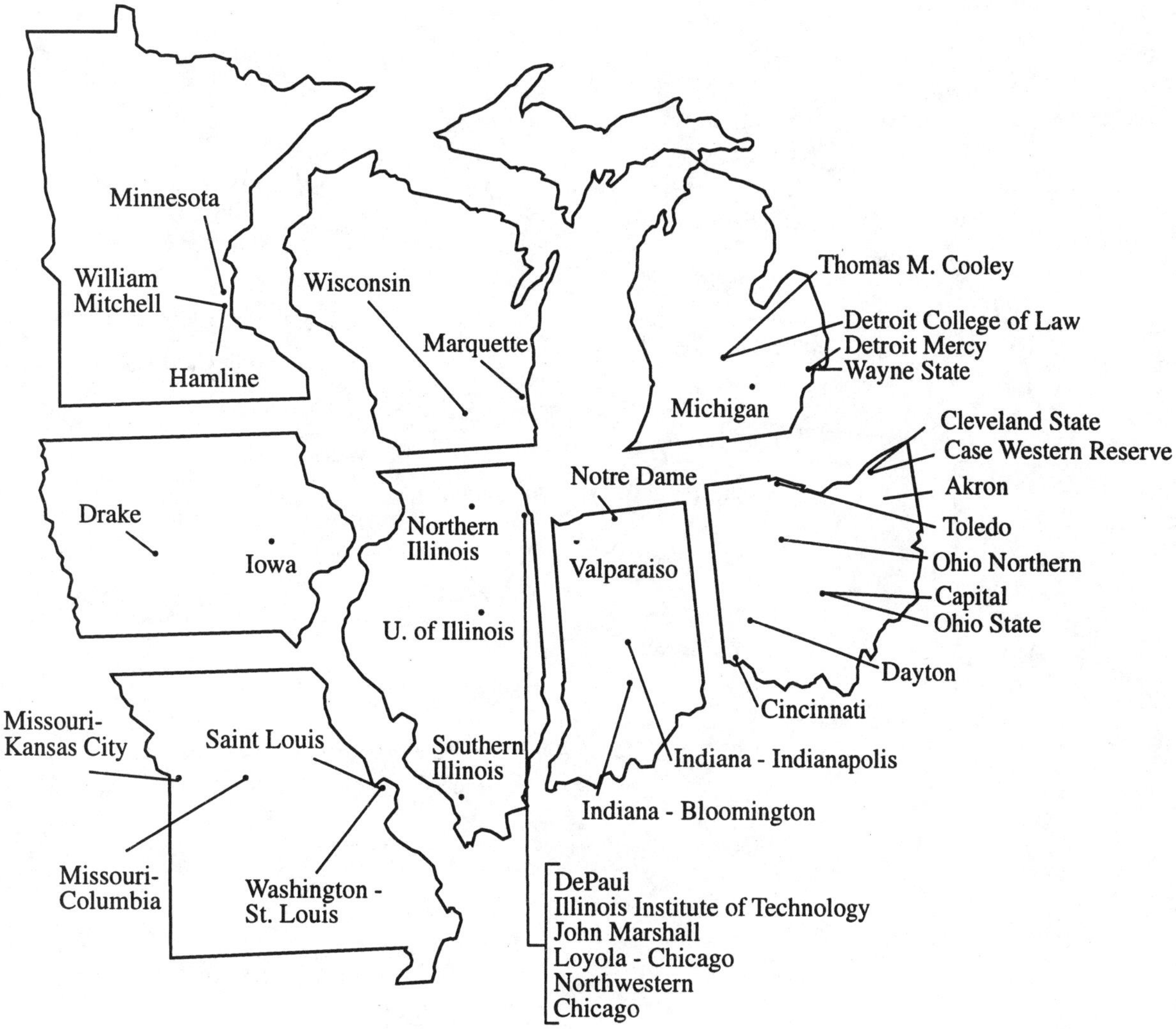

Minnesota
William Mitchell
Hamline
Wisconsin
Marquette
Michigan
Thomas M. Cooley
Detroit College of Law
Detroit Mercy
Wayne State
Cleveland State
Case Western Reserve
Akron
Toledo
Ohio Northern
Capital
Ohio State
Dayton
Cincinnati
Drake
Iowa
Northern Illinois
U. of Illinois
Southern Illinois
Notre Dame
Valparaiso
Indiana - Indianapolis
Indiana - Bloomington
Missouri-Kansas City
Saint Louis
Missouri-Columbia
Washington - St. Louis
DePaul
Illinois Institute of Technology
John Marshall
Loyola - Chicago
Northwestern
Chicago

Southeast

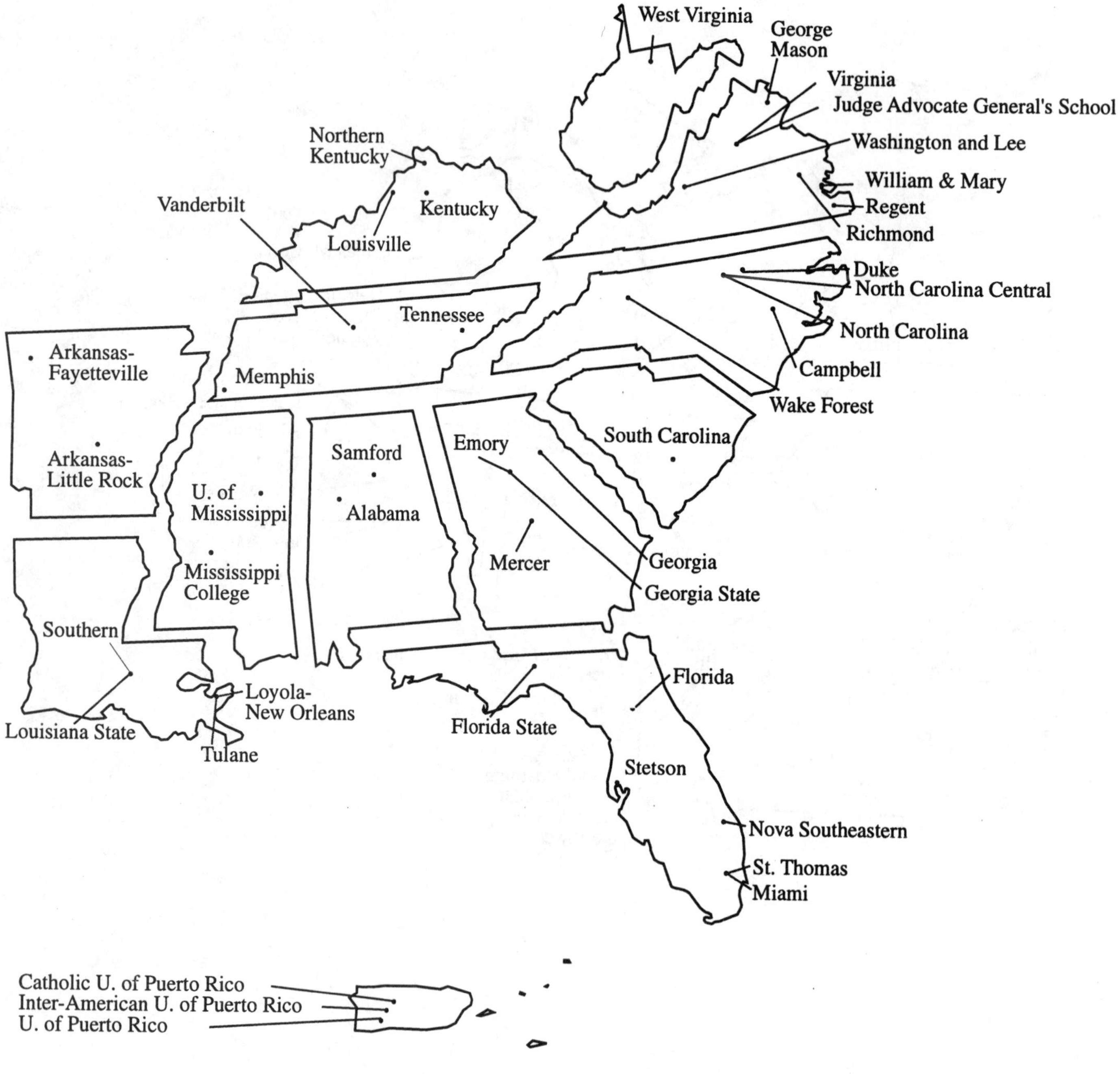

West Virginia
George Mason
Virginia
Judge Advocate General's School
Washington and Lee
William & Mary
Regent
Richmond
Northern Kentucky
Kentucky
Louisville
Vanderbilt
Duke
North Carolina Central
North Carolina
Campbell
Wake Forest
Tennessee
Memphis
Arkansas-Fayetteville
Arkansas-Little Rock
U. of Mississippi
Mississippi College
Samford
Alabama
Emory
South Carolina
Mercer
Georgia
Georgia State
Southern
Louisiana State
Loyola-New Orleans
Tulane
Florida
Florida State
Stetson
Nova Southeastern
St. Thomas
Miami
Catholic U. of Puerto Rico
Inter-American U. of Puerto Rico
U. of Puerto Rico

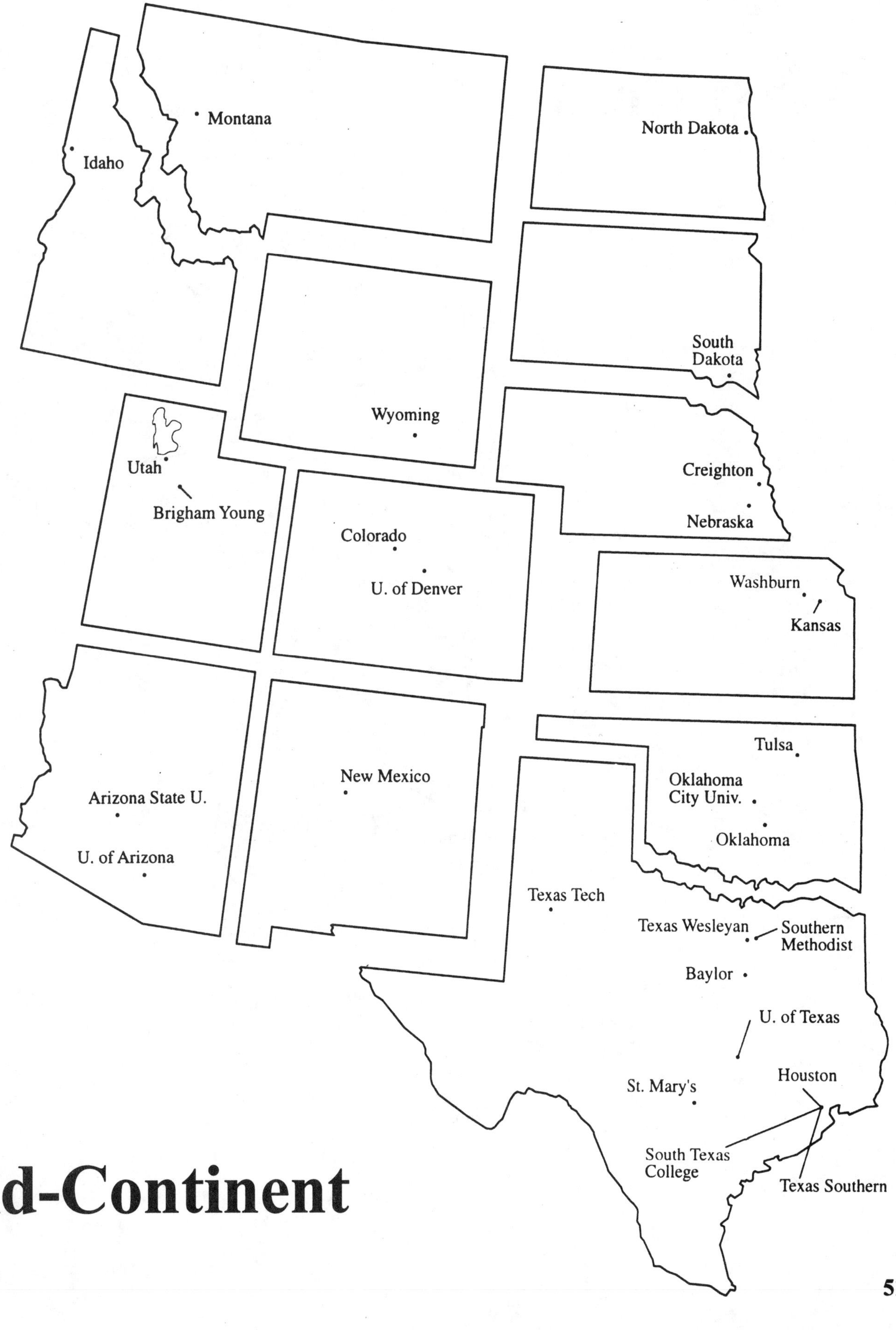

Mid-Continent

West Coast

U. of Washington
Seattle
Gonzaga
Willamette
Lewis and Clark
U. of Oregon
California-Davis
California-Berkeley
California-Hastings
Golden Gate
McGeorge
U. of San Francisco
Santa Clara
Stanford
California-Los Angeles
Loyola Marymount
Pepperdine
Southwestern
Whittier
Southern California
San Diego
California Western
Thomas Jefferson
University of Hawaii

Chapter Ten

About the Data

The purpose of this book is to provide consumers with basic information about approved schools in a similar format. However, it should be noted that applicants should not use this book as the sole source of information regarding application and admission. Rather, this book should supplement other avenues of evaluating respective schools including making direct contact with admission offices, professors, students, alumni or a prelaw advisor.

The information made available through this publication was collected from questionnaires completed during the Fall 1996 academic semester and submitted by American Bar Association ("ABA") approved law schools to the ABA's Consultant on Legal Education as part of the accreditation process. The completed questionnaires provided to the Consultant's Office are certified by the Dean of each law school. Each certification is submitted to the Consultant's Office as an assurance that the information provided accurately reflects prevailing conditions at the law school for which the certification is given. However, the Consultant's Office conducts no audit to verify the accuracy of the information submitted by the respective institutions.

The information contained in this book is only a small portion of what is collected in the questionnaire for accreditation purposes. Standard 509 of the *ABA Standards for Approval of Law Schools* and the Department of Education mandate as a minimum what basic information should be available to consumers. As a result of these requirements, this book contains a two-page spread on each law school approved by the ABA. Each page is divided into different segments as discussed below. In addition, much of the same data are displayed on three charts to facilitate side by side comparisons.

SCHOOL NAME

The law schools are arranged in alphabetical order by their main institutional name. Please note that some schools are known by more than one name. If the school is provisionally approved as of October 1, 1996 it will be stated next to the name of the school. The students at provisionally approved law schools and persons who graduate while a school is provisionally approved are entitled to the same recognition accorded under the ABA Standards to students and graduates of fully approved law schools.

In addition to listing the name, the two-page spread also contains contact information for each school. Currently, two schools are in the process of moving locations; and hence, they will have new addresses. Whittier College is currently in the process of moving from its Los Angeles, California campus to a new campus in Orange County California. The Detroit College of Law has affiliated itself with Michigan State University and is in the process of moving its campus from Detroit to Lansing, Michigan.

THE BASICS

The "Basic" section of the spread contains a variety of basic information.

Type of School: All ABA approved law schools are either public or private. "Public" means that the school receives money from the state in which the school resides. "Private" indicates the school is not operated by the state.

Application Deadline: Application deadline for the 1996-97 academic year. Not all schools have specific deadlines for admission applications. If the item is left blank it means that the school does not have a deadline. If the date has "pr" next to it, it means that the school prefers the application by the date stated.

Financial Aid Deadline: Financial Aid deadline for the 1996-97 academic year. Indicates the deadline for the school's financial aid form. The school deadline may not be the same as Federal and State deadlines. If the item is left blank it means that the school does not have a deadline. If the date has "pr" next to it, it means that the school prefers the application by the date stated.

Student Faculty Ratio: A formula indicating the relative number of students per instructor. The formula is used and developed as part of the *ABA Standards for Approval of Law Schools*. The ratio is calculated by comparing faculty full-time equivalency (FTE) to FTE of JD enrollment. A general definition of Faculty FTE is as follows: Total "Full-time" faculty, plus "Additional Instructional Resources." Additional instructional resources include administrators who teach, and part-time faculty. Teaching administrators and part-time faculty are included in the faculty FTE at differing weighted factors ranging from .2 to .7. FTE of JD enrollment is calculated as follows: Full-time JD enrollment plus two-thirds of part-time JD enrollment less enrollment in semester-abroad programs.

First Year Can Start Other Than Fall: This indicates whether the school has an entering class other than in the fall term.

Student Housing: This indicates whether student housing is available on campus and whether it is specifically reserved for law students.

Term: This indicates whether the school operates on a semester, quarter or trimester system.

FACULTY

This section of the two-page spread contains detail information on the number, gender, and race of the teachers at the school as of October 1, 1996. Hence, teachers present in the spring academic year but not in the fall are not counted. The five categories of faculty are mutually exclusive. Teachers on "leave" or sabbatical during the Fall 1996 term are not included in the full-time faculty count. The "Full-time" row indicates tenured or tenure-track faculty. "Other full-time"

indicates nontenured Professional Skills Instructors and nontenured Legal Writing Instructors. "Deans, librarians, & others who teach" are law school administrators who teach at least halftime. Administrators who teach are typically at the school and available to students during the entire year. For this reason they are included regardless of whether their teaching load is in the fall or spring. Part-time during the fall semester includes: Adjuncts, Permanent Part-time, Faculty from Another Unit, Part-time Professional Skills, and Emeritus Part-time. It should be noted that some schools may have low part-time numbers in the fall semester because at their school most of the part-time instruction occurs in the spring semester. The "Total" row combines figures from the "Full-time" row through the "Part-time" row. "Deans, librarians, & others who teach < half" are law school administrators who teach less than halftime in the fall or spring.

LIBRARY

This section of the two-page spread contains basic information about the law library. In addition, it contains a little information about the physical size of the school.

Number of volume & volume equivalents: "Volumes" refers to the total number of law and law-related books held by the law school at the end of the 1995-96 fiscal year. "Volume equivalents" is also the number held at the end of the 1995-96 fiscal year. Volume equivalents are computed as follows: Microfiche, Six fiche = 1 volume. Microfilm, 1 roll = 5 volumes.

Title: Each item for which a separate shelf bibliographic unit record has been made.

Active serial subscription: Subscriptions where pieces/parts/updates have been received on a regular or irregular basis during the last two years.

Study seating capacity inside the library: This indicates the number of study seats available for library users.

Square feet of law library: This is the total square footage of the law library.

Square feet of law school (Excluding Library): This is the square footage of the law school, excluding the library.

Number of professional staff: This is the number of professional librarians, including teaching librarians.

Hours per week with professional staff: This indicates the number of hours per week that professional staff are on duty in the library.

Hours per week without professional staff: This indicates the number of hours per week the library is open (regular schedule) minus the number of hours per week professional staff are on duty. Please note that many schools also allow students to have access to the library twenty-four hours a day.

Number of student computer workstations: This indicates the number of workstations (networked or stand alone) inside the library and elsewhere in the law school that are available to students. Please note that some ABA approved law schools require their students to possess their own personal computer -- which would not be counted for these purposes.

Number of additional networked connections: This number indicates the number of additional network ports (excluding those listed above) available to students inside the library and elsewhere in the law school. Please note that this is not a computer workstation; this number represents the number of network ports.

ENROLLMENT & ATTRITION

This section represents the JD enrollment by each class, year and division. Students are classified for purposes of enrollment statistics on the basis of whether they are carrying a full load in the division in which they are enrolled. Minority group enrollment is the total enrollment of students who classify themselves as African American, American Indian or Alaskan Native; Asian or Pacific Islander; Mexican American; Puerto Rican; and other Hispanic-American. Although Puerto Rican law students enrolled in the three approved law schools in Puerto Rico are not classified as minority students in the "Survey of Minority Group Students Enrolled in J.D. Programs in Approved Law Schools," they are counted as minorities in all other areas. Nonresident alien students are not included as minority students. Attrition percentages were based on Fall 1995 enrollment.

JD Degrees Awarded: This indicates the total number of JD degrees awarded during the 1995-96 academic year. The number of degrees awarded to graduates of each division is stated separately. Note: Thomas Jefferson School of Law was not on the approved list of ABA law schools during the 1995-96 academic year.

CURRICULUM

All information in this category should be based on the 12-month period beginning at the close of the prior academic year (e.g. June 1995 through May 1996). In courses where there was enrollment by both full-time and part-time students, schools were asked to classify each of those courses as "full-time" or "part-time" based on time of day and relative enrollment of full-time and part-time students. Some schools which have a part-time program experienced difficulty providing curriculum information distinguished between full-time and part-time. In those cases, the part-time column contains zeros. A "small section" means a section of a substantive law course, which may include a legal writing component; "small section" does not mean a legal writing section standing alone. A simulation course is one in which a substantial portion of the instruction is accomplished through the use of role playing or drafting exercises, e.g., trial advocacy, corporate planning and drafting, negotiations, and estate planning and drafting. The number of course titles, beyond the first year curriculum, offered the previous year refers only to classroom courses, not to clinical or field placement possibilities. If a title is offered in both the full-time program and part-time program, the school could count it once in both columns. Seminars are defined as courses requiring a written work product and having an enrollment limited to no more than 25. "Faculty-supervised clinics" are those courses or placements with other agencies in which full-time faculty have primary professional responsibility for all cases on which students are working. "Field placements" is a term in which someone other than full-time faculty has primary responsibility to the client; they are frequently called "externships or internships." Schools were also asked not to double count a single course by classifying it both as full-time and part-time. Law journal activities, advanced moot court or trial competitions reflected those students beyond the first year who participated in those activities during the previous year regardless of whether the student received credit.

GPA & LSAT SCORES

This section of the two-page spread contains statistics on the 1996 entering class. All persons in the particular category, regardless of whether that person was admitted through any special admissions program rather than through the normal admissions process was included. The admissions year was calculated from October 1, 1995 through September 30, 1996. Schools which admit in the spring and/or summer were to include those students in the totals. Figures on matriculants include all students who attended at least one class during the first week of the term in which they were admitted. All persons were counted, including those in any special admissions category, who were in that category from October 1, 1995 through September 30, 1996. For schools with part-time programs, where applications and admitted applicants could not be distinguished from full-time applications and admitted applicants, N/A's appear under the full-time and part-time columns and the total application and admission offers were entered under the total column.

Percentiles of GPA and LSAT: The GPA and LSAT scores represent the 75th and 25th percentile of the entering class. For example, if the entering class has 100 students, the 75th and 25th percentile could be determined by ranking the students with the best scores first and the worst scores last. The 25th highest score would indicate the 75th percentile; whereas, the 25th lowest score would indicate the 25th percentile. This computation is done separately for both the LSAT and the GPA. In theory, the 75th and 25th percentiles are a better indication of the quality of a class as compared to a median.

FINANCIAL AID

This indicates the number and percentage of students receiving internal grants or scholarships from law school or university sources. External grants such as state grants are not included. The percentage for full-time and part-time are based on the total number of full-time and part-time students, respectively. The total column percentage is based on total enrollment. All ABA approved law schools give away grants of some kind. However, a few schools did not submit any data for financial aid. Thus, if a school has reported $0 for the median grant amount, the school should be contacted directly to ascertain the correct figure.

TUITION

Full-time tuition: This represents the full-time tuition (plus annual fees) for the academic year for a typical first year student.

Part-time tuition: This represents the part-time tuition (plus annual fees) for the academic year for a typical first year student. Please note that some schools elected to report part-time tuition on a "per credit hour" basis.

Living Expenses: This represents the 1996-97 academic year total living expenses (room, board, etc.) and book expenses for full-time, single, resident students for "Living on campus," "Living off campus," and "Living at home." Tuition and fee charges are not included. The figures are used in analyzing law student budgets for loan purposes. Many schools use the same budget amount for all three categories.

CAREER PLACEMENT

This section represents statistics on the employment status of the 1995 graduating class six months after gradation. The employment percentages are based on the graduates whose employment status was "known." Hence, for the schools reporting a large percentage of graduates in which the employment status is unknown, the actual percentage employed may be significantly different -- higher or lower.

BAR PASSAGE

This section refers to numbers and percentages of 1995 graduates who took the Summer 1995 examination. The states' overall pass rate for first time takers and from ABA approved schools were obtained by an independent survey of each state bar authority. Please, note that bar exam rates often vary slightly because of the varying methodology utilized. For this book, schools reported data for the jurisdiction(s) in which a third or more of their students sat for the summer bar exam. If a third of the graduating class did not sit for one exam the school was required to report the state in which the highest number sat for the exam. Some schools opted to report statistics on more than one exam even though the they did not represent a third of the graduating class.

Please note, for the state of Georgia the state pass rate is a combination of the February 1995 test and the Summer 1995 test. In addition, please note that Wisconsin allows graduates of the University of Wisconsin School of Law and Marquette University School of Law to exercise the "diploma privilege" and be admitted to the bar without taking the examination.

Chapter Eleven

Comparison Charts

Please note that this book contains information concerning those law schools that were approved by the ABA as of October 1, 1996. The approval status of an individual law school could change, however. Therefore, if you would like to confirm whether an individual law school is approved by the ABA at a specific time after October 1, you should contact the ABA directly. Or you can access this information on the Section of Legal Education and Admissions to the Bar's Website. http://www.abanet.org/legaled

SECTION OF LEGAL EDUCATION AND ADMISSIONS TO THE BAR • ESTABLISHED 1893 • ABA

	CAREER PLACEMENT														BAR PASSAGE			
						Type of Employment						Location						
School	% Employment Status Known	% Employed	% Pursuing Graduate Degree	% Unemployed - Seeking	% Unemployed - Not Seeking	% in Law Firms	% in Business & Industry	% in Government	% in Public Interest	% in Judicial Clerkships	% in Academia	% Employed in State	# of States where Employed	% Employed in Foreign Nations	State where most take exam	Pass Rate for first-time test takers	State's Overall Pass Rate for first-time test takers	State's Pass Rate for first-time test takers from ABA Schools
Alabama																		
Alabama, U. of	98.9	90.9	3.4	5.1	0.6	60.4	8.2	10.1	1.9	17.0	2.5	78.0	12	1	AL	90.0	83.1	89.8
Samford U.	95.3	85.7	5.0	3.3	6.0	68.6	5.1	14.7	0.0	10.9	0.0	51.9	18	0	AL	94.0	83.1	89.8
Arizona																		
Arizona State U.	82.9	93.1	1.5	4.6	0.8	61.5	9.0	17.2	1.6	10.7	0.0	82.8	8	0	AZ	85.0	83.9	83.5
Arizona, U. of	99.4	83.1	4.6	8.4	3.9	43.8	12.5	21.1	5.5	15.6	1.6	68.8	18	0	AZ	90.3	83.9	83.5
Arkansas																		
Arkansas, U. of Fayetteville	96.6	87.6	3.5	3.5	5.3	67.7	12.1	14.1	0.0	5.1	1.0	42.4	9	1	AR	84.0	84.0	84.0
Arkansas, U. of Little Rock	32.5	92.1	2.6	2.6	2.6	48.6	28.6	11.4	2.9	5.7	2.9	77.1	3	0	AR	85.1	84.0	84.0
California																		
California Western School of Law	86.0	80.9	4.3	10.5	4.3	52.1	16.0	20.1	1.8	4.7	1.8	65.1	24	0	CA	81.6	73.4	83.1
California-Hastings	92.0	71.1	2.4	11.1	15.4	60.5	11.4	12.6	3.8	8.8	3.4	64.6	21	0	CA	79.2	73.4	83.1
California-Los Angeles	98.9	91.8	0.8	6.0	1.5	75.1	2.9	9.4	3.7	8.2	0.8	82.9	9	0	CA	88.8	73.4	83.1
California-Berkeley	97.7	93.3	2.2	3.7	0.8	74.5	4.4	7.2	2.4	11.2	0.4	69.7	19	1	CA	90.4	73.4	83.1
California-Davis	95.1	82.5	1.3	15.6	0.7	52.0	8.7	21.3	3.9	12.6	1.6	90.6	11	0	CA	92.9	73.4	83.1
Golden Gate U.	52.6	75.8	3.3	16.5	4.4	50.7	23.2	13.0	8.7	1.5	2.9	79.7	10	0	CA	76.5	73.4	83.1
Loyola Marymount U.	85.0	83.3	2.2	12.0	2.5	67.6	16.2	8.7	2.6	3.4	1.5	77.7	6	0	CA	83.4	73.4	83.1
McGeorge	75.8	71.8	3.2	24.2	0.8	58.4	11.2	20.8	1.1	7.9	0.6	78.1	14	2	CA	82.8	73.4	83.1
Pepperdine U.	75.0	87.6	3.4	5.7	3.4	70.3	19.4	6.5	0.0	3.9	0.0	81.3	10	0	CA	86.2	73.4	83.1
San Diego, U. of	89.3	88.8	3.2	5.9	1.8	70.1	12.2	10.9	1.8	4.5	0.5	83.7	20	1	CA	78.6	73.4	83.1
San Francisco, U. of	63.2	80.3	2.5	13.9	3.3	46.9	30.6	14.3	3.1	3.1	2.0	89.8	6	1	CA	81.0	73.4	83.1
Santa Clara U.	91.2	88.8	0.4	6.8	4.0	57.9	24.9	8.6	2.7	4.5	1.4	72.4	11	0	CA	82.3	73.4	83.1
Southern California, U.	95.1	97.4	0.0	2.1	0.5	78.2	1.1	4.3	4.3	11.2	1.1	82.5	11	0	CA	84.0	73.4	83.1
Southwestern U.	96.7	86.4	0.3	6.2	7.1	59.6	27.9	8.2	0.7	2.9	0.7	90.7	17	1	CA	80.0	73.4	83.1

SECTION OF LEGAL EDUCATION AND ADMISSIONS TO THE BAR • ESTABLISHED 1893 • ABA

	CAREER PLACEMENT														BAR PASSAGE			
						Type of Employment						Location						
	% Employment Status Known	% Employed	% Pursuing Graduate Degree	% Unemployed - Seeking	% Unemployed - Not Seeking	% in Law Firms	% in Business & Industry	% in Government	% in Public Interest	% in Judicial Clerkships	% in Academia	% Employed in State	# of States where Employed	% Employed in Foreign Nations	State where most take exam	Pass Rate for first-time test takers	State's Overall Pass Rate for first-time test takers	State's Pass Rate for first-time test takers from ABA Schools
California																		
Stanford U.	97.5	96.2	1.3	1.3	1.3	52.0	6.0	4.7	6.0	30.7	0.7	50.0	25	3	CA	91.1	73.4	83.1
Thomas Jefferson School of Law	48.8	93.8	1.2	1.2	3.7	61.8	14.5	10.5	0.0	0.0	1.3	0.0	0	0	CA	48.4	73.4	83.1
Whittier College	89.7	71.8	7.1	10.9	10.3	59.8	27.7	8.0	1.8	0.9	1.8	89.3	11	0	CA	72.2	73.4	83.1
Colorado																		
Colorado, U. of	95.6	81.5	0.7	16.6	1.3	48.8	17.1	13.0	4.9	11.4	4.9	69.9	16	0	CO	92.0	0.0	0.0
Denver, U. of	88.6	85.7	2.3	9.1	3.0	56.8	5.3	22.9	2.2	11.9	0.9	85.0	22	0	CO	87.0	0.0	0.0
Connecticut																		
Connecticut, U. of	98.0	89.6	0.5	9.3	0.5	46.2	28.3	13.9	0.6	8.7	2.3	80.4	13	0	CT	95.0	83.0	78.0
Quinnipiac College	87.7	81.3	6.4	10.5	1.8	46.8	24.5	19.4	1.4	7.9	0.0	49.6	14	0	CT	76.4	83.0	78.0
Yale U.	97.6	95.6	3.9	0.5	0.0	42.6	3.6	4.1	2.6	45.1	2.1	4.1	36	0	NY	96.5	78.0	0.0
Delaware																		
Widener U.	93.2	82.6	2.1	14.3	1.0	42.6	26.3	9.1	2.2	18.8	0.9	19.8	16	0	PA	65.0	72.5	72.5
District of Columbia																		
American U.	77.7	78.3	8.1	13.6	0.0	51.2	11.3	35.2	4.7	23.0	2.4	79.3	40	0	MD	67.0	75.0	75.0
Catholic U. of America	99.3	87.0	1.8	8.7	2.5	46.9	18.7	10.8	3.3	19.5	0.8	51.5	21	0	MD	70.2	75.0	75.0
District of Columbia	28.6	86.4	4.6	9.1	0.0	0.0	0.0	0.0	0.0	0.0	0.0	0.0	0	0	MD	16.0	75.0	75.0
George Washington U.	95.6	94.3	0.5	5.3	0.0	60.5	7.8	18.5	3.4	9.0	0.7	49.0	31	0	MD	89.0	75.0	75.0
Georgetown U.	98.8	96.3	1.0	2.0	0.7	60.9	7.9	10.9	4.1	15.9	0.4	48.1	40	0	NY	90.5	78.0	0.0
Howard U.	76.7	90.9	5.1	4.0	0.0	50.0	13.3	17.8	3.3	13.3	2.2	28.9	25	2	MD	29.0	75.0	75.0
Florida																		
Florida State U.	96.9	85.2	1.9	11.6	1.4	60.9	2.2	29.9	3.3	3.8	0.0	84.2	6	0	FL	82.1	84.4	84.4
Florida, U. of	90.5	79.6	6.1	10.5	3.9	62.5	8.0	22.2	0.0	7.3	0.0	82.6	11	0	FL	92.4	84.4	84.4
Miami, U. of	96.3	80.2	1.6	16.2	2.1	56.0	19.0	16.4	1.9	6.1	0.6	77.2	23	1	FL	89.2	84.4	84.4
Nova Southeastern U.	83.3	83.3	3.4	12.9	0.5	70.7	8.1	16.7	1.2	1.7	1.7	85.1	17	0	FL	81.6	84.4	84.4

SECTION OF LEGAL EDUCATION AND ADMISSIONS TO THE BAR • ESTABLISHED 1893 • ABA

	CAREER PLACEMENT														BAR PASSAGE			
						Type of Employment						Location						
	% Employment Status Known	% Employed	% Pursuing Graduate Degree	% Unemployed - Seeking	% Unemployed - Not Seeking	% in Law Firms	% in Business & Industry	% in Government	% in Public Interest	% in Judicial Clerkships	% in Academia	% Employed in State	# of States where Employed	% Employed in Foreign Nations	State where most take exam	Pass Rate for first-time test takers	State's Overall Pass Rate for first-time test takers	State's Pass Rate for first-time test takers from ABA Schools
Florida																		
St. Thomas U.	94.7	72.9	10.4	14.6	2.1	64.8	9.5	13.3	10.5	1.9	0.0	80.0	11	7	FL	68.6	84.4	84.4
Stetson U.	92.2	84.0	4.4	11.6	0.0	59.8	7.9	26.5	0.5	5.3	0.0	90.5	10	0	FL	85.2	84.4	84.4
Georgia																		
Emory U.	94.4	94.0	2.3	3.7	0.0	62.3	10.3	12.8	1.5	12.3	1.0	60.3	25	0	GA	81.1	80.8	84.3
Georgia State U.	97.0	88.3	0.6	7.4	3.7	56.9	22.2	13.9	0.7	5.6	0.7	92.4	9	0	GA	93.8	80.8	84.3
Georgia, U. of	92.8	96.1	1.7	1.7	0.6	66.9	5.8	13.4	1.7	10.5	1.7	79.7	17	1	GA	93.0	80.8	84.3
Mercer U.	98.4	90.9	3.3	4.1	1.7	69.1	3.6	21.8	0.0	3.6	1.8	70.9	7	0	GA	93.7	80.8	84.3
Hawaii																		
Hawaii, U. of	97.0	90.8	1.5	7.7	0.0	45.8	13.6	6.8	5.1	25.4	3.4	86.4	3	5	HI	86.0	0.0	0.0
Idaho																		
Idaho, U. of	95.8	81.3	7.7	7.7	3.3	52.7	6.8	18.9	2.7	18.9	0.0	67.6	11	0	ID	72.0	75.0	75.0
Illinois																		
Chicago, U. of	100.0	94.5	0.6	3.8	1.1	67.6	4.6	2.9	2.3	22.5	0.0	38.7	29	0	IL	97.0	87.0	87.0
Depaul U.	74.1	86.5	0.5	12.6	0.5	45.4	15.7	15.1	2.2	3.8	1.6	93.5	30	0	IL	92.0	87.0	87.0
Illinois Institute of Technology	97.7	83.0	0.8	5.1	11.2	51.9	21.2	14.4	4.5	4.8	3.2	85.9	28	0	IL	81.0	87.0	87.0
Illinois, U. of	97.3	93.3	2.8	3.9	0.0	53.9	17.4	16.8	1.2	8.4	1.8	73.7	18	0	IL	89.6	87.0	87.0
John Marshall Law School	89.0	85.8	0.8	11.6	1.9	51.7	21.3	20.4	0.9	5.2	0.4	87.4	18	0	IL	87.0	87.0	87.0
Loyola U.-Chicago	99.4	94.6	1.8	1.2	2.4	55.1	21.8	16.0	3.2	3.9	0.0	93.0	9	0	IL	93.9	87.0	87.0
Northern Illinois U.	91.2	82.8	5.4	11.8	0.0	42.9	6.5	28.6	18.2	3.9	0.0	85.7	9	1	IL	77.0	87.0	87.0
Northwestern U.	93.8	92.4	1.0	6.1	0.5	69.2	9.3	6.0	1.1	13.2	1.1	58.8	25	0	IL	94.7	87.0	87.0
Southern Illinois U.-Carbondale	86.0	89.1	2.2	7.6	1.1	68.3	9.8	18.3	0.0	3.7	0.0	74.4	11	13	IL	81.4	87.0	87.0

SECTION OF LEGAL EDUCATION • AND ADMISSIONS TO THE BAR • ESTABLISHED 1893 ABA	CAREER PLACEMENT														BAR PASSAGE			
						Type of Employment						Location						
	% Employment Status Known	% Employed	% Pursuing Graduate Degree	% Unemployed - Seeking	% Unemployed - Not Seeking	% in Law Firms	% in Business & Industry	% in Government	% in Public Interest	% in Judicial Clerkships	% in Academia	% Employed in State	# of States where Employed	% Employed in Foreign Nations	State where most take exam	Pass Rate for first-time test takers	State's Overall Pass Rate for first-time test takers	State's Pass Rate for first-time test takers from ABA Schools
Indiana																		
Indiana U.-Bloomington	91.8	92.0	3.3	5.0	0.0	60.2	13.3	10.8	2.4	11.5	1.8	46.4	24	1	IN	82.0	86.0	86.0
Indiana U.-Indianapolis	89.6	91.0	2.2	5.4	1.4	53.2	22.2	17.7	1.5	5.4	0.0	87.2	13	0	IN	86.3	86.0	86.0
Notre Dame, U. of	97.7	95.8	0.6	3.6	0.0	70.2	6.2	11.2	1.9	10.6	0.0	10.6	29	0	IN	97.1	86.0	86.0
Valparaiso U.	93.3	85.5	0.0	3.6	10.8	60.6	11.3	16.2	2.8	7.0	2.1	42.3	23	1	IN	82.4	86.0	86.0
Iowa																		
Drake U.	100.0	90.2	1.2	7.9	0.6	52.7	16.9	18.9	0.7	10.1	0.7	58.8	22	0	IA	87.0	87.0	87.0
Iowa, U. of	95.5	86.9	3.3	5.6	4.2	55.9	8.1	14.0	5.9	15.1	1.1	42.5	26	0	IA	79.0	87.0	87.0
Kansas																		
Kansas, U. of	94.3	81.1	4.1	12.2	2.7	60.8	10.0	14.2	5.0	7.5	0.0	47.5	14	0	KS	88.0	81.9	81.9
Washburn U.	96.1	78.2	4.8	11.6	5.4	54.8	14.8	22.6	2.6	5.2	0.0	61.7	21	0	KS	71.4	81.9	81.9
Kentucky																		
Kentucky, U. of	100.0	90.0	3.6	1.8	4.6	69.7	5.1	3.0	6.1	15.2	1.0	85.9	11	0	KY	92.0	88.0	88.0
Louisville, U. of	96.0	95.8	0.7	0.7	2.8	66.7	14.5	10.9	1.5	5.8	0.7	81.2	12	0	KY	88.0	88.0	88.0
Northern Kentucky U.	39.8	86.7	2.2	6.7	4.4	43.6	33.3	15.4	2.6	5.1	0.0	59.0	3	0	KY	82.5	88.0	88.0
Louisiana																		
Louisiana State U.	92.3	78.0	2.6	19.4	0.0	61.1	6.7	10.7	0.0	21.5	0.0	90.6	7	0	LA	79.0	55.0	67.0
Loyola U.-New Orleans	82.4	57.7	4.4	37.4	0.6	62.9	4.8	10.5	2.9	18.1	1.0	75.2	15	0	LA	56.0	55.0	67.0
Southern U.	95.8	78.0	17.6	4.4	0.0	52.1	2.8	33.8	0.0	14.1	25.4	**.*	4	0	LA	31.0	55.0	67.0
Tulane U.	95.2	76.8	3.5	12.1	7.6	46.9	10.4	13.3	0.4	14.9	0.0	31.1	28	1	LA	53.0	55.0	67.0
Maine																		
Maine, U. of	98.7	82.1	0.0	16.7	1.3	39.1	25.0	14.1	1.6	20.3	0.0	73.4	11	0	ME	75.0	0.0	0.0

SECTION OF LEGAL EDUCATION AND ADMISSIONS TO THE BAR
ESTABLISHED 1893
ABA

	CAREER PLACEMENT													BAR PASSAGE			
					Type of Employment						Location						
	% Employment Status Known	% Employed	% Pursuing Graduate Degree	% Unemployed - Seeking	% Unemployed - Not Seeking	% in Law Firms	% in Business & Industry	% in Government	% in Public Interest	% in Judicial Clerkships	% in Academia	% Employed in State	# of States where Employed	% Employed in Foreign Nations	State where most take exam	Pass Rate for first-time test takers	State's Overall Pass Rate for first-time test takers	State's Pass Rate for first-time test takers from ABA Schools
Maryland																		
Baltimore, U. of	88.3	85.4	1.4	11.8	1.4	36.8	18.0	19.3	0.8	23.0	1.3	80.8	11	0	MD	82.0	75.0	75.0
Maryland, U. of	97.9	85.2	0.8	12.7	1.3	34.7	19.3	22.3	4.0	17.8	2.0	43.1	17	0	MD	83.0	75.0	75.0
Massachusetts																		
Boston College	93.0	91.0	1.1	7.1	0.8	56.8	9.5	14.0	2.9	16.5	0.4	49.8	30	0	MA	91.9	82.5	84.8
Boston U.	96.2	82.4	3.4	11.5	2.8	66.3	9.9	11.6	2.4	9.2	0.7	35.7	26	1	MA	85.7	82.5	84.8
Harvard U.	98.5	96.9	0.7	2.2	0.2	59.9	7.5	2.3	2.9	26.6	1.0	12.6	35	2	NY	96.4	78.0	0.0
New England School of Law	78.1	84.9	2.7	12.0	0.4	45.6	22.5	23.6	0.5	5.8	2.1	77.5	15	0	MA	81.0	82.5	84.8
Northeastern U.	86.6	82.1	1.9	14.8	1.2	37.6	15.8	6.8	15.0	23.3	1.5	60.9	23	1	MA	84.7	82.5	84.8
Suffolk U.	87.2	85.5	2.3	10.4	1.8	41.5	32.1	15.4	1.6	7.6	1.9	78.4	23	1	MA	84.3	82.5	84.8
Western New England	90.0	84.1	2.4	9.7	3.9	41.4	23.0	21.8	5.2	6.3	2.3	32.2	21	0	MA	77.1	82.5	84.8
Michigan																		
Detroit College of Law At Michigan State U.	51.1	92.4	0.8	6.7	0.0	47.3	19.1	17.3	2.7	12.7	0.9	92.7	7	0	MI	76.0	70.0	70.0
Detroit Mercy, U. of	23.4	86.0	0.0	14.0	0.0	49.0	28.6	20.4	0.0	0.0	2.0	79.6	5	2	MI	57.0	70.0	70.0
Michigan, U. of	97.4	93.6	1.3	4.8	0.3	66.5	6.8	4.8	1.1	20.2	0.6	27.6	34	0	MI	89.0	70.0	70.0
Thomas Cooley Law School	48.7	84.8	4.7	8.9	1.6	75.3	16.7	17.3	0.0	7.4	1.2	55.6	30	0	MI	61.0	70.0	70.0
Wayne State U.	88.9	89.8	1.1	1.1	7.9	56.6	18.2	14.5	3.8	3.8	3.1	93.7	4	0	MI	83.0	70.0	70.0
Minnesota																		
Hamline U.	83.3	82.5	3.1	12.5	1.9	37.9	24.3	6.1	7.6	23.5	0.8	78.0	15	0	MN	82.7	89.9	89.9
Minnesota, U. of	99.6	91.3	1.5	3.5	3.5	46.6	15.5	5.6	3.0	26.7	2.6	78.0	18	1	MN	96.7	89.9	89.9
William Mitchell College of Law	89.5	92.7	0.4	6.6	0.4	42.1	25.2	13.4	2.8	10.6	5.9	91.3	11	0	MN	85.2	89.9	89.9

SECTION OF LEGAL EDUCATION AND ADMISSIONS TO THE BAR • ESTABLISHED 1893 • ABA

	CAREER PLACEMENT														BAR PASSAGE			
						Type of Employment						Location						
	% Employment Status Known	% Employed	% Pursuing Graduate Degree	% Unemployed - Seeking	% Unemployed - Not Seeking	% in Law Firms	% in Business & Industry	% in Government	% in Public Interest	% in Judicial Clerkships	% in Academia	% Employed in State	# of States where Employed	% Employed in Foreign Nations	State where most take exam	Pass Rate for first-time test takers	State's Overall Pass Rate for first-time test takers	State's Pass Rate for first-time test takers from ABA Schools
Mississippi																		
Mississippi College	92.7	82.4	6.9	6.9	3.9	71.4	6.0	7.1	0.0	15.5	0.0	51.2	17	0	MS	90.2	86.6	86.6
Mississippi, U. of	98.9	88.8	4.5	6.7	0.0	67.3	10.1	8.2	3.1	10.7	0.6	73.6	13	0	MS	86.0	86.6	86.6
Missouri																		
Missouri, U. of Kansas City	96.1	90.5	0.7	8.8	0.0	57.5	11.9	13.4	1.5	15.7	0.0	76.1	11	0	MO	95.0	92.0	92.0
Missouri, U. of Columbia	92.9	87.8	3.8	6.1	2.3	60.0	5.2	13.9	4.4	14.8	1.7	89.6	7	0	MO	89.8	92.0	92.0
St. Louis U.	92.5	91.9	0.5	6.7	1.0	51.6	20.8	11.5	1.0	9.4	2.6	87.0	16	0	MO	88.1	92.0	92.0
Washington U.	98.1	91.2	2.0	3.9	2.9	51.6	16.7	14.0	5.9	11.3	0.5	40.9	27	3	MO	94.3	92.0	92.0
Montana																		
Montana, U. of	87.3	88.4	5.8	4.4	1.5	44.3	6.6	13.1	1.6	32.8	1.6	86.9	6	0	MT	94.0	90.0	90.0
Nebraska																		
Creighton U.	96.5	84.7	1.2	12.3	1.8	50.7	23.2	16.7	1.5	7.3	0.7	52.9	22	0	NE	93.0	94.0	94.0
Nebraska, U. of	98.0	93.1	2.8	2.8	1.4	44.8	17.9	20.2	4.5	11.9	0.8	50.8	23	0	NE	98.9	94.0	94.0
New Hampshire																		
Franklin Pierce Law Center	97.7	79.4	1.6	15.1	4.0	65.0	19.0	7.0	2.0	3.0	3.0	32.0	19	1	NH	79.0	79.2	79.2
New Jersey																		
Rutgers U.-Newark	92.7	92.5	0.0	6.6	0.9	40.0	26.7	4.3	2.4	24.8	1.9	73.3	11	0	NJ	75.0	78.0	78.0
Rutgers U.-Camden	92.2	93.1	1.6	3.7	1.6	43.2	14.2	11.4	1.1	26.7	3.4	59.7	15	1	NJ	76.0	78.0	78.0
Seton Hall U.	94.6	90.7	0.6	6.9	1.9	33.9	13.3	10.3	0.6	41.8	0.0	73.6	30	0	NJ	78.0	78.0	78.0
New Mexico																		
New Mexico, U. of	98.0	77.3	4.1	15.5	3.1	57.3	10.7	14.7	2.7	9.3	5.3	84.0	4	1	NM	89.0	92.0	0.0
New York																		
Albany Law School	98.9	88.1	1.5	5.6	4.8	49.4	20.3	16.9	2.1	5.9	0.8	78.1	14	0	NY	92.9	78.0	0.0
Brooklyn Law School	97.1	83.5	0.2	16.3	0.0	58.1	17.6	15.4	3.9	3.9	1.1	91.7	13	0	NY	86.4	78.0	0.0
City U. of New York	67.2	72.8	0.0	20.7	6.5	34.3	7.5	22.4	56.7	7.5	9.0	79.1	10	0	NY	58.0	78.0	0.0
Columbia U.	99.1	94.2	2.9	2.6	0.3	69.3	5.2	1.5	2.8	17.8	3.4	64.7	26	3	NY	92.8	78.0	0.0
Cornell U.	96.8	93.4	3.9	1.7	1.1	66.5	7.7	7.1	1.8	13.5	0.6	32.9	22	0	NY	96.0	78.0	0.0

SECTION OF LEGAL EDUCATION AND ADMISSIONS TO THE BAR
ESTABLISHED 1893
ABA

	CAREER PLACEMENT														BAR PASSAGE			
						Type of Employment						Location						
	% Employment Status Known	% Employed	% Pursuing Graduate Degree	% Unemployed - Seeking	% Unemployed - Not Seeking	% in Law Firms	% in Business & Industry	% in Government	% in Public Interest	% in Judicial Clerkships	% in Academia	% Employed in State	# of States where Employed	% Employed in Foreign Nations	State where most take exam	Pass Rate for first-time test takers	State's Overall Pass Rate for first-time test takers	State's Pass Rate for first-time test takers from ABA Schools
New York																		
Fordham U.	89.2	91.8	1.6	5.0	1.6	65.0	17.5	11.8	0.6	4.3	0.9	90.8	18	0	NY	90.1	78.0	0.0
Hofstra U.	87.9	88.4	1.7	7.3	2.6	64.9	14.6	11.2	2.0	6.3	1.0	76.1	15	0	NY	79.4	78.0	0.0
New York Law School	92.6	91.2	2.1	5.4	1.3	59.7	19.1	13.5	1.5	5.0	1.2	81.5	12	0	NY	73.5	78.0	0.0
New York U.	99.3	96.2	1.7	2.2	0.0	74.1	3.5	3.2	3.0	16.2	0.0	75.4	29	0	NY	94.0	78.0	0.0
Pace U.	81.6	87.5	1.0	8.5	3.0	56.6	30.3	4.6	1.7	4.6	2.3	85.1	10	0	NY	80.0	78.0	0.0
St. John's U.	89.6	81.6	0.9	15.2	2.4	57.7	13.9	22.3	0.0	6.2	0.0	88.0	12	1	NY	85.0	78.0	0.0
State U. of New York at Buffalo	99.1	84.3	4.0	7.6	4.0	61.7	14.4	10.6	7.5	5.3	0.5	73.9	17	1	NY	72.3	78.0	0.0
Syracuse U.	96.4	80.8	1.7	16.7	0.8	56.7	19.1	15.5	1.6	6.2	1.0	53.1	24	1	NY	68.0	78.0	0.0
Touro College	86.5	72.4	0.5	24.6	2.5	60.4	24.3	9.0	3.5	2.8	0.0	91.0	8	0	NY	65.2	78.0	0.0
Yeshiva U.	74.8	89.6	0.9	9.5	0.0	57.3	16.1	11.1	3.0	9.1	3.5	81.4	0	0	NY	75.8	78.0	0.0
North Carolina																		
Campbell U.	95.9	97.9	2.1	0.0	0.0	92.4	1.1	4.4	1.1	3.3	0.0	91.3	8	0	NC	97.0	85.0	85.0
Duke U.	100.0	97.2	0.6	1.7	0.6	71.9	2.9	2.9	0.6	21.6	0.0	14.6	29	0	NY	94.0	78.0	0.0
North Carolina Central	84.0	96.8	0.0	3.2	0.0	55.7	23.0	9.8	6.6	6.6	1.6	90.2	6	0	NC	74.0	85.0	85.0
North Carolina, U. of	91.0	86.2	3.0	8.9	2.0	65.1	7.4	11.4	2.3	12.6	1.1	61.7	22	0	NC	94.0	85.0	85.0
Wake Forest U.	94.6	95.0	1.4	2.1	1.4	61.9	14.9	8.2	1.5	12.7	0.8	58.2	21	0	NC	90.0	85.0	85.0
North Dakota																		
North Dakota, U. of	59.5	97.7	0.0	2.3	0.0	39.5	16.3	11.6	0.0	34.9	0.0	53.5	7	0	ND	82.0	85.0	85.0
Ohio																		
Akron, U. of	98.6	90.2	2.8	3.5	3.5	49.6	17.1	17.1	7.0	7.8	1.6	77.5	15	0	OH	89.0	93.0	90.0
Capital U.	91.4	92.2	2.1	2.6	3.1	51.4	20.9	16.4	3.4	5.7	2.3	81.4	20	0	OH	94.0	93.0	90.0
Case Western Reserve U.	98.6	85.9	1.0	12.6	0.5	62.7	14.1	11.3	3.4	8.5	0.0	67.2	26	0	OH	94.0	93.0	90.0
Cincinnati, U. of	96.7	90.5	5.2	0.9	3.5	52.4	21.0	11.4	2.9	10.5	1.9	72.4	16	0	OH	95.0	93.0	90.0

SECTION OF LEGAL EDUCATION AND ADMISSIONS TO THE BAR • ESTABLISHED 1893 • ABA

	CAREER PLACEMENT														BAR PASSAGE			
						Type of Employment						Location						
	% Employment Status Known	% Employed	% Pursuing Graduate Degree	% Unemployed - Seeking	% Unemployed - Not Seeking	% in Law Firms	% in Business & Industry	% in Government	% in Public Interest	% in Judicial Clerkships	% in Academia	% Employed in State	# of States where Employed	% Employed in Foreign Nations	State where most take exam	Pass Rate for first-time test takers	State's Overall Pass Rate for first-time test takers	State's Pass Rate for first-time test takers from ABA Schools
Ohio																		
Cleveland State U.	40.4	86.0	1.9	12.2	0.0	68.5	12.0	10.9	2.2	4.4	2.2	88.0	9	0	OH	91.0	93.0	90.0
Dayton, U. of	94.4	83.8	0.7	12.5	2.9	51.8	26.3	8.8	0.9	6.1	0.0	44.7	23	0	OH	94.0	93.0	90.0
Ohio Northern U.	86.3	81.2	4.0	14.9	0.0	54.9	11.0	14.6	0.0	17.1	2.4	35.4	21	1	OH	89.7	93.0	90.0
Ohio State U.	96.7	87.7	1.0	10.3	1.0	52.3	15.7	20.2	0.0	10.1	1.7	66.9	23	0	OH	93.0	93.0	90.0
Toledo, U. of	78.3	77.3	4.2	9.2	9.2	52.2	17.4	14.1	2.2	10.9	3.3	66.3	12	1	OH	92.0	93.0	90.0
Oklahoma																		
Oklahoma City U.	62.0	80.2	1.9	11.3	6.6	65.9	15.3	12.9	0.0	4.7	1.2	54.1	18	0	OK	74.0	75.0	75.0
Oklahoma, U. of	89.0	84.0	5.2	10.8	0.0	62.6	14.7	16.6	1.8	3.1	1.2	68.7	20	0	OK	75.0	75.0	75.0
Tulsa, U. of	98.4	80.6	5.0	12.2	2.2	58.6	23.5	11.7	2.8	3.5	0.0	64.1	19	0	OK	78.0	75.0	75.0
Oregon																		
Lewis & Clark College	87.9	86.9	2.0	9.8	1.3	47.4	16.5	21.1	6.0	7.5	1.5	60.2	25	1	OR	86.0	85.0	0.0
Oregon, U. of	98.5	82.4	5.3	5.3	6.9	43.5	13.9	24.1	4.6	8.3	5.6	62.0	16	1	OR	77.0	85.0	0.0
Willamette U.	93.7	85.8	3.4	6.8	4.1	58.3	15.7	13.4	0.8	11.0	0.8	66.1	12	0	OR	90.7	85.0	0.0
Pennsylvania																		
Dickinson School of Law	93.4	91.0	1.3	7.7	0.0	46.8	10.6	14.2	1.4	26.2	0.7	75.2	14	0	PA	88.0	72.5	72.5
Duquesne U.	98.8	86.7	1.8	11.5	0.0	51.8	32.9	3.5	2.1	9.1	0.7	73.4	10	0	PA	73.0	72.5	72.5
Pennsylvania, U. of	98.4	94.6	0.8	3.8	0.8	71.4	4.4	4.0	2.2	17.6	0.4	27.8	21	0	NY	91.0	78.0	0.0
Pittsburgh, U. of	89.3	75.0	0.5	19.3	5.2	66.0	9.7	9.7	3.5	11.1	0.0	74.3	15	2	PA	81.5	72.5	72.5
Temple U.	91.2	90.0	1.1	6.3	2.6	47.3	21.9	8.9	4.1	17.1	0.6	67.0	15	0	PA	61.0	72.5	72.5
Villanova U.	86.9	95.9	2.3	1.2	0.6	58.2	12.1	6.1	0.6	23.0	0.0	80.0	0	0	PA	74.5	72.5	72.5
Widener U.	83.8	82.8	1.6	15.1	0.5	42.8	17.6	24.5	1.9	10.7	2.5	72.3	13	0	PA	57.0	72.5	72.5

SECTION OF LEGAL EDUCATION AND ADMISSIONS TO THE BAR • ESTABLISHED 1893 • ABA

	CAREER PLACEMENT														BAR PASSAGE			
						Type of Employment						Location						
	% Employment Status Known	% Employed	% Pursuing Graduate Degree	% Unemployed - Seeking	% Unemployed - Not Seeking	% in Law Firms	% in Business & Industry	% in Government	% in Public Interest	% in Judicial Clerkships	% in Academia	% Employed in State	# of States where Employed	% Employed in Foreign Nations	State where most take exam	Pass Rate for first-time test takers	State's Overall Pass Rate for first-time test takers	State's Pass Rate for first-time test takers from ABA Schools
Puerto Rico																		
Inter American U. of Puerto Rico	86.4	85.1	4.1	10.7	0.0	56.3	7.8	18.5	5.8	11.7	0.0	97.1	0	0	PR	60.0	68.0	69.0
Pontifical Catholic U. of Pruerto Rico	87.9	87.5	0.0	11.3	1.3	55.7	11.4	21.4	10.0	1.4	0.0	98.6	1	0	PR	63.0	68.0	69.0
Puerto Rico, U. of	0.0	0.0	0.0	0.0	0.0	0.0	0.0	0.0	0.0	0.0	0.0	0.0	0	0	PR	84.0	68.0	69.0
Rhode Island																		
Roger Williams U.	54.8	65.2	4.4	28.3	2.2	50.0	23.3	6.7	0.0	20.0	0.0	53.3	8	0	RI	53.0	71.0	75.0
South Carolina																		
South Carolina, U. of	95.5	88.4	3.4	6.0	2.2	61.2	4.4	12.6	0.0	21.8	0.5	90.8	11	0	SC	95.3	92.0	81.0
South Dakota																		
South Dakota, U. of	100.0	90.8	1.5	7.7	0.0	52.5	11.9	10.2	0.0	25.4	0.0	67.8	8	0	SD	96.0	91.0	91.0
Tennessee																		
Memphis, U. of	97.2	94.9	0.7	4.4	0.0	56.2	10.8	12.3	3.1	11.5	0.0	82.3	14	0	TN	81.3	79.0	91.3
Tennessee, U. of	99.3	91.9	0.0	6.1	2.0	68.4	6.6	8.1	2.9	13.2	0.7	75.7	13	0	TN	86.2	79.0	91.3
Vanderbilt U.	99.5	92.5	3.2	2.7	1.6	65.9	10.4	5.2	1.2	17.3	0.0	26.6	32	0	TN	90.0	79.0	91.3
Texas																		
Baylor U.	99.4	94.9	0.0	3.8	1.3	75.3	5.3	8.7	0.7	10.0	0.0	92.7	9	1	TX	94.5	82.3	82.3
Houston, U. of	91.7	86.2	2.0	9.1	2.7	64.8	15.2	9.0	1.2	8.6	1.2	90.6	12	1	TX	86.3	82.3	82.3
South Texas College of Law	94.3	79.4	0.5	19.6	0.5	63.2	23.4	9.2	0.0	3.6	0.7	94.4	12	0	TX	77.6	82.3	82.3
Southern Methodist U.	90.4	80.2	2.5	16.8	0.5	89.9	19.0	7.6	0.0	8.2	0.0	69.6	26	0	TX	84.0	82.3	82.3
St. Mary's U.	86.9	86.4	1.0	12.6	0.0	68.5	8.4	12.4	2.8	7.9	0.0	86.5	10	0	TX	80.4	82.3	82.3
Texas Southern U.	56.1	100.0	0.0	0.0	0.0	87.5	0.0	2.3	5.7	4.6	0.0	92.1	7	0	TX	68.0	82.3	82.3
Texas Tech U.	75.5	90.8	0.0	9.2	0.0	87.8	0.7	4.1	0.0	6.8	0.7	97.3	3	0	TX	91.8	82.3	82.3
Texas Wesleyan U.	41.4	84.4	0.0	15.6	0.0	52.3	38.5	4.6	4.6	0.0	0.0	**.*	1	0	TX	48.3	82.3	82.3
Texas, U. of at Austin	97.0	89.8	1.1	7.5	1.6	70.6	4.7	10.9	3.0	10.4	0.5	80.0	23	0	TX	91.9	82.3	82.3

	CAREER PLACEMENT														BAR PASSAGE			
						Type of Employment						Location						
SECTION OF LEGAL EDUCATION AND ADMISSIONS TO THE BAR • ESTABLISHED 1893 • ABA	% Employment Status Known	% Employed	% Pursuing Graduate Degree	% Unemployed - Seeking	% Unemployed - Not Seeking	% in Law Firms	% in Business & Industry	% in Government	% in Public Interest	% in Judicial Clerkships	% in Academia	% Employed in State	# of States where Employed	% Employed in Foreign Nations	State where most take exam	Pass Rate for first-time test takers	State's Overall Pass Rate for first-time test takers	State's Pass Rate for first-time test takers from ABA Schools
Utah																		
Brigham Young U.	99.3	92.6	2.7	2.7	2.0	52.6	17.5	10.2	0.7	15.3	3.7	44.5	16	0	UT	89.7	92.0	0.0
Utah, U. of	94.4	90.1	3.0	5.9	1.0	50.5	18.3	11.8	2.2	17.2	0.0	77.4	11	1	UT	91.0	92.0	0.0
Vermont																		
Vermont Law School	92.1	87.1	2.9	7.9	2.2	52.1	19.8	11.6	5.0	10.7	0.8	25.6	34	0	VT	80.6	78.0	77.0
Virginia																		
George Mason U.	92.7	86.3	1.3	10.5	2.0	33.3	18.2	29.6	2.3	16.7	0.0	52.3	11	0	VA	80.2	76.4	76.7
Regent U.	92.9	63.7	5.5	28.6	2.2	69.0	8.6	10.3	1.7	8.6	1.7	55.2	18	0	VA	59.0	76.4	76.7
Richmond, U. of	89.6	85.3	0.8	14.0	0.0	60.9	8.2	16.4	1.8	10.9	1.8	75.5	13	0	VA	86.0	76.4	76.7
Virginia, U. of	99.5	96.2	1.6	1.1	1.1	69.8	3.6	2.8	3.1	20.2	0.6	20.7	35	1	VA	87.7	76.4	76.7
Washington & Lee U.	98.3	87.6	2.7	9.7	0.0	69.7	5.1	5.1	3.0	17.2	0.0	32.3	22	1	VA	80.5	76.4	76.7
William and Mary School of Law	100.0	96.4	0.6	1.2	1.8	59.8	7.5	6.9	5.7	20.1	0.0	54.7	22	0	VA	87.0	76.4	76.7
Washington																		
Gonzaga U.	95.7	81.4	9.0	5.8	3.9	54.3	15.0	16.5	1.6	12.6	0.0	48.0	19	0	WA	83.0	83.0	0.0
Seattle U.	88.8	85.2	1.7	8.4	4.6	49.5	17.8	21.3	5.5	4.5	1.5	88.6	15	1	WA	86.0	83.0	0.0
Washington, U. of	94.0	89.4	2.1	8.5	0.0	51.2	15.7	15.0	1.6	14.2	2.4	74.0	14	0	WA	86.0	83.0	0.0
West Virginia																		
West Virginia U.	98.5	91.0	1.5	5.3	2.3	64.5	9.1	14.9	2.5	5.0	4.1	79.3	12	0	WV	91.0	89.0	89.0
Wisconsin																		
Marquette U.	98.1	88.2	2.6	5.9	3.3	64.9	14.2	14.2	1.5	5.2	0.0	79.9	14	0	IL	92.9	87.0	87.0
Wisconsin, U. of	96.5	89.1	0.4	9.4	1.1	60.6	9.8	11.8	4.5	9.8	0.8	65.0	20	2		0.0	0.0	0.0
Wyoming																		
Wyoming, U. of	97.1	85.1	4.5	9.0	1.5	64.9	8.8	10.5	7.0	8.8	0.0	61.4	12	0	WY	62.0	59.0	59.0

SECTION OF LEGAL EDUCATION AND ADMISSIONS TO THE BAR · ESTABLISHED 1893 · ABA	EXPENSES				FACULTY						STUDENT BODY					
	Res Non-Res Full-Time Tuition	Res Non-Res Part-Time Tuition	Expenses: on-campus	Expenses: off-campus	Student-Faculty Ratio	# Full-Time Faculty	# Part-Time Faculty	% Men	% Women	% Minorities	# of Full-Time Students	# of Part-Time Students	% Men	% Women	% Minorities	First Year Attrition Rate
Alabama																
Alabama, U. of	**$3,578 $7,712**	**$0 $0**	**$7,574**	**$8,230**	**19.2/1**	**24**	**23**	**75**	**25**	**4**	**553**	**0**	**58.8**	**41.2**	**9.6**	**8.2%**
Samford U.	**$16,480 $16,480**	**$0 $0**	**N/A**	**$10,800**	**19.6/1**	**28**	**14**	**82**	**18**	**11**	**633**	**0**	**65.2**	**34.8**	**9.2**	**8.6%**
Arizona																
Arizona State U.	**$4,010 $10,378**	**$0 $0**	**$10,440**	**$10,440**	**15.5/1**	**25**	**13**	**76**	**24**	**16**	**463**	**0**	**50.5**	**49.5**	**25.1**	**12%**
Arizona, U. of	**$4,010 $10,378**	**$0 $0**	**$8,094**	**$11,802**	**16.4/1**	**24**	**31**	**75**	**25**	**8**	**472**	**0**	**50.8**	**49.2**	**25.6**	**0.7%**
Arkansas																
Arkansas, U. of Fayetteville	**$3,363 $7,275**	**$0 $0**	**$10,464**	**$10,464**	**15.6/1**	**21**	**10**	**76**	**24**	**19**	**394**	**0**	**63.2**	**36.8**	**9.6**	**23%**
Arkansas, U. of Little Rock	**$3,891 $8,597**	**$3,011 $6,631**	**$8,900**	**$8,500**	**15.4/1**	**20**	**8**	**70**	**30**	**10**	**263**	**154**	**51.7**	**48.3**	**11.0**	**11%**
California																
California Western School of Law	**$19,170 $19,170**	**$0 $0**	**N/A**	**$13,120**	**16.4/1**	**35**	**24**	**54**	**46**	**17**	**690**	**0**	**52.9**	**47.1**	**23.9**	**27%**
California-Hastings	**$11,172 $19,564**	**$0 $0**	**$15,053**	**$15,053**	**24.5/1**	**44**	**78**	**73**	**27**	**18**	**1,292**	**0**	**52.4**	**47.6**	**30.3**	**5.8%**
California-Los Angeles	**$10,861 $19,255**	**$0 $0**	**$11,122**	**$13,445**	**15.5/1**	**51**	**8**	**71**	**29**	**6**	**919**	**0**	**50.5**	**49.5**	**41.0**	**7.5%**
California-Berkeley	**$10,800 $19,194**	**$0 $0**	**$10,917**	**$10,917**	**17.5/1**	**40**	**43**	**75**	**25**	**15**	**838**	**0**	**50.1**	**49.9**	**35.6**	**2.3%**
California-Davis	**$10,881 $19,275**	**$0 $0**	**$9,938**	**$9,885**	**15.1/1**	**29**	**9**	**66**	**34**	**24**	**489**	**0**	**54.2**	**45.8**	**32.3**	**0.7%**
Golden Gate U.	**$17,466 $17,466**	**$12,570 $12,570**	**N/A**	**$11,030**	**15.8/1**	**33**	**62**	**64**	**36**	**18**	**453**	**260**	**43.0**	**57.0**	**24.3**	**29%**
Loyola Marymount U.	**$19,646 $19,646**	**$13,210 $13,210**	**N/A**	**$14,470**	**22.0/1**	**46**	**33**	**65**	**35**	**24**	**947**	**404**	**54.6**	**45.4**	**40.8**	**8.6%**
McGeorge	**$16,864 $16,864**	**$10,006 $10,006**	**$13,300**	**$13,300**	**23.6/1**	**37**	**25**	**78**	**22**	**8**	**844**	**344**	**54.1**	**45.9**	**24.4**	**9.6%**
Pepperdine U.	**$20,900 $20,900**	**$0 $0**	**$15,732**	**$15,732**	**19.8/1**	**28**	**27**	**82**	**18**	**11**	**679**	**0**	**54.9**	**45.1**	**22.7**	**0.0%**
San Diego, U. of	**$18,940 $18,940**	**$13,440 $13,440**	**$10,000**	**$9,750**	**14.5/1**	**52**	**30**	**69**	**31**	**10**	**690**	**279**	**58.3**	**41.7**	**22.5**	**7.5%**
San Francisco, U. of	**$18,960 $18,960**	**$15,564 $15,564**	**$10,389**	**$10,650**	**21.5/1**	**25**	**38**	**72**	**28**	**20**	**556**	**135**	**48.4**	**51.6**	**25.9**	**10%**
Santa Clara U.	**$19,130 $19,130**	**$13,320 $13,320**	**$14,122**	**$14,122**	**22.4/1**	**30**	**28**	**53**	**47**	**23**	**640**	**252**	**51.1**	**48.9**	**35.2**	**1.4%**
Southern California, U.	**$22,620 $22,620**	**$0 $0**	**$10,978**	**$12,024**	**14.9/1**	**35**	**17**	**74**	**26**	**9**	**626**	**0**	**56.9**	**43.1**	**38.2**	**5.5%**
Southwestern U.	**$19,120 $19,120**	**$12,146 $12,146**	**N/A**	**$13,230**	**21.7/1**	**40**	**24**	**73**	**28**	**15**	**806**	**354**	**48.9**	**51.1**	**31.4**	**18%**
Stanford U.	**$23,360 $23,360**	**$0 $0**	**$10,845**	**$13,836**	**16.9/1**	**27**	**29**	**63**	**37**	**15**	**547**	**0**	**55.0**	**45.0**	**32.5**	**0.0%**
Thomas Jefferson School of Law	**$16,685 $16,685**	**$12,940 $12,940**	**N/A**	**$12,882**	**20.1/1**	**18**	**21**	**44**	**56**	**0**	**183**	**379**	**57.9**	**42.1**	**23.0**	**27%**

SECTION OF LEGAL EDUCATION • AND ADMISSIONS TO THE BAR • ESTABLISHED 1893 ABA	EXPENSES				FACULTY						STUDENT BODY					
	Full-Time Tuition (Res Non-Res)	Part-Time Tuition (Res Non-Res)	Expenses: on-campus	Expenses: off-campus	Student-Faculty Ratio	# Full-Time Faculty	# Part-Time Faculty	% Men	% Women	% Minorities	# of Full-Time Students	# of Part-Time Students	% Men	% Women	% Minorities	First Year Attrition Rate
California																
Whittier College	$18,934 $18,934	$11,374 $11,374	N/A	$14,958	21.1/1	22	24	73	27	14	406	229	50.0	50.0	36.0	29%
Colorado																
Colorado, U. of	$4,502 $15,260	$0 $0	$8,734	$10,637	15.7/1	27	10	85	15	15	497	0	56.5	43.5	19.3	1.2%
Denver, U. of	$17,160 $17,160	$12,870 $12,870	$9,312	$9,312	23.4/1	35	70	80	20	14	801	276	52.7	47.3	12.4	4.1%
Connecticut																
Connecticut, U. of	$10,492 $21,938	$7,372 $15,372	N/A	$12,848	14.0/1	33	20	79	21	12	443	188	53.7	46.3	15.1	2.6%
Quinnipiac College	$17,983 $17,983	$15,055 $15,055	N/A	$12,555	21.1/1	27	24	70	30	11	527	237	64.1	35.9	12.5	15%
Yale U.	$22,692 $22,692	$0 $0	$10,816	N/A	10.9/1	45	25	82	18	11	582	0	57.0	43.0	26.8	0.6%
Delaware																
Widener U.	$16,900 $16,900	$12,690 $12,690	$11,170	$11,170	23.9/1	39	35	56	44	3	818	454	55.3	44.7	5.6	10%
District of Columbia																
American U.	$20,868 $20,868	$15,444 $15,444	$12,649	$12,649	24.1/1	37	101	70	30	11	870	304	39.4	60.6	22.5	1.6%
Catholic U. of America	$21,468 $21,468	$15,339 $15,339	$12,454	$12,454	19.3/1	38	46	68	32	16	693	286	52.7	47.3	14.6	8.8%
District of Columbia	$7,135 $14,135	$0 $0	N/A	$18,900	15.7/1	12	6	58	42	33	226	0	49.1	50.9	62.8	36%
George Washington U.	$21,785 $21,785	$15,310 $15,310	N/A	$13,672	18.3/1	65	108	72	28	11	1,284	212	54.8	45.2	29.2	3.1%
Georgetown U.	$22,430 $22,430	$15,300 $15,300	$14,200	$14,200	18.2/1	89	89	72	28	11	1,626	486	53.4	46.6	24.7	0.5%
Howard U.	$12,065 $12,065	$0 $0	$9,815	$12,416	15.4/1	23	16	70	30	83	421	0	47.3	52.7	91.2	2.7%
Florida																
Florida State U.	$3,687 $11,583	$0 $0	$10,704	$10,704	22.0/1	24	12	71	29	13	633	1	55.5	44.5	25.8	5.9%
Florida, U. of	$3,605 $11,501	$0 $0	$7,590	$8,890	19.9/1	46	12	76	24	15	1,104	0	59.1	40.9	23.5	1.9%
Miami, U. of	$21,160 $21,160	$15,534 $15,534	$14,565	$14,565	23.7/1	46	107	76	24	15	1,125	276	56.5	43.5	31.6	2.6%
Nova Southeastern U.	$18,850 $18,850	$14,140 $14,140	$13,119	$14,142	20.5/1	38	35	58	42	18	876	88	59.2	40.8	24.4	18%
St. Thomas U.	$17,760 $17,760	$0 $0	$13,300	$13,300	23.3/1	19	18	74	26	26	531	0	61.4	38.6	33.7	21%
Stetson U.	$18,310 $18,310	$0 $0	$10,270	$12,050	19.3/1	29	23	76	24	10	673	0	48.3	51.7	14.9	8.0%

SECTION OF LEGAL EDUCATION AND ADMISSIONS TO THE BAR • ESTABLISHED 1893 • ABA	EXPENSES				FACULTY						STUDENT BODY					
	Res Non-Res Full-Time Tuition	Res Non-Res Part-Time Tuition	Expenses: on-campus	Expenses: off-campus	Student-Faculty Ratio	# Full-Time Faculty	# Part-Time Faculty	% Men	% Women	% Minorities	# of Full-Time Students	# of Part-Time Students	% Men	% Women	% Minorities	First Year Attrition Rate
Georgia																
Emory U.	$20,890 $20,890	$0 $0	$9,736	$9,736	22.1/1	26	42	85	15	8	691	0	58.0	42.0	19.2	2.0%
Georgia State U.	$2,903 $9,147	$2,175 $6,635	$11,170	$12,129	17.2/1	31	7	68	32	10	412	256	49.8	50.2	22.8	18%
Georgia, U. of	$3,315 $10,017	$0 $0	$6,679	$8,984	18.8/1	28	9	79	21	11	631	0	57.1	42.9	13.3	5.7%
Mercer U.	$17,490 $17,490	$8,745 $8,745	$11,000	$11,000	15.2/1	22	6	73	27	9	400	0	64.0	36.0	12.5	14%
Hawaii																
Hawaii, U. of	$4,907 $12,981	$0 $0	$7,000	$9,600	12.7/1	15	13	67	33	20	228	0	47.4	52.6	65.8	8.1%
Idaho																
Idaho, U. of	$3,308 $8,960	$0 $0	$10,106	$10,106	13.9/1	16	5	81	19	0	266	0	57.9	42.1	9.8	13%
Illinois																
Chicago, U. of	$22,755 $22,755	$0 $0	$13,693	$13,693	19.3/1	26	7	81	19	8	542	0	60.0	40.0	21.6	3.4%
Depaul U.	$17,620 $17,620	$11,420 $11,420	$12,224	$12,224	21.8/1	37	57	65	35	14	750	331	54.1	45.9	11.3	2.0%
Illinois Institute of Technology	$18,930 $18,930	$13,680 $13,680	$11,437	$11,437	21.8/1	41	95	68	32	12	853	334	52.3	47.7	16.2	8.7%
Illinois, U. of	$6,752 $16,345	$0 $0	$9,306	$9,306	16.6/1	31	18	71	29	16	616	0	61.4	38.6	27.6	2.8%
John Marshall Law School	$15,890 $15,890	$11,370 $11,370	N/A	$13,410	16.5/1	50	95	72	28	8	753	357	59.5	40.5	13.9	8.0%
Loyola U.-Chicago	$19,500 $19,500	$14,650 $14,650	N/A	$13,250	21.9/1	26	72	81	19	12	556	195	43.5	56.5	16.9	4.3%
Northern Illinois U.	$5,467 $10,099	$0 $0	$6,957	$7,757	14.8/1	17	7	76	24	24	294	0	57.8	42.2	20.1	9.3%
Northwestern U.	$21,316 $21,316	$0 $0	$13,094	$14,399	15.2/1	34	21	79	21	6	619	0	58.6	41.4	20.5	0.0%
Southern Illinois U.-Carbondale	$4,970 $12,978	$0 $0	$8,040	$8,040	13.0/1	24	3	71	29	8	358	0	57.8	42.2	17.6	10%
Indiana																
Indiana U.-Bloomington	$5,350 $14,142	$0 $0	$5,372	$5,372	16.6/1	33	10	79	21	6	651	7	57.0	43.0	18.4	5.2%
Indiana U.-Indianapolis	$5,151 $12,279	$3,727 $8,818	$7,866	$11,232	18.5/1	33	15	73	27	3	539	294	55.8	44.2	11.9	9.9%
Notre Dame, U. of	$19,427 $19,427	$0 $0	$5,150	$5,150	15.4/1	27	22	78	22	11	537	0	53.8	46.2	17.7	1.2%
Valparaiso U.	$16,110 $16,110	$6,080 $6,080	N/A	$10,370	22.7/1	16	16	63	38	6	398	57	55.8	44.2	17.1	5.3%

SECTION OF LEGAL EDUCATION AND ADMISSIONS TO THE BAR • ESTABLISHED 1893 • ABA	EXPENSES				FACULTY						STUDENT BODY					
	Res Non-Res Full-Time Tuition	Res Non-Res Part-Time Tuition	Expenses: on-campus	Expenses: off-campus	Student-Faculty Ratio	# Full-Time Faculty	# Part-Time Faculty	% Men	% Women	% Minorities	# of Full-Time Students	# of Part-Time Students	% Men	% Women	% Minorities	First Year Attrition Rate
Iowa																
Drake U.	**$15,550 $15,550**	**$525 $525**	**N/A**	**$10,579**	**20.9/1**	**18**	**16**	**72**	**28**	**6**	**444**	**10**	**58.6**	**41.4**	**10.1**	**11%**
Iowa, U. of	**$5,400 $14,254**	**$0 $0**	**$7,740**	**$7,740**	**13.2/1**	**46**	**10**	**72**	**28**	**11**	**661**	**0**	**55.5**	**44.5**	**21.6**	**3.6%**
Kansas																
Kansas, U. of	**$4,442 $10,892**	**$0 $0**	**$10,101**	**$10,101**	**17.6/1**	**23**	**20**	**87**	**13**	**13**	**486**	**0**	**61.9**	**38.1**	**12.8**	**3.0%**
Washburn U.	**$6,116 $9,140**	**$0 $0**	**$10,918**	**$10,918**	**16.8/1**	**22**	**12**	**64**	**36**	**23**	**442**	**0**	**57.5**	**42.5**	**11.1**	**8.8%**
Kentucky																
Kentucky, U. of	**$4,776 $12,396**	**$0 $0**	**$9,212**	**$9,212**	**15.3/1**	**23**	**18**	**74**	**26**	**9**	**421**	**0**	**62.7**	**37.3**	**5.7**	**4.0%**
Louisville, U. of	**$4,670 $12,270**	**$3,910 $10,240**	**$7,152**	**$8,868**	**18.2/1**	**22**	**13**	**77**	**23**	**14**	**416**	**88**	**52.2**	**47.8**	**6.3**	**8.4%**
Northern Kentucky U.	**$4,980 $12,580**	**$4,140 $10,480**	**$6,084**	**$12,799**	**15.6/1**	**18**	**24**	**72**	**28**	**6**	**210**	**192**	**60.5**	**39.5**	**7.1**	**5.2%**
Louisiana																
Louisiana State U.	**$3,936 $8,556**	**$2,634 $6,002**	**$10,550**	**$18,950**	**20.6/1**	**26**	**16**	**92**	**8**	**8**	**637**	**0**	**54.5**	**45.5**	**9.1**	**32%**
Loyola U.- New Orleans	**$16,230 $16,230**	**$11,014 $11,014**	**$11,089**	**$11,089**	**18.0/1**	**30**	**17**	**70**	**30**	**27**	**511**	**174**	**53.0**	**47.0**	**24.5**	**17%**
Southern U.	**$3,088 $6,288**	**$0 $0**	**$9,544**	**$9,544**	**13.1/1**	**23**	**8**	**70**	**30**	**61**	**335**	**0**	**53.1**	**46.9**	**65.7**	**3.2%**
Tulane U.	**$22,076 $22,076**	**$0 $0**	**$11,200**	**$11,200**	**17.6/1**	**47**	**48**	**74**	**26**	**13**	**990**	**3**	**52.0**	**48.0**	**19.6**	**8.9%**
Maine																
Maine, U. of	**$8,070 $15,686**	**$5,790 $11,230**	**$7,830**	**$7,830**	**18.8/1**	**13**	**7**	**77**	**23**	**0**	**284**	**5**	**57.0**	**43.0**	**4.6**	**7.5%**
Maryland																
Baltimore, U. of	**$7,596 $13,218**	**$6,258 $10,338**	**N/A**	**$10,100**	**19.3/1**	**39**	**57**	**64**	**36**	**13**	**645**	**389**	**52.9**	**47.1**	**15.5**	**6.4%**
Maryland, U. of	**$8,815 $15,881**	**$6,613 $11,910**	**$8,455**	**$10,020**	**14.4/1**	**45**	**34**	**62**	**38**	**16**	**598**	**258**	**48.0**	**52.0**	**29.9**	**7.5%**
Massachusetts																
Boston College	**$21,290 $21,290**	**$0 $0**	**N/A**	**$11,605**	**17.4/1**	**39**	**34**	**77**	**23**	**18**	**814**	**0**	**53.3**	**46.7**	**17.2**	**0.0%**
Boston U.	**$20,834 $20,834**	**$0 $0**	**$12,165**	**$12,165**	**19.3/1**	**46**	**84**	**70**	**30**	**7**	**1,064**	**0**	**52.4**	**47.6**	**18.0**	**6.2%**
Harvard U.	**$22,354 $22,354**	**$0 $0**	**$12,300**	**$12,300**	**21.1/1**	**65**	**12**	**88**	**12**	**12**	**1,646**	**0**	**59.3**	**40.7**	**28.3**	**0.2%**
New England School of Law	**$13,500 $13,500**	**$10,160 $10,160**	**N/A**	**$11,250**	**20.3/1**	**34**	**42**	**71**	**29**	**9**	**558**	**410**	**51.4**	**48.6**	**17.0**	**14%**
Northeastern U.	**$20,145 $20,145**	**$0 $0**	**$14,900**	**$14,900**	**23.4/1**	**23**	**10**	**65**	**35**	**4**	**614**	**0**	**33.1**	**66.9**	**26.2**	**4.1%**
Suffolk U.	**$17,820 $17,820**	**$13,366 $13,366**	**N/A**	**$14,158**	**22.8/1**	**55**	**59**	**82**	**18**	**9**	**1,010**	**747**	**48.9**	**51.1**	**8.6**	**5.3%**

SECTION OF LEGAL EDUCATION AND ADMISSIONS TO THE BAR · ESTABLISHED 1893 · ABA	EXPENSES				FACULTY						STUDENT BODY					
	Res Non-Res Full-Time Tuition	Res Non-Res Part-Time Tuition	Expenses: on-campus	Expenses: off-campus	Student-Faculty Ratio	# Full-Time Faculty	# Part-Time Faculty	% Men	% Women	% Minorities	# of Full-Time Students	# of Part-Time Students	% Men	% Women	% Minorities	First Year Attrition Rate
Massachusetts																
Western New England	**$15,506 $15,506**	**$11,592 $11,592**	**$7,695**	**$8,413**	**20.0/1**	**26**	**16**	**81**	**19**	**8**	**420**	**265**	**53.1**	**46.9**	**11.0**	**2.2%**
Michigan																
Detroit College of Law At Michigan State U.	**$14,140 $14,140**	**$10,100 $10,100**	**$9,700**	**$15,980**	**19.5/1**	**25**	**31**	**64**	**36**	**8**	**433**	**231**	**61.4**	**38.6**	**11.5**	**7.9%**
Detroit Mercy, U. of	**$13,740 $13,740**	**$9,818 $9,818**	**N/A**	**$11,712**	**22.3/1**	**19**	**28**	**79**	**21**	**5**	**375**	**238**	**52.3**	**47.7**	**12.8**	**20%**
Michigan, U. of	**$16,678 $22,678**	**$0 $0**	**$12,450**	**$11,800**	**16.4/1**	**54**	**15**	**67**	**33**	**7**	**1,068**	**0**	**58.4**	**41.6**	**21.3**	**0.6%**
Thomas Cooley Law School	**$0 $0**	**$0 $14,260**	**N/A**	**$15,571**	**24.3/1**	**43**	**104**	**74**	**26**	**9**	**154**	**1667**	**72.1**	**27.9**	**14.9**	**35%**
Wayne State U.	**$6,052 $13,080**	**$4,364 $9,384**	**$14,001**	**$14,001**	**26.2/1**	**21**	**23**	**71**	**29**	**10**	**518**	**215**	**51.9**	**48.1**	**14.9**	**12%**
Minnesota																
Hamline U.	**$14,513 $14,513**	**$0 $0**	**$7,260**	**$9,672**	**18.4/1**	**26**	**35**	**62**	**38**	**8**	**573**	**0**	**49.9**	**50.1**	**10.5**	**11%**
Minnesota, U. of	**$8,923 $14,819**	**$0 $0**	**$8,640**	**$8,640**	**16.7/1**	**39**	**59**	**69**	**31**	**10**	**787**	**0**	**55.3**	**44.7**	**16.8**	**5.7%**
William Mitchell College of Law	**$15,360 $15,360**	**$11,160 $11,160**	**N/A**	**$11,060**	**23.4/1**	**31**	**62**	**68**	**32**	**10**	**535**	**511**	**51.8**	**48.2**	**11.0**	**4.7%**
Mississippi																
Mississippi College	**$11,462 $11,462**	**$0 $0**	**$10,030**	**$13,850**	**22.2/1**	**16**	**7**	**63**	**38**	**13**	**418**	**0**	**64.6**	**35.4**	**11.5**	**8.6%**
Mississippi, U. of	**$3,081 $7,003**	**$118 $314**	**$9,085**	**$9,085**	**26.5/1**	**17**	**5**	**82**	**18**	**18**	**515**	**0**	**61.9**	**38.1**	**14.8**	**17%**
Missouri																
Missouri, U. of Kansas City	**$8,271 $16,061**	**$5,956 $11,520**	**$9,430**	**$11,450**	**19.4/1**	**22**	**11**	**73**	**27**	**0**	**481**	**22**	**54.5**	**45.5**	**12.1**	**3.4%**
Missouri, U. of Columbia	**$8,272 $16,062**	**$0 $0**	**$8,856**	**$11,330**	**16.8/1**	**25**	**4**	**80**	**20**	**8**	**485**	**0**	**62.3**	**37.7**	**9.5**	**11%**
St. Louis U.	**$17,175 $17,175**	**$12,810 $12,810**	**$8,520**	**$9,280**	**20.1/1**	**30**	**18**	**77**	**23**	**7**	**546**	**269**	**55.5**	**44.5**	**18.1**	**5.5%**
Washington U.	**$20,390 $20,390**	**$0 $0**	**N/A**	**$9,000**	**18.6/1**	**29**	**42**	**66**	**34**	**14**	**647**	**0**	**60.6**	**39.4**	**18.1**	**7.3%**
Montana																
Montana, U. of	**$5,656 $10,314**	**$0 $0**	**$7,440**	**$7,440**	**16.0/1**	**12**	**6**	**58**	**42**	**8**	**230**	**0**	**56.5**	**43.5**	**6.5**	**1.3%**
Nebraska																
Creighton U.	**$14,790 $14,790**	**$8,686 $8,686**	**$10,722**	**$10,722**	**16.3/1**	**24**	**25**	**71**	**29**	**4**	**455**	**22**	**58.0**	**42.0**	**9.2**	**13%**
Nebraska, U. of	**$3,953 $8,535**	**$0 $0**	**$6,680**	**$8,765**	**14.6/1**	**22**	**15**	**82**	**18**	**9**	**384**	**2**	**57.3**	**42.7**	**8.6**	**18%**

SECTION OF LEGAL EDUCATION AND ADMISSIONS TO THE BAR • ESTABLISHED 1893 • ABA	EXPENSES				FACULTY						STUDENT BODY					
	Res Non-Res Full-Time Tuition	Res Non-Res Part-Time Tuition	Expenses: on-campus	Expenses: off-campus	Student-Faculty Ratio	# Full-Time Faculty	# Part-Time Faculty	% Men	% Women	% Minorities	# of Full-Time Students	# of Part-Time Students	% Men	% Women	% Minorities	First Year Attrition Rate
New Hampshire																
Franklin Pierce Law Center	**$14,980 $14,980**	**$0 $0**	**N/A**	**$14,161**	**18.1/1**	**19**	**23**	**74**	**26**	**0**	**412**	**0**	**64.1**	**35.9**	**11.9**	**0.0%**
New Jersey																
Rutgers U.-Newark	**$9,534 $13,528**	**$6,098 $8,790**	**$9,668**	**$11,295**	**19.1/1**	**31**	**21**	**77**	**23**	**16**	**564**	**224**	**53.0**	**47.0**	**29.1**	**7.7%**
Rutgers U.-Camden	**$9,559 $13,553**	**$7,528 $10,893**	**$8,995**	**$11,295**	**22.9/1**	**26**	**35**	**85**	**15**	**8**	**608**	**163**	**55.6**	**44.4**	**17.1**	**9.3%**
Seton Hall U.	**$17,682 $17,682**	**$12,621 $12,621**	**N/A**	**$15,075**	**23.8/1**	**39**	**92**	**74**	**26**	**23**	**905**	**316**	**53.9**	**46.1**	**18.0**	**1.8%**
New Mexico																
New Mexico, U. of	**$3,283 $11,015**	**$0 $0**	**$7,220**	**$10,164**	**11.3/1**	**25**	**20**	**52**	**48**	**24**	**339**	**0**	**51.9**	**48.1**	**39.2**	**6.5%**
New York																
Albany Law School	**$18,100 $18,100**	**$13,601 $13,601**	**$8,900**	**$9,970**	**23.8/1**	**26**	**19**	**69**	**31**	**15**	**720**	**36**	**48.9**	**51.1**	**17.9**	**10%**
Brooklyn Law School	**$19,760 $19,760**	**$14,845 $14,845**	**$16,506**	**$16,506**	**20.3/1**	**53**	**53**	**55**	**45**	**8**	**967**	**487**	**52.8**	**47.2**	**16.0**	**2.6%**
City U. of New York	**$6,452 $9,682**	**$0 $0**	**N/A**	**$9,500**	**13.8/1**	**28**	**10**	**46**	**54**	**39**	**465**	**0**	**40.2**	**59.8**	**35.9**	**3.7%**
Columbia U.	**$24,342 $24,342**	**$0 $0**	**$12,380**	**$13,410**	**15.6/1**	**57**	**42**	**74**	**26**	**11**	**1,073**	**0**	**56.2**	**43.8**	**33.0**	**0.0%**
Cornell U.	**$22,100 $22,100**	**$0 $0**	**$11,850**	**N/A**	**12.0/1**	**42**	**12**	**81**	**19**	**7**	**553**	**0**	**59.7**	**40.3**	**26.6**	**2.2%**
Fordham U.	**$21,694 $21,694**	**$16,274 $16,274**	**$15,665**	**$15,665**	**20.5/1**	**52**	**92**	**77**	**23**	**10**	**1,043**	**361**	**57.1**	**42.9**	**26.4**	**1.3%**
Hofstra U.	**$20,238 $20,238**	**$0 $0**	**$13,552**	**$17,082**	**23.2/1**	**29**	**14**	**86**	**14**	**14**	**808**	**0**	**56.3**	**43.7**	**17.0**	**0.7%**
New York Law School	**$20,055 $20,055**	**$15,041 $15,041**	**$13,945**	**$13,945**	**22.8/1**	**45**	**64**	**73**	**27**	**16**	**911**	**484**	**52.4**	**47.6**	**22.1**	**7.8%**
New York U.	**$24,191 $24,191**	**$0 $0**	**$14,274**	**$14,274**	**14.1/1**	**79**	**61**	**72**	**28**	**5**	**1,342**	**0**	**54.9**	**45.1**	**22.4**	**0.2%**
Pace U.	**$19,444 $19,444**	**$14,592 $14,592**	**$9,108**	**$12,800**	**15.6/1**	**37**	**34**	**65**	**35**	**8**	**492**	**307**	**44.1**	**55.9**	**14.6**	**7.3%**
St. John's U.	**$20,000 $20,000**	**$15,000 $15,000**	**N/A**	**$12,000**	**18.0/1**	**48**	**21**	**71**	**29**	**19**	**852**	**282**	**60.3**	**39.7**	**26.1**	**12%**
State U. of New York at Buffalo	**$6,775 $11,425**	**$0 $0**	**$9,529**	**$9,529**	**17.1/1**	**37**	**0**	**65**	**35**	**14**	**743**	**0**	**51.0**	**49.0**	**17.0**	**5.3%**
Syracuse U.	**$20,142 $20,142**	**$189 $189**	**$11,727**	**$11,727**	**17.2/1**	**36**	**22**	**64**	**36**	**11**	**723**	**15**	**56.4**	**43.6**	**22.3**	**0.7%**
Touro College	**$18,750 $18,750**	**$14,600 $14,600**	**$15,089**	**$15,089**	**16.5/1**	**35**	**12**	**63**	**37**	**9**	**448**	**331**	**60.7**	**39.3**	**24.6**	**12%**
Yeshiva U.	**$19,055 $19,055**	**$0 $0**	**N/A**	**$17,742**	**21.3/1**	**38**	**52**	**76**	**24**	**5**	**972**	**0**	**53.7**	**46.3**	**15.8**	**0.0%**

Section of Legal Education and Admissions to the Bar · ABA · Established 1893	EXPENSES				FACULTY						STUDENT BODY					
	Res Non-Res Full-Time Tuition	Res Non-Res Part-Time Tuition	Expenses: on-campus	Expenses: off-campus	Student-Faculty Ratio	# Full-Time Faculty	# Part-Time Faculty	% Men	% Women	% Minorities	# of Full-Time Students	# of Part-Time Students	% Men	% Women	% Minorities	First Year Attrition Rate
North Carolina																
Campbell U.	**$14,700 $14,700**	**$0 $0**	**$9,517**	**$12,337**	**19.9/1**	**14**	**7**	**93**	**7**	**0**	**330**	**0**	**55.8**	**44.2**	**4.2**	**3.4%**
Duke U.	**$23,414 $23,414**	**$0 $0**	**$10,904**	**$10,904**	**15.4/1**	**32**	**19**	**66**	**34**	**13**	**600**	**0**	**60.7**	**39.3**	**17.5**	**2.0%**
North Carolina Central	**$1,890 $10,842**	**$1,890 $10,842**	**$4,655**	**$6,850**	**20.0/1**	**13**	**10**	**46**	**54**	**62**	**243**	**104**	**44.4**	**55.6**	**60.9**	**8.0%**
North Carolina, U. of	**$2,717 $13,989**	**$0 $0**	**$8,382**	**$8,728**	**18.6/1**	**32**	**17**	**66**	**34**	**6**	**688**	**0**	**53.5**	**46.5**	**20.1**	**3.5%**
Wake Forest U.	**$18,200 $18,200**	**$0 $0**	**N/A**	**$11,000**	**15.3/1**	**25**	**18**	**68**	**32**	**4**	**460**	**0**	**62.0**	**38.0**	**9.6**	**12%**
North Dakota																
North Dakota, U. of	**$3,948 $8,174**	**$0 $0**	**$7,300**	**$7,300**	**15.7/1**	**11**	**6**	**55**	**45**	**0**	**202**	**0**	**61.9**	**38.1**	**5.9**	**9.0%**
Ohio																
Akron, U. of	**$5,916 $10,158**	**$4,262 $7,292**	**$10,320**	**$10,320**	**30.0/1**	**16**	**32**	**75**	**25**	**13**	**456**	**182**	**61.0**	**39.0**	**9.0**	**15%**
Capital U.	**$15,407 $15,407**	**$9,443 $9,443**	**$10,585**	**$10,585**	**19.7/1**	**29**	**24**	**69**	**31**	**14**	**463**	**336**	**54.6**	**45.4**	**11.2**	**22%**
Case Western Reserve U.	**$19,040 $19,040**	**$19,040 $19,040**	**$10,100**	**$10,100**	**16.3/1**	**32**	**38**	**81**	**19**	**6**	**619**	**13**	**58.0**	**42.0**	**13.4**	**9.5%**
Cincinnati, U. of	**$6,900 $13,407**	**$0 $0**	**$10,144**	**$10,144**	**13.9/1**	**22**	**23**	**68**	**32**	**9**	**360**	**10**	**50.8**	**49.2**	**10.6**	**1.7%**
Cleveland State U.	**$6,936 $13,830**	**$5,334 $10,636**	**$7,934**	**$9,760**	**18.8/1**	**34**	**32**	**71**	**29**	**12**	**563**	**310**	**54.9**	**45.1**	**11.2**	**12%**
Dayton, U. of	**$17,030 $17,030**	**$0 $0**	**$8,800**	**$8,800**	**20.5/1**	**20**	**26**	**75**	**25**	**5**	**493**	**0**	**57.4**	**42.6**	**13.4**	**11%**
Ohio Northern U.	**$20,510 $20,510**	**$0 $0**	**$6,800**	**$7,800**	**15.0/1**	**20**	**7**	**80**	**20**	**5**	**343**	**0**	**64.1**	**35.9**	**9.9**	**20%**
Ohio State U.	**$6,412 $14,932**	**$0 $0**	**$8,630**	**$8,630**	**17.6/1**	**32**	**24**	**78**	**22**	**13**	**673**	**6**	**55.7**	**44.3**	**16.8**	**4.8%**
Toledo, U. of	**$6,542 $12,442**	**$5,452 $10,370**	**N/A**	**$9,502**	**18.8/1**	**26**	**14**	**77**	**23**	**4**	**436**	**198**	**58.0**	**42.0**	**9.6**	**13%**
Oklahoma																
Oklahoma City U.	**$12,218 $12,218**	**$8,748 $8,748**	**$6,509**	**$8,791**	**16.7/1**	**26**	**11**	**77**	**23**	**8**	**399**	**187**	**61.7**	**38.3**	**12.3**	**18%**
Oklahoma, U. of	**$4,141 $11,779**	**$0 $0**	**$9,122**	**$10,497**	**15.2/1**	**30**	**12**	**77**	**23**	**13**	**542**	**0**	**58.9**	**41.1**	**13.7**	**0.0%**
Tulsa, U. of	**$14,760 $14,760**	**$9,860 $9,860**	**$4,260**	**$5,850**	**16.8/1**	**28**	**30**	**68**	**32**	**14**	**480**	**128**	**60.8**	**39.2**	**12.7**	**3.4%**
Oregon																
Lewis & Clark College	**$16,485 $16,485**	**$12,365 $12,365**	**N/A**	**$10,730**	**18.3/1**	**26**	**30**	**81**	**19**	**4**	**450**	**181**	**55.3**	**44.7**	**16.0**	**5.0%**
Oregon, U. of	**$9,090 $13,572**	**$0 $0**	**$6,608**	**$7,305**	**16.9/1**	**25**	**10**	**68**	**32**	**16**	**499**	**0**	**48.9**	**51.1**	**13.8**	**1.1%**
Willamette U.	**$16,350 $16,350**	**$0 $0**	**$10,820**	**$10,820**	**19.2/1**	**19**	**6**	**79**	**21**	**5**	**438**	**0**	**57.8**	**42.2**	**11.6**	**11%**

SECTION OF LEGAL EDUCATION • AND ADMISSIONS TO THE BAR • ESTABLISHED 1893 ABA	EXPENSES				FACULTY						STUDENT BODY					
	Res Non-Res Full-Time Tuition	Res Non-Res Part-Time Tuition	Expenses: on-campus	Expenses: off-campus	Student-Faculty Ratio	# Full-Time Faculty	# Part-Time Faculty	% Men	% Women	% Minorities	# of Full-Time Students	# of Part-Time Students	% Men	% Women	% Minorities	First Year Attrition Rate
Pennsylvania																
Dickinson School of Law	**$14,600 $14,600**	**$0 $0**	**$9,724**	**$12,224**	**23.9/1**	**18**	**20**	**67**	**33**	**22**	**516**	**2**	**55.8**	**44.2**	**9.1**	**7.4%**
Duquesne U.	**$13,635 $13,635**	**$10,433 $10,433**	**$7,885**	**$9,384**	**20.7/1**	**21**	**14**	**71**	**29**	**14**	**311**	**319**	**56.3**	**43.7**	**7.7**	**14%**
Pennsylvania, U. of	**$23,314 $23,314**	**$0 $0**	**$11,686**	**$11,686**	**18.3/1**	**36**	**27**	**78**	**22**	**6**	**788**	**2**	**58.8**	**41.2**	**25.5**	**2.2%**
Pittsburgh, U. of	**$11,354 $17,362**	**$0 $0**	**N/A**	**$9,900**	**21.0/1**	**29**	**21**	**62**	**38**	**17**	**723**	**10**	**59.8**	**40.2**	**9.7**	**5.4%**
Temple U.	**$8,432 $14,946**	**$6,796 $12,008**	**$13,360**	**$13,360**	**19.7/1**	**43**	**83**	**74**	**26**	**23**	**771**	**375**	**50.3**	**49.7**	**28.8**	**2.5%**
Villanova U.	**$17,780 $17,780**	**$0 $0**	**N/A**	**$12,700**	**21.1/1**	**27**	**24**	**89**	**11**	**4**	**685**	**0**	**57.1**	**42.9**	**13.0**	**4.7%**
Widener U.	**$16,900 $16,900**	**$12,690 $12,690**	**N/A**	**$11,170**	**18.5/1**	**22**	**16**	**64**	**36**	**5**	**389**	**149**	**60.4**	**39.6**	**3.3**	**9.6%**
Puerto Rico																
Inter American U. of Puerto Rico	**$9,622 $9,622**	**$7,222 $7,222**	**N/A**	**$8,900**	**20.4/1**	**22**	**18**	**59**	**41**	**100**	**332**	**313**	**43.4**	**56.6**	**100.0**	**14%**
Pontifical Catholic U. of Pruerto Rico	**$7,338 $7,338**	**$5,566 $5,566**	**$6,811**	**$8,927**	**21.2/1**	**17**	**14**	**65**	**35**	**100**	**324**	**165**	**45.4**	**54.6**	**100.0**	**19%**
Puerto Rico, U. of	**$2,320 $3,570**	**$1,570 $3,500**	**$9,975**	**$8,475**	**24.0/1**	**16**	**31**	**81**	**19**	**100**	**333**	**199**	**37.2**	**62.8**	**97.0**	**9.0%**
Rhode Island																
Roger Williams U.	**$17,100 $17,100**	**$13,091 $13,091**	**$11,970**	**$12,825**	**18.2/1**	**23**	**0**	**65**	**35**	**9**	**286**	**227**	**58.0**	**42.0**	**5.2**	**7.5%**
South Carolina																
South Carolina, U. of	**$6,536 $12,896**	**$0 $0**	**$3,714**	**$6,957**	**19.7/1**	**34**	**12**	**88**	**12**	**6**	**752**	**0**	**60.0**	**40.0**	**10.5**	**5.2%**
South Dakota																
South Dakota, U. of	**$4,235 $8,743**	**$0 $0**	**$5,709**	**$8,329**	**17.7/1**	**10**	**3**	**90**	**10**	**0**	**213**	**0**	**64.8**	**35.2**	**5.2**	**13%**
Tennessee																
Memphis, U. of	**$3,852 $9,680**	**$3,022 $7,576**	**$9,873**	**$9,873**	**18.4/1**	**21**	**20**	**71**	**29**	**5**	**447**	**24**	**58.6**	**41.4**	**10.7**	**15%**
Tennessee, U. of	**$3,794 $9,620**	**$0 $0**	**$10,292**	**$10,292**	**14.5/1**	**27**	**22**	**70**	**30**	**7**	**469**	**0**	**53.3**	**46.7**	**11.7**	**6.1%**
Vanderbilt U.	**$20,964 $20,964**	**$0 $0**	**$13,500**	**$13,500**	**20.1/1**	**23**	**21**	**83**	**17**	**4**	**554**	**0**	**63.0**	**37.0**	**17.5**	**0.0%**
Texas																
Baylor U.	**$11,234 $11,234**	**$0 $0**	**$7,906**	**$12,166**	**21.5/1**	**16**	**8**	**75**	**25**	**6**	**408**	**0**	**67.2**	**32.8**	**10.3**	**12%**
Houston, U. of	**$5,197 $9,397**	**$3,829 $6,829**	**$7,510**	**$9,350**	**19.8/1**	**39**	**51**	**82**	**18**	**8**	**793**	**205**	**60.2**	**39.8**	**20.1**	**5.2%**
South Texas College of Law	**$14,355 $14,355**	**$9,619 $9,619**	**N/A**	**$11,708**	**21.3/1**	**44**	**25**	**77**	**23**	**11**	**838**	**379**	**58.0**	**42.0**	**19.5**	**13%**
Southern Methodist U.	**$19,804 $19,804**	**$0 $0**	**$10,536**	**$9,000**	**20.8/1**	**31**	**58**	**77**	**23**	**13**	**762**	**18**	**55.1**	**44.9**	**22.8**	**0.0%**

SECTION OF LEGAL EDUCATION • AND ADMISSIONS TO THE BAR • ESTABLISHED 1893 ABA

	EXPENSES				FACULTY						STUDENT BODY					
	Full-Time Tuition (Res / Non-Res)	Part-Time Tuition (Res / Non-Res)	Expenses: on-campus	Expenses: off-campus	Student-Faculty Ratio	# Full-Time Faculty	# Part-Time Faculty	% Men	% Women	% Minorities	# of Full-Time Students	# of Part-Time Students	% Men	% Women	% Minorities	First Year Attrition Rate
Texas																
St. Mary's U.	$15,200 $15,200	$0 $0	$9,212	$12,296	20.2/1	32	37	75	25	25	776	0	51.8	48.2	35.8	4.1%
Texas Southern U.	$4,440 $8,080	$0 $0	$4,407	$9,693	22.8/1	22	8	73	27	77	603	0	55.1	44.9	82.4	36%
Texas Tech U.	$5,866 $9,616	$0 $0	$8,890	$8,890	27.5/1	20	6	80	20	10	640	0	63.3	36.7	14.2	7.4%
Texas Wesleyan U.	$11,234 $11,234	$8,074 $8,074	N/A	$8,257	23.4/1	21	31	81	19	10	376	323	53.7	46.3	19.1	19%
Texas, U. of at Austin	$5,340 $11,360	$0 $0	N/A	$10,044	18.7/1	67	47	79	21	7	1,542	0	56.7	43.3	24.7	2.9%
Utah																
Brigham Young U.	$4,780 $7,160	$264 $396	$10,550	$10,440	18.5/1	21	21	81	19	14	467	0	67.9	32.1	12.8	0.0%
Utah, U. of	$4,291 $9,587	$0 $0	$12,246	$12,246	14.8/1	21	9	71	29	14	359	0	62.4	37.6	13.9	7.0%
Vermont																
Vermont Law School	$18,025 $18,025	$0 $0	N/A	$12,670	20.9/1	19	13	68	32	5	475	0	55.6	44.4	6.5	0.0%
Virginia																
George Mason U.	$7,280 $17,948	$5,200 $12,820	N/A	$14,378	18.7/1	26	28	85	15	8	372	319	61.6	38.4	9.1	1.9%
Regent U.	$12,848 $12,848	$0 $0	N/A	$10,380	19.1/1	16	14	75	25	19	367	0	68.7	31.3	6.5	14%
Richmond, U. of	$17,170 $17,170	$0 $0	$7,730	$10,005	18.0/1	22	30	59	41	5	472	6	51.5	48.5	20.1	3.5%
Virginia, U. of	$12,030 $19,178	$0 $0	$10,420	$10,420	17.4/1	58	35	79	21	9	1,148	0	63.2	36.8	13.5	3.4%
Washington & Lee U.	$16,351 $16,351	$0 $0	$9,800	$9,800	9.8/1	33	8	82	18	6	359	0	59.6	40.4	11.1	5.4%
William and Mary School of Law	$6,674 $17,002	$0 $0	$10,230	$10,230	18.5/1	24	22	71	29	17	532	0	53.9	46.1	20.7	6.0%
Washington																
Gonzaga U.	$16,570 $16,570	$9,970 $9,970	$10,900	$10,900	20.0/1	22	15	73	27	5	517	18	63.6	36.4	14.3	19%
Seattle U.	$16,426 $16,426	$16,412 $16,412	N/A	$10,980	23.1/1	30	16	67	33	7	701	198	51.5	48.5	19.8	7.6%
Washington, U. of	$5,050 $12,500	$0 $0	$10,974	$10,974	13.9/1	32	13	63	38	13	498	0	50.8	49.2	35.9	0.0%
West Virginia																
West Virginia U.	$4,288 $11,168	$0 $0	$7,580	$9,500	14.3/1	26	14	65	35	8	419	13	51.3	48.7	4.8	4.2%

SECTION OF LEGAL EDUCATION AND ADMISSIONS TO THE BAR • ESTABLISHED 1893 • ABA	EXPENSES				FACULTY						STUDENT BODY					
	Res Non-Res Full-Time Tuition	Res Non-Res Part-Time Tuition	Expenses: on-campus	Expenses: off-campus	Student-Faculty Ratio	# Full-Time Faculty	# Part-Time Faculty	% Men	% Women	% Minorities	# of Full-Time Students	# of Part-Time Students	% Men	% Women	% Minorities	First Year Attrition Rate
Wisconsin																
Marquette U.	**$17,310** **$17,310**	**$650** **$650**	**$10,730**	**$10,730**	**18.2/1**	**21**	**24**	**62**	**38**	**14**	**454**	**8**	**58.6**	**41.4**	**13.0**	**0.0%**
Wisconsin, U. of	**$5,504** **$14,261**	**$4,586** **$11,882**	**$9,110**	**$9,110**	**20.4/1**	**34**	**52**	**71**	**29**	**9**	**788**	**79**	**54.1**	**45.9**	**24.5**	**4.6%**
Wyoming																
Wyoming, U. of	**$3,920** **$8,648**	**$0** **$0**	**$6,740**	**$8,500**	**14.7/1**	**12**	**7**	**58**	**42**	**0**	**211**	**0**	**56.4**	**43.6**	**6.2**	**21%**

SECTION OF LEGAL EDUCATION AND ADMISSIONS TO THE BAR · ESTABLISHED 1893 · ABA	ADMISSIONS																
			FULL-TIME						PART-TIME						TOTAL	
	Application Deadline	Application Fee	75% GPA	25% GPA	75% LSAT	25% LSAT	% Accepted	# of Matriculants	75% GPA	25% GPA	75% LSAT	25% LSAT	% Accepted	# of Matriculants	Total % Admitted	Total Matriculants
Alabama																
Alabama, U. of	3/1	$25	3.66	3.16	159	153	38	189	0.00	0.00	0	0	N/A	0	38	189
Samford U.	2/28	$40	3.30	2.81	155	150	57	214	0.00	0.00	0	0	N/A	0	57	214
Arizona																
Arizona State U.	3/1	$35	3.70	3.19	162	156	21	155	0.00	0.00	0	0	N/A	0	21	155
Arizona, U. of	3/1	$45	3.68	3.12	164	156	27	151	0.00	0.00	0	0	N/A	0	27	151
Arkansas																
Arkansas, U. of Fayetteville	4/1	$0	3.51	2.88	157	147	50	157	0.00	0.00	0	0	N/A	0	50	157
Arkansas, U. of Little Rock	4/1	$40	3.57	2.95	156	149	57	86	3.59	2.81	159	146	43	49	53	135
California																
California Western School of Law	4/1	$45	3.35	2.84	155	148	64	304	0.00	0.00	0	0	N/A	0	64	304
California-Hastings	2/15	$40	3.65	2.94	165	149	41	492	0.00	0.00	0	0	N/A	0	41	492
California-Los Angeles	1/16	$40	3.75	3.42	165	159	23	305	0.00	0.00	0	0	N/A	0	23	305
California-Berkeley	2/1	$40	3.85	3.55	170	161	18	263	0.00	0.00	0	0	N/A	0	18	263
California-Davis	2/1	$40	3.62	3.15	165	158	32	152	0.00	0.00	0	0	N/A	0	32	152
Golden Gate U.	4/15	$40	3.39	2.76	155	149	56	187	3.38	2.72	155	150	54	72	56	259
Loyola Marymount U.	2/1	$50	3.48	3.05	161	154	39	354	3.42	2.93	161	154	39	124	39	478
McGeorge	5/15	$40	3.28	2.75	155	150	55	310	3.31	2.70	155	150	N/A	107	63	417
Pepperdine U.	3/1	$50	3.53	3.03	160	154	41	207	0.00	0.00	0	0	N/A	0	41	207
San Diego, U. of	5/1	$35	3.36	2.84	161	157	35	225	3.28	2.68	158	154	N/A	85	35	310
San Francisco, U. of	4/1	$40	3.40	2.90	160	154	40	181	3.40	2.80	156	150	84	53	43	234
Santa Clara U.	3/1	$40	3.46	3.07	158	153	41	222	3.38	2.86	159	152	46	68	41	290
Southern California, U.	2/1	$60	3.58	3.22	166	162	23	205	0.00	0.00	0	0	N/A	0	23	205
Southwestern U.	6/30	$50	3.27	2.72	154	150	53	296	3.25	2.69	153	150	49	104	53	400
Stanford U.	2/15	$65	3.88	3.51	171	165	12	176	0.00	0.00	0	0	N/A	0	12	176
Thomas Jefferson School of Law	n/a	$35	2.98	2.48	150	145	67	70	3.01	2.55	152	146	68	61	67	131

	ADMISSIONS																
			FULL-TIME						PART-TIME						TOTAL	
	Application Deadline	Application Fee	75% GPA	25% GPA	75% LSAT	25% LSAT	% Accepted	# of Matriculants	75% GPA	25% GPA	75% LSAT	25% LSAT	% Accepted	# of Matriculants	Total % Admitted	Total Matriculants
California																
Whittier College	3/15	$50	3.16	2.65	153	147	49	186	3.32	2.65	154	148	48	70	49	256
Colorado																
Colorado, U. of	2/15	$40	3.73	3.30	165	160	30	167	0.00	0.00	0	0	N/A	0	30	167
Denver, U. of	5/1	$45	3.38	2.82	159	153	56	277	3.49	2.77	159	152	63	72	57	349
Connecticut																
Connecticut, U. of	3/1	$30	3.50	3.03	161	156	38	125	3.50	3.08	159	152	41	65	39	190
Quinnipiac College	rolling	$40	3.00	2.50	153	147	54	161	3.20	2.60	153	147	45	74	52	235
Yale U.	2/15	$65	3.94	3.73	175	168	7	198	0.00	0.00	0	0	N/A	0	7	198
Delaware																
Widener U.	5/15	$60	3.23	2.75	151	147	67	285	3.27	2.62	154	147	64	155	66	440
District of Columbia																
American U.	3/1	$55	3.51	3.07	160	155	41	286	3.34	2.66	159	149	44	88	41	374
Catholic U. of America	3/1	$55	3.40	2.80	157	151	49	221	3.20	2.60	155	148	48	79	49	300
District of Columbia	4/1	$35	2.88	2.36	147	141	28	76	0.00	0.00	0	0	N/A	0	28	76
George Washington U.	3/1	$55	3.63	3.24	163	159	N/A	395	3.32	2.90	161	155	N/A	54	N/A	449
Georgetown U.	3/1	$60	3.77	3.24	169	161	28	568	3.62	3.10	167	160	35	131	29	699
Howard U.	4/30	$60	3.29	2.70	153	148	29	128	0.00	0.00	0	0	N/A	0	29	128
Florida																
Florida State U.		$20	3.55	3.06	159	153	31	203	0.00	0.00	0	0	N/A	0	31	203
Florida, U. of	2/1	$20	3.73	3.26	163	155	33	218	0.00	0.00	0	0	N/A	0	33	218
Miami, U. of	3/7	$45	3.43	2.92	156	150	62	378	3.31	2.68	152	145	60	126	62	504
Nova Southeastern U.	5/31	$45	3.17	2.67	151	145	56	313	3.30	2.55	153	144	56	72	56	385
St. Thomas U.	4/30	$40	2.92	2.37	150	144	58	217	0.00	0.00	0	0	N/A	0	58	217
Stetson U.	3/1	$45	3.45	2.95	156	149	43	220	0.00	0.00	0	0	N/A	0	43	220

SECTION OF LEGAL EDUCATION AND ADMISSIONS TO THE BAR • ESTABLISHED 1893 ABA	ADMISSIONS															
			FULL-TIME						PART-TIME						TOTAL	
	Application Deadline	Application Fee	75% GPA	25% GPA	75% LSAT	25% LSAT	% Accepted	# of Matriculants	75% GPA	25% GPA	75% LSAT	25% LSAT	% Accepted	# of Matriculants	Total % Admitted	Total Matriculants
Georgia																
Emory U.	3/1	$50	3.60	3.20	164	158	40	208	0.00	0.00	0	0	N/A	0	40	208
Georgia State U.	3/15	$30	3.46	2.92	159	154	23	153	3.60	2.90	161	153	25	65	23	218
Georgia, U. of	3/1	$30	3.65	3.23	165	158	26	236	0.00	0.00	0	0	N/A	0	26	236
Mercer U.	3/15	$45	3.43	2.67	157	151	43	143	0.00	0.00	0	0	N/A	0	43	143
Hawaii																
Hawaii, U. of	3/1	$30	3.61	3.11	161	154	27	68	0.00	0.00	0	0	N/A	0	27	68
Idaho																
Idaho, U. of	2/1	$30	3.51	3.02	157	149	50	84	0.00	0.00	0	0	N/A	0	50	84
Illinois																
Chicago, U. of	none	$60	3.80	3.54	173	166	23	180	0.00	0.00	0	0	N/A	0	23	180
Depaul U.	4/1	$40	3.48	3.03	158	153	58	251	3.43	2.75	157	152	52	87	57	338
Illinois Institute of Technology	4/1	$40	3.41	2.88	156	150	71	302	3.29	2.68	155	147	65	111	70	413
Illinois, U. of	3/15	$30	3.68	3.07	164	158	33	182	0.00	0.00	0	0	N/A	0	33	182
John Marshall Law School	3/1	$50	3.19	2.62	153	145	58	179	3.20	2.51	154	145	78	54	62	233
Loyola U.-Chicago	4/1	$45	3.48	2.95	161	154	38	163	3.40	2.84	159	151	64	83	41	246
Northern Illinois U.	5/15	$35	3.31	2.67	157	153	36	104	0.00	0.00	0	0	N/A	0	36	104
Northwestern U.	2/13	$80	3.73	3.26	167	159	21	203	0.00	0.00	0	0	N/A	0	21	203
Southern Illinois U.-Carbondale	3/1	$25	3.57	2.63	159	147	49	125	0.00	0.00	0	0	N/A	0	49	125
Indiana																
Indiana U.-Bloomington	rolling	$35	3.70	3.13	162	155	45	226	0.00	0.00	0	0	100	1	45	227
Indiana U.-Indianapolis	3/1	$35	3.53	2.92	158	152	52	179	3.52	2.90	158	152	38	87	48	266
Notre Dame, U. of	3/1	$45	3.64	3.09	165	160	26	172	0.00	0.00	0	0	N/A	0	26	172
Valparaiso U.	4/15	$30	3.50	2.85	156	147	70	141	3.41	2.80	152	146	64	17	69	158

	ADMISSIONS															
SECTION OF LEGAL EDUCATION AND ADMISSIONS TO THE BAR · ESTABLISHED 1893 · ABA			FULL-TIME						PART-TIME						TOTAL	
	Application Deadline	Application Fee	75% GPA	25% GPA	75% LSAT	25% LSAT	% Accepted	# of Matriculants	75% GPA	25% GPA	75% LSAT	25% LSAT	% Accepted	# of Matriculants	Total % Admitted	Total Matriculants
Iowa																
Drake U.	3/1	$35	3.41	2.82	157	150	52	154	3.56	2.39	159	149	19	3	51	157
Iowa, U. of	3/1	$20	3.73	3.20	161	155	43	217	0.00	0.00	0	0	N/A	0	43	217
Kansas																
Kansas, U. of	3/15	$40	3.67	3.16	161	154	46	185	0.00	0.00	0	0	N/A	0	46	185
Washburn U.	3/15	$30	3.57	2.91	156	149	60	182	0.00	0.00	0	0	N/A	0	60	182
Kentucky																
Kentucky, U. of	3/1	$25	3.68	3.11	161	156	38	133	0.00	0.00	0	0	N/A	0	38	133
Louisville, U. of	2/15	$30	3.66	3.01	158	152	40	123	3.48	2.80	159	152	52	43	42	166
Northern Kentucky U.	5/15	$30	3.40	2.87	157	151	39	72	3.34	2.79	157	151	48	55	41	127
Louisiana																
Louisiana State U.	2/1	$25	3.55	3.12	156	148	57	262	0.00	0.00	0	0	N/A	0	57	262
Loyola U.- New Orleans	none	$20	3.20	2.73	153	148	60	159	3.33	2.71	156	148	54	47	60	206
Southern U.	3/31	$0	2.99	2.43	147	143	18	125	0.00	0.00	0	0	N/A	0	18	125
Tulane U.		$45	3.52	3.03	161	156	51	327	0.00	0.00	0	0	N/A	0	51	327
Maine																
Maine, U. of	2/15	$25	3.45	3.09	158	150	50	101	3.16	2.90	156	142	N/A	4	50	105
Maryland																
Baltimore, U. of	4/1	$35	3.23	2.80	154	149	55	224	3.31	2.63	155	147	45	86	53	310
Maryland, U. of	2/15	$40	3.53	3.02	161	152	39	200	3.65	2.99	161	153	33	67	38	267
Massachusetts																
Boston College	3/1	$50	3.61	3.17	165	159	26	268	0.00	0.00	0	0	N/A	0	26	268
Boston U.	3/1	$50	3.60	3.14	163	159	34	340	0.00	0.00	0	0	N/A	0	34	340
Harvard U.	2/1	$65	3.93	3.70	173	166	13	555	0.00	0.00	0	0	N/A	0	13	555
New England School of Law	3/15 &	$50	3.18	2.59	151	146	65	171	3.12	2.55	152	146	68	82	65	253
Northeastern U.	3/1	$55	3.51	3.04	159	151	36	215	0.00	0.00	0	0	N/A	0	36	215
Suffolk U.	3/3	$50	3.39	2.91	156	148	71	365	3.38	2.82	156	150	61	209	69	574

	ADMISSIONS															
			FULL-TIME						PART-TIME						TOTAL	
	Application Deadline	Application Fee	75% GPA	25% GPA	75% LSAT	25% LSAT	% Accepted	# of Matriculants	75% GPA	25% GPA	75% LSAT	25% LSAT	% Accepted	# of Matriculants	Total % Admitted	Total Matriculants
Massachusetts																
Western New England	rolling	$35	3.25	2.71	153	147	61	134	3.27	2.69	153	146	69	74	63	208
Michigan																
Detroit College of Law At Michigan State U.	4/15	$50	3.10	2.74	154	149	65	148	3.16	2.51	151	147	57	37	64	185
Detroit Mercy, U. of	4/15	$50	3.35	2.79	155	146	63	108	3.15	2.66	154	147	34	50	51	158
Michigan, U. of	2/15	$70	3.68	3.34	170	164	31	319	0.00	0.00	0	0	N/A	0	31	319
Thomas Cooley Law School	rolling	$50	3.08	2.56	148	143	N/A	106	3.02	2.54	148	142	79	982	79	1,088
Wayne State U.	3/15	$20	3.56	3.07	158	152	52	150	3.47	2.94	158	151	34	77	47	227
Minnesota																
Hamline U.	5/15	$30	3.37	2.86	157	148	56	192	0.00	0.00	0	0	N/A	0	56	192
Minnesota, U. of	3/1	$40	3.77	3.27	164	158	37	253	0.00	0.00	0	0	N/A	0	37	253
William Mitchell College of Law	4/15	$35	3.40	2.90	158	150	67	168	3.38	2.82	158	148	N/A	126	67	294
Mississippi																
Mississippi College	5/1	$25	3.32	2.72	151	145	64	160	0.00	0.00	0	0	N/A	0	64	160
Mississippi, U. of	3/1	$20	3.56	3.02	156	147	44	224	0.00	0.00	0	0	N/A	0	44	224
Missouri																
Missouri, U. of Kansas City	none	$25	3.41	2.86	156	150	64	163	3.50	2.76	153	146	65	16	64	179
Missouri, U. of Columbia	3/1	$40	3.57	3.05	159	151	65	200	0.00	0.00	0	0	N/A	0	65	200
St. Louis U.	rolling	$40	3.64	3.12	158	149	53	179	3.51	2.73	157	149	62	77	54	256
Washington U.	3/1	$50	3.56	2.95	163	156	57	212	0.00	0.00	0	0	N/A	0	57	212
Montana																
Montana, U. of	3/1	$60	3.50	2.98	159	151	44	81	0.00	0.00	0	0	N/A	0	44	81
Nebraska																
Creighton U.	5/1	$40	3.48	2.95	154	147	65	162	2.97	2.64	150	147	79	5	66	167
Nebraska, U. of	3/1	$25	3.71	3.16	158	151	57	139	0.00	0.00	0	0	100	1	57	140

SECTION OF LEGAL EDUCATION AND ADMISSIONS TO THE BAR · ESTABLISHED 1893 · ABA	ADMISSIONS															
			FULL-TIME						PART-TIME						TOTAL	
	Application Deadline	Application Fee	75% GPA	25% GPA	75% LSAT	25% LSAT	% Accepted	# of Matriculants	75% GPA	25% GPA	75% LSAT	25% LSAT	% Accepted	# of Matriculants	Total % Admitted	Total Matriculants
New Hampshire																
Franklin Pierce Law Center	**5/1**	**$45**	**3.25**	**2.69**	**156**	**148**	**48**	**152**	**0.00**	**0.00**	**0**	**0**	**N/A**	**0**	**48**	**152**
New Jersey																
Rutgers U.-Newark	**3/15**	**$40**	**3.55**	**3.05**	**161**	**151**	**25**	**184**	**3.46**	**2.50**	**161**	**152**	**30**	**47**	**26**	**231**
Rutgers U.-Camden	**3/1**	**$40**	**3.41**	**2.95**	**157**	**151**	**45**	**192**	**3.37**	**2.71**	**159**	**151**	**N/A**	**42**	**45**	**234**
Seton Hall U.	**4/1**	**$50**	**3.36**	**2.88**	**156**	**151**	**52**	**272**	**3.24**	**2.70**	**157**	**152**	**35**	**80**	**49**	**352**
New Mexico																
New Mexico, U. of	**2/15**	**$40**	**3.57**	**2.91**	**160**	**150**	**29**	**112**	**0.00**	**0.00**	**0**	**0**	**N/A**	**0**	**29**	**112**
New York																
Albany Law School		**$50**	**3.35**	**2.78**	**154**	**147**	**67**	**247**	**0.00**	**0.00**	**0**	**0**	**N/A**	**0**	**67**	**247**
Brooklyn Law School	**none**	**$50**	**3.53**	**2.99**	**159**	**152**	**50**	**281**	**3.31**	**2.76**	**155**	**149**	**53**	**187**	**51**	**468**
City U. of New York	**3/15**	**$40**	**3.32**	**2.76**	**151**	**142**	**32**	**160**	**0.00**	**0.00**	**0**	**0**	**N/A**	**0**	**32**	**160**
Columbia U.	**2/15**	**$65**	**3.71**	**3.35**	**171**	**164**	**20**	**347**	**0.00**	**0.00**	**0**	**0**	**N/A**	**0**	**20**	**347**
Cornell U.	**2/1**	**$65**	**3.65**	**3.34**	**166**	**163**	**25**	**185**	**0.00**	**0.00**	**0**	**0**	**N/A**	**0**	**25**	**185**
Fordham U.	**3/1**	**$60**	**3.55**	**3.01**	**165**	**161**	**32**	**343**	**3.51**	**2.86**	**162**	**154**	**34**	**135**	**32**	**478**
Hofstra U.	**4/15**	**$60**	**3.50**	**2.97**	**158**	**150**	**43**	**256**	**0.00**	**0.00**	**0**	**0**	**N/A**	**0**	**43**	**256**
New York Law School	**4/1**	**$50**	**3.30**	**2.80**	**156**	**151**	**59**	**314**	**3.28**	**2.78**	**156**	**151**	**43**	**123**	**56**	**437**
New York U.	**2/1**	**$65**	**3.79**	**3.53**	**170**	**165**	**23**	**421**	**0.00**	**0.00**	**0**	**0**	**N/A**	**0**	**23**	**421**
Pace U.	**3/15**	**$55**	**3.46**	**3.00**	**155**	**146**	**44**	**165**	**3.52**	**2.67**	**157**	**149**	**41**	**81**	**44**	**246**
St. John's U.	**3/1**	**$50**	**3.34**	**2.71**	**157**	**152**	**51**	**348**	**3.09**	**2.64**	**156**	**151**	**40**	**77**	**49**	**425**
State U. of New York at Buffalo		**$50**	**3.56**	**2.99**	**159**	**148**	**52**	**208**	**0.00**	**0.00**	**0**	**0**	**N/A**	**0**	**52**	**208**
Syracuse U.	**4/1**	**$40**	**3.50**	**3.00**	**154**	**147**	**61**	**234**	**3.50**	**3.03**	**159**	**147**	**50**	**11**	**61**	**245**
Touro College	**rolling**	**$50**	**3.28**	**2.69**	**153**	**144**	**39**	**113**	**3.18**	**2.55**	**151**	**147**	**49**	**107**	**42**	**220**
Yeshiva U.	**4/1**	**$60**	**3.46**	**2.94**	**159**	**152**	**48**	**332**	**0.00**	**0.00**	**0**	**0**	**N/A**	**0**	**48**	**332**

Section of Legal Education and Admissions to the Bar • Established 1893 • ABA	ADMISSIONS															
			FULL-TIME						PART-TIME						TOTAL	
	Application Deadline	Application Fee	75% GPA	25% GPA	75% LSAT	25% LSAT	% Accepted	# of Matriculants	75% GPA	25% GPA	75% LSAT	25% LSAT	% Accepted	# of Matriculants	Total % Admitted	Total Matriculants
North Carolina																
Campbell U.	3/31	$40	3.42	2.62	158	152	26	119	0.00	0.00	0	0	N/A	0	26	119
Duke U.	1/15	$65	3.76	3.42	170	164	32	202	0.00	0.00	0	0	N/A	0	32	202
North Carolina Central		$30	3.20	2.60	154	146	19	101	3.40	2.70	158	151	19	32	19	133
North Carolina, U. of	2/1	$60	3.69	3.30	163	155	27	240	0.00	0.00	0	0	N/A	0	27	240
Wake Forest U.	3/15	$60	3.54	3.04	163	158	40	158	0.00	0.00	0	0	N/A	0	40	158
North Dakota																
North Dakota, U. of	4/1	$35	3.42	2.83	156	149	54	68	0.00	0.00	0	0	N/A	0	54	68
Ohio																
Akron, U. of	3/1pr	$35	3.37	2.78	156	150	48	153	3.57	2.71	156	150	43	66	47	219
Capital U.	none	$35	3.29	2.76	153	146	70	175	3.34	2.70	154	147	62	100	68	275
Case Western Reserve U.	4/1	$40	3.57	3.02	161	154	63	225	0.00	0.00	0	0	23	1	62	226
Cincinnati, U. of	4/1	$35	3.74	3.24	162	154	43	124	0.00	0.00	0	0	N/A	0	43	124
Cleveland State U.	4/1	$35	3.43	2.93	153	145	58	180	3.39	2.81	154	147	49	80	56	260
Dayton, U. of	5/1	$40	3.51	2.95	156	149	51	191	0.00	0.00	0	0	N/A	0	51	191
Ohio Northern U.	rolling	$40	3.29	2.64	152	144	64	125	0.00	0.00	0	0	N/A	0	64	125
Ohio State U.	3/15	$30	3.67	3.16	162	155	42	244	0.00	0.00	0	0	N/A	0	42	244
Toledo, U. of	3/15	$30	3.37	2.67	157	150	64	154	3.57	2.69	153	148	57	46	63	200
Oklahoma																
Oklahoma City U.	8/1	$35	3.24	2.66	152	144	58	131	3.47	2.66	152	145	77	51	60	182
Oklahoma, U. of	3/15	$50	3.43	3.05	155	150	41	167	0.00	0.00	0	0	N/A	0	41	167
Tulsa, U. of		$30	3.30	2.75	155	148	65	154	3.36	2.75	153	145	76	58	66	212
Oregon																
Lewis & Clark College		$50	3.45	3.01	164	158	46	135	3.34	2.78	161	156	57	36	47	171
Oregon, U. of	4/1	$50	3.60	3.13	161	155	41	162	0.00	0.00	0	0	N/A	0	41	162
Willamette U.	4/1	$40	3.44	2.84	158	152	53	136	0.00	0.00	0	0	N/A	0	53	136

Section of Legal Education and Admissions to the Bar • Established 1893 • ABA	ADMISSIONS																
			FULL-TIME						PART-TIME						TOTAL	
	Application Deadline	Application Fee	75% GPA	25% GPA	75% LSAT	25% LSAT	% Accepted	# of Matriculants	75% GPA	25% GPA	75% LSAT	25% LSAT	% Accepted	# of Matriculants	Total % Admitted	Total Matriculants
Pennsylvania																
Dickinson School of Law	3/1	$50	3.63	3.07	157	148	52	175	0.00	0.00	0	0	N/A	0	52	175
Duquesne U.	4/1	$50	3.53	2.92	156	150	61	113	3.18	2.59	156	148	59	85	60	198
Pennsylvania, U. of	3/1	$65	3.71	3.41	167	162	29	280	0.00	0.00	0	0	N/A	0	29	280
Pittsburgh, U. of	3/1	$40	3.42	2.89	158	152	64	263	0.00	0.00	0	0	31	3	63	266
Temple U.	3/1	$50	3.54	2.96	159	149	38	255	3.46	2.79	159	150	36	88	37	343
Villanova U.	1/31	$75	3.64	3.16	161	156	55	238	0.00	0.00	0	0	N/A	0	55	238
Widener U.	5/15	$60	3.25	2.64	151	145	70	107	3.31	2.68	154	149	65	48	69	155
Puerto Rico																
Inter American U. of Puerto Rico		$63	3.17	2.59	142	133	46	114	3.11	2.60	141	133	34	103	40	217
Pontifical Catholic U. of Pruerto Rico	4/15	$25	3.31	2.85	137	132	53	118	3.44	2.83	139	131	52	52	52	170
Puerto Rico, U. of	2/15	$15	3.66	3.26	150	143	30	114	3.60	2.95	150	142	16	46	25	160
Rhode Island																
Roger Williams U.	5/15	$60	3.38	2.75	151	143	61	91	3.28	2.70	152	142	62	82	61	173
South Carolina																
South Carolina, U. of	2/15	$25	3.59	2.98	160	154	32	250	0.00	0.00	0	0	N/A	0	32	250
South Dakota																
South Dakota, U. of	3/1pr	$15	3.50	2.80	154	149	61	73	0.00	0.00	0	0	N/A	0	61	73
Tennessee																
Memphis, U. of	2/15	$10	3.57	2.91	161	148	43	143	3.59	3.04	157	148	30	9	42	152
Tennessee, U. of	2/1	$15	3.71	3.14	160	153	36	165	0.00	0.00	0	0	N/A	0	36	165
Vanderbilt U.	2/1	$50	3.76	3.36	165	159	30	184	0.00	0.00	0	0	N/A	0	30	184
Texas																
Baylor U.	3/1	$40	3.76	3.28	163	157	43	75	0.00	0.00	0	0	N/A	0	43	75
Houston, U. of	2/1	$50	3.53	3.04	163	156	33	257	3.49	2.98	161	154	28	52	33	309
South Texas College of Law	3/1	$40	3.21	2.69	154	148	57	361	3.25	2.66	155	148	57	131	57	492
Southern Methodist U.	4/1	$45	3.47	2.85	159	154	41	255	3.15	2.91	158	154	12	6	40	261

	ADMISSIONS																	
SECTION OF LEGAL EDUCATION AND ADMISSIONS TO THE BAR · ESTABLISHED 1893 · ABA			FULL-TIME						PART-TIME						TOTAL	
	Application Deadline	Application Fee	75% GPA	25% GPA	75% LSAT	25% LSAT	% Accepted	# of Matriculants	75% GPA	25% GPA	75% LSAT	25% LSAT	% Accepted	# of Matriculants	Total % Admitted	Total Matriculants
Texas																
St. Mary's U.	3/1	$45	3.14	2.58	155	149	48	264	0.00	0.00	0	0	N/A	0	48	264
Texas Southern U.	4/11	$40	3.03	2.41	146	140	41	291	0.00	0.00	0	0	N/A	0	41	291
Texas Tech U.	2/1	$50	3.63	3.18	158	151	43	227	0.00	0.00	0	0	N/A	0	43	227
Texas Wesleyan U.	3/15pr	$50	3.23	2.59	150	143	53	144	3.22	2.69	151	144	62	105	55	249
Texas, U. of at Austin	2/1	$65	3.78	3.40	165	159	28	488	0.00	0.00	0	0	N/A	0	28	488
Utah																
Brigham Young U.	2/1	$30	3.78	3.40	163	156	31	160	0.00	0.00	0	0	N/A	0	31	160
Utah, U. of	2/1	$40	3.69	3.11	163	154	37	101	0.00	0.00	0	0	N/A	0	37	101
Vermont																
Vermont Law School	2/15	$50	3.38	2.83	158	152	78	176	0.00	0.00	0	0	N/A	0	78	176
Virginia																
George Mason U.	3/1	$35	3.34	2.87	161	157	39	148	3.24	2.71	162	158	34	68	38	216
Regent U.	4/1	$40	3.42	2.62	155	148	52	140	0.00	0.00	0	0	N/A	0	52	140
Richmond, U. of	2/10	$35	3.34	2.85	161	156	42	152	0.00	0.00	0	0	N/A	0	42	152
Virginia, U. of	1/15	$40	3.78	3.49	169	162	26	361	0.00	0.00	0	0	N/A	0	26	361
Washington & Lee U.	2/1	$40	3.75	3.11	166	161	28	120	0.00	0.00	0	0	N/A	0	28	120
William and Mary School of Law	3/1	$40	3.54	3.02	165	160	29	200	0.00	0.00	0	0	N/A	0	29	200
Washington																
Gonzaga U.	3/15	$40	3.28	2.70	154	148	67	169	0.00	0.00	0	0	N/A	0	67	169
Seattle U.	4/1	$50	3.52	3.00	159	153	56	215	3.53	2.85	157	150	63	73	57	288
Washington, U. of	1/15	$50	3.77	3.38	166	157	25	172	0.00	0.00	0	0	N/A	0	25	172
West Virginia																
West Virginia U.	2/1	$45	3.63	3.09	156	149	55	148	0.00	0.00	0	0	100	0	55	148

	ADMISSIONS															
			FULL-TIME						PART-TIME						TOTAL	
SECTION OF LEGAL EDUCATION AND ADMISSIONS TO THE BAR · ESTABLISHED 1893 · ABA	Application Deadline	Application Fee	75% GPA	25% GPA	75% LSAT	25% LSAT	% Accepted	# of Matriculants	75% GPA	25% GPA	75% LSAT	25% LSAT	% Accepted	# of Matriculants	Total % Admitted	Total Matriculants
Wisconsin																
Marquette U.	4/1	$35	3.33	2.87	160	153	47	150	3.52	2.82	160	153	15	7	45	157
Wisconsin, U. of	2/1	$38	3.64	3.13	161	153	39	267	0.00	0.00	0	0	N/A	0	39	267
Wyoming																
Wyoming, U. of	4/1	$35	3.59	3.06	157	150	47	78	0.00	0.00	0	0	N/A	0	47	78

Chapter Twelve

School Profiles

All ABA Approved Law Schools

pages 88-447

Please note that this book contains information concerning those law schools that were approved by the ABA as of October 1, 1996. The approval status of an individual law school could change, however. Therefore, if you would like to confirm whether an individual law school is approved by the ABA at a specific time after October 1, you should contact the ABA directly. Or you can access this information on the Section of Legal Education and Admissions to the Bar's Website. http://www.abanet.org/legaled

AKRON, UNIVERSITY OF

C. Blake McDowell Law Center
Akron, OH 44325-2901
800-4akron-u
http://www.uakron.edu/law/index.html

ABA Approved Since 1961

The Basics

Type of School: **PUBLIC**
Application deadline*: **3/1pr**
Application fee: **$35**
Financial Aid deadline*: **7/1pr**
Student faculty ratio: **30.0 to 1**
First year can start other than Fall: **No**
Student housing: **Yes**
--exclusively for law students: **No**
Term: **Semester**

*pr=preferred

Faculty

	Men #	Men %	Women #	Women %	Minorities #	Minorities %	Total
Full-time	12	75	4	25	2	13	16
Other full-time	0	0	0	0	0	0	0
Deans, librarians, & others who teach	3	60	2	40	1	20	5
Part-time	17	53	15	47	1	3	32
Total	32	60	21	40	4	8	53
Deans, librarians, & others who teach < 1/2	1	33	2	67	0	0	3

Library

# of volumes & volume equivalents	243,968	# of professional staff	6
# of titles	50,205	Hours per week with professional staff	79
# of active serial subscriptions	3,174	Hours per week without professional staff	19
Study seating capacity inside the library	295	# of student computer work stations for entire law school	48
Square feet of law library	34,634	# of additional networked connections	0
Square feet of law school (excl. Library)	31,937		

Curriculum

	Full time	Part time
Typical first-year section size	50	63
Is there typically a "small section" of the first year class, other than Legal Writing, taught by full-time faculty?	No	No
If yes, typical size offered last year	N/A	N/A
# of classroom course titles beyond 1st year curriculum	40	54
# of upper division courses, excluding seminars, with an enrollment:		
Under 25	26	21
25 - 49	15	24
50 - 74	11	2
75 - 99	2	0
100 +	0	0
# of seminars	12	14
# of seminar positions available	588	
# of seminar positions filled	207	249
# of positions available in simulation courses	192	
# of simulation positions filled	143	48
# of positions available in faculty supervised clinical courses	240	
# of fac. sup. clin. positions filled	96	0
# involved in field placements	93	7
# involved in law journals	51	0
# in moot court or trial competitions	38	11
# of credit hours required to graduate	88	

Enrollment & Attrition

	Full-Time Men #	Men %	Women #	Women %	Minorities #	Minorities %	Total #	Part-Time Men #	Men %	Women #	Women %	Minorities #	Minorities %	Total #	Attrition Academic #	Other #	Total #	Total %
1st Year	97	59.5	66	40.5	17	10.4	163	36	60.0	24	40.0	3	5.0	60	10	25	35	15
2nd Year	88	55.7	70	44.3	14	8.9	158	28	51.9	26	48.1	3	5.6	54	1	1	2	1.1
3rd Year	93	68.9	42	31.1	10	7.4	135	21	63.6	12	36.4	1	3.0	33	0	0	0	0.0
4th Year								20	57.1	15	42.9	2	5.7	35	0	0	0	0.0
Total	278	61.0	178	39.0	41	9.0	456	105	57.7	77	42.3	9	4.9	182	11	26	37	5.8
JD Degrees Awarded	81	60.4	53	39.6	11	8.2	134	21	55.3	17	44.7	2	5.3	38				

GPA & LSAT Scores

	Full Time	Part Time	Total
# of apps	1,194	224	1,418
# admits	575	96	671
# of matrics	153	66	219
75% GPA	3.37	3.57	
25% GPA	2.78	2.71	
75% LSAT	156	156	
25% LSAT	150	150	

Tuition/Living Expenses

	Resident	Non-resident
Full-Time	$5,916	$10,158
Part-Time	$4,262	$7,292

Estimated living expenses for Singles		
Living on campus	Living off campus	Living at home
$10,320	$10,320	$10,320

Career Placement

	Total	%
Employment status known	143	98.6
Employment status unknown	2	1.4
Employed	129	90.2
Pursuing graduate degrees	4	2.8
Unemployed seeking employment	5	3.5
Unemployed not seeking employment	5	3.5
Type of Employment		
# employed in law firms	64	49.6
# employed in business & industry	22	17.1
# employed in government	22	17.1
# employed in public interest	9	7.0
# employed as judicial clerks	10	7.8
# employed in academia	2	1.6
Geographic Location		
# employed in state	100	77.5
# employed in foreign countries	0	0.0
# of states where employed	15	

Financial Aid

	Full-time		Part-time		Total	
	#	%	#	%	#	%
Total # receiving grants	97	21.3	32	17.6	129	20.2
Less than 1/2 tuition	51	11.2	20	11.0	71	11.1
Half to full tuition	16	3.5	10	5.5	26	4.1
Full tuition	30	6.6	2	1.1	32	5.0
More than full tuition	0	0.0	0	0.0	0	0.0
Median Grant Amount	$3,000		$1,500			

Refunds

Refunds of Admissions or Seat Deposit prior to commencement of classes? Yes

66% refund from 04/15/96 to 05/31/96
33% refund from 06/01/96 to 06/30/96
0% refund from 07/01/96 to 08/19/96

Refunds of Pre-paid tuition prior to commencement of classes? Yes

If yes, fully refundable before the start of classes? Yes

Joint Degrees Offered

JD/MBA, JD/MTAX, JD/MPA

Advanced Degrees Offered

No Advanced Degrees

Bar Passage Rate

Jurisdiction	OH
# from school taking bar for the first time	95
School's pass rate for all first-time takers	89%
State's pass rate for all first-time takers	93%
State's pass rate for all first-time takers from ABA approved law schools	90%

ALABAMA, UNIVERSITY OF

P.O. Box 870382
Tuscaloosa, AL 35487
(205)348-5117
http://www.law.ua.edu

ABA Approved Since 1926

The Basics

Type of School: **PUBLIC**
Application deadline*: **3/1**
Application fee: **$25**
Financial Aid deadline*: **3/1**
Student faculty ratio: **19.2 to 1**

First year can start other than Fall: **No**
Student housing: **No**
--exclusively for law students: **No**
Term: **Semester**

*pr=preferred

Faculty

	Men #	Men %	Women #	Women %	Minorities #	Minorities %	Total
Full-time	18	75	6	25	1	4	24
Other full-time	0	0	0	0	0	0	0
Deans, librarians, & others who teach	3	100	0	0	1	33	3
Part-time	17	74	6	26	3	13	23
Total	38	76	12	24	5	10	50
Deans, librarians, & others who teach < 1/2	1	100	0	0	0	0	1

Library

# of volumes & volume equivalents	348,166	# of professional staff	7
# of titles	75,312	Hours per week with professional staff	57
# of active serial subscriptions	3,088	Hours per week without professional staff	53
Study seating capacity inside the library	559	# of student computer work stations for entire law school	58
Square feet of law library	65,950	# of additional networked connections	0
Square feet of law school (excl. Library)	75,982		

Curriculum

	Full time	Part time
Typical first-year section size	96	0
Is there typically a "small section" of the first year class, other than Legal Writing, taught by full-time faculty?	Yes	No
If yes, typical size offered last year	16	N/A
# of classroom course titles beyond 1st year curriculum	83	0
# of upper division courses, excluding seminars, with an enrollment:		
Under 25	36	0
25 - 49	28	0
50 - 74	13	0
75 - 99	8	0
100 +	4	0
# of seminars	17	0
# of seminar positions available	204	
# of seminar positions filled	183	0
# of positions available in simulation courses	272	
# of simulation positions filled	264	0
# of positions available in faculty supervised clinical courses	72	
# of fac. sup. clin. positions filled	52	0
# involved in field placements	38	0
# involved in law journals	85	0
# in moot court or trial competitions	114	0
# of credit hours required to graduate	90	

Enrollment & Attrition

	Full-Time Men #	Men %	Women #	Women %	Minorities #	Minorities %	Total #	Part-Time Men #	Men %	Women #	Women %	Minorities #	Minorities %	Total #	Attrition Academic #	Other #	Total #	Total %
1st Year	111	57.5	82	42.5	11	5.7	193	0	0.0	0	0.0	0	0.0	0	2	14	16	8.2
2nd Year	101	56.7	77	43.3	19	10.7	178	0	0.0	0	0.0	0	0.0	0	1	3	4	2.2
3rd Year	113	62.1	69	37.9	23	12.6	182	0	0.0	0	0.0	0	0.0	0	0	0	0	0.0
4th Year								0	0.0	0	0.0	0	0.0	0	0	0	0	0.0
Total	325	58.8	228	41.2	53	9.6	553	0	0.0	0	0.0	0	0.0	0	3	17	20	3.5
JD Degrees Awarded	108	58.7	76	41.3	22	12.0	184	0	0.0	0	0.0	0	0.0	0				

GPA & LSAT Scores

	Full Time	Part Time	Total
# of apps	798	0	798
# admits	304	0	304
# of matrics	189	0	189
75% GPA	3.66	0.00	
25% GPA	3.16	0.00	
75% LSAT	159	0	
25% LSAT	153	0	

Tuition/Living Expenses

	Resident	Non-resident
Full-Time	$3,578	$7,712
Part-Time	$0	$0

Estimated living expenses for Singles		
Living on campus	Living off campus	Living at home
$7,574	$8,230	$6,484

Financial Aid

	Full-time		Part-time		Total	
	#	%	#	%	#	%
Total # receiving grants	122	22.1	0	0.0	122	22.1
Less than 1/2 tuition	32	5.8	0	0.0	32	5.8
Half to full tuition	48	8.7	0	0.0	48	8.7
Full tuition	24	4.3	0	0.0	24	4.3
More than full tuition	18	3.3	0	0.0	18	3.3
Median Grant Amount	$2,000		$0			

Refunds

Refunds of Admissions or Seat Deposit prior to commencement of classes? No

Refunds of Pre-paid tuition prior to commencement of classes? Yes

If yes, fully refundable before the start of classes? Yes

Joint Degrees Offered

MBA/JD

Advanced Degrees Offered

LL.M.	In Taxation
M.C.L.	Comparative Law
LL.M.	General

Career Placement

	Total	%
Employment status known	175	98.9
Employment status unknown	2	1.1
Employed	159	90.9
Pursuing graduate degrees	6	3.4
Unemployed seeking employment	9	5.1
Unemployed not seeking employment	1	0.6
Type of Employment		
# employed in law firms	96	60.4
# employed in business & industry	13	8.2
# employed in government	16	10.1
# employed in public interest	3	1.9
# employed as judicial clerks	27	17.0
# employed in academia	4	2.5
Geographic Location		
# employed in state	124	78.0
# employed in foreign countries	2	1.3
# of states where employed	12	

Bar Passage Rate

Jurisdiction	AL
# from school taking bar for the first time	177
School's pass rate for all first-time takers	90%
State's pass rate for all first-time takers	83%
State's pass rate for all first-time takers from ABA approved law schools	90%

ALBANY LAW SCHOOL

80 New Scotland Avenue
Albany, NY 12208
(518)445-2311
http://www.als.edu

ABA Approved Since 1930

The Basics

Type of School: **PRIVATE**
Application deadline*:
Application fee: **$50**
Financial Aid deadline*:
Student faculty ratio: **23.8 to 1**

First year can start other than Fall: **No**
Student housing: **Yes**
--exclusively for law students: **Yes**
Term: **Semester**

*pr=preferred

Faculty

	Men		Women		Minorities		Total
	#	%	#	%	#	%	
Full-time	18	69	8	31	4	15	26
Other full-time	1	25	3	75	0	0	4
Deans, librarians, & others who teach	1	20	4	80	0	0	5
Part-time	13	68	6	32	2	11	19
Total	33	61	21	39	6	11	54
Deans, librarians, & others who teach < 1/2	4	100	0	0	0	0	4

Library

# of volumes & volume equivalents	489,398	# of professional staff	7
# of titles	71,652	Hours per week with professional staff	71
# of active serial subscriptions	3,819	Hours per week without professional staff	33
Study seating capacity inside the library	488	# of student computer work stations for entire law school	86
Square feet of law library	53,443	# of additional networked connections	18
Square feet of law school (excl. Library)	45,901		

Curriculum

	Full time	Part time
Typical first-year section size	92	0
Is there typically a "small section" of the first year class, other than Legal Writing, taught by full-time faculty?	Yes	No
If yes, typical size offered last year	53	N/A
# of classroom course titles beyond 1st year curriculum	104	0
# of upper division courses, excluding seminars, with an enrollment:		
Under 25	52	0
25 - 49	26	0
50 - 74	13	0
75 - 99	8	0
100 +	9	0
# of seminars	24	0
# of seminar positions available	610	
# of seminar positions filled	391	0
# of positions available in simulation courses	303	
# of simulation positions filled	258	0
# of positions available in faculty supervised clinical courses	89	
# of fac. sup. clin. positions filled	89	0
# involved in field placements	286	0
# involved in law journals	114	0
# in moot court or trial competitions	327	0
# of credit hours required to graduate	87	

Enrollment & Attrition

	Full-Time							Part-Time							Attrition			
	Men		Women		Minorities		Total	Men		Women		Minorities		Total	Academic	Other	Total	
	#	%	#	%	#	%	#	#	%	#	%	#	%	#	#	#	#	%
1st Year	99	42.7	133	57.3	37	15.9	232	11	57.9	8	42.1	2	10.5	19	2	25	27	10
2nd Year	123	51.5	116	48.5	45	18.8	239	3	42.9	4	57.1	0	0.0	7	0	1	1	0.4
3rd Year	130	52.2	119	47.8	47	18.9	249	2	40.0	3	60.0	1	20.0	5	0	1	1	0.4
4th Year								4	80.0	1	20.0	0	0.0	5	0	0	0	0.0
Total	352	48.9	368	51.1	129	17.9	720	20	55.6	16	44.4	3	8.3	36	2	27	29	3.7
JD Degrees Awarded	131	51.4	124	48.6	29	11.4	255	3	42.9	4	57.1	0	0.0	7				

GPA & LSAT Scores

	Full Time	Part Time	Total
# of apps	1,297	0	1,297
# admits	875	0	875
# of matrics	247	0	247
75% GPA	3.35	0.00	
25% GPA	2.78	0.00	
75% LSAT	154	0	
25% LSAT	147	0	

Tuition/Living Expenses

	Resident	Non-resident
Full-Time	$18,100	$18,100
Part-Time	$13,601	$13,601

Estimated living expenses for Singles		
Living on campus	Living off campus	Living at home
$8,900	$9,970	$6,250

Career Placement

	Total	%
Employment status known	269	98.9
Employment status unknown	3	1.1
Employed	237	88.1
Pursuing graduate degrees	4	1.5
Unemployed seeking employment	15	5.6
Unemployed not seeking employment	13	4.8
Type of Employment		
# employed in law firms	117	49.4
# employed in business & industry	48	20.3
# employed in government	40	16.9
# employed in public interest	5	2.1
# employed as judicial clerks	14	5.9
# employed in academia	2	0.8
Geographic Location		
# employed in state	185	78.1
# employed in foreign countries	2	0.8
# of states where employed	14	

Financial Aid

	Full-time		Part-time		Total	
	#	%	#	%	#	%
Total # receiving grants	347	48.2	10	27.8	357	47.2
Less than 1/2 tuition	272	37.8	9	25.0	281	37.2
Half to full tuition	72	10.0	1	2.8	73	9.7
Full tuition	3	0.4	0	0.0	3	0.4
More than full tuition	0	0.0	0	0.0	0	0.0
Median Grant Amount	$5,600		$3,400			

Refunds

Refunds of Admissions or Seat Deposit prior to commencement of classes? Yes

63% refund from 05/06/96 to 07/01/96
38% refund from 07/01/96 to 07/31/96

Refunds of Pre-paid tuition prior to commencement of classes? Yes

If yes, fully refundable before the start of classes? Yes

Joint Degrees Offered

JD/MBA, JD/MPA

Advanced Degrees Offered

No Advanced Degrees

Bar Passage Rate

Jurisdiction	NY
# from school taking bar for the first time	241
School's pass rate for all first-time takers	93%
State's pass rate for all first-time takers	78%
State's pass rate for all first-time takers from ABA approved law schools	

AMERICAN UNIVERSITY

4801 Massachusetts Ave, NW
Washington, DC 20016
(202)274-4004
http://www.wcl.american.edu

ABA Approved Since 1940

The Basics

Type of School: **PRIVATE**
Application deadline*: **3/1**
Application fee: **$55**
Financial Aid deadline*: **3/1**
Student faculty ratio: **24.1 to 1**

First year can start other than Fall: **No**
Student housing: **Yes**
--exclusively for law students: **No**
Term: **Semester**

*pr=preferred

Faculty

	Men		Women		Minorities		Total
	#	%	#	%	#	%	
Full-time	26	70	11	30	4	11	37
Other full-time	0	0	1	100	0	0	1
Deans, librarians, & others who teach	6	60	4	40	0	0	10
Part-time	69	68	32	32	10	10	101
Total	**101**	**68**	**48**	**32**	**14**	**9**	**149**
Deans, librarians, & others who teach < 1/2	1	100	0	0	1	100	1

Library

# of volumes & volume equivalents	404,893	# of professional staff	9
# of titles	153,619	Hours per week with professional staff	82
# of active serial subscriptions	6,181	Hours per week without professional staff	37
Study seating capacity inside the library	623	# of student computer work stations for entire law school	48
Square feet of law library	55,000	# of additional networked connections	600
Square feet of law school (excl. Library)	84,420		

Curriculum

	Full time	Part time
Typical first-year section size	95	88
Is there typically a "small section" of the first year class, other than Legal Writing, taught by full-time faculty?	No	No
If yes, typical size offered last year	N/A	N/A
# of classroom course titles beyond 1st year curriculum	81	0
# of upper division courses, excluding seminars, with an enrollment:		
Under 25	40	0
25 - 49	14	0
50 - 74	9	0
75 - 99	5	0
100 +	13	0
# of seminars	94	0
# of seminar positions available	2,029	
# of seminar positions filled	1,708	116
# of positions available in simulation courses	423	
# of simulation positions filled	273	77
# of positions available in faculty supervised clinical courses	109	
# of fac. sup. clin. positions filled	101	8
# involved in field placements	230	8
# involved in law journals	261	35
# in moot court or trial competitions	105	6
# of credit hours required to graduate	86	

Enrollment & Attrition

	Full-Time							Part-Time							Attrition			
	Men		Women		Minorities		Total	Men		Women		Minorities		Total	Academic	Other	Total	
	#	%	#	%	#	%	#	#	%	#	%	#	%	#	#	#	#	%
1st Year	109	38.5	174	61.5	61	21.6	283	36	40.9	52	59.1	29	33.0	88	0	6	6	1.6
2nd Year	111	35.5	202	64.5	74	23.6	313	41	58.6	29	41.4	12	17.1	70	1	13	14	4.2
3rd Year	123	44.9	151	55.1	61	22.3	274	39	60.0	26	40.0	15	23.1	65	0	2	2	0.6
4th Year								51	63.0	30	37.0	18	22.2	81	0	0	0	0.0
Total	343	39.4	527	60.6	196	22.5	870	167	54.9	137	45.1	74	24.3	304	1	21	22	1.9
JD Degrees Awarded	118	41.4	167	58.6	83	29.1	285	25	39.7	38	60.3	18	28.6	63				

GPA & LSAT Scores

	Full Time	Part Time	Total
# of apps	4,054	512	4,566
# admits	1,643	225	1,868
# of matrics	286	88	374
75% GPA	3.51	3.34	
25% GPA	3.07	2.66	
75% LSAT	160	159	
25% LSAT	155	149	

Tuition/Living Expenses

	Resident	Non-resident
Full-Time	$20,868	$20,868
Part-Time	$15,444	$15,444

Estimated living expenses for Singles		
Living on campus	Living off campus	Living at home
$12,649	$12,649	$12,649

Career Placement

	Total	%
Employment status known	272	77.7
Employment status unknown	78	22.3
Employed	213	78.3
Pursuing graduate degrees	22	8.1
Unemployed seeking employment	37	13.6
Unemployed not seeking employment	0	0.0
Type of Employment		
# employed in law firms	109	51.2
# employed in business & industry	24	11.3
# employed in government	75	35.2
# employed in public interest	10	4.7
# employed as judicial clerks	49	23.0
# employed in academia	5	2.4
Geographic Location		
# employed in state	169	79.3
# employed in foreign countries	1	0.5
# of states where employed	40	

Financial Aid

	Full-time		Part-time		Total	
	#	%	#	%	#	%
Total # receiving grants	299	34.4	0	0.0	299	25.5
Less than 1/2 tuition	254	29.2	0	0.0	254	21.6
Half to full tuition	45	5.2	0	0.0	45	3.8
Full tuition	0	0.0	0	0.0	0	0.0
More than full tuition	0	0.0	0	0.0	0	0.0
Median Grant Amount	$6,587		$0			

Refunds

Refunds of Admissions or Seat Deposit prior to commencement of classes? Yes

0% refund from 04/15/96 to 06/16/96
50% refund from 06/17/96 to 07/31/96
0% refund from 08/01/96 to 08/31/96

Refunds of Pre-paid tuition prior to commencement of classes? Yes

If yes, fully refundable before the start of classes? Yes

Joint Degrees Offered

JD/MA, JD/MS, JD/MBA

Advanced Degrees Offered

LL.M. International Legal Studies

Bar Passage Rate

Jurisdiction	MD	VA	NY
# from school taking bar for the first time	144	63	89
School's pass rate for all first-time takers	67%	68%	70%
State's pass rate for all first-time takers	75%	76%	78%
State's pass rate for all first-time takers from ABA approved law schools	75%	77%	

ARIZONA STATE UNIVERSITY

P.O. Box 877906
Tempe, AZ 85287-7906
(602)965-6181
http://www.asu.edu/law

ABA Approved Since 1969

The Basics

Type of School: **PUBLIC**
Application deadline*: **3/1**
Application fee: **$35**
Financial Aid deadline*: **3/1**
Student faculty ratio: **15.5 to 1**
First year can start other than Fall: **No**
Student housing: **Yes**
--exclusively for law students: **No**
Term: **Semester**

*pr=preferred

Faculty

	Men #	Men %	Women #	Women %	Minorities #	Minorities %	Total
Full-time	19	76	6	24	4	16	25
Other full-time	0	0	1	100	0	0	1
Deans, librarians, & others who teach	2	67	1	33	0	0	3
Part-time	11	85	2	15	0	0	13
Total	32	76	10	24	4	10	42
Deans, librarians, & others who teach < 1/2	2	100	0	0	0	0	2

Library

# of volumes & volume equivalents	351,639	# of professional staff	8
# of titles	106,643	Hours per week with professional staff	63
# of active serial subscriptions	6,423	Hours per week without professional staff	47
Study seating capacity inside the library	558	# of student computer work stations for entire law school	15
Square feet of law library	60,000	# of additional networked connections	28
Square feet of law school (excl. Library)	59,645		

Curriculum

	Full time	Part time
Typical first-year section size	125	0
Is there typically a "small section" of the first year class, other than Legal Writing, taught by full-time faculty?	Yes	No
If yes, typical size offered last year	30	N/A
# of classroom course titles beyond 1st year curriculum	107	0
# of upper division courses, excluding seminars, with an enrollment:		
Under 25	39	0
25 - 49	25	0
50 - 74	10	0
75 - 99	3	0
100 +	1	0
# of seminars	36	0
# of seminar positions available	556	
# of seminar positions filled	429	0
# of positions available in simulation courses	152	
# of simulation positions filled	147	0
# of positions available in faculty supervised clinical courses	85	
# of fac. sup. clin. positions filled	85	0
# involved in field placements	71	0
# involved in law journals	56	0
# in moot court or trial competitions	58	0
# of credit hours required to graduate	87	

Enrollment & Attrition

	Full-Time							Part-Time							Attrition			
	Men		Women		Minorities		Total	Men		Women		Minorities		Total	Academic	Other	Total	
	#	%	#	%	#	%	#	#	%	#	%	#	%	#	#	#	#	%
1st Year	75	48.4	80	51.6	29	18.7	155	0	0.0	0	0.0	0	0.0	0	7	12	19	12
2nd Year	72	51.1	69	48.9	41	29.1	141	0	0.0	0	0.0	0	0.0	0	0	1	1	0.6
3rd Year	87	52.1	80	47.9	46	27.5	167	0	0.0	0	0.0	0	0.0	0	0	2	2	1.2
4th Year								0	0.0	0	0.0	0	0.0	0	0	0	0	0.0
Total	234	50.5	229	49.5	116	25.1	463	0	0.0	0	0.0	0	0.0	0	7	15	22	4.6
JD Degrees Awarded	78	55.7	62	44.3	36	25.7	140	0	0.0	0	0.0	0	0.0	0				

GPA & LSAT Scores

	Full Time	Part Time	Total
# of apps	1,765	0	1,765
# admits	378	0	378
# of matrics	155	0	155
75% GPA	3.70	0.00	
25% GPA	3.19	0.00	
75% LSAT	162	0	
25% LSAT	156	0	

Tuition/Living Expenses

	Resident	Non-resident
Full-Time	$4,010	$10,378
Part-Time	$0	$0

Estimated living expenses for Singles		
Living on campus	Living off campus	Living at home
$10,440	$10,440	$10,440

Financial Aid

	Full-time #	Full-time %	Part-time #	Part-time %	Total #	Total %
Total # receiving grants	210	45.4	0	0.0	210	45.4
Less than 1/2 tuition	98	21.2	0	0.0	98	21.2
Half to full tuition	35	7.6	0	0.0	35	7.6
Full tuition	50	10.8	0	0.0	50	10.8
More than full tuition	27	5.8	0	0.0	27	5.8
Median Grant Amount	$3,184		$0			

Refunds

Refunds of Admissions or Seat Deposit prior to commencement of classes? Yes

Refunds of Pre-paid tuition prior to commencement of classes? Yes

If yes, fully refundable before the start of classes? Yes

Joint Degrees Offered

JD/MBA, JD/MHSA, JD/Ph.D, Justice Stds

Advanced Degrees Offered

No Advanced Degrees

Career Placement

	Total	%
Employment status known	131	82.9
Employment status unknown	27	17.1
Employed	122	93.1
Pursuing graduate degrees	2	1.5
Unemployed seeking employment	6	4.6
Unemployed not seeking employment	1	0.8
Type of Employment		
# employed in law firms	75	61.5
# employed in business & industry	11	9.0
# employed in government	21	17.2
# employed in public interest	2	1.6
# employed as judicial clerks	13	10.7
# employed in academia	0	0.0
Geographic Location		
# employed in state	101	82.8
# employed in foreign countries	0	0.0
# of states where employed	8	

Bar Passage Rate

Jurisdiction	AZ
# from school taking bar for the first time	142
School's pass rate for all first-time takers	85%
State's pass rate for all first-time takers	84%
State's pass rate for all first-time takers from ABA approved law schools	84%

ARIZONA, UNIVERSITY OF

Tucson, AZ 85721
(520)621-1373
http://www.law.arizona.edu

ABA Approved Since 1930

The Basics

Type of School: **PUBLIC**
Application deadline*: **3/1**
Application fee: **$45**
Financial Aid deadline*: **3/1**
Student faculty ratio: **16.4 to 1**

First year can start other than Fall: **No**
Student housing: **No**
--exclusively for law students: **No**
Term: **Semester**

*pr=preferred

Faculty

	Men #	Men %	Women #	Women %	Minorities #	Minorities %	Total
Full-time	18	75	6	25	2	8	24
Other full-time	1	100	0	0	0	0	1
Deans, librarians, & others who teach	1	50	1	50	0	0	2
Part-time	18	58	13	42	3	10	31
Total	38	66	20	34	5	9	58
Deans, librarians, & others who teach < 1/2	1	100	0	0	0	0	1

Library

# of volumes & volume equivalents	362,220	# of professional staff	6
# of titles	61,712	Hours per week with professional staff	71
# of active serial subscriptions	4,121	Hours per week without professional staff	38
Study seating capacity inside the library	368	# of student computer work stations for entire law school	28
Square feet of law library	41,953	# of additional networked connections	8
Square feet of law school (excl. Library)	32,094		

Curriculum

	Full time	Part time
Typical first-year section size	75	0
Is there typically a "small section" of the first year class, other than Legal Writing, taught by full-time faculty?	Yes	No
If yes, typical size offered last year	25	N/A
# of classroom course titles beyond 1st year curriculum	83	0
# of upper division courses, excluding seminars, with an enrollment:		
Under 25	57	0
25 - 49	23	0
50 - 74	9	0
75 - 99	4	0
100 +	1	0
# of seminars	20	0
# of seminar positions available	322	
# of seminar positions filled	201	0
# of positions available in simulation courses	295	
# of simulation positions filled	255	0
# of positions available in faculty supervised clinical courses	48	
# of fac. sup. clin. positions filled	36	0
# involved in field placements	89	0
# involved in law journals	86	0
# in moot court or trial competitions	72	0
# of credit hours required to graduate	85	

Enrollment & Attrition

	Full-Time							Part-Time							Attrition			
	Men		Women		Minorities		Total	Men		Women		Minorities		Total	Academic	Other	Total	
	#	%	#	%	#	%	#	#	%	#	%	#	%	#	#	#	#	%
1st Year	69	45.7	82	54.3	36	23.8	151	0	0.0	0	0.0	0	0.0	0	0	1	1	0.7
2nd Year	79	52.3	72	47.7	34	22.5	151	0	0.0	0	0.0	0	0.0	0	0	5	5	3.2
3rd Year	92	54.1	78	45.9	51	30.0	170	0	0.0	0	0.0	0	0.0	0	1	1	2	1.2
4th Year								0	0.0	0	0.0	0	0.0	0	0	0	0	0.0
Total	240	50.8	232	49.2	121	25.6	472	0	0.0	0	0.0	0	0.0	0	1	7	8	1.7
JD Degrees Awarded	79	50.3	78	49.7	46	29.3	157	0	0.0	0	0.0	0	0.0	0				

GPA & LSAT Scores

	Full Time	Part Time	Total
# of apps	1,773	0	1,773
# admits	478	0	478
# of matrics	151	0	151
75% GPA	3.68	0.00	
25% GPA	3.12	0.00	
75% LSAT	164	0	
25% LSAT	156	0	

Tuition/Living Expenses

	Resident	Non-resident
Full-Time	$4,010	$10,378
Part-Time	$0	$0

Estimated living expenses for Singles		
Living on campus	Living off campus	Living at home
$8,094	$11,802	$4,950

Financial Aid

	Full-time		Part-time		Total	
	#	%	#	%	#	%
Total # receiving grants	261	55.3	0	0.0	261	55.3
Less than 1/2 tuition	48	10.2	0	0.0	48	10.2
Half to full tuition	165	35.0	0	0.0	165	35.0
Full tuition	31	6.6	0	0.0	31	6.6
More than full tuition	17	3.6	0	0.0	17	3.6
Median Grant Amount	$2,000		$0			

Refunds

Refunds of Admissions or Seat Deposit prior to commencement of classes? No

Refunds of Pre-paid tuition prior to commencement of classes? Yes

If yes, fully refundable before the start of classes? Yes

Joint Degrees Offered

JD/PhD, Economics, Philosophy, Psychology, JD/MBA, JD/MPA, JD/MA, Economics, Am Ind Stds

Advanced Degrees Offered

LLM International Trade Law

Career Placement

	Total	%
Employment status known	154	99.4
Employment status unknown	1	0.7
Employed	128	83.1
Pursuing graduate degrees	7	4.6
Unemployed seeking employment	13	8.4
Unemployed not seeking employment	6	3.9
Type of Employment		
# employed in law firms	56	43.8
# employed in business & industry	16	12.5
# employed in government	27	21.1
# employed in public interest	7	5.5
# employed as judicial clerks	20	15.6
# employed in academia	2	1.6
Geographic Location		
# employed in state	88	68.8
# employed in foreign countries	0	0.0
# of states where employed	18	

Bar Passage Rate

Jurisdiction	AZ
# from school taking bar for the first time	113
School's pass rate for all first-time takers	90%
State's pass rate for all first-time takers	84%
State's pass rate for all first-time takers from ABA approved law schools	84%

ARKANSAS, FAYETTEVILLE, UNIVERSITY OF

Waterman Hall
Leflar Law Center
Fayetteville, AR 72701-1201
(501)575-5601
http://law-gopher.uark.edu/arklaw

ABA Approved Since 1926

The Basics

Type of School: **PUBLIC**
Application deadline*: **4/1**
Application fee: **$0**
Financial Aid deadline*: **5/1**
Student faculty ratio: **15.6 to 1**

First year can start other than Fall: **No**
Student housing: **No**
--exclusively for law students: **No**
Term: **Semester**

***pr=preferred**

Faculty

	Men #	Men %	Women #	Women %	Minorities #	Minorities %	Total
Full-time	16	76	5	24	4	19	21
Other full-time	2	67	1	33	0	0	3
Deans, librarians, & others who teach	2	50	2	50	0	0	4
Part-time	9	90	1	10	1	10	10
Total	**29**	**76**	**9**	**24**	**5**	**13**	**38**
Deans, librarians, & others who teach < 1/2	2	100	0	0	0	0	2

Library

# of volumes & volume equivalents	238,650	# of professional staff	5
# of titles	84,768	Hours per week with professional staff	60
# of active serial subscriptions	2,218	Hours per week without professional staff	47
Study seating capacity inside the library	355	# of student computer work stations for entire law school	48
Square feet of law library	25,500	# of additional networked connections	55
Square feet of law school (excl. Library)	54,500		

Curriculum

	Full time	Part time
Typical first-year section size	75	0
Is there typically a "small section" of the first year class, other than Legal Writing, taught by full-time faculty?	Yes	No
If yes, typical size offered last year	25	N/A
# of classroom course titles beyond 1st year curriculum	84	0
# of upper division courses, excluding seminars, with an enrollment:		
Under 25	52	0
25 - 49	18	0
50 - 74	8	0
75 - 99	6	0
100 +	0	0
# of seminars	19	0
# of seminar positions available	150	
# of seminar positions filled	137	0
# of positions available in simulation courses	150	
# of simulation positions filled	147	0
# of positions available in faculty supervised clinical courses	100	
# of fac. sup. clin. positions filled	97	0
# involved in field placements	9	0
# involved in law journals	40	0
# in moot court or trial competitions	143	0
# of credit hours required to graduate	90	

Enrollment & Attrition

	Full-Time Men #	Men %	Women #	Women %	Minorities #	Minorities %	Total #	Part-Time Men #	Men %	Women #	Women %	Minorities #	Minorities %	Total #	Attrition Academic #	Other #	Total #	%
1st Year	105	67.3	51	32.7	19	12.2	156	0	0.0	0	0.0	0	0.0	0	7	24	31	23
2nd Year	64	57.1	48	42.9	12	10.7	112	0	0.0	0	0.0	0	0.0	0	2	1	3	2.2
3rd Year	80	63.5	46	36.5	7	5.6	126	0	0.0	0	0.0	0	0.0	0	0	0	0	0.0
4th Year								0	0.0	0	0.0	0	0.0	0	0	0	0	0.0
Total	249	63.2	145	36.8	38	9.6	394	0	0.0	0	0.0	0	0.0	0	9	25	34	8.6
JD Degrees Awarded	70	59.8	47	40.2	11	9.4	117	0	0.0	0	0.0	0	0.0	0				

GPA & LSAT Scores

	Full Time	Part Time	Total
# of apps	716	0	716
# admits	356	0	356
# of matrics	157	0	157
75% GPA	3.51	0.00	
25% GPA	2.88	0.00	
75% LSAT	157	0	
25% LSAT	147	0	

Tuition/Living Expenses

	Resident	Non-resident
Full-Time	$3,363	$7,275
Part-Time	$0	$0

Estimated living expenses for Singles		
Living on campus	Living off campus	Living at home
$10,464	$10,464	$10,464

Career Placement

	Total	%
Employment status known	113	96.6
Employment status unknown	4	3.4
Employed	99	87.6
Pursuing graduate degrees	4	3.5
Unemployed seeking employment	4	3.5
Unemployed not seeking employment	6	5.3
Type of Employment		
# employed in law firms	67	67.7
# employed in business & industry	12	12.1
# employed in government	14	14.1
# employed in public interest	0	0.0
# employed as judicial clerks	5	5.1
# employed in academia	1	1.0
Geographic Location		
# employed in state	42	42.4
# employed in foreign countries	1	1.0
# of states where employed	9	

Financial Aid

	Full-time		Part-time		Total	
	#	%	#	%	#	%
Total # receiving grants	97	24.6	0	0.0	97	24.6
Less than 1/2 tuition	40	10.2	0	0.0	40	10.2
Half to full tuition	22	5.6	0	0.0	22	5.6
Full tuition	1	0.3	0	0.0	1	0.3
More than full tuition	34	8.6	0	0.0	34	8.6
Median Grant Amount	$2,250		$0			

Refunds

Refunds of Admissions or Seat Deposit prior to commencement of classes? No

Refunds of Pre-paid tuition prior to commencement of classes? Yes

If yes, fully refundable before the start of classes? Yes

Joint Degrees Offered

No Joint Degrees

Advanced Degrees Offered

LL.M. Agricultural Law

Bar Passage Rate

Jurisdiction	AR
# from school taking bar for the first time	110
School's pass rate for all first-time takers	84%
State's pass rate for all first-time takers	84%
State's pass rate for all first-time takers from ABA approved law schools	84%

ARKANSAS, LITTLE ROCK, UNIVERSITY OF

1201 McAlmont Street
Little Rock, AR 72202-5142
(501)324-9434
http://www.ualr.edu/~lawlib

ABA Approved Since 1969

The Basics

Type of School: **PUBLIC**
Application deadline*: **4/1**
Application fee: **$40**
Financial Aid deadline*: **5/1**
Student faculty ratio: **15.4 to 1**

First year can start other than Fall: **No**
Student housing: **No**
--exclusively for law students: **No**
Term: **Semester**

*pr=preferred

Faculty

	Men #	Men %	Women #	Women %	Minorities #	Minorities %	Total
Full-time	14	70	6	30	2	10	20
Other full-time	0	0	2	100	1	50	2
Deans, librarians, & others who teach	1	50	1	50	0	0	2
Part-time	6	75	2	25	1	13	8
Total	**21**	**66**	**11**	**34**	**4**	**13**	**32**
Deans, librarians, & others who teach < 1/2	0	0	0	0	0	0	0

Library

# of volumes & volume equivalents	248,966	# of professional staff	5
# of titles	26,302	Hours per week with professional staff	78
# of active serial subscriptions	3,183	Hours per week without professional staff	21
Study seating capacity inside the library	385	# of student computer work stations for entire law school	64
Square feet of law library	52,973	# of additional networked connections	26
Square feet of law school (excl. Library)	50,166		

Curriculum

	Full time	Part time
Typical first-year section size	75	50
Is there typically a "small section" of the first year class, other than Legal Writing, taught by full-time faculty?	No	No
If yes, typical size offered last year	N/A	N/A
# of classroom course titles beyond 1st year curriculum	44	34
# of upper division courses, excluding seminars, with an enrollment:		
Under 25	13	17
25 - 49	12	14
50 - 74	6	1
75 - 99	6	0
100 +	0	0
# of seminars	7	2
# of seminar positions available	112	
# of seminar positions filled	62	17
# of positions available in simulation courses	200	
# of simulation positions filled	130	42
# of positions available in faculty supervised clinical courses	42	
# of fac. sup. clin. positions filled	34	0
# involved in field placements	0	0
# involved in law journals	60	20
# in moot court or trial competitions	34	3
# of credit hours required to graduate	87	

Enrollment & Attrition

	Full-Time							Part-Time							Attrition			
	Men		Women		Minorities		Total	Men		Women		Minorities		Total	Academic	Other	Total	
	#	%	#	%	#	%	#	#	%	#	%	#	%	#	#	#	#	%
1st Year	52	55.3	42	44.7	10	10.6	94	30	45.5	36	54.5	12	18.2	66	1	15	16	11
2nd Year	36	44.4	45	55.6	10	12.3	81	21	56.8	16	43.2	4	10.8	37	8	5	13	9.8
3rd Year	48	54.5	40	45.5	9	10.2	88	14	53.8	12	46.2	4	15.4	26	0	0	0	0.0
4th Year								14	56.0	11	44.0	3	12.0	25	0	0	0	0.0
Total	136	51.7	127	48.3	29	11.0	263	79	51.3	75	48.7	23	14.9	154	9	20	29	6.8
JD Degrees Awarded	66	60.6	43	39.4	14	12.8	109	13	65.0	7	35.0	3	15.0	20				

ARKANSAS, LITTLE ROCK, UNIVERSITY OF

GPA & LSAT Scores

	Full Time	Part Time	Total
# of apps	317	150	467
# admits	181	65	246
# of matrics	86	49	135
75% GPA	3.57	3.59	
25% GPA	2.95	2.81	
75% LSAT	156	159	
25% LSAT	149	146	

Tuition/Living Expenses

	Resident	Non-resident
Full-Time	$3,891	$8,597
Part-Time	$3,011	$6,631

Estimated living expenses for Singles		
Living on campus	Living off campus	Living at home
$8,900	$8,500	$4,550

Career Placement

	Total	%
Employment status known	38	32.5
Employment status unknown	79	67.5
Employed	35	92.1
Pursuing graduate degrees	1	2.6
Unemployed seeking employment	1	2.6
Unemployed not seeking employment	1	2.6
Type of Employment		
# employed in law firms	17	48.6
# employed in business & industry	10	28.6
# employed in government	4	11.4
# employed in public interest	1	2.9
# employed as judicial clerks	2	5.7
# employed in academia	1	2.9
Geographic Location		
# employed in state	27	77.1
# employed in foreign countries	0	0.0
# of states where employed	3	

Financial Aid

	Full-time		Part-time		Total	
	#	%	#	%	#	%
Total # receiving grants	58	22.1	4	2.6	62	14.9
Less than 1/2 tuition	31	11.8	2	1.3	33	7.9
Half to full tuition	14	5.3	2	1.3	16	3.8
Full tuition	4	1.5	0	0.0	4	1.0
More than full tuition	9	3.4	0	0.0	9	2.2
Median Grant Amount	$1,500		$1,135			

Refunds

Refunds of Admissions or Seat Deposit prior to commencement of classes? No

Refunds of Pre-paid tuition prior to commencement of classes? Yes

If yes, fully refundable before the start of classes? Yes

Joint Degrees Offered

J.D./M.B.A.

Advanced Degrees Offered

No Advanced Degrees

Bar Passage Rate

Jurisdiction	AR
# from school taking bar for the first time	67
School's pass rate for all first-time takers	85%
State's pass rate for all first-time takers	84%
State's pass rate for all first-time takers from ABA approved law schools	84%

BALTIMORE, UNIVERSITY OF

1420 North Charles Street
Baltimore, MD 21201
(410)837-4458
http://www.ubalt.edu/www/law

ABA Approved Since 1972

The Basics

Type of School: **PUBLIC**
Application deadline*: **4/1**
Application fee: **$35**
Financial Aid deadline*: **4/1**
Student faculty ratio: **19.3 to 1**
First year can start other than Fall: **No**
Student housing: **No**
--exclusively for law students: **No**
Term: **Semester**

*pr=preferred

Faculty

	Men #	Men %	Women #	Women %	Minorities #	Minorities %	Total
Full-time	25	64	14	36	5	13	39
Other full-time	0	0	3	100	0	0	3
Deans, librarians, & others who teach	3	100	0	0	0	0	3
Part-time	38	67	19	33	7	12	57
Total	**66**	**65**	**36**	**35**	**12**	**12**	**102**
Deans, librarians, & others who teach < 1/2	1	100	0	0	0	0	1

Library

# of volumes & volume equivalents	279,153	# of professional staff	7
# of titles	26,404	Hours per week with professional staff	86
# of active serial subscriptions	3,272	Hours per week without professional staff	24
Study seating capacity inside the library	329	# of student computer work stations for entire law school	55
Square feet of law library	30,000	# of additional networked connections	0
Square feet of law school (excl. Library)	88,095		

Curriculum

	Full time	Part time
Typical first-year section size	75	75
Is there typically a "small section" of the first year class, other than Legal Writing, taught by full-time faculty?	No	No
If yes, typical size offered last year	N/A	N/A
# of classroom course titles beyond 1st year curriculum	95	89
# of upper division courses, excluding seminars, with an enrollment:		
Under 25	22	24
25 - 49	18	16
50 - 74	4	4
75 - 99	3	2
100 +	0	0
# of seminars	35	28
# of seminar positions available	1,260	
# of seminar positions filled	860	359
# of positions available in simulation courses	640	
# of simulation positions filled	458	182
# of positions available in faculty supervised clinical courses	110	
# of fac. sup. clin. positions filled	99	11
# involved in field placements	77	29
# involved in law journals	164	56
# in moot court or trial competitions	25	5
# of credit hours required to graduate	90	

Enrollment & Attrition

	Full-Time							Part-Time							Attrition			
	Men		Women		Minorities		Total	Men		Women		Minorities		Total	Academic	Other	Total	
	#	%	#	%	#	%	#	#	%	#	%	#	%	#	#	#	#	%
1st Year	121	54.0	103	46.0	48	21.4	224	38	44.2	48	55.8	25	29.1	86	5	15	20	6.4
2nd Year	104	51.5	98	48.5	31	15.3	202	61	59.8	41	40.2	20	19.6	102	0	5	5	1.5
3rd Year	116	53.0	103	47.0	21	9.6	219	58	54.2	49	45.8	27	25.2	107	0	2	2	0.6
4th Year								47	50.0	47	50.0	19	20.2	94	1	0	1	1.1
Total	341	52.9	304	47.1	100	15.5	645	204	52.4	185	47.6	91	23.4	389	6	22	28	2.6
JD Degrees Awarded	116	53.0	103	47.0	36	16.4	219	44	53.7	38	46.3	17	20.7	82				

GPA & LSAT Scores

	Full Time	Part Time	Total
# of apps	1,484	378	1,862
# admits	821	171	992
# of matrics	224	86	310
75% GPA	3.23	3.31	
25% GPA	2.80	2.63	
75% LSAT	154	155	
25% LSAT	149	147	

Tuition/Living Expenses

	Resident	Non-resident
Full-Time	$7,596	$13,218
Part-Time	$6,258	$10,338

Estimated living expenses for Singles		
Living on campus	Living off campus	Living at home
N/A	$10,100	$7,100

Career Placement

	Total	%
Employment status known	280	88.3
Employment status unknown	37	11.7
Employed	239	85.4
Pursuing graduate degrees	4	1.4
Unemployed seeking employment	33	11.8
Unemployed not seeking employment	4	1.4
Type of Employment		
# employed in law firms	88	36.8
# employed in business & industry	43	18.0
# employed in government	46	19.3
# employed in public interest	2	0.8
# employed as judicial clerks	55	23.0
# employed in academia	3	1.3
Geographic Location		
# employed in state	193	80.8
# employed in foreign countries	0	0.0
# of states where employed	11	

Financial Aid

	Full-time		Part-time		Total	
	#	%	#	%	#	%
Total # receiving grants	59	9.2	51	13.1	110	10.6
Less than 1/2 tuition	57	8.8	49	12.6	106	10.3
Half to full tuition	2	0.3	2	0.5	4	0.4
Full tuition	0	0.0	0	0.0	0	0.0
More than full tuition	0	0.0	0	0.0	0	0.0
Median Grant Amount	$1,500		$1,200			

Refunds

Refunds of Admissions or Seat Deposit prior to commencement of classes? Yes

100% refund from 04/01/96 to 06/30/96
0% refund from 07/01/96 to 08/26/96

Refunds of Pre-paid tuition prior to commencement of classes? Yes

If yes, fully refundable before the start of classes? Yes

100% refund from 07/01/96 to 09/01/96
80% refund from 09/02/96 to 09/09/96
60% refund from 09/10/96 to 09/16/96

Joint Degrees Offered

JD/MS, JD/MBA, JD/MPA, JD/Ph.D

Advanced Degrees Offered

LL.M. TAXATION

Bar Passage Rate

Jurisdiction	MD
# from school taking bar for the first time	223
School's pass rate for all first-time takers	82%
State's pass rate for all first-time takers	75%
State's pass rate for all first-time takers from ABA approved law schools	75%

BAYLOR UNIVERSITY

P.O. Box 97288
1400 S. 5th Street
Waco, TX 76798-7288
(817)755-1911
http://www.baylor.edu

ABA Approved Since 1931

The Basics

Type of School: **PRIVATE**
Application deadline*: **3/1**
Application fee: **$40**
Financial Aid deadline*: **5/31**
Student faculty ratio: **21.5 to 1**
First year can start other than Fall: **Yes**
Student housing: **Yes**
--exclusively for law students: **No**
Term: **Quarter**

*pr=preferred

Faculty

	Men #	Men %	Women #	Women %	Minorities #	Minorities %	Total
Full-time	12	75	4	25	1	6	16
Other full-time	0	0	0	0	0	0	0
Deans, librarians, & others who teach	1	50	1	50	0	0	2
Part-time	7	88	1	13	0	0	8
Total	20	77	6	23	1	4	26
Deans, librarians, & others who teach < 1/2	1	50	1	50	0	0	2

Library

# of volumes & volume equivalents	173,103	# of professional staff	6
# of titles	19,753	Hours per week with professional staff	55
# of active serial subscriptions	2,113	Hours per week without professional staff	28
Study seating capacity inside the library	303	# of student computer work stations for entire law school	30
Square feet of law library	17,861	# of additional networked connections	0
Square feet of law school (excl. Library)	37,413		

Curriculum

	Full time	Part time
Typical first-year section size	45	0
Is there typically a "small section" of the first year class, other than Legal Writing, taught by full-time faculty?	No	No
If yes, typical size offered last year	N/A	N/A
# of classroom course titles beyond 1st year curriculum	63	0
# of upper division courses, excluding seminars, with an enrollment:		
Under 25	47	0
25 - 49	19	0
50 - 74	15	0
75 - 99	4	0
100 +	5	0
# of seminars	14	0
# of seminar positions available	245	
# of seminar positions filled	244	0
# of positions available in simulation courses	1,185	
# of simulation positions filled	1,185	0
# of positions available in faculty supervised clinical courses	3	
# of fac. sup. clin. positions filled	3	0
# involved in field placements	67	0
# involved in law journals	90	0
# in moot court or trial competitions	39	0
# of credit hours required to graduate	120	

Enrollment & Attrition

	Full-Time							Part-Time							Attrition			
	Men		Women		Minorities		Total	Men		Women		Minorities		Total	Academic	Other	Total	
	#	%	#	%	#	%	#	#	%	#	%	#	%	#	#	#	#	%
1st Year	134	67.0	66	33.0	17	8.5	200	0	0.0	0	0.0	0	0.0	0	4	18	22	12
2nd Year	69	71.9	27	28.1	9	9.4	96	0	0.0	0	0.0	0	0.0	0	0	4	4	3.0
3rd Year	71	63.4	41	36.6	16	14.3	112	0	0.0	0	0.0	0	0.0	0	0	0	0	0.0
4th Year								0	0.0	0	0.0	0	0.0	0	0	0	0	0.0
Total	274	67.2	134	32.8	42	10.3	408	0	0.0	0	0.0	0	0.0	0	4	22	26	6.5
JD Degrees Awarded	84	58.7	59	41.3	27	18.9	143	0	0.0	0	0.0	0	0.0	0				

GPA & LSAT Scores

	Full Time	Part Time	Total
# of apps	1,174	0	1,174
# admits	501	0	501
# of matrics	75	0	75
75% GPA	3.76	0.00	
25% GPA	3.28	0.00	
75% LSAT	163	0	
25% LSAT	157	0	

Tuition/Living Expenses

	Resident	Non-resident
Full-Time	$11,234	$11,234
Part-Time	$0	$0

Estimated living expenses for Singles		
Living on campus	Living off campus	Living at home
$7,906	$12,166	$7,906

Career Placement

	Total	%
Employment status known	158	99.4
Employment status unknown	1	0.6
Employed	150	94.9
Pursuing graduate degrees	0	0.0
Unemployed seeking employment	6	3.8
Unemployed not seeking employment	2	1.3
Type of Employment		
# employed in law firms	113	75.3
# employed in business & industry	8	5.3
# employed in government	13	8.7
# employed in public interest	1	0.7
# employed as judicial clerks	15	10.0
# employed in academia	0	0.0
Geographic Location		
# employed in state	139	92.7
# employed in foreign countries	2	1.3
# of states where employed	9	

Financial Aid

	Full-time		Part-time		Total	
	#	%	#	%	#	%
Total # receiving grants	350	85.8	0	0.0	350	85.8
Less than 1/2 tuition	281	68.9	0	0.0	281	68.9
Half to full tuition	45	11.0	0	0.0	45	11.0
Full tuition	0	0.0	0	0.0	0	0.0
More than full tuition	25	6.1	0	0.0	25	6.1
Median Grant Amount	$2,745		$0			

Refunds

Refunds of Admissions or Seat Deposit prior to commencement of classes? Yes

50% refund to 06/01/96

Refunds of Pre-paid tuition prior to commencement of classes? Yes

If yes, fully refundable before the start of classes? Yes

Joint Degrees Offered

JD/MTAX, JD/MBA, JD/MPPA

Advanced Degrees Offered

No Advanced Degrees

Bar Passage Rate

Jurisdiction	TX
# from school taking bar for the first time	37
School's pass rate for all first-time takers	95%
State's pass rate for all first-time takers	82%
State's pass rate for all first-time takers from ABA approved law schools	82%

BOSTON COLLEGE

885 Centre Street
Newton, MA 02159
(617)552-4340
http://www.bc.edu

ABA Approved Since 1932

The Basics

Type of School: PRIVATE
Application deadline*: 3/1
Application fee: $50
Financial Aid deadline*: 3/1
Student faculty ratio: 17.4 to 1

First year can start other than Fall: No
Student housing: No
--exclusively for law students: No
Term: Semester

*pr=preferred

Faculty

	Men		Women		Minorities		Total
	#	%	#	%	#	%	
Full-time	30	77	9	23	7	18	39
Other full-time	0	0	6	100	1	17	6
Deans, librarians, & others who teach	1	50	1	50	0	0	2
Part-time	28	82	6	18	1	3	34
Total	59	73	22	27	9	11	81
Deans, librarians, & others who teach < 1/2	2	25	6	75	0	0	8

Library

# of volumes & volume equivalents	362,111	# of professional staff	9
# of titles	50,020	Hours per week with professional staff	76
# of active serial subscriptions	5,706	Hours per week without professional staff	30
Study seating capacity inside the library	605	# of student computer work stations for entire law school	95
Square feet of law library	49,488	# of additional networked connections	437
Square feet of law school (excl. Library)	57,784		

Curriculum

	Full time	Part time
Typical first-year section size	100	0
Is there typically a "small section" of the first year class, other than Legal Writing, taught by full-time faculty?	Yes	No
If yes, typical size offered last year	35	N/A
# of classroom course titles beyond 1st year curriculum	134	0
# of upper division courses, excluding seminars, with an enrollment:		
Under 25	100	0
25 - 49	29	0
50 - 74	9	0
75 - 99	3	0
100 +	9	0
# of seminars	45	0
# of seminar positions available	923	
# of seminar positions filled	549	0
# of positions available in simulation courses	463	
# of simulation positions filled	366	0
# of positions available in faculty supervised clinical courses	220	
# of fac. sup. clin. positions filled	181	0
# involved in field placements	127	0
# involved in law journals	95	0
# in moot court or trial competitions	187	0
# of credit hours required to graduate	85	

Enrollment & Attrition

	Full-Time							Part-Time							Attrition			
	Men		Women		Minorities		Total	Men		Women		Minorities		Total	Academic	Other	Total	
	#	%	#	%	#	%	#	#	%	#	%	#	%	#	#	#	#	%
1st Year	128	47.8	140	52.2	57	21.3	268	0	0.0	0	0.0	0	0.0	0	0	0	0	0.0
2nd Year	147	54.6	122	45.4	45	16.7	269	0	0.0	0	0.0	0	0.0	0	0	19	19	6.8
3rd Year	159	57.4	118	42.6	38	13.7	277	0	0.0	0	0.0	0	0.0	0	0	12	12	4.4
4th Year								0	0.0	0	0.0	0	0.0	0	0	0	0	0.0
Total	434	53.3	380	46.7	140	17.2	814	0	0.0	0	0.0	0	0.0	0	0	31	31	3.7
JD Degrees Awarded	147	55.1	120	44.9	46	17.2	267	0	0.0	0	0.0	0	0.0	0				

GPA & LSAT Scores

	Full Time	Part Time	Total
# of apps	4,644	0	4,644
# admits	1,224	0	1,224
# of matrics	268	0	268
75% GPA	3.61	0.00	
25% GPA	3.17	0.00	
75% LSAT	165	0	
25% LSAT	159	0	

Tuition/Living Expenses

	Resident	Non-resident
Full-Time	$21,290	$21,290
Part-Time	$0	$0

Estimated living expenses for Singles		
Living on campus	Living off campus	Living at home
N/A	$11,605	$11,605

Financial Aid

	Full-time		Part-time		Total	
	#	%	#	%	#	%
Total # receiving grants	289	35.5	0	0.0	289	35.5
Less than 1/2 tuition	212	26.0	0	0.0	212	26.0
Half to full tuition	77	9.5	0	0.0	77	9.5
Full tuition	0	0.0	0	0.0	0	0.0
More than full tuition	0	0.0	0	0.0	0	0.0
Median Grant Amount	$7,944		$0			

Refunds

Refunds of Admissions or Seat Deposit prior to commencement of classes? Yes

66% refund from 06/01/96 to 07/01/96

Refunds of Pre-paid tuition prior to commencement of classes? Yes

If yes, fully refundable before the start of classes? Yes

Joint Degrees Offered

JD/MSW, JD/MBA, JD/M.Ed.

Advanced Degrees Offered

No Advanced Degrees

Career Placement

	Total	%
Employment status known	267	93.0
Employment status unknown	20	7.0
Employed	243	91.0
Pursuing graduate degrees	3	1.1
Unemployed seeking employment	19	7.1
Unemployed not seeking employment	2	0.8
Type of Employment		
# employed in law firms	138	56.8
# employed in business & industry	23	9.5
# employed in government	34	14.0
# employed in public interest	7	2.9
# employed as judicial clerks	40	16.5
# employed in academia	1	0.4
Geographic Location		
# employed in state	121	49.8
# employed in foreign countries	1	0.4
# of states where employed	30	

Bar Passage Rate

Jurisdiction	MA
# from school taking bar for the first time	185
School's pass rate for all first-time takers	92%
State's pass rate for all first-time takers	83%
State's pass rate for all first-time takers from ABA approved law schools	85%

BOSTON UNIVERSITY

765 Commonwealth Ave
Boston, MA 02215
(617)353-3112
http://www.bu.edu/law

ABA Approved Since 1925

The Basics

Type of School: **PRIVATE**
Application deadline*: **3/1**
Application fee: **$50**
Financial Aid deadline*: **4/1**
Student faculty ratio: **19.3 to 1**
First year can start other than Fall: **No**
Student housing: **No**
--exclusively for law students: **No**
Term: **Semester**

*pr=preferred

Faculty

	Men #	Men %	Women #	Women %	Minorities #	Minorities %	Total
Full-time	32	70	14	30	3	7	46
Other full-time	0	0	1	100	0	0	1
Deans, librarians, & others who teach	2	100	0	0	0	0	2
Part-time	61	73	23	27	7	8	84
Total	95	71	38	29	10	8	133
Deans, librarians, & others who teach < 1/2	2	100	0	0	0	0	2

Library

# of volumes & volume equivalents	507,561	# of professional staff	10
# of titles	65,490	Hours per week with professional staff	77
# of active serial subscriptions	6,308	Hours per week without professional staff	25
Study seating capacity inside the library	797	# of student computer work stations for entire law school	101
Square feet of law library	38,113	# of additional networked connections	0
Square feet of law school (excl. Library)	79,940		

Curriculum

	Full time	Part time
Typical first-year section size	85	0
Is there typically a "small section" of the first year class, other than Legal Writing, taught by full-time faculty?	No	No
If yes, typical size offered last year	N/A	N/A
# of classroom course titles beyond 1st year curriculum	102	0
# of upper division courses, excluding seminars, with an enrollment:		
Under 25	41	0
25 - 49	24	0
50 - 74	13	0
75 - 99	15	0
100 +	9	0
# of seminars	43	0
# of seminar positions available	769	
# of seminar positions filled	607	0
# of positions available in simulation courses	192	
# of simulation positions filled	167	0
# of positions available in faculty supervised clinical courses	166	
# of fac. sup. clin. positions filled	156	0
# involved in field placements	36	0
# involved in law journals	338	0
# in moot court or trial competitions	274	0
# of credit hours required to graduate	84	

Enrollment & Attrition

	Full-Time							Part-Time							Attrition			
	Men		Women		Minorities		Total	Men		Women		Minorities		Total	Academic	Other	Total	
	#	%	#	%	#	%	#	#	%	#	%	#	%	#	#	#	#	%
1st Year	180	53.4	157	46.6	48	14.2	337	0	0.0	0	0.0	0	0.0	0	2	21	23	6.2
2nd Year	190	52.8	170	47.2	62	17.2	360	0	0.0	0	0.0	0	0.0	0	0	5	5	1.4
3rd Year	188	51.2	179	48.8	82	22.3	367	0	0.0	0	0.0	0	0.0	0	3	2	5	1.4
4th Year								0	0.0	0	0.0	0	0.0	0	0	0	0	0.0
Total	558	52.4	506	47.6	192	18.0	1,064	0	0.0	0	0.0	0	0.0	0	5	28	33	3.0
JD Degrees Awarded	201	57.1	151	42.9	75	21.3	352	0	0.0	0	0.0	0	0.0	0				

GPA & LSAT Scores

	Full Time	Part Time	Total
# of apps	4,585	0	4,585
# admits	1,576	0	1,576
# of matrics	340	0	340
75% GPA	3.60	0.00	
25% GPA	3.14	0.00	
75% LSAT	163	0	
25% LSAT	159	0	

Tuition/Living Expenses

	Resident	Non-resident
Full-Time	$20,834	$20,834
Part-Time	$0	$0

Estimated living expenses for Singles		
Living on campus	Living off campus	Living at home
$12,165	$12,165	$8,209

Career Placement

	Total	%
Employment status known	357	96.2
Employment status unknown	14	3.8
Employed	294	82.4
Pursuing graduate degrees	12	3.4
Unemployed seeking employment	41	11.5
Unemployed not seeking employment	10	2.8
Type of Employment		
# employed in law firms	195	66.3
# employed in business & industry	29	9.9
# employed in government	34	11.6
# employed in public interest	7	2.4
# employed as judicial clerks	27	9.2
# employed in academia	2	0.7
Geographic Location		
# employed in state	105	35.7
# employed in foreign countries	3	1.0
# of states where employed	26	

Financial Aid

	Full-time		Part-time		Total	
	#	%	#	%	#	%
Total # receiving grants	494	46.4	0	0.0	494	46.4
Less than 1/2 tuition	317	29.8	0	0.0	317	29.8
Half to full tuition	176	16.5	0	0.0	176	16.5
Full tuition	0	0.0	0	0.0	0	0.0
More than full tuition	1	0.1	0	0.0	1	0.1
Median Grant Amount	$9,000		$0			

Refunds

Refunds of Admissions or Seat Deposit prior to commencement of classes? No

Refunds of Pre-paid tuition prior to commencement of classes? Yes

If yes, fully refundable before the start of classes? Yes

Joint Degrees Offered

J.D./B.A., JD/MBA, JD/MPH, JD/MS, JD/MA

Advanced Degrees Offered

LL.M. Taxation
LL.M. Banking
LL.M. American Law

Bar Passage Rate

Jurisdiction	MA	NY
# from school taking bar for the first time	168	116
School's pass rate for all first-time takers	86%	83%
State's pass rate for all first-time takers	83%	78%
State's pass rate for all first-time takers from ABA approved law schools	85%	

BRIGHAM YOUNG UNIVERSITY

Provo, UT 84602
(801)378-4274
http://www.law.byu.edu

ABA
Approved
Since
1974

The Basics

Type of School: PRIVATE
Application deadline: 2/1
Application fee: $30
Financial Aid deadline: 5/1
Student faculty ratio: 18.5 to 1

First year can start other than Fall: No
Student housing: No
--exclusively for law students: No
Term: Semester

Faculty

	Men #	Men %	Women #	Women %	Minorities #	Minorities %	Total
Full-time	17	81	4	19	3	14	21
Other full-time	0	0	0	0	0	0	0
Deans, librarians, & others who teach	2	100	0	0	0	0	2
Part-time	18	86	3	14	0	0	21
Total	37	84	7	16	3	7	44
Deans, librarians, & others who teach < 1/2	0	0	1	100	0	0	1

Library

# of volumes & volume equivalents	395,780	# of professional staff	7
# of titles	141,279	Hours per week with professional staff	45
# of active serial subscriptions	5,987	Hours per week without professional staff	65
Study seating capacity inside the library	550	# of student computer work stations for entire law school	63
Square feet of law library	89,086	# of additional networked connections	470
Square feet of law school (excl. Library)	21,396		

Curriculum

	Full time	Part time
Typical first-year section size	125	0
Is there typically a "small section" of the first year class, other than Legal Writing, taught by full-time faculty?	Yes	No
If yes, typical size offered last year	25	N/A
# of classroom course titles beyond 1st year curriculum	53	0
# of upper division courses, excluding seminars, with an enrollment:		
Under 25	15	0
25 - 49	16	0
50 - 74	7	0
75 - 99	3	0
100 +	5	0
# of seminars	49	0
# of seminar positions available	1,342	
# of seminar positions filled	859	0
# of positions available in simulation courses	431	
# of simulation positions filled	305	0
# of positions available in faculty supervised clinical courses	225	
# of fac. sup. clin. positions filled	78	0
# involved in field placements	164	0
# involved in law journals	106	0
# in moot court or trial competitions	70	0
# of credit hours required to graduate	90	

Enrollment & Attrition

	Full-Time Men #	Men %	Women #	Women %	Minorities #	Minorities %	Total #	Part-Time Men #	Men %	Women #	Women %	Minorities #	Minorities %	Total #	Attrition Academic #	Other #	Total #	%
1st Year	105	66.0	54	34.0	22	13.8	159	0	0.0	0	0.0	0	0.0	0	0	0	0	0.0
2nd Year	104	71.2	42	28.8	20	13.7	146	0	0.0	0	0.0	0	0.0	0	1	1	2	1.2
3rd Year	108	66.7	54	33.3	18	11.1	162	0	0.0	0	0.0	0	0.0	0	0	0	0	0.0
4th Year								0	0.0	0	0.0	0	0.0	0	0	0	0	0.0
Total	317	67.9	150	32.1	60	12.8	467	0	0.0	0	0.0	0	0.0	0	1	1	2	0.4
JD Degrees Awarded	110	70.5	46	29.5	19	12.2	156	0	0.0	0	0.0	0	0.0	0				

GPA & LSAT Scores

	Full Time	Part Time	Total
# of apps	710	0	710
# admits	222	0	222
# of matrics	160	0	160
75% GPA	3.78	0.00	
25% GPA	3.40	0.00	
75% LSAT	163	0	
25% LSAT	156	0	

Tuition/Living Expenses

	LDS	Non-LDS
Full-Time	$4,780	$7,160
Part-Time	$264	$396

Estimated living expenses for Singles		
Living on campus	Living off campus	Living at home
$10,550	$10,440	$7,625

Career Placement

	Total	%
Employment status known	148	99.3
Employment status unknown	1	0.7
Employed	137	92.6
Pursuing graduate degrees	4	2.7
Unemployed seeking employment	4	2.7
Unemployed not seeking employment	3	2.0
Type of Employment		
# employed in law firms	72	52.6
# employed in business & industry	24	17.5
# employed in government	14	10.2
# employed in public interest	1	0.7
# employed as judicial clerks	21	15.3
# employed in academia	5	3.7
Geographic Location		
# employed in state	61	44.5
# employed in foreign countries	1	0.7
# of states where employed	16	

Financial Aid

	Full-time		Part-time		Total	
	#	%	#	%	#	%
Total # receiving grants	242	51.8	0	0.0	242	51.8
Less than 1/2 tuition	188	40.3	0	0.0	188	40.3
Half to full tuition	47	10.1	0	0.0	47	10.1
Full tuition	2	0.4	0	0.0	2	0.4
More than full tuition	5	1.1	0	0.0	5	1.1
Median Grant Amount	$1,500		$0			

Refunds

Refunds of Admissions or Seat Deposit prior to commencement of classes? Yes

100% refund to 08/01/96

Refunds of Pre-paid tuition prior to commencement of classes? Yes

If yes, fully refundable before the start of classes? Yes

Joint Degrees Offered

MBA, MPA, M-Acc, M.Ed, Ph.D., MOB, Ed.D

Advanced Degrees Offered

LL.M. Comparative Law for Foreign Lawyers

Bar Passage Rate

Jurisdiction	UT
# from school taking bar for the first time	78
School's pass rate for all first-time takers	90%
State's pass rate for all first-time takers	90%
State's pass rate for all first-time takers from ABA approved law schools	

BROOKLYN LAW SCHOOL

250 Joralemon Street
Brooklyn, NY 11201
(718)625-2200
http://www.brooklaw.edu

ABA Approved Since 1937

The Basics

Type of School: **PRIVATE**
Application deadline*: **none**
Application fee: **$50**
Financial Aid deadline*: **3/1**
Student faculty ratio: **20.3 to 1**

First year can start other than Fall: **No**
Student housing: **Yes**
--exclusively for law students: **Yes**
Term: **Semester**

*pr=preferred

Faculty

	Men		Women		Minorities		Total
	#	%	#	%	#	%	
Full-time	29	55	24	45	4	8	53
Other full-time	1	33	2	67	0	0	3
Deans, librarians, & others who teach	2	67	1	33	0	0	3
Part-time	29	55	24	45	3	6	53
Total	61	54	51	46	7	6	112
Deans, librarians, & others who teach < 1/2	2	33	4	67	0	0	6

Library

# of volumes & volume equivalents	453,182	# of professional staff	10
# of titles	63,288	Hours per week with professional staff	86
# of active serial subscriptions	4,875	Hours per week without professional staff	20
Study seating capacity inside the library	702	# of student computer work stations for entire law school	80
Square feet of law library	78,082	# of additional networked connections	313
Square feet of law school (excl. Library)	191,798		

Curriculum

	Full time	Part time
Typical first-year section size	87	97
Is there typically a "small section" of the first year class, other than Legal Writing, taught by full-time faculty?	Yes	No
If yes, typical size offered last year	31	N/A
# of classroom course titles beyond 1st year curriculum	73	64
# of upper division courses, excluding seminars, with an enrollment:		
Under 25	54	47
25 - 49	27	20
50 - 74	20	16
75 - 99	9	4
100 +	9	2
# of seminars	12	3
# of seminar positions available	325	
# of seminar positions filled	168	37
# of positions available in simulation courses	805	
# of simulation positions filled	565	165
# of positions available in faculty supervised clinical courses	181	
# of fac. sup. clin. positions filled	170	11
# involved in field placements	470	25
# involved in law journals	142	37
# in moot court or trial competitions	59	12
# of credit hours required to graduate	86	

Enrollment & Attrition

	Full-Time							Part-Time							Attrition			
	Men		Women		Minorities		Total	Men		Women		Minorities		Total	Academic	Other	Total	
	#	%	#	%	#	%	#	#	%	#	%	#	%	#	#	#	#	%
1st Year	145	52.2	133	47.8	47	16.9	278	97	51.9	90	48.1	39	20.9	187	1	11	12	2.6
2nd Year	184	55.3	149	44.7	57	17.1	333	62	53.9	53	46.1	22	19.1	115	8	15	23	5.0
3rd Year	182	51.1	174	48.9	51	14.3	356	51	53.7	44	46.3	14	14.7	95	4	4	8	1.8
4th Year								55	61.1	35	38.9	15	16.7	90	0	0	0	0.0
Total	511	52.8	456	47.2	155	16.0	967	265	54.4	222	45.6	90	18.5	487	13	30	43	3.0
JD Degrees Awarded	213	62.5	128	37.5	41	12.0	341	59	63.4	34	36.6	13	14.0	93				

GPA & LSAT Scores

	Full Time	Part Time	Total
# of apps	2,229	776	3,005
# admits	1,125	411	1,536
# of matrics	281	187	468
75% GPA	3.53	3.31	
25% GPA	2.99	2.76	
75% LSAT	159	155	
25% LSAT	152	149	

Tuition/Living Expenses

	Resident	Non-resident
Full-Time	$19,760	$19,760
Part-Time	$14,845	$14,845

Estimated living expenses for Singles		
Living on campus	Living off campus	Living at home
$16,506	$16,506	$10,296

Financial Aid

	Full-time		Part-time		Total	
	#	%	#	%	#	%
Total # receiving grants	433	44.8	93	19.1	526	36.2
Less than 1/2 tuition	384	39.7	83	17.0	467	32.1
Half to full tuition	47	4.9	10	2.1	57	3.9
Full tuition	2	0.2	0	0.0	2	0.1
More than full tuition	0	0.0	0	0.0	0	0.0
Median Grant Amount	$5,254		$4,138			

Refunds

Refunds of Admissions or Seat Deposit prior to commencement of classes? Yes

100% refund from 01/01/96 to 04/01/96
50% refund from 04/02/96 to 04/15/96
33% refund from 04/16/96 to 04/30/96

Refunds of Pre-paid tuition prior to commencement of classes? Yes

If yes, fully refundable before the start of classes? Yes

Joint Degrees Offered

MA(pol. Sci), MBA(Bus.Adm), MPA(Pub.Adm), MS(L.Inf.Sc), MS(planning), MUP(Urb.Pln)

Advanced Degrees Offered

No Advanced Degrees

Career Placement

	Total	%
Employment status known	435	97.1
Employment status unknown	13	2.9
Employed	363	83.5
Pursuing graduate degrees	1	0.2
Unemployed seeking employment	71	16.3
Unemployed not seeking employment	0	0.0
Type of Employment		
# employed in law firms	211	58.1
# employed in business & industry	64	17.6
# employed in government	56	15.4
# employed in public interest	14	3.9
# employed as judicial clerks	14	3.9
# employed in academia	4	1.1
Geographic Location		
# employed in state	333	91.7
# employed in foreign countries	2	0.6
# of states where employed	13	

Bar Passage Rate

Jurisdiction	NY
# from school taking bar for the first time	417
School's pass rate for all first-time takers	86%
State's pass rate for all first-time takers	78%
State's pass rate for all first-time takers from ABA approved law schools	

CALIFORNIA WESTERN SCHOOL OF LAW

225 Cedar Street
San Diego, CA 92101-3046
(619)239-0391
http://www.cwsl.edu

ABA Approved Since 1962

The Basics

Type of School: **PRIVATE**
Application deadline*: **4/1**
Application fee: **$45**
Financial Aid deadline*: **3/20**
Student faculty ratio: **16.4 to 1**

First year can start other than Fall: **Yes**
Student housing: **No**
--exclusively for law students: **No**
Term: **Trimester**

*pr=preferred

Faculty

	Men		Women		Minorities		Total
	#	%	#	%	#	%	
Full-time	19	54	16	46	6	17	35
Other full-time	1	25	3	75	0	0	4
Deans, librarians, & others who teach	0	0	0	0	0	0	0
Part-time	15	63	9	38	3	13	24
Total	35	56	28	44	9	14	63
Deans, librarians, & others who teach < 1/2	3	75	1	25	0	0	4

Library

# of volumes & volume equivalents	240,120	# of professional staff	8
# of titles	38,824	Hours per week with professional staff	90
# of active serial subscriptions	3,223	Hours per week without professional staff	20
Study seating capacity inside the library	508	# of student computer work stations for entire law school	46
Square feet of law library	27,370	# of additional networked connections	54
Square feet of law school (excl. Library)	111,974		

Curriculum

	Full time	Part time
Typical first-year section size	85	0
Is there typically a "small section" of the first year class, other than Legal Writing, taught by full-time faculty?	No	No
If yes, typical size offered last year	N/A	N/A
# of classroom course titles beyond 1st year curriculum	90	0
# of upper division courses, excluding seminars, with an enrollment:		
Under 25	87	0
25 - 49	29	0
50 - 74	19	0
75 - 99	11	0
100 +	2	0
# of seminars	20	0
# of seminar positions available	393	
# of seminar positions filled	233	0
# of positions available in simulation courses	1,119	
# of simulation positions filled	900	0
# of positions available in faculty supervised clinical courses	0	
# of fac. sup. clin. positions filled	0	0
# involved in field placements	218	0
# involved in law journals	76	0
# in moot court or trial competitions	52	0
# of credit hours required to graduate	89	

Enrollment & Attrition

	Full-Time							Part-Time							Attrition			
	Men		Women		Minorities		Total	Men		Women		Minorities		Total	Academic	Other	Total	
	#	%	#	%	#	%	#	#	%	#	%	#	%	#	#	#	#	%
1st Year	127	51.8	118	48.2	68	27.8	245	0	0.0	0	0.0	0	0.0	0	51	26	77	27
2nd Year	119	50.2	118	49.8	56	23.6	237	0	0.0	0	0.0	0	0.0	0	0	5	5	2.1
3rd Year	119	57.2	89	42.8	41	19.7	208	0	0.0	0	0.0	0	0.0	0	0	1	1	0.4
4th Year								0	0.0	0	0.0	0	0.0	0	0	0	0	0.0
Total	365	52.9	325	47.1	165	23.9	690	0	0.0	0	0.0	0	0.0	0	51	32	83	11
JD Degrees Awarded	163	53.8	140	46.2	48	15.8	303	0	0.0	0	0.0	0	0.0	0				

CALIFORNIA WESTERN SCHOOL OF LAW

GPA & LSAT Scores

	Full Time	Part Time	Total
# of apps	2,143	0	2,143
# admits	1,366	0	1,366
# of matrics	304	0	304
75% GPA	3.35	0.00	
25% GPA	2.84	0.00	
75% LSAT	155	0	
25% LSAT	148	0	

Tuition/Living Expenses

	Resident	Non-resident
Full-Time	$19,170	$19,170
Part-Time	$0	$0

Estimated living expenses for Singles		
Living on campus	Living off campus	Living at home
N/A	$13,120	$8,520

Financial Aid

	Full-time		Part-time		Total	
	#	%	#	%	#	%
Total # receiving grants	235	34.1	0	0.0	235	34.1
Less than 1/2 tuition	51	7.4	0	0.0	51	7.4
Half to full tuition	117	17.0	0	0.0	117	17.0
Full tuition	67	9.7	0	0.0	67	9.7
More than full tuition	0	0.0	0	0.0	0	0.0
Median Grant Amount	$9,125		$0			

Refunds

Refunds of Admissions or Seat Deposit prior to commencement of classes? No

Refunds of Pre-paid tuition prior to commencement of classes? Yes

If yes, fully refundable before the start of classes? Yes

Career Placement

	Total	%
Employment status known	209	86.0
Employment status unknown	34	14.0
Employed	169	80.9
Pursuing graduate degrees	9	4.3
Unemployed seeking employment	22	10.5
Unemployed not seeking employment	9	4.3
Type of Employment		
# employed in law firms	88	52.1
# employed in business & industry	27	16.0
# employed in government	34	20.1
# employed in public interest	3	1.8
# employed as judicial clerks	8	4.7
# employed in academia	3	1.8
Geographic Location		
# employed in state	110	65.1
# employed in foreign countries	0	0.0
# of states where employed	24	

Joint Degrees Offered

JD/MSW

Advanced Degrees Offered

No Advanced Degrees

Bar Passage Rate

Jurisdiction	CA
# from school taking bar for the first time	114
School's pass rate for all first-time takers	82%
State's pass rate for all first-time takers	73%
State's pass rate for all first-time takers from ABA approved law schools	83%

CALIFORNIA-BERKELEY, UNIVERSITY OF

221 Boalt Hall
Berkeley, CA 94720
(510)642-1741
http://www.law.berkeley.edu

ABA Approved Since 1923

The Basics

Type of School: **PUBLIC**
Application deadline*: **2/1**
Application fee: **$40**
Financial Aid deadline*: **3/2**
Student faculty ratio: **17.5 to 1**

First year can start other than Fall: **No**
Student housing: **Yes**
--exclusively for law students: **No**
Term: **Semester**

*pr=preferred

Faculty

	Men		Women		Minorities		Total
	#	%	#	%	#	%	
Full-time	30	75	10	25	6	15	40
Other full-time	1	25	3	75	1	25	4
Deans, librarians, & others who teach	5	71	2	29	1	14	7
Part-time	32	74	11	26	3	7	43
Total	68	72	26	28	11	12	94
Deans, librarians, & others who teach < 1/2	1	50	1	50	1	50	2

Library

# of volumes & volume equivalents	745,875	# of professional staff	17
# of titles	201,509	Hours per week with professional staff	70
# of active serial subscriptions	7,544	Hours per week without professional staff	21
Study seating capacity inside the library	397	# of student computer work stations for entire law school	79
Square feet of law library	88,902	# of additional networked connections	0
Square feet of law school (excl. Library)	85,833		

Curriculum

	Full time	Part time
Typical first-year section size	90	0
Is there typically a "small section" of the first year class, other than Legal Writing, taught by full-time faculty?	Yes	No
If yes, typical size offered last year	30	N/A
# of classroom course titles beyond 1st year curriculum	118	0
# of upper division courses, excluding seminars, with an enrollment:		
Under 25	47	0
25 - 49	25	0
50 - 74	19	0
75 - 99	11	0
100 +	7	0
# of seminars	31	0
# of seminar positions available	679	
# of seminar positions filled	488	0
# of positions available in simulation courses	275	
# of simulation positions filled	252	0
# of positions available in faculty supervised clinical courses	146	
# of fac. sup. clin. positions filled	105	0
# involved in field placements	79	0
# involved in law journals	354	0
# in moot court or trial competitions	129	0
# of credit hours required to graduate	85	

Enrollment & Attrition

	Full-Time							Part-Time							Attrition			
	Men		Women		Minorities		Total	Men		Women		Minorities		Total	Academic	Other	Total	
	#	%	#	%	#	%	#	#	%	#	%	#	%	#	#	#	#	%
1st Year	127	48.3	136	51.7	88	33.5	263	0	0.0	0	0.0	0	0.0	0	0	6	6	2.3
2nd Year	129	48.0	140	52.0	93	34.6	269	0	0.0	0	0.0	0	0.0	0	0	11	11	3.9
3rd Year	164	53.6	142	46.4	117	38.2	306	0	0.0	0	0.0	0	0.0	0	2	5	7	2.3
4th Year								0	0.0	0	0.0	0	0.0	0	0	0	0	0.0
Total	420	50.1	418	49.9	298	35.6	838	0	0.0	0	0.0	0	0.0	0	2	22	24	2.8
JD Degrees Awarded	136	49.5	139	50.5	102	37.1	275	0	0.0	0	0.0	0	0.0	0				

CALIFORNIA-BERKELEY, UNIVERSITY OF

GPA & LSAT Scores

	Full Time	Part Time	Total
# of apps	4,684	0	4,684
# admits	855	0	855
# of matrics	263	0	263
75% GPA	3.85	0.00	
25% GPA	3.55	0.00	
75% LSAT	170	0	
25% LSAT	161	0	

Tuition/Living Expenses

	Resident	Non-resident
Full-Time	$10,800	$19,194
Part-Time	$0	$0

Estimated living expenses for Singles		
Living on campus	Living off campus	Living at home
$10,917	$10,917	$10,917

Career Placement

	Total	%
Employment status known	269	97.7
Employment status unknown	6	2.1
Employed	251	93.3
Pursuing graduate degrees	6	2.2
Unemployed seeking employment	10	3.7
Unemployed not seeking employment	2	0.8
Type of Employment		
# employed in law firms	187	74.5
# employed in business & industry	11	4.4
# employed in government	18	7.2
# employed in public interest	6	2.4
# employed as judicial clerks	28	11.2
# employed in academia	1	0.4
Geographic Location		
# employed in state	175	69.7
# employed in foreign countries	3	1.2
# of states where employed	19	

Financial Aid

	Full-time		Part-time		Total	
	#	%	#	%	#	%
Total # receiving grants	487	58.1	0	0.0	487	58.1
Less than 1/2 tuition	350	41.8	0	0.0	350	41.8
Half to full tuition	94	11.2	0	0.0	94	11.2
Full tuition	6	0.7	0	0.0	6	0.7
More than full tuition	37	4.4	0	0.0	37	4.4
Median Grant Amount	$6,000		$0			

Refunds

Refunds of Admissions or Seat Deposit prior to commencement of classes? No

Refunds of Pre-paid tuition prior to commencement of classes? Yes

If yes, fully refundable before the start of classes? Yes

Joint Degrees Offered

JD-M ASIAN S, JD-MBA, JD-MCRP, JD-MA ECON, JD-M JOURN, JD-MPP, JD-MS AGR EC, JD-MSW, JD-PhD HIST, JD-PhD ECON, JD-PhD JSP, JD-MA RHETOR

Advanced Degrees Offered

LLM	General
JSD	General
Ph.D	Jurisprudence and Social Policy

Bar Passage Rate

Jurisdiction	CA
# from school taking bar for the first time	209
School's pass rate for all first-time takers	90%
State's pass rate for all first-time takers	73%
State's pass rate for all first-time takers from ABA approved law schools	83%

CALIFORNIA-DAVIS, UNIVERSITY OF

King Hall
Davis, CA 95616-5201
(916)752-0243
http://www.kinghall.ucdavis.edu

ABA Approved Since 1968

The Basics

Type of School: **PUBLIC**
Application deadline*: **2/1**
Application fee: **$40**
Financial Aid deadline*: **3/1**
Student faculty ratio: **15.1 to 1**

First year can start other than Fall: **No**
Student housing: **Yes**
--exclusively for law students: **No**
Term: **Semester**

*pr=preferred

Faculty

	Men		Women		Minorities		Total
	#	%	#	%	#	%	
Full-time	19	66	10	34	7	24	29
Other full-time	0	0	0	0	0	0	0
Deans, librarians, & others who teach	1	100	0	0	0	0	1
Part-time	5	56	4	44	3	33	9
Total	25	64	14	36	10	26	39
Deans, librarians, & others who teach < 1/2	2	100	0	0	0	0	2

Library

# of volumes & volume equivalents	392,497	# of professional staff	4
# of titles	80,861	Hours per week with professional staff	78
# of active serial subscriptions	5,476	Hours per week without professional staff	0
Study seating capacity inside the library	375	# of student computer work stations for entire law school	59
Square feet of law library	35,452	# of additional networked connections	0
Square feet of law school (excl. Library)	29,347		

Curriculum

	Full time	Part time
Typical first-year section size	80	0
Is there typically a "small section" of the first year class, other than Legal Writing, taught by full-time faculty?	Yes	No
If yes, typical size offered last year	22	N/A
# of classroom course titles beyond 1st year curriculum	68	0
# of upper division courses, excluding seminars, with an enrollment:		
Under 25	31	0
25 - 49	16	0
50 - 74	8	0
75 - 99	7	0
100 +	2	0
# of seminars	11	0
# of seminar positions available	194	
# of seminar positions filled	149	0
# of positions available in simulation courses	447	
# of simulation positions filled	442	0
# of positions available in faculty supervised clinical courses	230	
# of fac. sup. clin. positions filled	150	0
# involved in field placements	85	0
# involved in law journals	95	0
# in moot court or trial competitions	92	0
# of credit hours required to graduate	88	

Enrollment & Attrition

	Full-Time							Part-Time							Attrition			
	Men		Women		Minorities		Total	Men		Women		Minorities		Total	Academic	Other	Total	
	#	%	#	%	#	%	#	#	%	#	%	#	%	#	#	#	#	%
1st Year	87	56.9	66	43.1	42	27.5	153	0	0.0	0	0.0	0	0.0	0	0	1	1	0.7
2nd Year	84	55.3	68	44.7	57	37.5	152	0	0.0	0	0.0	0	0.0	0	1	9	10	5.6
3rd Year	94	51.1	90	48.9	59	32.1	184	0	0.0	0	0.0	0	0.0	0	0	3	3	2.0
4th Year								0	0.0	0	0.0	0	0.0	0	0	0	0	0.0
Total	265	54.2	224	45.8	158	32.3	489	0	0.0	0	0.0	0	0.0	0	1	13	14	3.0
JD Degrees Awarded	74	50.3	73	49.7	49	33.3	147	0	0.0	0	0.0	0	0.0	0				

GPA & LSAT Scores

	Full Time	Part Time	Total
# of apps	2,621	0	2,621
# admits	833	0	833
# of matrics	152	0	152
75% GPA	3.62	0.00	
25% GPA	3.15	0.00	
75% LSAT	165	0	
25% LSAT	158	0	

Tuition/Living Expenses

	Resident	Non-resident
Full-Time	$10,881	$19,275
Part-Time	$0	$0

Estimated living expenses for Singles		
Living on campus	Living off campus	Living at home
$9,938	$9,885	N/A

Career Placement

	Total	%
Employment status known	154	95.1
Employment status unknown	8	4.9
Employed	127	82.5
Pursuing graduate degrees	2	1.3
Unemployed seeking employment	24	15.6
Unemployed not seeking employment	1	0.7
Type of Employment		
# employed in law firms	66	52.0
# employed in business & industry	11	8.7
# employed in government	27	21.3
# employed in public interest	5	3.9
# employed as judicial clerks	16	12.6
# employed in academia	2	1.6
Geographic Location		
# employed in state	115	90.6
# employed in foreign countries	1	0.8
# of states where employed	11	

Financial Aid

	Full-time		Part-time		Total	
	#	%	#	%	#	%
Total # receiving grants	323	66.1	0	0.0	323	66.1
Less than 1/2 tuition	304	62.2	0	0.0	304	62.2
Half to full tuition	0	0.0	0	0.0	0	0.0
Full tuition	19	3.9	0	0.0	19	3.9
More than full tuition	0	0.0	0	0.0	0	0.0
Median Grant Amount	$3,776		$0			

Refunds

Refunds of Admissions or Seat Deposit prior to commencement of classes? No

Refunds of Pre-paid tuition prior to commencement of classes? No

If yes, fully refundable before the start of classes? No

Joint Degrees Offered

MBA, MS

Advanced Degrees Offered

No Advanced Degrees

Bar Passage Rate

Jurisdiction	CA
# from school taking bar for the first time	156
School's pass rate for all first-time takers	93%
State's pass rate for all first-time takers	73%
State's pass rate for all first-time takers from ABA approved law schools	83%

CALIFORNIA-HASTINGS, UNIVERSITY OF

200 McAllister Street
San Francisco, CA 94102
(415)565-4600
http://www.uchastings.edu

ABA Approved Since 1939

The Basics

Type of School: **PUBLIC**
Application deadline*: **2/15**
Application fee: **$40**
Financial Aid deadline*: **2/15**
Student faculty ratio: **24.5 to 1**

First year can start other than Fall: **No**
Student housing: **Yes**
--exclusively for law students: **Yes**
Term: **Semester**

*pr=preferred

Faculty

	Men #	Men %	Women #	Women %	Minorities #	Minorities %	Total
Full-time	32	73	12	27	8	18	44
Other full-time	0	0	0	0	0	0	0
Deans, librarians, & others who teach	3	75	1	25	1	25	4
Part-time	45	58	33	42	9	12	78
Total	80	63	46	37	18	14	126
Deans, librarians, & others who teach < 1/2	0	0	2	100	0	0	2

Library

# of volumes & volume equivalents	575,608	# of professional staff	8
# of titles	178,273	Hours per week with professional staff	53
# of active serial subscriptions	8,378	Hours per week without professional staff	49
Study seating capacity inside the library	1,295	# of student computer work stations for entire law school	98
Square feet of law library	82,750	# of additional networked connections	0
Square feet of law school (excl. Library)	120,070		

Curriculum

	Full time	Part time
Typical first-year section size	85	0
Is there typically a "small section" of the first year class, other than Legal Writing, taught by full-time faculty?	Yes	No
If yes, typical size offered last year	42	N/A
# of classroom course titles beyond 1st year curriculum	127	0
# of upper division courses, excluding seminars, with an enrollment:		
Under 25	74	0
25 - 49	43	0
50 - 74	19	0
75 - 99	12	0
100 +	12	0
# of seminars	52	0
# of seminar positions available	1,202	
# of seminar positions filled	776	0
# of positions available in simulation courses	918	
# of simulation positions filled	739	0
# of positions available in faculty supervised clinical courses	197	
# of fac. sup. clin. positions filled	144	0
# involved in field placements	126	0
# involved in law journals	425	0
# in moot court or trial competitions	145	0
# of credit hours required to graduate	86	

Enrollment & Attrition

	Full-Time							Part-Time							Attrition			
	Men		Women		Minorities		Total	Men		Women		Minorities		Total	Academic	Other	Total	
	#	%	#	%	#	%	#	#	%	#	%	#	%	#	#	#	#	%
1st Year	269	53.8	231	46.2	179	35.8	500	0	0.0	0	0.0	0	0.0	0	7	17	24	5.8
2nd Year	213	53.7	184	46.3	90	22.7	397	0	0.0	0	0.0	0	0.0	0	1	2	3	0.7
3rd Year	195	49.4	200	50.6	123	31.1	395	0	0.0	0	0.0	0	0.0	0	1	3	4	1.0
4th Year								0	0.0	0	0.0	0	0.0	0	0	0	0	0.0
Total	677	52.4	615	47.6	392	30.3	1,292	0	0.0	0	0.0	0	0.0	0	9	22	31	2.6
JD Degrees Awarded	191	50.1	190	49.9	148	38.8	381	0	0.0	0	0.0	0	0.0	0				

GPA & LSAT Scores

	Full Time	Part Time	Total
# of apps	4,352	0	4,352
# admits	1,773	0	1,773
# of matrics	492	0	492
75% GPA	3.65	0.00	
25% GPA	2.94	0.00	
75% LSAT	165	0	
25% LSAT	149	0	

Tuition/Living Expenses

	Resident	Non-resident
Full-Time	$11,172	$19,564
Part-Time	$0	$0

Estimated living expenses for Singles		
Living on campus	Living off campus	Living at home
$15,053	$15,053	$15,053

Financial Aid

	Full-time		Part-time		Total	
	#	%	#	%	#	%
Total # receiving grants	1048	81.1	0	0.0	1048	81.1
Less than 1/2 tuition	1041	80.6	0	0.0	1041	80.6
Half to full tuition	5	0.4	0	0.0	5	0.4
Full tuition	2	0.2	0	0.0	2	0.2
More than full tuition	0	0.0	0	0.0	0	0.0
Median Grant Amount	$3,350		$0			

Refunds

Refunds of Admissions or Seat Deposit prior to commencement of classes? No

Refunds of Pre-paid tuition prior to commencement of classes? Yes

If yes, fully refundable before the start of classes? Yes

Joint Degrees Offered

LL.M., MBA, MPPM, M.Ed.

Advanced Degrees Offered

No Advanced Degrees

Career Placement

	Total	%
Employment status known	370	92.0
Employment status unknown	32	8.0
Employed	263	71.1
Pursuing graduate degrees	9	2.4
Unemployed seeking employment	41	11.1
Unemployed not seeking employment	57	15.4
Type of Employment		
# employed in law firms	159	60.5
# employed in business & industry	30	11.4
# employed in government	33	12.6
# employed in public interest	10	3.8
# employed as judicial clerks	23	8.8
# employed in academia	9	3.4
Geographic Location		
# employed in state	170	64.6
# employed in foreign countries	1	0.4
# of states where employed	21	

Bar Passage Rate

Jurisdiction	CA
# from school taking bar for the first time	322
School's pass rate for all first-time takers	79%
State's pass rate for all first-time takers	73%
State's pass rate for all first-time takers from ABA approved law schools	83%

CALIFORNIA-LOS ANGELES, UNIVERSITY OF

405 Hilgard Avenue
Los Angeles, CA 90095
(310)825-4841
http://www.law.ucla.edu

ABA Approved Since 1950

The Basics

Type of School: **PUBLIC**
Application deadline*: **1/16**
Application fee: **$40**
Financial Aid deadline*: **3/2**
Student faculty ratio: **15.5 to 1**

First year can start other than Fall: **No**
Student housing: **Yes**
--exclusively for law students: **No**
Term: **Semester**

*pr=preferred

Faculty

	Men #	Men %	Women #	Women %	Minorities #	Minorities %	Total
Full-time	36	71	15	29	3	6	51
Other full-time	3	43	4	57	0	0	7
Deans, librarians, & others who teach	1	100	0	0	0	0	1
Part-time	7	88	1	13	0	0	8
Total	47	70	20	30	3	4	67
Deans, librarians, & others who teach < 1/2	0	0	3	100	0	0	3

Library

# of volumes & volume equivalents	524,296	# of professional staff	9
# of titles	177,204	Hours per week with professional staff	61
# of active serial subscriptions	6,885	Hours per week without professional staff	37
Study seating capacity inside the library	271	# of student computer work stations for entire law school	100
Square feet of law library	42,346	# of additional networked connections	35
Square feet of law school (excl. Library)	64,750		

Curriculum

	Full time	Part time
Typical first-year section size	67	0
Is there typically a "small section" of the first year class, other than Legal Writing, taught by full-time faculty?	Yes	No
If yes, typical size offered last year	27	N/A
# of classroom course titles beyond 1st year curriculum	103	0
# of upper division courses, excluding seminars, with an enrollment:		
Under 25	16	0
25 - 49	28	0
50 - 74	14	0
75 - 99	12	0
100 +	10	0
# of seminars	29	0
# of seminar positions available	403	
# of seminar positions filled	358	0
# of positions available in simulation courses	83	
# of simulation positions filled	83	0
# of positions available in faculty supervised clinical courses	164	
# of fac. sup. clin. positions filled	163	0
# involved in field placements	69	0
# involved in law journals	418	0
# in moot court or trial competitions	234	0
# of credit hours required to graduate	87	

Enrollment & Attrition

	Full-Time							Part-Time							Attrition			
	Men		Women		Minorities		Total	Men		Women		Minorities		Total	Academic	Other	Total	
	#	%	#	%	#	%	#	#	%	#	%	#	%	#	#	#	#	%
1st Year	164	53.8	141	46.2	109	35.7	305	0	0.0	0	0.0	0	0.0	0	0	20	20	7.5
2nd Year	132	46.8	150	53.2	101	35.8	282	0	0.0	0	0.0	0	0.0	0	1	3	4	1.2
3rd Year	168	50.6	164	49.4	167	50.3	332	0	0.0	0	0.0	0	0.0	0	0	0	0	0.0
4th Year								0	0.0	0	0.0	0	0.0	0	0	0	0	0.0
Total	464	50.5	455	49.5	377	41.0	919	0	0.0	0	0.0	0	0.0	0	1	23	24	2.6
JD Degrees Awarded	171	51.4	162	48.6	131	39.3	333	0	0.0	0	0.0	0	0.0	0				

CALIFORNIA-LOS ANGELES, UNIVERSITY OF

GPA & LSAT Scores

	Full Time	Part Time	Total
# of apps	4,417	0	4,417
# admits	1,009	0	1,009
# of matrics	305	0	305
75% GPA	3.75	0.00	
25% GPA	3.42	0.00	
75% LSAT	165	0	
25% LSAT	159	0	

Tuition/Living Expenses

	Resident	Non-resident
Full-Time	$10,861	$19,255
Part-Time	$0	$0

Estimated living expenses for Singles		
Living on campus	Living off campus	Living at home
$11,122	$13,445	$7,007

Financial Aid

	Full-time		Part-time		Total	
	#	%	#	%	#	%
Total # receiving grants	471	51.3	0	0.0	471	51.3
Less than 1/2 tuition	291	31.7	0	0.0	291	31.7
Half to full tuition	116	12.6	0	0.0	116	12.6
Full tuition	0	0.0	0	0.0	0	0.0
More than full tuition	64	7.0	0	0.0	64	7.0
Median Grant Amount	$4,250		$0			

Refunds

Refunds of Admissions or Seat Deposit prior to commencement of classes? No

Refunds of Pre-paid tuition prior to commencement of classes? Yes

If yes, fully refundable before the start of classes? Yes

Joint Degrees Offered

JD/MA, Urban Planng, JD/MA, JD/MBA

Advanced Degrees Offered

J.D.	Varies, depending on the interest of the student
LL.M.	Varies. Our program is aimed at non-U.S. students, who plan to return to their home countries after graduation.

Career Placement

	Total	%
Employment status known	267	98.9
Employment status unknown	3	1.1
Employed	245	91.8
Pursuing graduate degrees	2	0.8
Unemployed seeking employment	16	6.0
Unemployed not seeking employment	4	1.5
Type of Employment		
# employed in law firms	184	75.1
# employed in business & industry	7	2.9
# employed in government	23	9.4
# employed in public interest	9	3.7
# employed as judicial clerks	20	8.2
# employed in academia	2	0.8
Geographic Location		
# employed in state	203	82.9
# employed in foreign countries	0	0.0
# of states where employed	9	

Bar Passage Rate

Jurisdiction	CA	NY
# from school taking bar for the first time	241	11
School's pass rate for all first-time takers	89%	100%
State's pass rate for all first-time takers	73%	78%
State's pass rate for all first-time takers from ABA approved law schools	83%	

CAMPBELL UNIVERSITY

P.O. Box 158
Buies Creek, NC 27506
(910)893-1750
http://webster.campbell.edu/culawsch

ABA Approved Since 1979

The Basics

Type of School: **PRIVATE**
Application deadline*: **3/31**
Application fee: **$40**
Financial Aid deadline*:
Student faculty ratio: **19.9 to 1**

First year can start other than Fall: **No**
Student housing: **No**
--exclusively for law students: **No**
Term: **Semester**

*pr=preferred

Faculty

	Men #	Men %	Women #	Women %	Minorities #	Minorities %	Total
Full-time	13	93	1	7	0	0	14
Other full-time	0	0	0	0	0	0	0
Deans, librarians, & others who teach	2	100	0	0	0	0	2
Part-time	6	86	1	14	0	0	7
Total	21	91	2	9	0	0	23
Deans, librarians, & others who teach < 1/2	1	100	0	0	0	0	1

Library

# of volumes & volume equivalents	156,579	# of professional staff	4
# of titles	17,729	Hours per week with professional staff	45
# of active serial subscriptions	2,346	Hours per week without professional staff	61
Study seating capacity inside the library	412	# of student computer work stations for entire law school	52
Square feet of law library	28,143	# of additional networked connections	0
Square feet of law school (excl. Library)	50,140		

Curriculum

	Full time	Part time
Typical first-year section size	50	0
Is there typically a "small section" of the first year class, other than Legal Writing, taught by full-time faculty?	Yes	No
If yes, typical size offered last year	37	N/A
# of classroom course titles beyond 1st year curriculum	61	0
# of upper division courses, excluding seminars, with an enrollment:		
Under 25	27	0
25 - 49	14	0
50 - 74	7	0
75 - 99	4	0
100 +	2	0
# of seminars	8	0
# of seminar positions available	336	
# of seminar positions filled	196	0
# of positions available in simulation courses	103	
# of simulation positions filled	103	0
# of positions available in faculty supervised clinical courses	0	
# of fac. sup. clin. positions filled	0	0
# involved in field placements	30	0
# involved in law journals	90	0
# in moot court or trial competitions	48	0
# of credit hours required to graduate	90	

Enrollment & Attrition

	Full-Time							Part-Time							Attrition			
	Men		Women		Minorities		Total	Men		Women		Minorities		Total	Academic	Other	Total	
	#	%	#	%	#	%	#	#	%	#	%	#	%	#	#	#	#	%
1st Year	72	60.5	47	39.5	2	1.7	119	0	0.0	0	0.0	0	0.0	0	2	2	4	3.4
2nd Year	56	50.9	54	49.1	5	4.5	110	0	0.0	0	0.0	0	0.0	0	6	1	7	6.9
3rd Year	56	55.4	45	44.6	7	6.9	101	0	0.0	0	0.0	0	0.0	0	0	0	0	0.0
4th Year								0	0.0	0	0.0	0	0.0	0	0	0	0	0.0
Total	184	55.8	146	44.2	14	4.2	330	0	0.0	0	0.0	0	0.0	0	8	3	11	3.4
JD Degrees Awarded	58	56.3	45	43.7	2	1.9	103	0	0.0	0	0.0	0	0.0	0				

GPA & LSAT Scores

	Full Time	Part Time	Total
# of apps	800	0	800
# admits	206	0	206
# of matrics	119	0	119
75% GPA	3.42	0.00	
25% GPA	2.62	0.00	
75% LSAT	158	0	
25% LSAT	152	0	

Tuition/Living Expenses

	Resident	Non-resident
Full-Time	$14,700	$14,700
Part-Time	$0	$0

Estimated living expenses for Singles		
Living on campus	Living off campus	Living at home
$9,517	$12,337	N/A

Financial Aid

	Full-time		Part-time		Total	
	#	%	#	%	#	%
Total # receiving grants	110	33.3	0	0.0	110	33.3
Less than 1/2 tuition	93	28.2	0	0.0	93	28.2
Half to full tuition	9	2.7	0	0.0	9	2.7
Full tuition	8	2.4	0	0.0	8	2.4
More than full tuition	0	0.0	0	0.0	0	0.0
Median Grant Amount	$2,500		$0			

Refunds

Refunds of Admissions or Seat Deposit prior to commencement of classes? No

Refunds of Pre-paid tuition prior to commencement of classes? Yes

If yes, fully refundable before the start of classes? Yes

Joint Degrees Offered

JD/MBA

Advanced Degrees Offered

No Advanced Degrees

Career Placement

	Total	%
Employment status known	94	95.9
Employment status unknown	4	4.1
Employed	92	97.9
Pursuing graduate degrees	2	2.1
Unemployed seeking employment	0	0.0
Unemployed not seeking employment	0	0.0
Type of Employment		
# employed in law firms	85	92.4
# employed in business & industry	1	1.1
# employed in government	4	4.4
# employed in public interest	1	1.1
# employed as judicial clerks	3	3.3
# employed in academia	0	0.0
Geographic Location		
# employed in state	84	91.3
# employed in foreign countries	0	0.0
# of states where employed	8	

Bar Passage Rate

Jurisdiction	NC
# from school taking bar for the first time	91
School's pass rate for all first-time takers	97%
State's pass rate for all first-time takers	85%
State's pass rate for all first-time takers from ABA approved law schools	85%

CAPITAL UNIVERSITY

665 South High Street
Columbus, OH 43215
(614)445-8836
http://www.capital.edu

ABA Approved Since 1950

The Basics

Type of School: **PRIVATE**
Application deadline*: **none**
Application fee: **$35**
Financial Aid deadline*: **4/1**
Student faculty ratio: **19.7 to 1**
First year can start other than Fall: **No**
Student housing: **No**
--exclusively for law students: **No**
Term: **Semester**

*pr=preferred

Faculty

	Men #	Men %	Women #	Women %	Minorities #	Minorities %	Total
Full-time	20	69	9	31	4	14	29
Other full-time	1	100	0	0	0	0	1
Deans, librarians, & others who teach	2	67	1	33	0	0	3
Part-time	21	88	3	13	1	4	24
Total	44	77	13	23	5	9	57
Deans, librarians, & others who teach < 1/2	1	100	0	0	0	0	1

Library

# of volumes & volume equivalents	237,892	# of professional staff	6
# of titles	45,124	Hours per week with professional staff	56
# of active serial subscriptions	2,023	Hours per week without professional staff	41
Study seating capacity inside the library	380	# of student computer work stations for entire law school	30
Square feet of law library	35,000	# of additional networked connections	3
Square feet of law school (excl. Library)	65,000		

Curriculum

	Full time	Part time
Typical first-year section size	88	95
Is there typically a "small section" of the first year class, other than Legal Writing, taught by full-time faculty?	No	No
If yes, typical size offered last year	N/A	N/A
# of classroom course titles beyond 1st year curriculum	32	67
# of upper division courses, excluding seminars, with an enrollment:		
Under 25	26	47
25 - 49	8	9
50 - 74	7	9
75 - 99	11	6
100 +	0	0
# of seminars	5	6
# of seminar positions available	176	
# of seminar positions filled	79	67
# of positions available in simulation courses	391	
# of simulation positions filled	217	76
# of positions available in faculty supervised clinical courses	65	
# of fac. sup. clin. positions filled	51	9
# involved in field placements	100	20
# involved in law journals	35	10
# in moot court or trial competitions	9	3
# of credit hours required to graduate	86	

Enrollment & Attrition

	Full-Time							Part-Time							Attrition			
	Men		Women		Minorities		Total	Men		Women		Minorities		Total	Academic	Other	Total	
	#	%	#	%	#	%	#	#	%	#	%	#	%	#	#	#	#	%
1st Year	92	52.9	82	47.1	24	13.8	174	52	53.6	45	46.4	11	11.3	97	18	39	57	22
2nd Year	80	57.6	59	42.4	16	11.5	139	49	62.0	30	38.0	9	11.4	79	1	12	13	5.4
3rd Year	81	54.0	69	46.0	12	8.0	150	48	52.7	43	47.3	10	11.0	91	0	0	0	0.0
4th Year								41	59.4	28	40.6	5	7.2	69	0	0	0	0.0
Total	253	54.6	210	45.4	52	11.2	463	190	56.5	146	43.5	35	10.4	336	19	51	70	8.7
JD Degrees Awarded	86	54.4	72	45.6	7	4.4	158	44	61.1	28	38.9	6	8.3	72				

GPA & LSAT Scores

	Full Time	Part Time	Total
# of apps	754	201	955
# admits	528	125	653
# of matrics	175	100	275
75% GPA	3.29	3.34	
25% GPA	2.76	2.70	
75% LSAT	153	154	
25% LSAT	146	147	

Tuition/Living Expenses

	Resident	Non-resident
Full-Time	$15,407	$15,407
Part-Time	$9,443	$9,443

Estimated living expenses for Singles		
Living on campus	Living off campus	Living at home
$10,585	$10,585	$10,585

Financial Aid

	Full-time		Part-time		Total	
	#	%	#	%	#	%
Total # receiving grants	166	35.9	87	25.9	253	31.7
Less than 1/2 tuition	152	32.8	59	17.6	211	26.4
Half to full tuition	8	1.7	18	5.4	26	3.3
Full tuition	6	1.3	10	3.0	16	2.0
More than full tuition	0	0.0	0	0.0	0	0.0
Median Grant Amount	$3,000		$2,500			

Refunds

Refunds of Admissions or Seat Deposit prior to commencement of classes? Yes

100% refund from 01/01/97 to 04/01/97
50% refund from 04/02/97 to 08/01/97
0% refund from 08/02/97 to 09/25/97

Refunds of Pre-paid tuition prior to commencement of classes? Yes

If yes, fully refundable before the start of classes? Yes

Joint Degrees Offered

JD/MBA, JD/MSA, JD/LLM

Advanced Degrees Offered

LL.M. Taxation
LL.M. Business and Taxation

Career Placement

	Total	%
Employment status known	192	91.4
Employment status unknown	18	8.6
Employed	177	92.2
Pursuing graduate degrees	4	2.1
Unemployed seeking employment	5	2.6
Unemployed not seeking employment	6	3.1
Type of Employment		
# employed in law firms	91	51.4
# employed in business & industry	37	20.9
# employed in government	29	16.4
# employed in public interest	6	3.4
# employed as judicial clerks	10	5.7
# employed in academia	4	2.3
Geographic Location		
# employed in state	144	81.4
# employed in foreign countries	0	0.0
# of states where employed	20	

Bar Passage Rate

Jurisdiction	OH
# from school taking bar for the first time	175
School's pass rate for all first-time takers	94%
State's pass rate for all first-time takers	93%
State's pass rate for all first-time takers from ABA approved law schools	90%

CASE WESTERN RESERVE UNIVERSITY

Gund Hall
11075 East Blvd
Cleveland, OH 44106-7148
(216)368-6350
http://lawwww.cwru.edu

ABA Approved Since 1923

The Basics

Type of School: PRIVATE
Application deadline*: 4/1
Application fee: $40
Financial Aid deadline*: 5/1
Student faculty ratio: 16.3 to 1

First year can start other than Fall: No
Student housing: Yes
--exclusively for law students: No
Term: Semester

*pr=preferred

Faculty

	Men		Women		Minorities		Total
	#	%	#	%	#	%	
Full-time	26	81	6	19	2	6	32
Other full-time	5	56	4	44	0	0	9
Deans, librarians, & others who teach	2	100	0	0	0	0	2
Part-time	29	76	9	24	1	3	38
Total	62	77	19	23	3	4	81
Deans, librarians, & others who teach < 1/2	2	67	1	33	0	0	3

Library

# of volumes & volume equivalents	347,789	# of professional staff	10
# of titles	81,355	Hours per week with professional staff	63
# of active serial subscriptions	4,600	Hours per week without professional staff	45
Study seating capacity inside the library	446	# of student computer work stations for entire law school	62
Square feet of law library	31,495	# of additional networked connections	10
Square feet of law school (excl. Library)	64,909		

Curriculum

	Full time	Part time
Typical first-year section size	75	0
Is there typically a "small section" of the first year class, other than Legal Writing, taught by full-time faculty?	No	No
If yes, typical size offered last year	N/A	N/A
# of classroom course titles beyond 1st year curriculum	139	0
# of upper division courses, excluding seminars, with an enrollment:		
Under 25	91	0
25 - 49	25	0
50 - 74	17	0
75 - 99	9	0
100 +	1	0
# of seminars	16	0
# of seminar positions available	192	
# of seminar positions filled	165	0
# of positions available in simulation courses	320	
# of simulation positions filled	294	0
# of positions available in faculty supervised clinical courses	64	
# of fac. sup. clin. positions filled	64	0
# involved in field placements	36	0
# involved in law journals	115	0
# in moot court or trial competitions	92	0
# of credit hours required to graduate	88	

Enrollment & Attrition

	Full-Time							Part-Time							Attrition			
	Men		Women		Minorities		Total	Men		Women		Minorities		Total	Academic	Other	Total	
	#	%	#	%	#	%	#	#	%	#	%	#	%	#	#	#	#	%
1st Year	124	55.4	100	44.6	27	12.1	224	4	66.7	2	33.3	1	16.7	6	1	20	21	9.5
2nd Year	110	55.6	88	44.4	31	15.7	198	2	40.0	3	60.0	0	0.0	5	0	1	1	0.5
3rd Year	125	63.5	72	36.5	25	12.7	197	1	50.0	1	50.0	1	50.0	2	0	0	0	0.0
4th Year								0	0.0	0	0.0	0	0.0	0	0	0	0	0.0
Total	359	58.0	260	42.0	83	13.4	619	7	53.8	6	46.2	2	15.4	13	1	21	22	3.4
JD Degrees Awarded	113	53.6	98	46.4	25	11.8	211	3	60.0	2	40.0	0	0.0	5				

CASE WESTERN RESERVE UNIVERSITY

GPA & LSAT Scores

	Full Time	Part Time	Total
# of apps	1,420	30	1,450
# admits	890	7	897
# of matrics	225	1	226
75% GPA	3.57	0.00	
25% GPA	3.02	0.00	
75% LSAT	161	0	
25% LSAT	154	0	

Tuition/Living Expenses

	Resident	Non-resident
Full-Time	$19,040	$19,040
Part-Time	$19,040	$19,040

Estimated living expenses for Singles		
Living on campus	Living off campus	Living at home
$10,100	$10,100	$7,300

Financial Aid

	Full-time		Part-time		Total	
	#	%	#	%	#	%
Total # receiving grants	229	37.0	0	0.0	229	36.2
Less than 1/2 tuition	103	16.6	0	0.0	103	16.3
Half to full tuition	98	15.8	0	0.0	98	15.5
Full tuition	28	4.5	0	0.0	28	4.4
More than full tuition	0	0.0	0	0.0	0	0.0
Median Grant Amount	$9,700		$0			

Refunds

Refunds of Admissions or Seat Deposit prior to commencement of classes? No

Refunds of Pre-paid tuition prior to commencement of classes? Yes

If yes, fully refundable before the start of classes? Yes

Joint Degrees Offered

JD/MBA, JD/MSSA, JD/MNO, JD/MA (Hist)

Advanced Degrees Offered

LL.M. TAXATION
LL.M. UNITED STATES LEGAL STUDIES

Career Placement

	Total	%
Employment status known	206	98.6
Employment status unknown	3	1.4
Employed	177	85.9
Pursuing graduate degrees	2	1.0
Unemployed seeking employment	26	12.6
Unemployed not seeking employment	1	0.5
Type of Employment		
# employed in law firms	111	62.7
# employed in business & industry	25	14.1
# employed in government	20	11.3
# employed in public interest	6	3.4
# employed as judicial clerks	15	8.5
# employed in academia	0	0.0
Geographic Location		
# employed in state	119	67.2
# employed in foreign countries	1	0.6
# of states where employed	26	

Bar Passage Rate

Jurisdiction	OH
# from school taking bar for the first time	132
School's pass rate for all first-time takers	94%
State's pass rate for all first-time takers	93%
State's pass rate for all first-time takers from ABA approved law schools	90%

CATHOLIC UNIVERSITY OF AMERICA

Washington, DC 20064
(319)319-5140
http://www.law.cua.edu

ABA Approved Since 1925

The Basics

Type of School: **PRIVATE**
Application deadline*: **3/1**
Application fee: **$55**
Financial Aid deadline*: **3/1**
Student faculty ratio: **19.3 to 1**
First year can start other than Fall: **No**
Student housing: **Yes**
--exclusively for law students: **No**
Term: **Semester**

*pr=preferred

Faculty

	Men #	Men %	Women #	Women %	Minorities #	Minorities %	Total
Full-time	26	68	12	32	6	16	38
Other full-time	3	60	2	40	0	0	5
Deans, librarians, & others who teach	2	100	0	0	0	0	2
Part-time	33	72	13	28	2	4	46
Total	64	70	27	30	8	9	91
Deans, librarians, & others who teach < 1/2	2	100	0	0	0	0	2

Library

# of volumes & volume equivalents	264,408	# of professional staff	8
# of titles	75,360	Hours per week with professional staff	86
# of active serial subscriptions	5,291	Hours per week without professional staff	27
Study seating capacity inside the library	502	# of student computer work stations for entire law school	33
Square feet of law library	54,311	# of additional networked connections	477
Square feet of law school (excl. Library)	64,264		

Curriculum

	Full time	Part time
Typical first-year section size	70	70
Is there typically a "small section" of the first year class, other than Legal Writing, taught by full-time faculty?	Yes	Yes
If yes, typical size offered last year	35	35
# of classroom course titles beyond 1st year curriculum	79	72
# of upper division courses, excluding seminars, with an enrollment:		
Under 25	48	29
25 - 49	17	17
50 - 74	8	9
75 - 99	14	1
100 +	0	0
# of seminars	7	3
# of seminar positions available	173	
# of seminar positions filled	74	29
# of positions available in simulation courses	452	
# of simulation positions filled	256	93
# of positions available in faculty supervised clinical courses	120	
# of fac. sup. clin. positions filled	99	16
# involved in field placements	235	25
# involved in law journals	112	37
# in moot court or trial competitions	39	13
# of credit hours required to graduate	84	

Enrollment & Attrition

	Full-Time Men #	Men %	Women #	Women %	Minorities #	Minorities %	Total #	Part-Time Men #	Men %	Women #	Women %	Minorities #	Minorities %	Total #	Attrition Academic #	Other #	Total #	Total %
1st Year	113	51.4	107	48.6	34	15.5	220	49	62.0	30	38.0	20	25.3	79	3	24	27	8.8
2nd Year	113	50.9	109	49.1	37	16.7	222	46	62.2	28	37.8	16	21.6	74	0	6	6	1.9
3rd Year	139	55.4	112	44.6	30	12.0	251	37	56.1	29	43.9	11	16.7	66	0	0	0	0.0
4th Year								32	47.8	35	52.2	10	14.9	67	0	0	0	0.0
Total	365	52.7	328	47.3	101	14.6	693	164	57.3	122	42.7	57	19.9	286	3	30	33	3.5
JD Degrees Awarded	109	52.2	100	47.8	33	15.8	209	34	64.2	19	35.8	11	20.8	53				

CATHOLIC UNIVERSITY OF AMERICA

GPA & LSAT Scores

	Full Time	Part Time	Total
# of apps	1,848	425	2,273
# admits	911	205	1,116
# of matrics	221	79	300
75% GPA	3.40	3.20	
25% GPA	2.80	2.60	
75% LSAT	157	155	
25% LSAT	151	148	

Tuition/Living Expenses

	Resident	Non-resident
Full-Time	$21,468	$21,468
Part-Time	$15,339	$15,339

Estimated living expenses for Singles		
Living on campus	Living off campus	Living at home
$12,454	$12,454	$12,454

Career Placement

	Total	%
Employment status known	277	99.3
Employment status unknown	2	0.7
Employed	241	87.0
Pursuing graduate degrees	5	1.8
Unemployed seeking employment	24	8.7
Unemployed not seeking employment	7	2.5
Type of Employment		
# employed in law firms	113	46.9
# employed in business & industry	45	18.7
# employed in government	26	10.8
# employed in public interest	8	3.3
# employed as judicial clerks	47	19.5
# employed in academia	2	0.8
Geographic Location		
# employed in state	124	51.5
# employed in foreign countries	2	0.8
# of states where employed	21	

Financial Aid

	Full-time		Part-time		Total	
	#	%	#	%	#	%
Total # receiving grants	235	33.9	7	2.5	242	24.7
Less than 1/2 tuition	231	33.3	7	2.5	238	24.3
Half to full tuition	1	0.1	0	0.0	1	0.1
Full tuition	3	0.4	0	0.0	3	0.3
More than full tuition	0	0.0	0	0.0	0	0.0
Median Grant Amount	$3,500		$1,500			

Refunds

Refunds of Admissions or Seat Deposit prior to commencement of classes? No

Refunds of Pre-paid tuition prior to commencement of classes? Yes

If yes, fully refundable before the start of classes? Yes

Joint Degrees Offered

JD/MA Pol., JD/MA Phil., JD/JCL Canon, JD/MA Hist., JD/MSW, JD/MLS, JD/MA Econ.

Bar Passage Rate

Jurisdiction	MD
# from school taking bar for the first time	104
School's pass rate for all first-time takers	70%
State's pass rate for all first-time takers	75%
State's pass rate for all first-time takers from ABA approved law schools	75%

Advanced Degrees Offered

No Advanced Degrees

CHICAGO, UNIVERSITY OF

1111 East 60th Street
Chicago, IL 60637
(773)702-9494
http://www.lib.uchicago.edu/law

ABA Approved Since 1923

The Basics

Type of School: **PRIVATE**
Application deadline*: **none**
Application fee: **$60**
Financial Aid deadline*: **4/1**
Student faculty ratio: **19.3 to 1**

First year can start other than Fall: **No**
Student housing: **Yes**
--exclusively for law students: **No**
Term: **Quarter**

*pr=preferred

Faculty

	Men		Women		Minorities		Total
	#	%	#	%	#	%	
Full-time	21	81	5	19	2	8	26
Other full-time	0	0	0	0	0	0	0
Deans, librarians, & others who teach	2	100	0	0	1	50	2
Part-time	5	71	2	29	1	14	7
Total	28	80	7	20	4	11	35
Deans, librarians, & others who teach < 1/2	0	0	0	0	0	0	0

Library

# of volumes & volume equivalents	608,415	# of professional staff	9
# of titles	236,226	Hours per week with professional staff	57
# of active serial subscriptions	7,437	Hours per week without professional staff	33
Study seating capacity inside the library	445	# of student computer work stations for entire law school	43
Square feet of law library	75,002	# of additional networked connections	247
Square feet of law school (excl. Library)	64,859		

Curriculum

	Full time	Part time
Typical first-year section size	88	0
Is there typically a "small section" of the first year class, other than Legal Writing, taught by full-time faculty?	No	No
If yes, typical size offered last year	N/A	N/A
# of classroom course titles beyond 1st year curriculum	66	0
# of upper division courses, excluding seminars, with an enrollment:		
Under 25	13	0
25 - 49	23	0
50 - 74	10	0
75 - 99	4	0
100 +	16	0
# of seminars	70	0
# of seminar positions available	0	
# of seminar positions filled	0	0
# of positions available in simulation courses	0	
# of simulation positions filled	0	0
# of positions available in faculty supervised clinical courses	0	
# of fac. sup. clin. positions filled	0	0
# involved in field placements	0	0
# involved in law journals	0	0
# in moot court or trial competitions	0	0
# of credit hours required to graduate	105	

Enrollment & Attrition

	Full-Time							Part-Time							Attrition			
	Men		Women		Minorities		Total	Men		Women		Minorities		Total	Academic	Other	Total	
	#	%	#	%	#	%	#	#	%	#	%	#	%	#	#	#	#	%
1st Year	104	57.8	76	42.2	46	25.6	180	0	0.0	0	0.0	0	0.0	0	0	6	6	3.4
2nd Year	110	61.1	70	38.9	39	21.7	180	0	0.0	0	0.0	0	0.0	0	0	2	2	1.1
3rd Year	111	61.0	71	39.0	32	17.6	182	0	0.0	0	0.0	0	0.0	0	0	0	0	0.0
4th Year								0	0.0	0	0.0	0	0.0	0	0	0	0	0.0
Total	325	60.0	217	40.0	117	21.6	542	0	0.0	0	0.0	0	0.0	0	0	8	8	1.5
JD Degrees Awarded	95	51.9	88	48.1	42	23.0	183	0	0.0	0	0.0	0	0.0	0				

GPA & LSAT Scores

	Full Time	Part Time	Total
# of apps	2,773	0	2,773
# admits	642	0	642
# of matrics	180	0	180
75% GPA	3.80	0.00	
25% GPA	3.54	0.00	
75% LSAT	173	0	
25% LSAT	166	0	

Tuition/Living Expenses

	Resident	Non-resident
Full-Time	$22,755	$22,755
Part-Time	$0	$0

Estimated living expenses for Singles		
Living on campus	Living off campus	Living at home
$13,693	$13,693	$13,693

Career Placement

	Total	%
Employment status known	183	100.0
Employment status unknown	0	0.0
Employed	173	94.5
Pursuing graduate degrees	1	0.6
Unemployed seeking employment	7	3.8
Unemployed not seeking employment	2	1.1
Type of Employment		
# employed in law firms	117	67.6
# employed in business & industry	8	4.6
# employed in government	5	2.9
# employed in public interest	4	2.3
# employed as judicial clerks	39	22.5
# employed in academia	0	0.0
Geographic Location		
# employed in state	67	38.7
# employed in foreign countries	0	0.0
# of states where employed	29	

Financial Aid

	Full-time		Part-time		Total	
	#	%	#	%	#	%
Total # receiving grants	247	45.6	0	0.0	247	45.6
Less than 1/2 tuition	189	34.9	0	0.0	189	34.9
Half to full tuition	54	10.0	0	0.0	54	10.0
Full tuition	0	0.0	0	0.0	0	0.0
More than full tuition	4	0.7	0	0.0	4	0.7
Median Grant Amount	$8,000		$0			

Refunds

Refunds of Admissions or Seat Deposit prior to commencement of classes? No

Refunds of Pre-paid tuition prior to commencement of classes? No

If yes, fully refundable before the start of classes? No

Joint Degrees Offered

JD/MBA, JD/MPP, JD/MA Econ., JD/MA Hist., JD/MA INR, JD/PHD Econ., JD/PHD Hist.

Advanced Degrees Offered

LL.M
M.Comp
D.Comp
J.S.D.

Bar Passage Rate

Jurisdiction	IL
# from school taking bar for the first time	77
School's pass rate for all first-time takers	97%
State's pass rate for all first-time takers	87%
State's pass rate for all first-time takers from ABA approved law schools	87%

CINCINNATI, UNIVERSITY OF

P.O. Box 210040
Cincinnati, OH 45221-0040
(513)556-6805
http://www.law.uc.edu

ABA Approved Since 1923

The Basics

Type of School: **PUBLIC**
Application deadline*: **4/1**
Application fee: **$35**
Financial Aid deadline*: **3/1**
Student faculty ratio: **13.9 to 1**

First year can start other than Fall: **No**
Student housing: **Yes**
--exclusively for law students: **No**
Term: **Semester**

*pr=preferred

Faculty

	Men		Women		Minorities		Total
	#	%	#	%	#	%	
Full-time	15	68	7	32	2	9	22
Other full-time	0	0	3	100	0	0	3
Deans, librarians, & others who teach	0	0	1	100	0	0	1
Part-time	21	91	2	9	0	0	23
Total	36	73	13	27	2	4	49
Deans, librarians, & others who teach < 1/2	1	50	1	50	0	0	2

Library

# of volumes & volume equivalents	361,586	# of professional staff	10
# of titles	168,004	Hours per week with professional staff	61
# of active serial subscriptions	2,441	Hours per week without professional staff	46
Study seating capacity inside the library	439	# of student computer work stations for entire law school	44
Square feet of law library	49,227	# of additional networked connections	0
Square feet of law school (excl. Library)	48,836		

Curriculum

	Full time	Part time
Typical first-year section size	22	0
Is there typically a "small section" of the first year class, other than Legal Writing, taught by full-time faculty?	Yes	No
If yes, typical size offered last year	22	N/A
# of classroom course titles beyond 1st year curriculum	90	0
# of upper division courses, excluding seminars, with an enrollment:		
Under 25	34	0
25 - 49	17	0
50 - 74	8	0
75 - 99	1	0
100 +	3	0
# of seminars	22	0
# of seminar positions available	306	
# of seminar positions filled	203	0
# of positions available in simulation courses	171	
# of simulation positions filled	171	0
# of positions available in faculty supervised clinical courses	0	
# of fac. sup. clin. positions filled	0	0
# involved in field placements	110	0
# involved in law journals	50	0
# in moot court or trial competitions	18	0
# of credit hours required to graduate	88	

Enrollment & Attrition

	Full-Time							Part-Time							Attrition			
	Men		Women		Minorities		Total	Men		Women		Minorities		Total	Academic	Other	Total	
	#	%	#	%	#	%	#	#	%	#	%	#	%	#	#	#	#	%
1st Year	52	43.3	68	56.7	11	9.2	120	1	50.0	1	50.0	0	0.0	2	0	2	2	1.7
2nd Year	55	47.0	62	53.0	10	8.5	117	0	0.0	0	0.0	0	0.0	0	0	0	0	0.0
3rd Year	76	61.8	47	38.2	17	13.8	123	2	25.0	6	75.0	0	0.0	8	0	0	0	0.0
4th Year								0	0.0	0	0.0	0	0.0	0	0	0	0	0.0
Total	183	50.8	177	49.2	38	10.6	360	3	30.0	7	70.0	0	0.0	10	0	2	2	0.5
JD Degrees Awarded	71	56.3	55	43.7	22	17.5	126	0	0.0	0	0.0	0	0.0	0				

GPA & LSAT Scores

	Full Time	Part Time	Total
# of apps	995	0	995
# admits	424	0	424
# of matrics	124	0	124
75% GPA	3.74	0.00	
25% GPA	3.24	0.00	
75% LSAT	162	0	
25% LSAT	154	0	

Tuition/Living Expenses

	Resident	Non-resident
Full-Time	$6,900	$13,407
Part-Time	$0	$0

Estimated living expenses for Singles		
Living on campus	Living off campus	Living at home
$10,144	$10,144	$10,144

Career Placement

	Total	%
Employment status known	116	96.7
Employment status unknown	4	3.3
Employed	105	90.5
Pursuing graduate degrees	6	5.2
Unemployed seeking employment	1	0.9
Unemployed not seeking employment	4	3.5
Type of Employment		
# employed in law firms	55	52.4
# employed in business & industry	22	21.0
# employed in government	12	11.4
# employed in public interest	3	2.9
# employed as judicial clerks	11	10.5
# employed in academia	2	1.9
Geographic Location		
# employed in state	76	72.4
# employed in foreign countries	1	1.0
# of states where employed	16	

Financial Aid

	Full-time		Part-time		Total	
	#	%	#	%	#	%
Total # receiving grants	232	64.4	0	0.0	232	62.7
Less than 1/2 tuition	144	40.0	0	0.0	144	38.9
Half to full tuition	52	14.4	0	0.0	52	14.1
Full tuition	30	8.3	0	0.0	30	8.1
More than full tuition	6	1.7	0	0.0	6	1.6
Median Grant Amount	$3,000		$0			

Refunds

Refunds of Admissions or Seat Deposit prior to commencement of classes? Yes

67% refund from 02/03/96 to 05/15/96

Refunds of Pre-paid tuition prior to commencement of classes? No

If yes, fully refundable before the start of classes? No

Joint Degrees Offered

JD/MBA, JD/MCP, JD/WomensStu

Advanced Degrees Offered

No Advanced Degrees

Bar Passage Rate

Jurisdiction	OH
# from school taking bar for the first time	88
School's pass rate for all first-time takers	95%
State's pass rate for all first-time takers	93%
State's pass rate for all first-time takers from ABA approved law schools	90%

CITY UNIVERSITY OF NEW YORK

65-21 Main Street
Flushing, NY 11367
(718)575-4200
http://www.cuny.edu

ABA Approved Since 1985

The Basics

Type of School: **PUBLIC**
Application deadline*: **3/15**
Application fee: **$40**
Financial Aid deadline*: **7/1**
Student faculty ratio: **13.8 to 1**

First year can start other than Fall: **No**
Student housing: **No**
--exclusively for law students: **No**
Term: **Semester**

*pr=preferred

Faculty

	Men #	Men %	Women #	Women %	Minorities #	Minorities %	Total
Full-time	13	46	15	54	11	39	28
Other full-time	1	17	5	83	2	33	6
Deans, librarians, & others who teach	0	0	0	0	0	0	0
Part-time	6	60	4	40	2	20	10
Total	20	45	24	55	15	34	44
Deans, librarians, & others who teach < 1/2	2	25	6	75	2	25	8

Library

# of volumes & volume equivalents	226,557	# of professional staff	7
# of titles	23,892	Hours per week with professional staff	49
# of active serial subscriptions	2,537	Hours per week without professional staff	46
Study seating capacity inside the library	397	# of student computer work stations for entire law school	64
Square feet of law library	33,475	# of additional networked connections	0
Square feet of law school (excl. Library)	62,977		

Curriculum

	Full time	Part time
Typical first-year section size	80	0
Is there typically a "small section" of the first year class, other than Legal Writing, taught by full-time faculty?	Yes	No
If yes, typical size offered last year	20	N/A
# of classroom course titles beyond 1st year curriculum	68	0
# of upper division courses, excluding seminars, with an enrollment:		
Under 25	36	0
25 - 49	10	0
50 - 74	5	0
75 - 99	7	0
100 +	2	0
# of seminars	7	0
# of seminar positions available	140	
# of seminar positions filled	120	0
# of positions available in simulation courses	480	
# of simulation positions filled	480	0
# of positions available in faculty supervised clinical courses	74	
# of fac. sup. clin. positions filled	74	0
# involved in field placements	60	0
# involved in law journals	35	0
# in moot court or trial competitions	30	0
# of credit hours required to graduate	91	

Enrollment & Attrition

	Full-Time							Part-Time							Attrition			
	Men		Women		Minorities		Total	Men		Women		Minorities		Total	Academic	Other	Total	
	#	%	#	%	#	%	#	#	%	#	%	#	%	#	#	#	#	%
1st Year	64	39.5	98	60.5	73	45.1	162	0	0.0	0	0.0	0	0.0	0	0	6	6	3.7
2nd Year	67	43.8	86	56.2	47	30.7	153	0	0.0	0	0.0	0	0.0	0	0	5	5	3.4
3rd Year	56	37.3	94	62.7	47	31.3	150	0	0.0	0	0.0	0	0.0	0	1	1	2	1.3
4th Year								0	0.0	0	0.0	0	0.0	0	0	0	0	0.0
Total	187	40.2	278	59.8	167	35.9	465	0	0.0	0	0.0	0	0.0	0	1	12	13	2.8
JD Degrees Awarded	79	54.5	66	45.5	52	35.9	145	0	0.0	0	0.0	0	0.0	0				

GPA & LSAT Scores

	Full Time	Part Time	Total
# of apps	1,647	0	1,647
# admits	521	0	521
# of matrics	160	0	160
75% GPA	3.32	0.00	
25% GPA	2.76	0.00	
75% LSAT	151	0	
25% LSAT	142	0	

Tuition/Living Expenses

	Resident	Non-resident
Full-Time	$6,452	$9,682
Part-Time	$0	$0

Estimated living expenses for Singles		
Living on campus	Living off campus	Living at home
N/A	$9,500	$5,024

Career Placement

	Total	%
Employment status known	92	67.2
Employment status unknown	45	32.9
Employed	67	72.8
Pursuing graduate degrees	0	0.0
Unemployed seeking employment	19	20.7
Unemployed not seeking employment	6	6.5
Type of Employment		
# employed in law firms	23	34.3
# employed in business & industry	5	7.5
# employed in government	15	22.4
# employed in public interest	38	56.7
# employed as judicial clerks	5	7.5
# employed in academia	6	9.0
Geographic Location		
# employed in state	53	79.1
# employed in foreign countries	0	0.0
# of states where employed	10	

Financial Aid

	Full-time		Part-time		Total	
	#	%	#	%	#	%
Total # receiving grants	237	51.0	0	0.0	237	51.0
Less than 1/2 tuition	237	51.0	0	0.0	237	51.0
Half to full tuition	0	0.0	0	0.0	0	0.0
Full tuition	5	1.1	0	0.0	5	1.1
More than full tuition	0	0.0	0	0.0	0	0.0
Median Grant Amount	$1,575		$0			

Refunds

Refunds of Admissions or Seat Deposit prior to commencement of classes? No

Refunds of Pre-paid tuition prior to commencement of classes? Yes

If yes, fully refundable before the start of classes? Yes

Joint Degrees Offered

No Joint Degrees

Advanced Degrees Offered

No Advanced Degrees

Bar Passage Rate

Jurisdiction	NY	CT
# from school taking bar for the first time	103	17
School's pass rate for all first-time takers	58%	59%
State's pass rate for all first-time takers	78%	83%
State's pass rate for all first-time takers from ABA approved law schools		78%

CLEVELAND STATE UNIVERSITY

Cleveland-Marshall College of Law
1801 Euclid Avenue
Cleveland, OH 44115
(216)687-2344
http://www.law.csuohio.edu

ABA Approved Since 1957

The Basics

Type of School: **PUBLIC**
Application deadline*: **4/1**
Application fee: **$35**
Financial Aid deadline*: **4/1**
Student faculty ratio: **18.8 to 1**

First year can start other than Fall: **No**
Student housing: **Yes**
--exclusively for law students: **Yes**
Term: **Semester**

*pr=preferred

Faculty

	Men		Women		Minorities		Total
	#	%	#	%	#	%	
Full-time	24	71	10	29	4	12	34
Other full-time	1	20	4	80	0	0	5
Deans, librarians, & others who teach	4	67	2	33	0	0	6
Part-time	23	72	9	28	3	9	32
Total	52	68	25	32	7	9	77
Deans, librarians, & others who teach < 1/2	3	75	1	25	1	25	4

Library

# of volumes & volume equivalents	410,904	# of professional staff	14
# of titles	117,844	Hours per week with professional staff	94
# of active serial subscriptions	2,141	Hours per week without professional staff	6
Study seating capacity inside the library	324	# of student computer work stations for entire law school	20
Square feet of law library	27,524	# of additional networked connections	0
Square feet of law school (excl. Library)	48,092		

Curriculum

	Full time	Part time
Typical first-year section size	70	40
Is there typically a "small section" of the first year class, other than Legal Writing, taught by full-time faculty?	No	No
If yes, typical size offered last year	N/A	N/A
# of classroom course titles beyond 1st year curriculum	46	45
# of upper division courses, excluding seminars, with an enrollment:		
Under 25	36	38
25 - 49	17	24
50 - 74	9	7
75 - 99	2	3
100 +	0	0
# of seminars	11	9
# of seminar positions available	372	
# of seminar positions filled	118	90
# of positions available in simulation courses	270	
# of simulation positions filled	166	63
# of positions available in faculty supervised clinical courses	80	
# of fac. sup. clin. positions filled	52	6
# involved in field placements	25	4
# involved in law journals	31	10
# in moot court or trial competitions	36	8
# of credit hours required to graduate	87	

Enrollment & Attrition

	Full-Time							Part-Time							Attrition			
	Men		Women		Minorities		Total	Men		Women		Minorities		Total	Academic	Other	Total	
	#	%	#	%	#	%	#	#	%	#	%	#	%	#	#	#	#	%
1st Year	93	51.7	87	48.3	19	10.6	180	37	46.3	43	53.8	15	18.8	80	7	28	35	12
2nd Year	105	56.8	80	43.2	16	8.6	185	44	53.0	39	47.0	8	9.6	83	3	7	10	4.5
3rd Year	111	56.1	87	43.9	28	14.1	198	42	64.6	23	35.4	8	12.3	65	2	5	7	2.8
4th Year								37	45.1	45	54.9	10	12.2	82	0	0	0	0.0
Total	309	54.9	254	45.1	63	11.2	563	160	51.6	150	48.4	41	13.2	310	12	40	52	6.0
JD Degrees Awarded	112	60.9	72	39.1	17	9.2	184	43	59.7	29	40.3	8	11.1	72				

GPA & LSAT Scores

	Full Time	Part Time	Total
# of apps	1,136	265	1,401
# admits	655	131	786
# of matrics	180	80	260
75% GPA	3.43	3.39	
25% GPA	2.93	2.81	
75% LSAT	153	154	
25% LSAT	145	147	

Tuition/Living Expenses

	Resident	Non-resident
Full-Time	$6,936	$13,830
Part-Time	$5,334	$10,636

Estimated living expenses for Singles		
Living on campus	Living off campus	Living at home
$7,934	$9,760	$9,760

Career Placement

	Total	%
Employment status known	107	40.4
Employment status unknown	158	59.6
Employed	92	86.0
Pursuing graduate degrees	2	1.9
Unemployed seeking employment	13	12.2
Unemployed not seeking employment	0	0.0
Type of Employment		
# employed in law firms	63	68.5
# employed in business & industry	11	12.0
# employed in government	10	10.9
# employed in public interest	2	2.2
# employed as judicial clerks	4	4.4
# employed in academia	2	2.2
Geographic Location		
# employed in state	81	88.0
# employed in foreign countries	0	0.0
# of states where employed	9	

Financial Aid

	Full-time		Part-time		Total	
	#	%	#	%	#	%
Total # receiving grants	281	49.9	69	22.3	350	40.1
Less than 1/2 tuition	273	48.5	68	21.9	341	39.1
Half to full tuition	3	0.5	1	0.3	4	0.5
Full tuition	5	0.9	0	0.0	5	0.6
More than full tuition	0	0.0	0	0.0	0	0.0
Median Grant Amount	$700		$700			

Refunds

Refunds of Admissions or Seat Deposit prior to commencement of classes? Yes

83% refund to 04/15/96
67% refund from 04/16/96 to 05/15/96
50% refund from 05/16/96 to 06/15/96

Refunds of Pre-paid tuition prior to commencement of classes? Yes

If yes, fully refundable before the start of classes? Yes

Joint Degrees Offered

J.D./MBA, J.D./MPA

Advanced Degrees Offered

LL.M. General, but student must take half of credit in area of concentration selected by student.

Bar Passage Rate

Jurisdiction	OH
# from school taking bar for the first time	174
School's pass rate for all first-time takers	91%
State's pass rate for all first-time takers	93%
State's pass rate for all first-time takers from ABA approved law schools	90%

COLORADO, UNIVERSITY OF

Campus Box 401
Boulder, CO 80309-0401
(303)492-7203
http://www.colorado.edu/law

ABA Approved Since 1923

The Basics

Type of School: **PUBLIC**	First year can start other than Fall: **No**
Application deadline*: **2/15**	Student housing: **No**
Application fee: **$40**	--exclusively for law students: **No**
Financial Aid deadline*: **asap**	Term: **Semester**
Student faculty ratio: **15.7 to 1**	

*pr=preferred

Faculty

	Men		Women		Minorities		Total
	#	%	#	%	#	%	
Full-time	23	85	4	15	4	15	27
Other full-time	0	0	0	0	0	0	0
Deans, librarians, & others who teach	4	80	1	20	1	20	5
Part-time	8	80	2	20	1	10	10
Total	35	83	7	17	6	14	42
Deans, librarians, & others who teach < 1/2	0	0	2	100	0	0	2

Library

# of volumes & volume equivalents	346,303	# of professional staff	7
# of titles	118,006	Hours per week with professional staff	64
# of active serial subscriptions	3,316	Hours per week without professional staff	45
Study seating capacity inside the library	323	# of student computer work stations for entire law school	2
Square feet of law library	36,000	# of additional networked connections	23
Square feet of law school (excl. Library)	68,185		

Curriculum

	Full time	Part time
Typical first-year section size	83	0
Is there typically a "small section" of the first year class, other than Legal Writing, taught by full-time faculty?	Yes	No
If yes, typical size offered last year	28	N/A
# of classroom course titles beyond 1st year curriculum	89	0
# of upper division courses, excluding seminars, with an enrollment:		
Under 25	60	0
25 - 49	22	0
50 - 74	17	0
75 - 99	0	0
100 +	0	0
# of seminars	17	0
# of seminar positions available	219	
# of seminar positions filled	191	0
# of positions available in simulation courses	294	
# of simulation positions filled	284	0
# of positions available in faculty supervised clinical courses	92	
# of fac. sup. clin. positions filled	71	0
# involved in field placements	29	0
# involved in law journals	96	0
# in moot court or trial competitions	69	0
# of credit hours required to graduate	89	

Enrollment & Attrition

	Full-Time							Part-Time							Attrition			
	Men		Women		Minorities		Total	Men		Women		Minorities		Total	Academic	Other	Total	
	#	%	#	%	#	%	#	#	%	#	%	#	%	#	#	#	#	%
1st Year	94	57.7	69	42.3	29	17.8	163	0	0.0	0	0.0	0	0.0	0	0	2	2	1.2
2nd Year	82	49.7	83	50.3	35	21.2	165	0	0.0	0	0.0	0	0.0	0	0	2	2	1.2
3rd Year	105	62.1	64	37.9	32	18.9	169	0	0.0	0	0.0	0	0.0	0	0	2	2	1.2
4th Year								0	0.0	0	0.0	0	0.0	0	0	0	0	0.0
Total	281	56.5	216	43.5	96	19.3	497	0	0.0	0	0.0	0	0.0	0	0	6	6	1.2
JD Degrees Awarded	81	53.6	70	46.4	33	21.9	151	0	0.0	0	0.0	0	0.0	0				

GPA & LSAT Scores

	Full Time	Part Time	Total
# of apps	2,299	0	2,299
# admits	680	0	680
# of matrics	167	0	167
75% GPA	3.73	0.00	
25% GPA	3.30	0.00	
75% LSAT	165	0	
25% LSAT	160	0	

Tuition/Living Expenses

	Resident	Non-resident
Full-Time	$4,502	$15,260
Part-Time	$0	$0

Estimated living expenses for Singles		
Living on campus	Living off campus	Living at home
$8,734	$10,637	$6,695

Career Placement

	Total	%
Employment status known	151	95.6
Employment status unknown	7	4.4
Employed	123	81.5
Pursuing graduate degrees	1	0.7
Unemployed seeking employment	25	16.6
Unemployed not seeking employment	2	1.3
Type of Employment		
# employed in law firms	60	48.8
# employed in business & industry	21	17.1
# employed in government	16	13.0
# employed in public interest	6	4.9
# employed as judicial clerks	14	11.4
# employed in academia	6	4.9
Geographic Location		
# employed in state	86	69.9
# employed in foreign countries	1	0.8
# of states where employed	16	

Financial Aid

	Full-time		Part-time		Total	
	#	%	#	%	#	%
Total # receiving grants	251	50.5	0	0.0	251	50.5
Less than 1/2 tuition	150	30.2	0	0.0	150	30.2
Half to full tuition	23	4.6	0	0.0	23	4.6
Full tuition	60	12.1	0	0.0	60	12.1
More than full tuition	18	3.6	0	0.0	18	3.6
Median Grant Amount	$1,750		$0			

Refunds

Refunds of Admissions or Seat Deposit prior to commencement of classes? No

Refunds of Pre-paid tuition prior to commencement of classes? No

If yes, fully refundable before the start of classes? No

Joint Degrees Offered

JD/MBA, JD/MPA

Advanced Degrees Offered

No Advanced Degrees

Bar Passage Rate

Jurisdiction	CO
# from school taking bar for the first time	113
School's pass rate for all first-time takers	92%
State's pass rate for all first-time takers	
State's pass rate for all first-time takers from ABA approved law schools	

COLUMBIA UNIVERSITY

435 West 116th Street
New York, NY 10027
(212)854-2640
http://www.columbia.edu/cu/law

ABA Approved Since 1923

The Basics

Type of School: **PRIVATE**
Application deadline*: **2/15**
Application fee: **$65**
Financial Aid deadline*: **3/1**
Student faculty ratio: **15.6 to 1**
First year can start other than Fall: **No**
Student housing: **Yes**
--exclusively for law students: **Yes**
Term: **Semester**

*pr=preferred

Faculty

	Men #	Men %	Women #	Women %	Minorities #	Minorities %	Total
Full-time	42	74	15	26	6	11	57
Other full-time	3	30	7	70	2	20	10
Deans, librarians, & others who teach	5	83	1	17	1	17	6
Part-time	38	90	4	10	2	5	42
Total	**88**	**77**	**27**	**23**	**11**	**10**	**115**
Deans, librarians, & others who teach < 1/2	0	0	2	100	0	0	2

Library

# of volumes & volume equivalents	949,810	# of professional staff	19
# of titles	330,928	Hours per week with professional staff	72
# of active serial subscriptions	6,822	Hours per week without professional staff	30
Study seating capacity inside the library	327	# of student computer work stations for entire law school	84
Square feet of law library	63,988	# of additional networked connections	415
Square feet of law school (excl. Library)	102,367		

Curriculum

	Full time	Part time
Typical first-year section size	116	0
Is there typically a "small section" of the first year class, other than Legal Writing, taught by full-time faculty?	Yes	No
If yes, typical size offered last year	30	N/A
# of classroom course titles beyond 1st year curriculum	64	0
# of upper division courses, excluding seminars, with an enrollment:		
Under 25	10	0
25 - 49	25	0
50 - 74	15	0
75 - 99	4	0
100 +	17	0
# of seminars	95	0
# of seminar positions available	18	
# of seminar positions filled	1,710	0
# of positions available in simulation courses	655	
# of simulation positions filled	645	0
# of positions available in faculty supervised clinical courses	156	
# of fac. sup. clin. positions filled	154	0
# involved in field placements	73	0
# involved in law journals	540	0
# in moot court or trial competitions	88	0
# of credit hours required to graduate	83	

Enrollment & Attrition

	Full-Time							Part-Time							Attrition			
	Men		Women		Minorities		Total	Men		Women		Minorities		Total	Academic	Other	Total	
	#	%	#	%	#	%	#	#	%	#	%	#	%	#	#	#	#	%
1st Year	193	55.5	155	44.5	120	34.5	348	0	0.0	0	0.0	0	0.0	0	0	0	0	0.0
2nd Year	204	55.9	161	44.1	126	34.5	365	0	0.0	0	0.0	0	0.0	0	0	3	3	0.8
3rd Year	206	57.2	154	42.8	108	30.0	360	0	0.0	0	0.0	0	0.0	0	0	0	0	0.0
4th Year								0	0.0	0	0.0	0	0.0	0	0	0	0	0.0
Total	603	56.2	470	43.8	354	33.0	1,073	0	0.0	0	0.0	0	0.0	0	0	3	3	0.3
JD Degrees Awarded	220	60.1	146	39.9	103	28.1	366	0	0.0	0	0.0	0	0.0	0				

GPA & LSAT Scores

	Full Time	Part Time	Total
# of apps	5,510	0	5,510
# admits	1,087	0	1,087
# of matrics	347	0	347
75% GPA	3.71	0.00	
25% GPA	3.35	0.00	
75% LSAT	171	0	
25% LSAT	164	0	

Tuition/Living Expenses

	Resident	Non-resident
Full-Time	$24,342	$24,342
Part-Time	$0	$0

Estimated living expenses for Singles		
Living on campus	Living off campus	Living at home
$12,380	$13,410	$3,605

Career Placement

	Total	%
Employment status known	346	99.1
Employment status unknown	3	0.9
Employed	326	94.2
Pursuing graduate degrees	10	2.9
Unemployed seeking employment	9	2.6
Unemployed not seeking employment	1	0.3
Type of Employment		
# employed in law firms	226	69.3
# employed in business & industry	17	5.2
# employed in government	5	1.5
# employed in public interest	9	2.8
# employed as judicial clerks	58	17.8
# employed in academia	11	3.4
Geographic Location		
# employed in state	211	64.7
# employed in foreign countries	10	3.1
# of states where employed	26	

Financial Aid

	Full-time		Part-time		Total	
	#	%	#	%	#	%
Total # receiving grants	235	21.9	0	0.0	235	21.9
Less than 1/2 tuition	152	14.2	0	0.0	152	14.2
Half to full tuition	82	7.6	0	0.0	82	7.6
Full tuition	1	0.1	0	0.0	1	0.1
More than full tuition	0	0.0	0	0.0	0	0.0
Median Grant Amount	$9,125		$0			

Refunds

Refunds of Admissions or Seat Deposit prior to commencement of classes? Yes

100% refund to 07/01/96

Refunds of Pre-paid tuition prior to commencement of classes? Yes

If yes, fully refundable before the start of classes? Yes

Joint Degrees Offered

MA ANTH, MA ECON, MA HIST, MA PHIL, MA POL, MA PSY, MA SOC, MBA, MFA, MIA, MPA, MPH, MS JOUR, MS URB PLAN, MSW, PHD ANTH, PHD HIST, PHD PHIL, PHD POL, PHD SOC, PHD ECON, MPHIL

Advanced Degrees Offered

LLM There are no concentrations.
JSD There are no concentrations.

Bar Passage Rate

Jurisdiction	NY
# from school taking bar for the first time	251
School's pass rate for all first-time takers	93%
State's pass rate for all first-time takers	78%
State's pass rate for all first-time takers from ABA approved law schools	

CONNECTICUT, UNIVERSITY OF

55 Elizabeth Street
Hartford, CT 06105
(860)570-5127
http://www.uconn.law

ABA Approved Since 1933

The Basics

Type of School: **PUBLIC**
Application deadline*: **3/1**
Application fee: **$30**
Financial Aid deadline*: **3/1**
Student faculty ratio: **14.0 to 1**

First year can start other than Fall: **No**
Student housing: **No**
--exclusively for law students: **No**
Term: **Semester**

*pr=preferred

Faculty

	Men #	Men %	Women #	Women %	Minorities #	Minorities %	Total
Full-time	26	79	7	21	4	12	33
Other full-time	1	33	2	67	0	0	3
Deans, librarians, & others who teach	1	100	0	0	0	0	1
Part-time	14	70	6	30	1	5	20
Total	42	74	15	26	5	9	57
Deans, librarians, & others who teach < 1/2	1	50	1	50	0	0	2

Library

# of volumes & volume equivalents	433,030	# of professional staff	14
# of titles	140,976	Hours per week with professional staff	62
# of active serial subscriptions	6,165	Hours per week without professional staff	26
Study seating capacity inside the library	797	# of student computer work stations for entire law school	57
Square feet of law library	94,724	# of additional networked connections	0
Square feet of law school (excl. Library)	60,813		

Curriculum

	Full time	Part time
Typical first-year section size	70	70
Is there typically a "small section" of the first year class, other than Legal Writing, taught by full-time faculty?	Yes	Yes
If yes, typical size offered last year	25	30
# of classroom course titles beyond 1st year curriculum	64	35
# of upper division courses, excluding seminars, with an enrollment:		
Under 25	31	12
25 - 49	17	10
50 - 74	13	8
75 - 99	0	1
100 +	0	0
# of seminars	31	12
# of seminar positions available	655	
# of seminar positions filled	409	164
# of positions available in simulation courses	132	
# of simulation positions filled	58	68
# of positions available in faculty supervised clinical courses	88	
# of fac. sup. clin. positions filled	74	0
# involved in field placements	27	1
# involved in law journals	100	5
# in moot court or trial competitions	235	66
# of credit hours required to graduate	86	

Enrollment & Attrition

	Full-Time Men #	Men %	Women #	Women %	Minorities #	Minorities %	Total #	Part-Time Men #	Men %	Women #	Women %	Minorities #	Minorities %	Total #	Attrition Academic #	Other #	Total #	%
1st Year	71	58.2	51	41.8	21	17.2	122	33	50.0	33	50.0	6	9.1	66	0	5	5	2.6
2nd Year	80	51.3	76	48.7	24	15.4	156	17	45.9	20	54.1	9	24.3	37	0	1	1	0.5
3rd Year	87	52.7	78	47.3	22	13.3	165	21	55.3	17	44.7	2	5.3	38	0	1	1	0.5
4th Year								27	57.4	20	42.6	7	14.9	47	0	0	0	0.0
Total	238	53.7	205	46.3	67	15.1	443	98	52.1	90	47.9	24	12.8	188	0	7	7	1.1
JD Degrees Awarded	70	46.4	81	53.6	25	16.6	151	29	64.4	16	35.6	4	8.9	45				

GPA & LSAT Scores

	Full Time	Part Time	Total
# of apps	939	412	1,351
# admits	359	167	526
# of matrics	125	65	190
75% GPA	3.50	3.50	
25% GPA	3.03	3.08	
75% LSAT	161	159	
25% LSAT	156	152	

Tuition/Living Expenses

	Resident	Non-resident
Full-Time	$10,492	$21,938
Part-Time	$7,372	$15,372

Estimated living expenses for Singles		
Living on campus	Living off campus	Living at home
N/A	$12,848	$6,714

Career Placement

	Total	%
Employment status known	193	98.0
Employment status unknown	4	2.0
Employed	173	89.6
Pursuing graduate degrees	1	0.5
Unemployed seeking employment	18	9.3
Unemployed not seeking employment	1	0.5
Type of Employment		
# employed in law firms	80	46.2
# employed in business & industry	49	28.3
# employed in government	24	13.9
# employed in public interest	1	0.6
# employed as judicial clerks	15	8.7
# employed in academia	4	2.3
Geographic Location		
# employed in state	139	80.4
# employed in foreign countries	1	0.6
# of states where employed	13	

Financial Aid

	Full-time		Part-time		Total	
	#	%	#	%	#	%
Total # receiving grants	144	32.5	0	0.0	144	22.8
Less than 1/2 tuition	44	9.9	0	0.0	44	7.0
Half to full tuition	51	11.5	0	0.0	51	8.1
Full tuition	25	5.6	0	0.0	25	4.0
More than full tuition	24	5.4	0	0.0	24	3.8
Median Grant Amount	$9,000		$0			

Refunds

Refunds of Admissions or Seat Deposit prior to commencement of classes? Yes

50% refund from 01/01/95 to 05/31/95
0% refund from 06/01/95 to 09/01/95

Refunds of Pre-paid tuition prior to commencement of classes? Yes

If yes, fully refundable before the start of classes? Yes

Joint Degrees Offered

JD/MA Public, Policy, JD/MBA, JD/MLS, JD/MPA, JD/MPH, JD/MSW

Advanced Degrees Offered

LL.M. U.S. Legal Studies

Bar Passage Rate

Jurisdiction	CT
# from school taking bar for the first time	139
School's pass rate for all first-time takers	95%
State's pass rate for all first-time takers	83%
State's pass rate for all first-time takers from ABA approved law schools	78%

CORNELL UNIVERSITY

Myron Taylor Hall
Ithaca, NY 14853-4901
(607)255-3527
www.law.cornell.edu/admit/admit.htm

ABA Approved Since 1923

The Basics

Type of School: **PRIVATE**
Application deadline*: **2/1**
Application fee: **$65**
Financial Aid deadline*: **3/15**
Student faculty ratio: **12.0 to 1**
First year can start other than Fall: **No**
Student housing: **Yes**
--exclusively for law students: **Yes**
Term: **Semester**

*pr=preferred

Faculty

	Men #	Men %	Women #	Women %	Minorities #	Minorities %	Total
Full-time	34	81	8	19	3	7	42
Other full-time	0	0	0	0	0	0	0
Deans, librarians, & others who teach	2	50	2	50	0	0	4
Part-time	10	83	2	17	0	0	12
Total	46	79	12	21	3	5	58
Deans, librarians, & others who teach < 1/2	0	0	0	0	0	0	0

Library

# of volumes & volume equivalents	571,707	# of professional staff	8
# of titles	169,682	Hours per week with professional staff	61
# of active serial subscriptions	6,021	Hours per week without professional staff	24
Study seating capacity inside the library	409	# of student computer work stations for entire law school	43
Square feet of law library	51,534	# of additional networked connections	8
Square feet of law school (excl. Library)	96,956		

Curriculum

	Full time	Part time
Typical first-year section size	80	0
Is there typically a "small section" of the first year class, other than Legal Writing, taught by full-time faculty?	Yes	No
If yes, typical size offered last year	27	N/A
# of classroom course titles beyond 1st year curriculum	90	0
# of upper division courses, excluding seminars, with an enrollment:		
Under 25	21	0
25 - 49	22	0
50 - 74	17	0
75 - 99	4	0
100 +	5	0
# of seminars	33	0
# of seminar positions available	515	
# of seminar positions filled	478	0
# of positions available in simulation courses	112	
# of simulation positions filled	98	0
# of positions available in faculty supervised clinical courses	168	
# of fac. sup. clin. positions filled	153	0
# involved in field placements	12	0
# involved in law journals	131	0
# in moot court or trial competitions	32	0
# of credit hours required to graduate	84	

Enrollment & Attrition

	Full-Time							Part-Time							Attrition			
	Men		Women		Minorities		Total	Men		Women		Minorities		Total	Academic	Other	Total	
	#	%	#	%	#	%	#	#	%	#	%	#	%	#	#	#	#	%
1st Year	111	61.3	70	38.7	53	29.3	181	0	0.0	0	0.0	0	0.0	0	1	3	4	2.2
2nd Year	109	58.0	79	42.0	53	28.2	188	0	0.0	0	0.0	0	0.0	0	0	0	0	0.0
3rd Year	110	59.8	74	40.2	41	22.3	184	0	0.0	0	0.0	0	0.0	0	0	0	0	0.0
4th Year								0	0.0	0	0.0	0	0.0	0	0	0	0	0.0
Total	330	59.7	223	40.3	147	26.6	553	0	0.0	0	0.0	0	0.0	0	1	3	4	0.7
JD Degrees Awarded	108	59.7	73	40.3	28	15.5	181	0	0.0	0	0.0	0	0.0	0				

GPA & LSAT Scores

	Full Time	Part Time	Total
# of apps	3,369	0	3,369
# admits	834	0	834
# of matrics	185	0	185
75% GPA	3.65	0.00	
25% GPA	3.34	0.00	
75% LSAT	166	0	
25% LSAT	163	0	

Tuition/Living Expenses

	Resident	Non-resident
Full-Time	$22,100	$22,100
Part-Time	$0	$0

Estimated living expenses for Singles		
Living on campus	Living off campus	Living at home
$11,850	N/A	N/A

Career Placement

	Total	%
Employment status known	182	96.8
Employment status unknown	6	3.2
Employed	170	93.4
Pursuing graduate degrees	7	3.9
Unemployed seeking employment	3	1.7
Unemployed not seeking employment	2	1.1
Type of Employment		
# employed in law firms	113	66.5
# employed in business & industry	13	7.7
# employed in government	12	7.1
# employed in public interest	3	1.8
# employed as judicial clerks	23	13.5
# employed in academia	1	0.6
Geographic Location		
# employed in state	56	32.9
# employed in foreign countries	0	0.0
# of states where employed	22	

Financial Aid

	Full-time		Part-time		Total	
	#	%	#	%	#	%
Total # receiving grants	247	44.7	0	0.0	247	44.7
Less than 1/2 tuition	198	35.8	0	0.0	198	35.8
Half to full tuition	45	8.1	0	0.0	45	8.1
Full tuition	3	0.5	0	0.0	3	0.5
More than full tuition	1	0.2	0	0.0	1	0.2
Median Grant Amount	$7,600		$0			

Refunds

Refunds of Admissions or Seat Deposit prior to commencement of classes? Yes

Refunds of Pre-paid tuition prior to commencement of classes? Yes

If yes, fully refundable before the start of classes? Yes

Joint Degrees Offered

JD/MBA, JD/LLM, JD/MILR, JD/MRP, JD/MA, JD/PhD

Advanced Degrees Offered

LLM	Law - Specialty determined by student
JSD	Law - Specialty determined by student
JD/LLM	LLM in International and Comparative Law
FRENCH	JD/Maitrise en droit (french law degree)

Bar Passage Rate

Jurisdiction	NY
# from school taking bar for the first time	101
School's pass rate for all first-time takers	96%
State's pass rate for all first-time takers	78%
State's pass rate for all first-time takers from ABA approved law schools	

CREIGHTON UNIVERSITY

2500 California Plaza
Omaha, NE 68178
(402)280-2872
http://www.creighton.edu/culaw

ABA Approved Since 1924

The Basics

Type of School: **PRIVATE**
Application deadline*: **5/1**
Application fee: **$40**
Financial Aid deadline*: **4/1**
Student faculty ratio: **16.3 to 1**
First year can start other than Fall: **No**
Student housing: **Yes**
--exclusively for law students: **No**
Term: **Semester**

*pr=preferred

Faculty

	Men		Women		Minorities		Total
	#	%	#	%	#	%	
Full-time	17	71	7	29	1	4	24
Other full-time	0	0	1	100	0	0	1
Deans, librarians, & others who teach	2	67	1	33	0	0	3
Part-time	15	60	10	40	0	0	25
Total	34	64	19	36	1	2	53
Deans, librarians, & others who teach < 1/2	1	100	0	0	0	0	1

Library

# of volumes & volume equivalents	232,583	# of professional staff	6
# of titles	34,501	Hours per week with professional staff	71
# of active serial subscriptions	4,230	Hours per week without professional staff	33
Study seating capacity inside the library	330	# of student computer work stations for entire law school	41
Square feet of law library	28,325	# of additional networked connections	0
Square feet of law school (excl. Library)	52,250		

Curriculum

	Full time	Part time
Typical first-year section size	75	0
Is there typically a "small section" of the first year class, other than Legal Writing, taught by full-time faculty?	Yes	No
If yes, typical size offered last year	26	N/A
# of classroom course titles beyond 1st year curriculum	66	0
# of upper division courses, excluding seminars, with an enrollment:		
Under 25	44	0
25 - 49	26	0
50 - 74	12	0
75 - 99	7	0
100 +	1	0
# of seminars	10	0
# of seminar positions available	158	
# of seminar positions filled	152	0
# of positions available in simulation courses	330	
# of simulation positions filled	322	0
# of positions available in faculty supervised clinical courses	32	
# of fac. sup. clin. positions filled	29	0
# involved in field placements	76	0
# involved in law journals	37	0
# in moot court or trial competitions	45	0
# of credit hours required to graduate	94	

Enrollment & Attrition

	Full-Time							Part-Time							Attrition			
	Men		Women		Minorities		Total	Men		Women		Minorities		Total	Academic	Other	Total	
	#	%	#	%	#	%	#	#	%	#	%	#	%	#	#	#	#	%
1st Year	94	58.0	68	42.0	20	12.3	162	8	72.7	3	27.3	0	0.0	11	12	9	21	13
2nd Year	77	56.6	59	43.4	13	9.6	136	2	50.0	2	50.0	0	0.0	4	1	2	3	1.8
3rd Year	93	59.2	64	40.8	9	5.7	157	3	42.9	4	57.1	0	0.0	7	0	0	0	0.0
4th Year								0	0.0	0	0.0	0	0.0	0	0	0	0	0.0
Total	264	58.0	191	42.0	42	9.2	455	13	59.1	9	40.9	0	0.0	22	13	11	24	4.8
JD Degrees Awarded	91	54.2	77	45.8	14	8.3	168	0	0.0	2	100.0	0	0.0	2				

GPA & LSAT Scores

	Full Time	Part Time	Total
# of apps	697	14	711
# admits	455	11	466
# of matrics	162	5	167
75% GPA	3.48	2.97	
25% GPA	2.95	2.64	
75% LSAT	154	150	
25% LSAT	147	147	

Tuition/Living Expenses

	Resident	Non-resident
Full-Time	$14,790	$14,790
Part-Time	$8,686	$8,686

Estimated living expenses for Singles		
Living on campus	Living off campus	Living at home
$10,722	$10,722	$10,722

Career Placement

	Total	%
Employment status known	163	96.5
Employment status unknown	6	3.6
Employed	138	84.7
Pursuing graduate degrees	2	1.2
Unemployed seeking employment	20	12.3
Unemployed not seeking employment	3	1.8
Type of Employment		
# employed in law firms	70	50.7
# employed in business & industry	32	23.2
# employed in government	23	16.7
# employed in public interest	2	1.5
# employed as judicial clerks	10	7.3
# employed in academia	1	0.7
Geographic Location		
# employed in state	73	52.9
# employed in foreign countries	0	0.0
# of states where employed	22	

Financial Aid

	Full-time		Part-time		Total	
	#	%	#	%	#	%
Total # receiving grants	166	36.5	0	0.0	166	34.8
Less than 1/2 tuition	99	21.8	0	0.0	99	20.8
Half to full tuition	48	10.6	0	0.0	48	10.1
Full tuition	16	3.5	0	0.0	16	3.4
More than full tuition	3	0.7	0	0.0	3	0.6
Median Grant Amount	$6,500		$0			

Refunds

Refunds of Admissions or Seat Deposit prior to commencement of classes? Yes

60% refund from 04/15/96 to 06/01/96

Refunds of Pre-paid tuition prior to commencement of classes? Yes

If yes, fully refundable before the start of classes? Yes

Joint Degrees Offered

No Joint Degrees

Advanced Degrees Offered

No Advanced Degrees

Bar Passage Rate

Jurisdiction	NE
# from school taking bar for the first time	98
School's pass rate for all first-time takers	93%
State's pass rate for all first-time takers	94%
State's pass rate for all first-time takers from ABA approved law schools	94%

DAYTON, UNIVERSITY OF

300 College Park Ave.
Dayton, OH 45469-1320
(513)229-3211
http://www.udayton.edu/~law

ABA Approved Since 1975

The Basics

Type of School: **PRIVATE**
Application deadline*: **5/1**
Application fee: **$40**
Financial Aid deadline*: **3/1**
Student faculty ratio: **20.5 to 1**
First year can start other than Fall: **No**
Student housing: **Yes**
--exclusively for law students: **Yes**
Term: **Semester**

*pr=preferred

Faculty

	Men #	Men %	Women #	Women %	Minorities #	Minorities %	Total
Full-time	15	75	5	25	1	5	20
Other full-time	0	0	3	100	1	33	3
Deans, librarians, & others who teach	2	100	0	0	0	0	2
Part-time	18	69	8	31	1	4	26
Total	35	69	16	31	3	6	51
Deans, librarians, & others who teach < 1/2	0	0	0	0	0	0	0

Library

# of volumes & volume equivalents	252,171	# of professional staff	4
# of titles	35,168	Hours per week with professional staff	49
# of active serial subscriptions	4,214	Hours per week without professional staff	53
Study seating capacity inside the library	319	# of student computer work stations for entire law school	42
Square feet of law library	21,053	# of additional networked connections	0
Square feet of law school (excl. Library)	25,904		

Curriculum

	Full time	Part time
Typical first-year section size	90	0
Is there typically a "small section" of the first year class, other than Legal Writing, taught by full-time faculty?	No	No
If yes, typical size offered last year	N/A	N/A
# of classroom course titles beyond 1st year curriculum	62	0
# of upper division courses, excluding seminars, with an enrollment:		
Under 25	52	0
25 - 49	18	0
50 - 74	12	0
75 - 99	6	0
100 +	1	0
# of seminars	15	0
# of seminar positions available	240	
# of seminar positions filled	156	0
# of positions available in simulation courses	308	
# of simulation positions filled	249	0
# of positions available in faculty supervised clinical courses	24	
# of fac. sup. clin. positions filled	24	0
# involved in field placements	56	0
# involved in law journals	47	0
# in moot court or trial competitions	29	0
# of credit hours required to graduate	87	

Enrollment & Attrition

	Full-Time							Part-Time							Attrition			
	Men		Women		Minorities		Total	Men		Women		Minorities		Total	Academic	Other	Total	
	#	%	#	%	#	%	#	#	%	#	%	#	%	#	#	#	#	%
1st Year	107	55.7	85	44.3	35	18.2	192	0	0.0	0	0.0	0	0.0	0	6	12	18	11
2nd Year	86	59.7	58	40.3	16	11.1	144	0	0.0	0	0.0	0	0.0	0	2	1	3	1.8
3rd Year	90	57.3	67	42.7	15	9.6	157	0	0.0	0	0.0	0	0.0	0	0	1	1	0.6
4th Year								0	0.0	0	0.0	0	0.0	0	0	0	0	0.0
Total	283	57.4	210	42.6	66	13.4	493	0	0.0	0	0.0	0	0.0	0	8	14	22	4.5
JD Degrees Awarded	95	59.4	65	40.6	11	6.9	160	0	0.0	0	0.0	0	0.0	0				

GPA & LSAT Scores

	Full Time	Part Time	Total
# of apps	1,559	0	1,559
# admits	790	0	790
# of matrics	191	0	191
75% GPA	3.51	0.00	
25% GPA	2.95	0.00	
75% LSAT	156	0	
25% LSAT	149	0	

Tuition/Living Expenses

	Resident	Non-resident
Full-Time	$17,030	$17,030
Part-Time	$0	$0

Estimated living expenses for Singles		
Living on campus	Living off campus	Living at home
$8,800	$8,800	$8,800

Career Placement

	Total	%
Employment status known	136	94.4
Employment status unknown	8	5.6
Employed	114	83.8
Pursuing graduate degrees	1	0.7
Unemployed seeking employment	17	12.5
Unemployed not seeking employment	4	2.9
Type of Employment		
# employed in law firms	59	51.8
# employed in business & industry	30	26.3
# employed in government	10	8.8
# employed in public interest	1	0.9
# employed as judicial clerks	7	6.1
# employed in academia	0	0.0
Geographic Location		
# employed in state	51	44.7
# employed in foreign countries	0	0.0
# of states where employed	23	

Financial Aid

	Full-time		Part-time		Total	
	#	%	#	%	#	%
Total # receiving grants	192	39.0	0	0.0	192	38.9
Less than 1/2 tuition	83	16.8	0	0.0	83	16.8
Half to full tuition	97	19.7	0	0.0	97	19.7
Full tuition	10	2.0	0	0.0	10	2.0
More than full tuition	2	0.4	0	0.0	2	0.4
Median Grant Amount	$10,000		$0			

Refunds

Refunds of Admissions or Seat Deposit prior to commencement of classes? No

Refunds of Pre-paid tuition prior to commencement of classes? Yes

If yes, fully refundable before the start of classes? Yes

Joint Degrees Offered

JD/MBA, JD/MS MEDA, JD/MPA, JD/MAIA

Advanced Degrees Offered

No Advanced Degrees

Bar Passage Rate

Jurisdiction	OH
# from school taking bar for the first time	54
School's pass rate for all first-time takers	94%
State's pass rate for all first-time takers	93%
State's pass rate for all first-time takers from ABA approved law schools	90%

DENVER, UNIVERSITY OF

7039 East 18th Street
Denver, CO 80220
(303)871-6000
gopher://gopher.cair.du.edu/1

ABA Approved Since 1928

The Basics

Type of School: **PRIVATE**
Application deadline*: **5/1**
Application fee: **$45**
Financial Aid deadline*: **2/15**
Student faculty ratio: **23.4 to 1**
First year can start other than Fall: **No**
Student housing: **Yes**
--exclusively for law students: **Yes**
Term: **Semester**

*pr=preferred

Faculty

	Men #	Men %	Women #	Women %	Minorities #	Minorities %	Total
Full-time	28	80	7	20	5	14	35
Other full-time	0	0	4	100	0	0	4
Deans, librarians, & others who teach	2	67	1	33	1	33	3
Part-time	41	59	29	41	3	4	70
Total	71	63	41	37	9	8	112
Deans, librarians, & others who teach < 1/2	1	100	0	0	0	0	1

Library

# of volumes & volume equivalents	303,543	# of professional staff	6
# of titles	108,987	Hours per week with professional staff	82
# of active serial subscriptions	4,367	Hours per week without professional staff	28
Study seating capacity inside the library	624	# of student computer work stations for entire law school	90
Square feet of law library	55,000	# of additional networked connections	0
Square feet of law school (excl. Library)	126,160		

Curriculum

	Full time	Part time
Typical first-year section size	83	84
Is there typically a "small section" of the first year class, other than Legal Writing, taught by full-time faculty?	No	No
If yes, typical size offered last year	N/A	N/A
# of classroom course titles beyond 1st year curriculum	64	35
# of upper division courses, excluding seminars, with an enrollment:		
Under 25	31	31
25 - 49	17	16
50 - 74	11	6
75 - 99	13	2
100 +	2	2
# of seminars	12	4
# of seminar positions available	337	
# of seminar positions filled	126	76
# of positions available in simulation courses	354	
# of simulation positions filled	220	78
# of positions available in faculty supervised clinical courses	130	
# of fac. sup. clin. positions filled	103	27
# involved in field placements	220	69
# involved in law journals	145	20
# in moot court or trial competitions	190	50
# of credit hours required to graduate	90	

Enrollment & Attrition

	Full-Time Men #	Men %	Women #	Women %	Minorities #	Minorities %	Total #	Part-Time Men #	Men %	Women #	Women %	Minorities #	Minorities %	Total #	Attrition Academic #	Other #	Total #	Total %
1st Year	136	50.6	133	49.4	19	7.1	269	32	45.7	38	54.3	9	12.9	70	3	11	14	4.1
2nd Year	149	55.4	120	44.6	45	16.7	269	45	59.2	31	40.8	7	9.2	76	3	11	14	4.3
3rd Year	137	52.1	126	47.9	35	13.3	263	35	57.4	26	42.6	8	13.1	61	1	11	12	4.1
4th Year								36	52.2	33	47.8	11	15.9	69	0	0	0	0.0
Total	422	52.7	379	47.3	99	12.4	801	148	53.6	128	46.4	35	12.7	276	7	33	40	3.8
JD Degrees Awarded	106	51.0	102	49.0	21	10.1	208	43	52.4	39	47.6	12	14.6	82				

GPA & LSAT Scores

	Full Time	Part Time	Total
# of apps	1,905	183	2,088
# admits	1,068	115	1,183
# of matrics	277	72	349
75% GPA	3.38	3.49	
25% GPA	2.82	2.77	
75% LSAT	159	159	
25% LSAT	153	152	

Tuition/Living Expenses

	Resident	Non-resident
Full-Time	$17,160	$17,160
Part-Time	$12,870	$12,870

Estimated living expenses for Singles		
Living on campus	Living off campus	Living at home
$9,312	$9,312	$9,312

Career Placement

	Total	%
Employment status known	265	88.6
Employment status unknown	34	11.4
Employed	227	85.7
Pursuing graduate degrees	6	2.3
Unemployed seeking employment	24	9.1
Unemployed not seeking employment	8	3.0
Type of Employment		
# employed in law firms	129	56.8
# employed in business & industry	12	5.3
# employed in government	52	22.9
# employed in public interest	5	2.2
# employed as judicial clerks	27	11.9
# employed in academia	2	0.9
Geographic Location		
# employed in state	193	85.0
# employed in foreign countries	0	0.0
# of states where employed	22	

Financial Aid

	Full-time		Part-time		Total	
	#	%	#	%	#	%
Total # receiving grants	229	28.6	71	25.7	300	27.9
Less than 1/2 tuition	163	20.4	40	14.5	203	18.8
Half to full tuition	34	4.2	21	7.6	55	5.1
Full tuition	32	4.0	10	3.6	42	3.9
More than full tuition	0	0.0	0	0.0	0	0.0
Median Grant Amount	$6,000		$6,000			

Refunds

Refunds of Admissions or Seat Deposit prior to commencement of classes? Yes

100% refund to 08/01/96

Refunds of Pre-paid tuition prior to commencement of classes? Yes

If yes, fully refundable before the start of classes? Yes

Joint Degrees Offered

MBA/JD, IS/JD, SWK/JD, PHIL/JD, ECON/JD, MIM/JD

Advanced Degrees Offered

LLM Taxation

Bar Passage Rate

Jurisdiction	CO
# from school taking bar for the first time	191
School's pass rate for all first-time takers	87%
State's pass rate for all first-time takers	
State's pass rate for all first-time takers from ABA approved law schools	

DEPAUL UNIVERSITY

25 East Jackson Boulevard
Chicago, IL 60604-2287
(312)362-8701
http://www.law.depaul.edu

ABA Approved Since 1925

The Basics

Type of School: **PRIVATE**
Application deadline*: **4/1**
Application fee: **$40**
Financial Aid deadline*: **3/1**
Student faculty ratio: **21.8 to 1**

First year can start other than Fall: **No**
Student housing: **No**
--exclusively for law students: **No**
Term: **Semester**

*pr=preferred

Faculty

	Men		Women		Minorities		Total
	#	%	#	%	#	%	
Full-time	24	65	13	35	5	14	37
Other full-time	1	50	1	50	0	0	2
Deans, librarians, & others who teach	3	50	3	50	0	0	6
Part-time	38	67	19	33	4	7	57
Total	66	65	36	35	9	9	102
Deans, librarians, & others who teach < 1/2	1	50	1	50	0	0	2

Library

# of volumes & volume equivalents	326,663	# of professional staff	8
# of titles	55,317	Hours per week with professional staff	76
# of active serial subscriptions	4,938	Hours per week without professional staff	19
Study seating capacity inside the library	439	# of student computer work stations for entire law school	52
Square feet of law library	36,690	# of additional networked connections	0
Square feet of law school (excl. Library)	40,063		

Curriculum

	Full time	Part time
Typical first-year section size	85	83
Is there typically a "small section" of the first year class, other than Legal Writing, taught by full-time faculty?	Yes	Yes
If yes, typical size offered last year	20	20
# of classroom course titles beyond 1st year curriculum	79	62
# of upper division courses, excluding seminars, with an enrollment:		
Under 25	7	10
25 - 49	4	18
50 - 74	10	1
75 - 99	7	0
100 +	0	0
# of seminars	7	3
# of seminar positions available	180	
# of seminar positions filled	116	44
# of positions available in simulation courses	446	
# of simulation positions filled	89	261
# of positions available in faculty supervised clinical courses	30	
# of fac. sup. clin. positions filled	24	8
# involved in field placements	32	8
# involved in law journals	37	7
# in moot court or trial competitions	6	1
# of credit hours required to graduate	86	

Enrollment & Attrition

	Full-Time							Part-Time							Attrition			
	Men		Women		Minorities		Total	Men		Women		Minorities		Total	Academic	Other	Total	
	#	%	#	%	#	%	#	#	%	#	%	#	%	#	#	#	#	%
1st Year	139	53.9	119	46.1	30	11.6	258	49	50.5	48	49.5	20	20.6	97	0	8	8	2.0
2nd Year	137	51.9	127	48.1	30	11.4	264	51	56.7	39	43.3	10	11.1	90	7	19	26	8.3
3rd Year	130	57.0	98	43.0	25	11.0	228	34	52.3	31	47.7	13	20.0	65	2	1	3	0.9
4th Year								43	54.4	36	45.6	10	12.7	79	0	0	0	0.0
Total	406	54.1	344	45.9	85	11.3	750	177	53.5	154	46.5	53	16.0	331	9	28	37	3.3
JD Degrees Awarded	144	52.6	130	47.4	44	16.1	274	41	57.7	30	42.3	12	16.9	71				

GPA & LSAT Scores

	Full Time	Part Time	Total
# of apps	2,031	418	2,449
# admits	1,180	216	1,396
# of matrics	251	87	338
75% GPA	3.48	3.43	
25% GPA	3.03	2.75	
75% LSAT	158	157	
25% LSAT	153	152	

Tuition/Living Expenses

	Resident	Non-resident
Full-Time	$17,620	$17,620
Part-Time	$11,420	$11,420

Estimated living expenses for Singles		
Living on campus	Living off campus	Living at home
$12,224	$12,224	$12,224

Financial Aid

	Full-time		Part-time		Total	
	#	%	#	%	#	%
Total # receiving grants	507	67.6	26	7.9	533	49.3
Less than 1/2 tuition	502	66.9	26	7.9	528	48.8
Half to full tuition	5	0.7	0	0.0	5	0.5
Full tuition	0	0.0	0	0.0	0	0.0
More than full tuition	0	0.0	0	0.0	0	0.0
Median Grant Amount	$1,736		$1,736			

Refunds

Refunds of Admissions or Seat Deposit prior to commencement of classes? No

Refunds of Pre-paid tuition prior to commencement of classes? Yes

If yes, fully refundable before the start of classes? Yes

Joint Degrees Offered

J.D./M.B.A.

Advanced Degrees Offered

LL.M.	Taxation
LL.M.	Health Law

Career Placement

	Total	%
Employment status known	214	74.1
Employment status unknown	75	26.0
Employed	185	86.5
Pursuing graduate degrees	1	0.5
Unemployed seeking employment	27	12.6
Unemployed not seeking employment	1	0.5
Type of Employment		
# employed in law firms	84	45.4
# employed in business & industry	29	15.7
# employed in government	28	15.1
# employed in public interest	4	2.2
# employed as judicial clerks	7	3.8
# employed in academia	3	1.6
Geographic Location		
# employed in state	173	93.5
# employed in foreign countries	0	0.0
# of states where employed	30	

Bar Passage Rate

Jurisdiction	IL	CA
# from school taking bar for the first time	216	4
School's pass rate for all first-time takers	92%	100%
State's pass rate for all first-time takers	87%	73%
State's pass rate for all first-time takers from ABA approved law schools	87%	82%

DETROIT COLLEGE AT MICHIGAN STATE UNIV.

N-210 N. Business Complex
East Lansing, MI 48824
(313)226-0100
http://www.dcl.edu

ABA Approved Since 1941

The Basics

Type of School: **PRIVATE**
Application deadline*: **4/15**
Application fee: **$50**
Financial Aid deadline*: **3/15**
Student faculty ratio: **19.5 to 1**

First year can start other than Fall: **No**
Student housing: **No**
--exclusively for law students: **No**
Term: **Semester**

*pr=preferred

Faculty

	Men #	Men %	Women #	Women %	Minorities #	Minorities %	Total
Full-time	16	64	9	36	2	8	25
Other full-time	1	25	3	75	0	0	4
Deans, librarians, & others who teach	2	67	1	33	1	33	3
Part-time	27	87	4	13	6	19	31
Total	46	73	17	27	9	14	63
Deans, librarians, & others who teach < 1/2	0	0	0	0	0	0	0

Library

# of volumes & volume equivalents	224,134	# of professional staff	7
# of titles	100,691	Hours per week with professional staff	64
# of active serial subscriptions	3,480	Hours per week without professional staff	40
Study seating capacity inside the library	289	# of student computer work stations for entire law school	23
Square feet of law library	15,565	# of additional networked connections	0
Square feet of law school (excl. Library)	54,975		

Curriculum

	Full time	Part time
Typical first-year section size	78	39
Is there typically a "small section" of the first year class, other than Legal Writing, taught by full-time faculty?	No	No
If yes, typical size offered last year	N/A	N/A
# of classroom course titles beyond 1st year curriculum	73	83
# of upper division courses, excluding seminars, with an enrollment:		
Under 25	39	44
25 - 49	15	27
50 - 74	5	5
75 - 99	7	0
100 +	0	0
# of seminars	0	0
# of seminar positions available	405	
# of seminar positions filled	211	70
# of positions available in simulation courses	93	
# of simulation positions filled	61	32
# of positions available in faculty supervised clinical courses	185	
# of fac. sup. clin. positions filled	89	58
# involved in field placements	89	58
# involved in law journals	28	8
# in moot court or trial competitions	31	17
# of credit hours required to graduate	85	

Enrollment & Attrition

	Full-Time							Part-Time							Attrition			
	Men		Women		Minorities		Total	Men		Women		Minorities		Total	Academic	Other	Total	
	#	%	#	%	#	%	#	#	%	#	%	#	%	#	#	#	#	%
1st Year	92	63.9	52	36.1	21	14.6	144	18	51.4	17	48.6	3	8.6	35	1	22	23	7.9
2nd Year	99	55.9	78	44.1	15	8.5	177	53	64.6	29	35.4	15	18.3	82	4	9	13	7.1
3rd Year	75	67.0	37	33.0	14	12.5	112	39	66.1	20	33.9	10	16.9	59	0	2	2	1.1
4th Year								37	67.3	18	32.7	12	21.8	55	0	1	1	1.6
Total	266	61.4	167	38.6	50	11.5	433	147	63.6	84	36.4	40	17.3	231	5	34	39	5.5
JD Degrees Awarded	98	69.0	44	31.0	9	6.3	142	38	65.5	20	34.5	10	17.2	58				

DETROIT COLLEGE AT MICHIGAN STATE UNIV.

GPA & LSAT Scores

	Full Time	Part Time	Total
# of apps	740	141	881
# admits	484	80	564
# of matrics	148	37	185
75% GPA	3.10	3.16	
25% GPA	2.74	2.51	
75% LSAT	154	151	
25% LSAT	149	147	

Tuition/Living Expenses

	Resident	Non-resident
Full-Time	$14,140	$14,140
Part-Time	$10,100	$10,100

Estimated living expenses for Singles		
Living on campus	Living off campus	Living at home
$9,700	$15,980	$10,260

Financial Aid

	Full-time		Part-time		Total	
	#	%	#	%	#	%
Total # receiving grants	50	11.6	20	8.7	70	10.5
Less than 1/2 tuition	0	0.0	0	0.0	0	0.0
Half to full tuition	31	7.2	7	3.0	38	5.7
Full tuition	19	4.4	13	5.6	32	4.8
More than full tuition	0	0.0	0	0.0	0	0.0
Median Grant Amount	$10,160		$8,850			

Refunds

Refunds of Admissions or Seat Deposit prior to commencement of classes? No

Refunds of Pre-paid tuition prior to commencement of classes? Yes

If yes, fully refundable before the start of classes? Yes

Joint Degrees Offered

JD/MBA

Advanced Degrees Offered

No Advanced Degrees

Career Placement

	Total	%
Employment status known	119	51.1
Employment status unknown	114	48.9
Employed	110	92.4
Pursuing graduate degrees	1	0.8
Unemployed seeking employment	8	6.7
Unemployed not seeking employment	0	0.0
Type of Employment		
# employed in law firms	52	47.3
# employed in business & industry	21	19.1
# employed in government	19	17.3
# employed in public interest	3	2.7
# employed as judicial clerks	14	12.7
# employed in academia	1	0.9
Geographic Location		
# employed in state	102	92.7
# employed in foreign countries	1	0.9
# of states where employed	7	

Bar Passage Rate

Jurisdiction	MI
# from school taking bar for the first time	194
School's pass rate for all first-time takers	76%
State's pass rate for all first-time takers	70%
State's pass rate for all first-time takers from ABA approved law schools	70%

DETROIT MERCY, UNIVERSITY OF

651 E. Jefferson
Detroit, MI 48226
(313)596-0200
website is currently under construction

ABA Approved Since 1933

The Basics

Type of School: **PRIVATE**
Application deadline*: **4/15**
Application fee: **$50**
Financial Aid deadline*: **3/1**
Student faculty ratio: **22.3 to 1**

First year can start other than Fall: **No**
Student housing: **No**
--exclusively for law students: **No**
Term: **Semester**

*pr=preferred

Faculty

	Men		Women		Minorities		Total
	#	%	#	%	#	%	
Full-time	15	79	4	21	1	5	19
Other full-time	0	0	3	100	1	33	3
Deans, librarians, & others who teach	4	80	1	20	0	0	5
Part-time	24	86	4	14	1	4	28
Total	43	78	12	22	3	5	55
Deans, librarians, & others who teach < 1/2	1	100	0	0	0	0	1

Library

# of volumes & volume equivalents	286,533	# of professional staff	8
# of titles	117,403	Hours per week with professional staff	92
# of active serial subscriptions	3,295	Hours per week without professional staff	0
Study seating capacity inside the library	406	# of student computer work stations for entire law school	39
Square feet of law library	23,839	# of additional networked connections	3
Square feet of law school (excl. Library)	47,241		

Curriculum

	Full time	Part time
Typical first-year section size	70	57
Is there typically a "small section" of the first year class, other than Legal Writing, taught by full-time faculty?	No	No
If yes, typical size offered last year	N/A	N/A
# of classroom course titles beyond 1st year curriculum	59	56
# of upper division courses, excluding seminars, with an enrollment:		
Under 25	32	24
25 - 49	12	20
50 - 74	8	5
75 - 99	5	4
100 +	2	0
# of seminars	14	12
# of seminar positions available	400	
# of seminar positions filled	118	150
# of positions available in simulation courses	248	
# of simulation positions filled	197	37
# of positions available in faculty supervised clinical courses	36	
# of fac. sup. clin. positions filled	31	3
# involved in field placements	70	13
# involved in law journals	53	4
# in moot court or trial competitions	41	3
# of credit hours required to graduate	90	

Enrollment & Attrition

	Full-Time							Part-Time							Attrition			
	Men		Women		Minorities		Total	Men		Women		Minorities		Total	Academic	Other	Total	
	#	%	#	%	#	%	#	#	%	#	%	#	%	#	#	#	#	%
1st Year	47	46.5	54	53.5	12	11.9	101	28	50.0	28	50.0	4	7.1	56	32	10	42	20
2nd Year	62	57.4	46	42.6	8	7.4	108	34	52.3	31	47.7	9	13.8	65	4	0	4	1.8
3rd Year	87	52.4	79	47.6	28	16.9	166	24	48.0	26	52.0	19	38.0	50	0	0	0	0.0
4th Year								36	53.7	31	46.3	8	11.9	67	0	1	1	1.4
Total	196	52.3	179	47.7	48	12.8	375	122	51.3	116	48.7	40	16.8	238	36	11	47	6.4
JD Degrees Awarded	95	58.3	68	41.7	6	3.7	163	46	56.1	36	43.9	16	19.5	82				

GPA & LSAT Scores

	Full Time	Part Time	Total
# of apps	481	310	791
# admits	302	104	406
# of matrics	108	50	158
75% GPA	3.35	3.15	
25% GPA	2.79	2.66	
75% LSAT	155	154	
25% LSAT	146	147	

Tuition/Living Expenses

	Resident	Non-resident
Full-Time	$13,740	$13,740
Part-Time	$9,818	$9,818

Estimated living expenses for Singles		
Living on campus	Living off campus	Living at home
N/A	$11,712	$6,784

Financial Aid

	Full-time		Part-time		Total	
	#	%	#	%	#	%
Total # receiving grants	356	94.9	142	59.7	498	81.2
Less than 1/2 tuition	306	81.6	117	49.2	423	69.0
Half to full tuition	48	12.8	21	8.8	69	11.3
Full tuition	2	0.5	2	0.8	4	0.7
More than full tuition	0	0.0	2	0.8	2	0.3
Median Grant Amount	$2,172		$2,172			

Refunds

Refunds of Admissions or Seat Deposit prior to commencement of classes? No

Refunds of Pre-paid tuition prior to commencement of classes? Yes

If yes, fully refundable before the start of classes? Yes

Joint Degrees Offered

JD/MBA

Advanced Degrees Offered

No Advanced Degrees

Career Placement

	Total	%
Employment status known	57	23.4
Employment status unknown	187	76.6
Employed	49	86.0
Pursuing graduate degrees	0	0.0
Unemployed seeking employment	8	14.0
Unemployed not seeking employment	0	0.0
Type of Employment		
# employed in law firms	24	49.0
# employed in business & industry	14	28.6
# employed in government	10	20.4
# employed in public interest	0	0.0
# employed as judicial clerks	0	0.0
# employed in academia	1	2.0
Geographic Location		
# employed in state	39	79.6
# employed in foreign countries	1	2.0
# of states where employed	5	

Bar Passage Rate

Jurisdiction	MI
# from school taking bar for the first time	142
School's pass rate for all first-time takers	57%
State's pass rate for all first-time takers	70%
State's pass rate for all first-time takers from ABA approved law schools	70%

DICKINSON SCHOOL OF LAW

of Penn. State Univ. (as of 7/1/97)
150 S. College Street
Carlisle, PA 17013-2899
(717)240-5000
http://www.dsl.edu

ABA Approved Since 1931

The Basics

Type of School: **PRIVATE**
Application deadline*: **3/1**
Application fee: **$50**
Financial Aid deadline*: **2/15**
Student faculty ratio: **23.9 to 1**

First year can start other than Fall: **No**
Student housing: **Yes**
--exclusively for law students: **No**
Term: **Semester**

*pr=preferred

Faculty

	Men		Women		Minorities		Total
	#	%	#	%	#	%	
Full-time	12	67	6	33	4	22	18
Other full-time	3	60	2	40	0	0	5
Deans, librarians, & others who teach	6	86	1	14	0	0	7
Part-time	18	90	2	10	1	5	20
Total	39	78	11	22	5	10	50
Deans, librarians, & others who teach < 1/2	0	0	0	0	0	0	0

Library

# of volumes & volume equivalents	380,278	# of professional staff	10
# of titles	79,431	Hours per week with professional staff	81
# of active serial subscriptions	4,185	Hours per week without professional staff	5
Study seating capacity inside the library	444	# of student computer work stations for entire law school	59
Square feet of law library	33,134	# of additional networked connections	82
Square feet of law school (excl. Library)	41,550		

Curriculum

	Full time	Part time
Typical first-year section size	60	0
Is there typically a "small section" of the first year class, other than Legal Writing, taught by full-time faculty?	Yes	No
If yes, typical size offered last year	23	N/A
# of classroom course titles beyond 1st year curriculum	93	0
# of upper division courses, excluding seminars, with an enrollment:		
Under 25	31	0
25 - 49	20	0
50 - 74	15	0
75 - 99	7	0
100 +	0	0
# of seminars	20	0
# of seminar positions available	426	
# of seminar positions filled	339	0
# of positions available in simulation courses	363	
# of simulation positions filled	337	0
# of positions available in faculty supervised clinical courses	25	
# of fac. sup. clin. positions filled	25	0
# involved in field placements	94	0
# involved in law journals	110	0
# in moot court or trial competitions	32	0
# of credit hours required to graduate	88	

Enrollment & Attrition

	Full-Time							Part-Time							Attrition			
	Men		Women		Minorities		Total	Men		Women		Minorities		Total	Academic	Other	Total	
	#	%	#	%	#	%	#	#	%	#	%	#	%	#	#	#	#	%
1st Year	99	56.6	76	43.4	19	10.9	175	0	0.0	0	0.0	0	0.0	0	3	10	13	7.4
2nd Year	100	60.2	66	39.8	13	7.8	166	0	0.0	0	0.0	0	0.0	0	0	3	3	1.6
3rd Year	89	50.9	86	49.1	15	8.6	175	0	0.0	2	100.0	0	0.0	2	1	0	1	0.6
4th Year								0	0.0	0	0.0	0	0.0	0	0	0	0	0.0
Total	288	55.8	228	44.2	47	9.1	516	0	0.0	2	100.0	0	0.0	2	4	13	17	3.3
JD Degrees Awarded	81	50.0	81	50.0	5	3.1	162	0	0.0	0	0.0	0	0.0	0				

GPA & LSAT Scores

	Full Time	Part Time	Total
# of apps	1,287	0	1,287
# admits	663	0	663
# of matrics	175	0	175
75% GPA	3.63	0.00	
25% GPA	3.07	0.00	
75% LSAT	157	0	
25% LSAT	148	0	

Tuition/Living Expenses

	Resident	Non-resident
Full-Time	$14,600	$14,600
Part-Time	$0	$0

Estimated living expenses for Singles		
Living on campus	Living off campus	Living at home
$9,724	$12,224	$10,224

Career Placement

	Total	%
Employment status known	155	93.4
Employment status unknown	11	6.6
Employed	141	91.0
Pursuing graduate degrees	2	1.3
Unemployed seeking employment	12	7.7
Unemployed not seeking employment	0	0.0
Type of Employment		
# employed in law firms	66	46.8
# employed in business & industry	15	10.6
# employed in government	20	14.2
# employed in public interest	2	1.4
# employed as judicial clerks	37	26.2
# employed in academia	1	0.7
Geographic Location		
# employed in state	106	75.2
# employed in foreign countries	0	0.0
# of states where employed	14	

Financial Aid

	Full-time		Part-time		Total	
	#	%	#	%	#	%
Total # receiving grants	144	27.9	0	0.0	144	27.8
Less than 1/2 tuition	134	26.0	0	0.0	134	25.9
Half to full tuition	2	0.4	0	0.0	2	0.4
Full tuition	6	1.2	0	0.0	6	1.2
More than full tuition	2	0.4	0	0.0	2	0.4
Median Grant Amount	$2,893		$0			

Refunds

Refunds of Admissions or Seat Deposit prior to commencement of classes? Yes

33% refund from 01/01/96 to 05/31/96
17% refund from 06/01/96 to 06/30/96
0% refund from 07/01/96 to / /

Refunds of Pre-paid tuition prior to commencement of classes? Yes

If yes, fully refundable before the start of classes? Yes

90% refund from 08/26/96 to 09/09/96
60% refund from 09/09/96 to 09/23/96
40% refund from 09/23/96 to 10/07/96

Joint Degrees Offered

JD/MPA

Advanced Degrees Offered

LL.M. Comparative Law (formerly Master of Comparative Law, since 1969).

Bar Passage Rate

Jurisdiction	PA
# from school taking bar for the first time	128
School's pass rate for all first-time takers	88%
State's pass rate for all first-time takers	73%
State's pass rate for all first-time takers from ABA approved law schools	73%

DISTRICT OF COLUMBIA (Provisional)

4250 Connecticut Ave., NW
Washington, DC 20008
(202)274-7400

ABA Approved Since 1991

The Basics

Type of School: **PUBLIC**	First year can start other than Fall: **No**
Application deadline*: **4/1**	Student housing: **No**
Application fee: **$35**	--exclusively for law students: **No**
Financial Aid deadline*: **5/30**	Term: **Semester**
Student faculty ratio: **15.7 to 1**	

*pr=preferred

Faculty

	Men		Women		Minorities		Total
	#	%	#	%	#	%	
Full-time	7	58	5	42	4	33	12
Other full-time	1	33	2	67	1	33	3
Deans, librarians, & others who teach	1	50	1	50	1	50	2
Part-time	6	100	0	0	3	50	6
Total	15	65	8	35	9	39	23
Deans, librarians, & others who teach < 1/2	0	0	1	100	0	0	1

Library

# of volumes & volume equivalents	169,159	# of professional staff	3
# of titles	14,039	Hours per week with professional staff	53
# of active serial subscriptions	2,450	Hours per week without professional staff	40
Study seating capacity inside the library	143	# of student computer work stations for entire law school	8
Square feet of law library	16,000	# of additional networked connections	3
Square feet of law school (excl. Library)	24,550		

Curriculum

	Full time	Part time
Typical first-year section size	52	0
Is there typically a "small section" of the first year class, other than Legal Writing, taught by full-time faculty?	Yes	No
If yes, typical size offered last year	37	N/A
# of classroom course titles beyond 1st year curriculum	10	0
# of upper division courses, excluding seminars, with an enrollment:		
Under 25	10	0
25 - 49	10	0
50 - 74	5	0
75 - 99	1	0
100 +	0	0
# of seminars	1	0
# of seminar positions available	20	
# of seminar positions filled	6	0
# of positions available in simulation courses	44	
# of simulation positions filled	41	0
# of positions available in faculty supervised clinical courses	124	
# of fac. sup. clin. positions filled	116	0
# involved in field placements	6	0
# involved in law journals	9	0
# in moot court or trial competitions	0	0
# of credit hours required to graduate	85	

Enrollment & Attrition

	Full-Time							Part-Time							Attrition			
	Men		Women		Minorities		Total	Men		Women		Minorities		Total	Academic	Other	Total	
	#	%	#	%	#	%	#	#	%	#	%	#	%	#	#	#	#	%
1st Year	36	49.3	37	50.7	43	58.9	73	0	0.0	0	0.0	0	0.0	0	17	29	46	36
2nd Year	42	48.3	45	51.7	62	71.3	87	0	0.0	0	0.0	0	0.0	0	6	3	9	12
3rd Year	33	50.0	33	50.0	37	56.1	66	0	0.0	0	0.0	0	0.0	0	1	0	1	1.3
4th Year								0	0.0	0	0.0	0	0.0	0	0	0	0	0.0
Total	111	49.1	115	50.9	142	62.8	226	0	0.0	0	0.0	0	0.0	0	24	32	56	20
JD Degrees Awarded	31	45.6	37	54.4	26	38.2	68	0	0.0	0	0.0	0	0.0	0				

GPA & LSAT Scores

	Full Time	Part Time	Total
# of apps	503	0	503
# admits	143	0	143
# of matrics	76	0	76
75% GPA	2.88	0.00	
25% GPA	2.36	0.00	
75% LSAT	147	0	
25% LSAT	141	0	

Tuition/Living Expenses

	Resident	Non-resident
Full-Time	$7,135	$14,135
Part-Time	$0	$0

Estimated living expenses for Singles		
Living on campus	Living off campus	Living at home
N/A	$18,900	$9,800

Career Placement

	Total	%
Employment status known	22	28.6
Employment status unknown	55	71.4
Employed	19	86.4
Pursuing graduate degrees	1	4.6
Unemployed seeking employment	2	9.1
Unemployed not seeking employment	0	0.0
Type of Employment		
# employed in law firms	0	0.0
# employed in business & industry	0	0.0
# employed in government	0	0.0
# employed in public interest	0	0.0
# employed as judicial clerks	0	0.0
# employed in academia	0	0.0
Geographic Location		
# employed in state	0	0.0
# employed in foreign countries	0	0.0
# of states where employed	0	

Financial Aid

	Full-time		Part-time		Total	
	#	%	#	%	#	%
Total # receiving grants	143	63.3	0	0.0	143	63.3
Less than 1/2 tuition	72	31.9	0	0.0	72	31.9
Half to full tuition	70	31.0	0	0.0	70	31.0
Full tuition	0	0.0	0	0.0	0	0.0
More than full tuition	1	0.4	0	0.0	1	0.4
Median Grant Amount	$5,000		$0			

Refunds

Refunds of Admissions or Seat Deposit prior to commencement of classes? No

Refunds of Pre-paid tuition prior to commencement of classes? Yes

If yes, fully refundable before the start of classes? Yes

Joint Degrees Offered

No Joint Degrees

Advanced Degrees Offered

No Advanced Degrees

Bar Passage Rate

Jurisdiction	MD
# from school taking bar for the first time	25
School's pass rate for all first-time takers	16%
State's pass rate for all first-time takers	75%
State's pass rate for all first-time takers from ABA approved law schools	75%

DRAKE UNIVERSITY

2507 University Avenue
Des Moines, IA 50311
(515)271-2824
http://www.drake.edu

ABA Approved Since 1923

The Basics

Type of School: **PRIVATE**
Application deadline*: **3/1**
Application fee: **$35**
Financial Aid deadline*: **3/1**
Student faculty ratio: **20.9 to 1**

First year can start other than Fall: **No**
Student housing: **Yes**
--exclusively for law students: **No**
Term: **Semester**

*pr=preferred

Faculty

	Men #	Men %	Women #	Women %	Minorities #	Minorities %	Total
Full-time	13	72	5	28	1	6	18
Other full-time	2	67	1	33	0	0	3
Deans, librarians, & others who teach	4	100	0	0	0	0	4
Part-time	12	75	4	25	1	6	16
Total	31	76	10	24	2	5	41
Deans, librarians, & others who teach < 1/2	0	0	0	0	0	0	0

Library

# of volumes & volume equivalents	257,471	# of professional staff	5
# of titles	31,725	Hours per week with professional staff	60
# of active serial subscriptions	3,040	Hours per week without professional staff	49
Study seating capacity inside the library	705	# of student computer work stations for entire law school	104
Square feet of law library	50,541	# of additional networked connections	5
Square feet of law school (excl. Library)	62,341		

Curriculum

	Full time	Part time
Typical first-year section size	73	0
Is there typically a "small section" of the first year class, other than Legal Writing, taught by full-time faculty?	No	No
If yes, typical size offered last year	N/A	N/A
# of classroom course titles beyond 1st year curriculum	106	0
# of upper division courses, excluding seminars, with an enrollment:		
Under 25	43	0
25 - 49	25	0
50 - 74	12	0
75 - 99	10	0
100 +	0	0
# of seminars	15	0
# of seminar positions available	295	
# of seminar positions filled	235	6
# of positions available in simulation courses	1,240	
# of simulation positions filled	766	25
# of positions available in faculty supervised clinical courses	104	
# of fac. sup. clin. positions filled	91	2
# involved in field placements	157	2
# involved in law journals	84	0
# in moot court or trial competitions	68	1
# of credit hours required to graduate	90	

Enrollment & Attrition

	Full-Time Men #	Men %	Women #	Women %	Minorities #	Minorities %	Total #	Part-Time Men #	Men %	Women #	Women %	Minorities #	Minorities %	Total #	Attrition Academic #	Other #	Total #	%
1st Year	81	52.9	72	47.1	19	12.4	153	3	75.0	1	25.0	2	50.0	4	1	15	16	11
2nd Year	89	63.6	51	36.4	9	6.4	140	1	100.0	0	0.0	0	0.0	1	1	1	2	1.2
3rd Year	90	59.6	61	40.4	17	11.3	151	2	40.0	3	60.0	0	0.0	5	0	1	1	0.5
4th Year								0	0.0	0	0.0	0	0.0	0	0	0	0	0.0
Total	260	58.6	184	41.4	45	10.1	444	6	60.0	4	40.0	2	20.0	10	2	17	19	3.7
JD Degrees Awarded	122	61.6	76	38.4	11	5.6	198	1	33.3	2	66.7	0	0.0	3				

GPA & LSAT Scores

	Full Time	Part Time	Total
# of apps	917	27	944
# admits	481	5	486
# of matrics	154	3	157
75% GPA	3.41	3.56	
25% GPA	2.82	2.39	
75% LSAT	157	159	
25% LSAT	150	149	

Tuition/Living Expenses

	Resident	Non-resident
Full-Time	$15,550	$15,550
Part-Time	$525	$525

Estimated living expenses for Singles		
Living on campus	Living off campus	Living at home
N/A	$10,579	$5,654

Career Placement

	Total	%
Employment status known	164	100.0
Employment status unknown	0	0.0
Employed	148	90.2
Pursuing graduate degrees	2	1.2
Unemployed seeking employment	13	7.9
Unemployed not seeking employment	1	0.6
Type of Employment		
# employed in law firms	78	52.7
# employed in business & industry	25	16.9
# employed in government	28	18.9
# employed in public interest	1	0.7
# employed as judicial clerks	15	10.1
# employed in academia	1	0.7
Geographic Location		
# employed in state	87	58.8
# employed in foreign countries	0	0.0
# of states where employed	22	

Financial Aid

	Full-time		Part-time		Total	
	#	%	#	%	#	%
Total # receiving grants	297	66.9	0	0.0	297	65.4
Less than 1/2 tuition	208	46.9	0	0.0	208	45.8
Half to full tuition	63	14.2	0	0.0	63	13.9
Full tuition	24	5.4	0	0.0	24	5.3
More than full tuition	2	0.5	0	0.0	2	0.4
Median Grant Amount	$3,000		$0			

Refunds

Refunds of Admissions or Seat Deposit prior to commencement of classes? No

Refunds of Pre-paid tuition prior to commencement of classes? Yes

If yes, fully refundable before the start of classes? Yes

Joint Degrees Offered

JD/MBA, JD/MPA, JD/MAPol Sci, JD/MA AgEcon, JD/MAJournal, JD/MSW, JD/PharmD

Advanced Degrees Offered

No Advanced Degrees

Bar Passage Rate

Jurisdiction	IA	IL
# from school taking bar for the first time	99	8
School's pass rate for all first-time takers	87%	100%
State's pass rate for all first-time takers	87%	87%
State's pass rate for all first-time takers from ABA approved law schools	87%	87%

DUKE UNIVERSITY

P.O. Box 90362
Science Drive and Toweview Road
Durham, NC 27708-0362
(919)613-7001
http://www.law.duke.edu

ABA Approved Since 1931

The Basics

Type of School: **PRIVATE**
Application deadline*: **1/15**
Application fee: **$65**
Financial Aid deadline*: **1/15**
Student faculty ratio: **15.4 to 1**

First year can start other than Fall: **Yes**
Student housing: **No**
--exclusively for law students: **No**
Term: **Semester**

*pr=preferred

Faculty

	Men #	Men %	Women #	Women %	Minorities #	Minorities %	Total
Full-time	21	66	11	34	4	13	32
Other full-time	0	0	1	100	0	0	1
Deans, librarians, & others who teach	1	50	1	50	0	0	2
Part-time	15	79	4	21	1	5	19
Total	37	69	17	31	5	9	54
Deans, librarians, & others who teach < 1/2	3	43	4	57	0	0	7

Library

# of volumes & volume equivalents	494,413	# of professional staff	7
# of titles	181,959	Hours per week with professional staff	68
# of active serial subscriptions	7,351	Hours per week without professional staff	43
Study seating capacity inside the library	451	# of student computer work stations for entire law school	138
Square feet of law library	65,265	# of additional networked connections	169
Square feet of law school (excl. Library)	50,523		

Curriculum

	Full time	Part time
Typical first-year section size	80	0
Is there typically a "small section" of the first year class, other than Legal Writing, taught by full-time faculty?	Yes	No
If yes, typical size offered last year	25	N/A
# of classroom course titles beyond 1st year curriculum	101	0
# of upper division courses, excluding seminars, with an enrollment:		
Under 25	16	0
25 - 49	21	0
50 - 74	9	0
75 - 99	6	0
100 +	7	0
# of seminars	51	0
# of seminar positions available	796	
# of seminar positions filled	796	0
# of positions available in simulation courses	306	
# of simulation positions filled	280	0
# of positions available in faculty supervised clinical courses	42	
# of fac. sup. clin. positions filled	50	0
# involved in field placements	26	0
# involved in law journals	175	0
# in moot court or trial competitions	40	0
# of credit hours required to graduate	86	

Enrollment & Attrition

	Full-Time							Part-Time							Attrition			
	Men		Women		Minorities		Total	Men		Women		Minorities		Total	Academic	Other	Total	
	#	%	#	%	#	%	#	#	%	#	%	#	%	#	#	#	#	%
1st Year	120	59.4	82	40.6	40	19.8	202	0	0.0	0	0.0	0	0.0	0	0	4	4	2.0
2nd Year	124	59.6	84	40.4	35	16.8	208	0	0.0	0	0.0	0	0.0	0	0	2	2	1.0
3rd Year	120	63.2	70	36.8	30	15.8	190	0	0.0	0	0.0	0	0.0	0	0	0	0	0.0
4th Year								0	0.0	0	0.0	0	0.0	0	0	0	0	0.0
Total	364	60.7	236	39.3	105	17.5	600	0	0.0	0	0.0	0	0.0	0	0	6	6	1.0
JD Degrees Awarded	107	54.9	88	45.1	22	11.3	195	0	0.0	0	0.0	0	0.0	0				

GPA & LSAT Scores

	Full Time	Part Time	Total
# of apps	2,744	0	2,744
# admits	867	0	867
# of matrics	202	0	202
75% GPA	3.76	0.00	
25% GPA	3.42	0.00	
75% LSAT	170	0	
25% LSAT	164	0	

Tuition/Living Expenses

	Resident	Non-resident
Full-Time	$23,414	$23,414
Part-Time	$0	$0

Estimated living expenses for Singles		
Living on campus	Living off campus	Living at home
$10,904	$10,904	$10,904

Career Placement

	Total	%
Employment status known	176	100.0
Employment status unknown	0	0.0
Employed	171	97.2
Pursuing graduate degrees	1	0.6
Unemployed seeking employment	3	1.7
Unemployed not seeking employment	1	0.6
Type of Employment		
# employed in law firms	123	71.9
# employed in business & industry	5	2.9
# employed in government	5	2.9
# employed in public interest	1	0.6
# employed as judicial clerks	37	21.6
# employed in academia	0	0.0
Geographic Location		
# employed in state	25	14.6
# employed in foreign countries	1	0.6
# of states where employed	29	

Financial Aid

	Full-time		Part-time		Total	
	#	%	#	%	#	%
Total # receiving grants	451	75.2	0	0.0	451	75.2
Less than 1/2 tuition	414	69.0	0	0.0	414	69.0
Half to full tuition	37	6.2	0	0.0	37	6.2
Full tuition	0	0.0	0	0.0	0	0.0
More than full tuition	0	0.0	0	0.0	0	0.0
Median Grant Amount	$5,426		$0			

Refunds

Refunds of Admissions or Seat Deposit prior to commencement of classes? No

Refunds of Pre-paid tuition prior to commencement of classes? Yes

If yes, fully refundable before the start of classes? Yes

Joint Degrees Offered

JD/MBA, JD/CUL ANTH, JD/POL SCI, JD/FORESTRY, JD/MEM, JD/ECON, JD/PHIL, JD/PUB POL, JD/HISTORY, JD/ENGLISH, JD/HUMAN, JD/MECH ENG, JD/ROM STDS, JD/PSYCHOLOY, JD/MD, JD/LLM, JD/MPP

Advanced Degrees Offered

SJD	RESEARCH
LLM	US LAW FOR INTERNATIONAL STUDENTS
	INTERNATIONAL & COMPARATIVE LAW FOR U.S.

Bar Passage Rate

Jurisdiction	NY	NC
# from school taking bar for the first time	34	25
School's pass rate for all first-time takers	94%	92%
State's pass rate for all first-time takers	78%	85%
State's pass rate for all first-time takers from ABA approved law schools		85%

DUQUESNE UNIVERSITY

900 Locust Street
Pittsburgh, PA 15282
(412)396-6280
http://www.duq.edu/law

ABA Approved Since 1960

The Basics

Type of School: **PRIVATE**
Application deadline*: **4/1**
Application fee: **$50**
Financial Aid deadline*: **5/1**
Student faculty ratio: **20.7 to 1**

First year can start other than Fall: **No**
Student housing: **No**
--exclusively for law students: **No**
Term: **Semester**

*pr=preferred

Faculty

	Men		Women		Minorities		Total
	#	%	#	%	#	%	
Full-time	15	71	6	29	3	14	21
Other full-time	1	100	0	0	0	0	1
Deans, librarians, & others who teach	3	100	0	0	0	0	3
Part-time	12	86	2	14	1	7	14
Total	31	79	8	21	4	10	39
Deans, librarians, & others who teach < 1/2	1	100	0	0	0	0	1

Library

# of volumes & volume equivalents	210,921	# of professional staff	6
# of titles	56,405	Hours per week with professional staff	86
# of active serial subscriptions	4,308	Hours per week without professional staff	16
Study seating capacity inside the library	313	# of student computer work stations for entire law school	40
Square feet of law library	16,914	# of additional networked connections	71
Square feet of law school (excl. Library)	116,256		

Curriculum

	Full time	Part time
Typical first-year section size	55	45
Is there typically a "small section" of the first year class, other than Legal Writing, taught by full-time faculty?	Yes	Yes
If yes, typical size offered last year	32	32
# of classroom course titles beyond 1st year curriculum	56	61
# of upper division courses, excluding seminars, with an enrollment:		
Under 25	34	40
25 - 49	10	7
50 - 74	4	7
75 - 99	4	5
100 +	4	2
# of seminars	4	7
# of seminar positions available	165	
# of seminar positions filled	56	85
# of positions available in simulation courses	262	
# of simulation positions filled	150	99
# of positions available in faculty supervised clinical courses	30	
# of fac. sup. clin. positions filled	9	5
# involved in field placements	88	38
# involved in law journals	66	51
# in moot court or trial competitions	133	95
# of credit hours required to graduate	87	

Enrollment & Attrition

	Full-Time							Part-Time							Attrition			
	Men		Women		Minorities		Total	Men		Women		Minorities		Total	Academic	Other	Total	
	#	%	#	%	#	%	#	#	%	#	%	#	%	#	#	#	#	%
1st Year	66	58.9	46	41.1	7	6.3	112	47	54.7	39	45.3	5	5.8	86	10	18	28	14
2nd Year	52	52.5	47	47.5	8	8.1	99	47	61.8	29	38.2	1	1.3	76	3	1	4	2.3
3rd Year	57	57.0	43	43.0	9	9.0	100	53	66.3	27	33.8	10	12.5	80	1	0	1	0.6
4th Year								42	54.5	35	45.5	3	3.9	77	0	0	0	0.0
Total	175	56.3	136	43.7	24	7.7	311	189	59.2	130	40.8	19	6.0	319	14	19	33	5.1
JD Degrees Awarded	54	54.5	45	45.5	10	10.1	99	47	55.3	38	44.7	0	0.0	85				

GPA & LSAT Scores

	Full Time	Part Time	Total
# of apps	656	202	858
# admits	398	120	518
# of matrics	113	85	198
75% GPA	3.53	3.18	
25% GPA	2.92	2.59	
75% LSAT	156	156	
25% LSAT	150	148	

Tuition/Living Expenses

	Resident	Non-resident
Full-Time	$13,635	$13,635
Part-Time	$10,433	$10,433

Estimated living expenses for Singles		
Living on campus	Living off campus	Living at home
$7,885	$9,384	$3,005

Career Placement

	Total	%
Employment status known	165	98.8
Employment status unknown	2	1.2
Employed	143	86.7
Pursuing graduate degrees	3	1.8
Unemployed seeking employment	19	11.5
Unemployed not seeking employment	0	0.0
Type of Employment		
# employed in law firms	74	51.8
# employed in business & industry	47	32.9
# employed in government	5	3.5
# employed in public interest	3	2.1
# employed as judicial clerks	13	9.1
# employed in academia	1	0.7
Geographic Location		
# employed in state	105	73.4
# employed in foreign countries	0	0.0
# of states where employed	10	

Financial Aid

	Full-time		Part-time		Total	
	#	%	#	%	#	%
Total # receiving grants	101	32.5	50	15.7	151	24.0
Less than 1/2 tuition	33	10.6	16	5.0	49	7.8
Half to full tuition	48	15.4	22	6.9	70	11.1
Full tuition	20	6.4	12	3.8	32	5.1
More than full tuition	0	0.0	0	0.0	0	0.0
Median Grant Amount	$6,500		$4,900			

Refunds

Refunds of Admissions or Seat Deposit prior to commencement of classes? Yes

Refunds of Pre-paid tuition prior to commencement of classes? Yes

If yes, fully refundable before the start of classes? No

Joint Degrees Offered

JD/MBA, JD/M.S.-ES.M, JD/M.D.

Advanced Degrees Offered

No Advanced Degrees

Bar Passage Rate

Jurisdiction	PA
# from school taking bar for the first time	147
School's pass rate for all first-time takers	73%
State's pass rate for all first-time takers	73%
State's pass rate for all first-time takers from ABA approved law schools	73%

EMORY UNIVERSITY

Gambrell Hall
1301 Clifton Road
Atlanta, GA 30322-2770
(404)727-6816
http://www.law.emory.edu

ABA Approved Since 1923

The Basics

Type of School: **PRIVATE**
Application deadline*: **3/1**
Application fee: **$50**
Financial Aid deadline*: **3/1**
Student faculty ratio: **22.1 to 1**

First year can start other than Fall: **No**
Student housing: **No**
--exclusively for law students: **No**
Term: **Semester**

*pr=preferred

Faculty

	Men #	Men %	Women #	Women %	Minorities #	Minorities %	Total
Full-time	22	85	4	15	2	8	26
Other full-time	0	0	0	0	0	0	0
Deans, librarians, & others who teach	6	60	4	40	0	0	10
Part-time	26	62	16	38	5	12	42
Total	54	69	24	31	7	9	78
Deans, librarians, & others who teach < 1/2	0	0	0	0	0	0	0

Library

# of volumes & volume equivalents	316,315	# of professional staff	8
# of titles	94,440	Hours per week with professional staff	60
# of active serial subscriptions	5,253	Hours per week without professional staff	54
Study seating capacity inside the library	451	# of student computer work stations for entire law school	80
Square feet of law library	70,000	# of additional networked connections	400
Square feet of law school (excl. Library)	61,000		

Curriculum

	Full time	Part time
Typical first-year section size	60	0
Is there typically a "small section" of the first year class, other than Legal Writing, taught by full-time faculty?	Yes	No
If yes, typical size offered last year	30	N/A
# of classroom course titles beyond 1st year curriculum	100	0
# of upper division courses, excluding seminars, with an enrollment:		
Under 25	37	0
25 - 49	28	0
50 - 74	19	0
75 - 99	9	0
100 +	7	0
# of seminars	17	0
# of seminar positions available	242	
# of seminar positions filled	160	0
# of positions available in simulation courses	730	
# of simulation positions filled	746	0
# of positions available in faculty supervised clinical courses	10	
# of fac. sup. clin. positions filled	6	0
# involved in field placements	271	0
# involved in law journals	150	0
# in moot court or trial competitions	145	0
# of credit hours required to graduate	88	

Enrollment & Attrition

	Full-Time							Part-Time							Attrition			
	Men		Women		Minorities		Total	Men		Women		Minorities		Total	Academic	Other	Total	
	#	%	#	%	#	%	#	#	%	#	%	#	%	#	#	#	#	%
1st Year	109	53.2	96	46.8	50	24.4	205	0	0.0	0	0.0	0	0.0	0	0	5	5	2.0
2nd Year	143	60.1	95	39.9	43	18.1	238	0	0.0	0	0.0	0	0.0	0	3	9	12	4.6
3rd Year	149	60.1	99	39.9	40	16.1	248	0	0.0	0	0.0	0	0.0	0	0	0	0	0.0
4th Year								0	0.0	0	0.0	0	0.0	0	0	0	0	0.0
Total	401	58.0	290	42.0	133	19.2	691	0	0.0	0	0.0	0	0.0	0	3	14	17	2.3
JD Degrees Awarded	117	53.2	103	46.8	53	24.1	220	0	0.0	0	0.0	0	0.0	0				

GPA & LSAT Scores

	Full Time	Part Time	Total
# of apps	2,668	0	2,668
# admits	1,059	0	1,059
# of matrics	208	0	208
75% GPA	3.60	0.00	
25% GPA	3.20	0.00	
75% LSAT	164	0	
25% LSAT	158	0	

Tuition/Living Expenses

	Resident	Non-resident
Full-Time	$20,890	$20,890
Part-Time	$0	$0

Estimated living expenses for Singles		
Living on campus	Living off campus	Living at home
$9,736	$9,736	$9,736

Career Placement

	Total	%
Employment status known	217	94.4
Employment status unknown	13	5.7
Employed	204	94.0
Pursuing graduate degrees	5	2.3
Unemployed seeking employment	8	3.7
Unemployed not seeking employment	0	0.0
Type of Employment		
# employed in law firms	127	62.3
# employed in business & industry	21	10.3
# employed in government	26	12.8
# employed in public interest	3	1.5
# employed as judicial clerks	25	12.3
# employed in academia	2	1.0
Geographic Location		
# employed in state	123	60.3
# employed in foreign countries	2	1.0
# of states where employed	25	

Financial Aid

	Full-time		Part-time		Total	
	#	%	#	%	#	%
Total # receiving grants	372	53.8	0	0.0	372	53.8
Less than 1/2 tuition	75	10.9	0	0.0	75	10.9
Half to full tuition	126	18.2	0	0.0	126	18.2
Full tuition	160	23.2	0	0.0	160	23.2
More than full tuition	11	1.6	0	0.0	11	1.6
Median Grant Amount	$11,330		$0			

Refunds

Refunds of Admissions or Seat Deposit prior to commencement of classes? No

Refunds of Pre-paid tuition prior to commencement of classes? Yes

If yes, fully refundable before the start of classes? Yes

Joint Degrees Offered

JD/MBA, JD/M.DIV., JD/MTS, JD/MPA, JD/SEES

Advanced Degrees Offered

LL.M. General

Bar Passage Rate

Jurisdiction	GA
# from school taking bar for the first time	69
School's pass rate for all first-time takers	81%
State's pass rate for all first-time takers	81%
State's pass rate for all first-time takers from ABA approved law schools	84%

FLORIDA STATE UNIVERSITY

425 W. Jefferson Street
Tallahassee, FL 32306-1034
(904)644-3400
http://www.law.fsu.edu

ABA Approved Since 1968

The Basics

Type of School: PUBLIC
Application deadline*:
Application fee: $20
Financial Aid deadline*:
Student faculty ratio: 22.0 to 1

First year can start other than Fall: No
Student housing: No
--exclusively for law students: No
Term: Semester

*pr=preferred

Faculty

	Men #	Men %	Women #	Women %	Minorities #	Minorities %	Total
Full-time	17	71	7	29	3	13	24
Other full-time	2	50	2	50	1	25	4
Deans, librarians, & others who teach	1	50	1	50	0	0	2
Part-time	11	92	1	8	2	17	12
Total	31	74	11	26	6	14	42
Deans, librarians, & others who teach < 1/2	1	100	0	0	0	0	1

Library

# of volumes & volume equivalents	382,784	# of professional staff	6
# of titles	106,955	Hours per week with professional staff	57
# of active serial subscriptions	5,797	Hours per week without professional staff	36
Study seating capacity inside the library	396	# of student computer work stations for entire law school	61
Square feet of law library	33,237	# of additional networked connections	0
Square feet of law school (excl. Library)	57,433		

Curriculum

	Full time	Part time
Typical first-year section size	70	0
Is there typically a "small section" of the first year class, other than Legal Writing, taught by full-time faculty?	No	No
If yes, typical size offered last year	N/A	N/A
# of classroom course titles beyond 1st year curriculum	90	0
# of upper division courses, excluding seminars, with an enrollment:		
Under 25	38	0
25 - 49	23	0
50 - 74	13	0
75 - 99	5	0
100 +	3	0
# of seminars	34	0
# of seminar positions available	540	
# of seminar positions filled	423	0
# of positions available in simulation courses	131	
# of simulation positions filled	119	0
# of positions available in faculty supervised clinical courses	48	
# of fac. sup. clin. positions filled	41	0
# involved in field placements	100	0
# involved in law journals	152	0
# in moot court or trial competitions	48	0
# of credit hours required to graduate	88	

Enrollment & Attrition

	Full-Time							Part-Time							Attrition			
	Men		Women		Minorities		Total	Men		Women		Minorities		Total	Academic	Other	Total	
	#	%	#	%	#	%	#	#	%	#	%	#	%	#	#	#	#	%
1st Year	114	56.7	87	43.3	57	28.4	201	0	0.0	0	0.0	0	0.0	0	2	11	13	5.9
2nd Year	122	56.5	94	43.5	49	22.7	216	0	0.0	1	100.0	0	0.0	1	0	0	0	0.0
3rd Year	115	53.2	101	46.8	57	26.4	216	0	0.0	0	0.0	0	0.0	0	0	0	0	0.0
4th Year								0	0.0	0	0.0	0	0.0	0	0	0	0	0.0
Total	351	55.5	282	44.5	163	25.8	633	0	0.0	1	100.0	0	0.0	1	2	11	13	2.1
JD Degrees Awarded	101	54.9	83	45.1	39	21.2	184	0	0.0	0	0.0	0	0.0	0				

GPA & LSAT Scores

	Full Time	Part Time	Total
# of apps	2,107	0	2,107
# admits	654	0	654
# of matrics	203	0	203
75% GPA	3.55	0.00	
25% GPA	3.06	0.00	
75% LSAT	159	0	
25% LSAT	153	0	

Tuition/Living Expenses

	Resident	Non-resident
Full-Time	$3,687	$11,583
Part-Time	$0	$0

Estimated living expenses for Singles		
Living on campus	Living off campus	Living at home
$10,704	$10,704	$10,704

Career Placement

	Total	%
Employment status known	216	96.9
Employment status unknown	7	3.1
Employed	184	85.2
Pursuing graduate degrees	4	1.9
Unemployed seeking employment	25	11.6
Unemployed not seeking employment	3	1.4
Type of Employment		
# employed in law firms	112	60.9
# employed in business & industry	4	2.2
# employed in government	55	29.9
# employed in public interest	6	3.3
# employed as judicial clerks	7	3.8
# employed in academia	0	0.0
Geographic Location		
# employed in state	155	84.2
# employed in foreign countries	0	0.0
# of states where employed	6	

Financial Aid

	Full-time		Part-time		Total	
	#	%	#	%	#	%
Total # receiving grants	59	9.3	0	0.0	59	9.3
Less than 1/2 tuition	35	5.5	0	0.0	35	5.5
Half to full tuition	17	2.7	0	0.0	17	2.7
Full tuition	4	0.6	0	0.0	4	0.6
More than full tuition	3	0.5	0	0.0	3	0.5
Median Grant Amount	$2,000		$0			

Refunds

Refunds of Admissions or Seat Deposit prior to commencement of classes? No

Refunds of Pre-paid tuition prior to commencement of classes? No

If yes, fully refundable before the start of classes? No

Joint Degrees Offered

JD - MBA, JD - MPA, JD - ECON., JD - INT.AFF, JD - URB REG

Advanced Degrees Offered

No Advanced Degrees

Bar Passage Rate

Jurisdiction	FL
# from school taking bar for the first time	156
School's pass rate for all first-time takers	82%
State's pass rate for all first-time takers	84%
State's pass rate for all first-time takers from ABA approved law schools	84%

FLORIDA, UNIVERSITY OF

P.O. Box 117620
Gainesville, FL 32611
(352)392-0421
http://nervp.nerdc.ufl.edu

ABA Approved Since 1925

The Basics

Type of School: **PUBLIC**
Application deadline*: **2/1**
Application fee: **$20**
Financial Aid deadline*: **4/1**
Student faculty ratio: **19.9 to 1**
First year can start other than Fall: **Yes**
Student housing: **No**
--exclusively for law students: **No**
Term: **Semester**

*pr=preferred

Faculty

	Men #	Men %	Women #	Women %	Minorities #	Minorities %	Total
Full-time	35	76	11	24	7	15	46
Other full-time	2	14	12	86	0	0	14
Deans, librarians, & others who teach	4	80	1	20	0	0	5
Part-time	12	100	0	0	1	8	12
Total	53	69	24	31	8	10	77
Deans, librarians, & others who teach < 1/2	3	75	1	25	0	0	4

Library

# of volumes & volume equivalents	568,644	# of professional staff	11
# of titles	155,139	Hours per week with professional staff	58
# of active serial subscriptions	7,956	Hours per week without professional staff	42
Study seating capacity inside the library	812	# of student computer work stations for entire law school	97
Square feet of law library	47,654	# of additional networked connections	0
Square feet of law school (excl. Library)	96,875		

Curriculum

	Full time	Part time
Typical first-year section size	103	0
Is there typically a "small section" of the first year class, other than Legal Writing, taught by full-time faculty?	No	No
If yes, typical size offered last year	N/A	N/A
# of classroom course titles beyond 1st year curriculum	75	0
# of upper division courses, excluding seminars, with an enrollment:		
Under 25	24	0
25 - 49	36	0
50 - 74	36	0
75 - 99	29	0
100 +	2	0
# of seminars	41	0
# of seminar positions available	615	
# of seminar positions filled	518	0
# of positions available in simulation courses	798	
# of simulation positions filled	795	0
# of positions available in faculty supervised clinical courses	148	
# of fac. sup. clin. positions filled	149	0
# involved in field placements	0	0
# involved in law journals	170	0
# in moot court or trial competitions	66	0
# of credit hours required to graduate	88	

Enrollment & Attrition

	Full-Time Men #	Men %	Women #	Women %	Minorities #	Minorities %	Total #	Part-Time Men #	Men %	Women #	Women %	Minorities #	Minorities %	Total #	Attrition Academic #	Other #	Total #	%
1st Year	256	60.7	166	39.3	101	23.9	422	0	0.0	0	0.0	0	0.0	0	1	7	8	1.9
2nd Year	204	57.6	150	42.4	92	26.0	354	0	0.0	0	0.0	0	0.0	0	2	4	6	1.7
3rd Year	192	58.5	136	41.5	66	20.1	328	0	0.0	0	0.0	0	0.0	0	0	0	0	0.0
4th Year								0	0.0	0	0.0	0	0.0	0	0	0	0	0.0
Total	652	59.1	452	40.9	259	23.5	1,104	0	0.0	0	0.0	0	0.0	0	3	11	14	1.3
JD Degrees Awarded	211	58.6	149	41.4	82	22.8	360	0	0.0	0	0.0	0	0.0	0				

GPA & LSAT Scores

	Full Time	Part Time	Total
# of apps	1,549	0	1,549
# admits	512	0	512
# of matrics	218	0	218
75% GPA	3.73	0.00	
25% GPA	3.26	0.00	
75% LSAT	163	0	
25% LSAT	155	0	

Tuition/Living Expenses

	Resident	Non-resident
Full-Time	$3,605	$11,501
Part-Time	$0	$0

Estimated living expenses for Singles		
Living on campus	Living off campus	Living at home
$7,590	$8,890	$4,260

Career Placement

	Total	%
Employment status known	362	90.5
Employment status unknown	38	9.5
Employed	288	79.6
Pursuing graduate degrees	22	6.1
Unemployed seeking employment	38	10.5
Unemployed not seeking employment	14	3.9
Type of Employment		
# employed in law firms	180	62.5
# employed in business & industry	23	8.0
# employed in government	64	22.2
# employed in public interest	0	0.0
# employed as judicial clerks	21	7.3
# employed in academia	0	0.0
Geographic Location		
# employed in state	238	82.6
# employed in foreign countries	0	0.0
# of states where employed	11	

Financial Aid

	Full-time		Part-time		Total	
	#	%	#	%	#	%
Total # receiving grants	196	17.8	0	0.0	196	17.8
Less than 1/2 tuition	48	4.4	0	0.0	48	4.3
Half to full tuition	25	2.3	0	0.0	25	2.3
Full tuition	0	0.0	0	0.0	0	0.0
More than full tuition	123	11.1	0	0.0	123	11.1
Median Grant Amount	$6,398		$0			

Refunds

Refunds of Admissions or Seat Deposit prior to commencement of classes? No

Refunds of Pre-paid tuition prior to commencement of classes? No

If yes, fully refundable before the start of classes? No

Joint Degrees Offered

JD/MSAccting, JD/MSBusAdmi, JD/MSPolSci-, JD/MSSociolo, JD/MSUrbPlan, JD/PHDHistor, JD/PHDPsycho

Advanced Degrees Offered

LL.M. Taxation
LL.M. Comparative Law

Bar Passage Rate

Jurisdiction	FL
# from school taking bar for the first time	208
School's pass rate for all first-time takers	92%
State's pass rate for all first-time takers	84%
State's pass rate for all first-time takers from ABA approved law schools	84%

FORDHAM UNIVERSITY

140 West 62nd Street
New York, NY 10023-7485
(212)636-6875
http://www.fordham.edu/law/cle/law_main

ABA Approved Since 1936

The Basics

Type of School: **PRIVATE**
Application deadline*: **3/1**
Application fee: **$60**
Financial Aid deadline*: **3/1**
Student faculty ratio: **20.5 to 1**

First year can start other than Fall: **No**
Student housing: **Yes**
--exclusively for law students: **No**
Term: **Semester**

*pr=preferred

Faculty

	Men #	Men %	Women #	Women %	Minorities #	Minorities %	Total
Full-time	40	77	12	23	5	10	52
Other full-time	0	0	5	100	1	20	5
Deans, librarians, & others who teach	0	0	1	100	0	0	1
Part-time	67	73	25	27	9	10	92
Total	107	71	43	29	15	10	150
Deans, librarians, & others who teach < 1/2	3	60	2	40	1	20	5

Library

# of volumes & volume equivalents	491,529	# of professional staff	13
# of titles	164,520	Hours per week with professional staff	86
# of active serial subscriptions	3,866	Hours per week without professional staff	36
Study seating capacity inside the library	465	# of student computer work stations for entire law school	94
Square feet of law library	43,266	# of additional networked connections	0
Square feet of law school (excl. Library)	124,050		

Curriculum

	Full time	Part time
Typical first-year section size	74	78
Is there typically a "small section" of the first year class, other than Legal Writing, taught by full-time faculty?	Yes	Yes
If yes, typical size offered last year	37	39
# of classroom course titles beyond 1st year curriculum	121	99
# of upper division courses, excluding seminars, with an enrollment:		
Under 25	25	20
25 - 49	23	18
50 - 74	13	8
75 - 99	9	7
100 +	12	6
# of seminars	35	33
# of seminar positions available	1,499	
# of seminar positions filled	689	211
# of positions available in simulation courses	639	
# of simulation positions filled	442	110
# of positions available in faculty supervised clinical courses	109	
# of fac. sup. clin. positions filled	105	2
# involved in field placements	389	46
# involved in law journals	313	65
# in moot court or trial competitions	456	0
# of credit hours required to graduate	83	

Enrollment & Attrition

	Full-Time Men #	%	Women #	%	Minorities #	%	Total #	Part-Time Men #	%	Women #	%	Minorities #	%	Total #	Attrition Academic #	Other #	Total #	%
1st Year	198	58.8	139	41.2	78	23.1	337	66	49.3	68	50.7	37	27.6	134	1	5	6	1.3
2nd Year	206	55.8	163	44.2	100	27.1	369	51	58.6	36	41.4	26	29.9	87	0	11	11	2.5
3rd Year	192	57.0	145	43.0	97	28.8	337	41	53.2	36	46.8	13	16.9	77	0	0	0	0.0
4th Year								40	63.5	23	36.5	18	28.6	63	0	0	0	0.0
Total	596	57.1	447	42.9	275	26.4	1,043	198	54.8	163	45.2	94	26.0	361	1	16	17	1.1
JD Degrees Awarded	259	60.5	169	39.5	103	24.1	428	57	62.6	34	37.4	16	17.6	91				

GPA & LSAT Scores

	Full Time	Part Time	Total
# of apps	3,916	677	4,593
# admits	1,257	227	1,484
# of matrics	343	135	478
75% GPA	3.55	3.51	
25% GPA	3.01	2.86	
75% LSAT	165	162	
25% LSAT	161	154	

Tuition/Living Expenses

	Resident	Non-resident
Full-Time	$21,694	$21,694
Part-Time	$16,274	$16,274

Estimated living expenses for Singles		
Living on campus	Living off campus	Living at home
$15,665	$15,665	$8,665

Career Placement

	Total	%
Employment status known	380	89.2
Employment status unknown	46	10.8
Employed	349	91.8
Pursuing graduate degrees	6	1.6
Unemployed seeking employment	19	5.0
Unemployed not seeking employment	6	1.6
Type of Employment		
# employed in law firms	227	65.0
# employed in business & industry	61	17.5
# employed in government	41	11.8
# employed in public interest	2	0.6
# employed as judicial clerks	15	4.3
# employed in academia	3	0.9
Geographic Location		
# employed in state	317	90.8
# employed in foreign countries	1	0.3
# of states where employed	18	

Financial Aid

	Full-time		Part-time		Total	
	#	%	#	%	#	%
Total # receiving grants	679	65.1	92	25.5	771	54.9
Less than 1/2 tuition	642	61.6	88	24.4	730	52.0
Half to full tuition	28	2.7	3	0.8	31	2.2
Full tuition	9	0.9	1	0.3	10	0.7
More than full tuition	0	0.0	0	0.0	0	0.0
Median Grant Amount	$3,200		$2,400			

Refunds

Refunds of Admissions or Seat Deposit prior to commencement of classes? Yes

73% refund from 06/01/95 to 07/01/95

Refunds of Pre-paid tuition prior to commencement of classes? Yes

If yes, fully refundable before the start of classes? Yes

Joint Degrees Offered

JD/MBA

Advanced Degrees Offered

LLM Banking Corporate and Finance Law
LLM International Business and Trade Law

Bar Passage Rate

Jurisdiction	NY
# from school taking bar for the first time	382
School's pass rate for all first-time takers	90%
State's pass rate for all first-time takers	78%
State's pass rate for all first-time takers from ABA approved law schools	

FRANKLIN PIERCE LAW CENTER

2 White Street
Concord, NH 03301
(603)228-1541
http://www.fplc.edu

ABA Approved Since 1974

The Basics

Type of School: PRIVATE
Application deadline*: 5/1
Application fee: $45
Financial Aid deadline*:
Student faculty ratio: 18.1 to 1
First year can start other than Fall: No
Student housing: No
--exclusively for law students: No
Term: Semester

*pr=preferred

Faculty

	Men		Women		Minorities		Total
	#	%	#	%	#	%	
Full-time	14	74	5	26	0	0	19
Other full-time	0	0	0	0	0	0	0
Deans, librarians, & others who teach	1	100	0	0	0	0	1
Part-time	18	78	5	22	1	4	23
Total	33	77	10	23	1	2	43
Deans, librarians, & others who teach < 1/2	2	40	3	60	0	0	5

Library

# of volumes & volume equivalents	200,024	# of professional staff	5
# of titles	46,618	Hours per week with professional staff	45
# of active serial subscriptions	2,409	Hours per week without professional staff	59
Study seating capacity inside the library	231	# of student computer work stations for entire law school	28
Square feet of law library	20,016	# of additional networked connections	325
Square feet of law school (excl. Library)	53,984		

Curriculum

	Full time	Part time
Typical first-year section size	152	0
Is there typically a "small section" of the first year class, other than Legal Writing, taught by full-time faculty?	Yes	No
If yes, typical size offered last year	25	N/A
# of classroom course titles beyond 1st year curriculum	81	0
# of upper division courses, excluding seminars, with an enrollment:		
Under 25	16	0
25 - 49	16	0
50 - 74	9	0
75 - 99	3	0
100 +	4	0
# of seminars	33	0
# of seminar positions available	408	
# of seminar positions filled	403	0
# of positions available in simulation courses	217	
# of simulation positions filled	217	0
# of positions available in faculty supervised clinical courses	156	
# of fac. sup. clin. positions filled	100	0
# involved in field placements	57	0
# involved in law journals	34	0
# in moot court or trial competitions	33	0
# of credit hours required to graduate	84	

Enrollment & Attrition

	Full-Time							Part-Time							Attrition			
	Men		Women		Minorities		Total	Men		Women		Minorities		Total	Academic	Other	Total	
	#	%	#	%	#	%	#	#	%	#	%	#	%	#	#	#	#	%
1st Year	94	61.8	58	38.2	24	15.8	152	0	0.0	0	0.0	0	0.0	0	0	0	0	0.0
2nd Year	81	64.8	44	35.2	15	12.0	125	0	0.0	0	0.0	0	0.0	0	0	21	21	16
3rd Year	89	65.9	46	34.1	10	7.4	135	0	0.0	0	0.0	0	0.0	0	0	3	3	2.3
4th Year								0	0.0	0	0.0	0	0.0	0	0	0	0	0.0
Total	264	64.1	148	35.9	49	11.9	412	0	0.0	0	0.0	0	0.0	0	0	24	24	6.0
JD Degrees Awarded	77	61.6	48	38.4	2	1.6	125	0	0.0	0	0.0	0	0.0	0				

GPA & LSAT Scores

	Full Time	Part Time	Total
# of apps	1,121	0	1,121
# admits	533	0	533
# of matrics	152	0	152
75% GPA	3.25	0.00	
25% GPA	2.69	0.00	
75% LSAT	156	0	
25% LSAT	148	0	

Tuition/Living Expenses

	Resident	Non-resident
Full-Time	$14,980	$14,980
Part-Time	$0	$0

Estimated living expenses for Singles		
Living on campus	Living off campus	Living at home
N/A	$14,161	$14,161

Career Placement

	Total	%
Employment status known	126	97.7
Employment status unknown	3	2.3
Employed	100	79.4
Pursuing graduate degrees	2	1.6
Unemployed seeking employment	19	15.1
Unemployed not seeking employment	5	4.0
Type of Employment		
# employed in law firms	65	65.0
# employed in business & industry	19	19.0
# employed in government	7	7.0
# employed in public interest	2	2.0
# employed as judicial clerks	3	3.0
# employed in academia	3	3.0
Geographic Location		
# employed in state	32	32.0
# employed in foreign countries	1	1.0
# of states where employed	19	

Financial Aid

	Full-time		Part-time		Total	
	#	%	#	%	#	%
Total # receiving grants	252	61.2	0	0.0	252	61.2
Less than 1/2 tuition	231	56.1	0	0.0	231	56.1
Half to full tuition	4	1.0	0	0.0	4	1.0
Full tuition	17	4.1	0	0.0	17	4.1
More than full tuition	0	0.0	0	0.0	0	0.0
Median Grant Amount	$1,948		$0			

Refunds

Refunds of Admissions or Seat Deposit prior to commencement of classes? No

Refunds of Pre-paid tuition prior to commencement of classes? Yes

If yes, fully refundable before the start of classes? Yes

Joint Degrees Offered

JD/MIP

Advanced Degrees Offered

LLM Intellectual Property

Bar Passage Rate

Jurisdiction	NH
# from school taking bar for the first time	47
School's pass rate for all first-time takers	79%
State's pass rate for all first-time takers	79%
State's pass rate for all first-time takers from ABA approved law schools	79%

GEORGE MASON UNIVERSITY

3401 North Fairfax Drive
Arlington, VA 22201-4498
(703)993-8000
http://www.gmu.edu/departments/law

ABA Approved Since 1980

The Basics

Type of School: PUBLIC
Application deadline*: 3/1
Application fee: $35
Financial Aid deadline*:
Student faculty ratio: 18.7 to 1
First year can start other than Fall: No
Student housing: No
--exclusively for law students: No
Term: Semester

*pr=preferred

Faculty

	Men #	Men %	Women #	Women %	Minorities #	Minorities %	Total
Full-time	22	85	4	15	2	8	26
Other full-time	0	0	0	0	0	0	0
Deans, librarians, & others who teach	0	0	0	0	0	0	0
Part-time	24	86	4	14	2	7	28
Total	46	85	8	15	4	7	54
Deans, librarians, & others who teach < 1/2	1	100	0	0	0	0	1

Library

# of volumes & volume equivalents	338,730	# of professional staff	5
# of titles	131,812	Hours per week with professional staff	66
# of active serial subscriptions	4,665	Hours per week without professional staff	25
Study seating capacity inside the library	250	# of student computer work stations for entire law school	21
Square feet of law library	26,277	# of additional networked connections	18
Square feet of law school (excl. Library)	25,970		

Curriculum

	Full time	Part time
Typical first-year section size	151	69
Is there typically a "small section" of the first year class, other than Legal Writing, taught by full-time faculty?	Yes	No
If yes, typical size offered last year	24	N/A
# of classroom course titles beyond 1st year curriculum	72	74
# of upper division courses, excluding seminars, with an enrollment:		
Under 25	40	35
25 - 49	20	24
50 - 74	4	4
75 - 99	5	4
100 +	1	1
# of seminars	14	9
# of seminar positions available	215	
# of seminar positions filled	120	68
# of positions available in simulation courses	303	
# of simulation positions filled	83	101
# of positions available in faculty supervised clinical courses	0	
# of fac. sup. clin. positions filled	0	0
# involved in field placements	63	11
# involved in law journals	149	47
# in moot court or trial competitions	11	2
# of credit hours required to graduate	90	

Enrollment & Attrition

	Full-Time Men #	Men %	Women #	Women %	Minorities #	Minorities %	Total #	Part-Time Men #	Men %	Women #	Women %	Minorities #	Minorities %	Total #	Attrition Academic #	Other #	Total #	%
1st Year	94	62.3	57	37.7	13	8.6	151	44	63.8	25	36.2	6	8.7	69	1	3	4	1.9
2nd Year	64	59.3	44	40.7	7	6.5	108	66	71.0	27	29.0	13	14.0	93	0	9	9	4.4
3rd Year	71	62.8	42	37.2	14	12.4	113	56	70.0	24	30.0	9	11.3	80	0	1	1	0.5
4th Year								45	58.4	32	41.6	5	6.5	77	0	0	0	0.0
Total	229	61.6	143	38.4	34	9.1	372	211	66.1	108	33.9	33	10.3	319	1	13	14	2.0
JD Degrees Awarded	72	52.6	65	47.4	17	12.4	137	43	70.5	18	29.5	4	6.6	61				

GPA & LSAT Scores

	Full Time	Part Time	Total
# of apps	1,540	483	2,023
# admits	608	163	771
# of matrics	148	68	216
75% GPA	3.34	3.24	
25% GPA	2.87	2.71	
75% LSAT	161	162	
25% LSAT	157	158	

Tuition/Living Expenses

	Resident	Non-resident
Full-Time	$7,280	$17,948
Part-Time	$5,200	$12,820

Estimated living expenses for Singles		
Living on campus	Living off campus	Living at home
N/A	$14,378	$4,943

Career Placement

	Total	%
Employment status known	153	92.7
Employment status unknown	12	7.3
Employed	132	86.3
Pursuing graduate degrees	2	1.3
Unemployed seeking employment	16	10.5
Unemployed not seeking employment	3	2.0
Type of Employment		
# employed in law firms	44	33.3
# employed in business & industry	24	18.2
# employed in government	39	29.6
# employed in public interest	3	2.3
# employed as judicial clerks	22	16.7
# employed in academia	0	0.0
Geographic Location		
# employed in state	69	52.3
# employed in foreign countries	0	0.0
# of states where employed	11	

Financial Aid

	Full-time		Part-time		Total	
	#	%	#	%	#	%
Total # receiving grants	16	4.3	12	3.8	28	4.1
Less than 1/2 tuition	7	1.9	6	1.9	13	1.9
Half to full tuition	5	1.3	5	1.6	10	1.4
Full tuition	0	0.0	0	0.0	0	0.0
More than full tuition	4	1.1	1	0.3	5	0.7
Median Grant Amount	$5,000		$3,750			

Refunds

Refunds of Admissions or Seat Deposit prior to commencement of classes? No

Refunds of Pre-paid tuition prior to commencement of classes? Yes

If yes, fully refundable before the start of classes? Yes

Joint Degrees Offered

No Joint Degrees

Advanced Degrees Offered

No Advanced Degrees

Bar Passage Rate

Jurisdiction	VA
# from school taking bar for the first time	131
School's pass rate for all first-time takers	80%
State's pass rate for all first-time takers	76%
State's pass rate for all first-time takers from ABA approved law schools	77%

GEORGE WASHINGTON UNIVERSITY

2000 H Street, N.W.
Washington, DC 20052
(202)994-7230
http://www.law.gwu.edu

ABA Approved Since 1923

The Basics

Type of School: **PRIVATE**
Application deadline: **3/1**
Application fee: **$55**
Financial Aid deadline:
Student faculty ratio: **18.3 to 1**

First year can start other than Fall: **No**
Student housing: **No**
--exclusively for law students: **No**
Term: **Semester**

Faculty

	Men #	Men %	Women #	Women %	Minorities #	Minorities %	Total
Full-time	47	72	18	28	7	11	65
Other full-time	0	0	0	0	0	0	0
Deans, librarians, & others who teach	1	100	0	0	0	0	1
Part-time	69	64	39	36	8	7	108
Total	117	67	57	33	15	9	174
Deans, librarians, & others who teach < 1/2	3	60	2	40	1	20	5

Library

# of volumes & volume equivalents	477,214	# of professional staff	15
# of titles	89,490	Hours per week with professional staff	81
# of active serial subscriptions	5,732	Hours per week without professional staff	29
Study seating capacity inside the library	828	# of student computer work stations for entire law school	123
Square feet of law library	47,501	# of additional networked connections	0
Square feet of law school (excl. Library)	70,696		

Curriculum

	Full time	Part time
Typical first-year section size	90	50
Is there typically a "small section" of the first year class, other than Legal Writing, taught by full-time faculty?	No	No
If yes, typical size offered last year	N/A	N/A
# of classroom course titles beyond 1st year curriculum	108	89
# of upper division courses, excluding seminars, with an enrollment:		
Under 25	56	55
25 - 49	33	32
50 - 74	17	5
75 - 99	10	2
100 +	16	4
# of seminars	17	9
# of seminar positions available	530	
# of seminar positions filled	263	143
# of positions available in simulation courses	782	
# of simulation positions filled	320	396
# of positions available in faculty supervised clinical courses	261	
# of fac. sup. clin. positions filled	234	20
# involved in field placements	249	33
# involved in law journals	340	41
# in moot court or trial competitions	278	21
# of credit hours required to graduate	84	

Enrollment & Attrition

	Full-Time							Part-Time							Attrition			
	Men		Women		Minorities		Total	Men		Women		Minorities		Total	Academic	Other	Total	
	#	%	#	%	#	%	#	#	%	#	%	#	%	#	#	#	#	%
1st Year	238	59.2	164	40.8	117	29.1	402	33	55.0	27	45.0	21	35.0	60	0	16	16	3.1
2nd Year	226	52.2	207	47.8	137	31.6	433	27	50.0	27	50.0	18	33.3	54	2	7	9	1.9
3rd Year	240	53.5	209	46.5	121	26.9	449	30	62.5	18	37.5	19	39.6	48	2	0	2	0.4
4th Year								32	64.0	18	36.0	12	24.0	50	0	0	0	0.0
Total	704	54.8	580	45.2	375	29.2	1,284	122	57.5	90	42.5	70	33.0	212	4	23	27	1.8
JD Degrees Awarded	218	58.0	158	42.0	79	21.0	376	58	67.4	28	32.6	18	20.9	86				

GEORGE WASHINGTON UNIVERSITY

GPA & LSAT Scores

	Full Time	Part Time	Total
# of apps	N/A	N/A	6,454
# admits	N/A	N/A	1,922
# of matrics	395	54	449
75% GPA	3.63	3.32	
25% GPA	3.24	2.90	
75% LSAT	163	161	
25% LSAT	159	155	

Tuition/Living Expenses

	Resident	Non-resident
Full-Time	$21,785	$21,785
Part-Time	$15,310	$15,310

Estimated living expenses for Singles		
Living on campus	Living off campus	Living at home
N/A	$13,672	$9,972

Financial Aid

	Full-time		Part-time		Total	
	#	%	#	%	#	%
Total # receiving grants	544	42.4	27	12.7	571	38.2
Less than 1/2 tuition	437	34.0	27	12.7	464	31.0
Half to full tuition	107	8.3	0	0.0	107	7.2
Full tuition	0	0.0	0	0.0	0	0.0
More than full tuition	0	0.0	0	0.0	0	0.0
Median Grant Amount	$8,000		$2,000			

Refunds

Refunds of Admissions or Seat Deposit prior to commencement of classes? No

Refunds of Pre-paid tuition prior to commencement of classes? Yes

If yes, fully refundable before the start of classes? Yes

Joint Degrees Offered

JD/MA, JD/MBA, JD/MPH, JD/MPA, JD/MHSA, LLM/MPH

Advanced Degrees Offered

LL.M.	General
LL.M.	Environmental Law
LL.M.	Intellectual Property Law
LL.M.	Government Procurement Law
LL.M.	International & Comparative Law
S.J.D.	various

Career Placement

	Total	%
Employment status known	435	95.6
Employment status unknown	20	4.4
Employed	410	94.3
Pursuing graduate degrees	2	0.5
Unemployed seeking employment	23	5.3
Unemployed not seeking employment	0	0.0
Type of Employment		
# employed in law firms	248	60.5
# employed in business & industry	32	7.8
# employed in government	76	18.5
# employed in public interest	14	3.4
# employed as judicial clerks	37	9.0
# employed in academia	3	0.7
Geographic Location		
# employed in state	201	49.0
# employed in foreign countries	1	0.2
# of states where employed	31	

Bar Passage Rate

Jurisdiction	MD	NY
# from school taking bar for the first time	127	81
School's pass rate for all first-time takers	89%	92%
State's pass rate for all first-time takers	75%	78%
State's pass rate for all first-time takers from ABA approved law schools	75%	

GEORGETOWN UNIVERSITY

600 New Jersey Avenue N.W.
Washington, DC 20001
(202)662-9000
http://www.law.georgetown.edu/lc

ABA Approved Since 1924

The Basics

Type of School: **PRIVATE**
Application deadline*: **3/1**
Application fee: **$60**
Financial Aid deadline*: **3/1**
Student faculty ratio: **18.2 to 1**
First year can start other than Fall: **No**
Student housing: **Yes**
--exclusively for law students: **Yes**
Term: **Semester**

*pr=preferred

Faculty

	Men #	Men %	Women #	Women %	Minorities #	Minorities %	Total
Full-time	64	72	25	28	10	11	89
Other full-time	1	20	4	80	1	20	5
Deans, librarians, & others who teach	2	100	0	0	0	0	2
Part-time	76	85	13	15	4	4	89
Total	143	77	42	23	15	8	185
Deans, librarians, & others who teach < 1/2	3	43	4	57	3	43	7

Library

# of volumes & volume equivalents	861,296	# of professional staff	22
# of titles	252,626	Hours per week with professional staff	76
# of active serial subscriptions	12,102	Hours per week without professional staff	31
Study seating capacity inside the library	1,260	# of student computer work stations for entire law school	125
Square feet of law library	119,743	# of additional networked connections	301
Square feet of law school (excl. Library)	392,358		

Curriculum

	Full time	Part time
Typical first-year section size	125	125
Is there typically a "small section" of the first year class, other than Legal Writing, taught by full-time faculty?	Yes	Yes
If yes, typical size offered last year	32	32
# of classroom course titles beyond 1st year curriculum	135	99
# of upper division courses, excluding seminars, with an enrollment:		
Under 25	51	38
25 - 49	31	20
50 - 74	18	11
75 - 99	11	6
100 +	20	4
# of seminars	70	51
# of seminar positions available	2,438	
# of seminar positions filled	928	777
# of positions available in simulation courses	576	
# of simulation positions filled	198	339
# of positions available in faculty supervised clinical courses	248	
# of fac. sup. clin. positions filled	230	13
# involved in field placements	0	0
# involved in law journals	723	78
# in moot court or trial competitions	246	58
# of credit hours required to graduate	83	

Enrollment & Attrition

	Full-Time							Part-Time							Attrition			
	Men		Women		Minorities		Total	Men		Women		Minorities		Total	Academic	Other	Total	
	#	%	#	%	#	%	#	#	%	#	%	#	%	#	#	#	#	%
1st Year	295	52.2	270	47.8	140	24.8	565	83	63.8	47	36.2	27	20.8	130	0	3	3	0.5
2nd Year	290	54.7	240	45.3	130	24.5	530	65	52.0	60	48.0	29	23.2	125	0	2	2	0.3
3rd Year	283	53.3	248	46.7	131	24.7	531	62	57.9	45	42.1	21	19.6	107	0	1	1	0.2
4th Year								76	61.3	48	38.7	28	22.6	124	0	0	0	0.0
Total	868	53.4	758	46.6	401	24.7	1,626	286	58.8	200	41.2	105	21.6	486	0	6	6	0.3
JD Degrees Awarded	257	52.6	232	47.4	128	26.2	489	56	52.8	50	47.2	20	18.9	106				

GPA & LSAT Scores

	Full Time	Part Time	Total
# of apps	6,870	660	7,530
# admits	1,924	230	2,154
# of matrics	568	131	699
75% GPA	3.77	3.62	
25% GPA	3.24	3.10	
75% LSAT	169	167	
25% LSAT	161	160	

Tuition/Living Expenses

	Resident	Non-resident
Full-Time	$22,430	$22,430
Part-Time	$15,300	$15,300

Estimated living expenses for Singles		
Living on campus	Living off campus	Living at home
$14,200	$14,200	$10,725

Career Placement

	Total	%
Employment status known	590	98.8
Employment status unknown	7	1.2
Employed	568	96.3
Pursuing graduate degrees	6	1.0
Unemployed seeking employment	12	2.0
Unemployed not seeking employment	4	0.7
Type of Employment		
# employed in law firms	346	60.9
# employed in business & industry	45	7.9
# employed in government	62	10.9
# employed in public interest	23	4.1
# employed as judicial clerks	90	15.9
# employed in academia	2	0.4
Geographic Location		
# employed in state	273	48.1
# employed in foreign countries	5	0.9
# of states where employed	40	

Financial Aid

	Full-time		Part-time		Total	
	#	%	#	%	#	%
Total # receiving grants	489	30.1	0	0.0	489	23.2
Less than 1/2 tuition	421	25.9	0	0.0	421	19.9
Half to full tuition	67	4.1	0	0.0	67	3.2
Full tuition	1	0.1	0	0.0	1	0.0
More than full tuition	0	0.0	0	0.0	0	0.0
Median Grant Amount	$7,700		$0			

Refunds

Refunds of Admissions or Seat Deposit prior to commencement of classes? Yes

100% refund to 06/14/96
50% refund from 06/15/96 to 07/01/96
0% refund from 07/02/96 to / /

Refunds of Pre-paid tuition prior to commencement of classes? Yes

If yes, fully refundable before the start of classes? Yes

100% refund to 08/21/96
0% refund from 08/22/96 to / /

Joint Degrees Offered

JD/MSFS, JD/MBA, JD/MPH, JD/Gov, JD/Phil

Advanced Degrees Offered

LL.M.	General program with approved course of study
LL.M.	Advocacy (clinical fellows)
LL.M.	International and Comparative Law
LL.M.	Labor and Employment Law
LL.M.	Securities and Financial Regulation
LL.M.	Taxation
LL.M.	Common Law Studies (foreign attorneys)
S.J.D.	Doctoral study as approved (U.S./foreign attys.)
Certif	Employee Benefits

Bar Passage Rate

Jurisdiction	NY	MD
# from school taking bar for the first time	158	129
School's pass rate for all first-time takers	91%	82%
State's pass rate for all first-time takers	78%	75%
State's pass rate for all first-time takers from ABA approved law schools		75%

GEORGIA STATE UNIVERSITY

P.O. Box 4037
Atlanta, GA 30302-4037
(404)651-2096
http://www.gsu.edu/~lawadmn/gsulaw

ABA Approved Since 1984

The Basics

Type of School: **PUBLIC**
Application deadline*: **3/15**
Application fee: **$30**
Financial Aid deadline*: **5/1**
Student faculty ratio: **17.2 to 1**

First year can start other than Fall: **No**
Student housing: **Yes**
--exclusively for law students: **No**
Term: **Semester**

*pr=preferred

Faculty

	Men #	Men %	Women #	Women %	Minorities #	Minorities %	Total
Full-time	21	68	10	32	3	10	31
Other full-time	0	0	0	0	0	0	0
Deans, librarians, & others who teach	1	50	1	50	1	50	2
Part-time	5	71	2	29	2	29	7
Total	27	68	13	33	6	15	40
Deans, librarians, & others who teach < 1/2	0	0	3	100	2	67	3

Library

# of volumes & volume equivalents	255,461	# of professional staff	4
# of titles	46,807	Hours per week with professional staff	68
# of active serial subscriptions	3,548	Hours per week without professional staff	82
Study seating capacity inside the library	335	# of student computer work stations for entire law school	16
Square feet of law library	37,010	# of additional networked connections	0
Square feet of law school (excl. Library)	43,323		

Curriculum

	Full time	Part time
Typical first-year section size	70	70
Is there typically a "small section" of the first year class, other than Legal Writing, taught by full-time faculty?	No	No
If yes, typical size offered last year	N/A	N/A
# of classroom course titles beyond 1st year curriculum	60	52
# of upper division courses, excluding seminars, with an enrollment:		
Under 25	33	45
25 - 49	20	13
50 - 74	13	3
75 - 99	0	4
100 +	0	0
# of seminars	8	4
# of seminar positions available	227	
# of seminar positions filled	93	40
# of positions available in simulation courses	693	
# of simulation positions filled	330	224
# of positions available in faculty supervised clinical courses	60	
# of fac. sup. clin. positions filled	28	4
# involved in field placements	104	26
# involved in law journals	58	15
# in moot court or trial competitions	106	31
# of credit hours required to graduate	90	

Enrollment & Attrition

	Full-Time							Part-Time							Attrition			
	Men		Women		Minorities		Total	Men		Women		Minorities		Total	Academic	Other	Total	
	#	%	#	%	#	%	#	#	%	#	%	#	%	#	#	#	#	%
1st Year	67	48.6	71	51.4	22	15.9	138	43	53.1	38	46.9	13	16.0	81	9	26	35	18
2nd Year	54	51.9	50	48.1	29	27.9	104	32	61.5	20	38.5	12	23.1	52	2	5	7	3.6
3rd Year	84	49.4	86	50.6	43	25.3	170	31	50.8	30	49.2	21	34.4	61	0	1	1	0.6
4th Year								32	51.6	30	48.4	11	17.7	62	0	0	0	0.0
Total	205	49.8	207	50.2	94	22.8	412	138	53.9	118	46.1	57	22.3	256	11	32	43	6.8
JD Degrees Awarded	44	48.4	47	51.6	15	16.5	91	25	45.5	30	54.5	9	16.4	55				

GPA & LSAT Scores

	Full Time	Part Time	Total
# of apps	2,020	338	2,358
# admits	466	84	550
# of matrics	153	65	218
75% GPA	3.46	3.60	
25% GPA	2.92	2.90	
75% LSAT	159	161	
25% LSAT	154	153	

Tuition/Living Expenses

	Resident	Non-resident
Full-Time	$2,903	$9,147
Part-Time	$2,175	$6,635

Estimated living expenses for Singles		
Living on campus	Living off campus	Living at home
$11,170	$12,129	$6,815

Career Placement

	Total	%
Employment status known	163	97.0
Employment status unknown	5	3.0
Employed	144	88.3
Pursuing graduate degrees	1	0.6
Unemployed seeking employment	12	7.4
Unemployed not seeking employment	6	3.7
Type of Employment		
# employed in law firms	82	56.9
# employed in business & industry	32	22.2
# employed in government	20	13.9
# employed in public interest	1	0.7
# employed as judicial clerks	8	5.6
# employed in academia	1	0.7
Geographic Location		
# employed in state	133	92.4
# employed in foreign countries	0	0.0
# of states where employed	9	

Financial Aid

	Full-time		Part-time		Total	
	#	%	#	%	#	%
Total # receiving grants	18	4.4	5	2.0	23	3.4
Less than 1/2 tuition	1	0.2	0	0.0	1	0.1
Half to full tuition	3	0.7	0	0.0	3	0.4
Full tuition	13	3.2	5	2.0	18	2.7
More than full tuition	1	0.2	0	0.0	1	0.1
Median Grant Amount	$1,634		$1,313			

Refunds

Refunds of Admissions or Seat Deposit prior to commencement of classes? Yes

100% refund from 01/01/96 to 04/15/96
67% refund from 04/16/96 to 05/15/96
33% refund from 05/16/96 to 07/01/96

Refunds of Pre-paid tuition prior to commencement of classes? No

If yes, fully refundable before the start of classes? No

Joint Degrees Offered

MBA/JD, MPA/JD

Advanced Degrees Offered

No Advanced Degrees

Bar Passage Rate

Jurisdiction	GA
# from school taking bar for the first time	130
School's pass rate for all first-time takers	94%
State's pass rate for all first-time takers	81%
State's pass rate for all first-time takers from ABA approved law schools	84%

GEORGIA, UNIVERSITY OF

Herty Drive
Athens, GA 30602
(706)542-7140
http://www.lawsch.uga.edu

ABA Approved Since 1930

The Basics

Type of School: PUBLIC
Application deadline*: 3/1
Application fee: $30
Financial Aid deadline*: 3/1
Student faculty ratio: 18.8 to 1

First year can start other than Fall: No
Student housing: No
--exclusively for law students: No
Term: Semester

*pr=preferred

Faculty

	Men #	Men %	Women #	Women %	Minorities #	Minorities %	Total
Full-time	22	79	6	21	3	11	28
Other full-time	1	20	4	80	0	0	5
Deans, librarians, & others who teach	5	83	1	17	0	0	6
Part-time	6	67	3	33	0	0	9
Total	34	71	14	29	3	6	48
Deans, librarians, & others who teach < 1/2	0	0	2	100	0	0	2

Library

# of volumes & volume equivalents	458,249	# of professional staff	9
# of titles	121,196	Hours per week with professional staff	76
# of active serial subscriptions	6,664	Hours per week without professional staff	39
Study seating capacity inside the library	480	# of student computer work stations for entire law school	68
Square feet of law library	45,381	# of additional networked connections	0
Square feet of law school (excl. Library)	75,197		

Curriculum

	Full time	Part time
Typical first-year section size	75	0
Is there typically a "small section" of the first year class, other than Legal Writing, taught by full-time faculty?	No	No
If yes, typical size offered last year	N/A	N/A
# of classroom course titles beyond 1st year curriculum	109	0
# of upper division courses, excluding seminars, with an enrollment:		
Under 25	64	0
25 - 49	42	0
50 - 74	11	0
75 - 99	12	0
100 +	5	0
# of seminars	24	0
# of seminar positions available	351	
# of seminar positions filled	339	0
# of positions available in simulation courses	300	
# of simulation positions filled	253	0
# of positions available in faculty supervised clinical courses	274	
# of fac. sup. clin. positions filled	222	0
# involved in field placements	52	0
# involved in law journals	155	0
# in moot court or trial competitions	218	0
# of credit hours required to graduate	88	

Enrollment & Attrition

	Full-Time							Part-Time							Attrition			
	Men		Women		Minorities		Total	Men		Women		Minorities		Total	Academic	Other	Total	
	#	%	#	%	#	%	#	#	%	#	%	#	%	#	#	#	#	%
1st Year	124	55.1	101	44.9	24	10.7	225	0	0.0	0	0.0	0	0.0	0	3	9	12	5.7
2nd Year	112	55.4	90	44.6	30	14.9	202	0	0.0	0	0.0	0	0.0	0	0	0	0	0.0
3rd Year	124	60.8	80	39.2	30	14.7	204	0	0.0	0	0.0	0	0.0	0	0	4	4	1.7
4th Year								0	0.0	0	0.0	0	0.0	0	0	0	0	0.0
Total	360	57.1	271	42.9	84	13.3	631	0	0.0	0	0.0	0	0.0	0	3	13	16	2.5
JD Degrees Awarded	130	58.0	94	42.0	28	12.5	224	0	0.0	0	0.0	0	0.0	0				

GPA & LSAT Scores

	Full Time	Part Time	Total
# of apps	2,314	0	2,314
# admits	591	0	591
# of matrics	236	0	236
75% GPA	3.65	0.00	
25% GPA	3.23	0.00	
75% LSAT	165	0	
25% LSAT	158	0	

Tuition/Living Expenses

	Resident	Non-resident
Full-Time	$3,315	$10,017
Part-Time	$0	$0

Estimated living expenses for Singles		
Living on campus	Living off campus	Living at home
$6,679	$8,984	$5,124

Career Placement

	Total	%
Employment status known	179	92.8
Employment status unknown	14	7.3
Employed	172	96.1
Pursuing graduate degrees	3	1.7
Unemployed seeking employment	3	1.7
Unemployed not seeking employment	1	0.6
Type of Employment		
# employed in law firms	115	66.9
# employed in business & industry	10	5.8
# employed in government	23	13.4
# employed in public interest	3	1.7
# employed as judicial clerks	18	10.5
# employed in academia	3	1.7
Geographic Location		
# employed in state	137	79.7
# employed in foreign countries	3	1.7
# of states where employed	17	

Financial Aid

	Full-time		Part-time		Total	
	#	%	#	%	#	%
Total # receiving grants	154	24.4	0	0.0	154	24.4
Less than 1/2 tuition	80	12.7	0	0.0	80	12.7
Half to full tuition	42	6.7	0	0.0	42	6.7
Full tuition	13	2.1	0	0.0	13	2.1
More than full tuition	19	3.0	0	0.0	19	3.0
Median Grant Amount	$2,500		$0			

Refunds

Refunds of Admissions or Seat Deposit prior to commencement of classes? No

Refunds of Pre-paid tuition prior to commencement of classes? No

If yes, fully refundable before the start of classes? No

Joint Degrees Offered

J.D./MBA, JD/M.HistPre

Advanced Degrees Offered

LL.M. General

Bar Passage Rate

Jurisdiction	GA
# from school taking bar for the first time	190
School's pass rate for all first-time takers	93%
State's pass rate for all first-time takers	81%
State's pass rate for all first-time takers from ABA approved law schools	84%

GOLDEN GATE UNIVERSITY

536 Mission Street
San Francisco, CA 94105-2968
(415)442-6600
http://www.ggu.edu/law/

ABA Approved Since 1956

The Basics

Type of School: **PRIVATE**
Application deadline*: **4/15**
Application fee: **$40**
Financial Aid deadline*: **3/1**
Student faculty ratio: **15.8 to 1**
First year can start other than Fall: **Yes**
Student housing: **No**
--exclusively for law students: **No**
Term: **Semester**

*pr=preferred

Faculty

	Men #	Men %	Women #	Women %	Minorities #	Minorities %	Total
Full-time	21	64	12	36	6	18	33
Other full-time	0	0	0	0	0	0	0
Deans, librarians, & others who teach	1	100	0	0	1	100	1
Part-time	37	60	25	40	8	13	62
Total	59	61	37	39	15	16	96
Deans, librarians, & others who teach < 1/2	3	75	1	25	0	0	4

Library

# of volumes & volume equivalents	226,159	# of professional staff	6
# of titles	29,268	Hours per week with professional staff	55
# of active serial subscriptions	3,244	Hours per week without professional staff	36
Study seating capacity inside the library	350	# of student computer work stations for entire law school	54
Square feet of law library	27,296	# of additional networked connections	14
Square feet of law school (excl. Library)	33,174		

Curriculum

	Full time	Part time
Typical first-year section size	58	39
Is there typically a "small section" of the first year class, other than Legal Writing, taught by full-time faculty?	Yes	No
If yes, typical size offered last year	26	N/A
# of classroom course titles beyond 1st year curriculum	95	38
# of upper division courses, excluding seminars, with an enrollment:		
Under 25	74	28
25 - 49	31	13
50 - 74	10	2
75 - 99	3	4
100 +	0	0
# of seminars	29	3
# of seminar positions available	527	
# of seminar positions filled	347	36
# of positions available in simulation courses	345	
# of simulation positions filled	247	21
# of positions available in faculty supervised clinical courses	260	
# of fac. sup. clin. positions filled	173	5
# involved in field placements	179	8
# involved in law journals	36	19
# in moot court or trial competitions	13	0
# of credit hours required to graduate	88	

Enrollment & Attrition

	Full-Time Men #	Men %	Women #	Women %	Minorities #	Minorities %	Total #	Part-Time Men #	Men %	Women #	Women %	Minorities #	Minorities %	Total #	Attrition Academic #	Other #	Total #	%
1st Year	82	42.9	109	57.1	54	28.3	191	47	55.3	38	44.7	12	14.1	85	48	33	81	29
2nd Year	44	38.6	70	61.4	30	26.3	114	30	53.6	26	46.4	11	19.6	56	5	4	9	4.5
3rd Year	69	46.6	79	53.4	26	17.6	148	36	48.6	38	51.4	12	16.2	74	0	0	0	0.0
4th Year								24	53.3	21	46.7	8	17.8	45	0	0	0	0.0
Total	195	43.0	258	57.0	110	24.3	453	137	52.7	123	47.3	43	16.5	260	53	37	90	13
JD Degrees Awarded	69	46.0	81	54.0	47	31.3	150	17	65.4	9	34.6	2	7.7	26				

GPA & LSAT Scores

	Full Time	Part Time	Total
# of apps	2,065	274	2,339
# admits	1,153	148	1,301
# of matrics	187	72	259
75% GPA	3.39	3.38	
25% GPA	2.76	2.72	
75% LSAT	155	155	
25% LSAT	149	150	

Tuition/Living Expenses

	Resident	Non-resident
Full-Time	$17,466	$17,466
Part-Time	$12,570	$12,570

Estimated living expenses for Singles		
Living on campus	Living off campus	Living at home
N/A	$11,030	$11,030

Career Placement

	Total	%
Employment status known	91	52.6
Employment status unknown	82	47.4
Employed	69	75.8
Pursuing graduate degrees	3	3.3
Unemployed seeking employment	15	16.5
Unemployed not seeking employment	4	4.4
Type of Employment		
# employed in law firms	35	50.7
# employed in business & industry	16	23.2
# employed in government	9	13.0
# employed in public interest	6	8.7
# employed as judicial clerks	1	1.5
# employed in academia	2	2.9
Geographic Location		
# employed in state	55	79.7
# employed in foreign countries	0	0.0
# of states where employed	10	

Financial Aid

	Full-time		Part-time		Total	
	#	%	#	%	#	%
Total # receiving grants	273	60.3	56	21.5	329	46.1
Less than 1/2 tuition	150	33.1	37	14.2	187	26.2
Half to full tuition	89	19.7	9	3.5	98	13.7
Full tuition	34	7.5	10	3.9	44	6.2
More than full tuition	0	0.0	0	0.0	0	0.0
Median Grant Amount	$2,100		$1,000			

Refunds

Refunds of Admissions or Seat Deposit prior to commencement of classes? No

Refunds of Pre-paid tuition prior to commencement of classes? No

If yes, fully refundable before the start of classes? No

Joint Degrees Offered

JD/MBAs:, Finance, Accounting, Health Servs, Hum Resource, Intl Mgmt, JD/MAs:, Intl Relatns, JD/MPAs:, Public Admin, Intl Pub Svc, Health Servs

Advanced Degrees Offered

LL.M. Taxation
LL.M. International Legal Studies

Bar Passage Rate

Jurisdiction	CA
# from school taking bar for the first time	115
School's pass rate for all first-time takers	77%
State's pass rate for all first-time takers	73%
State's pass rate for all first-time takers from ABA approved law schools	83%

GONZAGA UNIVERSITY

P.O. Box 3528
Spokane, WA 99220
(509)328-4220
http://www.law.gonzaga.edu

ABA Approved Since 1951

The Basics

Type of School: **PRIVATE**
Application deadline*: **3/15**
Application fee: **$40**
Financial Aid deadline*: **5/1**
Student faculty ratio: **20.0 to 1**
First year can start other than Fall: **No**
Student housing: **No**
--exclusively for law students: **No**
Term: **Semester**

*pr=preferred

Faculty

	Men		Women		Minorities		Total
	#	%	#	%	#	%	
Full-time	16	73	6	27	1	5	22
Other full-time	2	100	0	0	0	0	2
Deans, librarians, & others who teach	0	0	0	0	0	0	0
Part-time	11	73	4	27	0	0	15
Total	29	74	10	26	1	3	39
Deans, librarians, & others who teach < 1/2	2	100	0	0	0	0	2

Library

# of volumes & volume equivalents	214,437	# of professional staff	5
# of titles	30,572	Hours per week with professional staff	52
# of active serial subscriptions	2,879	Hours per week without professional staff	56
Study seating capacity inside the library	468	# of student computer work stations for entire law school	74
Square feet of law library	23,806	# of additional networked connections	0
Square feet of law school (excl. Library)	35,305		

Curriculum

	Full time	Part time
Typical first-year section size	80	0
Is there typically a "small section" of the first year class, other than Legal Writing, taught by full-time faculty?	Yes	No
If yes, typical size offered last year	50	N/A
# of classroom course titles beyond 1st year curriculum	82	0
# of upper division courses, excluding seminars, with an enrollment:		
Under 25	41	0
25 - 49	20	0
50 - 74	14	0
75 - 99	4	0
100 +	3	0
# of seminars	4	0
# of seminar positions available	57	
# of seminar positions filled	31	0
# of positions available in simulation courses	110	
# of simulation positions filled	79	0
# of positions available in faculty supervised clinical courses	37	
# of fac. sup. clin. positions filled	22	0
# involved in field placements	61	0
# involved in law journals	25	0
# in moot court or trial competitions	25	0
# of credit hours required to graduate	90	

Enrollment & Attrition

	Full-Time							Part-Time							Attrition			
	Men		Women		Minorities		Total	Men		Women		Minorities		Total	Academic	Other	Total	
	#	%	#	%	#	%	#	#	%	#	%	#	%	#	#	#	#	%
1st Year	103	61.7	64	38.3	22	13.2	167	1	50.0	1	50.0	0	0.0	2	12	34	46	19
2nd Year	122	65.2	65	34.8	32	17.1	187	0	0.0	0	0.0	0	0.0	0	0	1	1	0.6
3rd Year	104	63.8	59	36.2	20	12.3	163	2	50.0	2	50.0	0	0.0	4	0	4	4	2.4
4th Year								7	58.3	5	41.7	2	16.7	12	0	0	0	0.0
Total	329	63.6	188	36.4	74	14.3	517	10	55.6	8	44.4	2	11.1	18	12	39	51	8.7
JD Degrees Awarded	101	61.2	64	38.8	10	6.1	165	1	50.0	1	50.0	1	50.0	2				

GPA & LSAT Scores

	Full Time	Part Time	Total
# of apps	1,198	0	1,198
# admits	805	0	805
# of matrics	169	0	169
75% GPA	3.28	0.00	
25% GPA	2.70	0.00	
75% LSAT	154	0	
25% LSAT	148	0	

Tuition/Living Expenses

	Resident	Non-resident
Full-Time	$16,570	$16,570
Part-Time	$9,970	$9,970

Estimated living expenses for Singles		
Living on campus	Living off campus	Living at home
$10,900	$10,900	$5,900

Career Placement

	Total	%
Employment status known	156	95.7
Employment status unknown	7	4.3
Employed	127	81.4
Pursuing graduate degrees	14	9.0
Unemployed seeking employment	9	5.8
Unemployed not seeking employment	6	3.9
Type of Employment		
# employed in law firms	69	54.3
# employed in business & industry	19	15.0
# employed in government	21	16.5
# employed in public interest	2	1.6
# employed as judicial clerks	16	12.6
# employed in academia	0	0.0
Geographic Location		
# employed in state	61	48.0
# employed in foreign countries	1	0.8
# of states where employed	19	

Financial Aid

	Full-time		Part-time		Total	
	#	%	#	%	#	%
Total # receiving grants	94	18.2	0	0.0	94	17.6
Less than 1/2 tuition	54	10.4	0	0.0	54	10.1
Half to full tuition	5	1.0	0	0.0	5	0.9
Full tuition	31	6.0	0	0.0	31	5.8
More than full tuition	4	0.8	0	0.0	4	0.7
Median Grant Amount	$0		$0			

Refunds

Refunds of Admissions or Seat Deposit prior to commencement of classes? No

100% refund from 01/01/96 to 04/01/96
50% refund from 04/02/96 to 05/01/96
30% refund from 05/02/96 to 06/01/96

Refunds of Pre-paid tuition prior to commencement of classes? Yes

If yes, fully refundable before the start of classes? Yes

Joint Degrees Offered

MBA/JD, MACC/JD

Advanced Degrees Offered

No Advanced Degrees

Bar Passage Rate

Jurisdiction	WA
# from school taking bar for the first time	75
School's pass rate for all first-time takers	83%
State's pass rate for all first-time takers	83%
State's pass rate for all first-time takers from ABA approved law schools	

HAMLINE UNIVERSITY

1536 Hewitt Avenue
St. Paul, MN 55104
(612)641-2968
http://www.hamline.edu

ABA Approved Since 1975

The Basics

Type of School: **PRIVATE**
Application deadline*: **5/15**
Application fee: **$30**
Financial Aid deadline*:
Student faculty ratio: **18.4 to 1**
First year can start other than Fall: **No**
Student housing: **Yes**
--exclusively for law students: **No**
Term: **Semester**

*pr=preferred

Faculty

	Men #	Men %	Women #	Women %	Minorities #	Minorities %	Total
Full-time	16	62	10	38	2	8	26
Other full-time	0	0	4	100	1	25	4
Deans, librarians, & others who teach	1	100	0	0	0	0	1
Part-time	22	63	13	37	2	6	35
Total	39	59	27	41	5	8	66
Deans, librarians, & others who teach < 1/2	1	50	1	50	0	0	2

Library

# of volumes & volume equivalents	229,218	# of professional staff	5
# of titles	249,841	Hours per week with professional staff	60
# of active serial subscriptions	2,678	Hours per week without professional staff	47
Study seating capacity inside the library	374	# of student computer work stations for entire law school	23
Square feet of law library	28,000	# of additional networked connections	0
Square feet of law school (excl. Library)	74,669		

Curriculum

	Full time	Part time
Typical first-year section size	73	0
Is there typically a "small section" of the first year class, other than Legal Writing, taught by full-time faculty?	No	No
If yes, typical size offered last year	N/A	N/A
# of classroom course titles beyond 1st year curriculum	164	0
# of upper division courses, excluding seminars, with an enrollment:		
Under 25	117	0
25 - 49	26	0
50 - 74	10	0
75 - 99	11	0
100 +	0	0
# of seminars	13	0
# of seminar positions available	204	
# of seminar positions filled	171	0
# of positions available in simulation courses	1,226	
# of simulation positions filled	979	0
# of positions available in faculty supervised clinical courses	74	
# of fac. sup. clin. positions filled	68	0
# involved in field placements	70	0
# involved in law journals	119	0
# in moot court or trial competitions	47	0
# of credit hours required to graduate	88	

Enrollment & Attrition

	Full-Time Men #	Men %	Women #	Women %	Minorities #	Minorities %	Total #	Part-Time Men #	Men %	Women #	Women %	Minorities #	Minorities %	Total #	Attrition Academic #	Other #	Total #	Total %
1st Year	107	57.5	79	42.5	15	8.1	186	0	0.0	0	0.0	0	0.0	0	2	23	25	11
2nd Year	103	49.8	104	50.2	29	14.0	207	0	0.0	0	0.0	0	0.0	0	0	4	4	2.0
3rd Year	76	42.2	104	57.8	16	8.9	180	0	0.0	0	0.0	0	0.0	0	0	0	0	0.0
4th Year								0	0.0	0	0.0	0	0.0	0	0	0	0	0.0
Total	286	49.9	287	50.1	60	10.5	573	0	0.0	0	0.0	0	0.0	0	2	27	29	4.9
JD Degrees Awarded	97	55.7	77	44.3	11	6.3	174	0	0.0	0	0.0	0	0.0	0				

GPA & LSAT Scores

	Full Time	Part Time	Total
# of apps	1,162	0	1,162
# admits	647	0	647
# of matrics	192	0	192
75% GPA	3.37	0.00	
25% GPA	2.86	0.00	
75% LSAT	157	0	
25% LSAT	148	0	

Tuition/Living Expenses

	Resident	Non-resident
Full-Time	$14,513	$14,513
Part-Time	$0	$0

Estimated living expenses for Singles		
Living on campus	Living off campus	Living at home
$7,260	$9,672	N/A

Career Placement

	Total	%
Employment status known	160	83.3
Employment status unknown	32	16.7
Employed	132	82.5
Pursuing graduate degrees	5	3.1
Unemployed seeking employment	20	12.5
Unemployed not seeking employment	3	1.9
Type of Employment		
# employed in law firms	50	37.9
# employed in business & industry	32	24.3
# employed in government	8	6.1
# employed in public interest	10	7.6
# employed as judicial clerks	31	23.5
# employed in academia	1	0.8
Geographic Location		
# employed in state	103	78.0
# employed in foreign countries	1	0.8
# of states where employed	15	

Financial Aid

	Full-time		Part-time		Total	
	#	%	#	%	#	%
Total # receiving grants	130	22.7	0	0.0	130	22.7
Less than 1/2 tuition	102	17.8	0	0.0	102	17.8
Half to full tuition	14	2.4	0	0.0	14	2.4
Full tuition	14	2.4	0	0.0	14	2.4
More than full tuition	0	0.0	0	0.0	0	0.0
Median Grant Amount	$0		$0			

Refunds

Refunds of Admissions or Seat Deposit prior to commencement of classes? No

Refunds of Pre-paid tuition prior to commencement of classes? No

If yes, fully refundable before the start of classes? No

Joint Degrees Offered

JD/MAPA

Advanced Degrees Offered

LL.M. Foreign

Bar Passage Rate

Jurisdiction	MN	WI
# from school taking bar for the first time	127	7
School's pass rate for all first-time takers	83%	100%
State's pass rate for all first-time takers	90%	83%
State's pass rate for all first-time takers from ABA approved law schools	90%	83%

HARVARD UNIVERSITY

Cambridge, MA 02138
(617)495-1000
http://www.law.harvard.edu

ABA Approved Since 1923

The Basics

Type of School: **PRIVATE**
Application deadline*: **2/1**
Application fee: **$65**
Financial Aid deadline*: **3/1**
Student faculty ratio: **21.1 to 1**

First year can start other than Fall: **No**
Student housing: **Yes**
--exclusively for law students: **Yes**
Term: **Semester**

*pr=preferred

Faculty

	Men		Women		Minorities		Total
	#	%	#	%	#	%	
Full-time	57	88	8	12	8	12	65
Other full-time	5	24	16	76	12	57	21
Deans, librarians, & others who teach	0	0	1	100	1	100	1
Part-time	10	83	2	17	1	8	12
Total	72	73	27	27	22	22	99
Deans, librarians, & others who teach < 1/2	4	57	3	43	0	0	7

Library

# of volumes & volume equivalents	1,883,541	# of professional staff	30
# of titles	730,182	Hours per week with professional staff	69
# of active serial subscriptions	14,484	Hours per week without professional staff	30
Study seating capacity inside the library	901	# of student computer work stations for entire law school	77
Square feet of law library	92,907	# of additional networked connections	729
Square feet of law school (excl. Library)	261,698		

Curriculum

	Full time	Part time
Typical first-year section size	138	0
Is there typically a "small section" of the first year class, other than Legal Writing, taught by full-time faculty?	Yes	No
If yes, typical size offered last year	45	N/A
# of classroom course titles beyond 1st year curriculum	216	0
# of upper division courses, excluding seminars, with an enrollment:		
Under 25	45	0
25 - 49	38	0
50 - 74	24	0
75 - 99	10	0
100 +	49	0
# of seminars	57	0
# of seminar positions available	1,140	
# of seminar positions filled	921	0
# of positions available in simulation courses	405	
# of simulation positions filled	405	0
# of positions available in faculty supervised clinical courses	524	
# of fac. sup. clin. positions filled	524	0
# involved in field placements	524	0
# involved in law journals	962	0
# in moot court or trial competitions	80	0
# of credit hours required to graduate	80	

Enrollment & Attrition

	Full-Time							Part-Time							Attrition			
	Men		Women		Minorities		Total	Men		Women		Minorities		Total	Academic	Other	Total	
	#	%	#	%	#	%	#	#	%	#	%	#	%	#	#	#	#	%
1st Year	333	60.0	222	40.0	173	31.2	555	0	0.0	0	0.0	0	0.0	0	0	1	1	0.2
2nd Year	318	58.2	228	41.8	133	24.4	546	0	0.0	0	0.0	0	0.0	0	0	7	7	1.3
3rd Year	325	59.6	220	40.4	159	29.2	545	0	0.0	0	0.0	0	0.0	0	0	1	1	0.2
4th Year								0	0.0	0	0.0	0	0.0	0	0	0	0	0.0
Total	976	59.3	670	40.7	465	28.3	1,646	0	0.0	0	0.0	0	0.0	0	0	9	9	0.5
JD Degrees Awarded	334	60.4	219	39.6	137	24.8	553	0	0.0	0	0.0	0	0.0	0				

GPA & LSAT Scores

	Full Time	Part Time	Total
# of apps	6,493	0	6,493
# admits	841	0	841
# of matrics	555	0	555
75% GPA	3.93	0.00	
25% GPA	3.70	0.00	
75% LSAT	173	0	
25% LSAT	166	0	

Tuition/Living Expenses

	Resident	Non-resident
Full-Time	$22,354	$22,354
Part-Time	$0	$0

Estimated living expenses for Singles		
Living on campus	Living off campus	Living at home
$12,300	$12,300	N/A

Career Placement

	Total	%
Employment status known	540	98.5
Employment status unknown	8	1.5
Employed	523	96.9
Pursuing graduate degrees	4	0.7
Unemployed seeking employment	12	2.2
Unemployed not seeking employment	1	0.2
Type of Employment		
# employed in law firms	313	59.9
# employed in business & industry	39	7.5
# employed in government	12	2.3
# employed in public interest	15	2.9
# employed as judicial clerks	139	26.6
# employed in academia	5	1.0
Geographic Location		
# employed in state	66	12.6
# employed in foreign countries	12	2.3
# of states where employed	35	

Financial Aid

	Full-time		Part-time		Total	
	#	%	#	%	#	%
Total # receiving grants	505	30.7	0	0.0	505	30.7
Less than 1/2 tuition	300	18.2	0	0.0	300	18.2
Half to full tuition	189	11.5	0	0.0	189	11.5
Full tuition	16	1.0	0	0.0	16	1.0
More than full tuition	0	0.0	0	0.0	0	0.0
Median Grant Amount	$7,810		$0			

Refunds

Refunds of Admissions or Seat Deposit prior to commencement of classes? Yes

50% refund from 01/01/96 to 06/15/96
20% refund from 06/16/96 to 07/15/96
0% refund from 07/15/96 to / /

Refunds of Pre-paid tuition prior to commencement of classes? Yes

If yes, fully refundable before the start of classes? No

Joint Degrees Offered

JD/MBA, JD/MPP, JD/MALD, JD/MPA, JD/M.Div., JD/Ed.M.

Advanced Degrees Offered

LL.M.
S.J.D.

Bar Passage Rate

Jurisdiction	NY	MA	CA
# from school taking bar for the first time	224	77	79
School's pass rate for all first-time takers	96%	94%	95%
State's pass rate for all first-time takers	78%	83%	73%
State's pass rate for all first-time takers from ABA approved law schools		85%	82%

HAWAII, UNIVERSITY OF

2515 Dole Street
Honolulu, HI 96822
(808)956-8636
gopher://gopher.hawaii.edu/11/student/ca

ABA Approved Since 1974

The Basics

Type of School: **PUBLIC**
Application deadline*: **3/1**
Application fee: **$30**
Financial Aid deadline*: **3/1**
Student faculty ratio: **12.7 to 1**

First year can start other than Fall: **No**
Student housing: **Yes**
--exclusively for law students: **No**
Term: **Semester**

*pr=preferred

Faculty

	Men #	Men %	Women #	Women %	Minorities #	Minorities %	Total
Full-time	10	67	5	33	3	20	15
Other full-time	0	0	1	100	0	0	1
Deans, librarians, & others who teach	0	0	1	100	0	0	1
Part-time	11	85	2	15	4	31	13
Total	21	70	9	30	7	23	30
Deans, librarians, & others who teach < 1/2	1	50	1	50	1	50	2

Library

# of volumes & volume equivalents	240,807	# of professional staff	5
# of titles	28,810	Hours per week with professional staff	66
# of active serial subscriptions	2,665	Hours per week without professional staff	4
Study seating capacity inside the library	392	# of student computer work stations for entire law school	11
Square feet of law library	32,126	# of additional networked connections	0
Square feet of law school (excl. Library)	36,233		

Curriculum

	Full time	Part time
Typical first-year section size	74	0
Is there typically a "small section" of the first year class, other than Legal Writing, taught by full-time faculty?	Yes	No
If yes, typical size offered last year	18	N/A
# of classroom course titles beyond 1st year curriculum	56	0
# of upper division courses, excluding seminars, with an enrollment:		
Under 25	40	0
25 - 49	7	0
50 - 74	7	0
75 - 99	1	0
100 +	1	0
# of seminars	10	0
# of seminar positions available	132	
# of seminar positions filled	126	0
# of positions available in simulation courses	92	
# of simulation positions filled	86	0
# of positions available in faculty supervised clinical courses	63	
# of fac. sup. clin. positions filled	59	0
# involved in field placements	96	0
# involved in law journals	30	0
# in moot court or trial competitions	25	0
# of credit hours required to graduate	89	

Enrollment & Attrition

	Full-Time Men #	Men %	Women #	Women %	Minorities #	Minorities %	Total #	Part-Time Men #	Men %	Women #	Women %	Minorities #	Minorities %	Total #	Attrition Academic #	Other #	Total #	Total %
1st Year	30	44.1	38	55.9	42	61.8	68	0	0.0	0	0.0	0	0.0	0	2	4	6	8.1
2nd Year	39	50.6	38	49.4	52	67.5	77	0	0.0	0	0.0	0	0.0	0	0	1	1	1.3
3rd Year	39	47.0	44	53.0	56	67.5	83	0	0.0	0	0.0	0	0.0	0	0	0	0	0.0
4th Year								0	0.0	0	0.0	0	0.0	0	0	0	0	0.0
Total	108	47.4	120	52.6	150	65.8	228	0	0.0	0	0.0	0	0.0	0	2	5	7	3.0
JD Degrees Awarded	41	56.2	32	43.8	47	64.4	73	0	0.0	0	0.0	0	0.0	0				

GPA & LSAT Scores

	Full Time	Part Time	Total
# of apps	668	0	668
# admits	178	0	178
# of matrics	68	0	68
75% GPA	3.61	0.00	
25% GPA	3.11	0.00	
75% LSAT	161	0	
25% LSAT	154	0	

Tuition/Living Expenses

	Resident	Non-resident
Full-Time	$4,907	$12,981
Part-Time	$0	$0

Estimated living expenses for Singles		
Living on campus	Living off campus	Living at home
$7,000	$9,600	$4,600

Career Placement

	Total	%
Employment status known	65	97.0
Employment status unknown	2	3.0
Employed	59	90.8
Pursuing graduate degrees	1	1.5
Unemployed seeking employment	5	7.7
Unemployed not seeking employment	0	0.0
Type of Employment		
# employed in law firms	27	45.8
# employed in business & industry	8	13.6
# employed in government	4	6.8
# employed in public interest	3	5.1
# employed as judicial clerks	15	25.4
# employed in academia	2	3.4
Geographic Location		
# employed in state	51	86.4
# employed in foreign countries	3	5.1
# of states where employed	3	

Financial Aid

	Full-time		Part-time		Total	
	#	%	#	%	#	%
Total # receiving grants	111	48.7	0	0.0	111	48.7
Less than 1/2 tuition	39	17.1	0	0.0	39	17.1
Half to full tuition	31	13.6	0	0.0	31	13.6
Full tuition	20	8.8	0	0.0	20	8.8
More than full tuition	21	9.2	0	0.0	21	9.2
Median Grant Amount	$4,800		$0			

Refunds

Refunds of Admissions or Seat Deposit prior to commencement of classes? No

Refunds of Pre-paid tuition prior to commencement of classes? No

If yes, fully refundable before the start of classes? No

Joint Degrees Offered

No Joint Degrees

Advanced Degrees Offered

No Advanced Degrees

Bar Passage Rate

Jurisdiction	HI
# from school taking bar for the first time	59
School's pass rate for all first-time takers	86%
State's pass rate for all first-time takers	
State's pass rate for all first-time takers from ABA approved law schools	

HOFSTRA UNIVERSITY

121 Hofstra University
Hempstead, NY 11550-1090
(516)463-5858
http://www.hofstra.edu

ABA Approved Since 1971

The Basics

Type of School: **PRIVATE**
Application deadline*: **4/15**
Application fee: **$60**
Financial Aid deadline*: **5/15**
Student faculty ratio: **23.2 to 1**

First year can start other than Fall: **No**
Student housing: **Yes**
--exclusively for law students: **No**
Term: **Semester**

*pr=preferred

Faculty

	Men #	Men %	Women #	Women %	Minorities #	Minorities %	Total
Full-time	25	86	4	14	4	14	29
Other full-time	1	20	4	80	0	0	5
Deans, librarians, & others who teach	0	0	1	100	1	100	1
Part-time	12	86	2	14	0	0	14
Total	38	78	11	22	5	10	49
Deans, librarians, & others who teach < 1/2	1	33	2	67	0	0	3

Library

# of volumes & volume equivalents	456,946	# of professional staff	7
# of titles	114,309	Hours per week with professional staff	92
# of active serial subscriptions	6,110	Hours per week without professional staff	6
Study seating capacity inside the library	595	# of student computer work stations for entire law school	33
Square feet of law library	50,665	# of additional networked connections	0
Square feet of law school (excl. Library)	52,219		

Curriculum

	Full time	Part time
Typical first-year section size	114	0
Is there typically a "small section" of the first year class, other than Legal Writing, taught by full-time faculty?	Yes	No
If yes, typical size offered last year	28	N/A
# of classroom course titles beyond 1st year curriculum	107	0
# of upper division courses, excluding seminars, with an enrollment:		
Under 25	41	0
25 - 49	23	0
50 - 74	9	0
75 - 99	13	0
100 +	13	0
# of seminars	21	0
# of seminar positions available	427	
# of seminar positions filled	259	0
# of positions available in simulation courses	706	
# of simulation positions filled	653	0
# of positions available in faculty supervised clinical courses	87	
# of fac. sup. clin. positions filled	72	0
# involved in field placements	59	0
# involved in law journals	155	0
# in moot court or trial competitions	50	0
# of credit hours required to graduate	87	

Enrollment & Attrition

	Full-Time							Part-Time							Attrition			
	Men		Women		Minorities		Total	Men		Women		Minorities		Total	Academic	Other	Total	
	#	%	#	%	#	%	#	#	%	#	%	#	%	#	#	#	#	%
1st Year	140	55.1	114	44.9	45	17.7	254	0	0.0	0	0.0	0	0.0	0	0	2	2	0.7
2nd Year	155	56.8	118	43.2	49	17.9	273	0	0.0	0	0.0	0	0.0	0	2	16	18	6.3
3rd Year	160	56.9	121	43.1	43	15.3	281	0	0.0	0	0.0	0	0.0	0	1	2	3	1.1
4th Year								0	0.0	0	0.0	0	0.0	0	0	0	0	0.0
Total	455	56.3	353	43.7	137	17.0	808	0	0.0	0	0.0	0	0.0	0	3	20	23	2.7
JD Degrees Awarded	162	58.7	114	41.3	45	16.3	276	0	0.0	0	0.0	0	0.0	0				

GPA & LSAT Scores

	Full Time	Part Time	Total
# of apps	1,912	0	1,912
# admits	816	0	816
# of matrics	256	0	256
75% GPA	3.50	0.00	
25% GPA	2.97	0.00	
75% LSAT	158	0	
25% LSAT	150	0	

Tuition/Living Expenses

	Resident	Non-resident
Full-Time	$20,238	$20,238
Part-Time	$0	$0

Estimated living expenses for Singles		
Living on campus	Living off campus	Living at home
$13,552	$17,082	$7,812

Career Placement

	Total	%
Employment status known	232	87.9
Employment status unknown	32	12.1
Employed	205	88.4
Pursuing graduate degrees	4	1.7
Unemployed seeking employment	17	7.3
Unemployed not seeking employment	6	2.6
Type of Employment		
# employed in law firms	133	64.9
# employed in business & industry	30	14.6
# employed in government	23	11.2
# employed in public interest	4	2.0
# employed as judicial clerks	13	6.3
# employed in academia	2	1.0
Geographic Location		
# employed in state	156	76.1
# employed in foreign countries	2	1.0
# of states where employed	15	

Financial Aid

	Full-time		Part-time		Total	
	#	%	#	%	#	%
Total # receiving grants	407	50.4	0	0.0	407	50.4
Less than 1/2 tuition	378	46.8	0	0.0	378	46.8
Half to full tuition	15	1.9	0	0.0	15	1.9
Full tuition	10	1.2	0	0.0	10	1.2
More than full tuition	4	0.5	0	0.0	4	0.5
Median Grant Amount	$2,000		$0			

Refunds

Refunds of Admissions or Seat Deposit prior to commencement of classes? Yes

100% refund to 04/01/96

Refunds of Pre-paid tuition prior to commencement of classes? Yes

If yes, fully refundable before the start of classes? Yes

Joint Degrees Offered

JD/MBA

Advanced Degrees Offered

No Advanced Degrees

Bar Passage Rate

Jurisdiction	NY
# from school taking bar for the first time	214
School's pass rate for all first-time takers	79%
State's pass rate for all first-time takers	78%
State's pass rate for all first-time takers from ABA approved law schools	

HOUSTON, UNIVERSITY OF

4800 Calhoun
Entrance 19
Houston, TX 77004
(713)743-2100
http://www.law.uh.edu

ABA Approved Since 1950

The Basics

Type of School: **PUBLIC**
Application deadline*: **2/1**
Application fee: **$50**
Financial Aid deadline*: **4/1**
Student faculty ratio: **19.8 to 1**
First year can start other than Fall: **Yes**
Student housing: **No**
--exclusively for law students: **No**
Term: **Semester**

*pr=preferred

Faculty

	Men #	Men %	Women #	Women %	Minorities #	Minorities %	Total
Full-time	32	82	7	18	3	8	39
Other full-time	0	0	0	0	0	0	0
Deans, librarians, & others who teach	6	86	1	14	1	14	7
Part-time	42	82	9	18	1	2	51
Total	80	82	17	18	5	5	97
Deans, librarians, & others who teach < 1/2	2	100	0	0	0	0	2

Library

# of volumes & volume equivalents	428,445	# of professional staff	10
# of titles	81,587	Hours per week with professional staff	62
# of active serial subscriptions	2,801	Hours per week without professional staff	43
Study seating capacity inside the library	936	# of student computer work stations for entire law school	100
Square feet of law library	87,528	# of additional networked connections	450
Square feet of law school (excl. Library)	75,585		

Curriculum

	Full time	Part time
Typical first-year section size	80	55
Is there typically a "small section" of the first year class, other than Legal Writing, taught by full-time faculty?	No	No
If yes, typical size offered last year	N/A	N/A
# of classroom course titles beyond 1st year curriculum	203	0
# of upper division courses, excluding seminars, with an enrollment:		
Under 25	102	0
25 - 49	52	0
50 - 74	23	0
75 - 99	17	0
100 +	2	0
# of seminars	30	0
# of seminar positions available	500	
# of seminar positions filled	458	0
# of positions available in simulation courses	650	
# of simulation positions filled	600	0
# of positions available in faculty supervised clinical courses	75	
# of fac. sup. clin. positions filled	67	0
# involved in field placements	161	0
# involved in law journals	148	0
# in moot court or trial competitions	431	0
# of credit hours required to graduate	88	

Enrollment & Attrition

	Full-Time Men #	Men %	Women #	Women %	Minorities #	Minorities %	Total #	Part-Time Men #	Men %	Women #	Women %	Minorities #	Minorities %	Total #	Attrition Academic #	Other #	Total #	%
1st Year	149	60.6	97	39.4	53	21.5	246	28	58.3	20	41.7	10	20.8	48	0	15	15	5.2
2nd Year	135	57.4	100	42.6	46	19.6	235	23	53.5	20	46.5	12	27.9	43	3	22	25	6.7
3rd Year	193	61.9	119	38.1	60	19.2	312	39	59.1	27	40.9	12	18.2	66	1	9	10	3.3
4th Year								36	75.0	12	25.0	7	14.6	48	0	3	3	6.0
Total	477	60.2	316	39.8	159	20.1	793	126	61.5	79	38.5	41	20.0	205	4	49	53	5.2
JD Degrees Awarded	131	53.0	116	47.0	50	20.2	247	32	72.7	12	27.3	10	22.7	44				

GPA & LSAT Scores

	Full Time	Part Time	Total
# of apps	2,290	310	2,600
# admits	767	86	853
# of matrics	257	52	309
75% GPA	3.53	3.49	
25% GPA	3.04	2.98	
75% LSAT	163	161	
25% LSAT	156	154	

Tuition/Living Expenses

	Resident	Non-resident
Full-Time	$5,197	$9,397
Part-Time	$3,829	$6,829

Estimated living expenses for Singles		
Living on campus	Living off campus	Living at home
$7,510	$9,350	$6,000

Career Placement

	Total	%
Employment status known	297	91.7
Employment status unknown	27	8.3
Employed	256	86.2
Pursuing graduate degrees	6	2.0
Unemployed seeking employment	27	9.1
Unemployed not seeking employment	8	2.7
Type of Employment		
# employed in law firms	166	64.8
# employed in business & industry	39	15.2
# employed in government	23	9.0
# employed in public interest	3	1.2
# employed as judicial clerks	22	8.6
# employed in academia	3	1.2
Geographic Location		
# employed in state	232	90.6
# employed in foreign countries	3	1.2
# of states where employed	12	

Financial Aid

	Full-time		Part-time		Total	
	#	%	#	%	#	%
Total # receiving grants	201	25.4	0	0.0	201	20.1
Less than 1/2 tuition	158	19.9	0	0.0	158	15.8
Half to full tuition	44	5.6	0	0.0	44	4.4
Full tuition	0	0.0	0	0.0	0	0.0
More than full tuition	0	0.0	0	0.0	0	0.0
Median Grant Amount	$1,440		$0			

Refunds

Refunds of Admissions or Seat Deposit prior to commencement of classes? No

Refunds of Pre-paid tuition prior to commencement of classes? Yes

If yes, fully refundable before the start of classes? Yes

Joint Degrees Offered

JD/MBA, JD/MPH, JD/PHD, JD/MA-HIST

Advanced Degrees Offered

LL.M.	International Economic Law
LL.M.	Energy Environment and Natural Resources
LL.M.	Tax Law
LL.M.	Foreign Lawyer Program
LL.M.	Health Law
LL.M.	Intellectual Property Law

Bar Passage Rate

Jurisdiction	TX
# from school taking bar for the first time	212
School's pass rate for all first-time takers	86%
State's pass rate for all first-time takers	82%
State's pass rate for all first-time takers from ABA approved law schools	82%

HOWARD UNIVERSITY

2900 Van Ness Street
Washington, DC 20008
(202)806-8003
http://www.law.howard.edu

ABA Approved Since 1931

The Basics

Type of School: **PRIVATE**
Application deadline*: **4/30**
Application fee: **$60**
Financial Aid deadline*: **4/1**
Student faculty ratio: **15.4 to 1**

First year can start other than Fall: **No**
Student housing: **No**
--exclusively for law students: **No**
Term: **Semester**

*pr=preferred

Faculty

	Men #	Men %	Women #	Women %	Minorities #	Minorities %	Total
Full-time	16	70	7	30	19	83	23
Other full-time	0	0	0	0	0	0	0
Deans, librarians, & others who teach	0	0	0	0	0	0	0
Part-time	13	81	3	19	13	81	16
Total	29	74	10	26	32	82	39
Deans, librarians, & others who teach < 1/2	1	33	2	67	3	100	3

Library

# of volumes & volume equivalents	255,648	# of professional staff	8
# of titles	68,860	Hours per week with professional staff	66
# of active serial subscriptions	1,733	Hours per week without professional staff	35
Study seating capacity inside the library	173	# of student computer work stations for entire law school	60
Square feet of law library	29,110	# of additional networked connections	0
Square feet of law school (excl. Library)	125,610		

Curriculum

	Full time	Part time
Typical first-year section size	70	0
Is there typically a "small section" of the first year class, other than Legal Writing, taught by full-time faculty?	No	No
If yes, typical size offered last year	N/A	N/A
# of classroom course titles beyond 1st year curriculum	64	0
# of upper division courses, excluding seminars, with an enrollment:		
Under 25	36	0
25 - 49	12	0
50 - 74	12	0
75 - 99	3	0
100 +	1	0
# of seminars	30	0
# of seminar positions available	483	
# of seminar positions filled	389	0
# of positions available in simulation courses	120	
# of simulation positions filled	104	0
# of positions available in faculty supervised clinical courses	44	
# of fac. sup. clin. positions filled	44	0
# involved in field placements	23	0
# involved in law journals	28	0
# in moot court or trial competitions	43	0
# of credit hours required to graduate	88	

Enrollment & Attrition

	Full-Time							Part-Time							Attrition			
	Men		Women		Minorities		Total	Men		Women		Minorities		Total	Academic	Other	Total	
	#	%	#	%	#	%	#	#	%	#	%	#	%	#	#	#	#	%
1st Year	62	48.4	66	51.6	121	94.5	128	0	0.0	0	0.0	0	0.0	0	1	3	4	2.7
2nd Year	78	48.1	84	51.9	146	90.1	162	0	0.0	0	0.0	0	0.0	0	3	7	10	7.7
3rd Year	59	45.0	72	55.0	117	89.3	131	0	0.0	0	0.0	0	0.0	0	1	4	5	3.4
4th Year								0	0.0	0	0.0	0	0.0	0	0	0	0	0.0
Total	199	47.3	222	52.7	384	91.2	421	0	0.0	0	0.0	0	0.0	0	5	14	19	4.4
JD Degrees Awarded	54	39.7	82	60.3	120	88.2	136	0	0.0	0	0.0	0	0.0	0				

GPA & LSAT Scores

	Full Time	Part Time	Total
# of apps	1,350	0	1,350
# admits	392	0	392
# of matrics	128	0	128
75% GPA	3.29	0.00	
25% GPA	2.70	0.00	
75% LSAT	153	0	
25% LSAT	148	0	

Tuition/Living Expenses

	Resident	Non-resident
Full-Time	$12,065	$12,065
Part-Time	$0	$0

Estimated living expenses for Singles		
Living on campus	Living off campus	Living at home
$9,815	$12,416	$10,960

Career Placement

	Total	%
Employment status known	99	76.7
Employment status unknown	30	23.3
Employed	90	90.9
Pursuing graduate degrees	5	5.1
Unemployed seeking employment	4	4.0
Unemployed not seeking employment	0	0.0
Type of Employment		
# employed in law firms	45	50.0
# employed in business & industry	12	13.3
# employed in government	16	17.8
# employed in public interest	3	3.3
# employed as judicial clerks	12	13.3
# employed in academia	2	2.2
Geographic Location		
# employed in state	26	28.9
# employed in foreign countries	2	2.2
# of states where employed	25	

Financial Aid

	Full-time		Part-time		Total	
	#	%	#	%	#	%
Total # receiving grants	203	48.2	0	0.0	203	48.2
Less than 1/2 tuition	46	10.9	0	0.0	46	10.9
Half to full tuition	109	25.9	0	0.0	109	25.9
Full tuition	31	7.4	0	0.0	31	7.4
More than full tuition	13	3.1	0	0.0	13	3.1
Median Grant Amount	$9,064		$0			

Refunds

Refunds of Admissions or Seat Deposit prior to commencement of classes? No

Refunds of Pre-paid tuition prior to commencement of classes? Yes

If yes, fully refundable before the start of classes? Yes

Joint Degrees Offered

JD/MBA

Advanced Degrees Offered

LLM American Jurisprudence

Bar Passage Rate

Jurisdiction	MD	NY
# from school taking bar for the first time	40	17
School's pass rate for all first-time takers	29%	82%
State's pass rate for all first-time takers	75%	78%
State's pass rate for all first-time takers from ABA approved law schools	75%	

IDAHO, UNIVERSITY OF

6th & Rayburn
Moscow, ID 83844-2321
(208)885-6422
http://www.uidaho.edu/law

ABA Approved Since 1925

The Basics

Type of School: **PUBLIC**
Application deadline*: **2/1**
Application fee: **$30**
Financial Aid deadline*: **2/15**
Student faculty ratio: **13.9 to 1**

First year can start other than Fall: **No**
Student housing: **No**
--exclusively for law students: **No**
Term: **Semester**

*pr=preferred

Faculty

	Men		Women		Minorities		Total
	#	%	#	%	#	%	
Full-time	13	81	3	19	0	0	16
Other full-time	1	33	2	67	0	0	3
Deans, librarians, & others who teach	1	100	0	0	0	0	1
Part-time	4	80	1	20	0	0	5
Total	19	76	6	24	0	0	25
Deans, librarians, & others who teach < 1/2	1	50	1	50	1	50	2

Library

# of volumes & volume equivalents	164,853	# of professional staff	4
# of titles	23,158	Hours per week with professional staff	45
# of active serial subscriptions	2,565	Hours per week without professional staff	52
Study seating capacity inside the library	369	# of student computer work stations for entire law school	27
Square feet of law library	24,822	# of additional networked connections	25
Square feet of law school (excl. Library)	24,150		

Curriculum

	Full time	Part time
Typical first-year section size	50	0
Is there typically a "small section" of the first year class, other than Legal Writing, taught by full-time faculty?	No	No
If yes, typical size offered last year	N/A	N/A
# of classroom course titles beyond 1st year curriculum	50	0
# of upper division courses, excluding seminars, with an enrollment:		
Under 25	31	0
25 - 49	15	0
50 - 74	7	0
75 - 99	3	0
100 +	2	0
# of seminars	3	0
# of seminar positions available	75	
# of seminar positions filled	55	0
# of positions available in simulation courses	100	
# of simulation positions filled	99	0
# of positions available in faculty supervised clinical courses	40	
# of fac. sup. clin. positions filled	39	0
# involved in field placements	30	0
# involved in law journals	13	0
# in moot court or trial competitions	14	0
# of credit hours required to graduate	88	

Enrollment & Attrition

	Full-Time							Part-Time							Attrition			
	Men		Women		Minorities		Total	Men		Women		Minorities		Total	Academic	Other	Total	
	#	%	#	%	#	%	#	#	%	#	%	#	%	#	#	#	#	%
1st Year	57	67.9	27	32.1	9	10.7	84	0	0.0	0	0.0	0	0.0	0	8	4	12	13
2nd Year	45	53.6	39	46.4	8	9.5	84	0	0.0	0	0.0	0	0.0	0	0	2	2	1.9
3rd Year	52	53.1	46	46.9	9	9.2	98	0	0.0	0	0.0	0	0.0	0	0	0	0	0.0
4th Year								0	0.0	0	0.0	0	0.0	0	0	0	0	0.0
Total	154	57.9	112	42.1	26	9.8	266	0	0.0	0	0.0	0	0.0	0	8	6	14	5.1
JD Degrees Awarded	49	65.3	26	34.7	10	13.3	75	0	0.0	0	0.0	0	0.0	0				

GPA & LSAT Scores

	Full Time	Part Time	Total
# of apps	482	0	482
# admits	241	0	241
# of matrics	84	0	84
75% GPA	3.51	0.00	
25% GPA	3.02	0.00	
75% LSAT	157	0	
25% LSAT	149	0	

Tuition/Living Expenses

	Resident	Non-resident
Full-Time	$3,308	$8,960
Part-Time	$0	$0

Estimated living expenses for Singles		
Living on campus	Living off campus	Living at home
$10,106	$10,106	$5,328

Career Placement

	Total	%
Employment status known	91	95.8
Employment status unknown	4	4.2
Employed	74	81.3
Pursuing graduate degrees	7	7.7
Unemployed seeking employment	7	7.7
Unemployed not seeking employment	3	3.3
Type of Employment		
# employed in law firms	39	52.7
# employed in business & industry	5	6.8
# employed in government	14	18.9
# employed in public interest	2	2.7
# employed as judicial clerks	14	18.9
# employed in academia	0	0.0
Geographic Location		
# employed in state	50	67.6
# employed in foreign countries	0	0.0
# of states where employed	11	

Financial Aid

	Full-time		Part-time		Total	
	#	%	#	%	#	%
Total # receiving grants	136	51.1	0	0.0	136	51.1
Less than 1/2 tuition	86	32.3	0	0.0	86	32.3
Half to full tuition	44	16.5	0	0.0	44	16.5
Full tuition	0	0.0	0	0.0	0	0.0
More than full tuition	6	2.3	0	0.0	6	2.3
Median Grant Amount	$1,304		$0			

Refunds

Refunds of Admissions or Seat Deposit prior to commencement of classes? Yes

100% refund from 02/01/95 to 06/01/96
50% refund from 06/02/96 to 06/30/96

Refunds of Pre-paid tuition prior to commencement of classes? Yes

If yes, fully refundable before the start of classes? Yes

100% refund from 02/01/95 to 08/25/96

Joint Degrees Offered

No Joint Degrees

Advanced Degrees Offered

No Advanced Degrees

Bar Passage Rate

Jurisdiction	ID
# from school taking bar for the first time	61
School's pass rate for all first-time takers	72%
State's pass rate for all first-time takers	75%
State's pass rate for all first-time takers from ABA approved law schools	75%

ILLINOIS INSTITUTE OF TECHNOLOGY

Chicago-Kent College of Law
565 West Adams Street
Chicago, IL 60661
(312)906-5000
http://www.kentlaw.edu

ABA Approved Since 1936

The Basics

Type of School: **PRIVATE**
Application deadline*: **4/1**
Application fee: **$40**
Financial Aid deadline*: **4/1**
Student faculty ratio: **21.8 to 1**

First year can start other than Fall: **No**
Student housing: **No**
--exclusively for law students: **No**
Term: **Semester**

*pr=preferred

Faculty

	Men		Women		Minorities		Total
	#	%	#	%	#	%	
Full-time	28	68	13	32	5	12	41
Other full-time	5	38	8	62	1	8	13
Deans, librarians, & others who teach	2	67	1	33	0	0	3
Part-time	77	81	18	19	3	3	95
Total	112	74	40	26	9	6	152
Deans, librarians, & others who teach < 1/2	2	100	0	0	0	0	2

Library

# of volumes & volume equivalents	520,867	# of professional staff	9
# of titles	130,161	Hours per week with professional staff	95
# of active serial subscriptions	7,560	Hours per week without professional staff	7
Study seating capacity inside the library	689	# of student computer work stations for entire law school	126
Square feet of law library	60,916	# of additional networked connections	999
Square feet of law school (excl. Library)	190,720		

Curriculum

	Full time	Part time
Typical first-year section size	100	100
Is there typically a "small section" of the first year class, other than Legal Writing, taught by full-time faculty?	Yes	Yes
If yes, typical size offered last year	50	50
# of classroom course titles beyond 1st year curriculum	94	70
# of upper division courses, excluding seminars, with an enrollment:		
Under 25	87	65
25 - 49	24	16
50 - 74	15	5
75 - 99	8	7
100 +	3	1
# of seminars	21	12
# of seminar positions available	505	
# of seminar positions filled	262	145
# of positions available in simulation courses	688	
# of simulation positions filled	404	183
# of positions available in faculty supervised clinical courses	241	
# of fac. sup. clin. positions filled	209	13
# involved in field placements	109	9
# involved in law journals	46	6
# in moot court or trial competitions	42	6
# of credit hours required to graduate	84	

Enrollment & Attrition

	Full-Time							Part-Time							Attrition			
	Men		Women		Minorities		Total	Men		Women		Minorities		Total	Academic	Other	Total	
	#	%	#	%	#	%	#	#	%	#	%	#	%	#	#	#	#	%
1st Year	159	50.2	158	49.8	46	14.5	317	66	60.6	43	39.4	14	12.8	109	4	32	36	8.7
2nd Year	157	54.1	133	45.9	54	18.6	290	46	57.5	34	42.5	17	21.3	80	4	26	30	8.0
3rd Year	130	52.8	116	47.2	38	15.4	246	46	59.7	31	40.3	15	19.5	77	1	5	6	1.7
4th Year								38	55.9	30	44.1	9	13.2	68	0	2	2	2.3
Total	446	52.3	407	47.7	138	16.2	853	196	58.7	138	41.3	55	16.5	334	9	65	74	6.0
JD Degrees Awarded	149	49.0	155	51.0	43	14.1	304	49	53.8	42	46.2	11	12.1	91				

ILLINOIS INSTITUTE OF TECHNOLOGY

GPA & LSAT Scores

	Full Time	Part Time	Total
# of apps	1,692	396	2,088
# admits	1,202	257	1,459
# of matrics	302	111	413
75% GPA	3.41	3.29	
25% GPA	2.88	2.68	
75% LSAT	156	155	
25% LSAT	150	147	

Tuition/Living Expenses

	Resident	Non-resident
Full-Time	$18,930	$18,930
Part-Time	$13,680	$13,680

Estimated living expenses for Singles		
Living on campus	Living off campus	Living at home
$11,437	$11,437	$7,237

Career Placement

	Total	%
Employment status known	376	97.7
Employment status unknown	9	2.3
Employed	312	83.0
Pursuing graduate degrees	3	0.8
Unemployed seeking employment	19	5.1
Unemployed not seeking employment	42	11.2
Type of Employment		
# employed in law firms	162	51.9
# employed in business & industry	66	21.2
# employed in government	45	14.4
# employed in public interest	14	4.5
# employed as judicial clerks	15	4.8
# employed in academia	10	3.2
Geographic Location		
# employed in state	268	85.9
# employed in foreign countries	1	0.3
# of states where employed	28	

Financial Aid

	Full-time		Part-time		Total	
	#	%	#	%	#	%
Total # receiving grants	319	37.4	102	30.5	421	35.5
Less than 1/2 tuition	248	29.1	73	21.9	321	27.0
Half to full tuition	49	5.7	28	8.4	77	6.5
Full tuition	22	2.6	1	0.3	23	1.9
More than full tuition	0	0.0	0	0.0	0	0.0
Median Grant Amount	$3,900		$3,225			

Refunds

Refunds of Admissions or Seat Deposit prior to commencement of classes? No

Refunds of Pre-paid tuition prior to commencement of classes? Yes

If yes, fully refundable before the start of classes? Yes

Joint Degrees Offered

JD/MBA, JD/LLM in, Taxation, JD/MS in, Finan Mkts, JD/LLM in, Finan Svcs, JD/MS in, Environ Eng

Advanced Degrees Offered

LLM	Taxation
LLM	International and Comparative Law
LLM	Financial Services Law

Bar Passage Rate

Jurisdiction	IL
# from school taking bar for the first time	299
School's pass rate for all first-time takers	81%
State's pass rate for all first-time takers	87%
State's pass rate for all first-time takers from ABA approved law schools	87%

ILLINOIS, UNIVERSITY OF

504 East Pennsylvania Avenue
Champaign, IL 61820
(217)333-0931
http://www.law.uiuc.edu

ABA Approved Since 1923

The Basics

Type of School: PUBLIC
Application deadline*: 3/15
Application fee: $30
Financial Aid deadline*: 3/15
Student faculty ratio: 16.6 to 1

First year can start other than Fall: No
Student housing: No
--exclusively for law students: No
Term: Semester

*pr=preferred

Faculty

	Men #	Men %	Women #	Women %	Minorities #	Minorities %	Total
Full-time	22	71	9	29	5	16	31
Other full-time	4	67	2	33	0	0	6
Deans, librarians, & others who teach	1	100	0	0	0	0	1
Part-time	16	89	2	11	1	6	18
Total	43	77	13	23	6	11	56
Deans, librarians, & others who teach < 1/2	1	100	0	0	0	0	1

Library

# of volumes & volume equivalents	660,231	# of professional staff	5
# of titles	236,588	Hours per week with professional staff	52
# of active serial subscriptions	8,081	Hours per week without professional staff	53
Study seating capacity inside the library	429	# of student computer work stations for entire law school	93
Square feet of law library	59,617	# of additional networked connections	39
Square feet of law school (excl. Library)	65,283		

Curriculum

	Full time	Part time
Typical first-year section size	65	0
Is there typically a "small section" of the first year class, other than Legal Writing, taught by full-time faculty?	No	No
If yes, typical size offered last year	N/A	N/A
# of classroom course titles beyond 1st year curriculum	82	0
# of upper division courses, excluding seminars, with an enrollment:		
Under 25	22	0
25 - 49	22	0
50 - 74	11	0
75 - 99	7	0
100 +	7	0
# of seminars	17	0
# of seminar positions available	270	
# of seminar positions filled	258	0
# of positions available in simulation courses	256	
# of simulation positions filled	243	0
# of positions available in faculty supervised clinical courses	36	
# of fac. sup. clin. positions filled	32	0
# involved in field placements	79	0
# involved in law journals	105	0
# in moot court or trial competitions	164	0
# of credit hours required to graduate	90	

Enrollment & Attrition

	Full-Time Men #	Men %	Women #	Women %	Minorities #	Minorities %	Total #	Part-Time Men #	Men %	Women #	Women %	Minorities #	Minorities %	Total #	Attrition Academic #	Other #	Total #	%
1st Year	105	57.7	77	42.3	43	23.6	182	0	0.0	0	0.0	0	0.0	0	0	6	6	2.8
2nd Year	136	61.8	84	38.2	72	32.7	220	0	0.0	0	0.0	0	0.0	0	0	0	0	0.0
3rd Year	137	64.0	77	36.0	55	25.7	214	0	0.0	0	0.0	0	0.0	0	0	0	0	0.0
4th Year								0	0.0	0	0.0	0	0.0	0	0	0	0	0.0
Total	378	61.4	238	38.6	170	27.6	616	0	0.0	0	0.0	0	0.0	0	0	6	6	1.0
JD Degrees Awarded	101	55.2	82	44.8	41	22.4	183	0	0.0	0	0.0	0	0.0	0				

GPA & LSAT Scores

	Full Time	Part Time	Total
# of apps	1,792	0	1,792
# admits	593	0	593
# of matrics	182	0	182
75% GPA	3.68	0.00	
25% GPA	3.07	0.00	
75% LSAT	164	0	
25% LSAT	158	0	

Tuition/Living Expenses

	Resident	Non-resident
Full-Time	$6,752	$16,345
Part-Time	$0	$0

Estimated living expenses for Singles		
Living on campus	Living off campus	Living at home
$9,306	$9,306	$9,306

Career Placement

	Total	%
Employment status known	179	97.3
Employment status unknown	5	2.7
Employed	167	93.3
Pursuing graduate degrees	5	2.8
Unemployed seeking employment	7	3.9
Unemployed not seeking employment	0	0.0
Type of Employment		
# employed in law firms	90	53.9
# employed in business & industry	29	17.4
# employed in government	28	16.8
# employed in public interest	2	1.2
# employed as judicial clerks	14	8.4
# employed in academia	3	1.8
Geographic Location		
# employed in state	123	73.7
# employed in foreign countries	1	0.6
# of states where employed	18	

Financial Aid

	Full-time		Part-time		Total	
	#	%	#	%	#	%
Total # receiving grants	269	43.7	0	0.0	269	43.7
Less than 1/2 tuition	41	6.7	0	0.0	41	6.7
Half to full tuition	2	0.3	0	0.0	2	0.3
Full tuition	10	1.6	0	0.0	10	1.6
More than full tuition	216	35.1	0	0.0	216	35.1
Median Grant Amount	$5,242		$0			

Refunds

Refunds of Admissions or Seat Deposit prior to commencement of classes? No

Refunds of Pre-paid tuition prior to commencement of classes? Yes

If yes, fully refundable before the start of classes? Yes

Joint Degrees Offered

JD/MBA, JD/MALIR, JD/M.Ed., JD/Ph.D.Ed., JD/MD, JD/MUP, JD/DVM, JD/MAS

Advanced Degrees Offered

JSD	General
LL.M	General
SJD	General

Bar Passage Rate

Jurisdiction	IL
# from school taking bar for the first time	144
School's pass rate for all first-time takers	90%
State's pass rate for all first-time takers	87%
State's pass rate for all first-time takers from ABA approved law schools	87%

INDIANA UNIVERSITY - BLOOMINGTON

Third Street and Indiana Avenue
Bloomington, IN 47405
(812)855-7995
http://www.law.indiana.edu

ABA Approved Since 1923

The Basics

Type of School: **PUBLIC**
Application deadline*: **rolling**
Application fee: **$35**
Financial Aid deadline*: **3/1**
Student faculty ratio: **16.6 to 1**
First year can start other than Fall: **Yes**
Student housing: **No**
--exclusively for law students: **No**
Term: **Semester**

***pr=preferred**

Faculty

	Men		Women		Minorities		Total
	#	%	#	%	#	%	
Full-time	26	79	7	21	2	6	33
Other full-time	3	33	6	67	0	0	9
Deans, librarians, & others who teach	2	50	2	50	0	0	4
Part-time	8	80	2	20	0	0	10
Total	39	70	17	30	2	4	56
Deans, librarians, & others who teach < 1/2	1	100	0	0	0	0	1

Library

# of volumes & volume equivalents	563,150	# of professional staff	9
# of titles	173,121	Hours per week with professional staff	65
# of active serial subscriptions	6,995	Hours per week without professional staff	50
Study seating capacity inside the library	723	# of student computer work stations for entire law school	78
Square feet of law library	65,526	# of additional networked connections	0
Square feet of law school (excl. Library)	42,787		

Curriculum

	Full time	Part time
Typical first-year section size	90	0
Is there typically a "small section" of the first year class, other than Legal Writing, taught by full-time faculty?	Yes	No
If yes, typical size offered last year	27	N/A
# of classroom course titles beyond 1st year curriculum	94	0
# of upper division courses, excluding seminars, with an enrollment:		
Under 25	55	0
25 - 49	23	0
50 - 74	6	0
75 - 99	6	0
100 +	4	0
# of seminars	14	0
# of seminar positions available	285	
# of seminar positions filled	172	0
# of positions available in simulation courses	325	
# of simulation positions filled	276	0
# of positions available in faculty supervised clinical courses	175	
# of fac. sup. clin. positions filled	97	0
# involved in field placements	118	0
# involved in law journals	154	0
# in moot court or trial competitions	135	0
# of credit hours required to graduate	86	

Enrollment & Attrition

	Full-Time							Part-Time							Attrition			
	Men		Women		Minorities		Total	Men		Women		Minorities		Total	Academic	Other	Total	
	#	%	#	%	#	%	#	#	%	#	%	#	%	#	#	#	#	%
1st Year	126	55.5	101	44.5	38	16.7	227	1	50.0	1	50.0	0	0.0	2	3	8	11	5.2
2nd Year	116	58.6	82	41.4	41	20.7	198	0	0.0	2	100.0	0	0.0	2	1	4	5	2.2
3rd Year	129	57.1	97	42.9	41	18.1	226	0	0.0	3	100.0	0	0.0	3	2	1	3	1.6
4th Year								0	0.0	0	0.0	0	0.0	0	0	0	0	0.0
Total	371	57.0	280	43.0	120	18.4	651	1	14.3	6	85.7	0	0.0	7	6	13	19	3.1
JD Degrees Awarded	94	50.3	93	49.7	52	27.8	187	0	0.0	0	0.0	0	0.0	0				

INDIANA UNIVERSITY - BLOOMINGTON

GPA & LSAT Scores

	Full Time	Part Time	Total
# of apps	1,522	1	1,523
# admits	679	1	680
# of matrics	226	1	227
75% GPA	3.70	0.00	
25% GPA	3.13	0.00	
75% LSAT	162	0	
25% LSAT	155	0	

Tuition/Living Expenses

	Resident	Non-resident
Full-Time	$5,350	$14,142
Part-Time	$0	$0

Estimated living expenses for Singles		
Living on campus	Living off campus	Living at home
$5,372	$5,372	$1,500

Career Placement

	Total	%
Employment status known	181	91.8
Employment status unknown	15	8.2
Employed	166	92.0
Pursuing graduate degrees	6	3.3
Unemployed seeking employment	9	5.0
Unemployed not seeking employment	0	0.0
Type of Employment		
# employed in law firms	100	60.2
# employed in business & industry	22	13.3
# employed in government	18	10.8
# employed in public interest	4	2.4
# employed as judicial clerks	19	11.5
# employed in academia	3	1.8
Geographic Location		
# employed in state	77	46.4
# employed in foreign countries	2	1.2
# of states where employed	24	

Financial Aid

	Full-time		Part-time		Total	
	#	%	#	%	#	%
Total # receiving grants	229	35.2	0	0.0	229	34.8
Less than 1/2 tuition	178	27.3	0	0.0	178	27.1
Half to full tuition	32	4.9	0	0.0	32	4.9
Full tuition	8	1.2	0	0.0	8	1.2
More than full tuition	11	1.7	0	0.0	11	1.7
Median Grant Amount	$1,500		$0			

Refunds

Refunds of Admissions or Seat Deposit prior to commencement of classes? No

Refunds of Pre-paid tuition prior to commencement of classes? Yes

If yes, fully refundable before the start of classes? Yes

Joint Degrees Offered

JD/MBA, JD/MPA, JD/MSES, JD/MLS

Advanced Degrees Offered

LLM	Varies
MCL	Comparative Law
SJD	Research degree

Bar Passage Rate

Jurisdiction	IN
# from school taking bar for the first time	108
School's pass rate for all first-time takers	82%
State's pass rate for all first-time takers	86%
State's pass rate for all first-time takers from ABA approved law schools	86%

INDIANA UNIVERSITY - INDIANAPOLIS

735 West New York Street
Indianapolis, IN 46202-5194
(317)274-8523
http://www.iulaw.indy.indiana.edu

ABA Approved Since 1936

The Basics

Type of School: **PUBLIC**
Application deadline*: **3/1**
Application fee: **$35**
Financial Aid deadline*: **3/1**
Student faculty ratio: **18.5 to 1**

First year can start other than Fall: **Yes**
Student housing: **No**
--exclusively for law students: **No**
Term: **Semester**

*pr=preferred

Faculty

	Men		Women		Minorities		Total
	#	%	#	%	#	%	
Full-time	24	73	9	27	1	3	33
Other full-time	2	40	3	60	0	0	5
Deans, librarians, & others who teach	1	100	0	0	0	0	1
Part-time	11	73	4	27	1	7	15
Total	38	70	16	30	2	4	54
Deans, librarians, & others who teach < 1/2	2	100	0	0	0	0	2

Library

# of volumes & volume equivalents	479,397	# of professional staff	7
# of titles	173,418	Hours per week with professional staff	60
# of active serial subscriptions	6,881	Hours per week without professional staff	39
Study seating capacity inside the library	452	# of student computer work stations for entire law school	58
Square feet of law library	32,016	# of additional networked connections	0
Square feet of law school (excl. Library)	40,150		

Curriculum

	Full time	Part time
Typical first-year section size	90	70
Is there typically a "small section" of the first year class, other than Legal Writing, taught by full-time faculty?	No	No
If yes, typical size offered last year	N/A	N/A
# of classroom course titles beyond 1st year curriculum	67	48
# of upper division courses, excluding seminars, with an enrollment:		
Under 25	13	18
25 - 49	19	11
50 - 74	18	9
75 - 99	8	2
100 +	4	0
# of seminars	13	8
# of seminar positions available	436	
# of seminar positions filled	171	66
# of positions available in simulation courses	313	
# of simulation positions filled	224	66
# of positions available in faculty supervised clinical courses	177	
# of fac. sup. clin. positions filled	91	20
# involved in field placements	76	15
# involved in law journals	84	25
# in moot court or trial competitions	113	10
# of credit hours required to graduate	90	

Enrollment & Attrition

	Full-Time							Part-Time							Attrition			
	Men		Women		Minorities		Total	Men		Women		Minorities		Total	Academic	Other	Total	
	#	%	#	%	#	%	#	#	%	#	%	#	%	#	#	#	#	%
1st Year	97	51.1	93	48.9	26	13.7	190	73	50.0	73	50.0	10	6.8	146	10	23	33	9.9
2nd Year	101	56.4	78	43.6	23	12.8	179	40	51.9	37	48.1	5	6.5	77	5	3	8	3.2
3rd Year	103	60.6	67	39.4	15	8.8	170	43	60.6	28	39.4	9	12.7	71	0	0	0	0.0
4th Year								0	0.0	0	0.0	0	0.0	0	0	0	0	0.0
Total	301	55.8	238	44.2	64	11.9	539	156	53.1	138	46.9	24	8.2	294	15	26	41	4.9
JD Degrees Awarded	107	60.5	70	39.5	18	10.2	177	41	56.2	32	43.8	7	9.6	73				

GPA & LSAT Scores

	Full Time	Part Time	Total
# of apps	757	285	1,042
# admits	393	107	500
# of matrics	179	87	266
75% GPA	3.53	3.52	
25% GPA	2.92	2.90	
75% LSAT	158	158	
25% LSAT	152	152	

Tuition/Living Expenses

	Resident	Non-resident
Full-Time	$5,151	$12,279
Part-Time	$3,727	$8,818

Estimated living expenses for Singles		
Living on campus	Living off campus	Living at home
$7,866	$11,232	$7,254

Financial Aid

	Full-time		Part-time		Total	
	#	%	#	%	#	%
Total # receiving grants	74	13.7	33	11.2	107	12.8
Less than 1/2 tuition	43	8.0	12	4.1	55	6.6
Half to full tuition	20	3.7	15	5.1	35	4.2
Full tuition	6	1.1	3	1.0	9	1.1
More than full tuition	5	0.9	3	1.0	8	1.0
Median Grant Amount	$2,750		$2,200			

Refunds

Refunds of Admissions or Seat Deposit prior to commencement of classes? Yes

100% refund from 04/15/96 to 05/15/96

Refunds of Pre-paid tuition prior to commencement of classes? Yes

If yes, fully refundable before the start of classes? Yes

Joint Degrees Offered

JD/MBA, JD/MPA, JD/MHA

Advanced Degrees Offered

No Advanced Degrees

Career Placement

	Total	%
Employment status known	223	89.6
Employment status unknown	26	10.4
Employed	203	91.0
Pursuing graduate degrees	5	2.2
Unemployed seeking employment	12	5.4
Unemployed not seeking employment	3	1.4
Type of Employment		
# employed in law firms	108	53.2
# employed in business & industry	45	22.2
# employed in government	36	17.7
# employed in public interest	3	1.5
# employed as judicial clerks	11	5.4
# employed in academia	0	0.0
Geographic Location		
# employed in state	177	87.2
# employed in foreign countries	0	0.0
# of states where employed	13	

Bar Passage Rate

Jurisdiction	IN
# from school taking bar for the first time	177
School's pass rate for all first-time takers	86%
State's pass rate for all first-time takers	86%
State's pass rate for all first-time takers from ABA approved law schools	86%

INTER AMERICAN UNIVERSITY OF PUERTO RICO

P.O. Box 70351
San Juan, PR 00936-8351
(787)751-1912

ABA Approved Since 1969

The Basics

Type of School: **PRIVATE**
Application deadline*:
Application fee: **$63**
Financial Aid deadline*:
Student faculty ratio: **20.4 to 1**

First year can start other than Fall: **No**
Student housing: **No**
--exclusively for law students: **No**
Term: **Semester**

*pr=preferred

Faculty

	Men		Women		Minorities		Total
	#	%	#	%	#	%	
Full-time	13	59	9	41	22	100	22
Other full-time	1	100	0	0	1	100	1
Deans, librarians, & others who teach	4	100	0	0	4	100	4
Part-time	12	67	6	33	17	94	18
Total	30	67	15	33	44	98	45
Deans, librarians, & others who teach < 1/2	0	0	0	0	0	0	0

Library

# of volumes & volume equivalents	170,749	# of professional staff	14
# of titles	21,817	Hours per week with professional staff	76
# of active serial subscriptions	3,909	Hours per week without professional staff	27
Study seating capacity inside the library	329	# of student computer work stations for entire law school	31
Square feet of law library	35,136	# of additional networked connections	3
Square feet of law school (excl. Library)	174,864		

Curriculum

	Full time	Part time
Typical first-year section size	55	50
Is there typically a "small section" of the first year class, other than Legal Writing, taught by full-time faculty?	No	No
If yes, typical size offered last year	N/A	N/A
# of classroom course titles beyond 1st year curriculum	36	40
# of upper division courses, excluding seminars, with an enrollment:		
Under 25	30	14
25 - 49	15	21
50 - 74	8	10
75 - 99	0	0
100 +	0	0
# of seminars	9	11
# of seminar positions available	300	
# of seminar positions filled	80	102
# of positions available in simulation courses	220	
# of simulation positions filled	96	92
# of positions available in faculty supervised clinical courses	120	
# of fac. sup. clin. positions filled	66	0
# involved in field placements	0	0
# involved in law journals	30	9
# in moot court or trial competitions	3	0
# of credit hours required to graduate	92	

Enrollment & Attrition

	Full-Time							Part-Time							Attrition			
	Men		Women		Minorities		Total	Men		Women		Minorities		Total	Academic	Other	Total	
	#	%	#	%	#	%	#	#	%	#	%	#	%	#	#	#	#	%
1st Year	53	46.9	60	53.1	113	100.0	113	55	55.0	45	45.0	100	100.0	100	5	22	27	14
2nd Year	43	43.4	56	56.6	99	100.	99	49	59.0	34	41.0	83	100.0	83	4	7	11	6.5
3rd Year	48	40.0	72	60.0	120	100.0	120	41	53.2	36	46.8	77	100.0	77	0	4	4	2.0
4th Year								34	64.2	19	35.8	53	100.0	53	0	3	3	3.7
Total	144	43.4	188	56.6	332	100.	332	179	57.2	134	42.8	313	100.0	313	9	36	45	7.0
JD Degrees Awarded	55	49.5	56	50.5	111	100.0	111	49	62.0	30	38.0	79	100.0	79				

INTER AMERICAN UNIVERSITY OF PUERTO RICO

GPA & LSAT Scores

	Full Time	Part Time	Total
# of apps	447	407	854
# admits	207	137	344
# of matrics	114	103	217
75% GPA	3.17	3.11	
25% GPA	2.59	2.60	
75% LSAT	142	141	
25% LSAT	133	133	

Tuition/Living Expenses

	Resident	Non-resident
Full-Time	$9,622	$9,622
Part-Time	$7,222	$7,222

Estimated living expenses for Singles		
Living on campus	Living off campus	Living at home
N/A	$8,900	$5,400

Financial Aid

	Full-time		Part-time		Total	
	#	%	#	%	#	%
Total # receiving grants	82	24.7	88	28.1	170	26.4
Less than 1/2 tuition	26	7.8	20	6.4	46	7.1
Half to full tuition	56	16.9	68	21.7	124	19.2
Full tuition	0	0.0	0	0.0	0	0.0
More than full tuition	0	0.0	0	0.0	0	0.0
Median Grant Amount	$2,250		$1,545			

Refunds

Refunds of Admissions or Seat Deposit prior to commencement of classes? No

Refunds of Pre-paid tuition prior to commencement of classes? Yes

If yes, fully refundable before the start of classes? Yes

Joint Degrees Offered

No Joint Degrees

Advanced Degrees Offered

No Advanced Degrees

Career Placement

	Total	%
Employment status known	121	86.4
Employment status unknown	19	13.6
Employed	103	85.1
Pursuing graduate degrees	5	4.1
Unemployed seeking employment	13	10.7
Unemployed not seeking employment	0	0.0
Type of Employment		
# employed in law firms	58	56.3
# employed in business & industry	8	7.8
# employed in government	19	18.5
# employed in public interest	6	5.8
# employed as judicial clerks	12	11.7
# employed in academia	0	0.0
Geographic Location		
# employed in state	100	97.1
# employed in foreign countries	0	0.0
# of states where employed	0	

Bar Passage Rate

Jurisdiction	PR
# from school taking bar for the first time	105
School's pass rate for all first-time takers	60%
State's pass rate for all first-time takers	68%
State's pass rate for all first-time takers from ABA approved law schools	69%

IOWA, UNIVERSITY OF

Melrose and Byington
Iowa City, IA 52242
(319)335-9034
http://www.uiowa.edu/~/lawcoll

ABA Approved Since 1923

The Basics

Type of School: **PUBLIC**
Application deadline*: **3/1**
Application fee: **$20**
Financial Aid deadline*: **3/1**
Student faculty ratio: **13.2 to 1**

First year can start other than Fall: **Yes**
Student housing: **No**
--exclusively for law students: **No**
Term: **Semester**

*pr=preferred

Faculty

	Men		Women		Minorities		Total
	#	%	#	%	#	%	
Full-time	33	72	13	28	5	11	46
Other full-time	1	100	0	0	0	0	1
Deans, librarians, & others who teach	3	100	0	0	0	0	3
Part-time	8	80	2	20	0	0	10
Total	45	75	15	25	5	8	60
Deans, librarians, & others who teach < 1/2	0	0	0	0	0	0	0

Library

# of volumes & volume equivalents	836,637	# of professional staff	13
# of titles	335,638	Hours per week with professional staff	104
# of active serial subscriptions	7,843	Hours per week without professional staff	0
Study seating capacity inside the library	672	# of student computer work stations for entire law school	57
Square feet of law library	76,571	# of additional networked connections	0
Square feet of law school (excl. Library)	68,429		

Curriculum

	Full time	Part time
Typical first-year section size	75	0
Is there typically a "small section" of the first year class, other than Legal Writing, taught by full-time faculty?	Yes	No
If yes, typical size offered last year	25	N/A
# of classroom course titles beyond 1st year curriculum	79	0
# of upper division courses, excluding seminars, with an enrollment:		
Under 25	50	0
25 - 49	26	0
50 - 74	14	0
75 - 99	9	0
100 +	0	0
# of seminars	23	0
# of seminar positions available	190	
# of seminar positions filled	177	0
# of positions available in simulation courses	478	
# of simulation positions filled	475	0
# of positions available in faculty supervised clinical courses	84	
# of fac. sup. clin. positions filled	84	0
# involved in field placements	6	0
# involved in law journals	236	0
# in moot court or trial competitions	162	0
# of credit hours required to graduate	90	

Enrollment & Attrition

	Full-Time							Part-Time							Attrition			
	Men		Women		Minorities		Total	Men		Women		Minorities		Total	Academic	Other	Total	
	#	%	#	%	#	%	#	#	%	#	%	#	%	#	#	#	#	%
1st Year	121	56.5	93	43.5	46	21.5	214	0	0.0	0	0.0	0	0.0	0	2	6	8	3.6
2nd Year	106	56.4	82	43.6	49	26.1	188	0	0.0	0	0.0	0	0.0	0	0	6	6	2.8
3rd Year	140	54.1	119	45.9	48	18.5	259	0	0.0	0	0.0	0	0.0	0	0	1	1	0.4
4th Year								0	0.0	0	0.0	0	0.0	0	0	0	0	0.0
Total	367	55.5	294	44.5	143	21.6	661	0	0.0	0	0.0	0	0.0	0	2	13	15	2.2
JD Degrees Awarded	112	54.6	93	45.4	42	20.5	205	0	0.0	0	0.0	0	0.0	0				

GPA & LSAT Scores

	Full Time	Part Time	Total
# of apps	1,261	0	1,261
# admits	542	0	542
# of matrics	217	0	217
75% GPA	3.73	0.00	
25% GPA	3.20	0.00	
75% LSAT	161	0	
25% LSAT	155	0	

Tuition/Living Expenses

	Resident	Non-resident
Full-Time	$5,400	$14,254
Part-Time	$0	$0

Estimated living expenses for Singles		
Living on campus	Living off campus	Living at home
$7,740	$7,740	$5,530

Career Placement

	Total	%
Employment status known	214	95.5
Employment status unknown	10	4.5
Employed	186	86.9
Pursuing graduate degrees	7	3.3
Unemployed seeking employment	12	5.6
Unemployed not seeking employment	9	4.2
Type of Employment		
# employed in law firms	104	55.9
# employed in business & industry	15	8.1
# employed in government	26	14.0
# employed in public interest	11	5.9
# employed as judicial clerks	28	15.1
# employed in academia	2	1.1
Geographic Location		
# employed in state	79	42.5
# employed in foreign countries	1	0.5
# of states where employed	26	

Financial Aid

	Full-time		Part-time		Total	
	#	%	#	%	#	%
Total # receiving grants	276	41.8	0	0.0	276	41.8
Less than 1/2 tuition	80	12.1	0	0.0	80	12.1
Half to full tuition	77	11.7	0	0.0	77	11.6
Full tuition	104	15.7	0	0.0	104	15.7
More than full tuition	15	2.3	0	0.0	15	2.3
Median Grant Amount	$8,634		$0			

Refunds

Refunds of Admissions or Seat Deposit prior to commencement of classes? No

Refunds of Pre-paid tuition prior to commencement of classes? Yes

If yes, fully refundable before the start of classes? Yes

Joint Degrees Offered

Accounting, MBA, Educ. Admin., History, Library Sci, Philosophy, Psychology, Religion, Sociology, Geography, Hosp/Hlth Ad, Urb/Reg Plan, Afro/Am Stu., Comm. Stu.

Advanced Degrees Offered

LLM International & Comparative Law

Bar Passage Rate

Jurisdiction	IA
# from school taking bar for the first time	109
School's pass rate for all first-time takers	79%
State's pass rate for all first-time takers	87%
State's pass rate for all first-time takers from ABA approved law schools	87%

JOHN MARSHALL LAW SCHOOL

315 S. Plymouth Ct.
Chicago, IL 60604
(312)427-2737
http://www.jmls.edu

ABA Approved Since 1951

The Basics

Type of School: **PRIVATE**
Application deadline*: **3/1**
Application fee: **$50**
Financial Aid deadline*:
Student faculty ratio: **16.5 to 1**

First year can start other than Fall: **Yes**
Student housing: **No**
--exclusively for law students: **No**
Term: **Semester**

*pr=preferred

Faculty

	Men		Women		Minorities		Total
	#	%	#	%	#	%	
Full-time	36	72	14	28	4	8	50
Other full-time	0	0	0	0	0	0	0
Deans, librarians, & others who teach	0	0	0	0	0	0	0
Part-time	69	73	26	27	8	8	95
Total	105	72	40	28	12	8	145
Deans, librarians, & others who teach < 1/2	0	0	0	0	0	0	0

Library

# of volumes & volume equivalents	344,719	# of professional staff	9
# of titles	90,794	Hours per week with professional staff	67
# of active serial subscriptions	4,938	Hours per week without professional staff	33
Study seating capacity inside the library	624	# of student computer work stations for entire law school	2
Square feet of law library	50,000	# of additional networked connections	122
Square feet of law school (excl. Library)	76,729		

Curriculum

	Full time	Part time
Typical first-year section size	65	65
Is there typically a "small section" of the first year class, other than Legal Writing, taught by full-time faculty?	No	No
If yes, typical size offered last year	N/A	N/A
# of classroom course titles beyond 1st year curriculum	38	71
# of upper division courses, excluding seminars, with an enrollment:		
Under 25	16	33
25 - 49	6	16
50 - 74	16	11
75 - 99	0	0
100 +	0	0
# of seminars	12	17
# of seminar positions available	624	
# of seminar positions filled	250	237
# of positions available in simulation courses	966	
# of simulation positions filled	284	285
# of positions available in faculty supervised clinical courses	128	
# of fac. sup. clin. positions filled	125	3
# involved in field placements	125	3
# involved in law journals	97	21
# in moot court or trial competitions	14	4
# of credit hours required to graduate	90	

Enrollment & Attrition

	Full-Time							Part-Time							Attrition			
	Men		Women		Minorities		Total	Men		Women		Minorities		Total	Academic	Other	Total	
	#	%	#	%	#	%	#	#	%	#	%	#	%	#	#	#	#	%
1st Year	156	60.0	104	40.0	55	21.2	260	64	58.2	46	41.8	32	29.1	110	11	17	28	8.0
2nd Year	128	58.2	92	41.8	28	12.7	220	51	64.6	28	35.4	18	22.8	79	9	26	35	9.7
3rd Year	164	60.1	109	39.9	22	8.1	273	53	69.7	23	30.3	10	13.2	76	0	6	6	1.6
4th Year								60	65.2	32	34.8	11	12.0	92	0	0	0	0.0
Total	448	59.5	305	40.5	105	13.9	753	228	63.9	129	36.1	71	19.9	357	20	49	69	6.0
JD Degrees Awarded	180	65.7	94	34.3	34	12.4	274	49	65.3	26	34.7	15	20.0	75				

GPA & LSAT Scores

	Full Time	Part Time	Total
# of apps	1,305	332	1,637
# admits	755	260	1,015
# of matrics	179	54	233
75% GPA	3.19	3.20	
25% GPA	2.62	2.51	
75% LSAT	153	154	
25% LSAT	145	145	

Tuition/Living Expenses

	Resident	Non-resident
Full-Time	$15,890	$15,890
Part-Time	$11,370	$11,370

Estimated living expenses for Singles		
Living on campus	Living off campus	Living at home
N/A	$13,410	$13,410

Career Placement

	Total	%
Employment status known	268	89.0
Employment status unknown	33	11.0
Employed	230	85.8
Pursuing graduate degrees	2	0.8
Unemployed seeking employment	31	11.6
Unemployed not seeking employment	5	1.9
Type of Employment		
# employed in law firms	119	51.7
# employed in business & industry	49	21.3
# employed in government	47	20.4
# employed in public interest	2	0.9
# employed as judicial clerks	12	5.2
# employed in academia	1	0.4
Geographic Location		
# employed in state	201	87.4
# employed in foreign countries	1	0.4
# of states where employed	18	

Financial Aid

	Full-time		Part-time		Total	
	#	%	#	%	#	%
Total # receiving grants	125	16.6	50	14.0	175	15.8
Less than 1/2 tuition	97	12.9	34	9.5	131	11.8
Half to full tuition	26	3.5	13	3.6	39	3.5
Full tuition	2	0.3	3	0.8	5	0.5
More than full tuition	0	0.0	0	0.0	0	0.0
Median Grant Amount	$8,232		$4,740			

Refunds

Refunds of Admissions or Seat Deposit prior to commencement of classes? No

Refunds of Pre-paid tuition prior to commencement of classes? Yes

If yes, fully refundable before the start of classes? Yes

Joint Degrees Offered

MBA/JD, MPA/JD, MA/JD

Advanced Degrees Offered

LL.M.	Taxation
LL.M.	Intellectual Property
LL.M.	Comparative Legal Studies
LL.M.	Real Estate

Bar Passage Rate

Jurisdiction	IL
# from school taking bar for the first time	177
School's pass rate for all first-time takers	87%
State's pass rate for all first-time takers	87%
State's pass rate for all first-time takers from ABA approved law schools	87%

KANSAS, UNIVERSITY OF

Green Hall
Lawrence, KS 66045
(913)864-4550
http://www.law.ukans.edu

ABA Approved Since 1923

The Basics

Type of School: **PUBLIC**
Application deadline*: **3/15**
Application fee: **$40**
Financial Aid deadline*: **3/1**
Student faculty ratio: **17.6 to 1**
First year can start other than Fall: **Yes**
Student housing: **No**
--exclusively for law students: **No**
Term: **Semester**

*pr=preferred

Faculty

	Men #	Men %	Women #	Women %	Minorities #	Minorities %	Total
Full-time	20	87	3	13	3	13	23
Other full-time	0	0	0	0	0	0	0
Deans, librarians, & others who teach	2	33	4	67	1	17	6
Part-time	14	70	6	30	0	0	20
Total	36	73	13	27	4	8	49
Deans, librarians, & others who teach < 1/2	0	0	1	100	0	0	1

Library

# of volumes & volume equivalents	325,439	# of professional staff	6
# of titles	113,629	Hours per week with professional staff	66
# of active serial subscriptions	4,330	Hours per week without professional staff	23
Study seating capacity inside the library	276	# of student computer work stations for entire law school	51
Square feet of law library	34,655	# of additional networked connections	14
Square feet of law school (excl. Library)	30,009		

Curriculum

	Full time	Part time
Typical first-year section size	90	0
Is there typically a "small section" of the first year class, other than Legal Writing, taught by full-time faculty?	Yes	No
If yes, typical size offered last year	20	N/A
# of classroom course titles beyond 1st year curriculum	85	0
# of upper division courses, excluding seminars, with an enrollment:		
Under 25	58	0
25 - 49	18	0
50 - 74	8	0
75 - 99	5	0
100 +	3	0
# of seminars	9	0
# of seminar positions available	185	
# of seminar positions filled	89	0
# of positions available in simulation courses	192	
# of simulation positions filled	182	0
# of positions available in faculty supervised clinical courses	135	
# of fac. sup. clin. positions filled	108	0
# involved in field placements	66	0
# involved in law journals	85	0
# in moot court or trial competitions	37	0
# of credit hours required to graduate	90	

Enrollment & Attrition

	Full-Time Men #	Men %	Women #	Women %	Minorities #	Minorities %	Total #	Part-Time Men #	Men %	Women #	Women %	Minorities #	Minorities %	Total #	Attrition Academic #	Other #	Total #	%
1st Year	109	58.9	76	41.1	26	14.1	185	0	0.0	0	0.0	0	0.0	0	0	5	5	3.0
2nd Year	106	64.2	59	35.8	18	10.9	165	0	0.0	0	0.0	0	0.0	0	0	2	2	1.1
3rd Year	86	63.2	50	36.8	18	13.2	136	0	0.0	0	0.0	0	0.0	0	0	1	1	0.7
4th Year								0	0.0	0	0.0	0	0.0	0	0	0	0	0.0
Total	301	61.9	185	38.1	62	12.8	486	0	0.0	0	0.0	0	0.0	0	0	8	8	1.6
JD Degrees Awarded	92	56.8	70	43.2	15	9.3	162	0	0.0	0	0.0	0	0.0	0				

GPA & LSAT Scores

	Full Time	Part Time	Total
# of apps	819	0	819
# admits	379	0	379
# of matrics	185	0	185
75% GPA	3.67	0.00	
25% GPA	3.16	0.00	
75% LSAT	161	0	
25% LSAT	154	0	

Tuition/Living Expenses

	Resident	Non-resident
Full-Time	$4,442	$10,892
Part-Time	$0	$0

Estimated living expenses for Singles		
Living on campus	Living off campus	Living at home
$10,101	$10,101	$6,291

Financial Aid

	Full-time		Part-time		Total	
	#	%	#	%	#	%
Total # receiving grants	173	35.6	0	0.0	173	35.6
Less than 1/2 tuition	150	30.9	0	0.0	150	30.9
Half to full tuition	9	1.9	0	0.0	9	1.9
Full tuition	14	2.9	0	0.0	14	2.9
More than full tuition	0	0.0	0	0.0	0	0.0
Median Grant Amount	$2,531		$0			

Refunds

Refunds of Admissions or Seat Deposit prior to commencement of classes? No

Refunds of Pre-paid tuition prior to commencement of classes? No

If yes, fully refundable before the start of classes? No

Joint Degrees Offered

Business MBA, Economics, Health Serv., Philosophy, Pub. Admin., Soc. Welfare, Urban Plan.

Advanced Degrees Offered

No Advanced Degrees

Career Placement

	Total	%
Employment status known	148	94.3
Employment status unknown	9	5.7
Employed	120	81.1
Pursuing graduate degrees	6	4.1
Unemployed seeking employment	18	12.2
Unemployed not seeking employment	4	2.7
Type of Employment		
# employed in law firms	73	60.8
# employed in business & industry	12	10.0
# employed in government	17	14.2
# employed in public interest	6	5.0
# employed as judicial clerks	9	7.5
# employed in academia	0	0.0
Geographic Location		
# employed in state	57	47.5
# employed in foreign countries	0	0.0
# of states where employed	14	

Bar Passage Rate

Jurisdiction	KS
# from school taking bar for the first time	84
School's pass rate for all first-time takers	88%
State's pass rate for all first-time takers	82%
State's pass rate for all first-time takers from ABA approved law schools	82%

KENTUCKY, UNIVERSITY OF

209 Law Building
Lexington, KY 40506-0048
(606)257-1678
http://www.uky.edu/law

ABA Approved Since 1925

The Basics

Type of School: **PUBLIC**
Application deadline*: **3/1**
Application fee: **$25**
Financial Aid deadline*: **4/1**
Student faculty ratio: **15.3 to 1**

First year can start other than Fall: **No**
Student housing: **Yes**
--exclusively for law students: **No**
Term: **Semester**

*pr=preferred

Faculty

	Men		Women		Minorities		Total
	#	%	#	%	#	%	
Full-time	17	74	6	26	2	9	23
Other full-time	0	0	0	0	0	0	0
Deans, librarians, & others who teach	2	100	0	0	0	0	2
Part-time	12	67	6	33	1	6	18
Total	31	72	12	28	3	7	43
Deans, librarians, & others who teach < 1/2	1	100	0	0	0	0	1

Library

# of volumes & volume equivalents	374,676	# of professional staff	8
# of titles	48,475	Hours per week with professional staff	63
# of active serial subscriptions	3,623	Hours per week without professional staff	41
Study seating capacity inside the library	264	# of student computer work stations for entire law school	45
Square feet of law library	36,843	# of additional networked connections	40
Square feet of law school (excl. Library)	28,071		

Curriculum

	Full time	Part time
Typical first-year section size	70	0
Is there typically a "small section" of the first year class, other than Legal Writing, taught by full-time faculty?	Yes	No
If yes, typical size offered last year	35	N/A
# of classroom course titles beyond 1st year curriculum	73	0
# of upper division courses, excluding seminars, with an enrollment:		
Under 25	41	0
25 - 49	16	0
50 - 74	17	0
75 - 99	2	0
100 +	0	0
# of seminars	12	0
# of seminar positions available	192	
# of seminar positions filled	160	0
# of positions available in simulation courses	217	
# of simulation positions filled	153	0
# of positions available in faculty supervised clinical courses	10	
# of fac. sup. clin. positions filled	9	0
# involved in field placements	62	0
# involved in law journals	56	0
# in moot court or trial competitions	106	0
# of credit hours required to graduate	90	

Enrollment & Attrition

	Full-Time							Part-Time							Attrition			
	Men		Women		Minorities		Total	Men		Women		Minorities		Total	Academic	Other	Total	
	#	%	#	%	#	%	#	#	%	#	%	#	%	#	#	#	#	%
1st Year	76	57.6	56	42.4	4	3.0	132	0	0.0	0	0.0	0	0.0	0	1	5	6	4.0
2nd Year	86	58.5	61	41.5	11	7.5	147	0	0.0	0	0.0	0	0.0	0	3	5	8	5.6
3rd Year	102	71.8	40	28.2	9	6.3	142	0	0.0	0	0.0	0	0.0	0	0	0	0	0.0
4th Year								0	0.0	0	0.0	0	0.0	0	0	0	0	0.0
Total	264	62.7	157	37.3	24	5.7	421	0	0.0	0	0.0	0	0.0	0	4	10	14	3.2
JD Degrees Awarded	87	63.5	50	36.5	11	8.0	137	0	0.0	0	0.0	0	0.0	0				

GPA & LSAT Scores

	Full Time	Part Time	Total
# of apps	891	0	891
# admits	341	0	341
# of matrics	133	0	133
75% GPA	3.68	0.00	
25% GPA	3.11	0.00	
75% LSAT	161	0	
25% LSAT	156	0	

Tuition/Living Expenses

	Resident	Non-resident
Full-Time	$4,776	$12,396
Part-Time	$0	$0

Estimated living expenses for Singles		
Living on campus	Living off campus	Living at home
$9,212	$9,212	$4,158

Financial Aid

	Full-time		Part-time		Total	
	#	%	#	%	#	%
Total # receiving grants	112	26.6	0	0.0	112	26.6
Less than 1/2 tuition	68	16.2	0	0.0	68	16.2
Half to full tuition	5	1.2	0	0.0	5	1.2
Full tuition	28	6.7	0	0.0	28	6.7
More than full tuition	11	2.6	0	0.0	11	2.6
Median Grant Amount	$2,000		$0			

Refunds

Refunds of Admissions or Seat Deposit prior to commencement of classes? No

Refunds of Pre-paid tuition prior to commencement of classes? Yes

If yes, fully refundable before the start of classes? Yes

Joint Degrees Offered

JD/MBA, JD/MPA

Advanced Degrees Offered

No Advanced Degrees

Career Placement

	Total	%
Employment status known	110	100.0
Employment status unknown	0	0.0
Employed	99	90.0
Pursuing graduate degrees	4	3.6
Unemployed seeking employment	2	1.8
Unemployed not seeking employment	5	4.6
Type of Employment		
# employed in law firms	69	69.7
# employed in business & industry	5	5.1
# employed in government	3	3.0
# employed in public interest	6	6.1
# employed as judicial clerks	15	15.2
# employed in academia	1	1.0
Geographic Location		
# employed in state	85	85.9
# employed in foreign countries	0	0.0
# of states where employed	11	

Bar Passage Rate

Jurisdiction	KY
# from school taking bar for the first time	90
School's pass rate for all first-time takers	92%
State's pass rate for all first-time takers	88%
State's pass rate for all first-time takers from ABA approved law schools	88%

LEWIS AND CLARK COLLEGE

10015 S.W. Terwilliger Blvd.
Portland, OR 97219-7799
(503)768-6600
http://lclark.edu/law/index.htm

ABA Approved Since 1970

The Basics

Type of School: **PRIVATE**
Application deadline*:
Application fee: **$50**
Financial Aid deadline*:
Student faculty ratio: **18.3 to 1**

First year can start other than Fall: **No**
Student housing: **No**
--exclusively for law students: **No**
Term: **Semester**

*pr=preferred

Faculty

	Men #	Men %	Women #	Women %	Minorities #	Minorities %	Total
Full-time	21	81	5	19	1	4	26
Other full-time	2	29	5	71	1	14	7
Deans, librarians, & others who teach	1	50	1	50	0	0	2
Part-time	22	73	8	27	1	3	30
Total	46	71	19	29	3	5	65
Deans, librarians, & others who teach < 1/2	1	50	1	50	0	0	2

Library

# of volumes & volume equivalents	416,454	# of professional staff	7
# of titles	73,462	Hours per week with professional staff	69
# of active serial subscriptions	4,312	Hours per week without professional staff	44
Study seating capacity inside the library	194	# of student computer work stations for entire law school	53
Square feet of law library	27,939	# of additional networked connections	112
Square feet of law school (excl. Library)	59,361		

Curriculum

	Full time	Part time
Typical first-year section size	90	33
Is there typically a "small section" of the first year class, other than Legal Writing, taught by full-time faculty?	Yes	Yes
If yes, typical size offered last year	35	35
# of classroom course titles beyond 1st year curriculum	67	51
# of upper division courses, excluding seminars, with an enrollment:		
Under 25	17	15
25 - 49	17	10
50 - 74	11	6
75 - 99	5	1
100 +	1	1
# of seminars	16	18
# of seminar positions available	653	
# of seminar positions filled	328	141
# of positions available in simulation courses	237	
# of simulation positions filled	121	60
# of positions available in faculty supervised clinical courses	130	
# of fac. sup. clin. positions filled	65	42
# involved in field placements	40	12
# involved in law journals	67	22
# in moot court or trial competitions	102	31
# of credit hours required to graduate	86	

Enrollment & Attrition

	Full-Time							Part-Time							Attrition			
	Men		Women		Minorities		Total	Men		Women		Minorities		Total	Academic	Other	Total	
	#	%	#	%	#	%	#	#	%	#	%	#	%	#	#	#	#	%
1st Year	67	51.5	63	48.5	21	16.2	130	19	51.4	18	48.6	6	16.2	37	1	10	11	5.0
2nd Year	102	57.0	77	43.0	36	20.1	179	13	35.1	24	64.9	3	8.1	37	2	7	9	4.0
3rd Year	80	56.7	61	43.3	15	10.6	141	44	57.1	33	42.9	6	7.8	77	0	1	1	0.5
4th Year								13	43.3	17	56.7	4	13.3	30	2	2	4	11
Total	249	55.3	201	44.7	72	16.0	450	89	49.2	92	50.8	19	10.5	181	5	20	25	3.6
JD Degrees Awarded	95	58.3	68	41.7	20	12.3	163	31	55.4	25	44.6	8	14.3	56				

GPA & LSAT Scores

	Full Time	Part Time	Total
# of apps	1,637	143	1,780
# admits	761	81	842
# of matrics	135	36	171
75% GPA	3.45	3.34	
25% GPA	3.01	2.78	
75% LSAT	164	161	
25% LSAT	158	156	

Tuition/Living Expenses

	Resident	Non-resident
Full-Time	$16,485	$16,485
Part-Time	$12,365	$12,365

Estimated living expenses for Singles		
Living on campus	Living off campus	Living at home
N/A	$10,730	$10,730

Career Placement

	Total	%
Employment status known	153	87.9
Employment status unknown	21	12.1
Employed	133	86.9
Pursuing graduate degrees	3	2.0
Unemployed seeking employment	15	9.8
Unemployed not seeking employment	2	1.3
Type of Employment		
# employed in law firms	63	47.4
# employed in business & industry	22	16.5
# employed in government	28	21.1
# employed in public interest	8	6.0
# employed as judicial clerks	10	7.5
# employed in academia	2	1.5
Geographic Location		
# employed in state	80	60.2
# employed in foreign countries	2	1.5
# of states where employed	25	

Financial Aid

	Full-time		Part-time		Total	
	#	%	#	%	#	%
Total # receiving grants	167	37.1	54	29.8	221	35.0
Less than 1/2 tuition	162	36.0	46	25.4	208	33.0
Half to full tuition	4	0.9	8	4.4	12	1.9
Full tuition	1	0.2	0	0.0	1	0.2
More than full tuition	0	0.0	0	0.0	0	0.0
Median Grant Amount	$5,000		$4,000			

Refunds

Refunds of Admissions or Seat Deposit prior to commencement of classes? Yes

29% refund from 04/01/96 to 08/01/96

Refunds of Pre-paid tuition prior to commencement of classes? Yes

If yes, fully refundable before the start of classes? Yes

Joint Degrees Offered

MPA/JD

Advanced Degrees Offered

LL.M. Environmental/Natural Resources

Bar Passage Rate

Jurisdiction	OR
# from school taking bar for the first time	99
School's pass rate for all first-time takers	86%
State's pass rate for all first-time takers	85%
State's pass rate for all first-time takers from ABA approved law schools	

LOUISIANA STATE UNIVERSITY

210 Law Center
Baton Rouge, LA 70803
(504)388-8491
gopher://gopher.lsu.edu

ABA Approved Since 1926

The Basics

Type of School: **PUBLIC**
Application deadline*: **2/1**
Application fee: **$25**
Financial Aid deadline*: **3/1**
Student faculty ratio: **20.6 to 1**

First year can start other than Fall: **No**
Student housing: **No**
--exclusively for law students: **No**
Term: **Semester**

*pr=preferred

Faculty

	Men		Women		Minorities		Total
	#	%	#	%	#	%	
Full-time	24	92	2	8	2	8	26
Other full-time	0	0	0	0	0	0	0
Deans, librarians, & others who teach	3	100	0	0	0	0	3
Part-time	15	94	1	6	1	6	16
Total	42	93	3	7	3	7	45
Deans, librarians, & others who teach < 1/2	0	0	1	100	0	0	1

Library

# of volumes & volume equivalents	563,986	# of professional staff	18
# of titles	138,298	Hours per week with professional staff	65
# of active serial subscriptions	2,889	Hours per week without professional staff	34
Study seating capacity inside the library	464	# of student computer work stations for entire law school	13
Square feet of law library	71,056	# of additional networked connections	9
Square feet of law school (excl. Library)	112,947		

Curriculum

	Full time	Part time
Typical first-year section size	65	0
Is there typically a "small section" of the first year class, other than Legal Writing, taught by full-time faculty?	Yes	No
If yes, typical size offered last year	32	N/A
# of classroom course titles beyond 1st year curriculum	58	0
# of upper division courses, excluding seminars, with an enrollment:		
Under 25	8	0
25 - 49	12	0
50 - 74	2	0
75 - 99	12	0
100 +	16	0
# of seminars	8	0
# of seminar positions available	189	
# of seminar positions filled	172	0
# of positions available in simulation courses	717	
# of simulation positions filled	693	0
# of positions available in faculty supervised clinical courses	0	
# of fac. sup. clin. positions filled	0	0
# involved in field placements	0	0
# involved in law journals	48	0
# in moot court or trial competitions	24	0
# of credit hours required to graduate	97	

Enrollment & Attrition

	Full-Time							Part-Time							Attrition			
	Men		Women		Minorities		Total	Men		Women		Minorities		Total	Academic	Other	Total	
	#	%	#	%	#	%	#	#	%	#	%	#	%	#	#	#	#	%
1st Year	132	52.8	118	47.2	31	12.4	250	0	0.0	0	0.0	0	0.0	0	54	34	88	32
2nd Year	106	54.1	90	45.9	14	7.1	196	0	0.0	0	0.0	0	0.0	0	1	5	6	3.1
3rd Year	109	57.1	82	42.9	13	6.8	191	0	0.0	0	0.0	0	0.0	0	3	1	4	2.0
4th Year								0	0.0	0	0.0	0	0.0	0	0	0	0	0.0
Total	347	54.5	290	45.5	58	9.1	637	0	0.0	0	0.0	0	0.0	0	58	40	98	15
JD Degrees Awarded	103	52.8	92	47.2	10	5.1	195	0	0.0	0	0.0	0	0.0	0				

GPA & LSAT Scores

	Full Time	Part Time	Total
# of apps	947	0	947
# admits	541	0	541
# of matrics	262	0	262
75% GPA	3.55	0.00	
25% GPA	3.12	0.00	
75% LSAT	156	0	
25% LSAT	148	0	

Tuition/Living Expenses

	Resident	Non-resident
Full-Time	$3,936	$8,556
Part-Time	$2,634	$6,002

Estimated living expenses for Singles		
Living on campus	Living off campus	Living at home
$10,550	$18,950	$9,110

Financial Aid

	Full-time		Part-time		Total	
	#	%	#	%	#	%
Total # receiving grants	130	20.4	0	0.0	130	20.4
Less than 1/2 tuition	45	7.1	0	0.0	45	7.1
Half to full tuition	56	8.8	0	0.0	56	8.8
Full tuition	0	0.0	0	0.0	0	0.0
More than full tuition	29	4.6	0	0.0	29	4.6
Median Grant Amount	$3,500		$0			

Refunds

Refunds of Admissions or Seat Deposit prior to commencement of classes? No

Refunds of Pre-paid tuition prior to commencement of classes? Yes

If yes, fully refundable before the start of classes? No

90% refund from 06/30/96 to 08/16/96
75% refund from 08/19/96 to 08/30/96
50% refund from 09/02/96 to 10/04/96

Joint Degrees Offered

JD/MPA

Advanced Degrees Offered

LLM Approval of faculty
MCL Approval of faculty

Career Placement

	Total	%
Employment status known	191	92.3
Employment status unknown	16	7.7
Employed	149	78.0
Pursuing graduate degrees	5	2.6
Unemployed seeking employment	37	19.4
Unemployed not seeking employment	0	0.0
Type of Employment		
# employed in law firms	91	61.1
# employed in business & industry	10	6.7
# employed in government	16	10.7
# employed in public interest	0	0.0
# employed as judicial clerks	32	21.5
# employed in academia	0	0.0
Geographic Location		
# employed in state	135	90.6
# employed in foreign countries	0	0.0
# of states where employed	7	

Bar Passage Rate

Jurisdiction	LA
# from school taking bar for the first time	171
School's pass rate for all first-time takers	79%
State's pass rate for all first-time takers	55%
State's pass rate for all first-time takers from ABA approved law schools	67%

LOUISVILLE, UNIVERSITY OF

Louisville, KY 40292
(502)852-6879
http://www.louisville.edu/law/

ABA Approved Since 1931

The Basics

Type of School: **PUBLIC**
Application deadline*: **2/15**
Application fee: **$30**
Financial Aid deadline*:
Student faculty ratio: **18.2 to 1**
First year can start other than Fall: **No**
Student housing: **Yes**
--exclusively for law students: **No**
Term: **Semester**

*pr=preferred

Faculty

	Men #	Men %	Women #	Women %	Minorities #	Minorities %	Total
Full-time	17	77	5	23	3	14	22
Other full-time	0	0	0	0	0	0	0
Deans, librarians, & others who teach	2	67	1	33	0	0	3
Part-time	10	77	3	23	1	8	13
Total	29	76	9	24	4	11	38
Deans, librarians, & others who teach < 1/2	1	100	0	0	0	0	1

Library

# of volumes & volume equivalents	273,047	# of professional staff	4
# of titles	37,220	Hours per week with professional staff	82
# of active serial subscriptions	4,799	Hours per week without professional staff	6
Study seating capacity inside the library	372	# of student computer work stations for entire law school	29
Square feet of law library	53,060	# of additional networked connections	0
Square feet of law school (excl. Library)	62,850		

Curriculum

	Full time	Part time
Typical first-year section size	63	42
Is there typically a "small section" of the first year class, other than Legal Writing, taught by full-time faculty?	No	No
If yes, typical size offered last year	N/A	N/A
# of classroom course titles beyond 1st year curriculum	54	45
# of upper division courses, excluding seminars, with an enrollment:		
Under 25	40	14
25 - 49	54	9
50 - 74	8	0
75 - 99	3	1
100 +	0	0
# of seminars	15	4
# of seminar positions available	342	
# of seminar positions filled	236	68
# of positions available in simulation courses	140	
# of simulation positions filled	94	20
# of positions available in faculty supervised clinical courses	0	
# of fac. sup. clin. positions filled	0	0
# involved in field placements	120	16
# involved in law journals	77	5
# in moot court or trial competitions	26	6
# of credit hours required to graduate	90	

Enrollment & Attrition

	Full-Time Men #	Men %	Women #	Women %	Minorities #	Minorities %	Total #	Part-Time Men #	Men %	Women #	Women %	Minorities #	Minorities %	Total #	Attrition Academic #	Other #	Total #	Total %
1st Year	68	55.7	54	44.3	5	4.1	122	25	58.1	18	41.9	5	11.6	43	6	9	15	8.4
2nd Year	72	49.3	74	50.7	4	2.7	146	9	52.9	8	47.1	0	0.0	17	3	4	7	4.1
3rd Year	77	52.0	71	48.0	17	11.5	148	9	69.2	4	30.8	0	0.0	13	0	1	1	1.0
4th Year								7	46.7	8	53.3	0	0.0	15	0	0	0	0.0
Total	217	52.2	199	47.8	26	6.3	416	50	56.8	38	43.2	5	5.7	88	9	14	23	4.9
JD Degrees Awarded	45	48.9	47	51.1	7	7.6	92	8	50.0	8	50.0	2	12.5	16				

GPA & LSAT Scores

	Full Time	Part Time	Total
# of apps	798	124	922
# admits	320	65	385
# of matrics	123	43	166
75% GPA	3.66	3.48	
25% GPA	3.01	2.80	
75% LSAT	158	159	
25% LSAT	152	152	

Tuition/Living Expenses

	Resident	Non-resident
Full-Time	$4,670	$12,270
Part-Time	$3,910	$10,240

Estimated living expenses for Singles		
Living on campus	Living off campus	Living at home
$7,152	$8,868	$4,222

Career Placement

	Total	%
Employment status known	144	96.0
Employment status unknown	6	4.0
Employed	138	95.8
Pursuing graduate degrees	1	0.7
Unemployed seeking employment	1	0.7
Unemployed not seeking employment	4	2.8
Type of Employment		
# employed in law firms	92	66.7
# employed in business & industry	20	14.5
# employed in government	15	10.9
# employed in public interest	2	1.5
# employed as judicial clerks	8	5.8
# employed in academia	1	0.7
Geographic Location		
# employed in state	112	81.2
# employed in foreign countries	0	0.0
# of states where employed	12	

Financial Aid

	Full-time		Part-time		Total	
	#	%	#	%	#	%
Total # receiving grants	56	13.5	6	6.8	62	12.3
Less than 1/2 tuition	2	0.5	0	0.0	2	0.4
Half to full tuition	2	0.5	1	1.1	3	0.6
Full tuition	39	9.4	5	5.7	44	8.7
More than full tuition	13	3.1	0	0.0	13	2.6
Median Grant Amount	$4,670		$4,670			

Refunds

Refunds of Admissions or Seat Deposit prior to commencement of classes? Yes

100% refund to 06/01/96

Refunds of Pre-paid tuition prior to commencement of classes? Yes

If yes, fully refundable before the start of classes? Yes

100% refund from 08/19/96 to 08/23/96
60% refund from 08/26/96 to 08/30/96
30% refund from 09/02/96 to 09/13/96

Joint Degrees Offered

MBA/JD, JD/M.Div.

Advanced Degrees Offered

No Advanced Degrees

Bar Passage Rate

Jurisdiction	KY
# from school taking bar for the first time	141
School's pass rate for all first-time takers	88%
State's pass rate for all first-time takers	88%
State's pass rate for all first-time takers from ABA approved law schools	88%

LOYOLA MARYMOUNT UNIVERSITY-LOS ANGELES

919 South Albany Street
Los Angeles, CA 90015
(213)736-1000
http://www.law.lmu.edu

ABA Approved Since 1935

The Basics

Type of School: **PRIVATE**
Application deadline*: **2/1**
Application fee: **$50**
Financial Aid deadline*: **3/2**
Student faculty ratio: **22.0 to 1**

First year can start other than Fall: **No**
Student housing: **No**
--exclusively for law students: **No**
Term: **Semester**

*pr=preferred

Faculty

	Men #	Men %	Women #	Women %	Minorities #	Minorities %	Total
Full-time	30	65	16	35	11	24	46
Other full-time	2	40	3	60	0	0	5
Deans, librarians, & others who teach	0	0	0	0	0	0	0
Part-time	24	73	9	27	5	15	33
Total	**56**	**67**	**28**	**33**	**16**	**19**	**84**
Deans, librarians, & others who teach < 1/2	4	67	2	33	1	17	6

Library

# of volumes & volume equivalents	414,355	# of professional staff	12
# of titles	194,172	Hours per week with professional staff	84
# of active serial subscriptions	6,300	Hours per week without professional staff	28
Study seating capacity inside the library	683	# of student computer work stations for entire law school	56
Square feet of law library	46,802	# of additional networked connections	60
Square feet of law school (excl. Library)	65,615		

Curriculum

	Full time	Part time
Typical first-year section size	80	104
Is there typically a "small section" of the first year class, other than Legal Writing, taught by full-time faculty?	No	No
If yes, typical size offered last year	N/A	N/A
# of classroom course titles beyond 1st year curriculum	73	65
# of upper division courses, excluding seminars, with an enrollment:		
Under 25	31	39
25 - 49	34	27
50 - 74	7	5
75 - 99	9	4
100 +	8	2
# of seminars	12	9
# of seminar positions available	446	
# of seminar positions filled	146	207
# of positions available in simulation courses	764	
# of simulation positions filled	379	252
# of positions available in faculty supervised clinical courses	274	
# of fac. sup. clin. positions filled	169	53
# involved in field placements	324	56
# involved in law journals	404	102
# in moot court or trial competitions	276	89
# of credit hours required to graduate	87	

Enrollment & Attrition

	Full-Time Men #	Full-Time Men %	Full-Time Women #	Full-Time Women %	Full-Time Minorities #	Full-Time Minorities %	Full-Time Total #	Part-Time Men #	Part-Time Men %	Part-Time Women #	Part-Time Women %	Part-Time Minorities #	Part-Time Minorities %	Part-Time Total #	Attrition Academic #	Attrition Other #	Attrition Total #	Attrition %
1st Year	167	53.5	145	46.5	129	41.3	312	57	52.3	52	47.7	33	30.3	109	11	26	37	8.6
2nd Year	171	54.8	141	45.2	137	43.9	312	52	55.9	41	44.1	31	33.3	93	3	3	6	1.4
3rd Year	179	55.4	144	44.6	120	37.2	323	60	64.5	33	35.5	38	40.9	93	4	1	5	1.2
4th Year								64	58.7	45	41.3	38	34.9	109	1	0	1	1.0
Total	517	54.6	430	45.4	386	40.8	947	233	57.7	171	42.3	140	34.7	404	19	30	49	3.6
JD Degrees Awarded	169	52.5	153	47.5	110	34.2	322	54	59.3	37	40.7	18	19.8	91				

LOYOLA MARYMOUNT UNIVERSITY-LOS ANGELES

GPA & LSAT Scores

	Full Time	Part Time	Total
# of apps	2,588	433	3,021
# admits	999	168	1,167
# of matrics	354	124	478
75% GPA	3.48	3.42	
25% GPA	3.05	2.93	
75% LSAT	161	161	
25% LSAT	154	154	

Tuition/Living Expenses

	Resident	Non-resident
Full-Time	$19,646	$19,646
Part-Time	$13,210	$13,210

Estimated living expenses for Singles		
Living on campus	Living off campus	Living at home
N/A	$14,470	$9,170

Career Placement

	Total	%
Employment status known	318	85.0
Employment status unknown	56	15.0
Employed	265	83.3
Pursuing graduate degrees	7	2.2
Unemployed seeking employment	38	12.0
Unemployed not seeking employment	8	2.5
Type of Employment		
# employed in law firms	179	67.6
# employed in business & industry	43	16.2
# employed in government	23	8.7
# employed in public interest	7	2.6
# employed as judicial clerks	9	3.4
# employed in academia	4	1.5
Geographic Location		
# employed in state	206	77.7
# employed in foreign countries	0	0.0
# of states where employed	6	

Financial Aid

	Full-time		Part-time		Total	
	#	%	#	%	#	%
Total # receiving grants	130	13.7	50	12.4	180	13.3
Less than 1/2 tuition	32	3.4	34	8.4	66	4.9
Half to full tuition	53	5.6	12	3.0	65	4.8
Full tuition	23	2.4	2	0.5	25	1.9
More than full tuition	22	2.3	2	0.5	24	1.8
Median Grant Amount	$12,000		$3,075			

Refunds

Refunds of Admissions or Seat Deposit prior to commencement of classes? Yes

83% refund from 05/20/96 to 07/05/96

Refunds of Pre-paid tuition prior to commencement of classes? Yes

If yes, fully refundable before the start of classes? Yes

Joint Degrees Offered

JD/MBA

Advanced Degrees Offered

No Advanced Degrees

Bar Passage Rate

Jurisdiction	CA
# from school taking bar for the first time	319
School's pass rate for all first-time takers	83%
State's pass rate for all first-time takers	73%
State's pass rate for all first-time takers from ABA approved law schools	83%

LOYOLA UNIVERSITY-CHICAGO

One East Pearson Street
Chicago, IL 60611
(312)915-7120
gopher://gopher.luc.edu/11/loyola/colleg

ABA Approved Since 1925

The Basics

Type of School: **PRIVATE**
Application deadline*: **4/1**
Application fee: **$45**
Financial Aid deadline*: **3/1**
Student faculty ratio: **21.9 to 1**
First year can start other than Fall: **No**
Student housing: **No**
--exclusively for law students: **No**
Term: **Semester**

*pr=preferred

Faculty

	Men #	Men %	Women #	Women %	Minorities #	Minorities %	Total
Full-time	21	81	5	19	3	12	26
Other full-time	1	25	3	75	1	25	4
Deans, librarians, & others who teach	2	100	0	0	0	0	2
Part-time	43	60	29	40	2	3	72
Total	67	64	37	36	6	6	104
Deans, librarians, & others who teach < 1/2	0	0	1	100	0	0	1

Library

# of volumes & volume equivalents	324,021	# of professional staff	7
# of titles	49,267	Hours per week with professional staff	90
# of active serial subscriptions	3,499	Hours per week without professional staff	9
Study seating capacity inside the library	380	# of student computer work stations for entire law school	81
Square feet of law library	43,900	# of additional networked connections	0
Square feet of law school (excl. Library)	39,202		

Curriculum

	Full time	Part time
Typical first-year section size	55	60
Is there typically a "small section" of the first year class, other than Legal Writing, taught by full-time faculty?	No	No
If yes, typical size offered last year	N/A	N/A
# of classroom course titles beyond 1st year curriculum	59	60
# of upper division courses, excluding seminars, with an enrollment:		
Under 25	47	34
25 - 49	24	21
50 - 74	15	5
75 - 99	7	0
100 +	0	0
# of seminars	12	4
# of seminar positions available	277	
# of seminar positions filled	204	68
# of positions available in simulation courses	1,065	
# of simulation positions filled	702	125
# of positions available in faculty supervised clinical courses	105	
# of fac. sup. clin. positions filled	74	11
# involved in field placements	72	5
# involved in law journals	103	11
# in moot court or trial competitions	54	8
# of credit hours required to graduate	86	

Enrollment & Attrition

	Full-Time							Part-Time							Attrition			
	Men		Women		Minorities		Total	Men		Women		Minorities		Total	Academic	Other	Total	
	#	%	#	%	#	%	#	#	%	#	%	#	%	#	#	#	#	%
1st Year	66	40.7	96	59.3	33	20.4	162	41	48.2	44	51.8	15	17.6	85	0	10	10	4.3
2nd Year	74	42.0	102	58.0	16	9.1	176	21	47.7	23	52.3	4	9.1	44	0	1	1	0.4
3rd Year	102	46.8	116	53.2	45	20.6	218	23	54.8	19	45.2	10	23.8	42	0	0	0	0.0
4th Year								16	66.7	8	33.3	3	12.5	24	0	0	0	0.0
Total	242	43.5	314	56.5	94	16.9	556	101	51.8	94	48.2	32	16.4	195	0	11	11	1.4
JD Degrees Awarded	107	55.2	87	44.8	45	23.2	194	14	42.4	19	57.6	5	15.2	33				

LOYOLA UNIVERSITY-CHICAGO

GPA & LSAT Scores

	Full Time	Part Time	Total
# of apps	2,009	320	2,329
# admits	755	204	959
# of matrics	163	83	246
75% GPA	3.48	3.40	
25% GPA	2.95	2.84	
75% LSAT	161	159	
25% LSAT	154	151	

Tuition/Living Expenses

	Resident	Non-resident
Full-Time	$19,500	$19,500
Part-Time	$14,650	$14,650

Estimated living expenses for Singles		
Living on campus	Living off campus	Living at home
N/A	$13,250	$9,250

Career Placement

	Total	%
Employment status known	165	99.4
Employment status unknown	1	0.6
Employed	156	94.6
Pursuing graduate degrees	3	1.8
Unemployed seeking employment	2	1.2
Unemployed not seeking employment	4	2.4
Type of Employment		
# employed in law firms	86	55.1
# employed in business & industry	34	21.8
# employed in government	25	16.0
# employed in public interest	5	3.2
# employed as judicial clerks	6	3.9
# employed in academia	0	0.0
Geographic Location		
# employed in state	145	93.0
# employed in foreign countries	0	0.0
# of states where employed	9	

Financial Aid

	Full-time		Part-time		Total	
	#	%	#	%	#	%
Total # receiving grants	219	39.4	45	23.1	264	35.2
Less than 1/2 tuition	219	39.4	45	23.1	264	35.2
Half to full tuition	0	0.0	0	0.0	0	0.0
Full tuition	0	0.0	0	0.0	0	0.0
More than full tuition	0	0.0	0	0.0	0	0.0
Median Grant Amount	$2,136		$1,737			

Refunds

Refunds of Admissions or Seat Deposit prior to commencement of classes? No

Refunds of Pre-paid tuition prior to commencement of classes? Yes

If yes, fully refundable before the start of classes? Yes

Joint Degrees Offered

Poli. Sci., Indust.Rel, Social Work, MBA

Advanced Degrees Offered

LLM	Health Law
LLM	ChildLaw
S.J.D.	Doctor of Juridical Science in Health Law
M.J.	Health Law
M.J.	Child Law

Bar Passage Rate

Jurisdiction	IL
# from school taking bar for the first time	164
School's pass rate for all first-time takers	94%
State's pass rate for all first-time takers	87%
State's pass rate for all first-time takers from ABA approved law schools	87%

LOYOLA UNIVERSITY-NEW ORLEANS

7214 St. Charles Avenue
New Orleans, LA 70118
(504)861-5550
http://www.loyno.edu

ABA Approved Since 1931

The Basics

Type of School: **PRIVATE**
Application deadline*: **none**
Application fee: **$20**
Financial Aid deadline*:
Student faculty ratio: **18.0 to 1**
First year can start other than Fall: **No**
Student housing: **Yes**
--exclusively for law students: **Yes**
Term: **Semester**

*pr=preferred

Faculty

	Men #	Men %	Women #	Women %	Minorities #	Minorities %	Total
Full-time	21	70	9	30	8	27	30
Other full-time	0	0	0	0	0	0	0
Deans, librarians, & others who teach	2	100	0	0	0	0	2
Part-time	16	94	1	6	0	0	17
Total	39	80	10	20	8	16	49
Deans, librarians, & others who teach < 1/2	1	50	1	50	0	0	2

Library

# of volumes & volume equivalents	255,262	# of professional staff	7
# of titles	76,298	Hours per week with professional staff	67
# of active serial subscriptions	2,594	Hours per week without professional staff	37
Study seating capacity inside the library	521	# of student computer work stations for entire law school	14
Square feet of law library	52,168	# of additional networked connections	0
Square feet of law school (excl. Library)	45,715		

Curriculum

	Full time	Part time
Typical first-year section size	77	70
Is there typically a "small section" of the first year class, other than Legal Writing, taught by full-time faculty?	No	No
If yes, typical size offered last year	N/A	N/A
# of classroom course titles beyond 1st year curriculum	56	43
# of upper division courses, excluding seminars, with an enrollment:		
Under 25	19	26
25 - 49	10	12
50 - 74	14	6
75 - 99	9	2
100 +	0	0
# of seminars	12	6
# of seminar positions available	370	
# of seminar positions filled	140	95
# of positions available in simulation courses	149	
# of simulation positions filled	76	17
# of positions available in faculty supervised clinical courses	135	
# of fac. sup. clin. positions filled	76	3
# involved in field placements	44	0
# involved in law journals	74	8
# in moot court or trial competitions	8	0
# of credit hours required to graduate	90	

Enrollment & Attrition

	Full-Time Men #	Full-Time Men %	Full-Time Women #	Full-Time Women %	Full-Time Minorities #	Full-Time Minorities %	Full-Time Total #	Part-Time Men #	Part-Time Men %	Part-Time Women #	Part-Time Women %	Part-Time Minorities #	Part-Time Minorities %	Part-Time Total #	Attrition Academic #	Attrition Other #	Attrition Total #	Attrition %
1st Year	69	43.4	90	56.6	29	18.2	159	23	48.9	24	51.1	3	6.4	47	3	47	50	17
2nd Year	117	59.1	81	40.9	49	24.7	198	29	64.4	16	35.6	6	13.3	45	0	0	0	0.0
3rd Year	85	55.2	69	44.8	47	30.5	154	21	58.3	15	41.7	4	11.1	36	0	3	3	1.4
4th Year								17	37.0	29	63.0	2	4.3	46	0	1	1	2.0
Total	271	53.0	240	47.0	125	24.5	511	90	51.7	84	48.3	15	8.6	174	3	51	54	7.1
JD Degrees Awarded	94	56.3	73	43.7	38	22.8	167	35	68.6	16	31.4	11	21.6	51				

GPA & LSAT Scores

	Full Time	Part Time	Total
# of apps	1,205	136	1,341
# admits	726	74	800
# of matrics	159	47	206
75% GPA	3.20	3.33	
25% GPA	2.73	2.71	
75% LSAT	153	156	
25% LSAT	148	148	

Tuition/Living Expenses

	Resident	Non-resident
Full-Time	$16,230	$16,230
Part-Time	$11,014	$11,014

Estimated living expenses for Singles		
Living on campus	Living off campus	Living at home
$11,089	$11,089	$4,264

Career Placement

	Total	%
Employment status known	182	82.4
Employment status unknown	39	17.7
Employed	105	57.7
Pursuing graduate degrees	8	4.4
Unemployed seeking employment	68	37.4
Unemployed not seeking employment	1	0.6
Type of Employment		
# employed in law firms	66	62.9
# employed in business & industry	5	4.8
# employed in government	11	10.5
# employed in public interest	3	2.9
# employed as judicial clerks	19	18.1
# employed in academia	1	1.0
Geographic Location		
# employed in state	79	75.2
# employed in foreign countries	0	0.0
# of states where employed	15	

Financial Aid

	Full-time		Part-time		Total	
	#	%	#	%	#	%
Total # receiving grants	0	0.0	0	0.0	0	0.0
Less than 1/2 tuition	68	13.3	0	0.0	68	9.9
Half to full tuition	39	7.6	0	0.0	39	5.7
Full tuition	4	0.8	0	0.0	4	0.6
More than full tuition	0	0.0	0	0.0	0	0.0
Median Grant Amount	$0		$0			

Refunds

Refunds of Admissions or Seat Deposit prior to commencement of classes? Yes

67% refund from 05/01/96 to 06/01/96

Refunds of Pre-paid tuition prior to commencement of classes? Yes

If yes, fully refundable before the start of classes? Yes

100% refund from 08/19/96 to 08/27/96

Joint Degrees Offered

JD/MBA, JD/MA, Mass Comm., JD/MA, Religious, Studies, JD/MA, Urban, Planning, JD/MA, Public, Admin.

Advanced Degrees Offered

No Advanced Degrees

Bar Passage Rate

Jurisdiction	LA
# from school taking bar for the first time	126
School's pass rate for all first-time takers	56%
State's pass rate for all first-time takers	55%
State's pass rate for all first-time takers from ABA approved law schools	67%

MAINE, UNIVERSITY OF

246 Deering Avenue
Portland, ME 04102
(207)780-4355
http://www.law.usm.maine.edu

ABA Approved Since 1962

The Basics

Type of School: **PUBLIC**
Application deadline: **2/15**
Application fee: **$25**
Financial Aid deadline: **2/1**
Student faculty ratio: **18.8 to 1**
First year can start other than Fall: **No**
Student housing: **No**
--exclusively for law students: **No**
Term: **Semester**

Faculty

	Men		Women		Minorities		Total
	#	%	#	%	#	%	
Full-time	10	77	3	23	0	0	13
Other full-time	0	0	0	0	0	0	0
Deans, librarians, & others who teach	1	50	1	50	0	0	2
Part-time	4	57	3	43	0	0	7
Total	**15**	**68**	**7**	**32**	**0**	**0**	**22**
Deans, librarians, & others who teach < 1/2	1	100	0	0	0	0	1

Library

# of volumes & volume equivalents	298,675	# of professional staff	7
# of titles	48,557	Hours per week with professional staff	59
# of active serial subscriptions	3,578	Hours per week without professional staff	38
Study seating capacity inside the library	172	# of student computer work stations for entire law school	31
Square feet of law library	32,800	# of additional networked connections	0
Square feet of law school (excl. Library)	30,115		

Curriculum

	Full time	Part time
Typical first-year section size	95	0
Is there typically a "small section" of the first year class, other than Legal Writing, taught by full-time faculty?	No	No
If yes, typical size offered last year	N/A	N/A
# of classroom course titles beyond 1st year curriculum	46	0
# of upper division courses, excluding seminars, with an enrollment:		
Under 25	27	0
25 - 49	13	0
50 - 74	4	0
75 - 99	3	0
100 +	0	0
# of seminars	3	0
# of seminar positions available	56	
# of seminar positions filled	40	0
# of positions available in simulation courses	97	
# of simulation positions filled	91	0
# of positions available in faculty supervised clinical courses	47	
# of fac. sup. clin. positions filled	42	0
# involved in field placements	0	0
# involved in law journals	40	0
# in moot court or trial competitions	18	0
# of credit hours required to graduate	89	

Enrollment & Attrition

	Full-Time							Part-Time							Attrition			
	Men		Women		Minorities		Total	Men		Women		Minorities		Total	Academic	Other	Total	
	#	%	#	%	#	%	#	#	%	#	%	#	%	#	#	#	#	%
1st Year	57	57.0	43	43.0	3	3.0	100	1	25.0	3	75.0	0	0.0	4	0	7	7	7.5
2nd Year	51	56.0	40	44.0	6	6.6	91	0	0.0	0	0.0	0	0.0	0	0	2	2	2.1
3rd Year	54	58.1	39	41.9	4	4.3	93	1	100.0	0	0.0	0	0.0	1	0	0	0	0.0
4th Year								0	0.0	0	0.0	0	0.0	0	0	0	0	0.0
Total	162	57.0	122	43.0	13	4.6	284	2	40.0	3	60.0	0	0.0	5	0	9	9	3.2
JD Degrees Awarded	39	45.3	47	54.7	1	1.2	86	0	0.0	2	100.0	0	0.0	2				

GPA & LSAT Scores

	Full Time	Part Time	Total
# of apps	N/A	N/A	672
# admits	N/A	N/A	336
# of matrics	101	4	105
75% GPA	3.45	3.16	
25% GPA	3.09	2.90	
75% LSAT	158	156	
25% LSAT	150	142	

Tuition/Living Expenses

	Resident	Non-resident
Full-Time	$8,070	$15,686
Part-Time	$5,790	$11,230

Estimated living expenses for Singles		
Living on campus	Living off campus	Living at home
$7,830	$7,830	$4,875

Financial Aid

	Full-time		Part-time		Total	
	#	%	#	%	#	%
Total # receiving grants	98	34.5	0	0.0	98	33.9
Less than 1/2 tuition	88	31.0	0	0.0	88	30.4
Half to full tuition	0	0.0	0	0.0	0	0.0
Full tuition	10	3.5	0	0.0	10	3.5
More than full tuition	0	0.0	0	0.0	0	0.0
Median Grant Amount	$2,893		$0			

Refunds

Refunds of Admissions or Seat Deposit prior to commencement of classes? No

Refunds of Pre-paid tuition prior to commencement of classes? No

If yes, fully refundable before the start of classes? No

Joint Degrees Offered

JD/MA

Advanced Degrees Offered

No Advanced Degrees

Career Placement

	Total	%
Employment status known	78	98.7
Employment status unknown	1	1.3
Employed	64	82.1
Pursuing graduate degrees	0	0.0
Unemployed seeking employment	13	16.7
Unemployed not seeking employment	1	1.3
Type of Employment		
# employed in law firms	25	39.1
# employed in business & industry	16	25.0
# employed in government	9	14.1
# employed in public interest	1	1.6
# employed as judicial clerks	13	20.3
# employed in academia	0	0.0
Geographic Location		
# employed in state	47	73.4
# employed in foreign countries	0	0.0
# of states where employed	11	

Bar Passage Rate

Jurisdiction	ME
# from school taking bar for the first time	65
School's pass rate for all first-time takers	75%
State's pass rate for all first-time takers	
State's pass rate for all first-time takers from ABA approved law schools	

MARQUETTE UNIVERSITY

Sensenbrenner Hall
P.O. Box 1881
Milwaukee, WI 53201-1881
(414)288-7090
http://www.mu.edu/dept/law

ABA Approved Since 1925

The Basics

Type of School: **PRIVATE**
Application deadline*: **4/1**
Application fee: **$35**
Financial Aid deadline*: **3/1**
Student faculty ratio: **18.2 to 1**

First year can start other than Fall: **No**
Student housing: **Yes**
--exclusively for law students: **No**
Term: **Semester**

*pr=preferred

Faculty

	Men		Women		Minorities		Total
	#	%	#	%	#	%	
Full-time	13	62	8	38	3	14	21
Other full-time	0	0	0	0	0	0	0
Deans, librarians, & others who teach	3	100	0	0	0	0	3
Part-time	20	83	4	17	2	8	24
Total	36	75	12	25	5	10	48
Deans, librarians, & others who teach < 1/2	0	0	1	100	0	0	1

Library

# of volumes & volume equivalents	246,559	# of professional staff	8
# of titles	119,496	Hours per week with professional staff	76
# of active serial subscriptions	3,108	Hours per week without professional staff	30
Study seating capacity inside the library	345	# of student computer work stations for entire law school	19
Square feet of law library	32,911	# of additional networked connections	60
Square feet of law school (excl. Library)	30,098		

Curriculum

	Full time	Part time
Typical first-year section size	75	0
Is there typically a "small section" of the first year class, other than Legal Writing, taught by full-time faculty?	Yes	No
If yes, typical size offered last year	40	N/A
# of classroom course titles beyond 1st year curriculum	102	0
# of upper division courses, excluding seminars, with an enrollment:		
Under 25	47	0
25 - 49	28	0
50 - 74	10	0
75 - 99	7	0
100 +	2	0
# of seminars	21	0
# of seminar positions available	315	
# of seminar positions filled	260	0
# of positions available in simulation courses	368	
# of simulation positions filled	269	0
# of positions available in faculty supervised clinical courses	41	
# of fac. sup. clin. positions filled	39	0
# involved in field placements	114	0
# involved in law journals	41	0
# in moot court or trial competitions	12	0
# of credit hours required to graduate	90	

Enrollment & Attrition

	Full-Time							Part-Time							Attrition			
	Men		Women		Minorities		Total	Men		Women		Minorities		Total	Academic	Other	Total	
	#	%	#	%	#	%	#	#	%	#	%	#	%	#	#	#	#	%
1st Year	82	57.3	61	42.7	10	7.0	143	2	25.0	6	75.0	1	12.5	8	0	0	0	0.0
2nd Year	81	56.3	63	43.8	20	13.9	144	0	0.0	0	0.0	0	0.0	0	0	8	8	4.8
3rd Year	103	61.7	64	38.3	29	17.4	167	0	0.0	0	0.0	0	0.0	0	1	2	3	1.8
4th Year								0	0.0	0	0.0	0	0.0	0	0	0	0	0.0
Total	266	58.6	188	41.4	59	13.0	454	2	25.0	6	75.0	1	12.5	8	1	10	11	2.3
JD Degrees Awarded	93	58.1	67	41.9	17	10.6	160	0	0.0	0	0.0	0	0.0	0				

GPA & LSAT Scores

	Full Time	Part Time	Total
# of apps	972	59	1,031
# admits	459	9	468
# of matrics	150	7	157
75% GPA	3.33	3.52	
25% GPA	2.87	2.82	
75% LSAT	160	160	
25% LSAT	153	153	

Tuition/Living Expenses

	Resident	Non-resident
Full-Time	$17,310	$17,310
Part-Time	$650	$650

Estimated living expenses for Singles		
Living on campus	Living off campus	Living at home
$10,730	$10,730	$10,730

Career Placement

	Total	%
Employment status known	152	98.1
Employment status unknown	3	1.9
Employed	134	88.2
Pursuing graduate degrees	4	2.6
Unemployed seeking employment	9	5.9
Unemployed not seeking employment	5	3.3
Type of Employment		
# employed in law firms	87	64.9
# employed in business & industry	19	14.2
# employed in government	19	14.2
# employed in public interest	2	1.5
# employed as judicial clerks	7	5.2
# employed in academia	0	0.0
Geographic Location		
# employed in state	107	79.9
# employed in foreign countries	0	0.0
# of states where employed	14	

Financial Aid

	Full-time		Part-time		Total	
	#	%	#	%	#	%
Total # receiving grants	54	11.9	0	0.0	54	11.7
Less than 1/2 tuition	29	6.4	0	0.0	29	6.3
Half to full tuition	10	2.2	0	0.0	10	2.2
Full tuition	15	3.3	0	0.0	15	3.2
More than full tuition	0	0.0	0	0.0	0	0.0
Median Grant Amount	$7,948		$0			

Refunds

Refunds of Admissions or Seat Deposit prior to commencement of classes? Yes

100% refund from 04/25/96 to 06/30/96

Refunds of Pre-paid tuition prior to commencement of classes? Yes

If yes, fully refundable before the start of classes? Yes

Joint Degrees Offered

JD/MBA, JD/MPOLISCI, JD/POLISCI, JD/MA, Intl Affairs

Advanced Degrees Offered

No Advanced Degrees

Bar Passage Rate

Jurisdiction	IL	MI
# from school taking bar for the first time	14	2
School's pass rate for all first-time takers	93%	100%
State's pass rate for all first-time takers	87%	70%
State's pass rate for all first-time takers from ABA approved law schools	87%	70%

MARYLAND, UNIVERSITY OF

500 West Baltimore Street
Baltimore, MD 21201-1786
(410)706-3492
http://www.law.umab.edu

ABA Approved Since 1930

The Basics

Type of School: PUBLIC	First year can start other than Fall: No
Application deadline*: 2/15	Student housing: No
Application fee: $40	--exclusively for law students: No
Financial Aid deadline*: 3/15	Term: Semester
Student faculty ratio: 14.4 to 1	

*pr=preferred

Faculty

	Men		Women		Minorities		Total
	#	%	#	%	#	%	
Full-time	28	62	17	38	7	16	45
Other full-time	0	0	0	0	0	0	0
Deans, librarians, & others who teach	1	100	0	0	0	0	1
Part-time	24	71	10	29	1	3	34
Total	53	66	27	34	8	10	80
Deans, librarians, & others who teach < 1/2	1	50	1	50	0	0	2

Library

# of volumes & volume equivalents	364,212	# of professional staff	8
# of titles	87,768	Hours per week with professional staff	55
# of active serial subscriptions	4,084	Hours per week without professional staff	43
Study seating capacity inside the library	372	# of student computer work stations for entire law school	58
Square feet of law library	45,921	# of additional networked connections	0
Square feet of law school (excl. Library)	45,695		

Curriculum

	Full time	Part time
Typical first-year section size	63	76
Is there typically a "small section" of the first year class, other than Legal Writing, taught by full-time faculty?	Yes	Yes
If yes, typical size offered last year	23	34
# of classroom course titles beyond 1st year curriculum	105	35
# of upper division courses, excluding seminars, with an enrollment:		
Under 25	46	24
25 - 49	18	3
50 - 74	12	2
75 - 99	3	4
100 +	1	0
# of seminars	38	7
# of seminar positions available	655	
# of seminar positions filled	425	89
# of positions available in simulation courses	300	
# of simulation positions filled	116	141
# of positions available in faculty supervised clinical courses	245	
# of fac. sup. clin. positions filled	215	30
# involved in field placements	66	8
# involved in law journals	152	18
# in moot court or trial competitions	132	6
# of credit hours required to graduate	85	

Enrollment & Attrition

	Full-Time							Part-Time							Attrition			
	Men		Women		Minorities		Total	Men		Women		Minorities		Total	Academic	Other	Total	
	#	%	#	%	#	%	#	#	%	#	%	#	%	#	#	#	#	%
1st Year	91	45.5	109	54.5	50	25.0	200	37	55.2	30	44.8	12	17.9	67	0	21	21	7.5
2nd Year	97	48.0	105	52.0	66	32.7	202	41	58.6	29	41.4	23	32.9	70	0	8	8	3.0
3rd Year	99	50.5	97	49.5	63	32.1	196	31	50.8	30	49.2	13	21.3	61	0	8	8	3.1
4th Year								31	51.7	29	48.3	22	36.7	60	0	1	1	1.6
Total	287	48.0	311	52.0	179	29.9	598	140	54.3	118	45.7	70	27.1	258	0	38	38	4.4
JD Degrees Awarded	97	45.5	116	54.5	73	34.3	213	30	60.0	20	40.0	6	12.0	50				

GPA & LSAT Scores

	Full Time	Part Time	Total
# of apps	2,156	378	2,534
# admits	840	124	964
# of matrics	200	67	267
75% GPA	3.53	3.65	
25% GPA	3.02	2.99	
75% LSAT	161	161	
25% LSAT	152	153	

Tuition/Living Expenses

	Resident	Non-resident
Full-Time	$8,815	$15,881
Part-Time	$6,613	$11,910

Estimated living expenses for Singles		
Living on campus	Living off campus	Living at home
$8,455	$10,020	$4,500

Financial Aid

	Full-time		Part-time		Total	
	#	%	#	%	#	%
Total # receiving grants	301	50.3	30	11.6	331	38.7
Less than 1/2 tuition	301	50.3	30	11.6	331	38.7
Half to full tuition	0	0.0	0	0.0	0	0.0
Full tuition	0	0.0	0	0.0	0	0.0
More than full tuition	0	0.0	0	0.0	0	0.0
Median Grant Amount	$3,208		$2,906			

Refunds

Refunds of Admissions or Seat Deposit prior to commencement of classes? No

Refunds of Pre-paid tuition prior to commencement of classes? Yes

If yes, fully refundable before the start of classes? No

Joint Degrees Offered

JD/Phd, Pol Sci, JD/MA, Bus Admin, Crim Justice, Liberal Educ, Marine/Envir, Publc Mgmt, Social Work

Advanced Degrees Offered

No Advanced Degrees

Career Placement

	Total	%
Employment status known	237	97.9
Employment status unknown	5	2.1
Employed	202	85.2
Pursuing graduate degrees	2	0.8
Unemployed seeking employment	30	12.7
Unemployed not seeking employment	3	1.3
Type of Employment		
# employed in law firms	70	34.7
# employed in business & industry	39	19.3
# employed in government	45	22.3
# employed in public interest	8	4.0
# employed as judicial clerks	36	17.8
# employed in academia	4	2.0
Geographic Location		
# employed in state	87	43.1
# employed in foreign countries	1	0.5
# of states where employed	17	

Bar Passage Rate

Jurisdiction	MD
# from school taking bar for the first time	190
School's pass rate for all first-time takers	83%
State's pass rate for all first-time takers	75%
State's pass rate for all first-time takers from ABA approved law schools	75%

MCGEORGE SCHOOL OF LAW

University of the Pacific
5200 Fifth Avenue
Sacramento, CA 95817
(916)739-7169
http://www.mcgeorge.edu

ABA Approved Since 1969

The Basics

Type of School: **PRIVATE**
Application deadline*: **5/15**
Application fee: **$40**
Financial Aid deadline*:
Student faculty ratio: **23.6 to 1**

First year can start other than Fall: **No**
Student housing: **Yes**
--exclusively for law students: **Yes**
Term: **Semester**

***pr=preferred**

Faculty

	Men		Women		Minorities		Total
	#	%	#	%	#	%	
Full-time	29	78	8	22	3	8	37
Other full-time	3	38	5	63	1	13	8
Deans, librarians, & others who teach	2	40	3	60	0	0	5
Part-time	20	80	5	20	1	4	25
Total	54	72	21	28	5	7	75
Deans, librarians, & others who teach < 1/2	2	67	1	33	0	0	3

Library

# of volumes & volume equivalents	419,333	# of professional staff	7
# of titles	89,825	Hours per week with professional staff	86
# of active serial subscriptions	3,969	Hours per week without professional staff	24
Study seating capacity inside the library	615	# of student computer work stations for entire law school	89
Square feet of law library	48,161	# of additional networked connections	40
Square feet of law school (excl. Library)	144,423		

Curriculum

	Full time	Part time
Typical first-year section size	100	100
Is there typically a "small section" of the first year class, other than Legal Writing, taught by full-time faculty?	No	No
If yes, typical size offered last year	N/A	N/A
# of classroom course titles beyond 1st year curriculum	74	59
# of upper division courses, excluding seminars, with an enrollment:		
Under 25	24	16
25 - 49	23	22
50 - 74	15	15
75 - 99	9	4
100 +	12	6
# of seminars	9	5
# of seminar positions available	312	
# of seminar positions filled	166	51
# of positions available in simulation courses	646	
# of simulation positions filled	495	144
# of positions available in faculty supervised clinical courses	112	
# of fac. sup. clin. positions filled	87	21
# involved in field placements	141	40
# involved in law journals	70	24
# in moot court or trial competitions	280	80
# of credit hours required to graduate	88	

Enrollment & Attrition

	Full-Time							Part-Time							Attrition			
	Men		Women		Minorities		Total	Men		Women		Minorities		Total	Academic	Other	Total	
	#	%	#	%	#	%	#	#	%	#	%	#	%	#	#	#	#	%
1st Year	168	55.3	136	44.7	69	22.7	304	48	45.3	58	54.7	23	21.7	106	18	21	39	9.6
2nd Year	161	54.6	134	45.4	73	24.7	295	32	49.2	33	50.8	18	27.7	65	7	29	36	11
3rd Year	128	52.2	117	47.8	64	26.1	245	34	50.0	34	50.0	17	25.0	68	0	11	11	2.8
4th Year								59	56.2	46	43.8	8	7.6	105	0	0	0	0.0
Total	457	54.1	387	45.9	206	24.4	844	173	50.3	171	49.7	66	19.2	344	25	61	86	7.0
JD Degrees Awarded	163	56.8	124	43.2	57	19.9	287	51	58.6	36	41.4	9	10.3	87				

GPA & LSAT Scores

	Full Time	Part Time	Total
# of apps	2,073	0	2,073
# admits	1,150	149	1,299
# of matrics	310	107	417
75% GPA	3.28	3.31	
25% GPA	2.75	2.70	
75% LSAT	155	155	
25% LSAT	150	150	

Tuition/Living Expenses

	Resident	Non-resident
Full-Time	$16,864	$16,864
Part-Time	$10,006	$10,006

Estimated living expenses for Singles		
Living on campus	Living off campus	Living at home
$13,300	$13,300	$5,707

Career Placement

	Total	%
Employment status known	248	75.8
Employment status unknown	79	24.2
Employed	178	71.8
Pursuing graduate degrees	8	3.2
Unemployed seeking employment	60	24.2
Unemployed not seeking employment	2	0.8
Type of Employment		
# employed in law firms	104	58.4
# employed in business & industry	20	11.2
# employed in government	37	20.8
# employed in public interest	2	1.1
# employed as judicial clerks	14	7.9
# employed in academia	1	0.6
Geographic Location		
# employed in state	139	78.1
# employed in foreign countries	5	2.8
# of states where employed	14	

Financial Aid

	Full-time		Part-time		Total	
	#	%	#	%	#	%
Total # receiving grants	552	65.4	183	53.2	735	61.9
Less than 1/2 tuition	520	61.6	165	48.0	685	57.7
Half to full tuition	29	3.4	3	0.9	32	2.7
Full tuition	15	1.8	3	0.9	18	1.5
More than full tuition	0	0.0	0	0.0	0	0.0
Median Grant Amount	$2,524		$1,475			

Refunds

Refunds of Admissions or Seat Deposit prior to commencement of classes? No

Refunds of Pre-paid tuition prior to commencement of classes? Yes

If yes, fully refundable before the start of classes? Yes

Joint Degrees Offered

JD/MBA, JD/MPPA, JD/MS, JD/Acc't

Advanced Degrees Offered

LL.M. TRANSNATIONAL BUSINESS PRACTICE

Bar Passage Rate

Jurisdiction	CA
# from school taking bar for the first time	267
School's pass rate for all first-time takers	83%
State's pass rate for all first-time takers	73%
State's pass rate for all first-time takers from ABA approved law schools	83%

MEMPHIS, UNIVERSITY OF

The University of Memphis
School of Law
Memphis, TN 39152-6513
(901)678-2421
http://www.people.memphis.edu/~law

ABA Approved Since 1965

The Basics

Type of School: **PUBLIC**
Application deadline*: **2/15**
Application fee: **$10**
Financial Aid deadline*: **4/1**
Student faculty ratio: **18.4 to 1**
First year can start other than Fall: **No**
Student housing: **Yes**
--exclusively for law students: **Yes**
Term: **Semester**

*pr=preferred

Faculty

	Men #	Men %	Women #	Women %	Minorities #	Minorities %	Total
Full-time	15	71	6	29	1	5	21
Other full-time	1	33	2	67	0	0	3
Deans, librarians, & others who teach	1	100	0	0	0	0	1
Part-time	11	55	9	45	1	5	20
Total	**28**	**62**	**17**	**38**	**2**	**4**	**45**
Deans, librarians, & others who teach < 1/2	1	100	0	0	0	0	1

Library

# of volumes & volume equivalents	262,561	# of professional staff	6
# of titles	40,789	Hours per week with professional staff	56
# of active serial subscriptions	3,044	Hours per week without professional staff	44
Study seating capacity inside the library	299	# of student computer work stations for entire law school	56
Square feet of law library	29,465	# of additional networked connections	4
Square feet of law school (excl. Library)	27,918		

Curriculum

	Full time	Part time
Typical first-year section size	92	0
Is there typically a "small section" of the first year class, other than Legal Writing, taught by full-time faculty?	No	No
If yes, typical size offered last year	N/A	N/A
# of classroom course titles beyond 1st year curriculum	58	0
# of upper division courses, excluding seminars, with an enrollment:		
Under 25	21	0
25 - 49	11	0
50 - 74	8	0
75 - 99	2	0
100 +	9	0
# of seminars	7	0
# of seminar positions available	84	
# of seminar positions filled	78	0
# of positions available in simulation courses	184	
# of simulation positions filled	170	0
# of positions available in faculty supervised clinical courses	56	
# of fac. sup. clin. positions filled	49	0
# involved in field placements	13	0
# involved in law journals	22	0
# in moot court or trial competitions	65	0
# of credit hours required to graduate	90	

Enrollment & Attrition

	Full-Time Men #	Men %	Women #	Women %	Minorities #	Minorities %	Total #	Part-Time Men #	Men %	Women #	Women %	Minorities #	Minorities %	Total #	Attrition Academic #	Other #	Total #	Total %
1st Year	76	54.3	64	45.7	17	12.1	140	3	37.5	5	62.5	1	12.5	8	20	7	27	15
2nd Year	104	61.5	65	38.5	17	10.1	169	1	20.0	4	80.0	0	0.0	5	5	1	6	4.3
3rd Year	82	59.4	56	40.6	14	10.1	138	3	75.0	1	25.0	1	25.0	4	0	0	0	0.0
4th Year								5	71.4	2	28.6	1	14.3	7	0	0	0	0.0
Total	262	58.6	185	41.4	48	10.7	447	12	50.0	12	50.0	3	12.5	24	25	8	33	7.1
JD Degrees Awarded	74	57.8	54	42.2	4	3.1	128	1	33.3	2	66.7	0	0.0	3				

GPA & LSAT Scores

	Full Time	Part Time	Total
# of apps	944	56	1,000
# admits	403	17	420
# of matrics	143	9	152
75% GPA	3.57	3.59	
25% GPA	2.91	3.04	
75% LSAT	161	157	
25% LSAT	148	148	

Tuition/Living Expenses

	Resident	Non-resident
Full-Time	$3,852	$9,680
Part-Time	$3,022	$7,576

Estimated living expenses for Singles		
Living on campus	Living off campus	Living at home
$9,873	$9,873	$9,873

Career Placement

	Total	%
Employment status known	137	97.2
Employment status unknown	4	2.8
Employed	130	94.9
Pursuing graduate degrees	1	0.7
Unemployed seeking employment	6	4.4
Unemployed not seeking employment	0	0.0
Type of Employment		
# employed in law firms	73	56.2
# employed in business & industry	14	10.8
# employed in government	16	12.3
# employed in public interest	4	3.1
# employed as judicial clerks	15	11.5
# employed in academia	0	0.0
Geographic Location		
# employed in state	107	82.3
# employed in foreign countries	0	0.0
# of states where employed	14	

Financial Aid

	Full-time		Part-time		Total	
	#	%	#	%	#	%
Total # receiving grants	52	11.6	0	0.0	52	11.0
Less than 1/2 tuition	5	1.1	0	0.0	5	1.1
Half to full tuition	8	1.8	0	0.0	8	1.7
Full tuition	17	3.8	0	0.0	17	3.6
More than full tuition	22	4.9	0	0.0	22	4.7
Median Grant Amount	$3,100		$0			

Refunds

Refunds of Admissions or Seat Deposit prior to commencement of classes? Yes

100% refund from 04/01/96 to 05/15/96

Refunds of Pre-paid tuition prior to commencement of classes? Yes

If yes, fully refundable before the start of classes? Yes

Joint Degrees Offered

JD/MBA

Advanced Degrees Offered

No Advanced Degrees

Bar Passage Rate

Jurisdiction	TN
# from school taking bar for the first time	107
School's pass rate for all first-time takers	81%
State's pass rate for all first-time takers	79%
State's pass rate for all first-time takers from ABA approved law schools	91%

MERCER UNIVERSITY

1021 Georgia Avenue
Macon, GA 31207
(912)752-2601
http://www.mercer.edu/~law

ABA Approved Since 1925

The Basics

Type of School: **PRIVATE**
Application deadline*: **3/15**
Application fee: **$45**
Financial Aid deadline*: **4/1**
Student faculty ratio: **15.2 to 1**

First year can start other than Fall: **No**
Student housing: **Yes**
--exclusively for law students: **Yes**
Term: **Semester**

*pr=preferred

Faculty

	Men		Women		Minorities		Total
	#	%	#	%	#	%	
Full-time	16	73	6	27	2	9	22
Other full-time	2	67	1	33	0	0	3
Deans, librarians, & others who teach	1	50	1	50	0	0	2
Part-time	5	83	1	17	0	0	6
Total	24	73	9	27	2	6	33
Deans, librarians, & others who teach < 1/2	1	50	1	50	0	0	2

Library

# of volumes & volume equivalents	272,486	# of professional staff	6
# of titles	34,770	Hours per week with professional staff	73
# of active serial subscriptions	3,035	Hours per week without professional staff	2
Study seating capacity inside the library	326	# of student computer work stations for entire law school	41
Square feet of law library	35,000	# of additional networked connections	0
Square feet of law school (excl. Library)	48,800		

Curriculum

	Full time	Part time
Typical first-year section size	70	0
Is there typically a "small section" of the first year class, other than Legal Writing, taught by full-time faculty?	Yes	No
If yes, typical size offered last year	21	N/A
# of classroom course titles beyond 1st year curriculum	89	0
# of upper division courses, excluding seminars, with an enrollment:		
Under 25	53	0
25 - 49	25	0
50 - 74	12	0
75 - 99	5	0
100 +	1	0
# of seminars	13	0
# of seminar positions available	195	
# of seminar positions filled	163	0
# of positions available in simulation courses	759	
# of simulation positions filled	629	0
# of positions available in faculty supervised clinical courses	34	
# of fac. sup. clin. positions filled	34	0
# involved in field placements	31	0
# involved in law journals	44	0
# in moot court or trial competitions	26	0
# of credit hours required to graduate	90	

Enrollment & Attrition

	Full-Time							Part-Time							Attrition			
	Men		Women		Minorities		Total	Men		Women		Minorities		Total	Academic	Other	Total	
	#	%	#	%	#	%	#	#	%	#	%	#	%	#	#	#	#	%
1st Year	98	70.5	41	29.5	15	10.8	139	0	0.0	0	0.0	0	0.0	0	3	15	18	14
2nd Year	69	56.6	53	43.4	14	11.5	122	0	0.0	0	0.0	0	0.0	0	0	0	0	0.0
3rd Year	89	64.0	50	36.0	21	15.1	139	0	0.0	0	0.0	0	0.0	0	0	0	0	0.0
4th Year								0	0.0	0	0.0	0	0.0	0	0	0	0	0.0
Total	256	64.0	144	36.0	50	12.5	400	0	0.0	0	0.0	0	0.0	0	3	15	18	4.4
JD Degrees Awarded	88	62.4	53	37.6	23	16.3	141	0	0.0	0	0.0	0	0.0	0				

GPA & LSAT Scores

	Full Time	Part Time	Total
# of apps	1,117	0	1,117
# admits	481	0	481
# of matrics	143	0	143
75% GPA	3.43	0.00	
25% GPA	2.67	0.00	
75% LSAT	157	0	
25% LSAT	151	0	

Tuition/Living Expenses

	Resident	Non-resident
Full-Time	$17,490	$17,490
Part-Time	$8,745	$8,745

Estimated living expenses for Singles		
Living on campus	Living off campus	Living at home
$11,000	$11,000	$11,000

Financial Aid

	Full-time		Part-time		Total	
	#	%	#	%	#	%
Total # receiving grants	91	22.8	0	0.0	91	22.8
Less than 1/2 tuition	48	12.0	0	0.0	48	12.0
Half to full tuition	19	4.8	0	0.0	19	4.8
Full tuition	16	4.0	0	0.0	16	4.0
More than full tuition	8	2.0	0	0.0	8	2.0
Median Grant Amount	$7,000		$0			

Refunds

Refunds of Admissions or Seat Deposit prior to commencement of classes? No

Refunds of Pre-paid tuition prior to commencement of classes? Yes

If yes, fully refundable before the start of classes? Yes

Joint Degrees Offered

J.D.\M.B.A.

Advanced Degrees Offered

No Advanced Degrees

Career Placement

	Total	%
Employment status known	121	98.4
Employment status unknown	2	1.6
Employed	110	90.9
Pursuing graduate degrees	4	3.3
Unemployed seeking employment	5	4.1
Unemployed not seeking employment	2	1.7
Type of Employment		
# employed in law firms	76	69.1
# employed in business & industry	4	3.6
# employed in government	24	21.8
# employed in public interest	0	0.0
# employed as judicial clerks	4	3.6
# employed in academia	2	1.8
Geographic Location		
# employed in state	78	70.9
# employed in foreign countries	0	0.0
# of states where employed	7	

Bar Passage Rate

Jurisdiction	GA
# from school taking bar for the first time	112
School's pass rate for all first-time takers	94%
State's pass rate for all first-time takers	81%
State's pass rate for all first-time takers from ABA approved law schools	84%

MIAMI, UNIVERSITY OF

P.O. Box 248087
Coral Gables, FL 33124
(305)284-2394
http://www.law.miami.edu

ABA Approved Since 1941

The Basics

Type of School: **PRIVATE**
Application deadline*: **3/7**
Application fee: **$45**
Financial Aid deadline*: **3/1**
Student faculty ratio: **23.7 to 1**
First year can start other than Fall: **No**
Student housing: **Yes**
--exclusively for law students: **No**
Term: **Semester**

*pr=preferred

Faculty

	Men		Women		Minorities		Total
	#	%	#	%	#	%	
Full-time	35	76	11	24	7	15	46
Other full-time	1	50	1	50	0	0	2
Deans, librarians, & others who teach	2	67	1	33	1	33	3
Part-time	78	73	29	27	8	7	107
Total	116	73	42	27	16	10	158
Deans, librarians, & others who teach < 1/2	1	50	1	50	1	50	2

Library

# of volumes & volume equivalents	442,893	# of professional staff	12
# of titles	74,809	Hours per week with professional staff	84
# of active serial subscriptions	7,267	Hours per week without professional staff	35
Study seating capacity inside the library	663	# of student computer work stations for entire law school	169
Square feet of law library	77,446	# of additional networked connections	145
Square feet of law school (excl. Library)	119,486		

Curriculum

	Full time	Part time
Typical first-year section size	120	120
Is there typically a "small section" of the first year class, other than Legal Writing, taught by full-time faculty?	Yes	Yes
If yes, typical size offered last year	45	50
# of classroom course titles beyond 1st year curriculum	92	31
# of upper division courses, excluding seminars, with an enrollment:		
Under 25	17	8
25 - 49	38	16
50 - 74	17	3
75 - 99	11	2
100 +	9	2
# of seminars	54	54
# of seminar positions available	1,275	
# of seminar positions filled	972	175
# of positions available in simulation courses	481	
# of simulation positions filled	400	81
# of positions available in faculty supervised clinical courses	12	
# of fac. sup. clin. positions filled	12	0
# involved in field placements	150	15
# involved in law journals	297	0
# in moot court or trial competitions	336	0
# of credit hours required to graduate	88	

Enrollment & Attrition

	Full-Time							Part-Time							Attrition			
	Men		Women		Minorities		Total	Men		Women		Minorities		Total	Academic	Other	Total	
	#	%	#	%	#	%	#	#	%	#	%	#	%	#	#	#	#	%
1st Year	213	57.0	161	43.0	109	29.1	374	73	60.3	48	39.7	50	41.3	121	0	12	12	2.6
2nd Year	230	58.7	162	41.3	117	29.8	392	49	51.0	47	49.0	35	36.5	96	8	45	53	11
3rd Year	193	53.8	166	46.2	129	35.9	359	18	62.1	11	37.9	15	51.7	29	0	5	5	1.3
4th Year								14	46.7	16	53.3	16	53.3	30	0	0	0	0.0
Total	636	56.5	489	43.5	355	31.6	1,125	154	55.8	122	44.2	116	42.0	276	8	62	70	5.2
JD Degrees Awarded	195	59.3	134	40.7	84	25.5	329	31	58.5	22	41.5	18	34.0	53				

GPA & LSAT Scores

	Full Time	Part Time	Total
# of apps	2,043	333	2,376
# admits	1,269	200	1,469
# of matrics	378	126	504
75% GPA	3.43	3.31	
25% GPA	2.92	2.68	
75% LSAT	156	152	
25% LSAT	150	145	

Tuition/Living Expenses

	Resident	Non-resident
Full-Time	$21,160	$21,160
Part-Time	$15,534	$15,534

Estimated living expenses for Singles		
Living on campus	Living off campus	Living at home
$14,565	$14,565	$9,390

Career Placement

	Total	%
Employment status known	388	96.3
Employment status unknown	15	3.7
Employed	311	80.2
Pursuing graduate degrees	6	1.6
Unemployed seeking employment	63	16.2
Unemployed not seeking employment	8	2.1
Type of Employment		
# employed in law firms	174	56.0
# employed in business & industry	59	19.0
# employed in government	51	16.4
# employed in public interest	6	1.9
# employed as judicial clerks	19	6.1
# employed in academia	2	0.6
Geographic Location		
# employed in state	240	77.2
# employed in foreign countries	4	1.3
# of states where employed	23	

Financial Aid

	Full-time		Part-time		Total	
	#	%	#	%	#	%
Total # receiving grants	323	28.7	6	2.2	329	23.5
Less than 1/2 tuition	136	12.1	5	1.8	141	10.1
Half to full tuition	64	5.7	1	0.4	65	4.6
Full tuition	107	9.5	0	0.0	107	7.6
More than full tuition	16	1.4	0	0.0	16	1.1
Median Grant Amount	$11,262		$3,719			

Refunds

Refunds of Admissions or Seat Deposit prior to commencement of classes? Yes

66% refund from 01/02/96 to 05/14/96
50% refund from 05/15/96 to 06/30/96
33% refund from 07/01/96 to 08/05/96

Refunds of Pre-paid tuition prior to commencement of classes? Yes

If yes, fully refundable before the start of classes? Yes

Joint Degrees Offered

No Joint Degrees

Advanced Degrees Offered

LL.M.	(1) Taxation
LL.M.	(2) Estate Planning
LL.M.	(3) Ocean and Coastal Law
LL.M.	(4) International Law
LL.M.	(5) Inter-American Law
LL.M.	(6) Real Property Land Development & Finance Law
LL.M.	(7) Comparative Law
LL.M.	(8) General (For Foreign Law Graduates with a Law background)

Bar Passage Rate

Jurisdiction	FL
# from school taking bar for the first time	296
School's pass rate for all first-time takers	89%
State's pass rate for all first-time takers	84%
State's pass rate for all first-time takers from ABA approved law schools	84%

MICHIGAN, UNIVERSITY OF

Hutchins Hall
625 South State Street
Ann Arbor, MI 48109-1215
(313)764-1358
http://www.law.umich.edu

ABA Approved Since 1923

The Basics

Type of School: **PUBLIC**
Application deadline*: **2/15**
Application fee: **$70**
Financial Aid deadline*: **1/1**
Student faculty ratio: **16.4 to 1**

First year can start other than Fall: **Yes**
Student housing: **Yes**
--exclusively for law students: **Yes**
Term: **Semester**

*pr=preferred

Faculty

	Men #	Men %	Women #	Women %	Minorities #	Minorities %	Total
Full-time	36	67	18	33	4	7	54
Other full-time	9	69	4	31	4	31	13
Deans, librarians, & others who teach	1	50	1	50	0	0	2
Part-time	11	73	4	27	0	0	15
Total	57	68	27	32	8	10	84
Deans, librarians, & others who teach < 1/2	1	50	1	50	0	0	2

Library

# of volumes & volume equivalents	800,187	# of professional staff	9
# of titles	261,805	Hours per week with professional staff	71
# of active serial subscriptions	10,243	Hours per week without professional staff	41
Study seating capacity inside the library	856	# of student computer work stations for entire law school	75
Square feet of law library	107,994	# of additional networked connections	27
Square feet of law school (excl. Library)	83,632		

Curriculum

	Full time	Part time
Typical first-year section size	85	0
Is there typically a "small section" of the first year class, other than Legal Writing, taught by full-time faculty?	Yes	No
If yes, typical size offered last year	43	N/A
# of classroom course titles beyond 1st year curriculum	132	0
# of upper division courses, excluding seminars, with an enrollment:		
Under 25	34	0
25 - 49	25	0
50 - 74	20	0
75 - 99	11	0
100 +	20	0
# of seminars	48	0
# of seminar positions available	747	
# of seminar positions filled	640	0
# of positions available in simulation courses	169	
# of simulation positions filled	169	0
# of positions available in faculty supervised clinical courses	174	
# of fac. sup. clin. positions filled	170	0
# involved in field placements	46	0
# involved in law journals	396	0
# in moot court or trial competitions	204	0
# of credit hours required to graduate	86	

Enrollment & Attrition

	Full-Time Men #	Men %	Women #	Women %	Minorities #	Minorities %	Total #	Part-Time Men #	Men %	Women #	Women %	Minorities #	Minorities %	Total #	Attrition Academic #	Other #	Total #	%
1st Year	207	64.1	116	35.9	68	21.1	323	0	0.0	0	0.0	0	0.0	0	0	2	2	0.6
2nd Year	195	54.6	162	45.4	70	19.6	357	0	0.0	0	0.0	0	0.0	0	0	2	2	0.5
3rd Year	222	57.2	166	42.8	90	23.2	388	0	0.0	0	0.0	0	0.0	0	0	0	0	0.0
4th Year								0	0.0	0	0.0	0	0.0	0	0	0	0	0.0
Total	624	58.4	444	41.6	228	21.3	1,068	0	0.0	0	0.0	0	0.0	0	0	4	4	0.4
JD Degrees Awarded	227	59.0	158	41.0	76	19.7	385	0	0.0	0	0.0	0	0.0	0				

GPA & LSAT Scores

	Full Time	Part Time	Total
# of apps	3,636	0	3,636
# admits	1,123	0	1,123
# of matrics	319	0	319
75% GPA	3.68	0.00	
25% GPA	3.34	0.00	
75% LSAT	170	0	
25% LSAT	164	0	

Tuition/Living Expenses

	Resident	Non-resident
Full-Time	$16,678	$22,678
Part-Time	$0	$0

Estimated living expenses for Singles		
Living on campus	Living off campus	Living at home
$12,450	$11,800	$7,000

Career Placement

	Total	%
Employment status known	376	97.4
Employment status unknown	10	2.6
Employed	352	93.6
Pursuing graduate degrees	5	1.3
Unemployed seeking employment	18	4.8
Unemployed not seeking employment	1	0.3
Type of Employment		
# employed in law firms	234	66.5
# employed in business & industry	24	6.8
# employed in government	17	4.8
# employed in public interest	4	1.1
# employed as judicial clerks	71	20.2
# employed in academia	2	0.6
Geographic Location		
# employed in state	97	27.6
# employed in foreign countries	2	0.6
# of states where employed	34	

Financial Aid

	Full-time		Part-time		Total	
	#	%	#	%	#	%
Total # receiving grants	410	38.4	0	0.0	410	38.4
Less than 1/2 tuition	336	31.5	0	0.0	336	31.5
Half to full tuition	52	4.9	0	0.0	52	4.9
Full tuition	12	1.1	0	0.0	12	1.1
More than full tuition	10	0.9	0	0.0	10	0.9
Median Grant Amount	$6,300		$0			

Refunds

Refunds of Admissions or Seat Deposit prior to commencement of classes? No

Refunds of Pre-paid tuition prior to commencement of classes? No

If yes, fully refundable before the start of classes? No

Joint Degrees Offered

Bus Admin, Economics, Hlth Svcs Ad, Higher Ed, Mod Mideast, Nat Resource, Philosophy, Polit Sci, Public Pol, Russ/E Eur, World Pol

Advanced Degrees Offered

M.C.L. L.L.M. S.J.D.	Advanced degree students select from general Law School curriculum to build an area of concentration within their degree programs.

Bar Passage Rate

Jurisdiction	MI	IL
# from school taking bar for the first time	72	53
School's pass rate for all first-time takers	89%	98%
State's pass rate for all first-time takers	70%	87%
State's pass rate for all first-time takers from ABA approved law schools	70%	87%

MINNESOTA, UNIVERSITY OF

229 19 Ave S.
Minneapolis, MN 55455
(612)625-1000
http://www.umn.edu/law/

ABA Approved Since 1923

The Basics

Type of School: **PUBLIC**
Application deadline*: **3/1**
Application fee: **$40**
Financial Aid deadline*: **3/15**
Student faculty ratio: **16.7 to 1**
First year can start other than Fall: **No**
Student housing: **No**
--exclusively for law students: **No**
Term: **Semester**

*pr=preferred

Faculty

	Men #	Men %	Women #	Women %	Minorities #	Minorities %	Total
Full-time	27	69	12	31	4	10	39
Other full-time	0	0	1	100	0	0	1
Deans, librarians, & others who teach	2	25	6	75	1	13	8
Part-time	38	64	21	36	9	15	59
Total	67	63	40	37	14	13	107
Deans, librarians, & others who teach < 1/2	0	0	0	0	0	0	0

Library

# of volumes & volume equivalents	813,892	# of professional staff	12
# of titles	217,774	Hours per week with professional staff	67
# of active serial subscriptions	9,550	Hours per week without professional staff	14
Study seating capacity inside the library	934	# of student computer work stations for entire law school	32
Square feet of law library	95,000	# of additional networked connections	0
Square feet of law school (excl. Library)	265,000		

Curriculum

	Full time	Part time
Typical first-year section size	108	0
Is there typically a "small section" of the first year class, other than Legal Writing, taught by full-time faculty?	Yes	No
If yes, typical size offered last year	54	N/A
# of classroom course titles beyond 1st year curriculum	156	0
# of upper division courses, excluding seminars, with an enrollment:		
Under 25	54	0
25 - 49	25	0
50 - 74	10	0
75 - 99	10	0
100 +	9	0
# of seminars	48	0
# of seminar positions available	748	
# of seminar positions filled	708	0
# of positions available in simulation courses	208	
# of simulation positions filled	208	0
# of positions available in faculty supervised clinical courses	390	
# of fac. sup. clin. positions filled	370	0
# involved in field placements	50	0
# involved in law journals	143	0
# in moot court or trial competitions	221	0
# of credit hours required to graduate	88	

Enrollment & Attrition

	Full-Time Men #	Men %	Women #	Women %	Minorities #	Minorities %	Total #	Part-Time Men #	Men %	Women #	Women %	Minorities #	Minorities %	Total #	Attrition Academic #	Other #	Total #	Total %
1st Year	143	56.5	110	43.5	45	17.8	253	0	0.0	0	0.0	0	0.0	0	1	14	15	5.7
2nd Year	147	57.9	107	42.1	34	13.4	254	0	0.0	0	0.0	0	0.0	0	1	0	1	0.4
3rd Year	145	51.8	135	48.2	53	18.9	280	0	0.0	0	0.0	0	0.0	0	0	0	0	0.0
4th Year								0	0.0	0	0.0	0	0.0	0	0	0	0	0.0
Total	435	55.3	352	44.7	132	16.8	787	0	0.0	0	0.0	0	0.0	0	2	14	16	2.0
JD Degrees Awarded	159	59.1	110	40.9	32	11.9	269	0	0.0	0	0.0	0	0.0	0				

GPA & LSAT Scores

	Full Time	Part Time	Total
# of apps	1,798	0	1,798
# admits	670	0	670
# of matrics	253	0	253
75% GPA	3.77	0.00	
25% GPA	3.27	0.00	
75% LSAT	164	0	
25% LSAT	158	0	

Tuition/Living Expenses

	Resident	Non-resident
Full-Time	$8,923	$14,819
Part-Time	$0	$0

Estimated living expenses for Singles		
Living on campus	Living off campus	Living at home
$8,640	$8,640	$5,760

Career Placement

	Total	%
Employment status known	254	99.6
Employment status unknown	1	0.4
Employed	232	91.3
Pursuing graduate degrees	4	1.5
Unemployed seeking employment	9	3.5
Unemployed not seeking employment	9	3.5
Type of Employment		
# employed in law firms	108	46.6
# employed in business & industry	36	15.5
# employed in government	13	5.6
# employed in public interest	7	3.0
# employed as judicial clerks	62	26.7
# employed in academia	6	2.6
Geographic Location		
# employed in state	181	78.0
# employed in foreign countries	3	1.3
# of states where employed	18	

Financial Aid

	Full-time		Part-time		Total	
	#	%	#	%	#	%
Total # receiving grants	284	36.1	0	0.0	284	36.1
Less than 1/2 tuition	58	7.4	0	0.0	58	7.4
Half to full tuition	98	12.5	0	0.0	98	12.5
Full tuition	7	0.9	0	0.0	7	0.9
More than full tuition	121	15.4	0	0.0	121	15.4
Median Grant Amount	$6,000		$0			

Refunds

Refunds of Admissions or Seat Deposit prior to commencement of classes? Yes

Refunds of Pre-paid tuition prior to commencement of classes? Yes

If yes, fully refundable before the start of classes? Yes

Joint Degrees Offered

JD/MA, JD/MPP, JD/MBA

Advanced Degrees Offered

LLM American Law (for foreign Lawyers)

Bar Passage Rate

Jurisdiction	MN
# from school taking bar for the first time	180
School's pass rate for all first-time takers	97%
State's pass rate for all first-time takers	90%
State's pass rate for all first-time takers from ABA approved law schools	90%

MISSISSIPPI COLLEGE

151 East Griffith Street
Jackson, MS 39201
(601)925-7105
http://www.mc.edu

ABA Approved Since 1980

The Basics

Type of School: **PRIVATE**
Application deadline*: **5/1**
Application fee: **$25**
Financial Aid deadline*: **5/1**
Student faculty ratio: **22.2 to 1**
First year can start other than Fall: **No**
Student housing: **No**
--exclusively for law students: **No**
Term: **Semester**

*pr=preferred

Faculty

	Men #	Men %	Women #	Women %	Minorities #	Minorities %	Total
Full-time	10	63	6	38	2	13	16
Other full-time	0	0	0	0	0	0	0
Deans, librarians, & others who teach	0	0	0	0	0	0	0
Part-time	4	57	3	43	0	0	7
Total	14	61	9	39	2	9	23
Deans, librarians, & others who teach < 1/2	2	50	2	50	0	0	4

Library

# of volumes & volume equivalents	240,990	# of professional staff	6
# of titles	80,991	Hours per week with professional staff	65
# of active serial subscriptions	3,333	Hours per week without professional staff	54
Study seating capacity inside the library	275	# of student computer work stations for entire law school	14
Square feet of law library	22,305	# of additional networked connections	0
Square feet of law school (excl. Library)	50,997		

Curriculum

	Full time	Part time
Typical first-year section size	80	0
Is there typically a "small section" of the first year class, other than Legal Writing, taught by full-time faculty?	No	No
If yes, typical size offered last year	N/A	N/A
# of classroom course titles beyond 1st year curriculum	43	0
# of upper division courses, excluding seminars, with an enrollment:		
Under 25	21	0
25 - 49	14	0
50 - 74	13	0
75 - 99	2	0
100 +	0	0
# of seminars	3	0
# of seminar positions available	45	
# of seminar positions filled	38	0
# of positions available in simulation courses	81	
# of simulation positions filled	78	0
# of positions available in faculty supervised clinical courses	0	
# of fac. sup. clin. positions filled	0	0
# involved in field placements	19	0
# involved in law journals	33	0
# in moot court or trial competitions	18	0
# of credit hours required to graduate	88	

Enrollment & Attrition

	Full-Time							Part-Time							Attrition			
	Men		Women		Minorities		Total	Men		Women		Minorities		Total	Academic	Other	Total	
	#	%	#	%	#	%	#	#	%	#	%	#	%	#	#	#	#	%
1st Year	103	65.2	55	34.8	19	12.0	158	0	0.0	0	0.0	0	0.0	0	1	12	13	8.6
2nd Year	83	60.6	54	39.4	18	13.1	137	0	0.0	0	0.0	0	0.0	0	0	0	0	0.0
3rd Year	84	68.3	39	31.7	11	8.9	123	0	0.0	0	0.0	0	0.0	0	0	0	0	0.0
4th Year								0	0.0	0	0.0	0	0.0	0	0	0	0	0.0
Total	270	64.6	148	35.4	48	11.5	418	0	0.0	0	0.0	0	0.0	0	1	12	13	3.4
JD Degrees Awarded	66	58.4	47	41.6	9	8.0	113	0	0.0	0	0.0	0	0.0	0				

GPA & LSAT Scores

	Full Time	Part Time	Total
# of apps	732	0	732
# admits	468	0	468
# of matrics	160	0	160
75% GPA	3.32	0.00	
25% GPA	2.72	0.00	
75% LSAT	151	0	
25% LSAT	145	0	

Tuition/Living Expenses

	Resident	Non-resident
Full-Time	$11,462	$11,462
Part-Time	$0	$0

Estimated living expenses for Singles		
Living on campus	Living off campus	Living at home
$10,030	$13,850	$13,850

Career Placement

	Total	%
Employment status known	102	92.7
Employment status unknown	8	7.3
Employed	84	82.4
Pursuing graduate degrees	7	6.9
Unemployed seeking employment	7	6.9
Unemployed not seeking employment	4	3.9
Type of Employment		
# employed in law firms	60	71.4
# employed in business & industry	5	6.0
# employed in government	6	7.1
# employed in public interest	0	0.0
# employed as judicial clerks	13	15.5
# employed in academia	0	0.0
Geographic Location		
# employed in state	43	51.2
# employed in foreign countries	0	0.0
# of states where employed	17	

Financial Aid

	Full-time		Part-time		Total	
	#	%	#	%	#	%
Total # receiving grants	93	22.3	0	0.0	93	22.2
Less than 1/2 tuition	29	6.9	0	0.0	29	6.9
Half to full tuition	20	4.8	0	0.0	20	4.8
Full tuition	39	9.3	0	0.0	39	9.3
More than full tuition	5	1.2	0	0.0	5	1.2
Median Grant Amount	$7,612		$0			

Refunds

Refunds of Admissions or Seat Deposit prior to commencement of classes? No

Refunds of Pre-paid tuition prior to commencement of classes? No

If yes, fully refundable before the start of classes? No

Joint Degrees Offered

No Joint Degrees

Advanced Degrees Offered

No Advanced Degrees

Bar Passage Rate

Jurisdiction	MS
# from school taking bar for the first time	46
School's pass rate for all first-time takers	90%
State's pass rate for all first-time takers	87%
State's pass rate for all first-time takers from ABA approved law schools	87%

MISSISSIPPI, UNIVERSITY OF

Law Center
University, MS 38677
(601)232-7631
http://www.olemiss.edu/depts/law_school

ABA Approved Since 1930

The Basics

Type of School: **PUBLIC**
Application deadline*: **3/1**
Application fee: **$20**
Financial Aid deadline*: **3/1**
Student faculty ratio: **26.5 to 1**

First year can start other than Fall: **Yes**
Student housing: **Yes**
--exclusively for law students: **No**
Term: **Semester**

*pr=preferred

Faculty

	Men		Women		Minorities		Total
	#	%	#	%	#	%	
Full-time	14	82	3	18	3	18	17
Other full-time	0	0	0	0	0	0	0
Deans, librarians, & others who teach	3	75	1	25	0	0	4
Part-time	4	80	1	20	1	20	5
Total	21	81	5	19	4	15	26
Deans, librarians, & others who teach < 1/2	0	0	0	0	0	0	0

Library

# of volumes & volume equivalents	281,529	# of professional staff	6
# of titles	60,856	Hours per week with professional staff	60
# of active serial subscriptions	3,355	Hours per week without professional staff	55
Study seating capacity inside the library	395	# of student computer work stations for entire law school	36
Square feet of law library	29,908	# of additional networked connections	0
Square feet of law school (excl. Library)	39,441		

Curriculum

	Full time	Part time
Typical first-year section size	57	0
Is there typically a "small section" of the first year class, other than Legal Writing, taught by full-time faculty?	No	No
If yes, typical size offered last year	N/A	N/A
# of classroom course titles beyond 1st year curriculum	57	0
# of upper division courses, excluding seminars, with an enrollment:		
Under 25	29	0
25 - 49	16	0
50 - 74	7	0
75 - 99	8	0
100 +	0	0
# of seminars	19	0
# of seminar positions available	340	
# of seminar positions filled	266	0
# of positions available in simulation courses	155	
# of simulation positions filled	142	0
# of positions available in faculty supervised clinical courses	40	
# of fac. sup. clin. positions filled	31	0
# involved in field placements	70	0
# involved in law journals	96	0
# in moot court or trial competitions	306	0
# of credit hours required to graduate	90	

Enrollment & Attrition

	Full-Time							Part-Time							Attrition			
	Men		Women		Minorities		Total	Men		Women		Minorities		Total	Academic	Other	Total	
	#	%	#	%	#	%	#	#	%	#	%	#	%	#	#	#	#	%
1st Year	135	60.5	88	39.5	39	17.5	223	0	0.0	0	0.0	0	0.0	0	21	8	29	17
2nd Year	85	57.0	64	43.0	20	13.4	149	0	0.0	0	0.0	0	0.0	0	2	4	6	3.8
3rd Year	99	69.2	44	30.8	17	11.9	143	0	0.0	0	0.0	0	0.0	0	0	0	0	0.0
4th Year								0	0.0	0	0.0	0	0.0	0	0	0	0	0.0
Total	319	61.9	196	38.1	76	14.8	515	0	0.0	0	0.0	0	0.0	0	23	12	35	7.5
JD Degrees Awarded	90	64.3	50	35.7	20	14.3	140	0	0.0	0	0.0	0	0.0	0				

GPA & LSAT Scores

	Full Time	Part Time	Total
# of apps	1,098	0	1,098
# admits	482	0	482
# of matrics	224	0	224
75% GPA	3.56	0.00	
25% GPA	3.02	0.00	
75% LSAT	156	0	
25% LSAT	147	0	

Tuition/Living Expenses

	Resident	Non-resident
Full-Time	$3,081	$7,003
Part-Time	$118	$314

Estimated living expenses for Singles		
Living on campus	Living off campus	Living at home
$9,085	$9,085	$9,085

Financial Aid

	Full-time		Part-time		Total	
	#	%	#	%	#	%
Total # receiving grants	63	12.2	0	0.0	63	12.2
Less than 1/2 tuition	0	0.0	0	0.0	0	0.0
Half to full tuition	0	0.0	0	0.0	0	0.0
Full tuition	63	12.2	0	0.0	63	12.2
More than full tuition	0	0.0	0	0.0	0	0.0
Median Grant Amount	$2,346		$0			

Refunds

Refunds of Admissions or Seat Deposit prior to commencement of classes? No

Refunds of Pre-paid tuition prior to commencement of classes? Yes

If yes, fully refundable before the start of classes? Yes

Joint Degrees Offered

JD/MBA

Advanced Degrees Offered

No Advanced Degrees

Career Placement

	Total	%
Employment status known	179	98.9
Employment status unknown	2	1.1
Employed	159	88.8
Pursuing graduate degrees	8	4.5
Unemployed seeking employment	12	6.7
Unemployed not seeking employment	0	0.0
Type of Employment		
# employed in law firms	107	67.3
# employed in business & industry	16	10.1
# employed in government	13	8.2
# employed in public interest	5	3.1
# employed as judicial clerks	17	10.7
# employed in academia	1	0.6
Geographic Location		
# employed in state	117	73.6
# employed in foreign countries	0	0.0
# of states where employed	13	

Bar Passage Rate

Jurisdiction	MS
# from school taking bar for the first time	92
School's pass rate for all first-time takers	86%
State's pass rate for all first-time takers	87%
State's pass rate for all first-time takers from ABA approved law schools	87%

MISSOURI-COLUMBIA, UNIVERSITY OF

203 Hulston Hall
University of Missouri-Columbia
Columbia, MO 65211
(573)882-6487
http://www.law.missouri.edu

ABA Approved Since 1923

The Basics

Type of School: **PUBLIC**
Application deadline*: **3/1**
Application fee: **$40**
Financial Aid deadline*: **3/1**
Student faculty ratio: **16.8 to 1**
First year can start other than Fall: **No**
Student housing: **Yes**
--exclusively for law students: **No**
Term: **Semester**

***pr=preferred**

Faculty

	Men #	Men %	Women #	Women %	Minorities #	Minorities %	Total
Full-time	20	80	5	20	2	8	25
Other full-time	0	0	1	100	0	0	1
Deans, librarians, & others who teach	1	100	0	0	0	0	1
Part-time	3	75	1	25	0	0	4
Total	24	77	7	23	2	6	31
Deans, librarians, & others who teach < 1/2	8	67	4	33	0	0	12

Library

# of volumes & volume equivalents	303,756	# of professional staff	6
# of titles	162,977	Hours per week with professional staff	69
# of active serial subscriptions	4,869	Hours per week without professional staff	20
Study seating capacity inside the library	378	# of student computer work stations for entire law school	29
Square feet of law library	61,851	# of additional networked connections	6
Square feet of law school (excl. Library)	30,699		

Curriculum

	Full time	Part time
Typical first-year section size	75	0
Is there typically a "small section" of the first year class, other than Legal Writing, taught by full-time faculty?	No	No
If yes, typical size offered last year	N/A	N/A
# of classroom course titles beyond 1st year curriculum	72	0
# of upper division courses, excluding seminars, with an enrollment:		
Under 25	47	0
25 - 49	16	0
50 - 74	10	0
75 - 99	8	0
100 +	0	0
# of seminars	4	0
# of seminar positions available	51	
# of seminar positions filled	36	0
# of positions available in simulation courses	204	
# of simulation positions filled	189	0
# of positions available in faculty supervised clinical courses	56	
# of fac. sup. clin. positions filled	55	0
# involved in field placements	20	0
# involved in law journals	96	0
# in moot court or trial competitions	200	0
# of credit hours required to graduate	89	

Enrollment & Attrition

	Full-Time Men #	Men %	Women #	Women %	Minorities #	Minorities %	Total #	Part-Time Men #	Men %	Women #	Women %	Minorities #	Minorities %	Total #	Attrition Academic #	Other #	Total #	%
1st Year	138	65.7	72	34.3	15	7.1	210	0	0.0	0	0.0	0	0.0	0	4	13	17	11
2nd Year	89	62.2	54	37.8	18	12.6	143	0	0.0	0	0.0	0	0.0	0	4	10	14	10
3rd Year	75	56.8	57	43.2	13	9.8	132	0	0.0	0	0.0	0	0.0	0	1	1	2	1.3
4th Year								0	0.0	0	0.0	0	0.0	0	0	0	0	0.0
Total	302	62.3	183	37.7	46	9.5	485	0	0.0	0	0.0	0	0.0	0	9	24	33	7.4
JD Degrees Awarded	95	63.3	55	36.7	9	6.0	150	0	0.0	0	0.0	0	0.0	0				

GPA & LSAT Scores

	Full Time	Part Time	Total
# of apps	750	0	750
# admits	490	0	490
# of matrics	200	0	200
75% GPA	3.57	0.00	
25% GPA	3.05	0.00	
75% LSAT	159	0	
25% LSAT	151	0	

Tuition/Living Expenses

	Resident	Non-resident
Full-Time	$8,272	$16,062
Part-Time	$0	$0

Estimated living expenses for Singles		
Living on campus	Living off campus	Living at home
$8,856	$11,330	$11,330

Career Placement

	Total	%
Employment status known	131	92.9
Employment status unknown	10	7.1
Employed	115	87.8
Pursuing graduate degrees	5	3.8
Unemployed seeking employment	8	6.1
Unemployed not seeking employment	3	2.3
Type of Employment		
# employed in law firms	69	60.0
# employed in business & industry	6	5.2
# employed in government	16	13.9
# employed in public interest	5	4.4
# employed as judicial clerks	17	14.8
# employed in academia	2	1.7
Geographic Location		
# employed in state	103	89.6
# employed in foreign countries	1	0.9
# of states where employed	7	

Financial Aid

	Full-time		Part-time		Total	
	#	%	#	%	#	%
Total # receiving grants	311	64.1	0	0.0	311	64.1
Less than 1/2 tuition	280	57.7	0	0.0	280	57.7
Half to full tuition	23	4.7	0	0.0	23	4.7
Full tuition	3	0.6	0	0.0	3	0.6
More than full tuition	5	1.0	0	0.0	5	1.0
Median Grant Amount	$1,000		$0			

Refunds

Refunds of Admissions or Seat Deposit prior to commencement of classes? No

Refunds of Pre-paid tuition prior to commencement of classes? Yes

If yes, fully refundable before the start of classes? Yes

Joint Degrees Offered

JD/MBA, JD/MPA

Advanced Degrees Offered

No Advanced Degrees

Bar Passage Rate

Jurisdiction	MO
# from school taking bar for the first time	127
School's pass rate for all first-time takers	90%
State's pass rate for all first-time takers	92%
State's pass rate for all first-time takers from ABA approved law schools	92%

MISSOURI-KANSAS CITY, UNIVERSITY OF

5100 Rockhill Road
Kansas City, MO 64110
(816)235-1644
http://www.law.umkc.edu

ABA Approved Since 1936

The Basics

Type of School: **PUBLIC**
Application deadline*: **none**
Application fee: **$25**
Financial Aid deadline*:
Student faculty ratio: **19.4 to 1**

First year can start other than Fall: **No**
Student housing: **No**
--exclusively for law students: **No**
Term: **Semester**

*pr=preferred

Faculty

	Men #	Men %	Women #	Women %	Minorities #	Minorities %	Total
Full-time	16	73	6	27	0	0	22
Other full-time	0	0	0	0	0	0	0
Deans, librarians, & others who teach	2	50	2	50	1	25	4
Part-time	9	82	2	18	1	9	11
Total	27	73	10	27	2	5	37
Deans, librarians, & others who teach < 1/2	0	0	0	0	0	0	0

Library

# of volumes & volume equivalents	263,989	# of professional staff	5
# of titles	47,144	Hours per week with professional staff	45
# of active serial subscriptions	3,857	Hours per week without professional staff	47
Study seating capacity inside the library	310	# of student computer work stations for entire law school	45
Square feet of law library	33,456	# of additional networked connections	0
Square feet of law school (excl. Library)	84,621		

Curriculum

	Full time	Part time
Typical first-year section size	56	0
Is there typically a "small section" of the first year class, other than Legal Writing, taught by full-time faculty?	No	No
If yes, typical size offered last year	N/A	N/A
# of classroom course titles beyond 1st year curriculum	84	0
# of upper division courses, excluding seminars, with an enrollment:		
Under 25	53	0
25 - 49	24	0
50 - 74	9	0
75 - 99	10	0
100 +	0	0
# of seminars	20	0
# of seminar positions available	221	
# of seminar positions filled	182	0
# of positions available in simulation courses	518	
# of simulation positions filled	366	0
# of positions available in faculty supervised clinical courses	0	
# of fac. sup. clin. positions filled	0	0
# involved in field placements	27	0
# involved in law journals	114	0
# in moot court or trial competitions	74	0
# of credit hours required to graduate	91	

Enrollment & Attrition

	Full-Time							Part-Time							Attrition			
	Men		Women		Minorities		Total	Men		Women		Minorities		Total	Academic	Other	Total	
	#	%	#	%	#	%	#	#	%	#	%	#	%	#	#	#	#	%
1st Year	85	52.8	76	47.2	20	12.4	161	5	35.7	9	64.3	0	0.0	14	0	6	6	3.4
2nd Year	90	55.2	73	44.8	19	11.7	163	2	40.0	3	60.0	0	0.0	5	2	11	13	8.3
3rd Year	87	55.4	70	44.6	19	12.1	157	1	33.3	2	66.7	0	0.0	3	0	1	1	0.7
4th Year								0	0.0	0	0.0	0	0.0	0	0	0	0	0.0
Total	262	54.5	219	45.5	58	12.1	481	8	36.4	14	63.6	0	0.0	22	2	18	20	4.2
JD Degrees Awarded	73	52.5	66	47.5	5	3.6	139	0	0.0	0	0.0	0	0.0	0				

MISSOURI-KANSAS CITY, UNIVERSITY OF

GPA & LSAT Scores

	Full Time	Part Time	Total
# of apps	726	40	766
# admits	465	26	491
# of matrics	163	16	179
75% GPA	3.41	3.50	
25% GPA	2.86	2.76	
75% LSAT	156	153	
25% LSAT	150	146	

Tuition/Living Expenses

	Resident	Non-resident
Full-Time	$8,271	$16,061
Part-Time	$5,956	$11,520

Estimated living expenses for Singles		
Living on campus	Living off campus	Living at home
$9,430	$11,450	$7,310

Career Placement

	Total	%
Employment status known	148	96.1
Employment status unknown	6	3.9
Employed	134	90.5
Pursuing graduate degrees	1	0.7
Unemployed seeking employment	13	8.8
Unemployed not seeking employment	0	0.0
Type of Employment		
# employed in law firms	77	57.5
# employed in business & industry	16	11.9
# employed in government	18	13.4
# employed in public interest	2	1.5
# employed as judicial clerks	21	15.7
# employed in academia	0	0.0
Geographic Location		
# employed in state	102	76.1
# employed in foreign countries	0	0.0
# of states where employed	11	

Financial Aid

	Full-time		Part-time		Total	
	#	%	#	%	#	%
Total # receiving grants	81	16.8	0	0.0	81	16.1
Less than 1/2 tuition	69	14.4	0	0.0	69	13.7
Half to full tuition	10	2.1	0	0.0	10	2.0
Full tuition	2	0.4	0	0.0	2	0.4
More than full tuition	0	0.0	0	0.0	0	0.0
Median Grant Amount	$3,862		$0			

Refunds

Refunds of Admissions or Seat Deposit prior to commencement of classes? No

Refunds of Pre-paid tuition prior to commencement of classes? Yes

If yes, fully refundable before the start of classes? Yes

Joint Degrees Offered

J.D./M.B.A.

Advanced Degrees Offered

L.L.M. General
L.L.M. Taxation
L.L.M. Urban Affairs (temporarily suspended)

Bar Passage Rate

Jurisdiction	MO
# from school taking bar for the first time	129
School's pass rate for all first-time takers	95%
State's pass rate for all first-time takers	92%
State's pass rate for all first-time takers from ABA approved law schools	92%

MONTANA, UNIVERSITY OF

Missoula, MT 59812
(406)243-4311
http://www.umt.edu/law

ABA Approved Since 1923

The Basics

Type of School: **PUBLIC**
Application deadline*: **3/1**
Application fee: **$60**
Financial Aid deadline*: **3/1**
Student faculty ratio: **16.0 to 1**

First year can start other than Fall: **No**
Student housing: **No**
--exclusively for law students: **No**
Term: **Semester**

*pr=preferred

Faculty

	Men #	Men %	Women #	Women %	Minorities #	Minorities %	Total
Full-time	7	58	5	42	1	8	12
Other full-time	1	100	0	0	0	0	1
Deans, librarians, & others who teach	1	50	1	50	0	0	2
Part-time	5	83	1	17	0	0	6
Total	14	67	7	33	1	5	21
Deans, librarians, & others who teach < 1/2	1	100	0	0	0	0	1

Library

# of volumes & volume equivalents	122,687	# of professional staff	3
# of titles	18,070	Hours per week with professional staff	40
# of active serial subscriptions	1,673	Hours per week without professional staff	53
Study seating capacity inside the library	127	# of student computer work stations for entire law school	35
Square feet of law library	19,641	# of additional networked connections	0
Square feet of law school (excl. Library)	39,109		

Curriculum

	Full time	Part time
Typical first-year section size	25	0
Is there typically a "small section" of the first year class, other than Legal Writing, taught by full-time faculty?	Yes	No
If yes, typical size offered last year	25	N/A
# of classroom course titles beyond 1st year curriculum	51	0
# of upper division courses, excluding seminars, with an enrollment:		
Under 25	4	0
25 - 49	11	0
50 - 74	8	0
75 - 99	2	0
100 +	0	0
# of seminars	24	0
# of seminar positions available	456	
# of seminar positions filled	286	0
# of positions available in simulation courses	383	
# of simulation positions filled	378	0
# of positions available in faculty supervised clinical courses	31	
# of fac. sup. clin. positions filled	30	0
# involved in field placements	39	0
# involved in law journals	29	0
# in moot court or trial competitions	27	0
# of credit hours required to graduate	90	

Enrollment & Attrition

	Full-Time Men #	Full-Time Men %	Full-Time Women #	Full-Time Women %	Full-Time Minorities #	Full-Time Minorities %	Full-Time Total #	Part-Time Men #	Part-Time Men %	Part-Time Women #	Part-Time Women %	Part-Time Minorities #	Part-Time Minorities %	Part-Time Total #	Attrition Academic #	Attrition Other #	Attrition Total #	Attrition %
1st Year	45	55.6	36	44.4	9	11.1	81	0	0.0	0	0.0	0	0.0	0	0	1	1	1.3
2nd Year	46	62.2	28	37.8	4	5.4	74	0	0.0	0	0.0	0	0.0	0	1	2	3	3.9
3rd Year	39	52.0	36	48.0	2	2.7	75	0	0.0	0	0.0	0	0.0	0	0	0	0	0.0
4th Year								0	0.0	0	0.0	0	0.0	0	0	0	0	0.0
Total	130	56.5	100	43.5	15	6.5	230	0	0.0	0	0.0	0	0.0	0	1	3	4	1.7
JD Degrees Awarded	50	67.6	24	32.4	3	4.1	74	0	0.0	0	0.0	0	0.0	0				

GPA & LSAT Scores

	Full Time	Part Time	Total
# of apps	478	0	478
# admits	208	0	208
# of matrics	81	0	81
75% GPA	3.50	0.00	
25% GPA	2.98	0.00	
75% LSAT	159	0	
25% LSAT	151	0	

Tuition/Living Expenses

	Resident	Non-resident
Full-Time	$5,656	$10,314
Part-Time	$0	$0

Estimated living expenses for Singles		
Living on campus	Living off campus	Living at home
$7,440	$7,440	$5,440

Financial Aid

	Full-time		Part-time		Total	
	#	%	#	%	#	%
Total # receiving grants	89	38.7	0	0.0	89	38.7
Less than 1/2 tuition	84	36.5	0	0.0	84	36.5
Half to full tuition	4	1.7	0	0.0	4	1.7
Full tuition	1	0.4	0	0.0	1	0.4
More than full tuition	0	0.0	0	0.0	0	0.0
Median Grant Amount	$1,482		$0			

Refunds

Refunds of Admissions or Seat Deposit prior to commencement of classes? Yes

50% refund to 07/15/96
0% refund from 07/15/96 to / /

Refunds of Pre-paid tuition prior to commencement of classes? Yes

If yes, fully refundable before the start of classes? Yes

90% refund from 08/21/96 to 08/27/96
75% refund from 08/28/96 to 09/04/96
50% refund from 09/05/96 to 09/11/96

Joint Degrees Offered

JD/MPA, JD/MS

Advanced Degrees Offered

No Advanced Degrees

Career Placement

	Total	%
Employment status known	69	87.3
Employment status unknown	10	12.7
Employed	61	88.4
Pursuing graduate degrees	4	5.8
Unemployed seeking employment	3	4.4
Unemployed not seeking employment	1	1.5
Type of Employment		
# employed in law firms	27	44.3
# employed in business & industry	4	6.6
# employed in government	8	13.1
# employed in public interest	1	1.6
# employed as judicial clerks	20	32.8
# employed in academia	1	1.6
Geographic Location		
# employed in state	53	86.9
# employed in foreign countries	0	0.0
# of states where employed	6	

Bar Passage Rate

Jurisdiction	MT
# from school taking bar for the first time	69
School's pass rate for all first-time takers	94%
State's pass rate for all first-time takers	90%
State's pass rate for all first-time takers from ABA approved law schools	90%

NEBRASKA, UNIVERSITY OF

P.O. Box 830902
Lincoln, NE 68583-0902
(402)472-2161
http://www.unl.edu/lawcoll

ABA Approved Since 1923

The Basics

Type of School: **PUBLIC**	First year can start other than Fall: **No**
Application deadline*: **3/1**	Student housing: **No**
Application fee: **$25**	--exclusively for law students: **No**
Financial Aid deadline*: **3/1**	Term: **Semester**
Student faculty ratio: **14.6 to 1**	

*pr=preferred

Faculty

	Men		Women		Minorities		Total
	#	%	#	%	#	%	
Full-time	18	82	4	18	2	9	22
Other full-time	0	0	1	100	0	0	1
Deans, librarians, & others who teach	1	100	0	0	0	0	1
Part-time	11	73	4	27	1	7	15
Total	30	77	9	23	3	8	39
Deans, librarians, & others who teach < 1/2	0	0	2	100	0	0	2

Library

# of volumes & volume equivalents	332,468	# of professional staff	6
# of titles	47,887	Hours per week with professional staff	64
# of active serial subscriptions	2,794	Hours per week without professional staff	44
Study seating capacity inside the library	339	# of student computer work stations for entire law school	58
Square feet of law library	30,872	# of additional networked connections	0
Square feet of law school (excl. Library)	77,628		

Curriculum

	Full time	Part time
Typical first-year section size	70	0
Is there typically a "small section" of the first year class, other than Legal Writing, taught by full-time faculty?	No	No
If yes, typical size offered last year	N/A	N/A
# of classroom course titles beyond 1st year curriculum	75	0
# of upper division courses, excluding seminars, with an enrollment:		
Under 25	27	0
25 - 49	21	0
50 - 74	5	0
75 - 99	5	0
100 +	5	0
# of seminars	13	0
# of seminar positions available	162	
# of seminar positions filled	157	0
# of positions available in simulation courses	330	
# of simulation positions filled	244	0
# of positions available in faculty supervised clinical courses	78	
# of fac. sup. clin. positions filled	70	0
# involved in field placements	0	0
# involved in law journals	20	0
# in moot court or trial competitions	49	0
# of credit hours required to graduate	96	

Enrollment & Attrition

	Full-Time							Part-Time							Attrition			
	Men		Women		Minorities		Total	Men		Women		Minorities		Total	Academic	Other	Total	
	#	%	#	%	#	%	#	#	%	#	%	#	%	#	#	#	#	%
1st Year	73	52.5	66	47.5	12	8.6	139	0	0.0	2	100.0	0	0.0	2	13	12	25	18
2nd Year	63	56.3	49	43.8	8	7.1	112	0	0.0	0	0.0	0	0.0	0	0	2	2	1.6
3rd Year	84	63.2	49	36.8	13	9.8	133	0	0.0	0	0.0	0	0.0	0	0	0	0	0.0
4th Year								0	0.0	0	0.0	0	0.0	0	0	0	0	0.0
Total	220	57.3	164	42.7	33	8.6	384	0	0.0	2	100.0	0	0.0	2	13	14	27	6.5
JD Degrees Awarded	83	56.1	65	43.9	9	6.1	148	0	0.0	0	0.0	0	0.0	0				

GPA & LSAT Scores

	Full Time	Part Time	Total
# of apps	684	1	685
# admits	387	1	388
# of matrics	139	1	140
75% GPA	3.71	0.00	
25% GPA	3.16	0.00	
75% LSAT	158	0	
25% LSAT	151	0	

Tuition/Living Expenses

	Resident	Non-resident
Full-Time	$3,953	$8,535
Part-Time	$0	$0

Estimated living expenses for Singles		
Living on campus	Living off campus	Living at home
$6,680	$8,765	$4,800

Financial Aid

	Full-time		Part-time		Total	
	#	%	#	%	#	%
Total # receiving grants	211	55.0	0	0.0	211	54.7
Less than 1/2 tuition	125	32.6	0	0.0	125	32.4
Half to full tuition	29	7.6	0	0.0	29	7.5
Full tuition	19	5.0	0	0.0	19	4.9
More than full tuition	38	9.9	0	0.0	38	9.8
Median Grant Amount	$2,598		$0			

Refunds

Refunds of Admissions or Seat Deposit prior to commencement of classes? Yes

75% refund from 04/01/96 to 05/15/96
50% refund from 05/15/96 to 07/01/96
25% refund from 07/01/96 to 08/01/96

Refunds of Pre-paid tuition prior to commencement of classes? Yes

If yes, fully refundable before the start of classes? Yes

Joint Degrees Offered

MA/Econ/Law, MPA/Law, MA Psych/Law, MBA Law, PhD Psych/Lw, Phd Ed/Law, Poly Sci/Law, Planning/Law

Advanced Degrees Offered

No Advanced Degrees

Career Placement

	Total	%
Employment status known	144	98.0
Employment status unknown	3	2.0
Employed	134	93.1
Pursuing graduate degrees	4	2.8
Unemployed seeking employment	4	2.8
Unemployed not seeking employment	2	1.4
Type of Employment		
# employed in law firms	60	44.8
# employed in business & industry	24	17.9
# employed in government	27	20.2
# employed in public interest	6	4.5
# employed as judicial clerks	16	11.9
# employed in academia	1	0.8
Geographic Location		
# employed in state	68	50.8
# employed in foreign countries	0	0.0
# of states where employed	23	

Bar Passage Rate

Jurisdiction	NE
# from school taking bar for the first time	90
School's pass rate for all first-time takers	99%
State's pass rate for all first-time takers	94%
State's pass rate for all first-time takers from ABA approved law schools	94%

NEW ENGLAND SCHOOL OF LAW

154 Stuart Street
Boston, MA 02116
(617)451-0010
http://www.nesl.edu

ABA Approved Since 1969

The Basics

Type of School: **PRIVATE**	First year can start other than Fall: **No**
Application deadline*: **3/15**	Student housing: **No**
Application fee: **$50**	--exclusively for law students: **No**
Financial Aid deadline*: **4/15**	Term: **Semester**
Student faculty ratio: **20.3 to 1**	

*pr=preferred

Faculty

	Men		Women		Minorities		Total
	#	%	#	%	#	%	
Full-time	24	71	10	29	3	9	34
Other full-time	0	0	0	0	0	0	0
Deans, librarians, & others who teach	0	0	0	0	0	0	0
Part-time	26	62	16	38	1	2	42
Total	50	66	26	34	4	5	76
Deans, librarians, & others who teach < 1/2	3	100	0	0	1	33	3

Library

# of volumes & volume equivalents	271,987	# of professional staff	9
# of titles	38,925	Hours per week with professional staff	78
# of active serial subscriptions	2,997	Hours per week without professional staff	23
Study seating capacity inside the library	435	# of student computer work stations for entire law school	72
Square feet of law library	28,087	# of additional networked connections	0
Square feet of law school (excl. Library)	48,355		

Curriculum

	Full time	Part time
Typical first-year section size	118	120
Is there typically a "small section" of the first year class, other than Legal Writing, taught by full-time faculty?	Yes	Yes
If yes, typical size offered last year	80	60
# of classroom course titles beyond 1st year curriculum	57	48
# of upper division courses, excluding seminars, with an enrollment:		
Under 25	27	28
25 - 49	19	12
50 - 74	14	8
75 - 99	11	11
100 +	1	0
# of seminars	15	6
# of seminar positions available	425	
# of seminar positions filled	211	95
# of positions available in simulation courses	340	
# of simulation positions filled	191	90
# of positions available in faculty supervised clinical courses	52	
# of fac. sup. clin. positions filled	34	6
# involved in field placements	130	21
# involved in law journals	74	29
# in moot court or trial competitions	15	1
# of credit hours required to graduate	84	

Enrollment & Attrition

	Full-Time							Part-Time							Attrition			
	Men		Women		Minorities		Total	Men		Women		Minorities		Total	Academic	Other	Total	
	#	%	#	%	#	%	#	#	%	#	%	#	%	#	#	#	#	%
1st Year	89	53.0	79	47.0	35	20.8	168	50	64.1	28	35.9	4	5.1	78	7	44	51	14
2nd Year	98	49.2	101	50.8	33	16.6	199	59	51.3	56	48.7	10	8.7	115	4	5	9	3.0
3rd Year	100	52.4	91	47.6	27	14.1	191	59	57.8	43	42.2	5	4.9	102	0	0	0	0.0
4th Year								61	53.0	54	47.0	3	2.6	115	0	0	0	0.0
Total	287	51.4	271	48.6	95	17.0	558	229	55.9	181	44.1	22	5.4	410	11	49	60	5.5
JD Degrees Awarded	130	58.3	93	41.7	10	4.5	223	59	58.4	42	41.6	8	7.9	101				

GPA & LSAT Scores

	Full Time	Part Time	Total
# of apps	2,038	370	2,408
# admits	1,318	252	1,570
# of matrics	171	82	253
75% GPA	3.18	3.12	
25% GPA	2.59	2.55	
75% LSAT	151	152	
25% LSAT	146	146	

Tuition/Living Expenses

	Resident	Non-resident
Full-Time	$13,500	$13,500
Part-Time	$10,160	$10,160

Estimated living expenses for Singles		
Living on campus	Living off campus	Living at home
N/A	$11,250	$7,730

Career Placement

	Total	%
Employment status known	225	78.1
Employment status unknown	63	21.9
Employed	191	84.9
Pursuing graduate degrees	6	2.7
Unemployed seeking employment	27	12.0
Unemployed not seeking employment	1	0.4
Type of Employment		
# employed in law firms	87	45.6
# employed in business & industry	43	22.5
# employed in government	45	23.6
# employed in public interest	1	0.5
# employed as judicial clerks	11	5.8
# employed in academia	4	2.1
Geographic Location		
# employed in state	148	77.5
# employed in foreign countries	0	0.0
# of states where employed	15	

Financial Aid

	Full-time		Part-time		Total	
	#	%	#	%	#	%
Total # receiving grants	271	48.6	55	13.4	326	33.7
Less than 1/2 tuition	259	46.4	44	10.7	303	31.3
Half to full tuition	6	1.1	9	2.2	15	1.5
Full tuition	6	1.1	2	0.5	8	0.8
More than full tuition	0	0.0	0	0.0	0	0.0
Median Grant Amount	$1,861		$2,064			

Refunds

Refunds of Admissions or Seat Deposit prior to commencement of classes? No

Refunds of Pre-paid tuition prior to commencement of classes? No

If yes, fully refundable before the start of classes? No

Joint Degrees Offered

No Joint Degrees

Advanced Degrees Offered

No Advanced Degrees

Bar Passage Rate

Jurisdiction	MA
# from school taking bar for the first time	210
School's pass rate for all first-time takers	81%
State's pass rate for all first-time takers	83%
State's pass rate for all first-time takers from ABA approved law schools	85%

NEW MEXICO, UNIVERSITY OF

1117 Stanford, N.E.
Albuquerque, NM 87131-1431
(505)277-2146
http://www.unm.edu/~unmlaw

ABA Approved Since 1948

The Basics

Type of School: **PUBLIC**
Application deadline*: **2/15**
Application fee: **$40**
Financial Aid deadline*: **3/1**
Student faculty ratio: **11.3 to 1**

First year can start other than Fall: **No**
Student housing: **No**
--exclusively for law students: **No**
Term: **Semester**

*pr=preferred

Faculty

	Men		Women		Minorities		Total
	#	%	#	%	#	%	
Full-time	13	52	12	48	6	24	25
Other full-time	0	0	1	100	0	0	1
Deans, librarians, & others who teach	2	67	1	33	2	67	3
Part-time	13	65	7	35	1	5	20
Total	28	57	21	43	9	18	49
Deans, librarians, & others who teach < 1/2	1	100	0	0	0	0	1

Library

# of volumes & volume equivalents	350,909	# of professional staff	4
# of titles	59,958	Hours per week with professional staff	56
# of active serial subscriptions	3,145	Hours per week without professional staff	52
Study seating capacity inside the library	329	# of student computer work stations for entire law school	36
Square feet of law library	32,443	# of additional networked connections	16
Square feet of law school (excl. Library)	36,005		

Curriculum

	Full time	Part time
Typical first-year section size	52	0
Is there typically a "small section" of the first year class, other than Legal Writing, taught by full-time faculty?	Yes	No
If yes, typical size offered last year	18	N/A
# of classroom course titles beyond 1st year curriculum	82	0
# of upper division courses, excluding seminars, with an enrollment:		
Under 25	43	0
25 - 49	13	0
50 - 74	5	0
75 - 99	2	0
100 +	0	0
# of seminars	20	0
# of seminar positions available	240	
# of seminar positions filled	167	0
# of positions available in simulation courses	184	
# of simulation positions filled	166	0
# of positions available in faculty supervised clinical courses	89	
# of fac. sup. clin. positions filled	71	0
# involved in field placements	34	0
# involved in law journals	122	0
# in moot court or trial competitions	25	0
# of credit hours required to graduate	86	

Enrollment & Attrition

	Full-Time							Part-Time							Attrition			
	Men		Women		Minorities		Total	Men		Women		Minorities		Total	Academic	Other	Total	
	#	%	#	%	#	%	#	#	%	#	%	#	%	#	#	#	#	%
1st Year	63	57.3	47	42.7	40	36.4	110	0	0.0	0	0.0	0	0.0	0	2	5	7	6.5
2nd Year	55	48.2	59	51.8	50	43.9	114	0	0.0	0	0.0	0	0.0	0	0	0	0	0.0
3rd Year	58	50.4	57	49.6	43	37.4	115	0	0.0	0	0.0	0	0.0	0	0	0	0	0.0
4th Year								0	0.0	0	0.0	0	0.0	0	0	0	0	0.0
Total	176	51.9	163	48.1	133	39.2	339	0	0.0	0	0.0	0	0.0	0	2	5	7	2.1
JD Degrees Awarded	55	47.4	61	52.6	59	50.9	116	0	0.0	0	0.0	0	0.0	0				

GPA & LSAT Scores

	Full Time	Part Time	Total
# of apps	825	0	825
# admits	236	0	236
# of matrics	112	0	112
75% GPA	3.57	0.00	
25% GPA	2.91	0.00	
75% LSAT	160	0	
25% LSAT	150	0	

Tuition/Living Expenses

	Resident	Non-resident
Full-Time	$3,283	$11,015
Part-Time	$0	$0

Estimated living expenses for Singles		
Living on campus	Living off campus	Living at home
$7,220	$10,164	$5,344

Career Placement

	Total	%
Employment status known	97	98.0
Employment status unknown	2	2.0
Employed	75	77.3
Pursuing graduate degrees	4	4.1
Unemployed seeking employment	15	15.5
Unemployed not seeking employment	3	3.1
Type of Employment		
# employed in law firms	43	57.3
# employed in business & industry	8	10.7
# employed in government	11	14.7
# employed in public interest	2	2.7
# employed as judicial clerks	7	9.3
# employed in academia	4	5.3
Geographic Location		
# employed in state	63	84.0
# employed in foreign countries	1	1.3
# of states where employed	4	

Financial Aid

	Full-time		Part-time		Total	
	#	%	#	%	#	%
Total # receiving grants	63	18.6	0	0.0	63	18.6
Less than 1/2 tuition	20	5.9	0	0.0	20	5.9
Half to full tuition	10	3.0	0	0.0	10	2.9
Full tuition	25	7.4	0	0.0	25	7.4
More than full tuition	8	2.4	0	0.0	8	2.4
Median Grant Amount	$3,284		$0			

Refunds

Refunds of Admissions or Seat Deposit prior to commencement of classes? Yes

Refunds of Pre-paid tuition prior to commencement of classes? Yes

If yes, fully refundable before the start of classes? Yes

Joint Degrees Offered

MBA, MPA, MLAS, Ph.D., MA - Phil.

Advanced Degrees Offered

No Advanced Degrees

Bar Passage Rate

Jurisdiction	NM
# from school taking bar for the first time	80
School's pass rate for all first-time takers	89%
State's pass rate for all first-time takers	92%
State's pass rate for all first-time takers from ABA approved law schools	

NEW YORK LAW SCHOOL

57 Worth Street
New York, NY 10013
(212)431-2100
http://www.nyls.edu

ABA Approved Since 1954

The Basics

Type of School: **PRIVATE**
Application deadline*: **4/1**
Application fee: **$50**
Financial Aid deadline*:
Student faculty ratio: **22.8 to 1**

First year can start other than Fall: **No**
Student housing: **Yes**
--exclusively for law students: **No**
Term: **Semester**

*pr=preferred

Faculty

	Men		Women		Minorities		Total
	#	%	#	%	#	%	
Full-time	33	73	12	27	7	16	45
Other full-time	0	0	0	0	0	0	0
Deans, librarians, & others who teach	0	0	1	100	0	0	1
Part-time	43	67	21	33	4	6	64
Total	76	69	34	31	11	10	110
Deans, librarians, & others who teach < 1/2	2	50	2	50	0	0	4

Library

# of volumes & volume equivalents	421,493	# of professional staff	13
# of titles	121,505	Hours per week with professional staff	79
# of active serial subscriptions	4,713	Hours per week without professional staff	19
Study seating capacity inside the library	616	# of student computer work stations for entire law school	105
Square feet of law library	48,464	# of additional networked connections	90
Square feet of law school (excl. Library)	101,036		

Curriculum

	Full time	Part time
Typical first-year section size	110	120
Is there typically a "small section" of the first year class, other than Legal Writing, taught by full-time faculty?	Yes	Yes
If yes, typical size offered last year	35	42
# of classroom course titles beyond 1st year curriculum	85	76
# of upper division courses, excluding seminars, with an enrollment:		
Under 25	19	21
25 - 49	19	23
50 - 74	11	8
75 - 99	13	7
100 +	12	4
# of seminars	39	27
# of seminar positions available	1,067	
# of seminar positions filled	465	355
# of positions available in simulation courses	232	
# of simulation positions filled	165	59
# of positions available in faculty supervised clinical courses	54	
# of fac. sup. clin. positions filled	40	6
# involved in field placements	264	40
# involved in law journals	143	48
# in moot court or trial competitions	48	11
# of credit hours required to graduate	86	

Enrollment & Attrition

	Full-Time							Part-Time							Attrition			
	Men		Women		Minorities		Total	Men		Women		Minorities		Total	Academic	Other	Total	
	#	%	#	%	#	%	#	#	%	#	%	#	%	#	#	#	#	%
1st Year	152	48.4	162	51.6	73	23.2	314	62	50.4	61	49.6	33	26.8	123	6	30	36	7.8
2nd Year	157	54.9	129	45.1	59	20.6	286	67	52.8	60	47.2	28	22.0	127	16	28	44	10
3rd Year	168	54.0	143	46.0	69	22.2	311	72	63.7	41	36.3	25	22.1	113	1	5	6	1.6
4th Year								67	55.4	54	44.6	41	33.9	121	0	1	1	1.0
Total	477	52.4	434	47.6	201	22.1	911	268	55.4	216	44.6	127	26.2	484	23	64	87	6.3
JD Degrees Awarded	162	59.6	110	40.4	55	20.2	272	65	63.7	37	36.3	24	23.5	102				

GPA & LSAT Scores

	Full Time	Part Time	Total
# of apps	3,288	825	4,113
# admits	1,929	356	2,285
# of matrics	314	123	437
75% GPA	3.30	3.28	
25% GPA	2.80	2.78	
75% LSAT	156	156	
25% LSAT	151	151	

Tuition/Living Expenses

	Resident	Non-resident
Full-Time	$20,055	$20,055
Part-Time	$15,041	$15,041

Estimated living expenses for Singles		
Living on campus	Living off campus	Living at home
$13,945	$13,945	$7,520

Career Placement

	Total	%
Employment status known	373	92.6
Employment status unknown	30	7.4
Employed	340	91.2
Pursuing graduate degrees	8	2.1
Unemployed seeking employment	20	5.4
Unemployed not seeking employment	5	1.3
Type of Employment		
# employed in law firms	203	59.7
# employed in business & industry	65	19.1
# employed in government	46	13.5
# employed in public interest	5	1.5
# employed as judicial clerks	17	5.0
# employed in academia	4	1.2
Geographic Location		
# employed in state	277	81.5
# employed in foreign countries	0	0.0
# of states where employed	12	

Financial Aid

	Full-time		Part-time		Total	
	#	%	#	%	#	%
Total # receiving grants	342	37.5	93	19.2	435	31.2
Less than 1/2 tuition	283	31.1	41	8.5	324	23.2
Half to full tuition	50	5.5	45	9.3	95	6.8
Full tuition	2	0.2	3	0.6	5	0.4
More than full tuition	7	0.8	4	0.8	11	0.8
Median Grant Amount	$6,180		$7,055			

Refunds

Refunds of Admissions or Seat Deposit prior to commencement of classes? Yes

100% refund from 04/01/96 to 06/20/96
50% refund from 06/21/96 to 07/11/96
25% refund from 07/12/96 to 08/01/96

Refunds of Pre-paid tuition prior to commencement of classes? Yes

If yes, fully refundable before the start of classes? Yes

Joint Degrees Offered

JD/MBA

Advanced Degrees Offered

No Advanced Degrees

Bar Passage Rate

Jurisdiction	NY
# from school taking bar for the first time	328
School's pass rate for all first-time takers	74%
State's pass rate for all first-time takers	78%
State's pass rate for all first-time takers from ABA approved law schools	

NEW YORK UNIVERSITY

40 Washington Square South
New York, NY 10012
(212)998-6000
http://www.nyu.edu/law

ABA Approved Since 1930

The Basics

Type of School: **PRIVATE**
Application deadline*: **2/1**
Application fee: **$65**
Financial Aid deadline*: **5/1**
Student faculty ratio: **14.1 to 1**
First year can start other than Fall: **No**
Student housing: **Yes**
--exclusively for law students: **Yes**
Term: **Semester**

*pr=preferred

Faculty

	Men #	Men %	Women #	Women %	Minorities #	Minorities %	Total
Full-time	57	72	22	28	4	5	79
Other full-time	8	35	15	65	6	26	23
Deans, librarians, & others who teach	3	100	0	0	0	0	3
Part-time	50	82	11	18	4	7	61
Total	118	71	48	29	14	8	166
Deans, librarians, & others who teach < 1/2	1	100	0	0	0	0	1

Library

# of volumes & volume equivalents	944,569	# of professional staff	16
# of titles	152,881	Hours per week with professional staff	65
# of active serial subscriptions	5,766	Hours per week without professional staff	36
Study seating capacity inside the library	897	# of student computer work stations for entire law school	100
Square feet of law library	82,000	# of additional networked connections	999
Square feet of law school (excl. Library)	183,500		

Curriculum

	Full time	Part time
Typical first-year section size	108	0
Is there typically a "small section" of the first year class, other than Legal Writing, taught by full-time faculty?	No	No
If yes, typical size offered last year	N/A	N/A
# of classroom course titles beyond 1st year curriculum	203	0
# of upper division courses, excluding seminars, with an enrollment:		
Under 25	33	0
25 - 49	40	0
50 - 74	25	0
75 - 99	23	0
100 +	25	0
# of seminars	85	0
# of seminar positions available	2,125	
# of seminar positions filled	1,648	0
# of positions available in simulation courses	146	
# of simulation positions filled	140	0
# of positions available in faculty supervised clinical courses	120	
# of fac. sup. clin. positions filled	114	0
# involved in field placements	56	0
# involved in law journals	285	0
# in moot court or trial competitions	104	0
# of credit hours required to graduate	82	

Enrollment & Attrition

	Full-Time							Part-Time							Attrition			
	Men		Women		Minorities		Total	Men		Women		Minorities		Total	Academic	Other	Total	
	#	%	#	%	#	%	#	#	%	#	%	#	%	#	#	#	#	%
1st Year	246	58.7	173	41.3	92	22.0	419	0	0.0	0	0.0	0	0.0	0	0	1	1	0.2
2nd Year	218	47.4	242	52.6	91	19.8	460	0	0.0	0	0.0	0	0.0	0	0	6	6	1.3
3rd Year	273	59.0	190	41.0	117	25.3	463	0	0.0	0	0.0	0	0.0	0	0	1	1	0.2
4th Year								0	0.0	0	0.0	0	0.0	0	0	0	0	0.0
Total	737	54.9	605	45.1	300	22.4	1,342	0	0.0	0	0.0	0	0.0	0	0	8	8	0.6
JD Degrees Awarded	233	53.7	201	46.3	85	19.6	434	0	0.0	0	0.0	0	0.0	0				

GPA & LSAT Scores

	Full Time	Part Time	Total
# of apps	6,525	0	6,525
# admits	1,480	0	1,480
# of matrics	421	0	421
75% GPA	3.79	0.00	
25% GPA	3.53	0.00	
75% LSAT	170	0	
25% LSAT	165	0	

Tuition/Living Expenses

	Resident	Non-resident
Full-Time	$24,191	$24,191
Part-Time	$0	$0

Estimated living expenses for Singles		
Living on campus	Living off campus	Living at home
$14,274	$14,274	$7,299

Career Placement

	Total	%
Employment status known	418	99.3
Employment status unknown	3	0.7
Employed	402	96.2
Pursuing graduate degrees	7	1.7
Unemployed seeking employment	9	2.2
Unemployed not seeking employment	0	0.0
Type of Employment		
# employed in law firms	298	74.1
# employed in business & industry	14	3.5
# employed in government	13	3.2
# employed in public interest	12	3.0
# employed as judicial clerks	65	16.2
# employed in academia	0	0.0
Geographic Location		
# employed in state	303	75.4
# employed in foreign countries	0	0.0
# of states where employed	29	

Financial Aid

	Full-time		Part-time		Total	
	#	%	#	%	#	%
Total # receiving grants	325	24.2	0	0.0	325	24.2
Less than 1/2 tuition	208	15.5	0	0.0	208	15.5
Half to full tuition	92	6.9	0	0.0	92	6.9
Full tuition	25	1.9	0	0.0	25	1.9
More than full tuition	0	0.0	0	0.0	0	0.0
Median Grant Amount	$8,424		$0			

Refunds

Refunds of Admissions or Seat Deposit prior to commencement of classes? No

Refunds of Pre-paid tuition prior to commencement of classes? Yes

If yes, fully refundable before the start of classes? Yes

Joint Degrees Offered

JD/MA, JD/MBA, JD/MPA, JD/MUP, JS/MSW

Advanced Degrees Offered

LL.M.	Corporate Law
LL.M.	International Legal Studies
LL.M.	Taxation
LL.M.	Trade Regulation
LL.M.	General Studies
L.L.M.	International Taxation
M.C.J.	Comparative Jurisprudence
J.S.D.	

Bar Passage Rate

Jurisdiction	NY
# from school taking bar for the first time	354
School's pass rate for all first-time takers	94%
State's pass rate for all first-time takers	78%
State's pass rate for all first-time takers from ABA approved law schools	

NORTH CAROLINA CENTRAL UNIVERSITY

1512 South Alston Avenue
Durham, NC 27707
(919)560-6333
http://www.nccu.edu/law

ABA Approved Since 1950

The Basics

Type of School: **PUBLIC**
Application deadline*:
Application fee: **$30**
Financial Aid deadline*:
Student faculty ratio: **20.0 to 1**
First year can start other than Fall: **No**
Student housing: **No**
--exclusively for law students: **No**
Term: **Semester**

*pr=preferred

Faculty

	Men		Women		Minorities		Total
	#	%	#	%	#	%	
Full-time	6	46	7	54	8	62	13
Other full-time	0	0	0	0	0	0	0
Deans, librarians, & others who teach	2	33	4	67	3	50	6
Part-time	5	50	5	50	2	20	10
Total	13	45	16	55	13	45	29
Deans, librarians, & others who teach < 1/2	1	100	0	0	1	100	1

Library

# of volumes & volume equivalents	270,228	# of professional staff	5
# of titles	184,977	Hours per week with professional staff	80
# of active serial subscriptions	2,375	Hours per week without professional staff	17
Study seating capacity inside the library	296	# of student computer work stations for entire law school	19
Square feet of law library	28,674	# of additional networked connections	0
Square feet of law school (excl. Library)	47,660		

Curriculum

	Full time	Part time
Typical first-year section size	50	30
Is there typically a "small section" of the first year class, other than Legal Writing, taught by full-time faculty?	No	No
If yes, typical size offered last year	N/A	N/A
# of classroom course titles beyond 1st year curriculum	42	13
# of upper division courses, excluding seminars, with an enrollment:		
Under 25	27	3
25 - 49	4	6
50 - 74	9	2
75 - 99	0	1
100 +	0	0
# of seminars	2	1
# of seminar positions available	68	
# of seminar positions filled	33	35
# of positions available in simulation courses	159	
# of simulation positions filled	128	31
# of positions available in faculty supervised clinical courses	35	
# of fac. sup. clin. positions filled	70	0
# involved in field placements	52	0
# involved in law journals	13	0
# in moot court or trial competitions	63	0
# of credit hours required to graduate	88	

Enrollment & Attrition

	Full-Time							Part-Time							Attrition			
	Men		Women		Minorities		Total	Men		Women		Minorities		Total	Academic	Other	Total	
	#	%	#	%	#	%	#	#	%	#	%	#	%	#	#	#	#	%
1st Year	46	45.5	55	54.5	65	64.4	101	19	59.4	13	40.6	14	43.8	32	5	4	9	8.0
2nd Year	30	40.5	44	59.5	42	56.8	74	10	35.7	18	64.3	8	28.6	28	1	2	3	3.1
3rd Year	32	47.1	36	52.9	41	60.3	68	12	50.0	12	50.0	8	33.3	24	0	0	0	0.0
4th Year								14	70.0	6	30.0	4	20.0	20	0	0	0	0.0
Total	108	44.4	135	55.6	148	60.9	243	55	52.9	49	47.1	34	32.7	104	6	6	12	3.7
JD Degrees Awarded	31	41.3	44	58.7	46	61.3	75	9	45.0	11	55.0	5	25.0	20				

NORTH CAROLINA CENTRAL UNIVERSITY

GPA & LSAT Scores

	Full Time	Part Time	Total
# of apps	1,152	252	1,404
# admits	223	49	272
# of matrics	101	32	133
75% GPA	3.20	3.40	
25% GPA	2.60	2.70	
75% LSAT	154	158	
25% LSAT	146	151	

Tuition/Living Expenses

	Resident	Non-resident
Full-Time	$1,890	$10,842
Part-Time	$1,890	$10,842

Estimated living expenses for Singles		
Living on campus	Living off campus	Living at home
$4,655	$6,850	$4,090

Career Placement

	Total	%
Employment status known	63	84.0
Employment status unknown	12	16.0
Employed	61	96.8
Pursuing graduate degrees	0	0.0
Unemployed seeking employment	2	3.2
Unemployed not seeking employment	0	0.0
Type of Employment		
# employed in law firms	34	55.7
# employed in business & industry	14	23.0
# employed in government	6	9.8
# employed in public interest	4	6.6
# employed as judicial clerks	4	6.6
# employed in academia	1	1.6
Geographic Location		
# employed in state	55	90.2
# employed in foreign countries	0	0.0
# of states where employed	6	

Financial Aid

	Full-time		Part-time		Total	
	#	%	#	%	#	%
Total # receiving grants	74	30.5	0	0.0	74	21.3
Less than 1/2 tuition	54	22.2	0	0.0	54	15.6
Half to full tuition	0	0.0	0	0.0	0	0.0
Full tuition	0	0.0	0	0.0	0	0.0
More than full tuition	20	8.2	0	0.0	20	5.8
Median Grant Amount	$400		$0			

Refunds

Refunds of Admissions or Seat Deposit prior to commencement of classes? Yes

100% refund from 10/01/95 to 05/01/96
75% refund from 05/02/96 to 05/15/96
50% refund from 05/16/96 to 06/15/96

Refunds of Pre-paid tuition prior to commencement of classes? Yes

If yes, fully refundable before the start of classes? Yes

Joint Degrees Offered

JD/MLS, JD/MBA

Advanced Degrees Offered

No Advanced Degrees

Bar Passage Rate

Jurisdiction	NC
# from school taking bar for the first time	57
School's pass rate for all first-time takers	74%
State's pass rate for all first-time takers	85%
State's pass rate for all first-time takers from ABA approved law schools	85%

NORTH CAROLINA, UNIVERSITY OF

Campus Box 3380
Van Hecke-Wettach Hall
Chapel Hill, NC 27599-3380
(919)962-5106
http://www.law.unc

ABA Approved Since 1923

The Basics

Type of School: **PUBLIC**
Application deadline*: **2/1**
Application fee: **$60**
Financial Aid deadline*: **3/1**
Student faculty ratio: **18.6 to 1**

First year can start other than Fall: **No**
Student housing: **No**
--exclusively for law students: **No**
Term: **Semester**

*pr=preferred

Faculty

	Men #	Men %	Women #	Women %	Minorities #	Minorities %	Total
Full-time	21	66	11	34	2	6	32
Other full-time	0	0	0	0	0	0	0
Deans, librarians, & others who teach	1	100	0	0	0	0	1
Part-time	13	76	4	24	2	12	17
Total	35	70	15	30	4	8	50
Deans, librarians, & others who teach < 1/2	1	25	3	75	0	0	4

Library

# of volumes & volume equivalents	420,532	# of professional staff	8
# of titles	74,939	Hours per week with professional staff	68
# of active serial subscriptions	5,718	Hours per week without professional staff	41
Study seating capacity inside the library	407	# of student computer work stations for entire law school	48
Square feet of law library	41,081	# of additional networked connections	55
Square feet of law school (excl. Library)	32,836		

Curriculum

	Full time	Part time
Typical first-year section size	80	0
Is there typically a "small section" of the first year class, other than Legal Writing, taught by full-time faculty?	Yes	No
If yes, typical size offered last year	25	N/A
# of classroom course titles beyond 1st year curriculum	80	0
# of upper division courses, excluding seminars, with an enrollment:		
Under 25	12	0
25 - 49	28	0
50 - 74	5	0
75 - 99	3	0
100 +	11	0
# of seminars	21	0
# of seminar positions available	301	
# of seminar positions filled	299	0
# of positions available in simulation courses	573	
# of simulation positions filled	467	0
# of positions available in faculty supervised clinical courses	48	
# of fac. sup. clin. positions filled	44	0
# involved in field placements	0	0
# involved in law journals	117	0
# in moot court or trial competitions	26	0
# of credit hours required to graduate	86	

Enrollment & Attrition

	Full-Time							Part-Time							Attrition			
	Men		Women		Minorities		Total	Men		Women		Minorities		Total	Academic	Other	Total	
	#	%	#	%	#	%	#	#	%	#	%	#	%	#	#	#	#	%
1st Year	121	50.6	118	49.4	53	22.2	239	0	0.0	0	0.0	0	0.0	0	2	6	8	3.5
2nd Year	119	53.4	104	46.6	48	21.5	223	0	0.0	0	0.0	0	0.0	0	0	0	0	0.0
3rd Year	128	56.6	98	43.4	37	16.4	226	0	0.0	0	0.0	0	0.0	0	0	2	2	0.8
4th Year								0	0.0	0	0.0	0	0.0	0	0	0	0	0.0
Total	368	53.5	320	46.5	138	20.1	688	0	0.0	0	0.0	0	0.0	0	2	8	10	1.4
JD Degrees Awarded	141	59.2	97	40.8	41	17.2	238	0	0.0	0	0.0	0	0.0	0				

GPA & LSAT Scores

	Full Time	Part Time	Total
# of apps	2,281	0	2,281
# admits	617	0	617
# of matrics	240	0	240
75% GPA	3.69	0.00	
25% GPA	3.30	0.00	
75% LSAT	163	0	
25% LSAT	155	0	

Tuition/Living Expenses

	Resident	Non-resident
Full-Time	$2,717	$13,989
Part-Time	$0	$0

Estimated living expenses for Singles		
Living on campus	Living off campus	Living at home
$8,382	$8,728	$4,469

Career Placement

	Total	%
Employment status known	203	91.0
Employment status unknown	20	9.0
Employed	175	86.2
Pursuing graduate degrees	6	3.0
Unemployed seeking employment	18	8.9
Unemployed not seeking employment	4	2.0
Type of Employment		
# employed in law firms	114	65.1
# employed in business & industry	13	7.4
# employed in government	20	11.4
# employed in public interest	4	2.3
# employed as judicial clerks	22	12.6
# employed in academia	2	1.1
Geographic Location		
# employed in state	108	61.7
# employed in foreign countries	0	0.0
# of states where employed	22	

Financial Aid

	Full-time		Part-time		Total	
	#	%	#	%	#	%
Total # receiving grants	127	18.5	0	0.0	127	18.5
Less than 1/2 tuition	17	2.5	0	0.0	17	2.5
Half to full tuition	67	9.7	0	0.0	67	9.7
Full tuition	0	0.0	0	0.0	0	0.0
More than full tuition	43	6.3	0	0.0	43	6.3
Median Grant Amount	$2,500		$0			

Refunds

Refunds of Admissions or Seat Deposit prior to commencement of classes? No

Refunds of Pre-paid tuition prior to commencement of classes? Yes

If yes, fully refundable before the start of classes? Yes

Joint Degrees Offered

JD/MBA, JD/MPA *, JD/MPP*, JD/MPH, JD/MRP, JD/MSW

Advanced Degrees Offered

No Advanced Degrees

Bar Passage Rate

Jurisdiction	NC
# from school taking bar for the first time	136
School's pass rate for all first-time takers	94%
State's pass rate for all first-time takers	85%
State's pass rate for all first-time takers from ABA approved law schools	85%

NORTH DAKOTA, UNIVERSITY OF

Centennial Drive
P.O. Box 9003
Grand Forks, ND 58202
(701)777-2104
http://www.law.und.nodak.edu

ABA Approved Since 1923

The Basics

Type of School: **PUBLIC**
Application deadline*: **4/1**
Application fee: **$35**
Financial Aid deadline*: **5/1**
Student faculty ratio: **15.7 to 1**

First year can start other than Fall: **No**
Student housing: **No**
--exclusively for law students: **No**
Term: **Semester**

***pr=preferred**

Faculty

	Men		Women		Minorities		Total
	#	%	#	%	#	%	
Full-time	6	55	5	45	0	0	11
Other full-time	0	0	0	0	0	0	0
Deans, librarians, & others who teach	0	0	0	0	0	0	0
Part-time	4	67	2	33	0	0	6
Total	10	59	7	41	0	0	17
Deans, librarians, & others who teach < 1/2	2	100	0	0	0	0	2

Library

# of volumes & volume equivalents	247,339	# of professional staff	4
# of titles	71,420	Hours per week with professional staff	45
# of active serial subscriptions	2,697	Hours per week without professional staff	61
Study seating capacity inside the library	279	# of student computer work stations for entire law school	68
Square feet of law library	21,582	# of additional networked connections	0
Square feet of law school (excl. Library)	19,409		

Curriculum

	Full time	Part time
Typical first-year section size	75	0
Is there typically a "small section" of the first year class, other than Legal Writing, taught by full-time faculty?	No	No
If yes, typical size offered last year	N/A	N/A
# of classroom course titles beyond 1st year curriculum	50	0
# of upper division courses, excluding seminars, with an enrollment:		
Under 25	25	0
25 - 49	13	0
50 - 74	8	0
75 - 99	3	0
100 +	0	0
# of seminars	1	0
# of seminar positions available	16	
# of seminar positions filled	13	0
# of positions available in simulation courses	76	
# of simulation positions filled	68	0
# of positions available in faculty supervised clinical courses	135	
# of fac. sup. clin. positions filled	44	0
# involved in field placements	22	0
# involved in law journals	49	0
# in moot court or trial competitions	58	0
# of credit hours required to graduate	90	

Enrollment & Attrition

	Full-Time							Part-Time							Attrition			
	Men		Women		Minorities		Total	Men		Women		Minorities		Total	Academic	Other	Total	
	#	%	#	%	#	%	#	#	%	#	%	#	%	#	#	#	#	%
1st Year	46	68.7	21	31.3	8	11.9	67	0	0.0	0	0.0	0	0.0	0	2	4	6	9.0
2nd Year	31	50.8	30	49.2	1	1.6	61	0	0.0	0	0.0	0	0.0	0	0	1	1	1.3
3rd Year	48	64.9	26	35.1	3	4.1	74	0	0.0	0	0.0	0	0.0	0	0	2	2	2.7
4th Year								0	0.0	0	0.0	0	0.0	0	0	0	0	0.0
Total	125	61.9	77	38.1	12	5.9	202	0	0.0	0	0.0	0	0.0	0	2	7	9	4.2
JD Degrees Awarded	36	52.9	32	47.1	4	5.9	68	0	0.0	0	0.0	0	0.0	0				

GPA & LSAT Scores

	Full Time	Part Time	Total
# of apps	315	0	315
# admits	171	0	171
# of matrics	68	0	68
75% GPA	3.42	0.00	
25% GPA	2.83	0.00	
75% LSAT	156	0	
25% LSAT	149	0	

Tuition/Living Expenses

	Resident	Non-resident
Full-Time	$3,948	$8,174
Part-Time	$0	$0

Estimated living expenses for Singles		
Living on campus	Living off campus	Living at home
$7,300	$7,300	$7,300

Career Placement

	Total	%
Employment status known	44	59.5
Employment status unknown	30	40.5
Employed	43	97.7
Pursuing graduate degrees	0	0.0
Unemployed seeking employment	1	2.3
Unemployed not seeking employment	0	0.0
Type of Employment		
# employed in law firms	17	39.5
# employed in business & industry	7	16.3
# employed in government	5	11.6
# employed in public interest	0	0.0
# employed as judicial clerks	15	34.9
# employed in academia	0	0.0
Geographic Location		
# employed in state	23	53.5
# employed in foreign countries	0	0.0
# of states where employed	7	

Financial Aid

	Full-time		Part-time		Total	
	#	%	#	%	#	%
Total # receiving grants	42	20.8	0	0.0	42	20.8
Less than 1/2 tuition	0	0.0	0	0.0	0	0.0
Half to full tuition	2	1.0	0	0.0	2	1.0
Full tuition	40	19.8	0	0.0	40	19.8
More than full tuition	0	0.0	0	0.0	0	0.0
Median Grant Amount	$2,530		$0			

Refunds

Refunds of Admissions or Seat Deposit prior to commencement of classes? No

Refunds of Pre-paid tuition prior to commencement of classes? No

If yes, fully refundable before the start of classes? No

Joint Degrees Offered

No Joint Degrees

Advanced Degrees Offered

No Advanced Degrees

Bar Passage Rate

Jurisdiction	ND	MN
# from school taking bar for the first time	50	28
School's pass rate for all first-time takers	82%	96%
State's pass rate for all first-time takers	85%	90%
State's pass rate for all first-time takers from ABA approved law schools	85%	90%

NORTHEASTERN UNIVERSITY

400 Huntington Avenue
Boston, MA 02115
(617)373-5149
http://www.slaw.neu.edu

ABA Approved Since 1969

The Basics

Type of School: PRIVATE
Application deadline*: 3/1
Application fee: $55
Financial Aid deadline*: 3/1
Student faculty ratio: 23.4 to 1
First year can start other than Fall: No
Student housing: Yes
--exclusively for law students: No
Term: Quarter

*pr=preferred

Faculty

	Men #	Men %	Women #	Women %	Minorities #	Minorities %	Total
Full-time	15	65	8	35	1	4	23
Other full-time	0	0	0	0	0	0	0
Deans, librarians, & others who teach	1	50	1	50	1	50	2
Part-time	4	40	6	60	2	20	10
Total	20	57	15	43	4	11	35
Deans, librarians, & others who teach < 1/2	0	0	1	100	0	0	1

Library

# of volumes & volume equivalents	219,654	# of professional staff	8
# of titles	30,202	Hours per week with professional staff	73
# of active serial subscriptions	2,509	Hours per week without professional staff	22
Study seating capacity inside the library	388	# of student computer work stations for entire law school	89
Square feet of law library	23,025	# of additional networked connections	1
Square feet of law school (excl. Library)	53,124		

Curriculum

	Full time	Part time
Typical first-year section size	65	0
Is there typically a "small section" of the first year class, other than Legal Writing, taught by full-time faculty?	No	No
If yes, typical size offered last year	N/A	N/A
# of classroom course titles beyond 1st year curriculum	86	0
# of upper division courses, excluding seminars, with an enrollment:		
Under 25	69	0
25 - 49	31	0
50 - 74	9	0
75 - 99	5	0
100 +	1	0
# of seminars	14	0
# of seminar positions available	202	
# of seminar positions filled	190	0
# of positions available in simulation courses	240	
# of simulation positions filled	212	0
# of positions available in faculty supervised clinical courses	126	
# of fac. sup. clin. positions filled	87	0
# involved in field placements	389	0
# involved in law journals	45	0
# in moot court or trial competitions	26	0
# of credit hours required to graduate	99	

Enrollment & Attrition

	Full-Time Men #	Men %	Women #	Women %	Minorities #	Minorities %	Total #	Part-Time Men #	Men %	Women #	Women %	Minorities #	Minorities %	Total #	Attrition Academic #	Other #	Total #	%
1st Year	68	31.2	150	68.8	56	25.7	218	0	0.0	0	0.0	0	0.0	0	3	5	8	4.1
2nd Year	64	33.5	127	66.5	53	27.7	191	0	0.0	0	0.0	0	0.0	0	0	9	9	4.4
3rd Year	71	34.6	134	65.4	52	25.4	205	0	0.0	0	0.0	0	0.0	0	0	0	0	0.0
4th Year								0	0.0	0	0.0	0	0.0	0	0	0	0	0.0
Total	203	33.1	411	66.9	161	26.2	614	0	0.0	0	0.0	0	0.0	0	3	14	17	2.8
JD Degrees Awarded	84	42.6	113	57.4	39	19.8	197	0	0.0	0	0.0	0	0.0	0				

GPA & LSAT Scores

	Full Time	Part Time	Total
# of apps	2,438	0	2,438
# admits	881	0	881
# of matrics	215	0	215
75% GPA	3.51	0.00	
25% GPA	3.04	0.00	
75% LSAT	159	0	
25% LSAT	151	0	

Tuition/Living Expenses

	Resident	Non-resident
Full-Time	$20,145	$20,145
Part-Time	$0	$0

Estimated living expenses for Singles		
Living on campus	Living off campus	Living at home
$14,900	$14,900	$7,700

Career Placement

	Total	%
Employment status known	162	86.6
Employment status unknown	25	13.4
Employed	133	82.1
Pursuing graduate degrees	3	1.9
Unemployed seeking employment	24	14.8
Unemployed not seeking employment	2	1.2
Type of Employment		
# employed in law firms	50	37.6
# employed in business & industry	21	15.8
# employed in government	9	6.8
# employed in public interest	20	15.0
# employed as judicial clerks	31	23.3
# employed in academia	2	1.5
Geographic Location		
# employed in state	81	60.9
# employed in foreign countries	2	1.5
# of states where employed	23	

Financial Aid

	Full-time		Part-time		Total	
	#	%	#	%	#	%
Total # receiving grants	274	44.6	0	0.0	274	44.6
Less than 1/2 tuition	199	32.4	0	0.0	199	32.4
Half to full tuition	62	10.1	0	0.0	62	10.1
Full tuition	14	2.3	0	0.0	14	2.3
More than full tuition	0	0.0	0	0.0	0	0.0
Median Grant Amount	$3,750		$0			

Refunds

Refunds of Admissions or Seat Deposit prior to commencement of classes? Yes

29% refund to 07/01/96

Refunds of Pre-paid tuition prior to commencement of classes? Yes

If yes, fully refundable before the start of classes? Yes

Joint Degrees Offered

J.D./M.B.A., J.D./Acct.

Advanced Degrees Offered

No Advanced Degrees

Bar Passage Rate

Jurisdiction	MA	NY
# from school taking bar for the first time	124	29
School's pass rate for all first-time takers	85%	72%
State's pass rate for all first-time takers	83%	78%
State's pass rate for all first-time takers from ABA approved law schools	85%	

NORTHERN ILLINOIS UNIVERSITY

Dekalb, IL 60115
(815)753-1068
http://www.niu.edu/claw

ABA Approved Since 1978

The Basics

Type of School: **PUBLIC**
Application deadline*: **5/15**
Application fee: **$35**
Financial Aid deadline*: **3/1**
Student faculty ratio: **14.8 to 1**

First year can start other than Fall: **No**
Student housing: **No**
--exclusively for law students: **No**
Term: **Semester**

*pr=preferred

Faculty

	Men #	Men %	Women #	Women %	Minorities #	Minorities %	Total
Full-time	13	76	4	24	4	24	17
Other full-time	0	0	0	0	0	0	0
Deans, librarians, & others who teach	2	100	0	0	0	0	2
Part-time	7	100	0	0	1	14	7
Total	22	85	4	15	5	19	26
Deans, librarians, & others who teach < 1/2	2	100	0	0	0	0	2

Library

# of volumes & volume equivalents	195,758	# of professional staff	4
# of titles	30,636	Hours per week with professional staff	53
# of active serial subscriptions	3,105	Hours per week without professional staff	46
Study seating capacity inside the library	210	# of student computer work stations for entire law school	25
Square feet of law library	24,700	# of additional networked connections	0
Square feet of law school (excl. Library)	18,600		

Curriculum

	Full time	Part time
Typical first-year section size	53	0
Is there typically a "small section" of the first year class, other than Legal Writing, taught by full-time faculty?	No	No
If yes, typical size offered last year	N/A	N/A
# of classroom course titles beyond 1st year curriculum	76	0
# of upper division courses, excluding seminars, with an enrollment:		
Under 25	54	0
25 - 49	17	0
50 - 74	11	0
75 - 99	1	0
100 +	0	0
# of seminars	10	0
# of seminar positions available	120	
# of seminar positions filled	106	0
# of positions available in simulation courses	208	
# of simulation positions filled	199	0
# of positions available in faculty supervised clinical courses	0	
# of fac. sup. clin. positions filled	0	0
# involved in field placements	37	0
# involved in law journals	36	0
# in moot court or trial competitions	60	0
# of credit hours required to graduate	85	

Enrollment & Attrition

	Full-Time Men #	Men %	Women #	Women %	Minorities #	Minorities %	Total #	Part-Time Men #	Men %	Women #	Women %	Minorities #	Minorities %	Total #	Attrition Academic #	Other #	Total #	%
1st Year	64	61.5	40	38.5	22	21.2	104	0	0.0	0	0.0	0	0.0	0	4	5	9	9.3
2nd Year	59	60.8	38	39.2	21	21.6	97	0	0.0	0	0.0	0	0.0	0	1	0	1	1.1
3rd Year	47	50.5	46	49.5	16	17.2	93	0	0.0	0	0.0	0	0.0	0	0	0	0	0.0
4th Year								0	0.0	0	0.0	0	0.0	0	0	0	0	0.0
Total	170	57.8	124	42.2	59	20.1	294	0	0.0	0	0.0	0	0.0	0	5	5	10	3.3
JD Degrees Awarded	72	67.3	35	32.7	20	18.7	107	0	0.0	0	0.0	0	0.0	0				

GPA & LSAT Scores

	Full Time	Part Time	Total
# of apps	1,073	0	1,073
# admits	381	0	381
# of matrics	104	0	104
75% GPA	3.31	0.00	
25% GPA	2.67	0.00	
75% LSAT	157	0	
25% LSAT	153	0	

Tuition/Living Expenses

	Resident	Non-resident
Full-Time	$5,467	$10,099
Part-Time	$0	$0

Estimated living expenses for Singles		
Living on campus	Living off campus	Living at home
$6,957	$7,757	$7,757

Career Placement

	Total	%
Employment status known	93	91.2
Employment status unknown	9	8.8
Employed	77	82.8
Pursuing graduate degrees	5	5.4
Unemployed seeking employment	11	11.8
Unemployed not seeking employment	0	0.0
Type of Employment		
# employed in law firms	33	42.9
# employed in business & industry	5	6.5
# employed in government	22	28.6
# employed in public interest	14	18.2
# employed as judicial clerks	3	3.9
# employed in academia	0	0.0
Geographic Location		
# employed in state	66	85.7
# employed in foreign countries	1	1.3
# of states where employed	9	

Financial Aid

	Full-time		Part-time		Total	
	#	%	#	%	#	%
Total # receiving grants	50	17.0	0	0.0	50	17.0
Less than 1/2 tuition	20	6.8	0	0.0	20	6.8
Half to full tuition	18	6.1	0	0.0	18	6.1
Full tuition	4	1.4	0	0.0	4	1.4
More than full tuition	8	2.7	0	0.0	8	2.7
Median Grant Amount	$2,316		$0			

Refunds

Refunds of Admissions or Seat Deposit prior to commencement of classes? No

Refunds of Pre-paid tuition prior to commencement of classes? Yes

If yes, fully refundable before the start of classes? Yes

Joint Degrees Offered

JD/MBA

Advanced Degrees Offered

No Advanced Degrees

Bar Passage Rate

Jurisdiction	IL
# from school taking bar for the first time	88
School's pass rate for all first-time takers	77%
State's pass rate for all first-time takers	87%
State's pass rate for all first-time takers from ABA approved law schools	87%

NORTHERN KENTUCKY UNIVERSITY

Nunn Drive
Highland Heights, KY 41099
(606)572-5340
http://www.eku.edu/~chase

ABA Approved Since 1954

The Basics

Type of School: **PUBLIC**
Application deadline*: **5/15**
Application fee: **$30**
Financial Aid deadline*: **2/1**
Student faculty ratio: **15.6 to 1**

First year can start other than Fall: **No**
Student housing: **Yes**
--exclusively for law students: **No**
Term: **Semester**

*pr=preferred

Faculty

	Men #	Men %	Women #	Women %	Minorities #	Minorities %	Total
Full-time	13	72	5	28	1	6	18
Other full-time	0	0	1	100	0	0	1
Deans, librarians, & others who teach	2	100	0	0	0	0	2
Part-time	20	83	4	17	0	0	24
Total	35	78	10	22	1	2	45
Deans, librarians, & others who teach < 1/2	1	50	1	50	0	0	2

Library

# of volumes & volume equivalents	241,873	# of professional staff	6
# of titles	32,481	Hours per week with professional staff	66
# of active serial subscriptions	2,328	Hours per week without professional staff	26
Study seating capacity inside the library	200	# of student computer work stations for entire law school	26
Square feet of law library	25,897	# of additional networked connections	0
Square feet of law school (excl. Library)	56,492		

Curriculum

	Full time	Part time
Typical first-year section size	60	50
Is there typically a "small section" of the first year class, other than Legal Writing, taught by full-time faculty?	No	No
If yes, typical size offered last year	N/A	N/A
# of classroom course titles beyond 1st year curriculum	32	65
# of upper division courses, excluding seminars, with an enrollment:		
Under 25	16	40
25 - 49	8	22
50 - 74	8	2
75 - 99	0	1
100 +	0	0
# of seminars	1	5
# of seminar positions available	0	
# of seminar positions filled	56	38
# of positions available in simulation courses	228	
# of simulation positions filled	168	60
# of positions available in faculty supervised clinical courses	30	
# of fac. sup. clin. positions filled	7	4
# involved in field placements	12	0
# involved in law journals	28	7
# in moot court or trial competitions	37	10
# of credit hours required to graduate	90	

Enrollment & Attrition

	Full-Time							Part-Time							Attrition			
	Men		Women		Minorities		Total	Men		Women		Minorities		Total	Academic	Other	Total	
	#	%	#	%	#	%	#	#	%	#	%	#	%	#	#	#	#	%
1st Year	40	55.6	32	44.4	5	6.9	72	36	64.3	20	35.7	7	12.5	56	3	3	6	5.2
2nd Year	40	61.5	25	38.5	2	3.1	65	30	63.8	17	36.2	4	8.5	47	1	5	6	5.2
3rd Year	47	64.4	26	35.6	8	11.0	73	33	67.3	16	32.7	1	2.0	49	1	1	2	1.4
4th Year								27	67.5	13	32.5	9	22.5	40	0	0	0	0.0
Total	127	60.5	83	39.5	15	7.1	210	126	65.6	66	34.4	21	10.9	192	5	9	14	3.4
JD Degrees Awarded	52	53.1	46	46.9	9	9.2	98	14	46.7	16	53.3	3	10.0	30				

NORTHERN KENTUCKY UNIVERSITY

GPA & LSAT Scores

	Full Time	Part Time	Total
# of apps	639	172	811
# admits	248	83	331
# of matrics	72	55	127
75% GPA	3.40	3.34	
25% GPA	2.87	2.79	
75% LSAT	157	157	
25% LSAT	151	151	

Tuition/Living Expenses

	Resident	Non-resident
Full-Time	$4,980	$12,580
Part-Time	$4,140	$10,480

Estimated living expenses for Singles		
Living on campus	Living off campus	Living at home
$6,084	$12,799	$12,799

Financial Aid

	Full-time		Part-time		Total	
	#	%	#	%	#	%
Total # receiving grants	60	28.6	59	30.7	119	29.6
Less than 1/2 tuition	28	13.3	43	22.4	71	17.7
Half to full tuition	3	1.4	4	2.1	7	1.7
Full tuition	29	13.8	12	6.3	41	10.2
More than full tuition	0	0.0	0	0.0	0	0.0
Median Grant Amount	$0		$0			

Refunds

Refunds of Admissions or Seat Deposit prior to commencement of classes? No

Refunds of Pre-paid tuition prior to commencement of classes? Yes

If yes, fully refundable before the start of classes? Yes

Joint Degrees Offered

JD/MBA

Advanced Degrees Offered

No Advanced Degrees

Career Placement

	Total	%
Employment status known	45	39.8
Employment status unknown	68	60.2
Employed	39	86.7
Pursuing graduate degrees	1	2.2
Unemployed seeking employment	3	6.7
Unemployed not seeking employment	2	4.4
Type of Employment		
# employed in law firms	17	43.6
# employed in business & industry	13	33.3
# employed in government	6	15.4
# employed in public interest	1	2.6
# employed as judicial clerks	2	5.1
# employed in academia	0	0.0
Geographic Location		
# employed in state	23	59.0
# employed in foreign countries	0	0.0
# of states where employed	3	

Bar Passage Rate

Jurisdiction	KY	OH
# from school taking bar for the first time	45	59
School's pass rate for all first-time takers	83%	92%
State's pass rate for all first-time takers	88%	93%
State's pass rate for all first-time takers from ABA approved law schools	88%	90%

NORTHWESTERN UNIVERSITY

357 East Chicago Avenue
Chicago, IL 60611
(312)503-8462

ABA Approved Since 1923

The Basics

Type of School: **PRIVATE**
Application deadline*: **2/13**
Application fee: **$80**
Financial Aid deadline*: **3/15**
Student faculty ratio: **15.2 to 1**

First year can start other than Fall: **No**
Student housing: **Yes**
--exclusively for law students: **No**
Term: **Semester**

*pr=preferred

Faculty

	Men #	Men %	Women #	Women %	Minorities #	Minorities %	Total
Full-time	27	79	7	21	2	6	34
Other full-time	6	43	8	57	0	0	14
Deans, librarians, & others who teach	2	100	0	0	0	0	2
Part-time	19	90	2	10	1	5	21
Total	54	76	17	24	3	4	71
Deans, librarians, & others who teach < 1/2	1	100	0	0	0	0	1

Library

# of volumes & volume equivalents	621,923	# of professional staff	9
# of titles	184,678	Hours per week with professional staff	79
# of active serial subscriptions	8,201	Hours per week without professional staff	26
Study seating capacity inside the library	747	# of student computer work stations for entire law school	25
Square feet of law library	93,900	# of additional networked connections	75
Square feet of law school (excl. Library)	69,961		

Curriculum

	Full time	Part time
Typical first-year section size	100	0
Is there typically a "small section" of the first year class, other than Legal Writing, taught by full-time faculty?	Yes	No
If yes, typical size offered last year	48	N/A
# of classroom course titles beyond 1st year curriculum	61	0
# of upper division courses, excluding seminars, with an enrollment:		
Under 25	27	0
25 - 49	24	0
50 - 74	12	0
75 - 99	9	0
100 +	3	0
# of seminars	37	0
# of seminar positions available	805	
# of seminar positions filled	512	0
# of positions available in simulation courses	324	
# of simulation positions filled	297	0
# of positions available in faculty supervised clinical courses	90	
# of fac. sup. clin. positions filled	64	0
# involved in field placements	42	0
# involved in law journals	160	0
# in moot court or trial competitions	41	0
# of credit hours required to graduate	86	

Enrollment & Attrition

	Full-Time							Part-Time							Attrition			
	Men		Women		Minorities		Total	Men		Women		Minorities		Total	Academic	Other	Total	
	#	%	#	%	#	%	#	#	%	#	%	#	%	#	#	#	#	%
1st Year	117	57.9	85	42.1	51	25.2	202	0	0.0	0	0.0	0	0.0	0	0	0	0	0.0
2nd Year	124	58.5	88	41.5	34	16.0	212	0	0.0	0	0.0	0	0.0	0	0	10	10	4.8
3rd Year	122	59.5	83	40.5	42	20.5	205	0	0.0	0	0.0	0	0.0	0	0	0	0	0.0
4th Year								0	0.0	0	0.0	0	0.0	0	0	0	0	0.0
Total	363	58.6	256	41.4	127	20.5	619	0	0.0	0	0.0	0	0.0	0	0	10	10	1.7
JD Degrees Awarded	97	48.5	103	51.5	51	25.5	200	0	0.0	0	0.0	0	0.0	0				

GPA & LSAT Scores

	Full Time	Part Time	Total
# of apps	4,098	0	4,098
# admits	842	0	842
# of matrics	203	0	203
75% GPA	3.73	0.00	
25% GPA	3.26	0.00	
75% LSAT	167	0	
25% LSAT	159	0	

Tuition/Living Expenses

	Resident	Non-resident
Full-Time	$21,316	$21,316
Part-Time	$0	$0

Estimated living expenses for Singles		
Living on campus	Living off campus	Living at home
$13,094	$14,399	$8,099

Career Placement

	Total	%
Employment status known	197	93.8
Employment status unknown	13	6.2
Employed	182	92.4
Pursuing graduate degrees	2	1.0
Unemployed seeking employment	12	6.1
Unemployed not seeking employment	1	0.5
Type of Employment		
# employed in law firms	126	69.2
# employed in business & industry	17	9.3
# employed in government	11	6.0
# employed in public interest	2	1.1
# employed as judicial clerks	24	13.2
# employed in academia	2	1.1
Geographic Location		
# employed in state	107	58.8
# employed in foreign countries	0	0.0
# of states where employed	25	

Financial Aid

	Full-time		Part-time		Total	
	#	%	#	%	#	%
Total # receiving grants	233	37.6	0	0.0	233	37.6
Less than 1/2 tuition	170	27.5	0	0.0	170	27.5
Half to full tuition	46	7.4	0	0.0	46	7.4
Full tuition	14	2.3	0	0.0	14	2.3
More than full tuition	3	0.5	0	0.0	3	0.5
Median Grant Amount	$9,500		$0			

Refunds

Refunds of Admissions or Seat Deposit prior to commencement of classes? No

Refunds of Pre-paid tuition prior to commencement of classes? Yes

If yes, fully refundable before the start of classes? Yes

Joint Degrees Offered

JDMM, JDPhD

Advanced Degrees Offered

SJD	Individual supervised research with faculty
LLM	Course work integrated with J.D. program

Bar Passage Rate

Jurisdiction	IL
# from school taking bar for the first time	115
School's pass rate for all first-time takers	95%
State's pass rate for all first-time takers	87%
State's pass rate for all first-time takers from ABA approved law schools	87%

NOTRE DAME, UNIVERSITY OF

103 Law Building
Notre Dame, IN 46556
(219)631-6627
http://www.nd.edu/~ndlaw

ABA Approved Since 1925

The Basics

Type of School: PRIVATE
Application deadline*: 3/1
Application fee: $45
Financial Aid deadline*: 3/1
Student faculty ratio: 15.4 to 1

First year can start other than Fall: No
Student housing: Yes
--exclusively for law students: No
Term: Semester

*pr=preferred

Faculty

	Men #	Men %	Women #	Women %	Minorities #	Minorities %	Total
Full-time	21	78	6	22	3	11	27
Other full-time	0	0	2	100	0	0	2
Deans, librarians, & others who teach	5	100	0	0	0	0	5
Part-time	19	86	3	14	0	0	22
Total	45	80	11	20	3	5	56
Deans, librarians, & others who teach < 1/2	2	67	1	33	0	0	3

Library

# of volumes & volume equivalents	405,356	# of professional staff	9
# of titles	78,433	Hours per week with professional staff	74
# of active serial subscriptions	5,144	Hours per week without professional staff	12
Study seating capacity inside the library	517	# of student computer work stations for entire law school	47
Square feet of law library	37,222	# of additional networked connections	0
Square feet of law school (excl. Library)	39,674		

Curriculum

	Full time	Part time
Typical first-year section size	90	0
Is there typically a "small section" of the first year class, other than Legal Writing, taught by full-time faculty?	No	No
If yes, typical size offered last year	N/A	N/A
# of classroom course titles beyond 1st year curriculum	104	0
# of upper division courses, excluding seminars, with an enrollment:		
Under 25	47	0
25 - 49	12	0
50 - 74	2	0
75 - 99	1	0
100 +	10	0
# of seminars	3	0
# of seminar positions available	24	
# of seminar positions filled	13	0
# of positions available in simulation courses	250	
# of simulation positions filled	236	0
# of positions available in faculty supervised clinical courses	250	
# of fac. sup. clin. positions filled	232	0
# involved in field placements	49	0
# involved in law journals	259	0
# in moot court or trial competitions	107	0
# of credit hours required to graduate	90	

Enrollment & Attrition

	Full-Time							Part-Time							Attrition			
	Men		Women		Minorities		Total	Men		Women		Minorities		Total	Academic	Other	Total	
	#	%	#	%	#	%	#	#	%	#	%	#	%	#	#	#	#	%
1st Year	91	52.9	81	47.1	38	22.1	172	0	0.0	0	0.0	0	0.0	0	0	2	2	1.2
2nd Year	84	52.5	76	47.5	25	15.6	160	0	0.0	0	0.0	0	0.0	0	0	8	8	4.2
3rd Year	114	55.6	91	44.4	32	15.6	205	0	0.0	0	0.0	0	0.0	0	0	0	0	0.0
4th Year								0	0.0	0	0.0	0	0.0	0	0	0	0	0.0
Total	289	53.8	248	46.2	95	17.7	537	0	0.0	0	0.0	0	0.0	0	0	10	10	1.9
JD Degrees Awarded	114	55.6	91	44.4	32	15.6	205	0	0.0	0	0.0	0	0.0	0				

GPA & LSAT Scores

	Full Time	Part Time	Total
# of apps	2,249	0	2,249
# admits	591	0	591
# of matrics	172	0	172
75% GPA	3.64	0.00	
25% GPA	3.09	0.00	
75% LSAT	165	0	
25% LSAT	160	0	

Tuition/Living Expenses

	Resident	Non-resident
Full-Time	$19,427	$19,427
Part-Time	$0	$0

Estimated living expenses for Singles		
Living on campus	Living off campus	Living at home
$5,150	$5,150	$5,150

Financial Aid

	Full-time		Part-time		Total	
	#	%	#	%	#	%
Total # receiving grants	196	36.5	0	0.0	196	36.5
Less than 1/2 tuition	153	28.5	0	0.0	153	28.5
Half to full tuition	29	5.4	0	0.0	29	5.4
Full tuition	12	2.2	0	0.0	12	2.2
More than full tuition	2	0.4	0	0.0	2	0.4
Median Grant Amount	$4,500		$0			

Refunds

Refunds of Admissions or Seat Deposit prior to commencement of classes? Yes

100% refund from 01/01/96 to 04/01/96
0% refund from 04/01/96 to 08/21/96

Refunds of Pre-paid tuition prior to commencement of classes? Yes

If yes, fully refundable before the start of classes? Yes

Joint Degrees Offered

JD/MBA, JD/MA, JD/PhD, JD/MS

Advanced Degrees Offered

LL.M. International and Comparative Law
LL.M. International Human Rights
J.S.D. International Human Rights

Career Placement

	Total	%
Employment status known	168	97.7
Employment status unknown	4	2.3
Employed	161	95.8
Pursuing graduate degrees	1	0.6
Unemployed seeking employment	6	3.6
Unemployed not seeking employment	0	0.0
Type of Employment		
# employed in law firms	113	70.2
# employed in business & industry	10	6.2
# employed in government	18	11.2
# employed in public interest	3	1.9
# employed as judicial clerks	17	10.6
# employed in academia	0	0.0
Geographic Location		
# employed in state	17	10.6
# employed in foreign countries	1	0.6
# of states where employed	29	

Bar Passage Rate

Jurisdiction	IN
# from school taking bar for the first time	35
School's pass rate for all first-time takers	97%
State's pass rate for all first-time takers	86%
State's pass rate for all first-time takers from ABA approved law schools	86%

NOVA SOUTHEASTERN UNIVERSITY

3305 College Avenue
Fort Lauderdale, FL 33314-7721
(954)262-6100
http://www.nsulaw.nova.edu

ABA Approved Since 1975

The Basics

Type of School: **PRIVATE**
Application deadline*: **5/31**
Application fee: **$45**
Financial Aid deadline*: **4/1**
Student faculty ratio: **20.5 to 1**

First year can start other than Fall: **No**
Student housing: **Yes**
--exclusively for law students: **No**
Term: **Semester**

*pr=preferred

Faculty

	Men		Women		Minorities		Total
	#	%	#	%	#	%	
Full-time	22	58	16	42	7	18	38
Other full-time	3	100	0	0	0	0	3
Deans, librarians, & others who teach	0	0	1	100	0	0	1
Part-time	24	69	11	31	2	6	35
Total	49	64	28	36	9	12	77
Deans, librarians, & others who teach < 1/2	2	50	2	50	0	0	4

Library

# of volumes & volume equivalents	288,783	# of professional staff	9
# of titles	116,688	Hours per week with professional staff	69
# of active serial subscriptions	5,470	Hours per week without professional staff	36
Study seating capacity inside the library	539	# of student computer work stations for entire law school	68
Square feet of law library	53,680	# of additional networked connections	172
Square feet of law school (excl. Library)	68,320		

Curriculum

	Full time	Part time
Typical first-year section size	49	0
Is there typically a "small section" of the first year class, other than Legal Writing, taught by full-time faculty?	No	No
If yes, typical size offered last year	N/A	N/A
# of classroom course titles beyond 1st year curriculum	84	0
# of upper division courses, excluding seminars, with an enrollment:		
Under 25	64	0
25 - 49	31	0
50 - 74	29	0
75 - 99	7	0
100 +	1	0
# of seminars	15	0
# of seminar positions available	300	
# of seminar positions filled	257	0
# of positions available in simulation courses	1,026	
# of simulation positions filled	877	0
# of positions available in faculty supervised clinical courses	40	
# of fac. sup. clin. positions filled	27	0
# involved in field placements	243	0
# involved in law journals	94	0
# in moot court or trial competitions	264	0
# of credit hours required to graduate	87	

Enrollment & Attrition

	Full-Time							Part-Time							Attrition			
	Men		Women		Minorities		Total	Men		Women		Minorities		Total	Academic	Other	Total	
	#	%	#	%	#	%	#	#	%	#	%	#	%	#	#	#	#	%
1st Year	186	60.4	122	39.6	75	24.4	308	47	67.1	23	32.9	17	24.3	70	21	33	54	18
2nd Year	164	63.3	95	36.7	63	24.3	259	3	75.0	1	25.0	0	0.0	4	10	3	13	3.9
3rd Year	169	54.7	140	45.3	76	24.6	309	1	16.7	5	83.3	2	33.3	6	0	1	1	0.4
4th Year								4	50.0	4	50.0	1	12.5	8	0	0	0	0.0
Total	519	59.2	357	40.8	214	24.4	876	55	62.5	33	37.5	20	22.7	88	31	37	68	7.5
JD Degrees Awarded	150	54.9	123	45.1	74	27.1	273	3	60.0	2	40.0	3	60.0	5				

GPA & LSAT Scores

	Full Time	Part Time	Total
# of apps	1,656	203	1,859
# admits	926	113	1,039
# of matrics	313	72	385
75% GPA	3.17	3.30	
25% GPA	2.67	2.55	
75% LSAT	151	153	
25% LSAT	145	144	

Tuition/Living Expenses

	Resident	Non-resident
Full-Time	$18,850	$18,850
Part-Time	$14,140	$14,140

Estimated living expenses for Singles		
Living on campus	Living off campus	Living at home
$13,119	$14,142	$7,914

Career Placement

	Total	%
Employment status known	209	83.3
Employment status unknown	42	16.7
Employed	174	83.3
Pursuing graduate degrees	7	3.4
Unemployed seeking employment	27	12.9
Unemployed not seeking employment	1	0.5
Type of Employment		
# employed in law firms	123	70.7
# employed in business & industry	14	8.1
# employed in government	29	16.7
# employed in public interest	2	1.2
# employed as judicial clerks	3	1.7
# employed in academia	3	1.7
Geographic Location		
# employed in state	148	85.1
# employed in foreign countries	0	0.0
# of states where employed	17	

Financial Aid

	Full-time		Part-time		Total	
	#	%	#	%	#	%
Total # receiving grants	252	28.8	5	5.7	257	26.7
Less than 1/2 tuition	224	25.6	5	5.7	229	23.8
Half to full tuition	20	2.3	0	0.0	20	2.1
Full tuition	8	0.9	0	0.0	8	0.8
More than full tuition	0	0.0	0	0.0	0	0.0
Median Grant Amount	$1,700		$3,535			

Refunds

Refunds of Admissions or Seat Deposit prior to commencement of classes? No

Refunds of Pre-paid tuition prior to commencement of classes? Yes

If yes, fully refundable before the start of classes? No

75% refund from 08/19/96 to 08/23/96
50% refund from 08/24/96 to 08/30/96
25% refund from 08/31/96 to 09/09/96

Joint Degrees Offered

JD/MBA, JD/MS(Psych), JD/MURP

Advanced Degrees Offered

No Advanced Degrees

Bar Passage Rate

Jurisdiction	FL	NY
# from school taking bar for the first time	190	13
School's pass rate for all first-time takers	82%	77%
State's pass rate for all first-time takers	84%	78%
State's pass rate for all first-time takers from ABA approved law schools	84%	

OHIO NORTHERN UNIVERSITY

525 S. Main Street
Ada, OH 45810
(419)772-2205
http://www.law.onu.edu

ABA Approved Since 1948

The Basics

Type of School: PRIVATE
Application deadline*: rolling
Application fee: $40
Financial Aid deadline*: 4/1
Student faculty ratio: 15.0 to 1
First year can start other than Fall: No
Student housing: Yes
--exclusively for law students: Yes
Term: Semester

*pr=preferred

Faculty

	Men #	Men %	Women #	Women %	Minorities #	Minorities %	Total
Full-time	16	80	4	20	1	5	20
Other full-time	0	0	0	0	0	0	0
Deans, librarians, & others who teach	4	100	0	0	0	0	4
Part-time	4	57	3	43	0	0	7
Total	24	77	7	23	1	3	31
Deans, librarians, & others who teach < 1/2	0	0	0	0	0	0	0

Library

# of volumes & volume equivalents	257,375	# of professional staff	4
# of titles	69,478	Hours per week with professional staff	59
# of active serial subscriptions	3,214	Hours per week without professional staff	49
Study seating capacity inside the library	261	# of student computer work stations for entire law school	36
Square feet of law library	27,027	# of additional networked connections	0
Square feet of law school (excl. Library)	16,335		

Curriculum

	Full time	Part time
Typical first-year section size	42	0
Is there typically a "small section" of the first year class, other than Legal Writing, taught by full-time faculty?	No	No
If yes, typical size offered last year	N/A	N/A
# of classroom course titles beyond 1st year curriculum	71	0
# of upper division courses, excluding seminars, with an enrollment:		
Under 25	40	0
25 - 49	17	0
50 - 74	11	0
75 - 99	0	0
100 +	0	0
# of seminars	10	0
# of seminar positions available	200	
# of seminar positions filled	161	0
# of positions available in simulation courses	211	
# of simulation positions filled	170	0
# of positions available in faculty supervised clinical courses	30	
# of fac. sup. clin. positions filled	26	0
# involved in field placements	71	0
# involved in law journals	51	0
# in moot court or trial competitions	86	0
# of credit hours required to graduate	87	

Enrollment & Attrition

	Full-Time Men #	Men %	Women #	Women %	Minorities #	Minorities %	Total #	Part-Time Men #	Men %	Women #	Women %	Minorities #	Minorities %	Total #	Attrition Academic #	Other #	Total #	Total %
1st Year	82	64.1	46	35.9	16	12.5	128	0	0.0	0	0.0	0	0.0	0	2	23	25	20
2nd Year	70	63.1	41	36.9	12	10.8	111	0	0.0	0	0.0	0	0.0	0	0	1	1	0.9
3rd Year	68	65.4	36	34.6	6	5.8	104	0	0.0	0	0.0	0	0.0	0	0	0	0	0.0
4th Year								0	0.0	0	0.0	0	0.0	0	0	0	0	0.0
Total	220	64.1	123	35.9	34	9.9	343	0	0.0	0	0.0	0	0.0	0	2	24	26	7.3
JD Degrees Awarded	78	61.4	49	38.6	11	8.7	127	0	0.0	0	0.0	0	0.0	0				

GPA & LSAT Scores

	Full Time	Part Time	Total
# of apps	861	0	861
# admits	549	0	549
# of matrics	125	0	125
75% GPA	3.29	0.00	
25% GPA	2.64	0.00	
75% LSAT	152	0	
25% LSAT	144	0	

Tuition/Living Expenses

	Resident	Non-resident
Full-Time	$20,510	$20,510
Part-Time	$0	$0

Estimated living expenses for Singles		
Living on campus	Living off campus	Living at home
$6,800	$7,800	$3,090

Financial Aid

	Full-time		Part-time		Total	
	#	%	#	%	#	%
Total # receiving grants	125	36.4	0	0.0	125	36.4
Less than 1/2 tuition	84	24.5	0	0.0	84	24.5
Half to full tuition	41	12.0	0	0.0	41	12.0
Full tuition	0	0.0	0	0.0	0	0.0
More than full tuition	0	0.0	0	0.0	0	0.0
Median Grant Amount	$8,000		$0			

Refunds

Refunds of Admissions or Seat Deposit prior to commencement of classes? No

Refunds of Pre-paid tuition prior to commencement of classes? No

If yes, fully refundable before the start of classes? No

Career Placement

	Total	%
Employment status known	101	86.3
Employment status unknown	16	13.7
Employed	82	81.2
Pursuing graduate degrees	4	4.0
Unemployed seeking employment	15	14.9
Unemployed not seeking employment	0	0.0
Type of Employment		
# employed in law firms	45	54.9
# employed in business & industry	9	11.0
# employed in government	12	14.6
# employed in public interest	0	0.0
# employed as judicial clerks	14	17.1
# employed in academia	2	2.4
Geographic Location		
# employed in state	29	35.4
# employed in foreign countries	1	1.2
# of states where employed	21	

Joint Degrees Offered

Pharm-Law

Advanced Degrees Offered

No Advanced Degrees

Bar Passage Rate

Jurisdiction	OH	PA	NY
# from school taking bar for the first time	39	21	15
School's pass rate for all first-time takers	90%	42%	73%
State's pass rate for all first-time takers	93%	73%	78%
State's pass rate for all first-time takers from ABA approved law schools	90%	73%	

OHIO STATE UNIVERSITY

55 W. 12th Avenue
Columbus, OH 43210
(614)292-2631
http://www.acs.ohio-state.edu/units/law

ABA Approved Since 1923

The Basics

Type of School: PUBLIC
Application deadline*: 3/15
Application fee: $30
Financial Aid deadline*: 3/1
Student faculty ratio: 17.6 to 1

First year can start other than Fall: No
Student housing: Yes
--exclusively for law students: No
Term: Semester

*pr=preferred

Faculty

	Men		Women		Minorities		Total
	#	%	#	%	#	%	
Full-time	25	78	7	22	4	13	32
Other full-time	0	0	0	0	0	0	0
Deans, librarians, & others who teach	3	50	3	50	3	50	6
Part-time	18	75	6	25	1	4	24
Total	46	74	16	26	8	13	62
Deans, librarians, & others who teach < 1/2	3	43	4	57	2	29	7

Library

# of volumes & volume equivalents	631,710	# of professional staff	7
# of titles	149,160	Hours per week with professional staff	68
# of active serial subscriptions	7,453	Hours per week without professional staff	39
Study seating capacity inside the library	660	# of student computer work stations for entire law school	69
Square feet of law library	81,340	# of additional networked connections	0
Square feet of law school (excl. Library)	78,009		

Curriculum

	Full time	Part time
Typical first-year section size	78	0
Is there typically a "small section" of the first year class, other than Legal Writing, taught by full-time faculty?	Yes	No
If yes, typical size offered last year	33	N/A
# of classroom course titles beyond 1st year curriculum	76	0
# of upper division courses, excluding seminars, with an enrollment:		
Under 25	24	0
25 - 49	26	0
50 - 74	19	0
75 - 99	4	0
100 +	3	0
# of seminars	25	0
# of seminar positions available	450	
# of seminar positions filled	365	0
# of positions available in simulation courses	128	
# of simulation positions filled	113	0
# of positions available in faculty supervised clinical courses	88	
# of fac. sup. clin. positions filled	75	0
# involved in field placements	38	0
# involved in law journals	139	0
# in moot court or trial competitions	180	0
# of credit hours required to graduate	91	

Enrollment & Attrition

	Full-Time							Part-Time							Attrition			
	Men		Women		Minorities		Total	Men		Women		Minorities		Total	Academic	Other	Total	
	#	%	#	%	#	%	#	#	%	#	%	#	%	#	#	#	#	%
1st Year	128	52.9	114	47.1	48	19.8	242	0	0.0	1	100.0	1	100.0	1	0	11	11	4.8
2nd Year	129	58.9	90	41.1	33	15.1	219	1	25.0	3	75.0	0	0.0	4	1	8	9	4.0
3rd Year	118	55.7	94	44.3	32	15.1	212	1	100.0	0	0.0	0	0.0	1	2	1	3	1.3
4th Year								0	0.0	0	0.0	0	0.0	0	0	0	0	0.0
Total	375	55.7	298	44.3	113	16.8	673	2	33.3	4	66.7	1	16.7	6	3	20	23	3.3
JD Degrees Awarded	125	57.1	94	42.9	33	15.1	219	0	0.0	0	0.0	0	0.0	0				

GPA & LSAT Scores

	Full Time	Part Time	Total
# of apps	1,387	0	1,387
# admits	582	0	582
# of matrics	244	0	244
75% GPA	3.67	0.00	
25% GPA	3.16	0.00	
75% LSAT	162	0	
25% LSAT	155	0	

Tuition/Living Expenses

	Resident	Non-resident
Full-Time	$6,412	$14,932
Part-Time	$0	$0

Estimated living expenses for Singles		
Living on campus	Living off campus	Living at home
$8,630	$8,630	$5,714

Career Placement

	Total	%
Employment status known	203	96.7
Employment status unknown	7	3.3
Employed	178	87.7
Pursuing graduate degrees	2	1.0
Unemployed seeking employment	21	10.3
Unemployed not seeking employment	2	1.0
Type of Employment		
# employed in law firms	93	52.3
# employed in business & industry	28	15.7
# employed in government	36	20.2
# employed in public interest	0	0.0
# employed as judicial clerks	18	10.1
# employed in academia	3	1.7
Geographic Location		
# employed in state	119	66.9
# employed in foreign countries	0	0.0
# of states where employed	23	

Financial Aid

	Full-time		Part-time		Total	
	#	%	#	%	#	%
Total # receiving grants	419	62.3	0	0.0	419	61.7
Less than 1/2 tuition	396	58.8	0	0.0	396	58.3
Half to full tuition	6	0.9	0	0.0	6	0.9
Full tuition	10	1.5	0	0.0	10	1.5
More than full tuition	7	1.0	0	0.0	7	1.0
Median Grant Amount	$1,500		$0			

Refunds

Refunds of Admissions or Seat Deposit prior to commencement of classes? Yes

100% refund from 10/01/95 to 04/15/96
0% refund from 04/15/96 to / /

Refunds of Pre-paid tuition prior to commencement of classes? Yes

If yes, fully refundable before the start of classes? Yes

100% refund from 08/22/96 to 08/27/96
75% refund from 08/28/96 to 09/05/96
50% refund from 09/06/96 to 09/20/96

Joint Degrees Offered

MBA, Ed & Pol, Pub Pol, HPER, MHA

Advanced Degrees Offered

No Advanced Degrees

Bar Passage Rate

Jurisdiction	OH
# from school taking bar for the first time	134
School's pass rate for all first-time takers	93%
State's pass rate for all first-time takers	93%
State's pass rate for all first-time takers from ABA approved law schools	90%

OKLAHOMA CITY UNIVERSITY

2501 North Blackwelder
Oklahoma City, OK 73106
(405)521-5337
http://frodo.okcu.edu/~law/home.htm

ABA Approved Since 1960

The Basics

Type of School: **PRIVATE**
Application deadline*: **8/1**
Application fee: **$35**
Financial Aid deadline*: **3/1**
Student faculty ratio: **16.7 to 1**
First year can start other than Fall: **No**
Student housing: **Yes**
--exclusively for law students: **No**
Term: **Semester**

*pr=preferred

Faculty

	Men		Women		Minorities		Total
	#	%	#	%	#	%	
Full-time	20	77	6	23	2	8	26
Other full-time	1	25	3	75	0	0	4
Deans, librarians, & others who teach	2	67	1	33	1	33	3
Part-time	10	91	1	9	1	9	11
Total	33	75	11	25	4	9	44
Deans, librarians, & others who teach < 1/2	1	100	0	0	1	100	1

Library

# of volumes & volume equivalents	242,009	# of professional staff	6
# of titles	54,092	Hours per week with professional staff	96
# of active serial subscriptions	3,768	Hours per week without professional staff	6
Study seating capacity inside the library	352	# of student computer work stations for entire law school	6
Square feet of law library	32,522	# of additional networked connections	20
Square feet of law school (excl. Library)	66,128		

Curriculum

	Full time	Part time
Typical first-year section size	82	75
Is there typically a "small section" of the first year class, other than Legal Writing, taught by full-time faculty?	No	No
If yes, typical size offered last year	N/A	N/A
# of classroom course titles beyond 1st year curriculum	39	34
# of upper division courses, excluding seminars, with an enrollment:		
Under 25	28	21
25 - 49	13	14
50 - 74	1	3
75 - 99	5	3
100 +	0	0
# of seminars	8	4
# of seminar positions available	204	
# of seminar positions filled	83	37
# of positions available in simulation courses	238	
# of simulation positions filled	93	123
# of positions available in faculty supervised clinical courses	66	
# of fac. sup. clin. positions filled	50	10
# involved in field placements	23	4
# involved in law journals	34	5
# in moot court or trial competitions	9	1
# of credit hours required to graduate	90	

Enrollment & Attrition

	Full-Time							Part-Time							Attrition			
	Men		Women		Minorities		Total	Men		Women		Minorities		Total	Academic	Other	Total	
	#	%	#	%	#	%	#	#	%	#	%	#	%	#	#	#	#	%
1st Year	76	59.8	51	40.2	19	15.0	127	26	52.0	24	48.0	6	12.0	50	16	25	41	18
2nd Year	91	62.3	55	37.7	18	12.3	146	32	68.1	15	31.9	3	6.4	47	7	8	15	7.4
3rd Year	79	62.7	47	37.3	12	9.5	126	55	61.1	35	38.9	13	14.4	90	0	1	1	0.5
4th Year								0	0.0	0	0.0	0	0.0	0	0	0	0	0.0
Total	246	61.7	153	38.3	49	12.3	399	113	60.4	74	39.6	22	11.8	187	23	34	57	8.9
JD Degrees Awarded	79	62.2	48	37.8	12	9.4	127	33	63.5	19	36.5	3	5.8	52				

GPA & LSAT Scores

	Full Time	Part Time	Total
# of apps	924	145	1,069
# admits	533	111	644
# of matrics	131	51	182
75% GPA	3.24	3.47	
25% GPA	2.66	2.66	
75% LSAT	152	152	
25% LSAT	144	145	

Tuition/Living Expenses

	Resident	Non-resident
Full-Time	$12,218	$12,218
Part-Time	$8,748	$8,748

Estimated living expenses for Singles		
Living on campus	Living off campus	Living at home
$6,509	$8,791	$5,952

Career Placement

	Total	%
Employment status known	106	62.0
Employment status unknown	65	38.0
Employed	85	80.2
Pursuing graduate degrees	2	1.9
Unemployed seeking employment	12	11.3
Unemployed not seeking employment	7	6.6
Type of Employment		
# employed in law firms	56	65.9
# employed in business & industry	13	15.3
# employed in government	11	12.9
# employed in public interest	0	0.0
# employed as judicial clerks	4	4.7
# employed in academia	1	1.2
Geographic Location		
# employed in state	46	54.1
# employed in foreign countries	0	0.0
# of states where employed	18	

Financial Aid

	Full-time		Part-time		Total	
	#	%	#	%	#	%
Total # receiving grants	49	12.3	19	10.2	68	11.6
Less than 1/2 tuition	25	6.3	19	10.2	44	7.5
Half to full tuition	12	3.0	0	0.0	12	2.0
Full tuition	0	0.0	0	0.0	0	0.0
More than full tuition	12	3.0	0	0.0	12	2.0
Median Grant Amount	$5,000		$3,000			

Refunds

Refunds of Admissions or Seat Deposit prior to commencement of classes? No

Refunds of Pre-paid tuition prior to commencement of classes? Yes

If yes, fully refundable before the start of classes? Yes

Joint Degrees Offered

JD/MBA, JD/MDiv

Advanced Degrees Offered

No Advanced Degrees

Bar Passage Rate

Jurisdiction	OK
# from school taking bar for the first time	69
School's pass rate for all first-time takers	74%
State's pass rate for all first-time takers	75%
State's pass rate for all first-time takers from ABA approved law schools	75%

OKLAHOMA, UNIVERSITY OF

300 Timberdell Road
Norman, OK 73019-5081
(405)325-4699
http://www.law.ou.edu

ABA Approved Since 1923

The Basics

Type of School: **PUBLIC**
Application deadline*: **3/15**
Application fee: **$50**
Financial Aid deadline*: **3/1**
Student faculty ratio: **15.2 to 1**
First year can start other than Fall: **No**
Student housing: **Yes**
--exclusively for law students: **No**
Term: **Semester**

*pr=preferred

Faculty

	Men #	Men %	Women #	Women %	Minorities #	Minorities %	Total
Full-time	23	77	7	23	4	13	30
Other full-time	0	0	2	100	0	0	2
Deans, librarians, & others who teach	2	100	0	0	0	0	2
Part-time	9	75	3	25	0	0	12
Total	34	74	12	26	4	9	46
Deans, librarians, & others who teach < 1/2	1	50	1	50	0	0	2

Library

# of volumes & volume equivalents	300,896	# of professional staff	8
# of titles	133,971	Hours per week with professional staff	54
# of active serial subscriptions	3,888	Hours per week without professional staff	47
Study seating capacity inside the library	368	# of student computer work stations for entire law school	49
Square feet of law library	28,733	# of additional networked connections	0
Square feet of law school (excl. Library)	58,063		

Curriculum

	Full time	Part time
Typical first-year section size	42	0
Is there typically a "small section" of the first year class, other than Legal Writing, taught by full-time faculty?	Yes	No
If yes, typical size offered last year	22	N/A
# of classroom course titles beyond 1st year curriculum	139	0
# of upper division courses, excluding seminars, with an enrollment:		
Under 25	57	0
25 - 49	37	0
50 - 74	23	0
75 - 99	6	0
100 +	0	0
# of seminars	16	0
# of seminar positions available	256	
# of seminar positions filled	244	0
# of positions available in simulation courses	190	
# of simulation positions filled	154	0
# of positions available in faculty supervised clinical courses	153	
# of fac. sup. clin. positions filled	141	0
# involved in field placements	98	0
# involved in law journals	78	0
# in moot court or trial competitions	32	0
# of credit hours required to graduate	90	

Enrollment & Attrition

	Full-Time Men #	Men %	Women #	Women %	Minorities #	Minorities %	Total #	Part-Time Men #	Men %	Women #	Women %	Minorities #	Minorities %	Total #	Attrition Academic #	Other #	Total #	%
1st Year	96	57.5	71	42.5	27	16.2	167	0	0.0	0	0.0	0	0.0	0	0	0	0	0.0
2nd Year	98	59.4	67	40.6	21	12.7	165	0	0.0	0	0.0	0	0.0	0	6	1	7	3.5
3rd Year	125	59.5	85	40.5	26	12.4	210	0	0.0	0	0.0	0	0.0	0	1	1	2	0.9
4th Year								0	0.0	0	0.0	0	0.0	0	0	0	0	0.0
Total	319	58.9	223	41.1	74	13.7	542	0	0.0	0	0.0	0	0.0	0	7	2	9	1.5
JD Degrees Awarded	122	60.7	79	39.3	22	10.9	201	0	0.0	0	0.0	0	0.0	0				

GPA & LSAT Scores

	Full Time	Part Time	Total
# of apps	704	0	704
# admits	291	0	291
# of matrics	167	0	167
75% GPA	3.43	0.00	
25% GPA	3.05	0.00	
75% LSAT	155	0	
25% LSAT	150	0	

Tuition/Living Expenses

	Resident	Non-resident
Full-Time	$4,141	$11,779
Part-Time	$0	$0

Estimated living expenses for Singles		
Living on campus	Living off campus	Living at home
$9,122	$10,497	$6,604

Career Placement

	Total	%
Employment status known	194	89.0
Employment status unknown	24	11.0
Employed	163	84.0
Pursuing graduate degrees	10	5.2
Unemployed seeking employment	21	10.8
Unemployed not seeking employment	0	0.0
Type of Employment		
# employed in law firms	102	62.6
# employed in business & industry	24	14.7
# employed in government	27	16.6
# employed in public interest	3	1.8
# employed as judicial clerks	5	3.1
# employed in academia	2	1.2
Geographic Location		
# employed in state	112	68.7
# employed in foreign countries	0	0.0
# of states where employed	20	

Financial Aid

	Full-time		Part-time		Total	
	#	%	#	%	#	%
Total # receiving grants	280	51.7	0	0.0	280	51.7
Less than 1/2 tuition	180	33.2	0	0.0	180	33.2
Half to full tuition	74	13.7	0	0.0	74	13.7
Full tuition	4	0.7	0	0.0	4	0.7
More than full tuition	22	4.1	0	0.0	22	4.1
Median Grant Amount	$1,000		$0			

Refunds

Refunds of Admissions or Seat Deposit prior to commencement of classes? No

Refunds of Pre-paid tuition prior to commencement of classes? No

If yes, fully refundable before the start of classes? No

Joint Degrees Offered

MBA, MPH, MS Occup. H, MS Envr.Mgmt

Advanced Degrees Offered

No Advanced Degrees

Bar Passage Rate

Jurisdiction	OK	TX
# from school taking bar for the first time	150	20
School's pass rate for all first-time takers	75%	75%
State's pass rate for all first-time takers	75%	82%
State's pass rate for all first-time takers from ABA approved law schools	75%	82%

OREGON, UNIVERSITY OF

1221 University of Oregon
Eugene, OR 97403-1221
(541)346-3852
http://www.law.uoregon.edu

ABA Approved Since 1923

The Basics

Type of School: **PUBLIC**	First year can start other than Fall: **No**
Application deadline*: **4/1**	Student housing: **No**
Application fee: **$50**	--exclusively for law students: **No**
Financial Aid deadline*: **3/1**	Term: **Semester**
Student faculty ratio: **16.9 to 1**	

*pr=preferred

Faculty

	Men		Women		Minorities		Total
	#	%	#	%	#	%	
Full-time	17	68	8	32	4	16	25
Other full-time	2	67	1	33	0	0	3
Deans, librarians, & others who teach	1	100	0	0	0	0	1
Part-time	8	80	2	20	0	0	10
Total	28	72	11	28	4	10	39
Deans, librarians, & others who teach < 1/2	0	0	0	0	0	0	0

Library

# of volumes & volume equivalents	330,438	# of professional staff	4
# of titles	44,625	Hours per week with professional staff	55
# of active serial subscriptions	3,216	Hours per week without professional staff	55
Study seating capacity inside the library	237	# of student computer work stations for entire law school	25
Square feet of law library	25,114	# of additional networked connections	350
Square feet of law school (excl. Library)	32,285		

Curriculum

	Full time	Part time
Typical first-year section size	53	0
Is there typically a "small section" of the first year class, other than Legal Writing, taught by full-time faculty?	No	No
If yes, typical size offered last year	N/A	N/A
# of classroom course titles beyond 1st year curriculum	79	0
# of upper division courses, excluding seminars, with an enrollment:		
Under 25	58	0
25 - 49	25	0
50 - 74	13	0
75 - 99	6	0
100 +	0	0
# of seminars	12	0
# of seminar positions available	246	
# of seminar positions filled	178	0
# of positions available in simulation courses	221	
# of simulation positions filled	147	0
# of positions available in faculty supervised clinical courses	169	
# of fac. sup. clin. positions filled	114	0
# involved in field placements	16	0
# involved in law journals	103	0
# in moot court or trial competitions	102	0
# of credit hours required to graduate	85	

Enrollment & Attrition

	Full-Time							Part-Time							Attrition			
	Men		Women		Minorities		Total	Men		Women		Minorities		Total	Academic	Other	Total	
	#	%	#	%	#	%	#	#	%	#	%	#	%	#	#	#	#	%
1st Year	73	45.1	89	54.9	19	11.7	162	0	0.0	0	0.0	0	0.0	0	0	2	2	1.1
2nd Year	95	53.4	83	46.6	29	16.3	178	0	0.0	0	0.0	0	0.0	0	0	7	7	4.4
3rd Year	76	47.8	83	52.2	21	13.2	159	0	0.0	0	0.0	0	0.0	0	1	0	1	0.7
4th Year								0	0.0	0	0.0	0	0.0	0	0	0	0	0.0
Total	244	48.9	255	51.1	69	13.8	499	0	0.0	0	0.0	0	0.0	0	1	9	10	2.1
JD Degrees Awarded	63	47.0	71	53.0	19	14.2	134	0	0.0	0	0.0	0	0.0	0				

GPA & LSAT Scores

	Full Time	Part Time	Total
# of apps	1,428	0	1,428
# admits	579	0	579
# of matrics	162	0	162
75% GPA	3.60	0.00	
25% GPA	3.13	0.00	
75% LSAT	161	0	
25% LSAT	155	0	

Tuition/Living Expenses

	Resident	Non-resident
Full-Time	$9,090	$13,572
Part-Time	$0	$0

Estimated living expenses for Singles		
Living on campus	Living off campus	Living at home
$6,608	$7,305	$4,065

Career Placement

	Total	%
Employment status known	131	98.5
Employment status unknown	2	1.5
Employed	108	82.4
Pursuing graduate degrees	7	5.3
Unemployed seeking employment	7	5.3
Unemployed not seeking employment	9	6.9
Type of Employment		
# employed in law firms	47	43.5
# employed in business & industry	15	13.9
# employed in government	26	24.1
# employed in public interest	5	4.6
# employed as judicial clerks	9	8.3
# employed in academia	6	5.6
Geographic Location		
# employed in state	67	62.0
# employed in foreign countries	2	1.9
# of states where employed	16	

Financial Aid

	Full-time		Part-time		Total	
	#	%	#	%	#	%
Total # receiving grants	220	44.1	0	0.0	220	44.1
Less than 1/2 tuition	208	41.7	0	0.0	208	41.7
Half to full tuition	12	2.4	0	0.0	12	2.4
Full tuition	0	0.0	0	0.0	0	0.0
More than full tuition	0	0.0	0	0.0	0	0.0
Median Grant Amount	$1,737		$0			

Refunds

Refunds of Admissions or Seat Deposit prior to commencement of classes? No

Refunds of Pre-paid tuition prior to commencement of classes? No

If yes, fully refundable before the start of classes? No

Joint Degrees Offered

No Joint Degrees

Advanced Degrees Offered

No Advanced Degrees

Bar Passage Rate

Jurisdiction	OR	WA
# from school taking bar for the first time	80	19
School's pass rate for all first-time takers	77%	95%
State's pass rate for all first-time takers	85%	83%
State's pass rate for all first-time takers from ABA approved law schools		

PACE UNIVERSITY

78 North Broadway
White Plains, NY 10603
(914)422-4205
http://www.law.pace.edu

ABA Approved Since 1978

The Basics

Type of School: **PRIVATE**
Application deadline*: **3/15**
Application fee: **$55**
Financial Aid deadline*: **2/1**
Student faculty ratio: **15.6 to 1**
First year can start other than Fall: **No**
Student housing: **Yes**
--exclusively for law students: **No**
Term: **Semester**

*pr=preferred

Faculty

	Men #	Men %	Women #	Women %	Minorities #	Minorities %	Total
Full-time	24	65	13	35	3	8	37
Other full-time	0	0	0	0	0	0	0
Deans, librarians, & others who teach	1	50	1	50	0	0	2
Part-time	21	62	13	38	1	3	34
Total	46	63	27	37	4	5	73
Deans, librarians, & others who teach < 1/2	4	80	1	20	0	0	5

Library

# of volumes & volume equivalents	311,203	# of professional staff	13
# of titles	122,474	Hours per week with professional staff	76
# of active serial subscriptions	3,580	Hours per week without professional staff	26
Study seating capacity inside the library	346	# of student computer work stations for entire law school	79
Square feet of law library	26,731	# of additional networked connections	95
Square feet of law school (excl. Library)	117,367		

Curriculum

	Full time	Part time
Typical first-year section size	85	90
Is there typically a "small section" of the first year class, other than Legal Writing, taught by full-time faculty?	No	No
If yes, typical size offered last year	N/A	N/A
# of classroom course titles beyond 1st year curriculum	74	68
# of upper division courses, excluding seminars, with an enrollment:		
Under 25	67	38
25 - 49	20	15
50 - 74	9	8
75 - 99	3	6
100 +	1	2
# of seminars	16	9
# of seminar positions available	293	
# of seminar positions filled	122	117
# of positions available in simulation courses	491	
# of simulation positions filled	148	226
# of positions available in faculty supervised clinical courses	66	
# of fac. sup. clin. positions filled	43	23
# involved in field placements	68	7
# involved in law journals	77	8
# in moot court or trial competitions	92	45
# of credit hours required to graduate	90	

Enrollment & Attrition

	Full-Time							Part-Time							Attrition			
	Men		Women		Minorities		Total	Men		Women		Minorities		Total	Academic	Other	Total	
	#	%	#	%	#	%	#	#	%	#	%	#	%	#	#	#	#	%
1st Year	64	40.5	94	59.5	25	15.8	158	47	61.8	29	38.2	12	15.8	76	4	16	20	7.3
2nd Year	84	46.9	95	53.1	27	15.1	179	49	54.4	41	45.6	13	14.4	90	7	9	16	6.6
3rd Year	69	44.5	86	55.5	20	12.9	155	43	58.9	30	41.1	16	21.9	73	0	2	2	1.0
4th Year								32	47.1	36	52.9	9	13.2	68	2	0	2	2.4
Total	217	44.1	275	55.9	72	14.6	492	171	55.7	136	44.3	50	16.3	307	13	27	40	5.0
JD Degrees Awarded	62	49.2	64	50.8	24	19.0	126	63	66.3	32	33.7	15	15.8	95				

GPA & LSAT Scores

	Full Time	Part Time	Total
# of apps	1,580	427	2,007
# admits	702	176	878
# of matrics	165	81	246
75% GPA	3.46	3.52	
25% GPA	3.00	2.67	
75% LSAT	155	157	
25% LSAT	146	149	

Tuition/Living Expenses

	Resident	Non-resident
Full-Time	$19,444	$19,444
Part-Time	$14,592	$14,592

Estimated living expenses for Singles		
Living on campus	Living off campus	Living at home
$9,108	$12,800	$5,250

Career Placement

	Total	%
Employment status known	200	81.6
Employment status unknown	45	18.4
Employed	175	87.5
Pursuing graduate degrees	2	1.0
Unemployed seeking employment	17	8.5
Unemployed not seeking employment	6	3.0
Type of Employment		
# employed in law firms	99	56.6
# employed in business & industry	53	30.3
# employed in government	8	4.6
# employed in public interest	3	1.7
# employed as judicial clerks	8	4.6
# employed in academia	4	2.3
Geographic Location		
# employed in state	149	85.1
# employed in foreign countries	0	0.0
# of states where employed	10	

Financial Aid

	Full-time		Part-time		Total	
	#	%	#	%	#	%
Total # receiving grants	284	57.7	46	15.0	330	41.3
Less than 1/2 tuition	259	52.6	36	11.7	295	36.9
Half to full tuition	21	4.3	8	2.6	29	3.6
Full tuition	4	0.8	2	0.7	6	0.8
More than full tuition	0	0.0	0	0.0	0	0.0
Median Grant Amount	$2,500		$4,000			

Refunds

Refunds of Admissions or Seat Deposit prior to commencement of classes? No

Refunds of Pre-paid tuition prior to commencement of classes? Yes

If yes, fully refundable before the start of classes? Yes

Joint Degrees Offered

JD/MBA, JD/MPA

Advanced Degrees Offered

LL.M. Environmental Law
S.J.D. Environmental Law

Bar Passage Rate

Jurisdiction	NY
# from school taking bar for the first time	194
School's pass rate for all first-time takers	80%
State's pass rate for all first-time takers	78%
State's pass rate for all first-time takers from ABA approved law schools	

PENNSYLVANIA, UNIVERSITY OF

3400 Chestnut Street
Philadelphia, PA 19104-6204
(215)898-7483
http://www.law.upenn.edu

ABA Approved Since 1923

The Basics

Type of School: PRIVATE	First year can start other than Fall: No
Application deadline*: 3/1	Student housing: Yes
Application fee: $65	--exclusively for law students: Yes
Financial Aid deadline*:	
Student faculty ratio: 18.3 to 1	Term: Semester

*pr=preferred

Faculty

	Men		Women		Minorities		Total
	#	%	#	%	#	%	
Full-time	28	78	8	22	2	6	36
Other full-time	0	0	4	100	0	0	4
Deans, librarians, & others who teach	2	100	0	0	0	0	2
Part-time	22	81	5	19	1	4	27
Total	52	75	17	25	3	4	69
Deans, librarians, & others who teach < 1/2	0	0	0	0	0	0	0

Library

# of volumes & volume equivalents	611,773	# of professional staff	14
# of titles	161,651	Hours per week with professional staff	76
# of active serial subscriptions	7,101	Hours per week without professional staff	34
Study seating capacity inside the library	550	# of student computer work stations for entire law school	96
Square feet of law library	72,000	# of additional networked connections	856
Square feet of law school (excl. Library)	75,300		

Curriculum

	Full time	Part time
Typical first-year section size	80	0
Is there typically a "small section" of the first year class, other than Legal Writing, taught by full-time faculty?	No	No
If yes, typical size offered last year	N/A	N/A
# of classroom course titles beyond 1st year curriculum	82	0
# of upper division courses, excluding seminars, with an enrollment:		
Under 25	47	0
25 - 49	29	0
50 - 74	14	0
75 - 99	10	0
100 +	5	0
# of seminars	36	0
# of seminar positions available	566	
# of seminar positions filled	466	0
# of positions available in simulation courses	252	
# of simulation positions filled	240	0
# of positions available in faculty supervised clinical courses	102	
# of fac. sup. clin. positions filled	78	0
# involved in field placements	21	0
# involved in law journals	181	0
# in moot court or trial competitions	179	0
# of credit hours required to graduate	89	

Enrollment & Attrition

	Full-Time							Part-Time							Attrition			
	Men		Women		Minorities		Total	Men		Women		Minorities		Total	Academic	Other	Total	
	#	%	#	%	#	%	#	#	%	#	%	#	%	#	#	#	#	%
1st Year	158	56.4	122	43.6	76	27.1	280	0	0.0	0	0.0	0	0.0	0	1	4	5	2.2
2nd Year	132	60.0	88	40.0	57	25.9	220	0	0.0	1	100.0	0	0.0	1	1	5	6	2.0
3rd Year	173	60.1	115	39.9	68	23.6	288	1	100.0	0	0.0	0	0.0	1	2	0	2	0.9
4th Year								0	0.0	0	0.0	0	0.0	0	0	0	0	0.0
Total	463	58.8	325	41.2	201	25.5	788	1	50.0	1	50.0	0	0.0	2	4	9	13	1.8
JD Degrees Awarded	135	61.6	84	38.4	35	16.0	219	0	0.0	0	0.0	0	0.0	0				

GPA & LSAT Scores

	Full Time	Part Time	Total
# of apps	3,956	0	3,956
# admits	1,158	0	1,158
# of matrics	280	0	280
75% GPA	3.71	0.00	
25% GPA	3.41	0.00	
75% LSAT	167	0	
25% LSAT	162	0	

Tuition/Living Expenses

	Resident	Non-resident
Full-Time	$23,314	$23,314
Part-Time	$0	$0

Estimated living expenses for Singles		
Living on campus	Living off campus	Living at home
$11,686	$11,686	$6,573

Career Placement

	Total	%
Employment status known	240	98.4
Employment status unknown	4	1.6
Employed	227	94.6
Pursuing graduate degrees	2	0.8
Unemployed seeking employment	9	3.8
Unemployed not seeking employment	2	0.8
Type of Employment		
# employed in law firms	162	71.4
# employed in business & industry	10	4.4
# employed in government	9	4.0
# employed in public interest	5	2.2
# employed as judicial clerks	40	17.6
# employed in academia	1	0.4
Geographic Location		
# employed in state	63	27.8
# employed in foreign countries	0	0.0
# of states where employed	21	

Financial Aid

	Full-time		Part-time		Total	
	#	%	#	%	#	%
Total # receiving grants	246	31.2	0	0.0	246	31.1
Less than 1/2 tuition	179	22.7	0	0.0	179	22.7
Half to full tuition	62	7.9	0	0.0	62	7.8
Full tuition	5	0.6	0	0.0	5	0.6
More than full tuition	0	0.0	0	0.0	0	0.0
Median Grant Amount	$7,400		$0			

Refunds

Refunds of Admissions or Seat Deposit prior to commencement of classes? No

Refunds of Pre-paid tuition prior to commencement of classes? Yes

If yes, fully refundable before the start of classes? Yes

Joint Degrees Offered

J.D./M.A, J.D./M.A, J.D./M.A., J.D./M.A., J.D./M.A., J.D./Ph.D., J.D./Ph.D., J.D./Ph.D., J.D./M.B.A., J.D./M.C.P., J.D./M.S., J.D./M.A., J.D./M.A., J.D./M.A., J.D./M.G.A.

Advanced Degrees Offered

LL.CM.	Individually structured
LL.M.	Individually structured
S.J.D.	Individually structured

Bar Passage Rate

Jurisdiction	NY	PA
# from school taking bar for the first time	108	67
School's pass rate for all first-time takers	91%	84%
State's pass rate for all first-time takers	78%	73%
State's pass rate for all first-time takers from ABA approved law schools		73%

PEPPERDINE UNIVERSITY

24255 Pacific Coast Highway
Malibu, CA 90263
(310)456-4611
http://www.law.pepperdine.edu

ABA Approved Since 1972

The Basics

Type of School: **PRIVATE**
Application deadline*: **3/1**
Application fee: **$50**
Financial Aid deadline*: **5/1**
Student faculty ratio: **19.8 to 1**
First year can start other than Fall: **No**
Student housing: **Yes**
--exclusively for law students: **No**
Term: **Semester**

*pr=preferred

Faculty

	Men		Women		Minorities		Total
	#	%	#	%	#	%	
Full-time	23	82	5	18	3	11	28
Other full-time	0	0	0	0	0	0	0
Deans, librarians, & others who teach	0	0	0	0	0	0	0
Part-time	14	52	13	48	0	0	27
Total	37	67	18	33	3	5	55
Deans, librarians, & others who teach < 1/2	6	67	3	33	1	11	9

Library

# of volumes & volume equivalents	262,908	# of professional staff	6
# of titles	109,407	Hours per week with professional staff	74
# of active serial subscriptions	3,496	Hours per week without professional staff	35
Study seating capacity inside the library	500	# of student computer work stations for entire law school	52
Square feet of law library	40,915	# of additional networked connections	0
Square feet of law school (excl. Library)	81,190		

Curriculum

	Full time	Part time
Typical first-year section size	70	0
Is there typically a "small section" of the first year class, other than Legal Writing, taught by full-time faculty?	No	No
If yes, typical size offered last year	N/A	N/A
# of classroom course titles beyond 1st year curriculum	92	0
# of upper division courses, excluding seminars, with an enrollment:		
Under 25	45	0
25 - 49	22	0
50 - 74	9	0
75 - 99	5	0
100 +	11	0
# of seminars	24	0
# of seminar positions available	510	
# of seminar positions filled	510	0
# of positions available in simulation courses	687	
# of simulation positions filled	687	0
# of positions available in faculty supervised clinical courses	27	
# of fac. sup. clin. positions filled	27	0
# involved in field placements	210	0
# involved in law journals	75	0
# in moot court or trial competitions	312	0
# of credit hours required to graduate	88	

Enrollment & Attrition

	Full-Time							Part-Time							Attrition			
	Men		Women		Minorities		Total	Men		Women		Minorities		Total	Academic	Other	Total	
	#	%	#	%	#	%	#	#	%	#	%	#	%	#	#	#	#	%
1st Year	118	58.1	85	41.9	38	18.7	203	0	0.0	0	0.0	0	0.0	0	0	0	0	0.0
2nd Year	130	58.0	94	42.0	44	19.6	224	0	0.0	0	0.0	0	0.0	0	9	13	22	8.7
3rd Year	125	49.6	127	50.4	72	28.6	252	0	0.0	0	0.0	0	0.0	0	0	0	0	0.0
4th Year								0	0.0	0	0.0	0	0.0	0	0	0	0	0.0
Total	373	54.9	306	45.1	154	22.7	679	0	0.0	0	0.0	0	0.0	0	9	13	22	3.1
JD Degrees Awarded	104	49.3	107	50.7	53	25.1	211	0	0.0	0	0.0	0	0.0	0				

GPA & LSAT Scores

	Full Time	Part Time	Total
# of apps	2,517	0	2,517
# admits	1,023	0	1,023
# of matrics	207	0	207
75% GPA	3.53	0.00	
25% GPA	3.03	0.00	
75% LSAT	160	0	
25% LSAT	154	0	

Tuition/Living Expenses

	Resident	Non-resident
Full-Time	$20,900	$20,900
Part-Time	$0	$0

Estimated living expenses for Singles		
Living on campus	Living off campus	Living at home
$15,732	$15,732	$15,732

Career Placement

	Total	%
Employment status known	177	75.0
Employment status unknown	59	25.0
Employed	155	87.6
Pursuing graduate degrees	6	3.4
Unemployed seeking employment	10	5.7
Unemployed not seeking employment	6	3.4
Type of Employment		
# employed in law firms	109	70.3
# employed in business & industry	30	19.4
# employed in government	10	6.5
# employed in public interest	0	0.0
# employed as judicial clerks	6	3.9
# employed in academia	0	0.0
Geographic Location		
# employed in state	126	81.3
# employed in foreign countries	0	0.0
# of states where employed	10	

Financial Aid

	Full-time		Part-time		Total	
	#	%	#	%	#	%
Total # receiving grants	510	75.1	0	0.0	510	75.1
Less than 1/2 tuition	265	39.0	0	0.0	265	39.0
Half to full tuition	213	31.4	0	0.0	213	31.4
Full tuition	2	0.3	0	0.0	2	0.3
More than full tuition	30	4.4	0	0.0	30	4.4
Median Grant Amount	$8,245		$0			

Refunds

Refunds of Admissions or Seat Deposit prior to commencement of classes? Yes

50% refund from 04/01/95 to 06/30/96

Refunds of Pre-paid tuition prior to commencement of classes? Yes

If yes, fully refundable before the start of classes? Yes

Joint Degrees Offered

JD/MBA

Advanced Degrees Offered

M.D.R. Masters in Dispute Resolution - ADR

Bar Passage Rate

Jurisdiction	CA
# from school taking bar for the first time	189
School's pass rate for all first-time takers	86%
State's pass rate for all first-time takers	73%
State's pass rate for all first-time takers from ABA approved law schools	83%

PITTSBURGH, UNIVERSITY OF

3900 Forbes Avenue
Pittsburgh, PA 15260
(412)648-1400
http://www.law.pitt.edu

ABA Approved Since 1923

The Basics

Type of School: **PUBLIC**
Application deadline*: **3/1**
Application fee: **$40**
Financial Aid deadline*: **3/1**
Student faculty ratio: **21.0 to 1**

First year can start other than Fall: **No**
Student housing: **No**
--exclusively for law students: **No**
Term: **Semester**

*pr=preferred

Faculty

	Men #	Men %	Women #	Women %	Minorities #	Minorities %	Total
Full-time	18	62	11	38	5	17	29
Other full-time	1	25	3	75	0	0	4
Deans, librarians, & others who teach	4	100	0	0	0	0	4
Part-time	14	67	7	33	3	14	21
Total	37	64	21	36	8	14	58
Deans, librarians, & others who teach < 1/2	0	0	0	0	0	0	0

Library

# of volumes & volume equivalents	364,397	# of professional staff	8
# of titles	101,354	Hours per week with professional staff	61
# of active serial subscriptions	5,154	Hours per week without professional staff	41
Study seating capacity inside the library	446	# of student computer work stations for entire law school	43
Square feet of law library	43,050	# of additional networked connections	0
Square feet of law school (excl. Library)	41,455		

Curriculum

	Full time	Part time
Typical first-year section size	81	0
Is there typically a "small section" of the first year class, other than Legal Writing, taught by full-time faculty?	Yes	No
If yes, typical size offered last year	27	N/A
# of classroom course titles beyond 1st year curriculum	111	0
# of upper division courses, excluding seminars, with an enrollment:		
Under 25	64	0
25 - 49	24	0
50 - 74	11	0
75 - 99	3	0
100 +	7	0
# of seminars	16	0
# of seminar positions available	240	
# of seminar positions filled	169	0
# of positions available in simulation courses	364	
# of simulation positions filled	299	0
# of positions available in faculty supervised clinical courses	112	
# of fac. sup. clin. positions filled	103	0
# involved in field placements	221	0
# involved in law journals	56	0
# in moot court or trial competitions	226	0
# of credit hours required to graduate	88	

Enrollment & Attrition

	Full-Time							Part-Time							Attrition			
	Men		Women		Minorities		Total	Men		Women		Minorities		Total	Academic	Other	Total	
	#	%	#	%	#	%	#	#	%	#	%	#	%	#	#	#	#	%
1st Year	152	58.7	107	41.3	14	5.4	259	1	33.3	2	66.7	0	0.0	3	2	11	13	5.4
2nd Year	135	59.0	94	41.0	28	12.2	229	0	0.0	2	100.0	0	0.0	2	0	8	8	3.2
3rd Year	145	61.7	90	38.3	28	11.9	235	1	25.0	3	75.0	0	0.0	4	0	21	21	11
4th Year								1	100.0	0	0.0	0	0.0	1	0	0	0	0.0
Total	432	59.8	291	40.2	70	9.7	723	3	30.0	7	70.0	0	0.0	10	2	40	42	6.0
JD Degrees Awarded	142	65.1	76	34.9	36	16.5	218	0	0.0	0	0.0	0	0.0	0				

GPA & LSAT Scores

	Full Time	Part Time	Total
# of apps	1,338	29	1,367
# admits	852	9	861
# of matrics	263	3	266
75% GPA	3.42	0.00	
25% GPA	2.89	0.00	
75% LSAT	158	0	
25% LSAT	152	0	

Tuition/Living Expenses

	Resident	Non-resident
Full-Time	$11,354	$17,362
Part-Time	$0	$0

Estimated living expenses for Singles		
Living on campus	Living off campus	Living at home
N/A	$9,900	$8,400

Career Placement

	Total	%
Employment status known	192	89.3
Employment status unknown	23	10.7
Employed	144	75.0
Pursuing graduate degrees	1	0.5
Unemployed seeking employment	37	19.3
Unemployed not seeking employment	10	5.2
Type of Employment		
# employed in law firms	95	66.0
# employed in business & industry	14	9.7
# employed in government	14	9.7
# employed in public interest	5	3.5
# employed as judicial clerks	16	11.1
# employed in academia	0	0.0
Geographic Location		
# employed in state	107	74.3
# employed in foreign countries	3	2.1
# of states where employed	15	

Financial Aid

	Full-time		Part-time		Total	
	#	%	#	%	#	%
Total # receiving grants	224	31.0	0	0.0	224	30.6
Less than 1/2 tuition	222	30.7	0	0.0	222	30.3
Half to full tuition	0	0.0	0	0.0	0	0.0
Full tuition	2	0.3	0	0.0	2	0.3
More than full tuition	0	0.0	0	0.0	0	0.0
Median Grant Amount	$3,760		$0			

Refunds

Refunds of Admissions or Seat Deposit prior to commencement of classes? No

Refunds of Pre-paid tuition prior to commencement of classes? Yes

If yes, fully refundable before the start of classes? Yes

Joint Degrees Offered

JD/MBA, JD/MPIA, JD/MSIA, JD/MPS, JD/MURP, JD/MPH, JD/MIA, JD/MS, JD/MAM, JD/MA

Advanced Degrees Offered

LLM INTERNATIONAL AND COMPARATIVE LAW

Bar Passage Rate

Jurisdiction	PA
# from school taking bar for the first time	152
School's pass rate for all first-time takers	82%
State's pass rate for all first-time takers	73%
State's pass rate for all first-time takers from ABA approved law schools	73%

PONTIFICAL CATHOLIC UNIVERSITY OF P.R.

2250 Las Americas Avenue Suite 543
Ponce, PR 00731-6382
(787)841-2000

ABA Approved Since 1967

The Basics

Type of School: **PRIVATE**
Application deadline*: **4/15**
Application fee: **$25**
Financial Aid deadline*: **9/30**
Student faculty ratio: **21.2 to 1**

First year can start other than Fall: **No**
Student housing: **No**
--exclusively for law students: **No**
Term: **Semester**

*pr=preferred

Faculty

	Men #	Men %	Women #	Women %	Minorities #	Minorities %	Total
Full-time	11	65	6	35	17	100	17
Other full-time	0	0	0	0	0	0	0
Deans, librarians, & others who teach	0	0	1	100	1	100	1
Part-time	12	86	2	14	14	100	14
Total	23	72	9	28	32	100	32
Deans, librarians, & others who teach < 1/2	1	33	2	67	3	100	3

Library

# of volumes & volume equivalents	171,806	# of professional staff	5
# of titles	21,601	Hours per week with professional staff	70
# of active serial subscriptions	2,202	Hours per week without professional staff	22
Study seating capacity inside the library	169	# of student computer work stations for entire law school	41
Square feet of law library	20,393	# of additional networked connections	0
Square feet of law school (excl. Library)	25,612		

Curriculum

	Full time	Part time
Typical first-year section size	60	50
Is there typically a "small section" of the first year class, other than Legal Writing, taught by full-time faculty?	Yes	Yes
If yes, typical size offered last year	20	20
# of classroom course titles beyond 1st year curriculum	29	26
# of upper division courses, excluding seminars, with an enrollment:		
Under 25	5	5
25 - 49	11	11
50 - 74	7	2
75 - 99	0	0
100 +	0	0
# of seminars	1	1
# of seminar positions available	40	
# of seminar positions filled	12	15
# of positions available in simulation courses	40	
# of simulation positions filled	0	32
# of positions available in faculty supervised clinical courses	60	
# of fac. sup. clin. positions filled	58	0
# involved in field placements	43	0
# involved in law journals	34	7
# in moot court or trial competitions	0	0
# of credit hours required to graduate	94	

Enrollment & Attrition

	Full-Time Men #	Men %	Women #	Women %	Minorities #	Minorities %	Total #	Part-Time Men #	Men %	Women #	Women %	Minorities #	Minorities %	Total #	Attrition Academic #	Other #	Total #	%
1st Year	54	45.8	64	54.2	118	100.0	118	20	38.5	32	61.5	52	100.0	52	17	13	30	19
2nd Year	34	41.0	49	59.0	83	100.	83	27	60.0	18	40.0	45	100.0	45	4	3	7	5.2
3rd Year	59	48.0	64	52.0	123	100.0	123	18	62.1	11	37.9	29	100.0	29	1	0	1	0.8
4th Year								22	56.4	17	43.6	39	100.0	39	0	0	0	0.0
Total	147	45.4	177	54.6	324	100.	324	87	52.7	78	47.3	165	100.0	165	22	16	38	8.4
JD Degrees Awarded	35	47.3	39	52.7	74	100.0	74	18	62.1	11	37.9	29	100.0	29				

PONTIFICAL CATHOLIC UNIVERSITY OF P.R.

GPA & LSAT Scores

	Full Time	Part Time	Total
# of apps	303	132	435
# admits	160	68	228
# of matrics	118	52	170
75% GPA	3.31	3.44	
25% GPA	2.85	2.83	
75% LSAT	137	139	
25% LSAT	132	131	

Tuition/Living Expenses

	Resident	Non-resident
Full-Time	$7,338	$7,338
Part-Time	$5,566	$5,566

Estimated living expenses for Singles		
Living on campus	Living off campus	Living at home
$6,811	$8,927	$6,227

Financial Aid

	Full-time		Part-time		Total	
	#	%	#	%	#	%
Total # receiving grants	26	8.0	9	5.5	35	7.2
Less than 1/2 tuition	25	7.7	9	5.5	34	7.0
Half to full tuition	0	0.0	0	0.0	0	0.0
Full tuition	1	0.3	0	0.0	1	0.2
More than full tuition	0	0.0	0	0.0	0	0.0
Median Grant Amount	$1,520		$0			

Refunds

Refunds of Admissions or Seat Deposit prior to commencement of classes? No

Refunds of Pre-paid tuition prior to commencement of classes? Yes

If yes, fully refundable before the start of classes? Yes

Joint Degrees Offered

JD/MBA

Advanced Degrees Offered

No Advanced Degrees

Career Placement

	Total	%
Employment status known	80	87.9
Employment status unknown	11	12.1
Employed	70	87.5
Pursuing graduate degrees	0	0.0
Unemployed seeking employment	9	11.3
Unemployed not seeking employment	1	1.3
Type of Employment		
# employed in law firms	39	55.7
# employed in business & industry	8	11.4
# employed in government	15	21.4
# employed in public interest	7	10.0
# employed as judicial clerks	1	1.4
# employed in academia	0	0.0
Geographic Location		
# employed in state	69	98.6
# employed in foreign countries	0	0.0
# of states where employed	1	

Bar Passage Rate

Jurisdiction	PR
# from school taking bar for the first time	83
School's pass rate for all first-time takers	63%
State's pass rate for all first-time takers	68%
State's pass rate for all first-time takers from ABA approved law schools	69%

PUERTO RICO, UNIVERSITY OF

P.O. Box 23349
San Juan, PR 00931-3349
(787)764-2680

ABA Approved Since 1945

The Basics

Type of School: **PUBLIC**
Application deadline*: **2/15**
Application fee: **$15**
Financial Aid deadline*: **4/15**
Student faculty ratio: **24.0 to 1**
First year can start other than Fall: **No**
Student housing: **No**
--exclusively for law students: **No**
Term: **Semester**

*pr=preferred

Faculty

	Men #	Men %	Women #	Women %	Minorities #	Minorities %	Total
Full-time	13	81	3	19	16	100	16
Other full-time	0	0	0	0	0	0	0
Deans, librarians, & others who teach	3	75	1	25	4	100	4
Part-time	14	45	17	55	30	97	31
Total	30	59	21	41	50	98	51
Deans, librarians, & others who teach < 1/2	3	100	0	0	2	67	3

Library

# of volumes & volume equivalents	290,387	# of professional staff	10
# of titles	59,831	Hours per week with professional staff	95
# of active serial subscriptions	4,247	Hours per week without professional staff	17
Study seating capacity inside the library	360	# of student computer work stations for entire law school	26
Square feet of law library	44,275	# of additional networked connections	0
Square feet of law school (excl. Library)	36,657		

Curriculum

	Full time	Part time
Typical first-year section size	50	50
Is there typically a "small section" of the first year class, other than Legal Writing, taught by full-time faculty?	No	No
If yes, typical size offered last year	N/A	N/A
# of classroom course titles beyond 1st year curriculum	60	38
# of upper division courses, excluding seminars, with an enrollment:		
Under 25	29	19
25 - 49	26	9
50 - 74	12	3
75 - 99	0	0
100 +	0	0
# of seminars	0	0
# of seminar positions available	135	
# of seminar positions filled	40	36
# of positions available in simulation courses	30	
# of simulation positions filled	25	5
# of positions available in faculty supervised clinical courses	140	
# of fac. sup. clin. positions filled	90	40
# involved in field placements	41	0
# involved in law journals	36	0
# in moot court or trial competitions	8	0
# of credit hours required to graduate	92	

Enrollment & Attrition

	Full-Time							Part-Time							Attrition			
	Men		Women		Minorities		Total	Men		Women		Minorities		Total	Academic	Other	Total	
	#	%	#	%	#	%	#	#	%	#	%	#	%	#	#	#	#	%
1st Year	47	41.2	67	58.8	111	97.4	114	25	54.3	21	45.7	46	100.0	46	4	12	16	9.0
2nd Year	39	36.1	69	63.9	108	100.	108	44	53.7	38	46.3	82	100.0	82	0	7	7	4.4
3rd Year	38	34.2	73	65.8	104	93.7	111	16	48.5	17	51.5	33	100.0	33	0	6	6	3.9
4th Year								21	55.3	17	44.7	38	100.0	38	0	2	2	5.7
Total	124	37.2	209	62.8	323	97.0	333	106	53.3	93	46.7	199	100.0	199	4	27	31	5.9
JD Degrees Awarded	40	42.1	55	57.9	95	100.0	95	19	63.3	11	36.7	30	100.0	30				

GPA & LSAT Scores

	Full Time	Part Time	Total
# of apps	449	290	739
# admits	136	47	183
# of matrics	114	46	160
75% GPA	3.66	3.60	
25% GPA	3.26	2.95	
75% LSAT	150	150	
25% LSAT	143	142	

Tuition/Living Expenses

	Resident	Non-resident
Full-Time	$2,320	$3,570
Part-Time	$1,570	$3,500

Estimated living expenses for Singles		
Living on campus	Living off campus	Living at home
$9,975	$8,475	$7,575

Career Placement

	Total	%
Employment status known	0	0.0
Employment status unknown	0	0.0
Employed	0	0.0
Pursuing graduate degrees	0	0.0
Unemployed seeking employment	0	0.0
Unemployed not seeking employment	0	0.0
Type of Employment		
# employed in law firms	0	0.0
# employed in business & industry	0	0.0
# employed in government	0	0.0
# employed in public interest	0	0.0
# employed as judicial clerks	0	0.0
# employed in academia	0	0.0
Geographic Location		
# employed in state	0	0.0
# employed in foreign countries	0	0.0
# of states where employed	0	

Financial Aid

	Full-time		Part-time		Total	
	#	%	#	%	#	%
Total # receiving grants	158	47.5	0	0.0	158	29.7
Less than 1/2 tuition	0	0.0	0	0.0	0	0.0
Half to full tuition	0	0.0	0	0.0	0	0.0
Full tuition	21	6.3	0	0.0	21	3.9
More than full tuition	137	41.1	0	0.0	137	25.8
Median Grant Amount	$0		$0			

Refunds

Refunds of Admissions or Seat Deposit prior to commencement of classes? No

Refunds of Pre-paid tuition prior to commencement of classes? Yes

If yes, fully refundable before the start of classes? No

Joint Degrees Offered

JD/MBA, Double deg., with Univ., of Barcelona

Advanced Degrees Offered

No Advanced Degrees

Bar Passage Rate

Jurisdiction	PR
# from school taking bar for the first time	121
School's pass rate for all first-time takers	84%
State's pass rate for all first-time takers	68%
State's pass rate for all first-time takers from ABA approved law schools	69%

QUINNIPIAC COLLEGE

275 Mount Carmel Avenue
Hamden, CT 06518-1950
(203)287-3200
http://www.quinnipiac.edu/law

ABA Approved Since 1992

The Basics

Type of School: **PRIVATE**
Application deadline*: **rolling**
Application fee: **$40**
Financial Aid deadline*: **4/1**
Student faculty ratio: **21.1 to 1**
First year can start other than Fall: **Yes**
Student housing: **No**
--exclusively for law students: **No**
Term: **Semester**

*pr=preferred

Faculty

	Men		Women		Minorities		Total
	#	%	#	%	#	%	
Full-time	19	70	8	30	3	11	27
Other full-time	2	25	6	75	0	0	8
Deans, librarians, & others who teach	1	100	0	0	0	0	1
Part-time	21	88	3	13	2	8	24
Total	43	72	17	28	5	8	60
Deans, librarians, & others who teach < 1/2	1	50	1	50	0	0	2

Library

# of volumes & volume equivalents	300,531	# of professional staff	7
# of titles	35,439	Hours per week with professional staff	63
# of active serial subscriptions	3,013	Hours per week without professional staff	33
Study seating capacity inside the library	400	# of student computer work stations for entire law school	130
Square feet of law library	46,000	# of additional networked connections	750
Square feet of law school (excl. Library)	84,000		

Curriculum

	Full time	Part time
Typical first-year section size	80	70
Is there typically a "small section" of the first year class, other than Legal Writing, taught by full-time faculty?	Yes	Yes
If yes, typical size offered last year	20	40
# of classroom course titles beyond 1st year curriculum	49	43
# of upper division courses, excluding seminars, with an enrollment:		
Under 25	37	31
25 - 49	13	14
50 - 74	6	4
75 - 99	10	5
100 +	1	0
# of seminars	7	3
# of seminar positions available	179	
# of seminar positions filled	91	32
# of positions available in simulation courses	304	
# of simulation positions filled	87	186
# of positions available in faculty supervised clinical courses	76	
# of fac. sup. clin. positions filled	73	0
# involved in field placements	104	0
# involved in law journals	80	40
# in moot court or trial competitions	20	10
# of credit hours required to graduate	86	

Enrollment & Attrition

	Full-Time							Part-Time							Attrition			
	Men		Women		Minorities		Total	Men		Women		Minorities		Total	Academic	Other	Total	
	#	%	#	%	#	%	#	#	%	#	%	#	%	#	#	#	#	%
1st Year	100	63.7	57	36.3	19	12.1	157	41	58.6	29	41.4	6	8.6	70	20	18	38	15
2nd Year	109	63.4	63	36.6	22	12.8	172	33	56.9	25	43.1	6	10.3	58	6	3	9	3.1
3rd Year	129	65.2	69	34.8	25	12.6	198	36	58.1	26	41.9	5	8.1	62	0	0	0	0.0
4th Year								29	61.7	18	38.3	6	12.8	47	0	0	0	0.0
Total	338	64.1	189	35.9	66	12.5	527	139	58.6	98	41.4	23	9.7	237	26	21	47	5.9
JD Degrees Awarded	130	68.1	61	31.9	23	12.0	191	24	72.7	9	27.3	1	3.0	33				

GPA & LSAT Scores

	Full Time	Part Time	Total
# of apps	1,703	325	2,028
# admits	917	145	1,062
# of matrics	161	74	235
75% GPA	3.00	3.20	
25% GPA	2.50	2.60	
75% LSAT	153	153	
25% LSAT	147	147	

Tuition/Living Expenses

	Resident	Non-resident
Full-Time	$17,983	$17,983
Part-Time	$15,055	$15,055

Estimated living expenses for Singles		
Living on campus	Living off campus	Living at home
N/A	$12,555	$8,175

Financial Aid

	Full-time		Part-time		Total	
	#	%	#	%	#	%
Total # receiving grants	152	28.8	46	19.4	198	25.9
Less than 1/2 tuition	105	19.9	30	12.7	135	17.7
Half to full tuition	38	7.2	15	6.3	53	6.9
Full tuition	9	1.7	1	0.4	10	1.3
More than full tuition	0	0.0	0	0.0	0	0.0
Median Grant Amount	$4,000		$2,500			

Refunds

Refunds of Admissions or Seat Deposit prior to commencement of classes? No

Refunds of Pre-paid tuition prior to commencement of classes? Yes

If yes, fully refundable before the start of classes? Yes

Joint Degrees Offered

JD/MBA, JD/MHA

Advanced Degrees Offered

No Advanced Degrees

Career Placement

	Total	%
Employment status known	171	87.7
Employment status unknown	24	12.3
Employed	139	81.3
Pursuing graduate degrees	11	6.4
Unemployed seeking employment	18	10.5
Unemployed not seeking employment	3	1.8
Type of Employment		
# employed in law firms	65	46.8
# employed in business & industry	34	24.5
# employed in government	27	19.4
# employed in public interest	2	1.4
# employed as judicial clerks	11	7.9
# employed in academia	0	0.0
Geographic Location		
# employed in state	69	49.6
# employed in foreign countries	1	0.7
# of states where employed	14	

Bar Passage Rate

Jurisdiction	CT	NY
# from school taking bar for the first time	106	94
School's pass rate for all first-time takers	76%	70%
State's pass rate for all first-time takers	83%	78%
State's pass rate for all first-time takers from ABA approved law schools	78%	

REGENT UNIVERSITY

1000 Regent University Drive
Virginia Beach, VA 23464
(757)579-4040
http://www.regent.edu/acad/schlaw

ABA Approved Since 1989

The Basics

Type of School: **PRIVATE**
Application deadline*: **4/1**
Application fee: **$40**
Financial Aid deadline*: **4/1**
Student faculty ratio: **19.1 to 1**

First year can start other than Fall: **No**
Student housing: **Yes**
--exclusively for law students: **No**
Term: **Semester**

*pr=preferred

Faculty

	Men		Women		Minorities		Total
	#	%	#	%	#	%	
Full-time	12	75	4	25	3	19	16
Other full-time	0	0	0	0	0	0	0
Deans, librarians, & others who teach	3	100	0	0	0	0	3
Part-time	8	57	6	43	0	0	14
Total	23	70	10	30	3	9	33
Deans, librarians, & others who teach < 1/2	1	100	0	0	0	0	1

Library

# of volumes & volume equivalents	299,146	# of professional staff	3
# of titles	40,231	Hours per week with professional staff	45
# of active serial subscriptions	4,367	Hours per week without professional staff	53
Study seating capacity inside the library	280	# of student computer work stations for entire law school	23
Square feet of law library	38,730	# of additional networked connections	0
Square feet of law school (excl. Library)	71,970		

Curriculum

	Full time	Part time
Typical first-year section size	69	0
Is there typically a "small section" of the first year class, other than Legal Writing, taught by full-time faculty?	No	No
If yes, typical size offered last year	N/A	N/A
# of classroom course titles beyond 1st year curriculum	53	0
# of upper division courses, excluding seminars, with an enrollment:		
Under 25	42	0
25 - 49	27	0
50 - 74	5	0
75 - 99	0	0
100 +	0	0
# of seminars	3	0
# of seminar positions available	65	
# of seminar positions filled	45	0
# of positions available in simulation courses	289	
# of simulation positions filled	266	0
# of positions available in faculty supervised clinical courses	0	
# of fac. sup. clin. positions filled	0	0
# involved in field placements	35	0
# involved in law journals	25	0
# in moot court or trial competitions	23	0
# of credit hours required to graduate	90	

Enrollment & Attrition

	Full-Time							Part-Time							Attrition			
	Men		Women		Minorities		Total	Men		Women		Minorities		Total	Academic	Other	Total	
	#	%	#	%	#	%	#	#	%	#	%	#	%	#	#	#	#	%
1st Year	94	66.2	48	33.8	15	10.6	142	0	0.0	0	0.0	0	0.0	0	10	9	19	14
2nd Year	83	68.0	39	32.0	7	5.7	122	0	0.0	0	0.0	0	0.0	0	0	0	0	0.0
3rd Year	75	72.8	28	27.2	2	1.9	103	0	0.0	0	0.0	0	0.0	0	0	0	0	0.0
4th Year								0	0.0	0	0.0	0	0.0	0	0	0	0	0.0
Total	252	68.7	115	31.3	24	6.5	367	0	0.0	0	0.0	0	0.0	0	10	9	19	5.5
JD Degrees Awarded	74	70.5	31	29.5	3	2.9	105	0	0.0	0	0.0	0	0.0	0				

GPA & LSAT Scores

	Full Time	Part Time	Total
# of apps	426	0	426
# admits	220	0	220
# of matrics	140	0	140
75% GPA	3.42	0.00	
25% GPA	2.62	0.00	
75% LSAT	155	0	
25% LSAT	148	0	

Tuition/Living Expenses

	Resident	Non-resident
Full-Time	$12,848	$12,848
Part-Time	$0	$0

Estimated living expenses for Singles		
Living on campus	Living off campus	Living at home
N/A	$10,380	$10,380

Career Placement

	Total	%
Employment status known	91	92.9
Employment status unknown	7	7.1
Employed	58	63.7
Pursuing graduate degrees	5	5.5
Unemployed seeking employment	26	28.6
Unemployed not seeking employment	2	2.2
Type of Employment		
# employed in law firms	40	69.0
# employed in business & industry	5	8.6
# employed in government	6	10.3
# employed in public interest	1	1.7
# employed as judicial clerks	5	8.6
# employed in academia	1	1.7
Geographic Location		
# employed in state	32	55.2
# employed in foreign countries	0	0.0
# of states where employed	18	

Financial Aid

	Full-time		Part-time		Total	
	#	%	#	%	#	%
Total # receiving grants	327	89.1	0	0.0	327	89.1
Less than 1/2 tuition	281	76.6	0	0.0	281	76.6
Half to full tuition	42	11.4	0	0.0	42	11.4
Full tuition	3	0.8	0	0.0	3	0.8
More than full tuition	1	0.3	0	0.0	1	0.3
Median Grant Amount	$2,840		$0			

Refunds

Refunds of Admissions or Seat Deposit prior to commencement of classes? No

Refunds of Pre-paid tuition prior to commencement of classes? Yes

If yes, fully refundable before the start of classes? No

100% refund from 08/21/96 to 09/04/96
50% refund from 09/05/96 to 09/18/96

Joint Degrees Offered

J.D/M.A.P.P, J.D./M.B.A., J.D./M.A.Mgt, J.D./M.A.Com

Advanced Degrees Offered

No Advanced Degrees

Bar Passage Rate

Jurisdiction	VA	FL	NC
# from school taking bar for the first time	21	10	4
School's pass rate for all first-time takers	59%	60%	100%
State's pass rate for all first-time takers	76%	84%	85%
State's pass rate for all first-time takers from ABA approved law schools	77%	84%	85%

RICHMOND, UNIVERSITY OF

Law School
University of Richmond
Richmond, VA 23173
(804)289-8740
http://www.urich.edu/~law/

ABA Approved Since 1928

The Basics

Type of School: **PRIVATE**
Application deadline*: **2/10**
Application fee: **$35**
Financial Aid deadline*: **2/25**
Student faculty ratio: **18.0 to 1**

First year can start other than Fall: **Yes**
Student housing: **Yes**
--exclusively for law students: **Yes**
Term: **Semester**

*pr=preferred

Faculty

	Men		Women		Minorities		Total
	#	%	#	%	#	%	
Full-time	13	59	9	41	1	5	22
Other full-time	0	0	1	100	0	0	1
Deans, librarians, & others who teach	2	100	0	0	0	0	2
Part-time	15	50	15	50	5	17	30
Total	30	55	25	45	6	11	55
Deans, librarians, & others who teach < 1/2	0	0	1	100	0	0	1

Library

# of volumes & volume equivalents	249,272	# of professional staff	5
# of titles	112,273	Hours per week with professional staff	77
# of active serial subscriptions	4,004	Hours per week without professional staff	29
Study seating capacity inside the library	602	# of student computer work stations for entire law school	460
Square feet of law library	49,000	# of additional networked connections	573
Square feet of law school (excl. Library)	41,745		

Curriculum

	Full time	Part time
Typical first-year section size	70	0
Is there typically a "small section" of the first year class, other than Legal Writing, taught by full-time faculty?	Yes	No
If yes, typical size offered last year	39	N/A
# of classroom course titles beyond 1st year curriculum	94	0
# of upper division courses, excluding seminars, with an enrollment:		
Under 25	42	0
25 - 49	26	0
50 - 74	10	0
75 - 99	4	0
100 +	0	0
# of seminars	13	0
# of seminar positions available	208	
# of seminar positions filled	129	0
# of positions available in simulation courses	498	
# of simulation positions filled	442	0
# of positions available in faculty supervised clinical courses	52	
# of fac. sup. clin. positions filled	32	0
# involved in field placements	65	0
# involved in law journals	95	0
# in moot court or trial competitions	370	0
# of credit hours required to graduate	86	

Enrollment & Attrition

	Full-Time							Part-Time							Attrition			
	Men		Women		Minorities		Total	Men		Women		Minorities		Total	Academic	Other	Total	
	#	%	#	%	#	%	#	#	%	#	%	#	%	#	#	#	#	%
1st Year	82	54.3	69	45.7	24	15.9	151	0	0.0	0	0.0	0	0.0	0	0	6	6	3.5
2nd Year	78	46.4	90	53.6	37	22.0	168	1	100.0	0	0.0	1	100.0	1	0	2	2	1.2
3rd Year	83	54.2	70	45.8	34	22.2	153	1	20.0	4	80.0	0	0.0	5	0	0	0	0.0
4th Year								0	0.0	0	0.0	0	0.0	0	0	0	0	0.0
Total	243	51.5	229	48.5	95	20.1	472	2	33.3	4	66.7	1	16.7	6	0	8	8	1.7
JD Degrees Awarded	82	53.2	72	46.8	28	18.2	154	0	0.0	0	0.0	0	0.0	0				

GPA & LSAT Scores

	Full Time	Part Time	Total
# of apps	1,296	0	1,296
# admits	542	0	542
# of matrics	152	0	152
75% GPA	3.34	0.00	
25% GPA	2.85	0.00	
75% LSAT	161	0	
25% LSAT	156	0	

Tuition/Living Expenses

	Resident	Non-resident
Full-Time	$17,170	$17,170
Part-Time	$0	$0

Estimated living expenses for Singles		
Living on campus	Living off campus	Living at home
$7,730	$10,005	$5,250

Career Placement

	Total	%
Employment status known	129	89.6
Employment status unknown	15	10.4
Employed	110	85.3
Pursuing graduate degrees	1	0.8
Unemployed seeking employment	18	14.0
Unemployed not seeking employment	0	0.0
Type of Employment		
# employed in law firms	67	60.9
# employed in business & industry	9	8.2
# employed in government	18	16.4
# employed in public interest	2	1.8
# employed as judicial clerks	12	10.9
# employed in academia	2	1.8
Geographic Location		
# employed in state	83	75.5
# employed in foreign countries	0	0.0
# of states where employed	13	

Financial Aid

	Full-time		Part-time		Total	
	#	%	#	%	#	%
Total # receiving grants	357	75.6	0	0.0	357	74.7
Less than 1/2 tuition	333	70.6	0	0.0	333	69.7
Half to full tuition	17	3.6	0	0.0	17	3.6
Full tuition	7	1.5	0	0.0	7	1.5
More than full tuition	0	0.0	0	0.0	0	0.0
Median Grant Amount	$3,200		$0			

Refunds

Refunds of Admissions or Seat Deposit prior to commencement of classes? No

Refunds of Pre-paid tuition prior to commencement of classes? Yes

If yes, fully refundable before the start of classes? Yes

Joint Degrees Offered

JD/MBA, JD/MSW, JD/Urban Pln, JD/Health Ad

Bar Passage Rate

Jurisdiction	VA
# from school taking bar for the first time	93
School's pass rate for all first-time takers	86%
State's pass rate for all first-time takers	76%
State's pass rate for all first-time takers from ABA approved law schools	77%

Advanced Degrees Offered

No Advanced Degrees

ROGER WILLIAMS UNIVERSITY (Provisional)

Ten Metacom Avenue
Bristol, RI 02809
(401)254-4500
website is currently under construction

ABA Approved Since 1995

The Basics

Type of School: **PRIVATE**
Application deadline*: **5/15**
Application fee: **$60**
Financial Aid deadline*:
Student faculty ratio: **18.2 to 1**

First year can start other than Fall: **No**
Student housing: **Yes**
--exclusively for law students: **No**
Term: **Semester**

*pr=preferred

Faculty

	Men		Women		Minorities		Total
	#	%	#	%	#	%	
Full-time	15	65	8	35	2	9	23
Other full-time	0	0	0	0	0	0	0
Deans, librarians, & others who teach	1	100	0	0	0	0	1
Part-time	0	0	0	0	0	0	0
Total	16	67	8	33	2	8	24
Deans, librarians, & others who teach < 1/2	1	100	0	0	0	0	1

Library

# of volumes & volume equivalents	175,406	# of professional staff	6
# of titles	78,533	Hours per week with professional staff	61
# of active serial subscriptions	3,022	Hours per week without professional staff	49
Study seating capacity inside the library	383	# of student computer work stations for entire law school	40
Square feet of law library	30,083	# of additional networked connections	109
Square feet of law school (excl. Library)	91,617		

Curriculum

	Full time	Part time
Typical first-year section size	50	75
Is there typically a "small section" of the first year class, other than Legal Writing, taught by full-time faculty?	No	No
If yes, typical size offered last year	N/A	N/A
# of classroom course titles beyond 1st year curriculum	40	21
# of upper division courses, excluding seminars, with an enrollment:		
Under 25	21	10
25 - 49	8	5
50 - 74	6	4
75 - 99	1	2
100 +	4	0
# of seminars	4	2
# of seminar positions available	108	
# of seminar positions filled	54	20
# of positions available in simulation courses	330	
# of simulation positions filled	225	92
# of positions available in faculty supervised clinical courses	42	
# of fac. sup. clin. positions filled	42	0
# involved in field placements	39	3
# involved in law journals	20	7
# in moot court or trial competitions	30	11
# of credit hours required to graduate	90	

Enrollment & Attrition

	Full-Time							Part-Time							Attrition			
	Men		Women		Minorities		Total	Men		Women		Minorities		Total	Academic	Other	Total	
	#	%	#	%	#	%	#	#	%	#	%	#	%	#	#	#	#	%
1st Year	52	59.1	36	40.9	7	8.0	88	47	60.3	31	39.7	10	12.8	78	12	1	13	7.5
2nd Year	54	58.7	38	41.3	4	4.3	92	36	67.9	17	32.1	1	1.9	53	8	1	9	5.5
3rd Year	60	56.6	46	43.4	4	3.8	106	29	56.9	22	43.1	3	5.9	51	0	0	0	0.0
4th Year								30	66.7	15	33.3	3	6.7	45	0	0	0	0.0
Total	166	58.0	120	42.0	15	5.2	286	142	62.6	85	37.4	17	7.5	227	20	2	22	4.6
JD Degrees Awarded	56	65.9	29	34.1	3	3.5	85	0	0.0	0	0.0	0	0.0	0				

ROGER WILLIAMS UNIVERSITY (Provisional)

GPA & LSAT Scores

	Full Time	Part Time	Total
# of apps	468	172	640
# admits	285	106	391
# of matrics	91	82	173
75% GPA	3.38	3.28	
25% GPA	2.75	2.70	
75% LSAT	151	152	
25% LSAT	143	142	

Tuition/Living Expenses

	Resident	Non-resident
Full-Time	$17,100	$17,100
Part-Time	$13,091	$13,091

Estimated living expenses for Singles		
Living on campus	Living off campus	Living at home
$11,970	$12,825	$12,825

Career Placement

	Total	%
Employment status known	46	54.8
Employment status unknown	38	45.2
Employed	30	65.2
Pursuing graduate degrees	2	4.4
Unemployed seeking employment	13	28.3
Unemployed not seeking employment	1	2.2
Type of Employment		
# employed in law firms	15	50.0
# employed in business & industry	7	23.3
# employed in government	2	6.7
# employed in public interest	0	0.0
# employed as judicial clerks	6	20.0
# employed in academia	0	0.0
Geographic Location		
# employed in state	16	53.3
# employed in foreign countries	0	0.0
# of states where employed	8	

Financial Aid

	Full-time		Part-time		Total	
	#	%	#	%	#	%
Total # receiving grants	14	4.9	6	2.6	20	3.9
Less than 1/2 tuition	14	4.9	6	2.6	20	3.9
Half to full tuition	0	0.0	0	0.0	0	0.0
Full tuition	0	0.0	0	0.0	0	0.0
More than full tuition	0	0.0	0	0.0	0	0.0
Median Grant Amount	$3,000		$3,000			

Refunds

Refunds of Admissions or Seat Deposit prior to commencement of classes? No

Refunds of Pre-paid tuition prior to commencement of classes? No

If yes, fully refundable before the start of classes? No

Joint Degrees Offered

J.D./M.C.P.

Advanced Degrees Offered

No Advanced Degrees

Bar Passage Rate

Jurisdiction	RI
# from school taking bar for the first time	53
School's pass rate for all first-time takers	53%
State's pass rate for all first-time takers	71%
State's pass rate for all first-time takers from ABA approved law schools	75%

RUTGERS UNIVERSITY-CAMDEN

Fifth and Penn Streets
Camden, NJ 08102
(609)225-6191
http://www-camlaw.rutgers.edu

ABA Approved Since 1951

The Basics

Type of School: PUBLIC
Application deadline: 3/1
Application fee: $40
Financial Aid deadline: 3/1
Student faculty ratio: 22.9 to 1

First year can start other than Fall: No
Student housing: Yes
--exclusively for law students: Yes
Term: Semester

Faculty

	Men #	Men %	Women #	Women %	Minorities #	Minorities %	Total
Full-time	22	85	4	15	2	8	26
Other full-time	0	0	0	0	0	0	0
Deans, librarians, & others who teach	2	40	3	60	0	0	5
Part-time	24	69	11	31	2	6	35
Total	48	73	18	27	4	6	66
Deans, librarians, & others who teach < 1/2	0	0	2	100	0	0	2

Library

# of volumes & volume equivalents	393,709	# of professional staff	7
# of titles	73,646	Hours per week with professional staff	64
# of active serial subscriptions	3,190	Hours per week without professional staff	36
Study seating capacity inside the library	431	# of student computer work stations for entire law school	44
Square feet of law library	47,163	# of additional networked connections	5
Square feet of law school (excl. Library)	42,727		

Curriculum

	Full time	Part time
Typical first-year section size	86	41
Is there typically a "small section" of the first year class, other than Legal Writing, taught by full-time faculty?	No	No
If yes, typical size offered last year	N/A	N/A
# of classroom course titles beyond 1st year curriculum	53	41
# of upper division courses, excluding seminars, with an enrollment:		
Under 25	18	42
25 - 49	25	16
50 - 74	15	2
75 - 99	5	2
100 +	2	0
# of seminars	14	5
# of seminar positions available	266	
# of seminar positions filled	176	61
# of positions available in simulation courses	732	
# of simulation positions filled	546	86
# of positions available in faculty supervised clinical courses	23	
# of fac. sup. clin. positions filled	18	5
# involved in field placements	66	3
# involved in law journals	53	3
# in moot court or trial competitions	187	10
# of credit hours required to graduate	84	

Enrollment & Attrition

	Full-Time							Part-Time							Attrition			
	Men		Women		Minorities		Total	Men		Women		Minorities		Total	Academic	Other	Total	
	#	%	#	%	#	%	#	#	%	#	%	#	%	#	#	#	#	%
1st Year	103	52.8	92	47.2	40	20.5	195	22	46.8	25	53.2	6	12.8	47	5	15	20	9.3
2nd Year	98	58.0	71	42.0	35	20.7	169	21	55.3	17	44.7	8	21.1	38	2	5	7	2.5
3rd Year	137	56.1	107	43.9	29	11.9	244	34	73.9	12	26.1	4	8.7	46	1	0	1	0.4
4th Year								15	46.9	17	53.1	7	21.9	32	0	0	0	0.0
Total	338	55.6	270	44.4	104	17.1	608	92	56.4	71	43.6	25	15.3	163	8	20	28	3.6
JD Degrees Awarded	114	60.0	76	40.0	55	28.9	190	16	66.7	8	33.3	4	16.7	24				

GPA & LSAT Scores

	Full Time	Part Time	Total
# of apps	N/A	N/A	1,656
# admits	N/A	N/A	742
# of matrics	192	42	234
75% GPA	3.41	3.37	
25% GPA	2.95	2.71	
75% LSAT	157	159	
25% LSAT	151	151	

Tuition/Living Expenses

	Resident	Non-resident
Full-Time	$9,559	$13,553
Part-Time	$7,528	$10,893

Estimated living expenses for Singles		
Living on campus	Living off campus	Living at home
$8,995	$11,295	$5,445

Career Placement

	Total	%
Employment status known	189	92.2
Employment status unknown	16	7.8
Employed	176	93.1
Pursuing graduate degrees	3	1.6
Unemployed seeking employment	7	3.7
Unemployed not seeking employment	3	1.6
Type of Employment		
# employed in law firms	76	43.2
# employed in business & industry	25	14.2
# employed in government	20	11.4
# employed in public interest	2	1.1
# employed as judicial clerks	47	26.7
# employed in academia	6	3.4
Geographic Location		
# employed in state	105	59.7
# employed in foreign countries	3	1.7
# of states where employed	15	

Financial Aid

	Full-time		Part-time		Total	
	#	%	#	%	#	%
Total # receiving grants	57	9.4	7	4.3	64	8.3
Less than 1/2 tuition	53	8.7	7	4.3	60	7.8
Half to full tuition	2	0.3	0	0.0	2	0.3
Full tuition	0	0.0	0	0.0	0	0.0
More than full tuition	2	0.3	0	0.0	2	0.3
Median Grant Amount	$1,200		$600			

Refunds

Refunds of Admissions or Seat Deposit prior to commencement of classes? Yes

66% refund from 01/01/96 to 07/01/96
33% refund from 07/02/96 to 08/01/96

Refunds of Pre-paid tuition prior to commencement of classes? Yes

If yes, fully refundable before the start of classes? Yes

Joint Degrees Offered

M.A., M.B.A., M.C.R.P.

Advanced Degrees Offered

No Advanced Degrees

Bar Passage Rate

Jurisdiction	NJ	PA
# from school taking bar for the first time	119	100
School's pass rate for all first-time takers	76%	68%
State's pass rate for all first-time takers	78%	73%
State's pass rate for all first-time takers from ABA approved law schools	78%	73%

RUTGERS UNIVERSITY-NEWARK

15 Washington Street
Newark, NJ 07102-3192
(201)648-5561
http://www.rutgers.edu/rusln

ABA Approved Since 1941

The Basics

Type of School: **PUBLIC**
Application deadline*: **3/15**
Application fee: **$40**
Financial Aid deadline*: **3/1**
Student faculty ratio: **19.1 to 1**

First year can start other than Fall: **No**
Student housing: **Yes**
--exclusively for law students: **No**
Term: **Semester**

*pr=preferred

Faculty

	Men		Women		Minorities		Total
	#	%	#	%	#	%	
Full-time	24	77	7	23	5	16	31
Other full-time	2	22	7	78	1	11	9
Deans, librarians, & others who teach	1	100	0	0	1	100	1
Part-time	16	76	5	24	3	14	21
Total	43	69	19	31	10	16	62
Deans, librarians, & others who teach < 1/2	1	33	2	67	0	0	3

Library

# of volumes & volume equivalents	415,240	# of professional staff	12
# of titles	111,926	Hours per week with professional staff	56
# of active serial subscriptions	3,065	Hours per week without professional staff	51
Study seating capacity inside the library	397	# of student computer work stations for entire law school	47
Square feet of law library	44,523	# of additional networked connections	0
Square feet of law school (excl. Library)	77,367		

Curriculum

	Full time	Part time
Typical first-year section size	90	60
Is there typically a "small section" of the first year class, other than Legal Writing, taught by full-time faculty?	Yes	Yes
If yes, typical size offered last year	30	30
# of classroom course titles beyond 1st year curriculum	65	21
# of upper division courses, excluding seminars, with an enrollment:		
Under 25	39	4
25 - 49	16	5
50 - 74	9	5
75 - 99	3	0
100 +	2	3
# of seminars	27	3
# of seminar positions available	448	
# of seminar positions filled	250	47
# of positions available in simulation courses	140	
# of simulation positions filled	90	106
# of positions available in faculty supervised clinical courses	210	
# of fac. sup. clin. positions filled	167	38
# involved in field placements	128	3
# involved in law journals	150	18
# in moot court or trial competitions	90	7
# of credit hours required to graduate	84	

Enrollment & Attrition

	Full-Time							Part-Time							Attrition			
	Men		Women		Minorities		Total	Men		Women		Minorities		Total	Academic	Other	Total	
	#	%	#	%	#	%	#	#	%	#	%	#	%	#	#	#	#	%
1st Year	96	53.0	85	47.0	61	33.7	181	32	68.1	15	31.9	15	31.9	47	0	19	19	7.7
2nd Year	94	53.1	83	46.9	46	26.0	177	43	74.1	15	25.9	15	25.9	58	0	12	12	4.5
3rd Year	109	52.9	97	47.1	57	27.7	206	30	45.5	36	54.5	19	28.8	66	0	1	1	0.5
4th Year								30	56.6	23	43.4	13	24.5	53	0	0	0	0.0
Total	299	53.0	265	47.0	164	29.1	564	135	60.3	89	39.7	62	27.7	224	0	32	32	4.0
JD Degrees Awarded	97	58.1	70	41.9	45	26.9	167	32	57.1	24	42.9	16	28.6	56				

GPA & LSAT Scores

	Full Time	Part Time	Total
# of apps	2,324	354	2,678
# admits	587	105	692
# of matrics	184	47	231
75% GPA	3.55	3.46	
25% GPA	3.05	2.50	
75% LSAT	161	161	
25% LSAT	151	152	

Tuition/Living Expenses

	Resident	Non-resident
Full-Time	$9,534	$13,528
Part-Time	$6,098	$8,790

Estimated living expenses for Singles		
Living on campus	Living off campus	Living at home
$9,668	$11,295	$5,445

Career Placement

	Total	%
Employment status known	227	92.7
Employment status unknown	18	7.4
Employed	210	92.5
Pursuing graduate degrees	0	0.0
Unemployed seeking employment	15	6.6
Unemployed not seeking employment	2	0.9
Type of Employment		
# employed in law firms	84	40.0
# employed in business & industry	56	26.7
# employed in government	9	4.3
# employed in public interest	5	2.4
# employed as judicial clerks	52	24.8
# employed in academia	4	1.9
Geographic Location		
# employed in state	154	73.3
# employed in foreign countries	0	0.0
# of states where employed	11	

Financial Aid

	Full-time		Part-time		Total	
	#	%	#	%	#	%
Total # receiving grants	100	17.7	30	13.4	130	16.5
Less than 1/2 tuition	85	15.1	30	13.4	115	14.6
Half to full tuition	5	0.9	0	0.0	5	0.6
Full tuition	2	0.4	0	0.0	2	0.3
More than full tuition	8	1.4	0	0.0	8	1.0
Median Grant Amount	$1,000		$500			

Refunds

Refunds of Admissions or Seat Deposit prior to commencement of classes? No

Refunds of Pre-paid tuition prior to commencement of classes? Yes

If yes, fully refundable before the start of classes? Yes

Joint Degrees Offered

JD-MA, JD MCRP, JD-PHD

Advanced Degrees Offered

No Advanced Degrees

Bar Passage Rate

Jurisdiction	NJ
# from school taking bar for the first time	193
School's pass rate for all first-time takers	75%
State's pass rate for all first-time takers	78%
State's pass rate for all first-time takers from ABA approved law schools	78%

SAMFORD UNIVERSITY

800 Lakeshore Drive
Birmingham, AL 35229
(205)870-2701
http://www.samford.edu/schools/law

ABA Approved Since 1949

The Basics

Type of School: PRIVATE
Application deadline*: 2/28
Application fee: $40
Financial Aid deadline*: 3/1
Student faculty ratio: 19.6 to 1

First year can start other than Fall: No
Student housing: No
--exclusively for law students: No
Term: Semester

*pr=preferred

Faculty

	Men #	Men %	Women #	Women %	Minorities #	Minorities %	Total
Full-time	23	82	5	18	3	11	28
Other full-time	0	0	0	0	0	0	0
Deans, librarians, & others who teach	1	50	1	50	1	50	2
Part-time	12	86	2	14	2	14	14
Total	36	82	8	18	6	14	44
Deans, librarians, & others who teach < 1/2	1	100	0	0	0	0	1

Library

# of volumes & volume equivalents	232,854	# of professional staff	7
# of titles	32,521	Hours per week with professional staff	54
# of active serial subscriptions	2,300	Hours per week without professional staff	53
Study seating capacity inside the library	474	# of student computer work stations for entire law school	28
Square feet of law library	42,500	# of additional networked connections	0
Square feet of law school (excl. Library)	72,900		

Curriculum

	Full time	Part time
Typical first-year section size	70	0
Is there typically a "small section" of the first year class, other than Legal Writing, taught by full-time faculty?	No	No
If yes, typical size offered last year	N/A	N/A
# of classroom course titles beyond 1st year curriculum	61	0
# of upper division courses, excluding seminars, with an enrollment:		
Under 25	15	0
25 - 49	34	0
50 - 74	28	0
75 - 99	11	0
100 +	0	0
# of seminars	23	0
# of seminar positions available	460	
# of seminar positions filled	337	0
# of positions available in simulation courses	465	
# of simulation positions filled	436	0
# of positions available in faculty supervised clinical courses	0	
# of fac. sup. clin. positions filled	0	0
# involved in field placements	157	0
# involved in law journals	117	0
# in moot court or trial competitions	325	0
# of credit hours required to graduate	90	

Enrollment & Attrition

	Full-Time							Part-Time							Attrition			
	Men		Women		Minorities		Total	Men		Women		Minorities		Total	Academic	Other	Total	
	#	%	#	%	#	%	#	#	%	#	%	#	%	#	#	#	#	%
1st Year	138	65.4	73	34.6	19	9.0	211	0	0.0	0	0.0	0	0.0	0	2	17	19	8.6
2nd Year	136	65.1	73	34.9	22	10.5	209	0	0.0	0	0.0	0	0.0	0	2	2	4	1.8
3rd Year	139	65.3	74	34.7	17	8.0	213	0	0.0	0	0.0	0	0.0	0	0	2	2	0.9
4th Year								0	0.0	0	0.0	0	0.0	0	0	0	0	0.0
Total	413	65.2	220	34.8	58	9.2	633	0	0.0	0	0.0	0	0.0	0	4	21	25	3.8
JD Degrees Awarded	132	62.3	80	37.7	13	6.1	212	0	0.0	0	0.0	0	0.0	0				

GPA & LSAT Scores

	Full Time	Part Time	Total
# of apps	1,030	0	1,030
# admits	591	0	591
# of matrics	214	0	214
75% GPA	3.30	0.00	
25% GPA	2.81	0.00	
75% LSAT	155	0	
25% LSAT	150	0	

Tuition/Living Expenses

	Resident	Non-resident
Full-Time	$16,480	$16,480
Part-Time	$0	$0

Estimated living expenses for Singles		
Living on campus	Living off campus	Living at home
N/A	$10,800	$5,095

Financial Aid

	Full-time		Part-time		Total	
	#	%	#	%	#	%
Total # receiving grants	166	26.2	0	0.0	166	26.2
Less than 1/2 tuition	89	14.1	0	0.0	89	14.1
Half to full tuition	22	3.5	0	0.0	22	3.5
Full tuition	23	3.6	0	0.0	23	3.6
More than full tuition	32	5.1	0	0.0	32	5.1
Median Grant Amount	$7,000		$0			

Refunds

Refunds of Admissions or Seat Deposit prior to commencement of classes? No

Refunds of Pre-paid tuition prior to commencement of classes? Yes

If yes, fully refundable before the start of classes? Yes

Joint Degrees Offered

J.D./M.P.H., J.D./M.B.A., J.D./M.A.E., J.D./M.P.A., J.D./M.Acc., J.D./M.Div., J.D./M.S. in, Env.Mgnt.

Advanced Degrees Offered

M.C.L. Master of Comparative Law

Career Placement

	Total	%
Employment status known	182	95.3
Employment status unknown	9	4.7
Employed	156	85.7
Pursuing graduate degrees	9	5.0
Unemployed seeking employment	6	3.3
Unemployed not seeking employment	11	6.0
Type of Employment		
# employed in law firms	107	68.6
# employed in business & industry	8	5.1
# employed in government	23	14.7
# employed in public interest	0	0.0
# employed as judicial clerks	17	10.9
# employed in academia	0	0.0
Geographic Location		
# employed in state	81	51.9
# employed in foreign countries	0	0.0
# of states where employed	18	

Bar Passage Rate

Jurisdiction	AL
# from school taking bar for the first time	101
School's pass rate for all first-time takers	94%
State's pass rate for all first-time takers	83%
State's pass rate for all first-time takers from ABA approved law schools	90%

SAN DIEGO, UNIVERSITY OF

5998 Alcala Park
San Diego, CA 92110-2492
(619)260-4527
http://www.acusd.edu/~usdlaw

ABA Approved Since 1961

The Basics

Type of School: **PRIVATE**
Application deadline: **5/1**
Application fee: **$35**
Financial Aid deadline: **3/3**
Student faculty ratio: **14.5 to 1**
First year can start other than Fall: **No**
Student housing: **Yes**
--exclusively for law students: **No**
Term: **Semester**

Faculty

	Men #	Men %	Women #	Women %	Minorities #	Minorities %	Total
Full-time	36	69	16	31	5	10	52
Other full-time	1	50	1	50	0	0	2
Deans, librarians, & others who teach	0	0	2	100	0	0	2
Part-time	20	67	10	33	5	17	30
Total	57	66	29	34	10	12	86
Deans, librarians, & others who teach < 1/2	0	0	1	100	0	0	1

Library

# of volumes & volume equivalents	394,864	# of professional staff	10
# of titles	174,121	Hours per week with professional staff	70
# of active serial subscriptions	5,182	Hours per week without professional staff	38
Study seating capacity inside the library	600	# of student computer work stations for entire law school	28
Square feet of law library	53,800	# of additional networked connections	0
Square feet of law school (excl. Library)	62,040		

Curriculum

	Full time	Part time
Typical first-year section size	80	80
Is there typically a "small section" of the first year class, other than Legal Writing, taught by full-time faculty?	Yes	Yes
If yes, typical size offered last year	40	40
# of classroom course titles beyond 1st year curriculum	123	76
# of upper division courses, excluding seminars, with an enrollment:		
Under 25	80	40
25 - 49	40	30
50 - 74	13	13
75 - 99	20	10
100 +	0	0
# of seminars	28	16
# of seminar positions available	860	
# of seminar positions filled	389	203
# of positions available in simulation courses	700	
# of simulation positions filled	392	134
# of positions available in faculty supervised clinical courses	250	
# of fac. sup. clin. positions filled	135	18
# involved in field placements	200	50
# involved in law journals	109	29
# in moot court or trial competitions	175	70
# of credit hours required to graduate	85	

Enrollment & Attrition

	Full-Time							Part-Time							Attrition			
	Men		Women		Minorities		Total	Men		Women		Minorities		Total	Academic	Other	Total	
	#	%	#	%	#	%	#	#	%	#	%	#	%	#	#	#	#	%
1st Year	142	62.0	87	38.0	49	21.4	229	50	65.8	26	34.2	16	21.1	76	12	12	24	7.5
2nd Year	145	58.5	103	41.5	54	21.8	248	42	64.6	23	35.4	10	15.4	65	1	2	3	0.9
3rd Year	115	54.0	98	46.0	52	24.4	213	58	54.2	49	45.8	16	15.0	107	0	1	1	0.3
4th Year								23	74.2	8	25.8	7	22.6	31	0	0	0	0.0
Total	402	58.3	288	41.7	155	22.5	690	173	62.0	106	38.0	49	17.6	279	13	15	28	2.8
JD Degrees Awarded	153	56.9	116	43.1	56	20.8	269	26	53.1	23	46.9	3	6.1	49				

GPA & LSAT Scores

	Full Time	Part Time	Total
# of apps	N/A	N/A	2,932
# admits	N/A	N/A	1,014
# of matrics	225	85	310
75% GPA	3.36	3.28	
25% GPA	2.84	2.68	
75% LSAT	161	158	
25% LSAT	157	154	

Tuition/Living Expenses

	Resident	Non-resident
Full-Time	$18,940	$18,940
Part-Time	$13,440	$13,440

Estimated living expenses for Singles		
Living on campus	Living off campus	Living at home
$10,000	$9,750	$4,800

Career Placement

	Total	%
Employment status known	249	89.3
Employment status unknown	30	10.8
Employed	221	88.8
Pursuing graduate degrees	7	3.2
Unemployed seeking employment	13	5.9
Unemployed not seeking employment	4	1.8
Type of Employment		
# employed in law firms	155	70.1
# employed in business & industry	27	12.2
# employed in government	24	10.9
# employed in public interest	4	1.8
# employed as judicial clerks	10	4.5
# employed in academia	1	0.5
Geographic Location		
# employed in state	185	83.7
# employed in foreign countries	3	1.4
# of states where employed	20	

Financial Aid

	Full-time		Part-time		Total	
	#	%	#	%	#	%
Total # receiving grants	277	40.1	58	20.8	335	34.6
Less than 1/2 tuition	83	12.0	17	6.1	100	10.3
Half to full tuition	165	23.9	35	12.5	200	20.6
Full tuition	7	1.0	5	1.8	12	1.2
More than full tuition	22	3.2	1	0.4	23	2.4
Median Grant Amount	$0		$0			

Refunds

Refunds of Admissions or Seat Deposit prior to commencement of classes? Yes

0% refund from 06/01/96 to 08/01/96

Refunds of Pre-paid tuition prior to commencement of classes? Yes

If yes, fully refundable before the start of classes? Yes

Joint Degrees Offered

JD/MBA, JD/MA, Int'l Bus, JD/MA, Int'l Rel

Advanced Degrees Offered

LL.M.	Taxation
LL.M.	General or "as approved" (various)
LL.M.	Comparative Law (for Foreign Lawyers)
LL.M.	International Law and Comparative Law

Bar Passage Rate

Jurisdiction	CA
# from school taking bar for the first time	243
School's pass rate for all first-time takers	79%
State's pass rate for all first-time takers	73%
State's pass rate for all first-time takers from ABA approved law schools	83%

SAN FRANCISCO, UNIVERSITY OF

2130 Fulton Street
San Francisco, CA 94117-1080
(415)422-6304
http://www.usfca.edu

ABA Approved Since 1935

The Basics

Type of School: **PRIVATE**
Application deadline*: **4/1**
Application fee: **$40**
Financial Aid deadline*: **4/1**
Student faculty ratio: **21.5 to 1**

First year can start other than Fall: **No**
Student housing: **Yes**
--exclusively for law students: **No**
Term: **Semester**

*pr=preferred

Faculty

	Men		Women		Minorities		Total
	#	%	#	%	#	%	
Full-time	18	72	7	28	5	20	25
Other full-time	0	0	0	0	0	0	0
Deans, librarians, & others who teach	2	100	0	0	0	0	2
Part-time	23	61	15	39	8	21	38
Total	43	66	22	34	13	20	65
Deans, librarians, & others who teach < 1/2	0	0	1	100	0	0	1

Library

# of volumes & volume equivalents	272,265	# of professional staff	6
# of titles	27,625	Hours per week with professional staff	65
# of active serial subscriptions	2,355	Hours per week without professional staff	35
Study seating capacity inside the library	293	# of student computer work stations for entire law school	41
Square feet of law library	21,708	# of additional networked connections	29
Square feet of law school (excl. Library)	30,792		

Curriculum

	Full time	Part time
Typical first-year section size	83	55
Is there typically a "small section" of the first year class, other than Legal Writing, taught by full-time faculty?	No	No
If yes, typical size offered last year	N/A	N/A
# of classroom course titles beyond 1st year curriculum	67	45
# of upper division courses, excluding seminars, with an enrollment:		
Under 25	31	19
25 - 49	11	9
50 - 74	9	8
75 - 99	7	5
100 +	0	1
# of seminars	9	3
# of seminar positions available	278	
# of seminar positions filled	174	6
# of positions available in simulation courses	472	
# of simulation positions filled	250	110
# of positions available in faculty supervised clinical courses	124	
# of fac. sup. clin. positions filled	89	7
# involved in field placements	134	8
# involved in law journals	75	1
# in moot court or trial competitions	77	0
# of credit hours required to graduate	86	

Enrollment & Attrition

	Full-Time							Part-Time							Attrition			
	Men		Women		Minorities		Total	Men		Women		Minorities		Total	Academic	Other	Total	
	#	%	#	%	#	%	#	#	%	#	%	#	%	#	#	#	#	%
1st Year	87	48.6	92	51.4	44	24.6	179	22	44.0	28	56.0	14	28.0	50	15	7	22	10
2nd Year	81	46.6	93	53.4	54	31.0	174	17	65.4	9	34.6	6	23.1	26	4	15	19	8.1
3rd Year	101	49.8	102	50.2	46	22.7	203	15	48.4	16	51.6	8	25.8	31	0	0	0	0.0
4th Year								11	39.3	17	60.7	7	25.0	28	0	0	0	0.0
Total	269	48.4	287	51.6	144	25.9	556	65	48.1	70	51.9	35	25.9	135	19	22	41	6.0
JD Degrees Awarded	82	45.6	98	54.4	42	23.3	180	12	60.0	8	40.0	2	10.0	20				

GPA & LSAT Scores

	Full Time	Part Time	Total
# of apps	2,661	235	2,896
# admits	1,053	198	1,251
# of matrics	181	53	234
75% GPA	3.40	3.40	
25% GPA	2.90	2.80	
75% LSAT	160	156	
25% LSAT	154	150	

Tuition/Living Expenses

	Resident	Non-resident
Full-Time	$18,960	$18,960
Part-Time	$15,564	$15,564

Estimated living expenses for Singles		
Living on campus	Living off campus	Living at home
$10,389	$10,650	$5,450

Career Placement

	Total	%
Employment status known	122	63.2
Employment status unknown	71	36.8
Employed	98	80.3
Pursuing graduate degrees	3	2.5
Unemployed seeking employment	17	13.9
Unemployed not seeking employment	4	3.3
Type of Employment		
# employed in law firms	46	46.9
# employed in business & industry	30	30.6
# employed in government	14	14.3
# employed in public interest	3	3.1
# employed as judicial clerks	3	3.1
# employed in academia	2	2.0
Geographic Location		
# employed in state	88	89.8
# employed in foreign countries	1	1.0
# of states where employed	6	

Financial Aid

	Full-time		Part-time		Total	
	#	%	#	%	#	%
Total # receiving grants	390	70.1	44	32.6	434	62.8
Less than 1/2 tuition	378	68.0	43	31.9	421	60.9
Half to full tuition	10	1.8	1	0.7	11	1.6
Full tuition	2	0.4	0	0.0	2	0.3
More than full tuition	0	0.0	0	0.0	0	0.0
Median Grant Amount	$1,400		$3,000			

Refunds

Refunds of Admissions or Seat Deposit prior to commencement of classes? No

Refunds of Pre-paid tuition prior to commencement of classes? Yes

If yes, fully refundable before the start of classes? Yes

100% refund from 08/02/00 to 09/20/00

Joint Degrees Offered

JD/MBA

Advanced Degrees Offered

LL.M. International Transactions & Comparative Law

Bar Passage Rate

Jurisdiction	CA
# from school taking bar for the first time	172
School's pass rate for all first-time takers	81%
State's pass rate for all first-time takers	73%
State's pass rate for all first-time takers from ABA approved law schools	83%

SANTA CLARA UNIVERSITY

500 El Camino Real
Santa Clara, CA 95053
(408)554-4767
http://www.scu.edu/law

ABA Approved Since 1937

The Basics

Type of School: **PRIVATE**
Application deadline*: **3/1**
Application fee: **$40**
Financial Aid deadline*:
Student faculty ratio: **22.4 to 1**

First year can start other than Fall: **No**
Student housing: **Yes**
--exclusively for law students: **No**
Term: **Semester**

*pr=preferred

Faculty

	Men		Women		Minorities		Total
	#	%	#	%	#	%	
Full-time	16	53	14	47	7	23	30
Other full-time	0	0	3	100	1	33	3
Deans, librarians, & others who teach	1	100	0	0	0	0	1
Part-time	18	64	10	36	3	11	28
Total	35	56	27	44	11	18	62
Deans, librarians, & others who teach < 1/2	1	50	1	50	0	0	2

Library

# of volumes & volume equivalents	258,756	# of professional staff	8
# of titles	105,151	Hours per week with professional staff	75
# of active serial subscriptions	3,457	Hours per week without professional staff	30
Study seating capacity inside the library	448	# of student computer work stations for entire law school	65
Square feet of law library	39,554	# of additional networked connections	470
Square feet of law school (excl. Library)	193,636		

Curriculum

	Full time	Part time
Typical first-year section size	70	60
Is there typically a "small section" of the first year class, other than Legal Writing, taught by full-time faculty?	Yes	No
If yes, typical size offered last year	35	N/A
# of classroom course titles beyond 1st year curriculum	72	40
# of upper division courses, excluding seminars, with an enrollment:		
Under 25	15	5
25 - 49	13	16
50 - 74	8	4
75 - 99	8	1
100 +	8	4
# of seminars	19	9
# of seminar positions available	599	
# of seminar positions filled	517	0
# of positions available in simulation courses	355	
# of simulation positions filled	333	0
# of positions available in faculty supervised clinical courses	200	
# of fac. sup. clin. positions filled	169	0
# involved in field placements	169	0
# involved in law journals	81	0
# in moot court or trial competitions	106	0
# of credit hours required to graduate	86	

Enrollment & Attrition

	Full-Time							Part-Time							Attrition			
	Men		Women		Minorities		Total	Men		Women		Minorities		Total	Academic	Other	Total	
	#	%	#	%	#	%	#	#	%	#	%	#	%	#	#	#	#	%
1st Year	114	53.0	101	47.0	68	31.6	215	36	53.7	31	46.3	19	28.4	67	0	4	4	1.4
2nd Year	97	46.6	111	53.4	79	38.0	208	44	67.7	21	32.3	13	20.0	65	3	12	15	5.5
3rd Year	116	53.5	101	46.5	78	35.9	217	31	53.4	27	46.6	21	36.2	58	2	2	4	1.5
4th Year								25	40.3	37	59.7	18	29.0	62	0	0	0	0.0
Total	327	51.1	313	48.9	225	35.2	640	136	54.0	116	46.0	71	28.2	252	5	18	23	2.7
JD Degrees Awarded	82	43.4	107	56.6	59	31.2	189	70	76.1	22	23.9	16	17.4	92				

GPA & LSAT Scores

	Full Time	Part Time	Total
# of apps	2,746	259	3,005
# admits	1,118	118	1,236
# of matrics	222	68	290
75% GPA	3.46	3.38	
25% GPA	3.07	2.86	
75% LSAT	158	159	
25% LSAT	153	152	

Tuition/Living Expenses

	Resident	Non-resident
Full-Time	$19,130	$19,130
Part-Time	$13,320	$13,320

Estimated living expenses for Singles		
Living on campus	Living off campus	Living at home
$14,122	$14,122	$14,122

Financial Aid

	Full-time		Part-time		Total	
	#	%	#	%	#	%
Total # receiving grants	241	37.7	31	12.3	272	30.5
Less than 1/2 tuition	168	26.3	27	10.7	195	21.9
Half to full tuition	67	10.5	3	1.2	70	7.8
Full tuition	6	0.9	1	0.4	7	0.8
More than full tuition	0	0.0	0	0.0	0	0.0
Median Grant Amount	$7,000		$6,000			

Refunds

Refunds of Admissions or Seat Deposit prior to commencement of classes? No

Refunds of Pre-paid tuition prior to commencement of classes? Yes

If yes, fully refundable before the start of classes? No

Joint Degrees Offered

JD/MBA

Advanced Degrees Offered

No Advanced Degrees

Career Placement

	Total	%
Employment status known	249	91.2
Employment status unknown	24	8.8
Employed	221	88.8
Pursuing graduate degrees	1	0.4
Unemployed seeking employment	17	6.8
Unemployed not seeking employment	10	4.0
Type of Employment		
# employed in law firms	128	57.9
# employed in business & industry	55	24.9
# employed in government	19	8.6
# employed in public interest	6	2.7
# employed as judicial clerks	10	4.5
# employed in academia	3	1.4
Geographic Location		
# employed in state	160	72.4
# employed in foreign countries	1	0.5
# of states where employed	11	

Bar Passage Rate

Jurisdiction	CA
# from school taking bar for the first time	232
School's pass rate for all first-time takers	82%
State's pass rate for all first-time takers	73%
State's pass rate for all first-time takers from ABA approved law schools	83%

SEATTLE UNIVERSITY

950 Broadway Plaza
Tacoma, WA 98402
(206)591-2275
http://www.law.seattleu.edu

ABA Approved Since 1994

The Basics

Type of School: **PRIVATE**
Application deadline*: **4/1**
Application fee: **$50**
Financial Aid deadline*: **3/1**
Student faculty ratio: **23.1 to 1**

First year can start other than Fall: **Yes**
Student housing: **No**
--exclusively for law students: **No**
Term: **Semester**

*pr=preferred

Faculty

	Men		Women		Minorities		Total
	#	%	#	%	#	%	
Full-time	20	67	10	33	2	7	30
Other full-time	3	33	6	67	2	22	9
Deans, librarians, & others who teach	1	50	1	50	0	0	2
Part-time	12	75	4	25	3	19	16
Total	36	63	21	37	7	12	57
Deans, librarians, & others who teach < 1/2	1	50	1	50	0	0	2

Library

# of volumes & volume equivalents	329,380	# of professional staff	8
# of titles	134,486	Hours per week with professional staff	61
# of active serial subscriptions	3,785	Hours per week without professional staff	58
Study seating capacity inside the library	599	# of student computer work stations for entire law school	137
Square feet of law library	40,397	# of additional networked connections	0
Square feet of law school (excl. Library)	59,290		

Curriculum

	Full time	Part time
Typical first-year section size	75	60
Is there typically a "small section" of the first year class, other than Legal Writing, taught by full-time faculty?	No	No
If yes, typical size offered last year	N/A	N/A
# of classroom course titles beyond 1st year curriculum	104	0
# of upper division courses, excluding seminars, with an enrollment:		
Under 25	45	0
25 - 49	32	0
50 - 74	17	0
75 - 99	16	0
100 +	5	0
# of seminars	12	0
# of seminar positions available	230	
# of seminar positions filled	237	0
# of positions available in simulation courses	264	
# of simulation positions filled	245	0
# of positions available in faculty supervised clinical courses	133	
# of fac. sup. clin. positions filled	118	0
# involved in field placements	24	0
# involved in law journals	39	0
# in moot court or trial competitions	15	0
# of credit hours required to graduate	90	

Enrollment & Attrition

	Full-Time							Part-Time							Attrition			
	Men		Women		Minorities		Total	Men		Women		Minorities		Total	Academic	Other	Total	
	#	%	#	%	#	%	#	#	%	#	%	#	%	#	#	#	#	%
1st Year	101	48.1	109	51.9	40	19.0	210	30	40.5	44	59.5	10	13.5	74	8	13	21	7.6
2nd Year	120	53.6	104	46.4	44	19.6	224	23	53.5	20	46.5	6	14.0	43	0	12	12	4.0
3rd Year	140	52.4	127	47.6	55	20.6	267	23	60.5	15	39.5	13	34.2	38	0	5	5	1.8
4th Year								18	41.9	25	58.1	5	11.6	43	0	0	0	0.0
Total	361	51.5	340	48.5	139	19.8	701	94	47.5	104	52.5	34	17.2	198	8	30	38	4.3
JD Degrees Awarded	131	57.7	96	42.3	32	14.1	227	27	60.0	18	40.0	3	6.7	45				

GPA & LSAT Scores

	Full Time	Part Time	Total
# of apps	1,223	145	1,368
# admits	684	92	776
# of matrics	215	73	288
75% GPA	3.52	3.53	
25% GPA	3.00	2.85	
75% LSAT	159	157	
25% LSAT	153	150	

Tuition/Living Expenses

	Resident	Non-resident
Full-Time	$16,426	$16,426
Part-Time	$16,412	$16,412

Estimated living expenses for Singles		
Living on campus	Living off campus	Living at home
N/A	$10,980	$6,096

Financial Aid

	Full-time		Part-time		Total	
	#	%	#	%	#	%
Total # receiving grants	303	43.2	47	23.7	350	38.9
Less than 1/2 tuition	278	39.7	43	21.7	321	35.7
Half to full tuition	25	3.6	4	2.0	29	3.2
Full tuition	0	0.0	0	0.0	0	0.0
More than full tuition	0	0.0	0	0.0	0	0.0
Median Grant Amount	$4,669		$0			

Refunds

Refunds of Admissions or Seat Deposit prior to commencement of classes? No

Refunds of Pre-paid tuition prior to commencement of classes? No

If yes, fully refundable before the start of classes? No

Joint Degrees Offered

No Joint Degrees

Advanced Degrees Offered

No Advanced Degrees

Career Placement

	Total	%
Employment status known	237	88.8
Employment status unknown	30	11.2
Employed	202	85.2
Pursuing graduate degrees	4	1.7
Unemployed seeking employment	20	8.4
Unemployed not seeking employment	11	4.6
Type of Employment		
# employed in law firms	100	49.5
# employed in business & industry	36	17.8
# employed in government	43	21.3
# employed in public interest	11	5.5
# employed as judicial clerks	9	4.5
# employed in academia	3	1.5
Geographic Location		
# employed in state	179	88.6
# employed in foreign countries	4	2.0
# of states where employed	15	

Bar Passage Rate

Jurisdiction	WA
# from school taking bar for the first time	199
School's pass rate for all first-time takers	86%
State's pass rate for all first-time takers	83%
State's pass rate for all first-time takers from ABA approved law schools	

SETON HALL UNIVERSITY

One Newark Center
Newark, NJ 07102
(201)642-8500
http://www.shu.edu/law

ABA Approved Since 1951

The Basics

Type of School: PRIVATE
Application deadline*: 4/1
Application fee: $50
Financial Aid deadline*: 5/15
Student faculty ratio: 23.8 to 1
First year can start other than Fall: No
Student housing: No
--exclusively for law students: No
Term: Semester

*pr=preferred

Faculty

	Men #	Men %	Women #	Women %	Minorities #	Minorities %	Total
Full-time	29	74	10	26	9	23	39
Other full-time	2	29	5	71	0	0	7
Deans, librarians, & others who teach	3	100	0	0	0	0	3
Part-time	73	79	19	21	6	7	92
Total	107	76	34	24	15	11	141
Deans, librarians, & others who teach < 1/2	0	0	2	100	0	0	2

Library

# of volumes & volume equivalents	367,565	# of professional staff	8
# of titles	56,770	Hours per week with professional staff	83
# of active serial subscriptions	5,068	Hours per week without professional staff	15
Study seating capacity inside the library	600	# of student computer work stations for entire law school	88
Square feet of law library	55,250	# of additional networked connections	2
Square feet of law school (excl. Library)	154,750		

Curriculum

	Full time	Part time
Typical first-year section size	70	70
Is there typically a "small section" of the first year class, other than Legal Writing, taught by full-time faculty?	Yes	Yes
If yes, typical size offered last year	35	35
# of classroom course titles beyond 1st year curriculum	121	80
# of upper division courses, excluding seminars, with an enrollment:		
Under 25	51	30
25 - 49	30	18
50 - 74	27	9
75 - 99	9	4
100 +	0	0
# of seminars	56	26
# of seminar positions available	1,566	
# of seminar positions filled	914	283
# of positions available in simulation courses	472	
# of simulation positions filled	332	83
# of positions available in faculty supervised clinical courses	272	
# of fac. sup. clin. positions filled	112	48
# involved in field placements	76	9
# involved in law journals	159	15
# in moot court or trial competitions	149	10
# of credit hours required to graduate	85	

Enrollment & Attrition

	Full-Time Men #	Men %	Women #	Women %	Minorities #	Minorities %	Total #	Part-Time Men #	Men %	Women #	Women %	Minorities #	Minorities %	Total #	Attrition Academic #	Other #	Total #	Total %
1st Year	138	50.7	134	49.3	50	18.4	272	43	57.3	32	42.7	8	10.7	75	2	6	8	1.8
2nd Year	183	53.2	161	46.8	60	17.4	344	45	57.0	34	43.0	9	11.4	79	27	10	37	10
3rd Year	167	57.8	122	42.2	53	18.3	289	55	68.8	25	31.3	12	15.0	80	3	1	4	1.0
4th Year								44	53.7	38	46.3	13	15.9	82	3	0	3	3.1
Total	488	53.9	417	46.1	163	18.0	905	187	59.2	129	40.8	42	13.3	316	35	17	52	4.0
JD Degrees Awarded	169	52.2	155	47.8	49	15.1	324	47	51.6	44	48.4	17	18.7	91				

GPA & LSAT Scores

	Full Time	Part Time	Total
# of apps	2,117	454	2,571
# admits	1,105	158	1,263
# of matrics	272	80	352
75% GPA	3.36	3.24	
25% GPA	2.88	2.70	
75% LSAT	156	157	
25% LSAT	151	152	

Tuition/Living Expenses

	Resident	Non-resident
Full-Time	$17,682	$17,682
Part-Time	$12,621	$12,621

Estimated living expenses for Singles		
Living on campus	Living off campus	Living at home
N/A	$15,075	N/A

Career Placement

	Total	%
Employment status known	364	94.6
Employment status unknown	21	5.5
Employed	330	90.7
Pursuing graduate degrees	2	0.6
Unemployed seeking employment	25	6.9
Unemployed not seeking employment	7	1.9
Type of Employment		
# employed in law firms	112	33.9
# employed in business & industry	44	13.3
# employed in government	34	10.3
# employed in public interest	2	0.6
# employed as judicial clerks	138	41.8
# employed in academia	0	0.0
Geographic Location		
# employed in state	243	73.6
# employed in foreign countries	0	0.0
# of states where employed	30	

Financial Aid

	Full-time		Part-time		Total	
	#	%	#	%	#	%
Total # receiving grants	473	52.3	237	75.0	710	58.1
Less than 1/2 tuition	463	51.2	233	73.7	696	57.0
Half to full tuition	10	1.1	4	1.3	14	1.1
Full tuition	0	0.0	0	0.0	0	0.0
More than full tuition	0	0.0	0	0.0	0	0.0
Median Grant Amount	$2,260		$1,850			

Refunds

Refunds of Admissions or Seat Deposit prior to commencement of classes? Yes

Refunds of Pre-paid tuition prior to commencement of classes? Yes

If yes, fully refundable before the start of classes? Yes

Joint Degrees Offered

MBA/JD

Advanced Degrees Offered

No Advanced Degrees

Bar Passage Rate

Jurisdiction	NJ	NY
# from school taking bar for the first time	304	157
School's pass rate for all first-time takers	78%	63%
State's pass rate for all first-time takers	78%	78%
State's pass rate for all first-time takers from ABA approved law schools	78%	

SOUTH CAROLINA, UNIVERSITY OF

Main and Greene Streets
Columbia, SC 29208
(803)777-6857
http://www.law.sc.edu

ABA Approved Since 1925

The Basics

Type of School: **PUBLIC**
Application deadline*: **2/15**
Application fee: **$25**
Financial Aid deadline*: **4/15**
Student faculty ratio: **19.7 to 1**
First year can start other than Fall: **No**
Student housing: **No**
--exclusively for law students: **No**
Term: **Semester**

*pr=preferred

Faculty

	Men		Women		Minorities		Total
	#	%	#	%	#	%	
Full-time	30	88	4	12	2	6	34
Other full-time	0	0	0	0	0	0	0
Deans, librarians, & others who teach	4	100	0	0	0	0	4
Part-time	11	92	1	8	0	0	12
Total	45	90	5	10	2	4	50
Deans, librarians, & others who teach < 1/2	0	0	0	0	0	0	0

Library

# of volumes & volume equivalents	383,179	# of professional staff	9
# of titles	66,650	Hours per week with professional staff	65
# of active serial subscriptions	2,925	Hours per week without professional staff	46
Study seating capacity inside the library	642	# of student computer work stations for entire law school	55
Square feet of law library	51,915	# of additional networked connections	40
Square feet of law school (excl. Library)	83,170		

Curriculum

	Full time	Part time
Typical first-year section size	85	0
Is there typically a "small section" of the first year class, other than Legal Writing, taught by full-time faculty?	No	No
If yes, typical size offered last year	N/A	N/A
# of classroom course titles beyond 1st year curriculum	91	0
# of upper division courses, excluding seminars, with an enrollment:		
Under 25	52	0
25 - 49	30	0
50 - 74	18	0
75 - 99	15	0
100 +	4	0
# of seminars	8	0
# of seminar positions available	160	
# of seminar positions filled	107	0
# of positions available in simulation courses	320	
# of simulation positions filled	257	0
# of positions available in faculty supervised clinical courses	50	
# of fac. sup. clin. positions filled	44	0
# involved in field placements	0	0
# involved in law journals	131	0
# in moot court or trial competitions	20	0
# of credit hours required to graduate	90	

Enrollment & Attrition

	Full-Time							Part-Time							Attrition			
	Men		Women		Minorities		Total	Men		Women		Minorities		Total	Academic	Other	Total	
	#	%	#	%	#	%	#	#	%	#	%	#	%	#	#	#	#	%
1st Year	150	60.2	99	39.8	22	8.8	249	0	0.0	0	0.0	0	0.0	0	5	8	13	5.2
2nd Year	155	59.4	106	40.6	24	9.2	261	0	0.0	0	0.0	0	0.0	0	0	4	4	1.7
3rd Year	146	60.3	96	39.7	33	13.6	242	0	0.0	0	0.0	0	0.0	0	0	0	0	0.0
4th Year								0	0.0	0	0.0	0	0.0	0	0	0	0	0.0
Total	451	60.0	301	40.0	79	10.5	752	0	0.0	0	0.0	0	0.0	0	5	12	17	2.2
JD Degrees Awarded	143	55.9	113	44.1	22	8.6	256	0	0.0	0	0.0	0	0.0	0				

GPA & LSAT Scores

	Full Time	Part Time	Total
# of apps	1,294	0	1,294
# admits	420	0	420
# of matrics	250	0	250
75% GPA	3.59	0.00	
25% GPA	2.98	0.00	
75% LSAT	160	0	
25% LSAT	154	0	

Tuition/Living Expenses

	Resident	Non-resident
Full-Time	$6,536	$12,896
Part-Time	$0	$0

Estimated living expenses for Singles		
Living on campus	Living off campus	Living at home
$3,714	$6,957	$5,643

Career Placement

	Total	%
Employment status known	233	95.5
Employment status unknown	11	4.5
Employed	206	88.4
Pursuing graduate degrees	8	3.4
Unemployed seeking employment	14	6.0
Unemployed not seeking employment	5	2.2
Type of Employment		
# employed in law firms	126	61.2
# employed in business & industry	9	4.4
# employed in government	26	12.6
# employed in public interest	0	0.0
# employed as judicial clerks	45	21.8
# employed in academia	1	0.5
Geographic Location		
# employed in state	187	90.8
# employed in foreign countries	0	0.0
# of states where employed	11	

Financial Aid

	Full-time		Part-time		Total	
	#	%	#	%	#	%
Total # receiving grants	271	36.0	0	0.0	271	36.0
Less than 1/2 tuition	251	33.4	0	0.0	251	33.4
Half to full tuition	6	0.8	0	0.0	6	0.8
Full tuition	6	0.8	0	0.0	6	0.8
More than full tuition	8	1.1	0	0.0	8	1.1
Median Grant Amount	$1,290		$0			

Refunds

Refunds of Admissions or Seat Deposit prior to commencement of classes? No

Refunds of Pre-paid tuition prior to commencement of classes? Yes

If yes, fully refundable before the start of classes? Yes

Joint Degrees Offered

MBA, MIBS, Crim. Just., Economics, Human Res.

Advanced Degrees Offered

No Advanced Degrees

Bar Passage Rate

Jurisdiction	SC
# from school taking bar for the first time	235
School's pass rate for all first-time takers	95%
State's pass rate for all first-time takers	92%
State's pass rate for all first-time takers from ABA approved law schools	81%

SOUTH DAKOTA, UNIVERSITY OF

414 E. Clark Street
Vermillion, SD 57069-2390
(605)677-5443
http://www.usd.edu/law

ABA Approved Since 1923

The Basics

Type of School: **PUBLIC**
Application deadline*: **3/1pr**
Application fee: **$15**
Financial Aid deadline*:
Student faculty ratio: **17.7 to 1**
First year can start other than Fall: **No**
Student housing: **No**
--exclusively for law students: **No**
Term: **Semester**

*pr=preferred

Faculty

	Men #	Men %	Women #	Women %	Minorities #	Minorities %	Total
Full-time	9	90	1	10	0	0	10
Other full-time	1	50	1	50	0	0	2
Deans, librarians, & others who teach	1	100	0	0	0	0	1
Part-time	3	100	0	0	0	0	3
Total	14	88	2	13	0	0	16
Deans, librarians, & others who teach < 1/2	1	50	1	50	0	0	2

Library

# of volumes & volume equivalents	176,950	# of professional staff	5
# of titles	35,429	Hours per week with professional staff	45
# of active serial subscriptions	1,282	Hours per week without professional staff	50
Study seating capacity inside the library	227	# of student computer work stations for entire law school	24
Square feet of law library	23,103	# of additional networked connections	12
Square feet of law school (excl. Library)	37,129		

Curriculum

	Full time	Part time
Typical first-year section size	75	0
Is there typically a "small section" of the first year class, other than Legal Writing, taught by full-time faculty?	Yes	No
If yes, typical size offered last year	37	N/A
# of classroom course titles beyond 1st year curriculum	42	0
# of upper division courses, excluding seminars, with an enrollment:		
Under 25	22	0
25 - 49	13	0
50 - 74	6	0
75 - 99	1	0
100 +	0	0
# of seminars	1	0
# of seminar positions available	18	
# of seminar positions filled	10	0
# of positions available in simulation courses	64	
# of simulation positions filled	64	0
# of positions available in faculty supervised clinical courses	0	
# of fac. sup. clin. positions filled	0	0
# involved in field placements	17	0
# involved in law journals	47	0
# in moot court or trial competitions	33	0
# of credit hours required to graduate	90	

Enrollment & Attrition

	Full-Time							Part-Time							Attrition			
	Men		Women		Minorities		Total	Men		Women		Minorities		Total	Academic	Other	Total	
	#	%	#	%	#	%	#	#	%	#	%	#	%	#	#	#	#	%
1st Year	49	67.1	24	32.9	8	11.0	73	0	0.0	0	0.0	0	0.0	0	2	8	10	13
2nd Year	41	63.1	24	36.9	1	1.5	65	0	0.0	0	0.0	0	0.0	0	0	0	0	0.0
3rd Year	48	64.0	27	36.0	2	2.7	75	0	0.0	0	0.0	0	0.0	0	1	0	1	1.4
4th Year								0	0.0	0	0.0	0	0.0	0	0	0	0	0.0
Total	138	64.8	75	35.2	11	5.2	213	0	0.0	0	0.0	0	0.0	0	3	8	11	4.9
JD Degrees Awarded	45	64.3	25	35.7	1	1.4	70	0	0.0	0	0.0	0	0.0	0				

GPA & LSAT Scores

	Full Time	Part Time	Total
# of apps	351	0	351
# admits	214	0	214
# of matrics	73	0	73
75% GPA	3.50	0.00	
25% GPA	2.80	0.00	
75% LSAT	154	0	
25% LSAT	149	0	

Tuition/Living Expenses

	Resident	Non-resident
Full-Time	$4,235	$8,743
Part-Time	$0	$0

Estimated living expenses for Singles		
Living on campus	Living off campus	Living at home
$5,709	$8,329	$4,866

Career Placement

	Total	%
Employment status known	65	100.0
Employment status unknown	0	0.0
Employed	59	90.8
Pursuing graduate degrees	1	1.5
Unemployed seeking employment	5	7.7
Unemployed not seeking employment	0	0.0
Type of Employment		
# employed in law firms	31	52.5
# employed in business & industry	7	11.9
# employed in government	6	10.2
# employed in public interest	0	0.0
# employed as judicial clerks	15	25.4
# employed in academia	0	0.0
Geographic Location		
# employed in state	40	67.8
# employed in foreign countries	0	0.0
# of states where employed	8	

Financial Aid

	Full-time		Part-time		Total	
	#	%	#	%	#	%
Total # receiving grants	90	42.3	0	0.0	90	42.3
Less than 1/2 tuition	109	51.2	0	0.0	109	51.2
Half to full tuition	4	1.9	0	0.0	4	1.9
Full tuition	6	2.8	0	0.0	6	2.8
More than full tuition	17	8.0	0	0.0	17	8.0
Median Grant Amount	$750		$0			

Refunds

Refunds of Admissions or Seat Deposit prior to commencement of classes? No

Refunds of Pre-paid tuition prior to commencement of classes? Yes

If yes, fully refundable before the start of classes? Yes

Joint Degrees Offered

MPAcc Acctg, MBA Bus Admn, MA Econ (Ag), MA Educ Admn, MA English, MA History, MA Pol Sci, MPA Pub Admn, MA Psych

Advanced Degrees Offered

No Advanced Degrees

Bar Passage Rate

Jurisdiction	SD
# from school taking bar for the first time	50
School's pass rate for all first-time takers	96%
State's pass rate for all first-time takers	91%
State's pass rate for all first-time takers from ABA approved law schools	91%

SOUTH TEXAS COLLEGE OF LAW

1303 San Jacinto
Houston, TX 77002-7000
(713)659-8040
http://www.stcl.edu

ABA Approved Since 1959

The Basics

Type of School: **PRIVATE**
Application deadline*: **3/1**
Application fee: **$40**
Financial Aid deadline*: **5/1**
Student faculty ratio: **21.3 to 1**
First year can start other than Fall: **Yes**
Student housing: **No**
--exclusively for law students: **No**
Term: **Semester**

*pr=preferred

Faculty

	Men #	Men %	Women #	Women %	Minorities #	Minorities %	Total
Full-time	34	77	10	23	5	11	44
Other full-time	0	0	0	0	0	0	0
Deans, librarians, & others who teach	1	50	1	50	0	0	2
Part-time	22	88	3	12	1	4	25
Total	57	80	14	20	6	8	71
Deans, librarians, & others who teach < 1/2	2	50	2	50	0	0	4

Library

# of volumes & volume equivalents	338,951	# of professional staff	12
# of titles	53,811	Hours per week with professional staff	83
# of active serial subscriptions	4,011	Hours per week without professional staff	20
Study seating capacity inside the library	594	# of student computer work stations for entire law school	66
Square feet of law library	43,767	# of additional networked connections	26
Square feet of law school (excl. Library)	101,984		

Curriculum

	Full time	Part time
Typical first-year section size	90	70
Is there typically a "small section" of the first year class, other than Legal Writing, taught by full-time faculty?	No	No
If yes, typical size offered last year	N/A	N/A
# of classroom course titles beyond 1st year curriculum	67	56
# of upper division courses, excluding seminars, with an enrollment:		
Under 25	12	20
25 - 49	21	20
50 - 74	21	9
75 - 99	13	7
100 +	0	0
# of seminars	4	16
# of seminar positions available	400	
# of seminar positions filled	77	271
# of positions available in simulation courses	840	
# of simulation positions filled	455	363
# of positions available in faculty supervised clinical courses	52	
# of fac. sup. clin. positions filled	39	10
# involved in field placements	107	27
# involved in law journals	142	36
# in moot court or trial competitions	78	20
# of credit hours required to graduate	90	

Enrollment & Attrition

	Full-Time Men #	Full-Time Men %	Full-Time Women #	Full-Time Women %	Full-Time Minorities #	Full-Time Minorities %	Full-Time Total #	Part-Time Men #	Part-Time Men %	Part-Time Women #	Part-Time Women %	Part-Time Minorities #	Part-Time Minorities %	Part-Time Total #	Attrition Academic #	Attrition Other #	Attrition Total #	Attrition Total %
1st Year	261	56.4	202	43.6	84	18.1	463	109	56.8	83	43.2	45	23.4	192	35	42	77	13
2nd Year	148	61.7	92	38.3	48	20.0	240	48	54.5	40	45.5	17	19.3	88	6	0	6	1.8
3rd Year	77	57.0	58	43.0	31	23.0	135	45	67.2	22	32.8	16	23.9	67	2	1	3	1.1
4th Year								21	65.6	11	34.4	9	28.1	32	0	0	0	0.0
Total	486	58.0	352	42.0	163	19.5	838	223	58.8	156	41.2	87	23.0	379	43	43	86	6.9
JD Degrees Awarded	114	55.3	92	44.7	30	14.6	206	163	79.9	41	20.1	44	21.6	204				

GPA & LSAT Scores

	Full Time	Part Time	Total
# of apps	1,429	613	2,042
# admits	818	350	1,168
# of matrics	361	131	492
75% GPA	3.21	3.25	
25% GPA	2.69	2.66	
75% LSAT	154	155	
25% LSAT	148	148	

Tuition/Living Expenses

	Resident	Non-resident
Full-Time	$14,355	$14,355
Part-Time	$9,619	$9,619

Estimated living expenses for Singles		
Living on campus	Living off campus	Living at home
N/A	$11,708	$8,154

Career Placement

	Total	%
Employment status known	383	94.3
Employment status unknown	23	5.7
Employed	304	79.4
Pursuing graduate degrees	2	0.5
Unemployed seeking employment	75	19.6
Unemployed not seeking employment	2	0.5
Type of Employment		
# employed in law firms	192	63.2
# employed in business & industry	71	23.4
# employed in government	28	9.2
# employed in public interest	0	0.0
# employed as judicial clerks	11	3.6
# employed in academia	2	0.7
Geographic Location		
# employed in state	287	94.4
# employed in foreign countries	1	0.3
# of states where employed	12	

Financial Aid

	Full-time		Part-time		Total	
	#	%	#	%	#	%
Total # receiving grants	335	40.0	112	29.6	447	36.7
Less than 1/2 tuition	323	38.5	106	28.0	429	35.3
Half to full tuition	11	1.3	4	1.1	15	1.2
Full tuition	0	0.0	0	0.0	0	0.0
More than full tuition	1	0.1	2	0.5	3	0.2
Median Grant Amount	$1,830		$1,375			

Refunds

Refunds of Admissions or Seat Deposit prior to commencement of classes? No

Refunds of Pre-paid tuition prior to commencement of classes? Yes

If yes, fully refundable before the start of classes? Yes

Joint Degrees Offered

No Joint Degrees

Advanced Degrees Offered

No Advanced Degrees

Bar Passage Rate

Jurisdiction	TX
# from school taking bar for the first time	334
School's pass rate for all first-time takers	78%
State's pass rate for all first-time takers	82%
State's pass rate for all first-time takers from ABA approved law schools	82%

SOUTHERN CALIFORNIA, UNIVERSITY OF

University Park
699 Exposition Boulevard
Los Angeles, CA 90089-0071
(213)740-7331
http://www.usc.edu/dept/law-lib

ABA Approved Since 1924

The Basics

Type of School: **PRIVATE**
Application deadline*: **2/1**
Application fee: **$60**
Financial Aid deadline*: **2/15**
Student faculty ratio: **14.9 to 1**

First year can start other than Fall: **No**
Student housing: **Yes**
--exclusively for law students: **Yes**
Term: **Semester**

*pr=preferred

Faculty

	Men		Women		Minorities		Total
	#	%	#	%	#	%	
Full-time	26	74	9	26	3	9	35
Other full-time	0	0	2	100	0	0	2
Deans, librarians, & others who teach	3	100	0	0	0	0	3
Part-time	16	94	1	6	1	6	17
Total	45	79	12	21	4	7	57
Deans, librarians, & others who teach < 1/2	4	57	3	43	0	0	7

Library

# of volumes & volume equivalents	344,741	# of professional staff	8
# of titles	146,819	Hours per week with professional staff	52
# of active serial subscriptions	4,091	Hours per week without professional staff	49
Study seating capacity inside the library	294	# of student computer work stations for entire law school	81
Square feet of law library	40,000	# of additional networked connections	68
Square feet of law school (excl. Library)	52,490		

Curriculum

	Full time	Part time
Typical first-year section size	70	0
Is there typically a "small section" of the first year class, other than Legal Writing, taught by full-time faculty?	No	No
If yes, typical size offered last year	N/A	N/A
# of classroom course titles beyond 1st year curriculum	89	0
# of upper division courses, excluding seminars, with an enrollment:		
Under 25	40	0
25 - 49	24	0
50 - 74	7	0
75 - 99	7	0
100 +	5	0
# of seminars	5	0
# of seminar positions available	124	
# of seminar positions filled	118	0
# of positions available in simulation courses	152	
# of simulation positions filled	134	0
# of positions available in faculty supervised clinical courses	41	
# of fac. sup. clin. positions filled	36	0
# involved in field placements	101	0
# involved in law journals	130	0
# in moot court or trial competitions	57	0
# of credit hours required to graduate	88	

Enrollment & Attrition

	Full-Time							Part-Time							Attrition			
	Men		Women		Minorities		Total	Men		Women		Minorities		Total	Academic	Other	Total	
	#	%	#	%	#	%	#	#	%	#	%	#	%	#	#	#	#	%
1st Year	107	52.2	98	47.8	77	37.6	205	0	0.0	0	0.0	0	0.0	0	0	12	12	5.5
2nd Year	131	61.2	83	38.8	91	42.5	214	0	0.0	0	0.0	0	0.0	0	0	3	3	1.4
3rd Year	118	57.0	89	43.0	71	34.3	207	0	0.0	0	0.0	0	0.0	0	0	0	0	0.0
4th Year								0	0.0	0	0.0	0	0.0	0	0	0	0	0.0
Total	356	56.9	270	43.1	239	38.2	626	0	0.0	0	0.0	0	0.0	0	0	15	15	2.4
JD Degrees Awarded	128	59.5	87	40.5	75	34.9	215	0	0.0	0	0.0	0	0.0	0				

SOUTHERN CALIFORNIA, UNIVERSITY OF

GPA & LSAT Scores

	Full Time	Part Time	Total
# of apps	3,674	0	3,674
# admits	854	0	854
# of matrics	205	0	205
75% GPA	3.58	0.00	
25% GPA	3.22	0.00	
75% LSAT	166	0	
25% LSAT	162	0	

Tuition/Living Expenses

	Resident	Non-resident
Full-Time	$22,620	$22,620
Part-Time	$0	$0

Estimated living expenses for Singles		
Living on campus	Living off campus	Living at home
$10,978	$12,024	$5,984

Financial Aid

	Full-time		Part-time		Total	
	#	%	#	%	#	%
Total # receiving grants	297	47.4	0	0.0	297	47.4
Less than 1/2 tuition	174	27.8	0	0.0	174	27.8
Half to full tuition	96	15.3	0	0.0	96	15.3
Full tuition	24	3.8	0	0.0	24	3.8
More than full tuition	3	0.5	0	0.0	3	0.5
Median Grant Amount	$10,000		$0			

Refunds

Refunds of Admissions or Seat Deposit prior to commencement of classes? Yes

40% refund from 06/01/96 to 07/01/96

Refunds of Pre-paid tuition prior to commencement of classes? Yes

If yes, fully refundable before the start of classes? Yes

Joint Degrees Offered

JD/MA ECON, JD/MA IR, JD/MPA, JD/MA REL, JD/MSW, JD/MBA, JD/MBT, JD/MA COMM, JD/MRED, JD/MA PHIL, JD/PhD ECON

Advanced Degrees Offered

No Advanced Degrees

Career Placement

	Total	%
Employment status known	193	95.1
Employment status unknown	10	4.9
Employed	188	97.4
Pursuing graduate degrees	0	0.0
Unemployed seeking employment	4	2.1
Unemployed not seeking employment	1	0.5
Type of Employment		
# employed in law firms	147	78.2
# employed in business & industry	2	1.1
# employed in government	8	4.3
# employed in public interest	8	4.3
# employed as judicial clerks	21	11.2
# employed in academia	2	1.1
Geographic Location		
# employed in state	155	82.5
# employed in foreign countries	0	0.0
# of states where employed	11	

Bar Passage Rate

Jurisdiction	CA
# from school taking bar for the first time	170
School's pass rate for all first-time takers	84%
State's pass rate for all first-time takers	73%
State's pass rate for all first-time takers from ABA approved law schools	83%

SOUTHERN ILLINOIS UNIVERSITY-CARBONDALE

Lesar Law Building
Carbondale, IL 62901-6804
(618)536-7711
http://www.siu.edu/~lawsch

ABA Approved Since 1974

The Basics

Type of School: **PUBLIC**
Application deadline*: **3/1**
Application fee: **$25**
Financial Aid deadline*: **3/15**
Student faculty ratio: **13.0 to 1**
First year can start other than Fall: **No**
Student housing: **No**
--exclusively for law students: **Yes**
Term: **Semester**

*pr=preferred

Faculty

	Men		Women		Minorities		Total
	#	%	#	%	#	%	
Full-time	17	71	7	29	2	8	24
Other full-time	0	0	0	0	0	0	0
Deans, librarians, & others who teach	4	57	3	43	0	0	7
Part-time	1	33	2	67	0	0	3
Total	22	65	12	35	2	6	34
Deans, librarians, & others who teach < 1/2	1	50	1	50	0	0	2

Library

# of volumes & volume equivalents	328,784	# of professional staff	7
# of titles	64,563	Hours per week with professional staff	52
# of active serial subscriptions	4,711	Hours per week without professional staff	34
Study seating capacity inside the library	364	# of student computer work stations for entire law school	49
Square feet of law library	34,613	# of additional networked connections	0
Square feet of law school (excl. Library)	36,833		

Curriculum

	Full time	Part time
Typical first-year section size	63	0
Is there typically a "small section" of the first year class, other than Legal Writing, taught by full-time faculty?	No	No
If yes, typical size offered last year	N/A	N/A
# of classroom course titles beyond 1st year curriculum	51	0
# of upper division courses, excluding seminars, with an enrollment:		
Under 25	26	0
25 - 49	18	0
50 - 74	18	0
75 - 99	0	0
100 +	0	0
# of seminars	8	0
# of seminar positions available	93	
# of seminar positions filled	81	0
# of positions available in simulation courses	284	
# of simulation positions filled	244	0
# of positions available in faculty supervised clinical courses	72	
# of fac. sup. clin. positions filled	34	0
# involved in field placements	46	0
# involved in law journals	60	0
# in moot court or trial competitions	48	0
# of credit hours required to graduate	90	

Enrollment & Attrition

	Full-Time							Part-Time							Attrition			
	Men		Women		Minorities		Total	Men		Women		Minorities		Total	Academic	Other	Total	
	#	%	#	%	#	%	#	#	%	#	%	#	%	#	#	#	#	%
1st Year	70	57.9	51	42.1	25	20.7	121	0	0.0	0	0.0	0	0.0	0	2	11	13	10
2nd Year	69	57.5	51	42.5	21	17.5	120	0	0.0	0	0.0	0	0.0	0	0	1	1	0.9
3rd Year	68	58.1	49	41.9	17	14.5	117	0	0.0	0	0.0	0	0.0	0	0	0	0	0.0
4th Year								0	0.0	0	0.0	0	0.0	0	0	0	0	0.0
Total	207	57.8	151	42.2	63	17.6	358	0	0.0	0	0.0	0	0.0	0	2	12	14	4.0
JD Degrees Awarded	66	60.6	43	39.4	11	10.1	109	0	0.0	0	0.0	0	0.0	0				

SOUTHERN ILLINOIS UNIVERSITY-CARBONDALE

GPA & LSAT Scores

	Full Time	Part Time	Total
# of apps	740	0	740
# admits	365	0	365
# of matrics	125	0	125
75% GPA	3.57	0.00	
25% GPA	2.63	0.00	
75% LSAT	159	0	
25% LSAT	147	0	

Tuition/Living Expenses

	Resident	Non-resident
Full-Time	$4,970	$12,978
Part-Time	$0	$0

Estimated living expenses for Singles		
Living on campus	Living off campus	Living at home
$8,040	$8,040	$4,220

Career Placement

	Total	%
Employment status known	92	86.0
Employment status unknown	15	14.0
Employed	82	89.1
Pursuing graduate degrees	2	2.2
Unemployed seeking employment	7	7.6
Unemployed not seeking employment	1	1.1
Type of Employment		
# employed in law firms	56	68.3
# employed in business & industry	8	9.8
# employed in government	15	18.3
# employed in public interest	0	0.0
# employed as judicial clerks	3	3.7
# employed in academia	0	0.0
Geographic Location		
# employed in state	61	74.4
# employed in foreign countries	11	13.4
# of states where employed	11	

Financial Aid

	Full-time		Part-time		Total	
	#	%	#	%	#	%
Total # receiving grants	131	36.6	0	0.0	131	36.6
Less than 1/2 tuition	49	13.7	0	0.0	49	13.7
Half to full tuition	23	6.4	0	0.0	23	6.4
Full tuition	1	0.3	0	0.0	1	0.3
More than full tuition	58	16.2	0	0.0	58	16.2
Median Grant Amount	$3,320		$0			

Refunds

Refunds of Admissions or Seat Deposit prior to commencement of classes? No

Refunds of Pre-paid tuition prior to commencement of classes? Yes

If yes, fully refundable before the start of classes? Yes

80% refund from 09/09/96 to 09/15/96
70% refund from 09/16/96 to 09/22/96
60% refund from 09/23/96 to 09/29/96

Joint Degrees Offered

JD/MBA, JD/MACC, JD/MPA, JD/MD

Advanced Degrees Offered

No Advanced Degrees

Bar Passage Rate

Jurisdiction	IL
# from school taking bar for the first time	70
School's pass rate for all first-time takers	81%
State's pass rate for all first-time takers	87%
State's pass rate for all first-time takers from ABA approved law schools	87%

SOUTHERN METHODIST UNIVERSITY

P.O. Box 750116
Dallas, TX 75275-0116
(214)768-2080
http://www.smu.edu/~law

ABA Approved Since 1927

The Basics

Type of School: **PRIVATE**
Application deadline*: **4/1**
Application fee: **$45**
Financial Aid deadline*: **5/1**
Student faculty ratio: **20.8 to 1**
First year can start other than Fall: **No**
Student housing: **Yes**
--exclusively for law students: **No**
Term: **Semester**

*pr=preferred

Faculty

	Men #	Men %	Women #	Women %	Minorities #	Minorities %	Total
Full-time	24	77	7	23	4	13	31
Other full-time	0	0	0	0	0	0	0
Deans, librarians, & others who teach	2	67	1	33	0	0	3
Part-time	44	76	14	24	4	7	58
Total	70	76	22	24	8	9	92
Deans, librarians, & others who teach < 1/2	0	0	1	100	0	0	1

Library

# of volumes & volume equivalents	478,378	# of professional staff	10
# of titles	143,842	Hours per week with professional staff	62
# of active serial subscriptions	5,052	Hours per week without professional staff	35
Study seating capacity inside the library	700	# of student computer work stations for entire law school	89
Square feet of law library	100,000	# of additional networked connections	13
Square feet of law school (excl. Library)	13,586		

Curriculum

	Full time	Part time
Typical first-year section size	85	0
Is there typically a "small section" of the first year class, other than Legal Writing, taught by full-time faculty?	Yes	No
If yes, typical size offered last year	18	N/A
# of classroom course titles beyond 1st year curriculum	114	0
# of upper division courses, excluding seminars, with an enrollment:		
Under 25	17	0
25 - 49	16	0
50 - 74	15	0
75 - 99	5	0
100 +	1	0
# of seminars	9	0
# of seminar positions available	180	
# of seminar positions filled	175	0
# of positions available in simulation courses	394	
# of simulation positions filled	393	0
# of positions available in faculty supervised clinical courses	44	
# of fac. sup. clin. positions filled	44	0
# involved in field placements	36	0
# involved in law journals	142	0
# in moot court or trial competitions	95	0
# of credit hours required to graduate	90	

Enrollment & Attrition

	Full-Time Men #	Men %	Women #	Women %	Minorities #	Minorities %	Total #	Part-Time Men #	Men %	Women #	Women %	Minorities #	Minorities %	Total #	Attrition Academic #	Other #	Total #	%
1st Year	150	54.7	124	45.3	73	26.6	274	2	40.0	3	60.0	1	20.0	5	0	0	0	0.0
2nd Year	136	53.1	120	46.9	56	21.9	256	5	83.3	1	16.7	0	0.0	6	0	0	0	0.0
3rd Year	134	57.8	98	42.2	45	19.4	232	5	71.4	2	28.6	4	57.1	7	0	0	0	0.0
4th Year								0	0.0	0	0.0	0	0.0	0	0	0	0	0.0
Total	420	55.1	342	44.9	174	22.8	762	12	66.7	6	33.3	5	27.8	18	0	0	0	0.0
JD Degrees Awarded	149	56.4	115	43.6	62	23.5	264	0	0.0	0	0.0	0	0.0	0				

GPA & LSAT Scores

	Full Time	Part Time	Total
# of apps	1,750	50	1,800
# admits	720	6	726
# of matrics	255	6	261
75% GPA	3.47	3.15	
25% GPA	2.85	2.91	
75% LSAT	159	158	
25% LSAT	154	154	

Tuition/Living Expenses

	Resident	Non-resident
Full-Time	$19,804	$19,804
Part-Time	$0	$0

Estimated living expenses for Singles		
Living on campus	Living off campus	Living at home
$10,536	$9,000	$4,500

Career Placement

	Total	%
Employment status known	197	90.4
Employment status unknown	21	9.6
Employed	158	80.2
Pursuing graduate degrees	5	2.5
Unemployed seeking employment	33	16.8
Unemployed not seeking employment	1	0.5
Type of Employment		
# employed in law firms	142	89.9
# employed in business & industry	30	19.0
# employed in government	12	7.6
# employed in public interest	0	0.0
# employed as judicial clerks	13	8.2
# employed in academia	0	0.0
Geographic Location		
# employed in state	110	69.6
# employed in foreign countries	0	0.0
# of states where employed	26	

Financial Aid

	Full-time		Part-time		Total	
	#	%	#	%	#	%
Total # receiving grants	214	28.1	0	0.0	214	27.4
Less than 1/2 tuition	91	11.9	0	0.0	91	11.7
Half to full tuition	103	13.5	0	0.0	103	13.2
Full tuition	0	0.0	0	0.0	0	0.0
More than full tuition	20	2.6	0	0.0	20	2.6
Median Grant Amount	$9,450		$0			

Refunds

Refunds of Admissions or Seat Deposit prior to commencement of classes? No

Refunds of Pre-paid tuition prior to commencement of classes? Yes

If yes, fully refundable before the start of classes? No

Joint Degrees Offered

JD/MBA, JD/MA

Advanced Degrees Offered

LL.M	General
LL.M	Comparative & International Law
S.J.D.	Doctor of Science of Law
LL.M	Taxation

Bar Passage Rate

Jurisdiction	TX
# from school taking bar for the first time	180
School's pass rate for all first-time takers	84%
State's pass rate for all first-time takers	82%
State's pass rate for all first-time takers from ABA approved law schools	82%

SOUTHERN UNIVERSITY

P. O. Box 9294
Baton Rouge, LA 70813
(504)771-2552
website is currently under construction

ABA Approved Since 1953

The Basics

Type of School: **PUBLIC**
Application deadline*: **3/31**
Application fee: **$0**
Financial Aid deadline*: **4/15**
Student faculty ratio: **13.1 to 1**

First year can start other than Fall: **No**
Student housing: **No**
--exclusively for law students: **No**
Term: **Semester**

*pr=preferred

Faculty

	Men		Women		Minorities		Total
	#	%	#	%	#	%	
Full-time	16	70	7	30	14	61	23
Other full-time	0	0	0	0	0	0	0
Deans, librarians, & others who teach	2	100	0	0	2	100	2
Part-time	7	88	1	13	7	88	8
Total	25	76	8	24	23	70	33
Deans, librarians, & others who teach < 1/2	0	0	0	0	0	0	0

Library

# of volumes & volume equivalents	378,926	# of professional staff	6
# of titles	54,281	Hours per week with professional staff	82
# of active serial subscriptions	4,351	Hours per week without professional staff	12
Study seating capacity inside the library	284	# of student computer work stations for entire law school	52
Square feet of law library	28,830	# of additional networked connections	15
Square feet of law school (excl. Library)	50,878		

Curriculum

	Full time	Part time
Typical first-year section size	41	0
Is there typically a "small section" of the first year class, other than Legal Writing, taught by full-time faculty?	No	No
If yes, typical size offered last year	N/A	N/A
# of classroom course titles beyond 1st year curriculum	57	0
# of upper division courses, excluding seminars, with an enrollment:		
Under 25	17	0
25 - 49	10	0
50 - 74	4	0
75 - 99	7	0
100 +	8	0
# of seminars	11	0
# of seminar positions available	250	
# of seminar positions filled	183	0
# of positions available in simulation courses	160	
# of simulation positions filled	125	0
# of positions available in faculty supervised clinical courses	66	
# of fac. sup. clin. positions filled	55	0
# involved in field placements	11	0
# involved in law journals	25	0
# in moot court or trial competitions	55	0
# of credit hours required to graduate	96	

Enrollment & Attrition

	Full-Time							Part-Time							Attrition			
	Men		Women		Minorities		Total	Men		Women		Minorities		Total	Academic	Other	Total	
	#	%	#	%	#	%	#	#	%	#	%	#	%	#	#	#	#	%
1st Year	58	47.9	63	52.1	76	62.8	121	0	0.0	0	0.0	0	0.0	0	0	4	4	3.2
2nd Year	60	54.1	51	45.9	77	69.4	111	0	0.0	0	0.0	0	0.0	0	5	7	12	11
3rd Year	60	58.3	43	41.7	67	65.0	103	0	0.0	0	0.0	0	0.0	0	0	1	1	1.1
4th Year								0	0.0	0	0.0	0	0.0	0	0	0	0	0.0
Total	178	53.1	157	46.9	220	65.7	335	0	0.0	0	0.0	0	0.0	0	5	12	17	5.2
JD Degrees Awarded	52	56.5	40	43.5	55	59.8	92	0	0.0	0	0.0	0	0.0	0				

GPA & LSAT Scores

	Full Time	Part Time	Total
# of apps	1,122	0	1,122
# admits	198	0	198
# of matrics	125	0	125
75% GPA	2.99	0.00	
25% GPA	2.43	0.00	
75% LSAT	147	0	
25% LSAT	143	0	

Tuition/Living Expenses

	Resident	Non-resident
Full-Time	$3,088	$6,288
Part-Time	$0	$0

Estimated living expenses for Singles		
Living on campus	Living off campus	Living at home
$9,544	$9,544	$9,544

Career Placement

	Total	%
Employment status known	91	95.8
Employment status unknown	4	4.2
Employed	71	78.0
Pursuing graduate degrees	16	17.6
Unemployed seeking employment	4	4.4
Unemployed not seeking employment	0	0.0
Type of Employment		
# employed in law firms	37	52.1
# employed in business & industry	2	2.8
# employed in government	24	33.8
# employed in public interest	0	0.0
# employed as judicial clerks	10	14.1
# employed in academia	18	25.4
Geographic Location		
# employed in state	75	105.6
# employed in foreign countries	0	0.0
# of states where employed	4	

Financial Aid

	Full-time		Part-time		Total	
	#	%	#	%	#	%
Total # receiving grants	64	19.1	0	0.0	64	19.1
Less than 1/2 tuition	0	0.0	0	0.0	0	0.0
Half to full tuition	9	2.7	0	0.0	9	2.7
Full tuition	6	1.8	0	0.0	6	1.8
More than full tuition	49	14.6	0	0.0	49	14.6
Median Grant Amount	$3,330		$0			

Refunds

Refunds of Admissions or Seat Deposit prior to commencement of classes? No

Refunds of Pre-paid tuition prior to commencement of classes? No

If yes, fully refundable before the start of classes? No

Joint Degrees Offered

No Joint Degrees

Advanced Degrees Offered

No Advanced Degrees

Bar Passage Rate

Jurisdiction	LA
# from school taking bar for the first time	87
School's pass rate for all first-time takers	31%
State's pass rate for all first-time takers	55%
State's pass rate for all first-time takers from ABA approved law schools	67%

SOUTHWESTERN UNIVERSITY

675 South Westmoreland Avenue
Los Angeles, CA 90005-3992
(213)738-6717
http://www.swlaw.edu

ABA Approved Since 1970

The Basics

Type of School: **PRIVATE**
Application deadline*: **6/30**
Application fee: **$50**
Financial Aid deadline*: **6/1**
Student faculty ratio: **21.7 to 1**

First year can start other than Fall: **No**
Student housing: **No**
--exclusively for law students: **No**
Term: **Semester**

*pr=preferred

Faculty

	Men #	Men %	Women #	Women %	Minorities #	Minorities %	Total
Full-time	29	73	11	28	6	15	40
Other full-time	1	33	2	67	1	33	3
Deans, librarians, & others who teach	0	0	2	100	0	0	2
Part-time	19	79	5	21	7	29	24
Total	**49**	**71**	**20**	**29**	**14**	**20**	**69**
Deans, librarians, & others who teach < 1/2	1	100	0	0	0	0	1

Library

# of volumes & volume equivalents	372,950	# of professional staff	9
# of titles	99,963	Hours per week with professional staff	86
# of active serial subscriptions	4,902	Hours per week without professional staff	21
Study seating capacity inside the library	610	# of student computer work stations for entire law school	85
Square feet of law library	80,000	# of additional networked connections	120
Square feet of law school (excl. Library)	79,638		

Curriculum

	Full time	Part time
Typical first-year section size	87	95
Is there typically a "small section" of the first year class, other than Legal Writing, taught by full-time faculty?	No	No
If yes, typical size offered last year	N/A	N/A
# of classroom course titles beyond 1st year curriculum	89	48
# of upper division courses, excluding seminars, with an enrollment:		
Under 25	16	18
25 - 49	21	10
50 - 74	8	12
75 - 99	7	3
100 +	9	2
# of seminars	18	7
# of seminar positions available	440	
# of seminar positions filled	170	81
# of positions available in simulation courses	520	
# of simulation positions filled	349	99
# of positions available in faculty supervised clinical courses	0	
# of fac. sup. clin. positions filled	0	0
# involved in field placements	258	45
# involved in law journals	84	9
# in moot court or trial competitions	63	14
# of credit hours required to graduate	87	

Enrollment & Attrition

	Full-Time							Part-Time							Attrition			
	Men		Women		Minorities		Total	Men		Women		Minorities		Total	Academic	Other	Total	
	#	%	#	%	#	%	#	#	%	#	%	#	%	#	#	#	#	%
1st Year	147	50.2	146	49.8	111	37.9	293	53	51.5	50	48.5	40	38.8	103	43	35	78	18
2nd Year	104	49.8	105	50.2	64	30.6	209	57	54.8	47	45.2	41	39.4	104	7	2	9	2.4
3rd Year	143	47.0	161	53.0	78	25.7	304	41	51.3	39	48.8	25	31.3	80	0	2	2	0.6
4th Year								39	58.2	28	41.8	21	31.3	67	0	0	0	0.0
Total	394	48.9	412	51.1	253	31.4	806	190	53.7	164	46.3	127	35.9	354	50	39	89	7.4
JD Degrees Awarded	131	51.4	124	48.6	62	24.3	255	43	51.2	41	48.8	25	29.8	84				

GPA & LSAT Scores

	Full Time	Part Time	Total
# of apps	2,252	436	2,688
# admits	1,200	213	1,413
# of matrics	296	104	400
75% GPA	3.27	3.25	
25% GPA	2.72	2.69	
75% LSAT	154	153	
25% LSAT	150	150	

Tuition/Living Expenses

	Resident	Non-resident
Full-Time	$19,120	$19,120
Part-Time	$12,146	$12,146

Estimated living expenses for Singles		
Living on campus	Living off campus	Living at home
N/A	$13,230	$4,770

Career Placement

	Total	%
Employment status known	324	96.7
Employment status unknown	11	3.3
Employed	280	86.4
Pursuing graduate degrees	1	0.3
Unemployed seeking employment	20	6.2
Unemployed not seeking employment	23	7.1
Type of Employment		
# employed in law firms	167	59.6
# employed in business & industry	78	27.9
# employed in government	23	8.2
# employed in public interest	2	0.7
# employed as judicial clerks	8	2.9
# employed in academia	2	0.7
Geographic Location		
# employed in state	254	90.7
# employed in foreign countries	4	1.4
# of states where employed	17	

Financial Aid

	Full-time		Part-time		Total	
	#	%	#	%	#	%
Total # receiving grants	69	8.6	38	10.7	107	9.2
Less than 1/2 tuition	22	2.7	8	2.3	30	2.6
Half to full tuition	32	4.0	23	6.5	55	4.7
Full tuition	15	1.9	7	2.0	22	1.9
More than full tuition	0	0.0	0	0.0	0	0.0
Median Grant Amount	$5,980		$6,110			

Refunds

Refunds of Admissions or Seat Deposit prior to commencement of classes? Yes

20% refund from 01/01/96 to 07/01/96

Refunds of Pre-paid tuition prior to commencement of classes? Yes

If yes, fully refundable before the start of classes? Yes

Joint Degrees Offered

No Joint Degrees

Advanced Degrees Offered

No Advanced Degrees

Bar Passage Rate

Jurisdiction	CA	NY
# from school taking bar for the first time	270	8
School's pass rate for all first-time takers	80%	88%
State's pass rate for all first-time takers	73%	78%
State's pass rate for all first-time takers from ABA approved law schools	83%	

ST. JOHN'S UNIVERSITY

8000 Utopia Parkway
Jamaica, NY 11439
(718)990-6600
http://www.stjohns.edu/law

ABA Approved Since 1937

The Basics

Type of School: **PRIVATE**
Application deadline*: **3/1**
Application fee: **$50**
Financial Aid deadline*: **4/1**
Student faculty ratio: **18.0 to 1**
First year can start other than Fall: **Yes**
Student housing: **No**
--exclusively for law students: **No**
Term: **Semester**

*pr=preferred

Faculty

	Men		Women		Minorities		Total
	#	%	#	%	#	%	
Full-time	34	71	14	29	9	19	48
Other full-time	2	40	3	60	0	0	5
Deans, librarians, & others who teach	1	33	2	67	0	0	3
Part-time	20	95	1	5	6	29	21
Total	57	74	20	26	15	19	77
Deans, librarians, & others who teach < 1/2	3	100	0	0	0	0	3

Library

# of volumes & volume equivalents	452,167	# of professional staff	7
# of titles	320,013	Hours per week with professional staff	77
# of active serial subscriptions	5,477	Hours per week without professional staff	34
Study seating capacity inside the library	607	# of student computer work stations for entire law school	60
Square feet of law library	56,000	# of additional networked connections	60
Square feet of law school (excl. Library)	96,100		

Curriculum

	Full time	Part time
Typical first-year section size	67	63
Is there typically a "small section" of the first year class, other than Legal Writing, taught by full-time faculty?	No	No
If yes, typical size offered last year	N/A	N/A
# of classroom course titles beyond 1st year curriculum	77	55
# of upper division courses, excluding seminars, with an enrollment:		
Under 25	46	28
25 - 49	37	14
50 - 74	18	7
75 - 99	20	12
100 +	9	7
# of seminars	5	9
# of seminar positions available	441	
# of seminar positions filled	100	203
# of positions available in simulation courses	771	
# of simulation positions filled	280	235
# of positions available in faculty supervised clinical courses	664	
# of fac. sup. clin. positions filled	386	0
# involved in field placements	369	0
# involved in law journals	161	13
# in moot court or trial competitions	442	60
# of credit hours required to graduate	85	

Enrollment & Attrition

	Full-Time							Part-Time							Attrition			
	Men		Women		Minorities		Total	Men		Women		Minorities		Total	Academic	Other	Total	
	#	%	#	%	#	%	#	#	%	#	%	#	%	#	#	#	#	%
1st Year	178	62.0	109	38.0	65	22.6	287	47	62.7	28	37.3	18	24.0	75	5	27	32	12
2nd Year	138	58.2	99	41.8	70	29.5	237	40	69.0	18	31.0	19	32.8	58	1	13	14	3.3
3rd Year	198	60.4	130	39.6	87	26.5	328	58	75.3	19	24.7	21	27.3	77	0	1	1	0.3
4th Year								51	70.8	21	29.2	13	18.1	72	0	0	0	0.0
Total	514	60.3	338	39.7	222	26.1	852	196	69.5	86	30.5	71	25.2	282	6	41	47	4.2
JD Degrees Awarded	166	59.5	113	40.5	36	12.9	279	46	61.3	29	38.7	23	30.7	75				

GPA & LSAT Scores

	Full Time	Part Time	Total
# of apps	2,026	446	2,472
# admits	1,033	180	1,213
# of matrics	348	77	425
75% GPA	3.34	3.09	
25% GPA	2.71	2.64	
75% LSAT	157	156	
25% LSAT	152	151	

Tuition/Living Expenses

	Resident	Non-resident
Full-Time	$20,000	$20,000
Part-Time	$15,000	$15,000

Estimated living expenses for Singles		
Living on campus	Living off campus	Living at home
N/A	$12,000	$6,500

Financial Aid

	Full-time		Part-time		Total	
	#	%	#	%	#	%
Total # receiving grants	265	31.1	67	23.8	332	29.3
Less than 1/2 tuition	194	22.8	49	17.4	243	21.4
Half to full tuition	10	1.2	4	1.4	14	1.2
Full tuition	36	4.2	10	3.6	46	4.1
More than full tuition	25	2.9	4	1.4	29	2.6
Median Grant Amount	$4,500		$4,000			

Refunds

Refunds of Admissions or Seat Deposit prior to commencement of classes? Yes

73% refund from 01/01/95 to 06/01/96

Refunds of Pre-paid tuition prior to commencement of classes? Yes

If yes, fully refundable before the start of classes? Yes

Joint Degrees Offered

M.A./J.D., M.B.A./J.D.

Advanced Degrees Offered

No Advanced Degrees

Career Placement

	Total	%
Employment status known	336	89.6
Employment status unknown	39	10.4
Employed	274	81.6
Pursuing graduate degrees	3	0.9
Unemployed seeking employment	51	15.2
Unemployed not seeking employment	8	2.4
Type of Employment		
# employed in law firms	158	57.7
# employed in business & industry	38	13.9
# employed in government	61	22.3
# employed in public interest	0	0.0
# employed as judicial clerks	17	6.2
# employed in academia	0	0.0
Geographic Location		
# employed in state	241	88.0
# employed in foreign countries	4	1.5
# of states where employed	12	

Bar Passage Rate

Jurisdiction	NY
# from school taking bar for the first time	356
School's pass rate for all first-time takers	85%
State's pass rate for all first-time takers	78%
State's pass rate for all first-time takers from ABA approved law schools	

ST. LOUIS UNIVERSITY

3700 Lindell Blvd.
St. Louis, MO 63108
(314)977-2766
http://lawlib.slu.edu

ABA Approved Since 1924

The Basics

Type of School: **PRIVATE**
Application deadline*: **rolling**
Application fee: **$40**
Financial Aid deadline*: **rolling**
Student faculty ratio: **20.1 to 1**

First year can start other than Fall: **No**
Student housing: **No**
--exclusively for law students: **No**
Term: **Semester**

***pr=preferred**

Faculty

	Men		Women		Minorities		Total
	#	%	#	%	#	%	
Full-time	23	77	7	23	2	7	30
Other full-time	4	57	3	43	0	0	7
Deans, librarians, & others who teach	1	100	0	0	0	0	1
Part-time	16	89	2	11	0	0	18
Total	44	79	12	21	2	4	56
Deans, librarians, & others who teach < 1/2	1	100	0	0	0	0	1

Library

# of volumes & volume equivalents	487,377	# of professional staff	8
# of titles	179,596	Hours per week with professional staff	79
# of active serial subscriptions	6,253	Hours per week without professional staff	25
Study seating capacity inside the library	439	# of student computer work stations for entire law school	66
Square feet of law library	39,000	# of additional networked connections	0
Square feet of law school (excl. Library)	67,057		

Curriculum

	Full time	Part time
Typical first-year section size	90	75
Is there typically a "small section" of the first year class, other than Legal Writing, taught by full-time faculty?	No	No
If yes, typical size offered last year	N/A	N/A
# of classroom course titles beyond 1st year curriculum	100	28
# of upper division courses, excluding seminars, with an enrollment:		
Under 25	18	6
25 - 49	30	7
50 - 74	10	5
75 - 99	8	4
100 +	5	1
# of seminars	30	7
# of seminar positions available	444	
# of seminar positions filled	265	100
# of positions available in simulation courses	675	
# of simulation positions filled	442	12
# of positions available in faculty supervised clinical courses	80	
# of fac. sup. clin. positions filled	52	4
# involved in field placements	46	0
# involved in law journals	98	12
# in moot court or trial competitions	92	10
# of credit hours required to graduate	88	

Enrollment & Attrition

	Full-Time							Part-Time							Attrition			
	Men		Women		Minorities		Total	Men		Women		Minorities		Total	Academic	Other	Total	
	#	%	#	%	#	%	#	#	%	#	%	#	%	#	#	#	#	%
1st Year	97	54.5	81	45.5	29	16.3	178	36	46.8	41	53.2	8	10.4	77	7	8	15	5.5
2nd Year	102	56.7	78	43.3	28	15.6	180	47	66.2	24	33.8	16	22.5	71	3	3	6	2.5
3rd Year	104	55.3	84	44.7	42	22.3	188	35	59.3	24	40.7	13	22.0	59	0	0	0	0.0
4th Year								37	59.7	25	40.3	15	24.2	62	0	0	0	0.0
Total	303	55.5	243	44.5	99	18.1	546	155	57.6	114	42.4	52	19.3	269	10	11	21	2.5
JD Degrees Awarded	94	50.3	93	49.7	30	16.0	187	36	72.0	14	28.0	7	14.0	50				

GPA & LSAT Scores

	Full Time	Part Time	Total
# of apps	970	170	1,140
# admits	511	106	617
# of matrics	179	77	256
75% GPA	3.64	3.51	
25% GPA	3.12	2.73	
75% LSAT	158	157	
25% LSAT	149	149	

Tuition/Living Expenses

	Resident	Non-resident
Full-Time	$17,175	$17,175
Part-Time	$12,810	$12,810

Estimated living expenses for Singles		
Living on campus	Living off campus	Living at home
$8,520	$9,280	$8,200

Career Placement

	Total	%
Employment status known	209	92.5
Employment status unknown	17	7.5
Employed	192	91.9
Pursuing graduate degrees	1	0.5
Unemployed seeking employment	14	6.7
Unemployed not seeking employment	2	1.0
Type of Employment		
# employed in law firms	99	51.6
# employed in business & industry	40	20.8
# employed in government	22	11.5
# employed in public interest	2	1.0
# employed as judicial clerks	18	9.4
# employed in academia	5	2.6
Geographic Location		
# employed in state	167	87.0
# employed in foreign countries	0	0.0
# of states where employed	16	

Financial Aid

	Full-time		Part-time		Total	
	#	%	#	%	#	%
Total # receiving grants	328	60.1	75	27.9	403	49.4
Less than 1/2 tuition	281	51.5	72	26.8	353	43.3
Half to full tuition	47	8.6	3	1.1	50	6.1
Full tuition	0	0.0	0	0.0	0	0.0
More than full tuition	0	0.0	0	0.0	0	0.0
Median Grant Amount	$5,000		$2,000			

Refunds

Refunds of Admissions or Seat Deposit prior to commencement of classes? Yes

Refunds of Pre-paid tuition prior to commencement of classes? Yes

If yes, fully refundable before the start of classes? Yes

Joint Degrees Offered

JD/MHA, JD/MBA, JD/MAUA, JD/MPA

Advanced Degrees Offered

LL.M. Health Law

LL.M. American Law for Foreign Lawyers

Bar Passage Rate

Jurisdiction	MO	IL
# from school taking bar for the first time	143	52
School's pass rate for all first-time takers	88%	70%
State's pass rate for all first-time takers	92%	87%
State's pass rate for all first-time takers from ABA approved law schools	92%	87%

ST. MARY'S UNIVERSITY

One Camino Santa Maria
San Antonio, TX 78228-8602
(210)436-3424
http://www.stmarylaw.edu

ABA Approved Since 1948

The Basics

Type of School: **PRIVATE**
Application deadline*: **3/1**
Application fee: **$45**
Financial Aid deadline*: **3/31**
Student faculty ratio: **20.2 to 1**

First year can start other than Fall: **No**
Student housing: **No**
--exclusively for law students: **No**
Term: **Semester**

*pr=preferred

Faculty

	Men		Women		Minorities		Total
	#	%	#	%	#	%	
Full-time	24	75	8	25	8	25	32
Other full-time	0	0	0	0	0	0	0
Deans, librarians, & others who teach	1	50	1	50	0	0	2
Part-time	25	68	12	32	4	11	37
Total	**50**	**70**	**21**	**30**	**12**	**17**	**71**
Deans, librarians, & others who teach < 1/2	0	0	0	0	0	0	0

Library

# of volumes & volume equivalents	312,211	# of professional staff	10
# of titles	30,230	Hours per week with professional staff	87
# of active serial subscriptions	3,442	Hours per week without professional staff	23
Study seating capacity inside the library	446	# of student computer work stations for entire law school	12
Square feet of law library	65,000	# of additional networked connections	128
Square feet of law school (excl. Library)	85,707		

Curriculum

	Full time	Part time
Typical first-year section size	86	0
Is there typically a "small section" of the first year class, other than Legal Writing, taught by full-time faculty?	No	No
If yes, typical size offered last year	N/A	N/A
# of classroom course titles beyond 1st year curriculum	139	0
# of upper division courses, excluding seminars, with an enrollment:		
Under 25	56	0
25 - 49	32	0
50 - 74	14	0
75 - 99	15	0
100 +	0	0
# of seminars	22	0
# of seminar positions available	176	
# of seminar positions filled	176	0
# of positions available in simulation courses	128	
# of simulation positions filled	128	0
# of positions available in faculty supervised clinical courses	50	
# of fac. sup. clin. positions filled	50	0
# involved in field placements	15	0
# involved in law journals	40	0
# in moot court or trial competitions	22	0
# of credit hours required to graduate	90	

Enrollment & Attrition

	Full-Time							Part-Time							Attrition			
	Men		Women		Minorities		Total	Men		Women		Minorities		Total	Academic	Other	Total	
	#	%	#	%	#	%	#	#	%	#	%	#	%	#	#	#	#	%
1st Year	134	50.8	130	49.2	107	40.5	264	0	0.0	0	0.0	0	0.0	0	2	9	11	4.1
2nd Year	131	50.8	127	49.2	91	35.3	258	0	0.0	0	0.0	0	0.0	0	0	13	13	5.3
3rd Year	137	53.9	117	46.1	80	31.5	254	0	0.0	0	0.0	0	0.0	0	0	0	0	0.0
4th Year								0	0.0	0	0.0	0	0.0	0	0	0	0	0.0
Total	402	51.8	374	48.2	278	35.8	776	0	0.0	0	0.0	0	0.0	0	2	22	24	3.1
JD Degrees Awarded	136	53.5	118	46.5	81	31.9	254	0	0.0	0	0.0	0	0.0	0				

GPA & LSAT Scores

	Full Time	Part Time	Total
# of apps	1,545	0	1,545
# admits	735	0	735
# of matrics	264	0	264
75% GPA	3.14	0.00	
25% GPA	2.58	0.00	
75% LSAT	155	0	
25% LSAT	149	0	

Tuition/Living Expenses

	Resident	Non-resident
Full-Time	$15,200	$15,200
Part-Time	$0	$0

Estimated living expenses for Singles		
Living on campus	Living off campus	Living at home
$9,212	$12,296	$12,296

Career Placement

	Total	%
Employment status known	206	86.9
Employment status unknown	31	13.1
Employed	178	86.4
Pursuing graduate degrees	2	1.0
Unemployed seeking employment	26	12.6
Unemployed not seeking employment	0	0.0
Type of Employment		
# employed in law firms	122	68.5
# employed in business & industry	15	8.4
# employed in government	22	12.4
# employed in public interest	5	2.8
# employed as judicial clerks	14	7.9
# employed in academia	0	0.0
Geographic Location		
# employed in state	154	86.5
# employed in foreign countries	1	0.6
# of states where employed	10	

Financial Aid

	Full-time		Part-time		Total	
	#	%	#	%	#	%
Total # receiving grants	264	34.0	0	0.0	264	34.0
Less than 1/2 tuition	248	32.0	0	0.0	248	32.0
Half to full tuition	2	0.3	0	0.0	2	0.3
Full tuition	13	1.7	0	0.0	13	1.7
More than full tuition	1	0.1	0	0.0	1	0.1
Median Grant Amount	$500		$0			

Refunds

Refunds of Admissions or Seat Deposit prior to commencement of classes? No

Refunds of Pre-paid tuition prior to commencement of classes? No

If yes, fully refundable before the start of classes? No

Joint Degrees Offered

JD/MBA, JD/EC, JD/EG, JD/IR, 1D/MPA, JD/TH, JD/EA, JD/CIS

Advanced Degrees Offered

LL.M.	International and Comparative Law
LL.M.	American Legal Studies

Bar Passage Rate

Jurisdiction	TX
# from school taking bar for the first time	173
School's pass rate for all first-time takers	80%
State's pass rate for all first-time takers	82%
State's pass rate for all first-time takers from ABA approved law schools	82%

ST. THOMAS UNIVERSITY

16400 N.W. 32 Avenue
Miami, FL 33054
(305)623-2320
http://www.law.stu.edu

ABA Approved Since 1988

The Basics

Type of School: **PRIVATE**
Application deadline*: **4/30**
Application fee: **$40**
Financial Aid deadline*: **3/1**
Student faculty ratio: **23.3 to 1**
First year can start other than Fall: **No**
Student housing: **Yes**
--exclusively for law students: **No**
Term: **Semester**

*pr=preferred

Faculty

	Men #	Men %	Women #	Women %	Minorities #	Minorities %	Total
Full-time	14	74	5	26	5	26	19
Other full-time	0	0	1	100	0	0	1
Deans, librarians, & others who teach	0	0	0	0	0	0	0
Part-time	13	72	5	28	1	6	18
Total	27	71	11	29	6	16	38
Deans, librarians, & others who teach < 1/2	2	100	0	0	0	0	2

Library

# of volumes & volume equivalents	247,387	# of professional staff	7
# of titles	36,072	Hours per week with professional staff	96
# of active serial subscriptions	1,725	Hours per week without professional staff	9
Study seating capacity inside the library	298	# of student computer work stations for entire law school	63
Square feet of law library	25,116	# of additional networked connections	0
Square feet of law school (excl. Library)	36,884		

Curriculum

	Full time	Part time
Typical first-year section size	65	0
Is there typically a "small section" of the first year class, other than Legal Writing, taught by full-time faculty?	No	No
If yes, typical size offered last year	N/A	N/A
# of classroom course titles beyond 1st year curriculum	104	0
# of upper division courses, excluding seminars, with an enrollment:		
Under 25	54	0
25 - 49	20	0
50 - 74	15	0
75 - 99	5	0
100 +	0	0
# of seminars	10	0
# of seminar positions available	160	
# of seminar positions filled	151	0
# of positions available in simulation courses	244	
# of simulation positions filled	229	0
# of positions available in faculty supervised clinical courses	124	
# of fac. sup. clin. positions filled	66	0
# involved in field placements	51	0
# involved in law journals	32	0
# in moot court or trial competitions	86	0
# of credit hours required to graduate	90	

Enrollment & Attrition

	Full-Time							Part-Time							Attrition			
	Men		Women		Minorities		Total	Men		Women		Minorities		Total	Academic	Other	Total	
	#	%	#	%	#	%	#	#	%	#	%	#	%	#	#	#	#	%
1st Year	135	62.8	80	37.2	78	36.3	215	0	0.0	0	0.0	0	0.0	0	17	26	43	21
2nd Year	93	58.5	66	41.5	52	32.7	159	0	0.0	0	0.0	0	0.0	0	5	4	9	5.4
3rd Year	98	62.4	59	37.6	49	31.2	157	0	0.0	0	0.0	0	0.0	0	0	0	0	0.0
4th Year								0	0.0	0	0.0	0	0.0	0	0	0	0	0.0
Total	326	61.4	205	38.6	179	33.7	531	0	0.0	0	0.0	0	0.0	0	22	30	52	10
JD Degrees Awarded	91	58.7	64	41.3	50	32.3	155	0	0.0	0	0.0	0	0.0	0				

GPA & LSAT Scores

	Full Time	Part Time	Total
# of apps	1,338	0	1,338
# admits	782	0	782
# of matrics	217	0	217
75% GPA	2.92	0.00	
25% GPA	2.37	0.00	
75% LSAT	150	0	
25% LSAT	144	0	

Tuition/Living Expenses

	Resident	Non-resident
Full-Time	$17,760	$17,760
Part-Time	$0	$0

Estimated living expenses for Singles		
Living on campus	Living off campus	Living at home
$13,300	$13,300	$13,300

Career Placement

	Total	%
Employment status known	144	94.7
Employment status unknown	8	5.3
Employed	105	72.9
Pursuing graduate degrees	15	10.4
Unemployed seeking employment	21	14.6
Unemployed not seeking employment	3	2.1
Type of Employment		
# employed in law firms	68	64.8
# employed in business & industry	10	9.5
# employed in government	14	13.3
# employed in public interest	11	10.5
# employed as judicial clerks	2	1.9
# employed in academia	0	0.0
Geographic Location		
# employed in state	84	80.0
# employed in foreign countries	8	7.6
# of states where employed	11	

Financial Aid

	Full-time		Part-time		Total	
	#	%	#	%	#	%
Total # receiving grants	133	25.1	0	0.0	133	25.0
Less than 1/2 tuition	112	21.1	0	0.0	112	21.1
Half to full tuition	20	3.8	0	0.0	20	3.8
Full tuition	1	0.2	0	0.0	1	0.2
More than full tuition	0	0.0	0	0.0	0	0.0
Median Grant Amount	$4,500		$0			

Refunds

Refunds of Admissions or Seat Deposit prior to commencement of classes? No

Refunds of Pre-paid tuition prior to commencement of classes? Yes

If yes, fully refundable before the start of classes? Yes

Joint Degrees Offered

No Joint Degrees

Advanced Degrees Offered

No Advanced Degrees

Bar Passage Rate

Jurisdiction	FL
# from school taking bar for the first time	121
School's pass rate for all first-time takers	69%
State's pass rate for all first-time takers	84%
State's pass rate for all first-time takers from ABA approved law schools	84%

STANFORD UNIVERSITY

Crown Quadrangle
Stanford, CA 94305-8610
(415)723-2465
http://www-leland.stanford.edu/group/law

ABA Approved Since 1923

The Basics

Type of School: **PRIVATE**
Application deadline*: **2/15**
Application fee: **$65**
Financial Aid deadline*: **3/15**
Student faculty ratio: **16.9 to 1**

First year can start other than Fall: **No**
Student housing: **No**
--exclusively for law students: **No**
Term: **Semester**

*pr=preferred

Faculty

	Men #	Men %	Women #	Women %	Minorities #	Minorities %	Total
Full-time	17	63	10	37	4	15	27
Other full-time	0	0	0	0	0	0	0
Deans, librarians, & others who teach	3	100	0	0	0	0	3
Part-time	16	55	13	45	5	17	29
Total	36	61	23	39	9	15	59
Deans, librarians, & others who teach < 1/2	1	100	0	0	0	0	1

Library

# of volumes & volume equivalents	447,506	# of professional staff	7
# of titles	163,562	Hours per week with professional staff	56
# of active serial subscriptions	7,030	Hours per week without professional staff	40
Study seating capacity inside the library	554	# of student computer work stations for entire law school	50
Square feet of law library	56,617	# of additional networked connections	0
Square feet of law school (excl. Library)	91,513		

Curriculum

	Full time	Part time
Typical first-year section size	60	0
Is there typically a "small section" of the first year class, other than Legal Writing, taught by full-time faculty?	Yes	No
If yes, typical size offered last year	30	N/A
# of classroom course titles beyond 1st year curriculum	147	0
# of upper division courses, excluding seminars, with an enrollment:		
Under 25	57	0
25 - 49	26	0
50 - 74	6	0
75 - 99	8	0
100 +	4	0
# of seminars	58	0
# of seminar positions available	349	
# of seminar positions filled	349	0
# of positions available in simulation courses	193	
# of simulation positions filled	193	0
# of positions available in faculty supervised clinical courses	33	
# of fac. sup. clin. positions filled	33	0
# involved in field placements	53	0
# involved in law journals	400	0
# in moot court or trial competitions	30	0
# of credit hours required to graduate	86	

Enrollment & Attrition

	Full-Time							Part-Time							Attrition			
	Men		Women		Minorities		Total	Men		Women		Minorities		Total	Academic	Other	Total	
	#	%	#	%	#	%	#	#	%	#	%	#	%	#	#	#	#	%
1st Year	97	55.1	79	44.9	55	31.3	176	0	0.0	0	0.0	0	0.0	0	0	0	0	0.0
2nd Year	110	59.1	76	40.9	60	32.3	186	0	0.0	0	0.0	0	0.0	0	0	3	3	1.6
3rd Year	94	50.8	91	49.2	63	34.1	185	0	0.0	0	0.0	0	0.0	0	0	0	0	0.0
4th Year								0	0.0	0	0.0	0	0.0	0	0	0	0	0.0
Total	301	55.0	246	45.0	178	32.5	547	0	0.0	0	0.0	0	0.0	0	0	3	3	0.5
JD Degrees Awarded	109	55.3	88	44.7	67	34.0	197	0	0.0	0	0.0	0	0.0	0				

GPA & LSAT Scores

	Full Time	Part Time	Total
# of apps	4,034	0	4,034
# admits	491	0	491
# of matrics	176	0	176
75% GPA	3.88	0.00	
25% GPA	3.51	0.00	
75% LSAT	171	0	
25% LSAT	165	0	

Tuition/Living Expenses

	Resident	Non-resident
Full-Time	$23,360	$23,360
Part-Time	$0	$0

Estimated living expenses for Singles		
Living on campus	Living off campus	Living at home
$10,845	$13,836	N/A

Career Placement

	Total	%
Employment status known	156	97.5
Employment status unknown	4	2.5
Employed	150	96.2
Pursuing graduate degrees	2	1.3
Unemployed seeking employment	2	1.3
Unemployed not seeking employment	2	1.3
Type of Employment		
# employed in law firms	78	52.0
# employed in business & industry	9	6.0
# employed in government	7	4.7
# employed in public interest	9	6.0
# employed as judicial clerks	46	30.7
# employed in academia	1	0.7
Geographic Location		
# employed in state	75	50.0
# employed in foreign countries	5	3.3
# of states where employed	25	

Financial Aid

	Full-time		Part-time		Total	
	#	%	#	%	#	%
Total # receiving grants	198	36.2	0	0.0	198	36.2
Less than 1/2 tuition	173	31.6	0	0.0	173	31.6
Half to full tuition	17	3.1	0	0.0	17	3.1
Full tuition	8	1.5	0	0.0	8	1.5
More than full tuition	0	0.0	0	0.0	0	0.0
Median Grant Amount	$6,718		$0			

Refunds

Refunds of Admissions or Seat Deposit prior to commencement of classes? Yes

50% refund from 04/15/96 to 05/01/96
20% refund from 06/30/96 to 08/01/96

Refunds of Pre-paid tuition prior to commencement of classes? Yes

If yes, fully refundable before the start of classes? Yes

Joint Degrees Offered

JD/MBA, JD/MA, JD/Phd

Advanced Degrees Offered

JSD	Doctor of the Science of Law - designed to meet individual student interest
JSM	Master of the Science of Law - designed to meet individual student interest

Bar Passage Rate

Jurisdiction	CA
# from school taking bar for the first time	90
School's pass rate for all first-time takers	91%
State's pass rate for all first-time takers	73%
State's pass rate for all first-time takers from ABA approved law schools	83%

STATE UNIVERSITY OF NEW YORK AT BUFFALO

319 O'Brian Hall
North Campus
Buffalo, NY 14260
(716)645-2053
MCook@MSMail.Buffalo.edu

ABA Approved Since 1936

The Basics

Type of School: **PUBLIC**
Application deadline*:
Application fee: **$50**
Financial Aid deadline*:
Student faculty ratio: **17.1 to 1**

First year can start other than Fall: **No**
Student housing: **No**
--exclusively for law students: **No**
Term: **Semester**

*pr=preferred

Faculty

	Men #	Men %	Women #	Women %	Minorities #	Minorities %	Total
Full-time	24	65	13	35	5	14	37
Other full-time	3	43	4	57	1	14	7
Deans, librarians, & others who teach	3	60	2	40	1	20	5
Part-time	0	0	0	0	0	0	0
Total	30	61	19	39	7	14	49
Deans, librarians, & others who teach < 1/2	0	0	0	0	0	0	0

Library

# of volumes & volume equivalents	488,571	# of professional staff	9
# of titles	101,655	Hours per week with professional staff	74
# of active serial subscriptions	5,291	Hours per week without professional staff	19
Study seating capacity inside the library	508	# of student computer work stations for entire law school	34
Square feet of law library	52,385	# of additional networked connections	10
Square feet of law school (excl. Library)	60,080		

Curriculum

	Full time	Part time
Typical first-year section size	100	0
Is there typically a "small section" of the first year class, other than Legal Writing, taught by full-time faculty?	Yes	No
If yes, typical size offered last year	25	N/A
# of classroom course titles beyond 1st year curriculum	146	0
# of upper division courses, excluding seminars, with an enrollment:		
Under 25	40	0
25 - 49	42	0
50 - 74	13	0
75 - 99	11	0
100 +	4	0
# of seminars	36	0
# of seminar positions available	587	
# of seminar positions filled	388	0
# of positions available in simulation courses	240	
# of simulation positions filled	203	0
# of positions available in faculty supervised clinical courses	120	
# of fac. sup. clin. positions filled	119	0
# involved in field placements	78	0
# involved in law journals	219	0
# in moot court or trial competitions	78	0
# of credit hours required to graduate	87	

Enrollment & Attrition

	Full-Time							Part-Time							Attrition			
	Men		Women		Minorities		Total	Men		Women		Minorities		Total	Academic	Other	Total	
	#	%	#	%	#	%	#	#	%	#	%	#	%	#	#	#	#	%
1st Year	109	52.4	99	47.6	41	19.7	208	0	0.0	0	0.0	0	0.0	0	0	14	14	5.3
2nd Year	140	52.0	129	48.0	43	16.0	269	0	0.0	0	0.0	0	0.0	0	0	12	12	4.5
3rd Year	130	48.9	136	51.1	42	15.8	266	0	0.0	0	0.0	0	0.0	0	0	1	1	0.4
4th Year								0	0.0	0	0.0	0	0.0	0	0	0	0	0.0
Total	379	51.0	364	49.0	126	17.0	743	0	0.0	0	0.0	0	0.0	0	0	27	27	3.3
JD Degrees Awarded	146	55.5	117	44.5	44	16.7	263	0	0.0	0	0.0	0	0.0	0				

STATE UNIVERSITY OF NEW YORK AT BUFFALO

GPA & LSAT Scores

	Full Time	Part Time	Total
# of apps	1,023	0	1,023
# admits	527	0	527
# of matrics	208	0	208
75% GPA	3.56	0.00	
25% GPA	2.99	0.00	
75% LSAT	159	0	
25% LSAT	148	0	

Tuition/Living Expenses

	Resident	Non-resident
Full-Time	$6,775	$11,425
Part-Time	$0	$0

Estimated living expenses for Singles		
Living on campus	Living off campus	Living at home
$9,529	$9,529	$9,529

Career Placement

	Total	%
Employment status known	223	99.1
Employment status unknown	2	0.9
Employed	188	84.3
Pursuing graduate degrees	9	4.0
Unemployed seeking employment	17	7.6
Unemployed not seeking employment	9	4.0
Type of Employment		
# employed in law firms	116	61.7
# employed in business & industry	27	14.4
# employed in government	20	10.6
# employed in public interest	14	7.5
# employed as judicial clerks	10	5.3
# employed in academia	1	0.5
Geographic Location		
# employed in state	139	73.9
# employed in foreign countries	2	1.1
# of states where employed	17	

Financial Aid

	Full-time		Part-time		Total	
	#	%	#	%	#	%
Total # receiving grants	399	53.7	0	0.0	399	53.7
Less than 1/2 tuition	201	27.1	0	0.0	201	27.1
Half to full tuition	146	19.7	0	0.0	146	19.7
Full tuition	52	7.0	0	0.0	52	7.0
More than full tuition	0	0.0	0	0.0	0	0.0
Median Grant Amount	$0		$0			

Refunds

Refunds of Admissions or Seat Deposit prior to commencement of classes? No

Refunds of Pre-paid tuition prior to commencement of classes? Yes

If yes, fully refundable before the start of classes? Yes

30% refund from 09/14/95 to 09/20/95
0% refund from 09/21/95 to / /

Joint Degrees Offered

No Joint Degrees

Advanced Degrees Offered

No Advanced Degrees

Bar Passage Rate

Jurisdiction	NY	CT	PA
# from school taking bar for the first time	184	7	5
School's pass rate for all first-time takers	72%	86%	80%
State's pass rate for all first-time takers	78%	83%	73%
State's pass rate for all first-time takers from ABA approved law schools		78%	73%

STETSON UNIVERSITY

1401 61st Street South
St. Petersburg, FL 33707
(813)562-7809
http://www.law.stetson.edu

ABA Approved Since 1930

The Basics

Type of School: **PRIVATE**
Application deadline*: **3/1**
Application fee: **$45**
Financial Aid deadline*: **3/1**
Student faculty ratio: **19.3 to 1**

First year can start other than Fall: **Yes**
Student housing: **Yes**
--exclusively for law students: **Yes**
Term: **Semester**

*pr=preferred

Faculty

	Men		Women		Minorities		Total
	#	%	#	%	#	%	
Full-time	22	76	7	24	3	10	29
Other full-time	1	33	2	67	0	0	3
Deans, librarians, & others who teach	1	50	1	50	0	0	2
Part-time	17	74	6	26	0	0	23
Total	41	72	16	28	3	5	57
Deans, librarians, & others who teach < 1/2	1	50	1	50	1	50	2

Library

# of volumes & volume equivalents	341,774	# of professional staff	7
# of titles	94,743	Hours per week with professional staff	80
# of active serial subscriptions	4,842	Hours per week without professional staff	31
Study seating capacity inside the library	375	# of student computer work stations for entire law school	47
Square feet of law library	31,886	# of additional networked connections	60
Square feet of law school (excl. Library)	99,614		

Curriculum

	Full time	Part time
Typical first-year section size	58	0
Is there typically a "small section" of the first year class, other than Legal Writing, taught by full-time faculty?	No	No
If yes, typical size offered last year	N/A	N/A
# of classroom course titles beyond 1st year curriculum	138	0
# of upper division courses, excluding seminars, with an enrollment:		
Under 25	82	0
25 - 49	39	0
50 - 74	19	0
75 - 99	7	0
100 +	1	0
# of seminars	11	0
# of seminar positions available	220	
# of seminar positions filled	186	0
# of positions available in simulation courses	776	
# of simulation positions filled	680	0
# of positions available in faculty supervised clinical courses	171	
# of fac. sup. clin. positions filled	150	0
# involved in field placements	145	0
# involved in law journals	109	0
# in moot court or trial competitions	62	0
# of credit hours required to graduate	88	

Enrollment & Attrition

	Full-Time							Part-Time							Attrition			
	Men		Women		Minorities		Total	Men		Women		Minorities		Total	Academic	Other	Total	
	#	%	#	%	#	%	#	#	%	#	%	#	%	#	#	#	#	%
1st Year	116	52.0	107	48.0	37	16.6	223	0	0.0	0	0.0	0	0.0	0	7	16	23	8.0
2nd Year	98	46.0	115	54.0	36	16.9	213	0	0.0	0	0.0	0	0.0	0	0	15	15	7.8
3rd Year	111	46.8	126	53.2	27	11.4	237	0	0.0	0	0.0	0	0.0	0	0	1	1	0.5
4th Year								0	0.0	0	0.0	0	0.0	0	0	0	0	0.0
Total	325	48.3	348	51.7	100	14.9	673	0	0.0	0	0.0	0	0.0	0	7	32	39	5.8
JD Degrees Awarded	98	48.3	105	51.7	38	18.7	203	0	0.0	0	0.0	0	0.0	0				

GPA & LSAT Scores

	Full Time	Part Time	Total
# of apps	1,702	0	1,702
# admits	726	0	726
# of matrics	220	0	220
75% GPA	3.45	0.00	
25% GPA	2.95	0.00	
75% LSAT	156	0	
25% LSAT	149	0	

Tuition/Living Expenses

	Resident	Non-resident
Full-Time	$18,310	$18,310
Part-Time	$0	$0

Estimated living expenses for Singles		
Living on campus	Living off campus	Living at home
$10,270	$12,050	$6,030

Career Placement

	Total	%
Employment status known	225	92.2
Employment status unknown	19	7.8
Employed	189	84.0
Pursuing graduate degrees	10	4.4
Unemployed seeking employment	26	11.6
Unemployed not seeking employment	0	0.0
Type of Employment		
# employed in law firms	113	59.8
# employed in business & industry	15	7.9
# employed in government	50	26.5
# employed in public interest	1	0.5
# employed as judicial clerks	10	5.3
# employed in academia	0	0.0
Geographic Location		
# employed in state	171	90.5
# employed in foreign countries	0	0.0
# of states where employed	10	

Financial Aid

	Full-time		Part-time		Total	
	#	%	#	%	#	%
Total # receiving grants	302	44.9	0	0.0	302	44.9
Less than 1/2 tuition	246	36.6	0	0.0	246	36.6
Half to full tuition	14	2.1	0	0.0	14	2.1
Full tuition	42	6.2	0	0.0	42	6.2
More than full tuition	0	0.0	0	0.0	0	0.0
Median Grant Amount	$3,875		$0			

Refunds

Refunds of Admissions or Seat Deposit prior to commencement of classes? No

Refunds of Pre-paid tuition prior to commencement of classes? Yes

If yes, fully refundable before the start of classes? Yes

Joint Degrees Offered

JD/MBA

Advanced Degrees Offered

No Advanced Degrees

Bar Passage Rate

Jurisdiction	FL
# from school taking bar for the first time	155
School's pass rate for all first-time takers	85%
State's pass rate for all first-time takers	84%
State's pass rate for all first-time takers from ABA approved law schools	84%

SUFFOLK UNIVERSITY

41 Temple Street
Boston, MA 02114-4280
(617)573-8155
http://www.suffolk.edu/law

ABA Approved Since 1953

The Basics

Type of School: **PRIVATE**	First year can start other than Fall: **No**
Application deadline*: **3/3**	Student housing: **No**
Application fee: **$50**	--exclusively for law students: **No**
Financial Aid deadline*: **2/28**	Term: **Semester**
Student faculty ratio: **22.8 to 1**	

*pr=preferred

Faculty

	Men		Women		Minorities		Total
	#	%	#	%	#	%	
Full-time	45	82	10	18	5	9	55
Other full-time	6	55	5	45	1	9	11
Deans, librarians, & others who teach	3	50	3	50	0	0	6
Part-time	38	64	21	36	6	10	59
Total	92	70	39	30	12	9	131
Deans, librarians, & others who teach < 1/2	1	50	1	50	0	0	2

Library

# of volumes & volume equivalents	300,080	# of professional staff	11
# of titles	111,566	Hours per week with professional staff	78
# of active serial subscriptions	5,830	Hours per week without professional staff	25
Study seating capacity inside the library	743	# of student computer work stations for entire law school	45
Square feet of law library	35,524	# of additional networked connections	9
Square feet of law school (excl. Library)	55,042		

Curriculum

	Full time	Part time
Typical first-year section size	96	100
Is there typically a "small section" of the first year class, other than Legal Writing, taught by full-time faculty?	Yes	No
If yes, typical size offered last year	45	N/A
# of classroom course titles beyond 1st year curriculum	138	123
# of upper division courses, excluding seminars, with an enrollment:		
Under 25	33	32
25 - 49	28	27
50 - 74	12	10
75 - 99	15	25
100 +	13	1
# of seminars	37	28
# of seminar positions available	1,183	
# of seminar positions filled	480	409
# of positions available in simulation courses	470	
# of simulation positions filled	265	163
# of positions available in faculty supervised clinical courses	127	
# of fac. sup. clin. positions filled	115	12
# involved in field placements	150	18
# involved in law journals	97	25
# in moot court or trial competitions	200	45
# of credit hours required to graduate	84	

Enrollment & Attrition

	Full-Time							Part-Time							Attrition			
	Men		Women		Minorities		Total	Men		Women		Minorities		Total	Academic	Other	Total	
	#	%	#	%	#	%	#	#	%	#	%	#	%	#	#	#	#	%
1st Year	188	51.5	177	48.5	31	8.5	365	113	54.1	96	45.9	16	7.7	209	13	18	31	5.3
2nd Year	156	45.0	191	55.0	32	9.2	347	111	55.0	91	45.0	20	9.9	202	2	21	23	4.8
3rd Year	150	50.3	148	49.7	24	8.1	298	90	54.2	76	45.8	24	14.5	166	1	2	3	0.6
4th Year								96	56.5	74	43.5	13	7.6	170	0	0	0	0.0
Total	494	48.9	516	51.1	87	8.6	1,010	410	54.9	337	45.1	73	9.8	747	16	41	57	3.3
JD Degrees Awarded	151	44.9	185	55.1	45	13.4	336	75	46.0	88	54.0	15	9.2	163				

GPA & LSAT Scores

	Full Time	Part Time	Total
# of apps	1,533	464	1,997
# admits	1,096	284	1,380
# of matrics	365	209	574
75% GPA	3.39	3.38	
25% GPA	2.91	2.82	
75% LSAT	156	156	
25% LSAT	148	150	

Tuition/Living Expenses

	Resident	Non-resident
Full-Time	$17,820	$17,820
Part-Time	$13,366	$13,366

Estimated living expenses for Singles		
Living on campus	Living off campus	Living at home
N/A	$14,158	$7,708

Financial Aid

	Full-time		Part-time		Total	
	#	%	#	%	#	%
Total # receiving grants	368	36.4	107	14.3	475	27.0
Less than 1/2 tuition	366	36.2	107	14.3	473	26.9
Half to full tuition	0	0.0	0	0.0	0	0.0
Full tuition	2	0.2	0	0.0	2	0.1
More than full tuition	0	0.0	0	0.0	0	0.0
Median Grant Amount	$1,500		$1,000			

Refunds

Refunds of Admissions or Seat Deposit prior to commencement of classes? Yes

50% refund from 04/15/96 to 06/02/96
60% refund from 06/03/96 to 08/15/96

Refunds of Pre-paid tuition prior to commencement of classes? Yes

If yes, fully refundable before the start of classes? Yes

Joint Degrees Offered

JD/MBA, JD/MPA, JD/MSF, JD/MSIE

Advanced Degrees Offered

No Advanced Degrees

Career Placement

	Total	%
Employment status known	434	87.2
Employment status unknown	64	12.9
Employed	371	85.5
Pursuing graduate degrees	10	2.3
Unemployed seeking employment	45	10.4
Unemployed not seeking employment	8	1.8
Type of Employment		
# employed in law firms	154	41.5
# employed in business & industry	119	32.1
# employed in government	57	15.4
# employed in public interest	6	1.6
# employed as judicial clerks	28	7.6
# employed in academia	7	1.9
Geographic Location		
# employed in state	291	78.4
# employed in foreign countries	4	1.1
# of states where employed	23	

Bar Passage Rate

Jurisdiction	MA
# from school taking bar for the first time	396
School's pass rate for all first-time takers	84%
State's pass rate for all first-time takers	83%
State's pass rate for all first-time takers from ABA approved law schools	85%

SYRACUSE UNIVERSITY

Syracuse, NY 13244-1030
(315)443-2524
http://www.law.syr.edu

ABA Approved Since 1923

The Basics

Type of School: **PRIVATE**
Application deadline*: **4/1**
Application fee: **$40**
Financial Aid deadline*: **3/1**
Student faculty ratio: **17.2 to 1**
First year can start other than Fall: **No**
Student housing: **Yes**
--exclusively for law students: **No**
Term: **Semester**

*pr=preferred

Faculty

	Men #	Men %	Women #	Women %	Minorities #	Minorities %	Total
Full-time	23	64	13	36	4	11	36
Other full-time	0	0	1	100	0	0	1
Deans, librarians, & others who teach	0	0	2	100	0	0	2
Part-time	20	91	2	9	2	9	22
Total	43	70	18	30	6	10	61
Deans, librarians, & others who teach < 1/2	1	33	2	67	0	0	3

Library

# of volumes & volume equivalents	358,842	# of professional staff	10
# of titles	64,906	Hours per week with professional staff	45
# of active serial subscriptions	5,865	Hours per week without professional staff	60
Study seating capacity inside the library	546	# of student computer work stations for entire law school	55
Square feet of law library	31,005	# of additional networked connections	0
Square feet of law school (excl. Library)	35,102		

Curriculum

	Full time	Part time
Typical first-year section size	90	0
Is there typically a "small section" of the first year class, other than Legal Writing, taught by full-time faculty?	Yes	No
If yes, typical size offered last year	40	N/A
# of classroom course titles beyond 1st year curriculum	127	0
# of upper division courses, excluding seminars, with an enrollment:		
Under 25	79	0
25 - 49	41	0
50 - 74	10	0
75 - 99	12	0
100 +	8	0
# of seminars	10	0
# of seminar positions available	160	
# of seminar positions filled	102	0
# of positions available in simulation courses	305	
# of simulation positions filled	285	0
# of positions available in faculty supervised clinical courses	40	
# of fac. sup. clin. positions filled	36	0
# involved in field placements	58	0
# involved in law journals	180	0
# in moot court or trial competitions	179	0
# of credit hours required to graduate	87	

Enrollment & Attrition

	Full-Time							Part-Time							Attrition			
	Men		Women		Minorities		Total	Men		Women		Minorities		Total	Academic	Other	Total	
	#	%	#	%	#	%	#	#	%	#	%	#	%	#	#	#	#	%
1st Year	120	51.9	111	48.1	60	26.0	231	6	50.0	6	50.0	0	0.0	12	0	2	2	0.7
2nd Year	139	54.3	117	45.7	55	21.5	256	1	100.0	0	0.0	0	0.0	1	3	10	13	5.2
3rd Year	149	63.1	87	36.9	46	19.5	236	2	100.0	0	0.0	1	50.0	2	1	15	16	5.9
4th Year								0	0.0	0	0.0	0	0.0	0	0	0	0	0.0
Total	408	56.4	315	43.6	161	22.3	723	9	60.0	6	40.0	1	6.7	15	4	27	31	3.9
JD Degrees Awarded	139	55.2	113	44.8	64	25.4	252	1	100.0	0	0.0	1	100.0	1				

GPA & LSAT Scores

	Full Time	Part Time	Total
# of apps	1,837	30	1,867
# admits	1,124	15	1,139
# of matrics	234	11	245
75% GPA	3.50	3.50	
25% GPA	3.00	3.03	
75% LSAT	154	159	
25% LSAT	147	147	

Tuition/Living Expenses

	Resident	Non-resident
Full-Time	$20,142	$20,142
Part-Time	$189	$189

Estimated living expenses for Singles		
Living on campus	Living off campus	Living at home
$11,727	$11,727	$11,727

Career Placement

	Total	%
Employment status known	240	96.4
Employment status unknown	9	3.6
Employed	194	80.8
Pursuing graduate degrees	4	1.7
Unemployed seeking employment	40	16.7
Unemployed not seeking employment	2	0.8
Type of Employment		
# employed in law firms	110	56.7
# employed in business & industry	37	19.1
# employed in government	30	15.5
# employed in public interest	3	1.6
# employed as judicial clerks	12	6.2
# employed in academia	2	1.0
Geographic Location		
# employed in state	103	53.1
# employed in foreign countries	2	1.0
# of states where employed	24	

Financial Aid

	Full-time		Part-time		Total	
	#	%	#	%	#	%
Total # receiving grants	415	57.4	0	0.0	415	56.2
Less than 1/2 tuition	337	46.6	0	0.0	337	45.7
Half to full tuition	41	5.7	0	0.0	41	5.6
Full tuition	33	4.6	0	0.0	33	4.5
More than full tuition	4	0.6	0	0.0	4	0.5
Median Grant Amount	$6,620		$0			

Refunds

Refunds of Admissions or Seat Deposit prior to commencement of classes? No

Refunds of Pre-paid tuition prior to commencement of classes? Yes

If yes, fully refundable before the start of classes? Yes

Joint Degrees Offered

JD/MS-Acct, JD/MBA-BusAd, JD/MA-Econ, JD/MS-EnvSci, MA/PhD-Hist, JD/MA-IntRel, JD/MA-Media, JD/MPA-PubAm, JD/MLS-InfoS, MA/PhD-Philo, JD/MA-Commun, JD/MS-Engin, JD/MS-PoliSi

Advanced Degrees Offered

No Advanced Degrees

Bar Passage Rate

Jurisdiction	NY
# from school taking bar for the first time	152
School's pass rate for all first-time takers	68%
State's pass rate for all first-time takers	78%
State's pass rate for all first-time takers from ABA approved law schools	

TEMPLE UNIVERSITY

1719 North Broad Street
Philadelphia, PA 19122
(215)204-7861
http://www.temple.edu/lawschool

ABA Approved Since 1933

The Basics

Type of School: **PUBLIC**
Application deadline*: **3/1**
Application fee: **$50**
Financial Aid deadline*: **3/1**
Student faculty ratio: **19.7 to 1**

First year can start other than Fall: **No**
Student housing: **Yes**
--exclusively for law students: **No**
Term: **Semester**

*pr=preferred

Faculty

	Men		Women		Minorities		Total
	#	%	#	%	#	%	
Full-time	32	74	11	26	10	23	43
Other full-time	1	25	3	75	0	0	4
Deans, librarians, & others who teach	8	57	6	43	2	14	14
Part-time	58	70	25	30	5	6	83
Total	**99**	**69**	**45**	**31**	**17**	**12**	**144**
Deans, librarians, & others who teach < 1/2	0	0	1	100	1	100	1

Library

# of volumes & volume equivalents	470,505	# of professional staff	10
# of titles	83,493	Hours per week with professional staff	78
# of active serial subscriptions	2,517	Hours per week without professional staff	18
Study seating capacity inside the library	644	# of student computer work stations for entire law school	88
Square feet of law library	80,000	# of additional networked connections	152
Square feet of law school (excl. Library)	32,432		

Curriculum

	Full time	Part time
Typical first-year section size	67	89
Is there typically a "small section" of the first year class, other than Legal Writing, taught by full-time faculty?	No	No
If yes, typical size offered last year	N/A	N/A
# of classroom course titles beyond 1st year curriculum	139	63
# of upper division courses, excluding seminars, with an enrollment:		
Under 25	72	45
25 - 49	50	21
50 - 74	12	7
75 - 99	11	1
100 +	3	2
# of seminars	42	11
# of seminar positions available	752	
# of seminar positions filled	529	154
# of positions available in simulation courses	983	
# of simulation positions filled	722	222
# of positions available in faculty supervised clinical courses	0	
# of fac. sup. clin. positions filled	0	0
# involved in field placements	364	23
# involved in law journals	152	7
# in moot court or trial competitions	56	0
# of credit hours required to graduate	83	

Enrollment & Attrition

	Full-Time							Part-Time							Attrition			
	Men		Women		Minorities		Total	Men		Women		Minorities		Total	Academic	Other	Total	
	#	%	#	%	#	%	#	#	%	#	%	#	%	#	#	#	#	%
1st Year	113	46.1	132	53.9	79	32.2	245	51	54.3	43	45.7	18	19.1	94	0	9	9	2.5
2nd Year	139	54.9	114	45.1	71	28.1	253	54	59.3	37	40.7	19	20.9	91	0	15	15	4.2
3rd Year	136	49.8	137	50.2	72	26.4	273	42	47.2	47	52.8	18	20.2	89	1	2	3	0.8
4th Year								63	62.4	38	37.6	16	15.8	101	0	0	0	0.0
Total	388	50.3	383	49.7	222	28.8	771	210	56.0	165	44.0	71	18.9	375	1	26	27	2.3
JD Degrees Awarded	152	55.1	124	44.9	65	23.6	276	43	57.3	32	42.7	11	14.7	75				

GPA & LSAT Scores

	Full Time	Part Time	Total
# of apps	2,384	394	2,778
# admits	894	143	1,037
# of matrics	255	88	343
75% GPA	3.54	3.46	
25% GPA	2.96	2.79	
75% LSAT	159	159	
25% LSAT	149	150	

Tuition/Living Expenses

	Resident	Non-resident
Full-Time	$8,432	$14,946
Part-Time	$6,796	$12,008

Estimated living expenses for Singles		
Living on campus	Living off campus	Living at home
$13,360	$13,360	$11,594

Financial Aid

	Full-time		Part-time		Total	
	#	%	#	%	#	%
Total # receiving grants	535	69.4	73	19.5	608	53.1
Less than 1/2 tuition	510	66.2	72	19.2	582	50.8
Half to full tuition	12	1.6	0	0.0	12	1.0
Full tuition	13	1.7	1	0.3	14	1.2
More than full tuition	0	0.0	0	0.0	0	0.0
Median Grant Amount	$1,497		$736			

Refunds

Refunds of Admissions or Seat Deposit prior to commencement of classes? No

Refunds of Pre-paid tuition prior to commencement of classes? Yes

If yes, fully refundable before the start of classes? Yes

Joint Degrees Offered

JD/MBA

Advanced Degrees Offered

LL.M.	General
LL.M.	Taxation
LL.M.	American Common Law Legal System; International and Comparative Law (foreign lawyers)
LL.M.	Law and Humanities; Clinical Legal Education (prospective law teachers)
LL.M.	Trial Advocacy

Career Placement

	Total	%
Employment status known	350	91.2
Employment status unknown	34	8.9
Employed	315	90.0
Pursuing graduate degrees	4	1.1
Unemployed seeking employment	22	6.3
Unemployed not seeking employment	9	2.6
Type of Employment		
# employed in law firms	149	47.3
# employed in business & industry	69	21.9
# employed in government	28	8.9
# employed in public interest	13	4.1
# employed as judicial clerks	54	17.1
# employed in academia	2	0.6
Geographic Location		
# employed in state	211	67.0
# employed in foreign countries	0	0.0
# of states where employed	15	

Bar Passage Rate

Jurisdiction	PA
# from school taking bar for the first time	301
School's pass rate for all first-time takers	61%
State's pass rate for all first-time takers	73%
State's pass rate for all first-time takers from ABA approved law schools	73%

TENNESSEE, UNIVERSITY OF

2221 Dunford Hall
915 Volunteer Blvd
Knoxville, TN 37996-4070
(423)974-4241
http://www.law.utk.edu

ABA Approved Since 1925

The Basics

Type of School: **PUBLIC**
Application deadline*: **2/1**
Application fee: **$15**
Financial Aid deadline*: **2/14**
Student faculty ratio: **14.5 to 1**

First year can start other than Fall: **No**
Student housing: **No**
--exclusively for law students: **No**
Term: **Semester**

*pr=preferred

Faculty

	Men #	Men %	Women #	Women %	Minorities #	Minorities %	Total
Full-time	19	70	8	30	2	7	27
Other full-time	0	0	0	0	0	0	0
Deans, librarians, & others who teach	3	100	0	0	0	0	3
Part-time	16	73	6	27	0	0	22
Total	38	73	14	27	2	4	52
Deans, librarians, & others who teach < 1/2	1	50	1	50	0	0	2

Library

# of volumes & volume equivalents	420,805	# of professional staff	6
# of titles	81,103	Hours per week with professional staff	71
# of active serial subscriptions	5,344	Hours per week without professional staff	41
Study seating capacity inside the library	286	# of student computer work stations for entire law school	57
Square feet of law library	59,425	# of additional networked connections	57
Square feet of law school (excl. Library)	46,975		

Curriculum

	Full time	Part time
Typical first-year section size	55	0
Is there typically a "small section" of the first year class, other than Legal Writing, taught by full-time faculty?	No	No
If yes, typical size offered last year	N/A	N/A
# of classroom course titles beyond 1st year curriculum	46	0
# of upper division courses, excluding seminars, with an enrollment:		
Under 25	44	0
25 - 49	17	0
50 - 74	17	0
75 - 99	3	0
100 +	0	0
# of seminars	12	0
# of seminar positions available	202	
# of seminar positions filled	165	0
# of positions available in simulation courses	448	
# of simulation positions filled	384	0
# of positions available in faculty supervised clinical courses	88	
# of fac. sup. clin. positions filled	85	0
# involved in field placements	0	0
# involved in law journals	60	0
# in moot court or trial competitions	109	0
# of credit hours required to graduate	89	

Enrollment & Attrition

	Full-Time Men #	Men %	Women #	Women %	Minorities #	Minorities %	Total #	Part-Time Men #	Men %	Women #	Women %	Minorities #	Minorities %	Total #	Attrition Academic #	Other #	Total #	%
1st Year	96	58.2	69	41.8	20	12.1	165	0	0.0	0	0.0	0	0.0	0	4	6	10	6.1
2nd Year	79	49.7	80	50.3	20	12.6	159	0	0.0	0	0.0	0	0.0	0	2	1	3	2.1
3rd Year	75	51.7	70	48.3	15	10.3	145	0	0.0	0	0.0	0	0.0	0	0	0	0	0.0
4th Year								0	0.0	0	0.0	0	0.0	0	0	0	0	0.0
Total	250	53.3	219	46.7	55	11.7	469	0	0.0	0	0.0	0	0.0	0	6	7	13	2.7
JD Degrees Awarded	86	52.8	77	47.2	15	9.2	163	0	0.0	0	0.0	0	0.0	0				

GPA & LSAT Scores

	Full Time	Part Time	Total
# of apps	1,062	0	1,062
# admits	384	0	384
# of matrics	165	0	165
75% GPA	3.71	0.00	
25% GPA	3.14	0.00	
75% LSAT	160	0	
25% LSAT	153	0	

Tuition/Living Expenses

	Resident	Non-resident
Full-Time	$3,794	$9,620
Part-Time	$0	$0

Estimated living expenses for Singles		
Living on campus	Living off campus	Living at home
$10,292	$10,292	$7,039

Career Placement

	Total	%
Employment status known	148	99.3
Employment status unknown	1	0.7
Employed	136	91.9
Pursuing graduate degrees	0	0.0
Unemployed seeking employment	9	6.1
Unemployed not seeking employment	3	2.0
Type of Employment		
# employed in law firms	93	68.4
# employed in business & industry	9	6.6
# employed in government	11	8.1
# employed in public interest	4	2.9
# employed as judicial clerks	18	13.2
# employed in academia	1	0.7
Geographic Location		
# employed in state	103	75.7
# employed in foreign countries	0	0.0
# of states where employed	13	

Financial Aid

	Full-time		Part-time		Total	
	#	%	#	%	#	%
Total # receiving grants	105	22.4	0	0.0	105	22.4
Less than 1/2 tuition	22	4.7	0	0.0	22	4.7
Half to full tuition	19	4.1	0	0.0	19	4.1
Full tuition	0	0.0	0	0.0	0	0.0
More than full tuition	64	13.7	0	0.0	64	13.6
Median Grant Amount	$4,000		$0			

Refunds

Refunds of Admissions or Seat Deposit prior to commencement of classes? No

Refunds of Pre-paid tuition prior to commencement of classes? Yes

If yes, fully refundable before the start of classes? Yes

Joint Degrees Offered

JD/MBA, JD/MPA

Advanced Degrees Offered

No Advanced Degrees

Bar Passage Rate

Jurisdiction	TN
# from school taking bar for the first time	109
School's pass rate for all first-time takers	86%
State's pass rate for all first-time takers	79%
State's pass rate for all first-time takers from ABA approved law schools	91%

TEXAS AT AUSTIN, UNIVERSITY OF

727 E. 26th Street
Austin, TX 78705
(512)471-4800
http://www.utexas.edu/law

ABA Approved Since 1923

The Basics

Type of School: **PUBLIC**
Application deadline*: **2/1**
Application fee: **$65**
Financial Aid deadline*: **3/31**
Student faculty ratio: **18.7 to 1**
First year can start other than Fall: **No**
Student housing: **No**
--exclusively for law students: **No**
Term: **Semester**

*pr=preferred

Faculty

	Men #	Men %	Women #	Women %	Minorities #	Minorities %	Total
Full-time	53	79	14	21	5	7	67
Other full-time	0	0	1	100	0	0	1
Deans, librarians, & others who teach	1	50	1	50	0	0	2
Part-time	31	66	16	34	5	11	47
Total	85	73	32	27	10	9	117
Deans, librarians, & others who teach < 1/2	0	0	1	100	0	0	1

Library

# of volumes & volume equivalents	907,417	# of professional staff	20
# of titles	236,449	Hours per week with professional staff	84
# of active serial subscriptions	9,515	Hours per week without professional staff	18
Study seating capacity inside the library	1,361	# of student computer work stations for entire law school	126
Square feet of law library	167,000	# of additional networked connections	0
Square feet of law school (excl. Library)	101,053		

Curriculum

	Full time	Part time
Typical first-year section size	100	0
Is there typically a "small section" of the first year class, other than Legal Writing, taught by full-time faculty?	No	No
If yes, typical size offered last year	N/A	N/A
# of classroom course titles beyond 1st year curriculum	111	0
# of upper division courses, excluding seminars, with an enrollment:		
Under 25	67	0
25 - 49	57	0
50 - 74	24	0
75 - 99	18	0
100 +	18	0
# of seminars	66	0
# of seminar positions available	792	
# of seminar positions filled	673	0
# of positions available in simulation courses	733	
# of simulation positions filled	561	0
# of positions available in faculty supervised clinical courses	236	
# of fac. sup. clin. positions filled	203	0
# involved in field placements	94	0
# involved in law journals	525	0
# in moot court or trial competitions	439	0
# of credit hours required to graduate	86	

Enrollment & Attrition

	Full-Time							Part-Time							Attrition			
	Men		Women		Minorities		Total	Men		Women		Minorities		Total	Academic	Other	Total	
	#	%	#	%	#	%	#	#	%	#	%	#	%	#	#	#	#	%
1st Year	273	54.4	229	45.6	115	22.9	502	0	0.0	0	0.0	0	0.0	0	2	13	15	2.9
2nd Year	283	55.5	227	44.5	136	26.7	510	0	0.0	0	0.0	0	0.0	0	0	6	6	1.1
3rd Year	318	60.0	212	40.0	130	24.5	530	0	0.0	0	0.0	0	0.0	0	0	4	4	0.8
4th Year								0	0.0	0	0.0	0	0.0	0	0	0	0	0.0
Total	874	56.7	668	43.3	381	24.7	1,542	0	0.0	0	0.0	0	0.0	0	2	23	25	1.6
JD Degrees Awarded	286	58.7	201	41.3	104	21.4	487	0	0.0	0	0.0	0	0.0	0				

GPA & LSAT Scores

	Full Time	Part Time	Total
# of apps	3,910	0	3,910
# admits	1,105	0	1,105
# of matrics	488	0	488
75% GPA	3.78	0.00	
25% GPA	3.40	0.00	
75% LSAT	165	0	
25% LSAT	159	0	

Tuition/Living Expenses

	Resident	Non-resident
Full-Time	$5,340	$11,360
Part-Time	$0	$0

Estimated living expenses for Singles		
Living on campus	Living off campus	Living at home
N/A	$10,044	N/A

Career Placement

	Total	%
Employment status known	451	97.0
Employment status unknown	14	3.0
Employed	405	89.8
Pursuing graduate degrees	5	1.1
Unemployed seeking employment	34	7.5
Unemployed not seeking employment	7	1.6
Type of Employment		
# employed in law firms	286	70.6
# employed in business & industry	19	4.7
# employed in government	44	10.9
# employed in public interest	12	3.0
# employed as judicial clerks	42	10.4
# employed in academia	2	0.5
Geographic Location		
# employed in state	324	80.0
# employed in foreign countries	1	0.3
# of states where employed	23	

Financial Aid

	Full-time		Part-time		Total	
	#	%	#	%	#	%
Total # receiving grants	1175	76.2	0	0.0	1175	76.2
Less than 1/2 tuition	1046	67.8	0	0.0	1046	67.8
Half to full tuition	16	1.0	0	0.0	16	1.0
Full tuition	63	4.1	0	0.0	63	4.1
More than full tuition	50	3.2	0	0.0	50	3.2
Median Grant Amount	$2,923		$0			

Refunds

Refunds of Admissions or Seat Deposit prior to commencement of classes? No

Refunds of Pre-paid tuition prior to commencement of classes? No

If yes, fully refundable before the start of classes? No

80% refund from 04/15/96 to 08/31/96

Joint Degrees Offered

JD/MBA, JD/MPA, JD/MA

Advanced Degrees Offered

LL.M. General

Bar Passage Rate

Jurisdiction	TX
# from school taking bar for the first time	356
School's pass rate for all first-time takers	92%
State's pass rate for all first-time takers	82%
State's pass rate for all first-time takers from ABA approved law schools	82%

TEXAS SOUTHERN UNIVERSITY

3100 Cleburne
Houston, TX 77004-3216
(713)313-1075
http://www.tsulaw.edu

ABA Approved Since 1949

The Basics

Type of School: **PUBLIC**
Application deadline*: **4/11**
Application fee: **$40**
Financial Aid deadline*: **5/11**
Student faculty ratio: **22.8 to 1**
First year can start other than Fall: **No**
Student housing: **Yes**
--exclusively for law students: **No**
Term: **Semester**

*pr=preferred

Faculty

	Men #	Men %	Women #	Women %	Minorities #	Minorities %	Total
Full-time	16	73	6	27	17	77	22
Other full-time	1	25	3	75	0	0	4
Deans, librarians, & others who teach	4	100	0	0	4	100	4
Part-time	5	63	3	38	6	75	8
Total	26	68	12	32	27	71	38
Deans, librarians, & others who teach < 1/2	1	50	1	50	2	100	2

Library

# of volumes & volume equivalents	371,147	# of professional staff	6
# of titles	60,032	Hours per week with professional staff	63
# of active serial subscriptions	2,448	Hours per week without professional staff	44
Study seating capacity inside the library	348	# of student computer work stations for entire law school	30
Square feet of law library	47,883	# of additional networked connections	40
Square feet of law school (excl. Library)	49,326		

Curriculum

	Full time	Part time
Typical first-year section size	65	0
Is there typically a "small section" of the first year class, other than Legal Writing, taught by full-time faculty?	No	No
If yes, typical size offered last year	N/A	N/A
# of classroom course titles beyond 1st year curriculum	68	0
# of upper division courses, excluding seminars, with an enrollment:		
Under 25	38	0
25 - 49	26	0
50 - 74	12	0
75 - 99	3	0
100 +	0	0
# of seminars	13	0
# of seminar positions available	260	
# of seminar positions filled	145	0
# of positions available in simulation courses	141	
# of simulation positions filled	141	0
# of positions available in faculty supervised clinical courses	21	
# of fac. sup. clin. positions filled	21	0
# involved in field placements	156	0
# involved in law journals	35	0
# in moot court or trial competitions	21	0
# of credit hours required to graduate	90	

Enrollment & Attrition

	Full-Time							Part-Time							Attrition			
	Men		Women		Minorities		Total	Men		Women		Minorities		Total	Academic	Other	Total	
	#	%	#	%	#	%	#	#	%	#	%	#	%	#	#	#	#	%
1st Year	162	54.9	133	45.1	250	84.7	295	0	0.0	0	0.0	0	0.0	0	65	27	92	36
2nd Year	86	51.8	80	48.2	135	81.3	166	0	0.0	0	0.0	0	0.0	0	2	10	12	7.8
3rd Year	84	59.2	58	40.8	112	78.9	142	0	0.0	0	0.0	0	0.0	0	0	0	0	0.0
4th Year								0	0.0	0	0.0	0	0.0	0	0	0	0	0.0
Total	332	55.1	271	44.9	497	82.4	603	0	0.0	0	0.0	0	0.0	0	67	37	104	19
JD Degrees Awarded	67	54.5	56	45.5	95	77.2	123	0	0.0	0	0.0	0	0.0	0				

GPA & LSAT Scores

	Full Time	Part Time	Total
# of apps	1,378	0	1,378
# admits	571	0	571
# of matrics	291	0	291
75% GPA	3.03	0.00	
25% GPA	2.41	0.00	
75% LSAT	146	0	
25% LSAT	140	0	

Tuition/Living Expenses

	Resident	Non-resident
Full-Time	$4,440	$8,080
Part-Time	$0	$0

Estimated living expenses for Singles		
Living on campus	Living off campus	Living at home
$4,407	$9,693	$2,678

Career Placement

	Total	%
Employment status known	88	56.1
Employment status unknown	69	44.0
Employed	88	100.0
Pursuing graduate degrees	0	0.0
Unemployed seeking employment	0	0.0
Unemployed not seeking employment	0	0.0
Type of Employment		
# employed in law firms	77	87.5
# employed in business & industry	0	0.0
# employed in government	2	2.3
# employed in public interest	5	5.7
# employed as judicial clerks	4	4.6
# employed in academia	0	0.0
Geographic Location		
# employed in state	81	92.1
# employed in foreign countries	0	0.0
# of states where employed	7	

Financial Aid

	Full-time		Part-time		Total	
	#	%	#	%	#	%
Total # receiving grants	250	41.5	0	0.0	250	41.5
Less than 1/2 tuition	250	41.5	0	0.0	250	41.5
Half to full tuition	0	0.0	0	0.0	0	0.0
Full tuition	0	0.0	0	0.0	0	0.0
More than full tuition	0	0.0	0	0.0	0	0.0
Median Grant Amount	$1,240		$0			

Refunds

Refunds of Admissions or Seat Deposit prior to commencement of classes? No

Refunds of Pre-paid tuition prior to commencement of classes? No

If yes, fully refundable before the start of classes? No

Joint Degrees Offered

No Joint Degrees

Advanced Degrees Offered

No Advanced Degrees

Bar Passage Rate

Jurisdiction	TX
# from school taking bar for the first time	117
School's pass rate for all first-time takers	68%
State's pass rate for all first-time takers	82%
State's pass rate for all first-time takers from ABA approved law schools	82%

TEXAS TECH UNIVERSITY

1802 Hartford
Lubbock, TX 79409-0004
(806)742-3793
http://www.law.ttu.edu

ABA Approved Since 1969

The Basics

Type of School: **PUBLIC**	First year can start other than Fall: **No**
Application deadline*: **2/1**	Student housing: **No**
Application fee: **$50**	--exclusively for law students: **No**
Financial Aid deadline*: **7/1**	Term: **Semester**
Student faculty ratio: **27.5 to 1**	

*pr=preferred

Faculty

	Men		Women		Minorities		Total
	#	%	#	%	#	%	
Full-time	16	80	4	20	2	10	20
Other full-time	0	0	0	0	0	0	0
Deans, librarians, & others who teach	3	60	2	40	0	0	5
Part-time	6	100	0	0	1	17	6
Total	25	81	6	19	3	10	31
Deans, librarians, & others who teach < 1/2	0	0	1	100	0	0	1

Library

# of volumes & volume equivalents	251,207	# of professional staff	5
# of titles	50,041	Hours per week with professional staff	40
# of active serial subscriptions	2,136	Hours per week without professional staff	53
Study seating capacity inside the library	380	# of student computer work stations for entire law school	232
Square feet of law library	49,302	# of additional networked connections	0
Square feet of law school (excl. Library)	40,436		

Curriculum

	Full time	Part time
Typical first-year section size	79	0
Is there typically a "small section" of the first year class, other than Legal Writing, taught by full-time faculty?	No	No
If yes, typical size offered last year	N/A	N/A
# of classroom course titles beyond 1st year curriculum	83	0
# of upper division courses, excluding seminars, with an enrollment:		
Under 25	27	0
25 - 49	23	0
50 - 74	13	0
75 - 99	7	0
100 +	5	0
# of seminars	8	0
# of seminar positions available	130	
# of seminar positions filled	130	0
# of positions available in simulation courses	112	
# of simulation positions filled	111	0
# of positions available in faculty supervised clinical courses	0	
# of fac. sup. clin. positions filled	0	0
# involved in field placements	38	0
# involved in law journals	64	0
# in moot court or trial competitions	57	0
# of credit hours required to graduate	90	

Enrollment & Attrition

	Full-Time							Part-Time							Attrition			
	Men		Women		Minorities		Total	Men		Women		Minorities		Total	Academic	Other	Total	
	#	%	#	%	#	%	#	#	%	#	%	#	%	#	#	#	#	%
1st Year	146	64.6	80	35.4	31	13.7	226	0	0.0	0	0.0	0	0.0	0	5	12	17	7.4
2nd Year	128	58.7	90	41.3	32	14.7	218	0	0.0	0	0.0	0	0.0	0	5	5	10	5.0
3rd Year	131	66.8	65	33.2	28	14.3	196	0	0.0	0	0.0	0	0.0	0	0	1	1	0.5
4th Year								0	0.0	0	0.0	0	0.0	0	0	0	0	0.0
Total	405	63.3	235	36.7	91	14.2	640	0	0.0	0	0.0	0	0.0	0	10	18	28	4.5
JD Degrees Awarded	124	65.3	66	34.7	31	16.3	190	0	0.0	0	0.0	0	0.0	0				

GPA & LSAT Scores

	Full Time	Part Time	Total
# of apps	1,345	0	1,345
# admits	578	0	578
# of matrics	227	0	227
75% GPA	3.63	0.00	
25% GPA	3.18	0.00	
75% LSAT	158	0	
25% LSAT	151	0	

Tuition/Living Expenses

	Resident	Non-resident
Full-Time	$5,866	$9,616
Part-Time	$0	$0

Estimated living expenses for Singles		
Living on campus	Living off campus	Living at home
$8,890	$8,890	$4,860

Career Placement

	Total	%
Employment status known	163	75.5
Employment status unknown	53	24.5
Employed	148	90.8
Pursuing graduate degrees	0	0.0
Unemployed seeking employment	15	9.2
Unemployed not seeking employment	0	0.0
Type of Employment		
# employed in law firms	130	87.8
# employed in business & industry	1	0.7
# employed in government	6	4.1
# employed in public interest	0	0.0
# employed as judicial clerks	10	6.8
# employed in academia	1	0.7
Geographic Location		
# employed in state	144	97.3
# employed in foreign countries	1	0.7
# of states where employed	3	

Financial Aid

	Full-time		Part-time		Total	
	#	%	#	%	#	%
Total # receiving grants	301	47.0	0	0.0	301	47.0
Less than 1/2 tuition	152	23.8	0	0.0	152	23.8
Half to full tuition	21	3.3	0	0.0	21	3.3
Full tuition	113	17.7	0	0.0	113	17.7
More than full tuition	15	2.3	0	0.0	15	2.3
Median Grant Amount	$2,000		$0			

Refunds

Refunds of Admissions or Seat Deposit prior to commencement of classes? Yes

50% refund from 10/01/95 to 05/01/96
0% refund from 05/01/96 to 09/01/96

Refunds of Pre-paid tuition prior to commencement of classes? Yes

If yes, fully refundable before the start of classes? Yes

Joint Degrees Offered

JD/MBA, JD/MPA, JD/AG ECO, JD/MS TAX

Advanced Degrees Offered

No Advanced Degrees

Bar Passage Rate

Jurisdiction	TX
# from school taking bar for the first time	158
School's pass rate for all first-time takers	92%
State's pass rate for all first-time takers	82%
State's pass rate for all first-time takers from ABA approved law schools	82%

TEXAS WESLEYAN UNIVERSITY (Provisional)

2535 E. Grauwyler Road
Irving, TX 75061
(972)579-5782
http://www.txwesleyan.edu

ABA Approved Since 1994

The Basics

Type of School: **PRIVATE**
Application deadline*: **3/15pr**
Application fee: **$50**
Financial Aid deadline*: **4/15pr**
Student faculty ratio: **23.4 to 1**

First year can start other than Fall: **No**
Student housing: **No**
--exclusively for law students: **No**
Term: **Semester**

*pr=preferred

Faculty

	Men #	Men %	Women #	Women %	Minorities #	Minorities %	Total
Full-time	17	81	4	19	2	10	21
Other full-time	0	0	0	0	0	0	0
Deans, librarians, & others who teach	1	50	1	50	0	0	2
Part-time	17	55	14	45	1	3	31
Total	35	65	19	35	3	6	54
Deans, librarians, & others who teach < 1/2	2	100	0	0	0	0	2

Library

# of volumes & volume equivalents	141,426	# of professional staff	6
# of titles	13,003	Hours per week with professional staff	89
# of active serial subscriptions	2,517	Hours per week without professional staff	23
Study seating capacity inside the library	218	# of student computer work stations for entire law school	20
Square feet of law library	15,112	# of additional networked connections	0
Square feet of law school (excl. Library)	67,583		

Curriculum

	Full time	Part time
Typical first-year section size	77	110
Is there typically a "small section" of the first year class, other than Legal Writing, taught by full-time faculty?	Yes	Yes
If yes, typical size offered last year	42	52
# of classroom course titles beyond 1st year curriculum	37	42
# of upper division courses, excluding seminars, with an enrollment:		
Under 25	26	29
25 - 49	9	14
50 - 74	5	7
75 - 99	1	2
100 +	0	0
# of seminars	6	4
# of seminar positions available	160	
# of seminar positions filled	72	38
# of positions available in simulation courses	295	
# of simulation positions filled	111	60
# of positions available in faculty supervised clinical courses	0	
# of fac. sup. clin. positions filled	0	0
# involved in field placements	15	6
# involved in law journals	27	18
# in moot court or trial competitions	11	9
# of credit hours required to graduate	88	

Enrollment & Attrition

	Full-Time Men #	Men %	Women #	Women %	Minorities #	Minorities %	Total #	Part-Time Men #	Men %	Women #	Women %	Minorities #	Minorities %	Total #	Attrition Academic #	Other #	Total #	Total %
1st Year	83	57.6	61	42.4	31	21.5	144	69	65.7	36	34.3	17	16.2	105	24	27	51	19
2nd Year	79	48.5	84	51.5	30	18.4	163	64	60.4	42	39.6	23	21.7	106	8	17	25	10
3rd Year	40	58.0	29	42.0	11	15.9	69	38	65.5	20	34.5	8	13.8	58	3	4	7	6.7
4th Year								34	63.0	20	37.0	10	18.5	54	0	0	0	0.0
Total	202	53.7	174	46.3	72	19.1	376	205	63.5	118	36.5	58	18.0	323	35	48	83	12
JD Degrees Awarded	41	74.5	14	25.5	3	5.5	55	49	57.0	37	43.0	12	14.0	86				

TEXAS WESLEYAN UNIVERSITY (Provisional)

GPA & LSAT Scores

	Full Time	Part Time	Total
# of apps	783	226	1,009
# admits	418	141	559
# of matrics	144	105	249
75% GPA	3.23	3.22	
25% GPA	2.59	2.69	
75% LSAT	150	151	
25% LSAT	143	144	

Tuition/Living Expenses

	Resident	Non-resident
Full-Time	$11,234	$11,234
Part-Time	$8,074	$8,074

Estimated living expenses for Singles		
Living on campus	Living off campus	Living at home
N/A	$8,257	$5,571

Financial Aid

	Full-time		Part-time		Total	
	#	%	#	%	#	%
Total # receiving grants	171	45.5	142	44.0	313	44.8
Less than 1/2 tuition	169	45.0	140	43.3	309	44.2
Half to full tuition	0	0.0	0	0.0	0	0.0
Full tuition	0	0.0	1	0.3	1	0.1
More than full tuition	2	0.5	1	0.3	3	0.4
Median Grant Amount	$1,100		$475			

Refunds

Refunds of Admissions or Seat Deposit prior to commencement of classes? No

Refunds of Pre-paid tuition prior to commencement of classes? Yes

If yes, fully refundable before the start of classes? Yes

Joint Degrees Offered

No Joint Degrees

Advanced Degrees Offered

No Advanced Degrees

Career Placement

	Total	%
Employment status known	77	41.4
Employment status unknown	109	58.6
Employed	65	84.4
Pursuing graduate degrees	0	0.0
Unemployed seeking employment	12	15.6
Unemployed not seeking employment	0	0.0
Type of Employment		
# employed in law firms	34	52.3
# employed in business & industry	25	38.5
# employed in government	3	4.6
# employed in public interest	3	4.6
# employed as judicial clerks	0	0.0
# employed in academia	0	0.0
Geographic Location		
# employed in state	65	100.0
# employed in foreign countries	0	0.0
# of states where employed	1	

Bar Passage Rate

Jurisdiction	TX
# from school taking bar for the first time	58
School's pass rate for all first-time takers	48%
State's pass rate for all first-time takers	82%
State's pass rate for all first-time takers from ABA approved law schools	82%

THOMAS JEFFERSON SCHOOL OF LAW (Provisional)

2121 San Diego Avenue
San Diego, CA 92101
(619)297-9700
http://www.jeffersonlaw.edu

ABA Approved Since 1996

The Basics

Type of School: **PRIVATE**
Application deadline*: **n/a**
Application fee: **$35**
Financial Aid deadline*:
Student faculty ratio: **20.1 to 1**

First year can start other than Fall: **Yes**
Student housing: **No**
--exclusively for law students: **No**
Term: **Semester**

*pr=preferred

Faculty

	Men		Women		Minorities		Total
	#	%	#	%	#	%	
Full-time	8	44	10	56	0	0	18
Other full-time	0	0	0	0	0	0	0
Deans, librarians, & others who teach	1	50	1	50	0	0	2
Part-time	17	81	4	19	1	5	21
Total	26	63	15	37	1	2	41
Deans, librarians, & others who teach < 1/2	0	0	1	100	0	0	1

Library

# of volumes & volume equivalents	107,971	# of professional staff	5
# of titles	10,653	Hours per week with professional staff	76
# of active serial subscriptions	2,413	Hours per week without professional staff	19
Study seating capacity inside the library	286	# of student computer work stations for entire law school	33
Square feet of law library	17,588	# of additional networked connections	0
Square feet of law school (excl. Library)	49,412		

Curriculum

	Full time	Part time
Typical first-year section size	30	30
Is there typically a "small section" of the first year class, other than Legal Writing, taught by full-time faculty?	No	No
If yes, typical size offered last year	N/A	N/A
# of classroom course titles beyond 1st year curriculum	34	33
# of upper division courses, excluding seminars, with an enrollment:		
Under 25	23	21
25 - 49	7	15
50 - 74	4	5
75 - 99	2	2
100 +	0	0
# of seminars	5	3
# of seminar positions available	80	
# of seminar positions filled	33	25
# of positions available in simulation courses	224	
# of simulation positions filled	28	117
# of positions available in faculty supervised clinical courses	0	
# of fac. sup. clin. positions filled	0	0
# involved in field placements	29	99
# involved in law journals	10	28
# in moot court or trial competitions	9	30
# of credit hours required to graduate	88	

Enrollment & Attrition

	Full-Time							Part-Time							Attrition			
	Men		Women		Minorities		Total	Men		Women		Minorities		Total	Academic	Other	Total	
	#	%	#	%	#	%	#	#	%	#	%	#	%	#	#	#	#	%
1st Year	51	53.1	45	46.9	24	25.0	96	62	61.4	39	38.6	21	20.8	101	33	25	58	27
2nd Year	35	63.6	20	36.4	12	21.8	55	52	68.4	24	31.6	14	18.4	76	21	4	25	18
3rd Year	20	62.5	12	37.5	6	18.8	32	40	55.6	32	44.4	6	8.3	72	2	0	2	1.6
4th Year								73	56.2	57	43.8	21	16.2	130	2	0	2	2.3
Total	106	57.9	77	42.1	42	23.0	183	227	59.9	152	40.1	62	16.4	379	58	29	87	15
JD Degrees Awarded	19	65.5	10	34.5	1	3.4	29	40	48.2	43	51.8	15	18.1	83				

THOMAS JEFFERSON SCHOOL OF LAW (Provisional)

GPA & LSAT Scores

	Full Time	Part Time	Total
# of apps	208	131	339
# admits	139	89	228
# of matrics	70	61	131
75% GPA	2.98	3.01	
25% GPA	2.48	2.55	
75% LSAT	150	152	
25% LSAT	145	146	

Tuition/Living Expenses

	Resident	Non-resident
Full-Time	$16,685	$16,685
Part-Time	$12,940	$12,940

Estimated living expenses for Singles		
Living on campus	Living off campus	Living at home
N/A	$12,882	$7,909

Career Placement

	Total	%
Employment status known	81	48.8
Employment status unknown	85	51.2
Employed	76	93.8
Pursuing graduate degrees	1	1.2
Unemployed seeking employment	1	1.2
Unemployed not seeking employment	3	3.7
Type of Employment		
# employed in law firms	47	61.8
# employed in business & industry	11	14.5
# employed in government	8	10.5
# employed in public interest	0	0.0
# employed as judicial clerks	0	0.0
# employed in academia	1	1.3
Geographic Location		
# employed in state	0	0.0
# employed in foreign countries	0	0.0
# of states where employed	0	

Financial Aid

	Full-time		Part-time		Total	
	#	%	#	%	#	%
Total # receiving grants	78	42.6	120	31.7	198	35.2
Less than 1/2 tuition	70	38.3	118	31.1	188	33.5
Half to full tuition	6	3.3	1	0.3	7	1.2
Full tuition	1	0.6	1	0.3	2	0.4
More than full tuition	1	0.6	0	0.0	1	0.2
Median Grant Amount	$4,000		$1,600			

Refunds

Refunds of Admissions or Seat Deposit prior to commencement of classes? Yes

100% refund to 04/01/96

Refunds of Pre-paid tuition prior to commencement of classes? Yes

If yes, fully refundable before the start of classes? Yes

90% refund from 08/29/96 to 09/03/96
80% refund from 09/04/96 to 09/17/96
70% refund from 09/18/96 to 09/24/96

Joint Degrees Offered

No Joint Degrees

Advanced Degrees Offered

No Advanced Degrees

Bar Passage Rate

Jurisdiction	CA
# from school taking bar for the first time	93
School's pass rate for all first-time takers	48%
State's pass rate for all first-time takers	73%
State's pass rate for all first-time takers from ABA approved law schools	83%

THOMAS M. COOLEY LAW SCHOOL

217 South Capitol Avenue
P.O. Box 13038
Lansing, MI 48901
(517)371-5140
http://www.cooley.edu

As of May, 1996, Thomas M. Cooley offers two full-time and two part-time scheduling options.

ABA Approved Since 1975

The Basics

Type of School: **PRIVATE**
Application deadline: **rolling**
Application fee: **$50**
Financial Aid deadline:
Student faculty ratio: **24.3 to 1**
First year can start other than Fall: **Yes**
Student housing: **No**
--exclusively for law students: **No**
Term: **Semester**

Faculty

	Men		Women		Minorities		Total
	#	%	#	%	#	%	
Full-time	32	74	11	26	4	9	43
Other full-time	1	33	2	67	0	0	3
Deans, librarians, & others who teach	3	60	2	40	0	0	5
Part-time	72	69	32	31	4	4	104
Total	108	70	47	30	8	5	155
Deans, librarians, & others who teach < 1/2	2	40	3	60	0	0	5

Library

# of volumes & volume equivalents	349,416	# of professional staff	11
# of titles	70,585	Hours per week with professional staff	80
# of active serial subscriptions	5,509	Hours per week without professional staff	31
Study seating capacity inside the library	530	# of student computer work stations for entire law school	58
Square feet of law library	65,000	# of additional networked connections	27
Square feet of law school (excl. Library)	149,924		

Curriculum

	Full time	Part time
Typical first-year section size	0	80
Is there typically a "small section" of the first year class, other than Legal Writing, taught by full-time faculty?	No	No
If yes, typical size offered last year	N/A	N/A
# of classroom course titles beyond 1st year curriculum	0	94
# of upper division courses, excluding seminars, with an enrollment:		
Under 25	0	54
25 - 49	0	63
50 - 74	0	26
75 - 99	0	46
100 +	0	4
# of seminars	0	199
# of seminar positions available	2,644	
# of seminar positions filled	0	2,037
# of positions available in simulation courses	984	
# of simulation positions filled	0	914
# of positions available in faculty supervised clinical courses	64	
# of fac. sup. clin. positions filled	0	64
# involved in field placements	0	75
# involved in law journals	0	135
# in moot court or trial competitions	0	70
# of credit hours required to graduate	90	

Enrollment & Attrition

	Full-Time							Part-Time							Attrition			
	Men		Women		Minorities		Total	Men		Women		Minorities		Total	Academic	Other	Total	
	#	%	#	%	#	%	#	#	%	#	%	#	%	#	#	#	#	%
1st Year	76	71.0	31	29.0	22	20.6	107	579	64.1	324	35.9	140	15.5	903	178	127	305	35
2nd Year	17	70.8	7	29.2	0	0.0	24	296	67.4	143	32.6	53	12.1	439	92	164	256	52
3rd Year	18	78.3	5	21.7	1	4.3	23	203	62.5	122	37.5	14	4.3	325	1	1	2	0.5
4th Year								0	0.0	0	0.0	0	0.0	0	0	0	0	0.0
Total	111	72.1	43	27.9	23	14.9	154	1078	64.7	589	35.3	207	12.4	1667	271	292	563	32
JD Degrees Awarded	37	71.2	15	28.8	4	7.7	52	278	69.5	122	30.5	16	4.0	400				

THOMAS M. COOLEY LAW SCHOOL

GPA & LSAT Scores

	Full Time	Part Time	Total
# of apps	0	1,934	1,934
# admits	0	1,529	1,529
# of matrics	106	982	1,088
75% GPA	3.08	3.02	
25% GPA	2.56	2.54	
75% LSAT	148	148	
25% LSAT	143	142	

Tuition/Living Expenses

	Resident	Non-resident
Full-Time	$0	$0
Part-Time	$0	$14,260

Estimated living expenses for Singles		
Living on campus	Living off campus	Living at home
N/A	$15,571	$7,431

Financial Aid

	Full-time		Part-time		Total	
	#	%	#	%	#	%
Total # receiving grants	0	0.0	21	1.3	21	1.2
Less than 1/2 tuition	0	0.0	10	0.6	10	0.5
Half to full tuition	0	0.0	0	0.0	0	0.0
Full tuition	0	0.0	11	0.7	11	0.6
More than full tuition	0	0.0	0	0.0	0	0.0
Median Grant Amount	$0		$4,687			

Refunds

Refunds of Admissions or Seat Deposit prior to commencement of classes? Yes

Refunds of Pre-paid tuition prior to commencement of classes? Yes

If yes, fully refundable before the start of classes? Yes

Joint Degrees Offered

No Joint Degrees

Advanced Degrees Offered

No Advanced Degrees

Career Placement

	Total	%
Employment status known	191	48.7
Employment status unknown	201	51.3
Employed	162	84.8
Pursuing graduate degrees	9	4.7
Unemployed seeking employment	17	8.9
Unemployed not seeking employment	3	1.6
Type of Employment		
# employed in law firms	122	75.3
# employed in business & industry	27	16.7
# employed in government	28	17.3
# employed in public interest	0	0.0
# employed as judicial clerks	12	7.4
# employed in academia	2	1.2
Geographic Location		
# employed in state	90	55.6
# employed in foreign countries	0	0.0
# of states where employed	30	

Bar Passage Rate

Jurisdiction	MI	NY
# from school taking bar for the first time	59	48
School's pass rate for all first-time takers	61%	63%
State's pass rate for all first-time takers	70%	78%
State's pass rate for all first-time takers from ABA approved law schools	70%	

TOLEDO, UNIVERSITY OF

2801 West Bancroft
Toledo, OH 43606
(419)530-2882
http://www.utoledo.edu/law

ABA Approved Since 1939

The Basics

Type of School: **PUBLIC**
Application deadline*: **3/15**
Application fee: **$30**
Financial Aid deadline*: **4/1**
Student faculty ratio: **18.8 to 1**

First year can start other than Fall: **No**
Student housing: **No**
--exclusively for law students: **No**
Term: **Semester**

*pr=preferred

Faculty

	Men #	Men %	Women #	Women %	Minorities #	Minorities %	Total
Full-time	20	77	6	23	1	4	26
Other full-time	0	0	0	0	0	0	0
Deans, librarians, & others who teach	1	100	0	0	0	0	1
Part-time	10	71	4	29	0	0	14
Total	31	76	10	24	1	2	41
Deans, librarians, & others who teach < 1/2	3	100	0	0	0	0	3

Library

# of volumes & volume equivalents	301,214	# of professional staff	6
# of titles	41,986	Hours per week with professional staff	82
# of active serial subscriptions	3,374	Hours per week without professional staff	31
Study seating capacity inside the library	533	# of student computer work stations for entire law school	63
Square feet of law library	41,900	# of additional networked connections	45
Square feet of law school (excl. Library)	59,972		

Curriculum

	Full time	Part time
Typical first-year section size	50	47
Is there typically a "small section" of the first year class, other than Legal Writing, taught by full-time faculty?	Yes	No
If yes, typical size offered last year	28	N/A
# of classroom course titles beyond 1st year curriculum	44	33
# of upper division courses, excluding seminars, with an enrollment:		
Under 25	22	15
25 - 49	15	13
50 - 74	13	9
75 - 99	5	3
100 +	0	0
# of seminars	8	4
# of seminar positions available	180	
# of seminar positions filled	81	53
# of positions available in simulation courses	312	
# of simulation positions filled	217	82
# of positions available in faculty supervised clinical courses	110	
# of fac. sup. clin. positions filled	88	10
# involved in field placements	36	3
# involved in law journals	54	3
# in moot court or trial competitions	49	0
# of credit hours required to graduate	87	

Enrollment & Attrition

	Full-Time Men #	Men %	Women #	Women %	Minorities #	Minorities %	Total #	Part-Time Men #	Men %	Women #	Women %	Minorities #	Minorities %	Total #	Attrition Academic #	Other #	Total #	%
1st Year	84	56.8	64	43.2	9	6.1	148	28	56.0	22	44.0	4	8.0	50	12	15	27	13
2nd Year	72	55.0	59	45.0	19	14.5	131	28	48.3	30	51.7	7	12.1	58	4	2	6	3.2
3rd Year	97	61.8	60	38.2	14	8.9	157	16	40.0	24	60.0	3	7.5	40	2	1	3	1.3
4th Year								31	62.0	19	38.0	4	8.0	50	0	0	0	0.0
Total	253	58.0	183	42.0	42	9.6	436	103	52.0	95	48.0	18	9.1	198	18	18	36	5.4
JD Degrees Awarded	105	64.8	57	35.2	23	14.2	162	23	57.5	17	42.5	3	7.5	40				

GPA & LSAT Scores

	Full Time	Part Time	Total
# of apps	765	163	928
# admits	488	93	581
# of matrics	154	46	200
75% GPA	3.37	3.57	
25% GPA	2.67	2.69	
75% LSAT	157	153	
25% LSAT	150	148	

Tuition/Living Expenses

	Resident	Non-resident
Full-Time	$6,542	$12,442
Part-Time	$5,452	$10,370

Estimated living expenses for Singles		
Living on campus	Living off campus	Living at home
N/A	$9,502	$6,543

Career Placement

	Total	%
Employment status known	119	78.3
Employment status unknown	33	21.7
Employed	92	77.3
Pursuing graduate degrees	5	4.2
Unemployed seeking employment	11	9.2
Unemployed not seeking employment	11	9.2
Type of Employment		
# employed in law firms	48	52.2
# employed in business & industry	16	17.4
# employed in government	13	14.1
# employed in public interest	2	2.2
# employed as judicial clerks	10	10.9
# employed in academia	3	3.3
Geographic Location		
# employed in state	61	66.3
# employed in foreign countries	1	1.1
# of states where employed	12	

Financial Aid

	Full-time		Part-time		Total	
	#	%	#	%	#	%
Total # receiving grants	108	24.8	16	8.1	124	19.6
Less than 1/2 tuition	11	2.5	13	6.6	24	3.8
Half to full tuition	15	3.4	1	0.5	16	2.5
Full tuition	4	0.9	1	0.5	5	0.8
More than full tuition	78	17.9	1	0.5	79	12.5
Median Grant Amount	$6,541		$315			

Refunds

Refunds of Admissions or Seat Deposit prior to commencement of classes? No

Refunds of Pre-paid tuition prior to commencement of classes? Yes

If yes, fully refundable before the start of classes? Yes

Joint Degrees Offered

JD/MBA

Advanced Degrees Offered

No Advanced Degrees

Bar Passage Rate

Jurisdiction	OH
# from school taking bar for the first time	60
School's pass rate for all first-time takers	92%
State's pass rate for all first-time takers	93%
State's pass rate for all first-time takers from ABA approved law schools	90%

TOURO COLLEGE

300 Nassau Road
Huntington, NY 11743
(516)421-2244
http://www.tourolaw.edu

ABA Approved Since 1983

The Basics

Type of School: **PRIVATE**
Application deadline*: **rolling**
Application fee: **$50**
Financial Aid deadline*: **5/1**
Student faculty ratio: **16.5 to 1**
First year can start other than Fall: **No**
Student housing: **Yes**
--exclusively for law students: **Yes**
Term: **Semester**

*pr=preferred

Faculty

	Men #	Men %	Women #	Women %	Minorities #	Minorities %	Total
Full-time	22	63	13	37	3	9	35
Other full-time	2	100	0	0	0	0	2
Deans, librarians, & others who teach	0	0	2	100	0	0	2
Part-time	11	92	1	8	1	8	12
Total	35	69	16	31	4	8	51
Deans, librarians, & others who teach < 1/2	1	100	0	0	0	0	1

Library

# of volumes & volume equivalents	336,636	# of professional staff	6
# of titles	53,419	Hours per week with professional staff	76
# of active serial subscriptions	3,408	Hours per week without professional staff	10
Study seating capacity inside the library	424	# of student computer work stations for entire law school	50
Square feet of law library	27,950	# of additional networked connections	0
Square feet of law school (excl. Library)	93,050		

Curriculum

	Full time	Part time
Typical first-year section size	55	73
Is there typically a "small section" of the first year class, other than Legal Writing, taught by full-time faculty?	Yes	No
If yes, typical size offered last year	55	N/A
# of classroom course titles beyond 1st year curriculum	47	35
# of upper division courses, excluding seminars, with an enrollment:		
Under 25	11	10
25 - 49	11	9
50 - 74	7	8
75 - 99	5	1
100 +	2	3
# of seminars	11	4
# of seminar positions available	300	
# of seminar positions filled	198	74
# of positions available in simulation courses	320	
# of simulation positions filled	229	78
# of positions available in faculty supervised clinical courses	160	
# of fac. sup. clin. positions filled	115	22
# involved in field placements	128	25
# involved in law journals	49	11
# in moot court or trial competitions	15	5
# of credit hours required to graduate	87	

Enrollment & Attrition

	Full-Time Men #	Men %	Women #	Women %	Minorities #	Minorities %	Total #	Part-Time Men #	Men %	Women #	Women %	Minorities #	Minorities %	Total #	Attrition Academic #	Other #	Total #	%
1st Year	63	55.3	51	44.7	28	24.6	114	61	59.8	41	40.2	23	22.5	102	6	22	28	12
2nd Year	82	55.8	65	44.2	40	27.2	147	44	62.9	26	37.1	14	20.0	70	8	4	12	4.6
3rd Year	127	67.9	60	32.1	42	22.5	187	45	57.0	34	43.0	24	30.4	79	2	0	2	0.9
4th Year								42	52.5	38	47.5	19	23.8	80	0	0	0	0.0
Total	272	60.7	176	39.3	110	24.6	448	192	58.0	139	42.0	80	24.2	331	16	26	42	5.3
JD Degrees Awarded	94	63.1	55	36.9	34	22.8	149	43	63.2	25	36.8	18	26.5	68				

GPA & LSAT Scores

	Full Time	Part Time	Total
# of apps	1,232	443	1,675
# admits	481	218	699
# of matrics	113	107	220
75% GPA	3.28	3.18	
25% GPA	2.69	2.55	
75% LSAT	153	151	
25% LSAT	144	147	

Tuition/Living Expenses

	Resident	Non-resident
Full-Time	$18,750	$18,750
Part-Time	$14,600	$14,600

Estimated living expenses for Singles		
Living on campus	Living off campus	Living at home
$15,089	$15,089	$7,946

Career Placement

	Total	%
Employment status known	199	86.5
Employment status unknown	31	13.5
Employed	144	72.4
Pursuing graduate degrees	1	0.5
Unemployed seeking employment	49	24.6
Unemployed not seeking employment	5	2.5
Type of Employment		
# employed in law firms	87	60.4
# employed in business & industry	35	24.3
# employed in government	13	9.0
# employed in public interest	5	3.5
# employed as judicial clerks	4	2.8
# employed in academia	0	0.0
Geographic Location		
# employed in state	131	91.0
# employed in foreign countries	0	0.0
# of states where employed	8	

Financial Aid

	Full-time		Part-time		Total	
	#	%	#	%	#	%
Total # receiving grants	186	41.5	87	26.3	273	35.0
Less than 1/2 tuition	157	35.0	72	21.8	229	29.4
Half to full tuition	22	4.9	10	3.0	32	4.1
Full tuition	5	1.1	5	1.5	10	1.3
More than full tuition	2	0.5	0	0.0	2	0.3
Median Grant Amount	$3,680		$2,000			

Refunds

Refunds of Admissions or Seat Deposit prior to commencement of classes? Yes

100% refund to 07/01/00

Refunds of Pre-paid tuition prior to commencement of classes? Yes

If yes, fully refundable before the start of classes? Yes

Joint Degrees Offered

JD/MS, JD/MBA, JD/MPA

Advanced Degrees Offered

LL.M. LL.M. Program in American Legal Studies

Bar Passage Rate

Jurisdiction	NY
# from school taking bar for the first time	198
School's pass rate for all first-time takers	65%
State's pass rate for all first-time takers	78%
State's pass rate for all first-time takers from ABA approved law schools	

TULANE UNIVERSITY

6329 Freret Street
New Orleans, LA 70118
(504)865-5939
http://www.law.tulane.edu/

ABA Approved Since 1925

The Basics

Type of School: **PRIVATE**
Application deadline*:
Application fee: **$45**
Financial Aid deadline*: **2/15**
Student faculty ratio: **17.6 to 1**

First year can start other than Fall: **No**
Student housing: **No**
--exclusively for law students: **No**
Term: **Semester**

*pr=preferred

Faculty

	Men		Women		Minorities		Total
	#	%	#	%	#	%	
Full-time	35	74	12	26	6	13	47
Other full-time	2	33	4	67	0	0	6
Deans, librarians, & others who teach	1	100	0	0	0	0	1
Part-time	36	75	12	25	3	6	48
Total	74	73	28	27	9	9	102
Deans, librarians, & others who teach < 1/2	1	33	2	67	0	0	3

Library

# of volumes & volume equivalents	484,443	# of professional staff	10
# of titles	263,073	Hours per week with professional staff	69
# of active serial subscriptions	5,584	Hours per week without professional staff	44
Study seating capacity inside the library	596	# of student computer work stations for entire law school	140
Square feet of law library	50,000	# of additional networked connections	350
Square feet of law school (excl. Library)	74,760		

Curriculum

	Full time	Part time
Typical first-year section size	96	0
Is there typically a "small section" of the first year class, other than Legal Writing, taught by full-time faculty?	Yes	No
If yes, typical size offered last year	41	N/A
# of classroom course titles beyond 1st year curriculum	125	0
# of upper division courses, excluding seminars, with an enrollment:		
Under 25	48	0
25 - 49	33	0
50 - 74	19	0
75 - 99	18	0
100 +	7	0
# of seminars	23	0
# of seminar positions available	511	
# of seminar positions filled	457	0
# of positions available in simulation courses	378	
# of simulation positions filled	355	0
# of positions available in faculty supervised clinical courses	132	
# of fac. sup. clin. positions filled	123	0
# involved in field placements	32	0
# involved in law journals	164	0
# in moot court or trial competitions	82	0
# of credit hours required to graduate	88	

Enrollment & Attrition

	Full-Time							Part-Time							Attrition			
	Men		Women		Minorities		Total	Men		Women		Minorities		Total	Academic	Other	Total	
	#	%	#	%	#	%	#	#	%	#	%	#	%	#	#	#	#	%
1st Year	155	47.7	170	52.3	55	16.9	325	0	0.0	0	0.0	0	0.0	0	5	25	30	8.9
2nd Year	183	54.3	154	45.7	62	18.4	337	0	0.0	1	100.0	1	100.0	1	5	7	12	3.6
3rd Year	177	54.0	151	46.0	77	23.5	328	0	0.0	2	100.0	0	0.0	2	0	0	0	0.0
4th Year								0	0.0	0	0.0	0	0.0	0	0	0	0	0.0
Total	515	52.0	475	48.0	194	19.6	990	0	0.0	3	100.0	1	33.3	3	10	32	42	4.1
JD Degrees Awarded	215	61.4	135	38.6	69	19.7	350	0	0.0	0	0.0	0	0.0	0				

GPA & LSAT Scores

	Full Time	Part Time	Total
# of apps	2,902	0	2,902
# admits	1,492	0	1,492
# of matrics	327	0	327
75% GPA	3.52	0.00	
25% GPA	3.03	0.00	
75% LSAT	161	0	
25% LSAT	156	0	

Tuition/Living Expenses

	Resident	Non-resident
Full-Time	$22,076	$22,076
Part-Time	$0	$0

Estimated living expenses for Singles		
Living on campus	Living off campus	Living at home
$11,200	$11,200	$5,895

Financial Aid

	Full-time		Part-time		Total	
	#	%	#	%	#	%
Total # receiving grants	392	39.6	0	0.0	392	39.5
Less than 1/2 tuition	320	32.3	0	0.0	320	32.2
Half to full tuition	63	6.4	0	0.0	63	6.3
Full tuition	6	0.6	0	0.0	6	0.6
More than full tuition	3	0.3	0	0.0	3	0.3
Median Grant Amount	$5,000		$0			

Refunds

Refunds of Admissions or Seat Deposit prior to commencement of classes? No

Refunds of Pre-paid tuition prior to commencement of classes? Yes

If yes, fully refundable before the start of classes? Yes

Joint Degrees Offered

JD-BS, JD-BA, JD-MBA, JD-MHA, JD-MSPH, LLM-MSPH, JD-MA Latin, Am. Studies, MCL-MA-Latin, Am. Studies

Advanced Degrees Offered

LLM	General
LLM	Admiralty
LLM	Energy & Environment
MCL	Comparative Law
MCL-MA	Comparative Law & Latin American Studies
SJD	General

Career Placement

	Total	%
Employment status known	314	95.2
Employment status unknown	16	4.9
Employed	241	76.8
Pursuing graduate degrees	11	3.5
Unemployed seeking employment	38	12.1
Unemployed not seeking employment	24	7.6
Type of Employment		
# employed in law firms	113	46.9
# employed in business & industry	25	10.4
# employed in government	32	13.3
# employed in public interest	1	0.4
# employed as judicial clerks	36	14.9
# employed in academia	0	0.0
Geographic Location		
# employed in state	75	31.1
# employed in foreign countries	3	1.2
# of states where employed	28	

Bar Passage Rate

Jurisdiction	LA
# from school taking bar for the first time	121
School's pass rate for all first-time takers	53%
State's pass rate for all first-time takers	55%
State's pass rate for all first-time takers from ABA approved law schools	67%

TULSA, UNIVERSITY OF

3120 East Fourth Place
Tulsa, OK 74104
(918)631-2401
http://www.utulsa.edu/

ABA Approved Since 1950

The Basics

Type of School: PRIVATE
Application deadline*:
Application fee: $30
Financial Aid deadline*:
Student faculty ratio: 16.8 to 1
First year can start other than Fall: No
Student housing: Yes
--exclusively for law students: No
Term: Semester

*pr=preferred

Faculty

	Men #	Men %	Women #	Women %	Minorities #	Minorities %	Total
Full-time	19	68	9	32	4	14	28
Other full-time	0	0	0	0	0	0	0
Deans, librarians, & others who teach	1	33	2	67	1	33	3
Part-time	24	80	6	20	1	3	30
Total	44	72	17	28	6	10	61
Deans, librarians, & others who teach < 1/2	2	67	1	33	0	0	3

Library

# of volumes & volume equivalents	263,700	# of professional staff	8
# of titles	49,638	Hours per week with professional staff	61
# of active serial subscriptions	3,869	Hours per week without professional staff	50
Study seating capacity inside the library	499	# of student computer work stations for entire law school	56
Square feet of law library	32,849	# of additional networked connections	0
Square feet of law school (excl. Library)	46,520		

Curriculum

	Full time	Part time
Typical first-year section size	76	76
Is there typically a "small section" of the first year class, other than Legal Writing, taught by full-time faculty?	No	No
If yes, typical size offered last year	N/A	N/A
# of classroom course titles beyond 1st year curriculum	78	39
# of upper division courses, excluding seminars, with an enrollment:		
Under 25	45	21
25 - 49	17	14
50 - 74	15	5
75 - 99	2	3
100 +	0	0
# of seminars	10	0
# of seminar positions available	158	
# of seminar positions filled	128	11
# of positions available in simulation courses	413	
# of simulation positions filled	335	37
# of positions available in faculty supervised clinical courses	32	
# of fac. sup. clin. positions filled	32	0
# involved in field placements	50	5
# involved in law journals	92	3
# in moot court or trial competitions	85	5
# of credit hours required to graduate	88	

Enrollment & Attrition

	Full-Time Men #	Full-Time Men %	Full-Time Women #	Full-Time Women %	Full-Time Minorities #	Full-Time Minorities %	Full-Time Total #	Part-Time Men #	Part-Time Men %	Part-Time Women #	Part-Time Women %	Part-Time Minorities #	Part-Time Minorities %	Part-Time Total #	Attrition Academic #	Attrition Other #	Attrition Total #	Attrition Total %
1st Year	89	58.2	64	41.8	25	16.3	153	32	55.2	26	44.8	19	32.8	58	0	7	7	3.4
2nd Year	108	61.7	67	38.3	24	13.7	175	25	62.5	15	37.5	8	20.0	40	9	7	16	7.7
3rd Year	95	62.5	57	37.5	12	7.9	152	8	57.1	6	42.9	2	14.3	14	0	3	3	1.6
4th Year								12	75.0	4	25.0	3	18.8	16	0	0	0	0.0
Total	292	60.8	188	39.2	61	12.7	480	77	60.2	51	39.8	32	25.0	128	9	17	26	4.2
JD Degrees Awarded	110	67.9	52	32.1	18	11.1	162	27	65.9	14	34.1	9	22.0	41				

GPA & LSAT Scores

	Full Time	Part Time	Total
# of apps	793	110	903
# admits	516	84	600
# of matrics	154	58	212
75% GPA	3.30	3.36	
25% GPA	2.75	2.75	
75% LSAT	155	153	
25% LSAT	148	145	

Tuition/Living Expenses

	Resident	Non-resident
Full-Time	$14,760	$14,760
Part-Time	$9,860	$9,860

Estimated living expenses for Singles		
Living on campus	Living off campus	Living at home
$4,260	$5,850	$1,800

Career Placement

	Total	%
Employment status known	180	98.4
Employment status unknown	3	1.6
Employed	145	80.6
Pursuing graduate degrees	9	5.0
Unemployed seeking employment	22	12.2
Unemployed not seeking employment	4	2.2
Type of Employment		
# employed in law firms	85	58.6
# employed in business & industry	34	23.5
# employed in government	17	11.7
# employed in public interest	4	2.8
# employed as judicial clerks	5	3.5
# employed in academia	0	0.0
Geographic Location		
# employed in state	93	64.1
# employed in foreign countries	0	0.0
# of states where employed	19	

Financial Aid

	Full-time		Part-time		Total	
	#	%	#	%	#	%
Total # receiving grants	166	34.6	36	28.1	202	33.2
Less than 1/2 tuition	99	20.6	18	14.1	117	19.2
Half to full tuition	42	8.8	12	9.4	54	8.9
Full tuition	25	5.2	6	4.7	31	5.1
More than full tuition	0	0.0	0	0.0	0	0.0
Median Grant Amount	$3,688		$5,000			

Refunds

Refunds of Admissions or Seat Deposit prior to commencement of classes? No

Refunds of Pre-paid tuition prior to commencement of classes? Yes

If yes, fully refundable before the start of classes? Yes

Joint Degrees Offered

JD/GEOLOGY, JD/ACCOUNT, JD BIOLOGY, JD/ENGLISH, JD/HISTORY, JD/MOD.LTRS., JD/PSYCH., JD/TAXATION, JD/ANTHROP., JD/MBA

Advanced Degrees Offered

No Advanced Degrees

Bar Passage Rate

Jurisdiction	OK	TX	MO
# from school taking bar for the first time	83	19	5
School's pass rate for all first-time takers	78%	63%	100%
State's pass rate for all first-time takers	75%	82%	92%
State's pass rate for all first-time takers from ABA approved law schools	75%	82%	92%

UTAH, UNIVERSITY OF

Salt Lake City, UT 84112
(801)581-6833
http://info.law.utah.edu

ABA Approved Since 1927

The Basics

Type of School: **PUBLIC**
Application deadline*: **2/1**
Application fee: **$40**
Financial Aid deadline*: **2/15**
Student faculty ratio: **14.8 to 1**
First year can start other than Fall: **No**
Student housing: **No**
--exclusively for law students: **No**
Term: **Semester**

*pr=preferred

Faculty

	Men		Women		Minorities		Total
	#	%	#	%	#	%	
Full-time	15	71	6	29	3	14	21
Other full-time	0	0	0	0	0	0	0
Deans, librarians, & others who teach	2	50	2	50	1	25	4
Part-time	7	78	2	22	0	0	9
Total	24	71	10	29	4	12	34
Deans, librarians, & others who teach < 1/2	0	0	0	0	0	0	0

Library

# of volumes & volume equivalents	286,354	# of professional staff	7
# of titles	94,446	Hours per week with professional staff	58
# of active serial subscriptions	4,395	Hours per week without professional staff	42
Study seating capacity inside the library	356	# of student computer work stations for entire law school	62
Square feet of law library	38,895	# of additional networked connections	404
Square feet of law school (excl. Library)	54,095		

Curriculum

	Full time	Part time
Typical first-year section size	45	0
Is there typically a "small section" of the first year class, other than Legal Writing, taught by full-time faculty?	No	No
If yes, typical size offered last year	N/A	N/A
# of classroom course titles beyond 1st year curriculum	71	0
# of upper division courses, excluding seminars, with an enrollment:		
Under 25	43	0
25 - 49	19	0
50 - 74	5	0
75 - 99	2	0
100 +	0	0
# of seminars	14	0
# of seminar positions available	210	
# of seminar positions filled	161	0
# of positions available in simulation courses	206	
# of simulation positions filled	206	0
# of positions available in faculty supervised clinical courses	0	
# of fac. sup. clin. positions filled	0	0
# involved in field placements	108	0
# involved in law journals	152	0
# in moot court or trial competitions	258	0
# of credit hours required to graduate	88	

Enrollment & Attrition

	Full-Time							Part-Time							Attrition			
	Men		Women		Minorities		Total	Men		Women		Minorities		Total	Academic	Other	Total	
	#	%	#	%	#	%	#	#	%	#	%	#	%	#	#	#	#	%
1st Year	69	70.4	29	29.6	13	13.3	98	0	0.0	0	0.0	0	0.0	0	0	9	9	7.0
2nd Year	82	63.1	48	36.9	20	15.4	130	0	0.0	0	0.0	0	0.0	0	0	0	0	0.0
3rd Year	73	55.7	58	44.3	17	13.0	131	0	0.0	0	0.0	0	0.0	0	0	0	0	0.0
4th Year								0	0.0	0	0.0	0	0.0	0	0	0	0	0.0
Total	224	62.4	135	37.6	50	13.9	359	0	0.0	0	0.0	0	0.0	0	0	9	9	2.5
JD Degrees Awarded	64	58.2	46	41.8	15	13.6	110	0	0.0	0	0.0	0	0.0	0				

GPA & LSAT Scores

	Full Time	Part Time	Total
# of apps	810	0	810
# admits	300	0	300
# of matrics	101	0	101
75% GPA	3.69	0.00	
25% GPA	3.11	0.00	
75% LSAT	163	0	
25% LSAT	154	0	

Tuition/Living Expenses

	Resident	Non-resident
Full-Time	$4,291	$9,587
Part-Time	$0	$0

Estimated living expenses for Singles		
Living on campus	Living off campus	Living at home
$12,246	$12,246	$7,071

Financial Aid

	Full-time		Part-time		Total	
	#	%	#	%	#	%
Total # receiving grants	147	41.0	0	0.0	147	40.9
Less than 1/2 tuition	112	31.2	0	0.0	112	31.2
Half to full tuition	21	5.9	0	0.0	21	5.8
Full tuition	0	0.0	0	0.0	0	0.0
More than full tuition	14	3.9	0	0.0	14	3.9
Median Grant Amount	$2,366		$0			

Refunds

Refunds of Admissions or Seat Deposit prior to commencement of classes? No

Refunds of Pre-paid tuition prior to commencement of classes? Yes

If yes, fully refundable before the start of classes? Yes

Joint Degrees Offered

JD/MBA, JD/MPA

Advanced Degrees Offered

LL.M. Environmental and Resource Law

Career Placement

	Total	%
Employment status known	102	94.4
Employment status unknown	5	5.6
Employed	93	90.1
Pursuing graduate degrees	3	3.0
Unemployed seeking employment	5	5.9
Unemployed not seeking employment	1	1.0
Type of Employment		
# employed in law firms	47	50.5
# employed in business & industry	17	18.3
# employed in government	11	11.8
# employed in public interest	2	2.2
# employed as judicial clerks	16	17.2
# employed in academia	0	0.0
Geographic Location		
# employed in state	72	77.4
# employed in foreign countries	1	1.1
# of states where employed	11	

Bar Passage Rate

Jurisdiction	UT
# from school taking bar for the first time	80
School's pass rate for all first-time takers	91%
State's pass rate for all first-time takers	92%
State's pass rate for all first-time takers from ABA approved law schools	

VALPARAISO UNIVERSITY

Valparaiso, IN 46383
(219)465-7829
http://www.valpo.edu/law

ABA Approved Since 1929

The Basics

Type of School: **PRIVATE**	First year can start other than Fall: **No**
Application deadline*: **4/15**	Student housing: **No**
Application fee: **$30**	--exclusively for law students: **No**
Financial Aid deadline*: **4/1**	Term: **Semester**
Student faculty ratio: **22.7 to 1**	

*pr=preferred

Faculty

	Men		Women		Minorities		Total
	#	%	#	%	#	%	
Full-time	10	63	6	38	1	6	16
Other full-time	2	67	1	33	0	0	3
Deans, librarians, & others who teach	1	100	0	0	0	0	1
Part-time	9	56	7	44	1	6	16
Total	22	61	14	39	2	6	36
Deans, librarians, & others who teach < 1/2	4	80	1	20	0	0	5

Library

# of volumes & volume equivalents	255,828	# of professional staff	6
# of titles	87,383	Hours per week with professional staff	65
# of active serial subscriptions	3,223	Hours per week without professional staff	49
Study seating capacity inside the library	347	# of student computer work stations for entire law school	41
Square feet of law library	29,370	# of additional networked connections	35
Square feet of law school (excl. Library)	49,825		

Curriculum

	Full time	Part time
Typical first-year section size	80	80
Is there typically a "small section" of the first year class, other than Legal Writing, taught by full-time faculty?	Yes	Yes
If yes, typical size offered last year	50	50
# of classroom course titles beyond 1st year curriculum	81	81
# of upper division courses, excluding seminars, with an enrollment:		
Under 25	60	60
25 - 49	22	22
50 - 74	11	11
75 - 99	5	5
100 +	3	3
# of seminars	11	11
# of seminar positions available	154	
# of seminar positions filled	139	5
# of positions available in simulation courses	834	
# of simulation positions filled	684	33
# of positions available in faculty supervised clinical courses	35	
# of fac. sup. clin. positions filled	35	0
# involved in field placements	72	3
# involved in law journals	19	0
# in moot court or trial competitions	32	0
# of credit hours required to graduate	90	

Enrollment & Attrition

	Full-Time							Part-Time							Attrition			
	Men		Women		Minorities		Total	Men		Women		Minorities		Total	Academic	Other	Total	
	#	%	#	%	#	%	#	#	%	#	%	#	%	#	#	#	#	%
1st Year	81	57.4	60	42.6	23	16.3	141	17	56.7	13	43.3	7	23.3	30	0	9	9	5.3
2nd Year	60	48.8	63	51.2	23	18.7	123	7	46.7	8	53.3	0	0.0	15	0	17	17	12
3rd Year	81	60.4	53	39.6	22	16.4	134	5	41.7	7	58.3	1	8.3	12	0	0	0	0.0
4th Year								0	0.0	0	0.0	0	0.0	0	0	0	0	0.0
Total	222	55.8	176	44.2	68	17.1	398	29	50.9	28	49.1	8	14.0	57	0	26	26	5.4
JD Degrees Awarded	87	52.7	78	47.3	14	8.5	165	2	100.0	0	0.0	0	0.0	2				

GPA & LSAT Scores

	Full Time	Part Time	Total
# of apps	736	47	783
# admits	514	30	544
# of matrics	141	17	158
75% GPA	3.50	3.41	
25% GPA	2.85	2.80	
75% LSAT	156	152	
25% LSAT	147	146	

Tuition/Living Expenses

	Resident	Non-resident
Full-Time	$16,110	$16,110
Part-Time	$6,080	$6,080

Estimated living expenses for Singles		
Living on campus	Living off campus	Living at home
N/A	$10,370	$5,270

Career Placement

	Total	%
Employment status known	166	93.3
Employment status unknown	12	6.7
Employed	142	85.5
Pursuing graduate degrees	0	0.0
Unemployed seeking employment	6	3.6
Unemployed not seeking employment	18	10.8
Type of Employment		
# employed in law firms	86	60.6
# employed in business & industry	16	11.3
# employed in government	23	16.2
# employed in public interest	4	2.8
# employed as judicial clerks	10	7.0
# employed in academia	3	2.1
Geographic Location		
# employed in state	60	42.3
# employed in foreign countries	2	1.4
# of states where employed	23	

Financial Aid

	Full-time		Part-time		Total	
	#	%	#	%	#	%
Total # receiving grants	260	65.3	17	29.8	277	60.9
Less than 1/2 tuition	227	57.0	17	29.8	244	53.6
Half to full tuition	7	1.8	0	0.0	7	1.5
Full tuition	10	2.5	0	0.0	10	2.2
More than full tuition	16	4.0	0	0.0	16	3.5
Median Grant Amount	$4,225		$4,009			

Refunds

Refunds of Admissions or Seat Deposit prior to commencement of classes? Yes

100% refund from 04/15/96 to 06/01/96

Refunds of Pre-paid tuition prior to commencement of classes? Yes

If yes, fully refundable before the start of classes? Yes

Joint Degrees Offered

No Joint Degrees

Advanced Degrees Offered

No Advanced Degrees

Bar Passage Rate

Jurisdiction	IN	IL
# from school taking bar for the first time	74	61
School's pass rate for all first-time takers	82%	77%
State's pass rate for all first-time takers	86%	87%
State's pass rate for all first-time takers from ABA approved law schools	86%	87%

VANDERBILT UNIVERSITY

21st Avenue South
Nashville, TN 37240
(615)322-2615
http://www.vanderbilt.edu/law

ABA Approved Since 1925

The Basics

Type of School: PRIVATE
Application deadline*: 2/1
Application fee: $50
Financial Aid deadline*: 3/1
Student faculty ratio: 20.1 to 1

First year can start other than Fall: No
Student housing: No
--exclusively for law students: No
Term: Semester

*pr=preferred

Faculty

	Men #	Men %	Women #	Women %	Minorities #	Minorities %	Total
Full-time	19	83	4	17	1	4	23
Other full-time	0	0	0	0	0	0	0
Deans, librarians, & others who teach	1	100	0	0	0	0	1
Part-time	14	67	7	33	1	5	21
Total	34	76	11	24	2	4	45
Deans, librarians, & others who teach < 1/2	1	50	1	50	1	50	2

Library

# of volumes & volume equivalents	499,859	# of professional staff	9
# of titles	103,522	Hours per week with professional staff	60
# of active serial subscriptions	6,050	Hours per week without professional staff	51
Study seating capacity inside the library	436	# of student computer work stations for entire law school	40
Square feet of law library	43,852	# of additional networked connections	0
Square feet of law school (excl. Library)	60,998		

Curriculum

	Full time	Part time
Typical first-year section size	91	0
Is there typically a "small section" of the first year class, other than Legal Writing, taught by full-time faculty?	No	No
If yes, typical size offered last year	N/A	N/A
# of classroom course titles beyond 1st year curriculum	77	0
# of upper division courses, excluding seminars, with an enrollment:		
Under 25	15	0
25 - 49	18	0
50 - 74	13	0
75 - 99	8	0
100 +	7	0
# of seminars	17	0
# of seminar positions available	272	
# of seminar positions filled	189	0
# of positions available in simulation courses	120	
# of simulation positions filled	120	0
# of positions available in faculty supervised clinical courses	48	
# of fac. sup. clin. positions filled	48	0
# involved in field placements	65	0
# involved in law journals	120	0
# in moot court or trial competitions	160	0
# of credit hours required to graduate	88	

Enrollment & Attrition

	Full-Time							Part-Time							Attrition			
	Men		Women		Minorities		Total	Men		Women		Minorities		Total	Academic	Other	Total	
	#	%	#	%	#	%	#	#	%	#	%	#	%	#	#	#	#	%
1st Year	111	61.0	71	39.0	33	18.1	182	0	0.0	0	0.0	0	0.0	0	0	0	0	0.0
2nd Year	112	62.2	68	37.8	29	16.1	180	0	0.0	0	0.0	0	0.0	0	0	5	5	2.6
3rd Year	126	65.6	66	34.4	35	18.2	192	0	0.0	0	0.0	0	0.0	0	0	0	0	0.0
4th Year								0	0.0	0	0.0	0	0.0	0	0	0	0	0.0
Total	349	63.0	205	37.0	97	17.5	554	0	0.0	0	0.0	0	0.0	0	0	5	5	0.9
JD Degrees Awarded	112	64.7	61	35.3	21	12.1	173	0	0.0	0	0.0	0	0.0	0				

VANDERBILT UNIVERSITY

GPA & LSAT Scores

	Full Time	Part Time	Total
# of apps	2,452	0	2,452
# admits	736	0	736
# of matrics	184	0	184
75% GPA	3.76	0.00	
25% GPA	3.36	0.00	
75% LSAT	165	0	
25% LSAT	159	0	

Tuition/Living Expenses

	Resident	Non-resident
Full-Time	$20,964	$20,964
Part-Time	$0	$0

Estimated living expenses for Singles		
Living on campus	Living off campus	Living at home
$13,500	$13,500	$13,500

Career Placement

	Total	%
Employment status known	187	99.5
Employment status unknown	1	0.5
Employed	173	92.5
Pursuing graduate degrees	6	3.2
Unemployed seeking employment	5	2.7
Unemployed not seeking employment	3	1.6
Type of Employment		
# employed in law firms	114	65.9
# employed in business & industry	18	10.4
# employed in government	9	5.2
# employed in public interest	2	1.2
# employed as judicial clerks	30	17.3
# employed in academia	0	0.0
Geographic Location		
# employed in state	46	26.6
# employed in foreign countries	1	0.6
# of states where employed	32	

Financial Aid

	Full-time		Part-time		Total	
	#	%	#	%	#	%
Total # receiving grants	284	51.3	0	0.0	284	51.3
Less than 1/2 tuition	202	36.5	0	0.0	202	36.5
Half to full tuition	71	12.8	0	0.0	71	12.8
Full tuition	11	2.0	0	0.0	11	2.0
More than full tuition	0	0.0	0	0.0	0	0.0
Median Grant Amount	$8,685		$0			

Refunds

Refunds of Admissions or Seat Deposit prior to commencement of classes? No

Refunds of Pre-paid tuition prior to commencement of classes? Yes

If yes, fully refundable before the start of classes? Yes

Joint Degrees Offered

JD/MBA, JD/MTS, JD/M.DIV., JD/MPP, JD/MA

Advanced Degrees Offered

No Advanced Degrees

Bar Passage Rate

Jurisdiction	TN
# from school taking bar for the first time	41
School's pass rate for all first-time takers	90%
State's pass rate for all first-time takers	79%
State's pass rate for all first-time takers from ABA approved law schools	91%

VERMONT LAW SCHOOL

Chelsea Street
P.O. Box 96
South Royalton, VT 05068-0096
(802)763-8303
http://www.vermontlaw.edu

ABA Approved Since 1975

The Basics

Type of School: **PRIVATE**
Application deadline*: **2/15**
Application fee: **$50**
Financial Aid deadline*: **2/15**
Student faculty ratio: **20.9 to 1**

First year can start other than Fall: **No**
Student housing: **Yes**
--exclusively for law students: **Yes**
Term: **Semester**

*pr=preferred

Faculty

	Men		Women		Minorities		Total
	#	%	#	%	#	%	
Full-time	13	68	6	32	1	5	19
Other full-time	0	0	0	0	0	0	0
Deans, librarians, & others who teach	3	75	1	25	0	0	4
Part-time	12	92	1	8	0	0	13
Total	28	78	8	22	1	3	36
Deans, librarians, & others who teach < 1/2	0	0	0	0	0	0	0

Library

# of volumes & volume equivalents	206,968	# of professional staff	6
# of titles	30,324	Hours per week with professional staff	45
# of active serial subscriptions	2,710	Hours per week without professional staff	65
Study seating capacity inside the library	389	# of student computer work stations for entire law school	20
Square feet of law library	35,143	# of additional networked connections	0
Square feet of law school (excl. Library)	73,919		

Curriculum

	Full time	Part time
Typical first-year section size	80	0
Is there typically a "small section" of the first year class, other than Legal Writing, taught by full-time faculty?	Yes	No
If yes, typical size offered last year	40	N/A
# of classroom course titles beyond 1st year curriculum	92	0
# of upper division courses, excluding seminars, with an enrollment:		
Under 25	42	0
25 - 49	16	0
50 - 74	10	0
75 - 99	4	0
100 +	0	0
# of seminars	20	0
# of seminar positions available	379	
# of seminar positions filled	257	0
# of positions available in simulation courses	180	
# of simulation positions filled	130	0
# of positions available in faculty supervised clinical courses	36	
# of fac. sup. clin. positions filled	24	0
# involved in field placements	136	0
# involved in law journals	58	0
# in moot court or trial competitions	124	0
# of credit hours required to graduate	84	

Enrollment & Attrition

	Full-Time							Part-Time							Attrition			
	Men		Women		Minorities		Total	Men		Women		Minorities		Total	Academic	Other	Total	
	#	%	#	%	#	%	#	#	%	#	%	#	%	#	#	#	#	%
1st Year	94	53.4	82	46.6	11	6.3	176	0	0.0	0	0.0	0	0.0	0	0	0	0	0.0
2nd Year	78	52.0	72	48.0	8	5.3	150	0	0.0	0	0.0	0	0.0	0	3	12	15	10
3rd Year	92	61.7	57	38.3	12	8.1	149	0	0.0	0	0.0	0	0.0	0	0	2	2	1.3
4th Year								0	0.0	0	0.0	0	0.0	0	0	0	0	0.0
Total	264	55.6	211	44.4	31	6.5	475	0	0.0	0	0.0	0	0.0	0	3	14	17	3.7
JD Degrees Awarded	82	51.9	76	48.1	11	7.0	158	0	0.0	0	0.0	0	0.0	0				

GPA & LSAT Scores

	Full Time	Part Time	Total
# of apps	992	0	992
# admits	773	0	773
# of matrics	176	0	176
75% GPA	3.38	0.00	
25% GPA	2.83	0.00	
75% LSAT	158	0	
25% LSAT	152	0	

Tuition/Living Expenses

	Resident	Non-resident
Full-Time	$18,025	$18,025
Part-Time	$0	$0

Estimated living expenses for Singles		
Living on campus	Living off campus	Living at home
N/A	$12,670	N/A

Career Placement

	Total	%
Employment status known	139	92.1
Employment status unknown	12	8.0
Employed	121	87.1
Pursuing graduate degrees	4	2.9
Unemployed seeking employment	11	7.9
Unemployed not seeking employment	3	2.2
Type of Employment		
# employed in law firms	63	52.1
# employed in business & industry	24	19.8
# employed in government	14	11.6
# employed in public interest	6	5.0
# employed as judicial clerks	13	10.7
# employed in academia	1	0.8
Geographic Location		
# employed in state	31	25.6
# employed in foreign countries	0	0.0
# of states where employed	34	

Financial Aid

	Full-time		Part-time		Total	
	#	%	#	%	#	%
Total # receiving grants	186	39.2	0	0.0	186	39.2
Less than 1/2 tuition	160	33.7	0	0.0	160	33.7
Half to full tuition	24	5.1	0	0.0	24	5.1
Full tuition	0	0.0	0	0.0	0	0.0
More than full tuition	2	0.4	0	0.0	2	0.4
Median Grant Amount	$5,500		$0			

Refunds

Refunds of Admissions or Seat Deposit prior to commencement of classes? No

Refunds of Pre-paid tuition prior to commencement of classes? Yes

If yes, fully refundable before the start of classes? Yes

Joint Degrees Offered

JD/MSEL

Advanced Degrees Offered

MSEL Master of Science in Environmental Law

Bar Passage Rate

Jurisdiction	VT	NY
# from school taking bar for the first time	31	16
School's pass rate for all first-time takers	81%	94%
State's pass rate for all first-time takers	78%	78%
State's pass rate for all first-time takers from ABA approved law schools	77%	

VILLANOVA UNIVERSITY

299 North Spring Mill Road
Villanova, PA 19085-1682
(610)519-7000
http://www.law.vill.edu/vls

ABA Approved Since 1954

The Basics

Type of School: **PRIVATE**
Application deadline*: **1/31**
Application fee: **$75**
Financial Aid deadline*: **3/1**
Student faculty ratio: **21.1 to 1**

First year can start other than Fall: **No**
Student housing: **No**
--exclusively for law students: **No**
Term: **Semester**

*pr=preferred

Faculty

	Men #	Men %	Women #	Women %	Minorities #	Minorities %	Total
Full-time	24	89	3	11	1	4	27
Other full-time	2	33	4	67	1	17	6
Deans, librarians, & others who teach	4	80	1	20	1	20	5
Part-time	17	71	7	29	1	4	24
Total	47	76	15	24	4	6	62
Deans, librarians, & others who teach < 1/2	0	0	0	0	0	0	0

Library

# of volumes & volume equivalents	421,535	# of professional staff	7
# of titles	128,749	Hours per week with professional staff	76
# of active serial subscriptions	3,915	Hours per week without professional staff	92
Study seating capacity inside the library	368	# of student computer work stations for entire law school	198
Square feet of law library	31,056	# of additional networked connections	64
Square feet of law school (excl. Library)	42,898		

Curriculum

	Full time	Part time
Typical first-year section size	117	0
Is there typically a "small section" of the first year class, other than Legal Writing, taught by full-time faculty?	Yes	No
If yes, typical size offered last year	30	N/A
# of classroom course titles beyond 1st year curriculum	113	0
# of upper division courses, excluding seminars, with an enrollment:		
Under 25	57	0
25 - 49	17	0
50 - 74	11	0
75 - 99	4	0
100 +	15	0
# of seminars	14	0
# of seminar positions available	210	
# of seminar positions filled	152	0
# of positions available in simulation courses	343	
# of simulation positions filled	310	0
# of positions available in faculty supervised clinical courses	85	
# of fac. sup. clin. positions filled	65	0
# involved in field placements	17	0
# involved in law journals	153	0
# in moot court or trial competitions	205	0
# of credit hours required to graduate	87	

Enrollment & Attrition

	Full-Time							Part-Time							Attrition			
	Men		Women		Minorities		Total	Men		Women		Minorities		Total	Academic	Other	Total	
	#	%	#	%	#	%	#	#	%	#	%	#	%	#	#	#	#	%
1st Year	142	60.7	92	39.3	29	12.4	234	0	0.0	0	0.0	0	0.0	0	1	10	11	4.7
2nd Year	122	57.0	92	43.0	27	12.6	214	0	0.0	0	0.0	0	0.0	0	1	7	8	3.4
3rd Year	127	53.6	110	46.4	33	13.9	237	0	0.0	0	0.0	0	0.0	0	0	1	1	0.5
4th Year								0	0.0	0	0.0	0	0.0	0	0	0	0	0.0
Total	391	57.1	294	42.9	89	13.0	685	0	0.0	0	0.0	0	0.0	0	2	18	20	2.9
JD Degrees Awarded	119	53.6	103	46.4	36	16.2	222	0	0.0	0	0.0	0	0.0	0				

GPA & LSAT Scores

	Full Time	Part Time	Total
# of apps	1,270	0	1,270
# admits	693	0	693
# of matrics	238	0	238
75% GPA	3.64	0.00	
25% GPA	3.16	0.00	
75% LSAT	161	0	
25% LSAT	156	0	

Tuition/Living Expenses

	Resident	Non-resident
Full-Time	$17,780	$17,780
Part-Time	$0	$0

Estimated living expenses for Singles		
Living on campus	Living off campus	Living at home
N/A	$12,700	$4,060

Career Placement

	Total	%
Employment status known	172	86.9
Employment status unknown	26	13.1
Employed	165	95.9
Pursuing graduate degrees	4	2.3
Unemployed seeking employment	2	1.2
Unemployed not seeking employment	1	0.6
Type of Employment		
# employed in law firms	96	58.2
# employed in business & industry	20	12.1
# employed in government	10	6.1
# employed in public interest	1	0.6
# employed as judicial clerks	38	23.0
# employed in academia	0	0.0
Geographic Location		
# employed in state	132	80.0
# employed in foreign countries	0	0.0
# of states where employed	0	

Financial Aid

	Full-time		Part-time		Total	
	#	%	#	%	#	%
Total # receiving grants	55	8.0	0	0.0	55	8.0
Less than 1/2 tuition	7	1.0	0	0.0	7	1.0
Half to full tuition	20	2.9	0	0.0	20	2.9
Full tuition	28	4.1	0	0.0	28	4.1
More than full tuition	0	0.0	0	0.0	0	0.0
Median Grant Amount	$8,875		$0			

Refunds

Refunds of Admissions or Seat Deposit prior to commencement of classes? No

Refunds of Pre-paid tuition prior to commencement of classes? No

If yes, fully refundable before the start of classes? No

Joint Degrees Offered

JD/PhD, JD/MBA

Advanced Degrees Offered

LLM Taxation

Bar Passage Rate

Jurisdiction	PA
# from school taking bar for the first time	117
School's pass rate for all first-time takers	75%
State's pass rate for all first-time takers	73%
State's pass rate for all first-time takers from ABA approved law schools	73%

VIRGINIA, UNIVERSITY OF

580 Massie Road
Charlottesville, VA 22903-1789
(804)924-7354
http://www.law.virginia.edu/index.htm

ABA Approved Since 1923

The Basics

Type of School: **PUBLIC**
Application deadline*: **1/15**
Application fee: **$40**
Financial Aid deadline*: **2/15**
Student faculty ratio: **17.4 to 1**
First year can start other than Fall: **No**
Student housing: **No**
--exclusively for law students: **No**
Term: **Semester**

*pr=preferred

Faculty

	Men #	Men %	Women #	Women %	Minorities #	Minorities %	Total
Full-time	46	79	12	21	5	9	58
Other full-time	0	0	0	0	0	0	0
Deans, librarians, & others who teach	0	0	0	0	0	0	0
Part-time	28	80	7	20	1	3	35
Total	74	80	19	20	6	6	93
Deans, librarians, & others who teach < 1/2	2	100	0	0	0	0	2

Library

# of volumes & volume equivalents	753,585	# of professional staff	12
# of titles	215,135	Hours per week with professional staff	69
# of active serial subscriptions	10,558	Hours per week without professional staff	41
Study seating capacity inside the library	709	# of student computer work stations for entire law school	112
Square feet of law library	72,142	# of additional networked connections	73
Square feet of law school (excl. Library)	111,012		

Curriculum

	Full time	Part time
Typical first-year section size	95	0
Is there typically a "small section" of the first year class, other than Legal Writing, taught by full-time faculty?	Yes	No
If yes, typical size offered last year	32	N/A
# of classroom course titles beyond 1st year curriculum	122	0
# of upper division courses, excluding seminars, with an enrollment:		
Under 25	38	0
25 - 49	27	0
50 - 74	22	0
75 - 99	14	0
100 +	21	0
# of seminars	78	0
# of seminar positions available	1,223	
# of seminar positions filled	1,023	0
# of positions available in simulation courses	806	
# of simulation positions filled	707	0
# of positions available in faculty supervised clinical courses	130	
# of fac. sup. clin. positions filled	106	0
# involved in field placements	65	0
# involved in law journals	422	0
# in moot court or trial competitions	182	0
# of credit hours required to graduate	86	

Enrollment & Attrition

	Full-Time Men #	Men %	Women #	Women %	Minorities #	Minorities %	Total #	Part-Time Men #	Men %	Women #	Women %	Minorities #	Minorities %	Total #	Attrition Academic #	Other #	Total #	%
1st Year	238	66.1	122	33.9	36	10.0	360	0	0.0	0	0.0	0	0.0	0	1	12	13	3.4
2nd Year	246	63.1	144	36.9	57	14.6	390	0	0.0	0	0.0	0	0.0	0	0	2	2	0.5
3rd Year	241	60.6	157	39.4	62	15.6	398	0	0.0	0	0.0	0	0.0	0	0	0	0	0.0
4th Year								0	0.0	0	0.0	0	0.0	0	0	0	0	0.0
Total	725	63.2	423	36.8	155	13.5	1,148	0	0.0	0	0.0	0	0.0	0	1	14	15	1.3
JD Degrees Awarded	228	60.5	149	39.5	55	14.6	377	0	0.0	0	0.0	0	0.0	0				

GPA & LSAT Scores

	Full Time	Part Time	Total
# of apps	3,782	0	3,782
# admits	980	0	980
# of matrics	361	0	361
75% GPA	3.78	0.00	
25% GPA	3.49	0.00	
75% LSAT	169	0	
25% LSAT	162	0	

Tuition/Living Expenses

	Resident	Non-resident
Full-Time	$12,030	$19,178
Part-Time	$0	$0

Estimated living expenses for Singles		
Living on campus	Living off campus	Living at home
$10,420	$10,420	$10,420

Career Placement

	Total	%
Employment status known	371	99.5
Employment status unknown	2	0.5
Employed	357	96.2
Pursuing graduate degrees	6	1.6
Unemployed seeking employment	4	1.1
Unemployed not seeking employment	4	1.1
Type of Employment		
# employed in law firms	249	69.8
# employed in business & industry	13	3.6
# employed in government	10	2.8
# employed in public interest	11	3.1
# employed as judicial clerks	72	20.2
# employed in academia	2	0.6
Geographic Location		
# employed in state	74	20.7
# employed in foreign countries	5	1.4
# of states where employed	35	

Financial Aid

	Full-time		Part-time		Total	
	#	%	#	%	#	%
Total # receiving grants	346	30.1	0	0.0	346	30.1
Less than 1/2 tuition	263	22.9	0	0.0	263	22.9
Half to full tuition	54	4.7	0	0.0	54	4.7
Full tuition	0	0.0	0	0.0	0	0.0
More than full tuition	29	2.5	0	0.0	29	2.5
Median Grant Amount	$6,500		$0			

Refunds

Refunds of Admissions or Seat Deposit prior to commencement of classes? No

Refunds of Pre-paid tuition prior to commencement of classes? Yes

If yes, fully refundable before the start of classes? Yes

Joint Degrees Offered

JD/MBA, JD/MA Hist, JD/MA Govt, JD/MP Plan, JD/MA Econ, JD/MA Eng, JD/MA Phil, JD/MA Soc, JD/MA Marine, JD/MS Acctg, JD/PhD Govt

Advanced Degrees Offered

LL.M.
S.J.D.
LL.M Judicial Process

Bar Passage Rate

Jurisdiction	VA
# from school taking bar for the first time	122
School's pass rate for all first-time takers	88%
State's pass rate for all first-time takers	76%
State's pass rate for all first-time takers from ABA approved law schools	77%

WAKE FOREST UNIVERSITY

P.O. Box 7206
Reynolda Station
Winston-Salem, NC 27109-7206
(910)759-5435
http://www.wfu.edu

ABA Approved Since 1935

The Basics

Type of School: PRIVATE
Application deadline*: 3/15
Application fee: $60
Financial Aid deadline*: 5/1
Student faculty ratio: 15.3 to 1

First year can start other than Fall: No
Student housing: No
--exclusively for law students: No
Term: Semester

*pr=preferred

Faculty

	Men #	Men %	Women #	Women %	Minorities #	Minorities %	Total
Full-time	17	68	8	32	1	4	25
Other full-time	0	0	3	100	1	33	3
Deans, librarians, & others who teach	2	50	2	50	0	0	4
Part-time	18	100	0	0	1	6	18
Total	37	74	13	26	3	6	50
Deans, librarians, & others who teach < 1/2	2	100	0	0	0	0	2

Library

# of volumes & volume equivalents	308,131	# of professional staff	6
# of titles	69,969	Hours per week with professional staff	57
# of active serial subscriptions	5,140	Hours per week without professional staff	52
Study seating capacity inside the library	552	# of student computer work stations for entire law school	99
Square feet of law library	43,000	# of additional networked connections	360
Square feet of law school (excl. Library)	41,573		

Curriculum

	Full time	Part time
Typical first-year section size	40	0
Is there typically a "small section" of the first year class, other than Legal Writing, taught by full-time faculty?	Yes	No
If yes, typical size offered last year	40	N/A
# of classroom course titles beyond 1st year curriculum	72	0
# of upper division courses, excluding seminars, with an enrollment:		
Under 25	51	0
25 - 49	29	0
50 - 74	12	0
75 - 99	5	0
100 +	0	0
# of seminars	16	0
# of seminar positions available	288	
# of seminar positions filled	226	0
# of positions available in simulation courses	380	
# of simulation positions filled	344	0
# of positions available in faculty supervised clinical courses	71	
# of fac. sup. clin. positions filled	56	0
# involved in field placements	7	0
# involved in law journals	63	0
# in moot court or trial competitions	41	0
# of credit hours required to graduate	89	

Enrollment & Attrition

	Full-Time Men #	Men %	Women #	Women %	Minorities #	Minorities %	Total #	Part-Time Men #	Men %	Women #	Women %	Minorities #	Minorities %	Total #	Attrition Academic #	Other #	Total #	%
1st Year	95	59.7	64	40.3	18	11.3	159	0	0.0	0	0.0	0	0.0	0	8	11	19	12
2nd Year	92	63.0	54	37.0	14	9.6	146	0	0.0	0	0.0	0	0.0	0	0	2	2	1.3
3rd Year	98	63.2	57	36.8	12	7.7	155	0	0.0	0	0.0	0	0.0	0	0	0	0	0.0
4th Year								0	0.0	0	0.0	0	0.0	0	0	0	0	0.0
Total	285	62.0	175	38.0	44	9.6	460	0	0.0	0	0.0	0	0.0	0	8	13	21	4.4
JD Degrees Awarded	91	57.2	68	42.8	15	9.4	159	0	0.0	0	0.0	0	0.0	0				

WAKE FOREST UNIVERSITY

GPA & LSAT Scores

	Full Time	Part Time	Total
# of apps	1,492	0	1,492
# admits	599	0	599
# of matrics	158	0	158
75% GPA	3.54	0.00	
25% GPA	3.04	0.00	
75% LSAT	163	0	
25% LSAT	158	0	

Tuition/Living Expenses

	Resident	Non-resident
Full-Time	$18,200	$18,200
Part-Time	$0	$0

Estimated living expenses for Singles		
Living on campus	Living off campus	Living at home
N/A	$11,000	N/A

Career Placement

	Total	%
Employment status known	141	94.6
Employment status unknown	8	5.4
Employed	134	95.0
Pursuing graduate degrees	2	1.4
Unemployed seeking employment	3	2.1
Unemployed not seeking employment	2	1.4
Type of Employment		
# employed in law firms	83	61.9
# employed in business & industry	20	14.9
# employed in government	11	8.2
# employed in public interest	2	1.5
# employed as judicial clerks	17	12.7
# employed in academia	1	0.8
Geographic Location		
# employed in state	78	58.2
# employed in foreign countries	0	0.0
# of states where employed	21	

Financial Aid

	Full-time		Part-time		Total	
	#	%	#	%	#	%
Total # receiving grants	114	24.8	0	0.0	114	24.8
Less than 1/2 tuition	54	11.7	0	0.0	54	11.7
Half to full tuition	4	0.9	0	0.0	4	0.9
Full tuition	44	9.6	0	0.0	44	9.6
More than full tuition	12	2.6	0	0.0	12	2.6
Median Grant Amount	$7,530		$0			

Refunds

Refunds of Admissions or Seat Deposit prior to commencement of classes? No

Refunds of Pre-paid tuition prior to commencement of classes? Yes

If yes, fully refundable before the start of classes? Yes

Joint Degrees Offered

JD/MBA

Advanced Degrees Offered

LL.M Master of Laws (LL.M) in American Law for Foreign Law Graduates

Bar Passage Rate

Jurisdiction	NC
# from school taking bar for the first time	104
School's pass rate for all first-time takers	90%
State's pass rate for all first-time takers	85%
State's pass rate for all first-time takers from ABA approved law schools	85%

WASHBURN UNIVERSITY

1700 College Avenue
Topeka, KS 66621
(913)231-1010
http://www.washburnlaw.wuacc.edu/school

ABA Approved Since 1923

The Basics

Type of School: **PUBLIC**
Application deadline*: **3/15**
Application fee: **$30**
Financial Aid deadline*: **3/15**
Student faculty ratio: **16.8 to 1**
First year can start other than Fall: **Yes**
Student housing: **Yes**
--exclusively for law students: **No**
Term: **Semester**

*pr=preferred

Faculty

	Men #	Men %	Women #	Women %	Minorities #	Minorities %	Total
Full-time	14	64	8	36	5	23	22
Other full-time	0	0	1	100	0	0	1
Deans, librarians, & others who teach	2	100	0	0	1	50	2
Part-time	9	75	3	25	0	0	12
Total	25	68	12	32	6	16	37
Deans, librarians, & others who teach < 1/2	1	100	0	0	0	0	1

Library

# of volumes & volume equivalents	289,820	# of professional staff	7
# of titles	184,958	Hours per week with professional staff	77
# of active serial subscriptions	3,666	Hours per week without professional staff	22
Study seating capacity inside the library	346	# of student computer work stations for entire law school	63
Square feet of law library	41,270	# of additional networked connections	80
Square feet of law school (excl. Library)	45,928		

Curriculum

	Full time	Part time
Typical first-year section size	77	0
Is there typically a "small section" of the first year class, other than Legal Writing, taught by full-time faculty?	Yes	No
If yes, typical size offered last year	25	N/A
# of classroom course titles beyond 1st year curriculum	72	0
# of upper division courses, excluding seminars, with an enrollment:		
Under 25	49	0
25 - 49	15	0
50 - 74	19	0
75 - 99	5	0
100 +	0	0
# of seminars	23	0
# of seminar positions available	547	
# of seminar positions filled	320	0
# of positions available in simulation courses	240	
# of simulation positions filled	237	0
# of positions available in faculty supervised clinical courses	74	
# of fac. sup. clin. positions filled	67	0
# involved in field placements	26	0
# involved in law journals	48	0
# in moot court or trial competitions	28	0
# of credit hours required to graduate	90	

Enrollment & Attrition

	Full-Time Men #	Men %	Women #	Women %	Minorities #	Minorities %	Total #	Part-Time Men #	Men %	Women #	Women %	Minorities #	Minorities %	Total #	Attrition Academic #	Other #	Total #	%
1st Year	106	58.6	75	41.4	16	8.8	181	0	0.0	0	0.0	0	0.0	0	2	11	13	8.8
2nd Year	76	58.5	54	41.5	15	11.5	130	0	0.0	0	0.0	0	0.0	0	2	2	4	3.3
3rd Year	72	55.0	59	45.0	18	13.7	131	0	0.0	0	0.0	0	0.0	0	0	0	0	0.0
4th Year								0	0.0	0	0.0	0	0.0	0	0	0	0	0.0
Total	254	57.5	188	42.5	49	11.1	442	0	0.0	0	0.0	0	0.0	0	4	13	17	4.1
JD Degrees Awarded	91	61.5	57	38.5	24	16.2	148	0	0.0	0	0.0	0	0.0	0				

GPA & LSAT Scores

	Full Time	Part Time	Total
# of apps	719	0	719
# admits	432	0	432
# of matrics	182	0	182
75% GPA	3.57	0.00	
25% GPA	2.91	0.00	
75% LSAT	156	0	
25% LSAT	149	0	

Tuition/Living Expenses

	Resident	Non-resident
Full-Time	$6,116	$9,140
Part-Time	$0	$0

Estimated living expenses for Singles		
Living on campus	Living off campus	Living at home
$10,918	$10,918	$10,918

Career Placement

	Total	%
Employment status known	147	96.1
Employment status unknown	6	3.9
Employed	115	78.2
Pursuing graduate degrees	7	4.8
Unemployed seeking employment	17	11.6
Unemployed not seeking employment	8	5.4
Type of Employment		
# employed in law firms	63	54.8
# employed in business & industry	17	14.8
# employed in government	26	22.6
# employed in public interest	3	2.6
# employed as judicial clerks	6	5.2
# employed in academia	0	0.0
Geographic Location		
# employed in state	71	61.7
# employed in foreign countries	0	0.0
# of states where employed	21	

Financial Aid

	Full-time		Part-time		Total	
	#	%	#	%	#	%
Total # receiving grants	160	36.2	0	0.0	160	36.2
Less than 1/2 tuition	100	22.6	0	0.0	100	22.6
Half to full tuition	31	7.0	0	0.0	31	7.0
Full tuition	24	5.4	0	0.0	24	5.4
More than full tuition	5	1.1	0	0.0	5	1.1
Median Grant Amount	$2,000		$0			

Refunds

Refunds of Admissions or Seat Deposit prior to commencement of classes? No

Refunds of Pre-paid tuition prior to commencement of classes? No

If yes, fully refundable before the start of classes? No

Joint Degrees Offered

No Joint Degrees

Advanced Degrees Offered

No Advanced Degrees

Bar Passage Rate

Jurisdiction	KS
# from school taking bar for the first time	77
School's pass rate for all first-time takers	71%
State's pass rate for all first-time takers	82%
State's pass rate for all first-time takers from ABA approved law schools	82%

WASHINGTON AND LEE UNIVERSITY

Sydney Lewis Hall
Lexington, VA 24450-0303
(540)463-8400
http://www.wlu.edu

ABA Approved Since 1923

The Basics

Type of School: **PRIVATE**
Application deadline*: **2/1**
Application fee: **$40**
Financial Aid deadline*: **3/1**
Student faculty ratio: **9.8 to 1**

First year can start other than Fall: **No**
Student housing: **Yes**
--exclusively for law students: **Yes**
Term: **Semester**

*pr=preferred

Faculty

	Men		Women		Minorities		Total
	#	%	#	%	#	%	
Full-time	27	82	6	18	2	6	33
Other full-time	0	0	1	100	0	0	1
Deans, librarians, & others who teach	2	50	2	50	1	25	4
Part-time	8	100	0	0	0	0	8
Total	37	80	9	20	3	7	46
Deans, librarians, & others who teach < 1/2	0	0	0	0	0	0	0

Library

# of volumes & volume equivalents	339,785	# of professional staff	7
# of titles	131,318	Hours per week with professional staff	60
# of active serial subscriptions	4,374	Hours per week without professional staff	108
Study seating capacity inside the library	551	# of student computer work stations for entire law school	73
Square feet of law library	58,155	# of additional networked connections	0
Square feet of law school (excl. Library)	45,143		

Curriculum

	Full time	Part time
Typical first-year section size	63	0
Is there typically a "small section" of the first year class, other than Legal Writing, taught by full-time faculty?	Yes	Yes
If yes, typical size offered last year	21	N/A
# of classroom course titles beyond 1st year curriculum	75	0
# of upper division courses, excluding seminars, with an enrollment:		
Under 25	38	0
25 - 49	14	0
50 - 74	11	0
75 - 99	3	0
100 +	0	0
# of seminars	24	0
# of seminar positions available	453	
# of seminar positions filled	226	0
# of positions available in simulation courses	341	
# of simulation positions filled	244	0
# of positions available in faculty supervised clinical courses	40	
# of fac. sup. clin. positions filled	40	0
# involved in field placements	41	0
# involved in law journals	74	0
# in moot court or trial competitions	75	0
# of credit hours required to graduate	85	

Enrollment & Attrition

	Full-Time							Part-Time							Attrition			
	Men		Women		Minorities		Total	Men		Women		Minorities		Total	Academic	Other	Total	
	#	%	#	%	#	%	#	#	%	#	%	#	%	#	#	#	#	%
1st Year	73	60.8	47	39.2	11	9.2	120	0	0.0	0	0.0	0	0.0	0	0	7	7	5.4
2nd Year	71	58.7	50	41.3	16	13.2	121	0	0.0	0	0.0	0	0.0	0	0	5	5	4.2
3rd Year	70	59.3	48	40.7	13	11.0	118	0	0.0	0	0.0	0	0.0	0	0	1	1	0.8
4th Year								0	0.0	0	0.0	0	0.0	0	0	0	0	0.0
Total	214	59.6	145	40.4	40	11.1	359	0	0.0	0	0.0	0	0.0	0	0	13	13	3.5
JD Degrees Awarded	74	60.2	49	39.8	22	17.9	123	0	0.0	0	0.0	0	0.0	0				

GPA & LSAT Scores

	Full Time	Part Time	Total
# of apps	1,844	0	1,844
# admits	513	0	513
# of matrics	120	0	120
75% GPA	3.75	0.00	
25% GPA	3.11	0.00	
75% LSAT	166	0	
25% LSAT	161	0	

Tuition/Living Expenses

	Resident	Non-resident
Full-Time	$16,351	$16,351
Part-Time	$0	$0

Estimated living expenses for Singles		
Living on campus	Living off campus	Living at home
$9,800	$9,800	$750

Financial Aid

	Full-time		Part-time		Total	
	#	%	#	%	#	%
Total # receiving grants	238	66.3	0	0.0	238	66.3
Less than 1/2 tuition	175	48.8	0	0.0	175	48.7
Half to full tuition	60	16.7	0	0.0	60	16.7
Full tuition	3	0.8	0	0.0	3	0.8
More than full tuition	0	0.0	0	0.0	0	0.0
Median Grant Amount	$5,200		$0			

Refunds

Refunds of Admissions or Seat Deposit prior to commencement of classes? No

Refunds of Pre-paid tuition prior to commencement of classes? Yes

If yes, fully refundable before the start of classes? Yes

Joint Degrees Offered

No Joint Degrees

Advanced Degrees Offered

No Advanced Degrees

Career Placement

	Total	%
Employment status known	113	98.3
Employment status unknown	2	1.7
Employed	99	87.6
Pursuing graduate degrees	3	2.7
Unemployed seeking employment	11	9.7
Unemployed not seeking employment	0	0.0
Type of Employment		
# employed in law firms	69	69.7
# employed in business & industry	5	5.1
# employed in government	5	5.1
# employed in public interest	3	3.0
# employed as judicial clerks	17	17.2
# employed in academia	0	0.0
Geographic Location		
# employed in state	32	32.3
# employed in foreign countries	1	1.0
# of states where employed	22	

Bar Passage Rate

Jurisdiction	VA
# from school taking bar for the first time	41
School's pass rate for all first-time takers	81%
State's pass rate for all first-time takers	76%
State's pass rate for all first-time takers from ABA approved law schools	77%

WASHINGTON UNIVERSITY

1 Brookings Drive
Campus Box 1120
St. Louis, MO 63130-4899
(314)935-6400
http://www.wulaw.wustl.edu

ABA Approved Since 1923

The Basics

Type of School: **PRIVATE**
Application deadline*: **3/1**
Application fee: **$50**
Financial Aid deadline*: **4/1**
Student faculty ratio: **18.6 to 1**

First year can start other than Fall: **No**
Student housing: **No**
--exclusively for law students: **No**
Term: **Semester**

*pr=preferred

Faculty

	Men #	Men %	Women #	Women %	Minorities #	Minorities %	Total
Full-time	19	66	10	34	4	14	29
Other full-time	1	33	2	67	0	0	3
Deans, librarians, & others who teach	1	33	2	67	0	0	3
Part-time	31	74	11	26	4	10	42
Total	52	68	25	32	8	10	77
Deans, librarians, & others who teach < 1/2	0	0	0	0	0	0	0

Library

# of volumes & volume equivalents	546,401	# of professional staff	4
# of titles	100,942	Hours per week with professional staff	43
# of active serial subscriptions	6,312	Hours per week without professional staff	77
Study seating capacity inside the library	275	# of student computer work stations for entire law school	56
Square feet of law library	31,360	# of additional networked connections	0
Square feet of law school (excl. Library)	31,426		

Curriculum

	Full time	Part time
Typical first-year section size	35	0
Is there typically a "small section" of the first year class, other than Legal Writing, taught by full-time faculty?	No	No
If yes, typical size offered last year	N/A	N/A
# of classroom course titles beyond 1st year curriculum	89	0
# of upper division courses, excluding seminars, with an enrollment:		
Under 25	28	0
25 - 49	25	0
50 - 74	11	0
75 - 99	5	0
100 +	4	0
# of seminars	16	0
# of seminar positions available	288	
# of seminar positions filled	220	0
# of positions available in simulation courses	352	
# of simulation positions filled	327	0
# of positions available in faculty supervised clinical courses	32	
# of fac. sup. clin. positions filled	32	0
# involved in field placements	97	0
# involved in law journals	128	0
# in moot court or trial competitions	217	0
# of credit hours required to graduate	85	

Enrollment & Attrition

	Full-Time							Part-Time							Attrition			
	Men		Women		Minorities		Total	Men		Women		Minorities		Total	Academic	Other	Total	
	#	%	#	%	#	%	#	#	%	#	%	#	%	#	#	#	#	%
1st Year	120	56.6	92	43.4	40	18.9	212	0	0.0	0	0.0	0	0.0	0	0	15	15	7.3
2nd Year	139	63.2	81	36.8	54	24.5	220	0	0.0	0	0.0	0	0.0	0	1	1	2	1.0
3rd Year	133	61.9	82	38.1	23	10.7	215	0	0.0	0	0.0	0	0.0	0	0	0	0	0.0
4th Year								0	0.0	0	0.0	0	0.0	0	0	0	0	0.0
Total	392	60.6	255	39.4	117	18.1	647	0	0.0	0	0.0	0	0.0	0	1	16	17	2.7
JD Degrees Awarded	105	55.9	83	44.1	26	13.8	188	0	0.0	0	0.0	0	0.0	0				

GPA & LSAT Scores

	Full Time	Part Time	Total
# of apps	1,665	0	1,665
# admits	949	0	949
# of matrics	212	0	212
75% GPA	3.56	0.00	
25% GPA	2.95	0.00	
75% LSAT	163	0	
25% LSAT	156	0	

Tuition/Living Expenses

	Resident	Non-resident
Full-Time	$20,390	$20,390
Part-Time	$0	$0

Estimated living expenses for Singles		
Living on campus	Living off campus	Living at home
N/A	$9,000	$2,000

Financial Aid

	Full-time		Part-time		Total	
	#	%	#	%	#	%
Total # receiving grants	272	42.0	0	0.0	272	42.0
Less than 1/2 tuition	190	29.4	0	0.0	190	29.4
Half to full tuition	39	6.0	0	0.0	39	6.0
Full tuition	30	4.6	0	0.0	30	4.6
More than full tuition	13	2.0	0	0.0	13	2.0
Median Grant Amount	$8,500		$0			

Refunds

Refunds of Admissions or Seat Deposit prior to commencement of classes? Yes

Refunds of Pre-paid tuition prior to commencement of classes? No

If yes, fully refundable before the start of classes? No

Joint Degrees Offered

Bus. Adm., East Asian, Social Work, Health Adm., European St., Eng.&Policy, Economics, Pol. Science, Islamic St., Int'l Aff.

Advanced Degrees Offered

LL.M.	Taxation
JSD	Research
LL.M.	Urban Studies
LL.M.	Master of Laws for International Students

Career Placement

	Total	%
Employment status known	204	98.1
Employment status unknown	4	1.9
Employed	186	91.2
Pursuing graduate degrees	4	2.0
Unemployed seeking employment	8	3.9
Unemployed not seeking employment	6	2.9
Type of Employment		
# employed in law firms	96	51.6
# employed in business & industry	31	16.7
# employed in government	26	14.0
# employed in public interest	11	5.9
# employed as judicial clerks	21	11.3
# employed in academia	1	0.5
Geographic Location		
# employed in state	76	40.9
# employed in foreign countries	6	3.2
# of states where employed	27	

Bar Passage Rate

Jurisdiction	MO	IL
# from school taking bar for the first time	87	46
School's pass rate for all first-time takers	94%	89%
State's pass rate for all first-time takers	92%	87%
State's pass rate for all first-time takers from ABA approved law schools	92%	87%

WASHINGTON, UNIVERSITY OF

1100 NE Campus Parkway
Seattle, WA 98105-6617
(206)543-4551
http:/www2.law.washington.edu

ABA Approved Since 1924

The Basics

Type of School: PUBLIC
Application deadline*: 1/15
Application fee: $50
Financial Aid deadline*: 2/28
Student faculty ratio: 13.9 to 1

First year can start other than Fall: No
Student housing: No
--exclusively for law students: No
Term: Quarter

*pr=preferred

Faculty

	Men		Women		Minorities		Total
	#	%	#	%	#	%	
Full-time	20	63	12	38	4	13	32
Other full-time	0	0	0	0	0	0	0
Deans, librarians, & others who teach	0	0	1	100	0	0	1
Part-time	7	54	6	46	2	15	13
Total	27	59	19	41	6	13	46
Deans, librarians, & others who teach < 1/2	2	100	0	0	0	0	2

Library

# of volumes & volume equivalents	462,076	# of professional staff	14
# of titles	115,506	Hours per week with professional staff	56
# of active serial subscriptions	7,686	Hours per week without professional staff	28
Study seating capacity inside the library	517	# of student computer work stations for entire law school	61
Square feet of law library	60,122	# of additional networked connections	704
Square feet of law school (excl. Library)	53,493		

Curriculum

	Full time	Part time
Typical first-year section size	101	0
Is there typically a "small section" of the first year class, other than Legal Writing, taught by full-time faculty?	Yes	No
If yes, typical size offered last year	29	N/A
# of classroom course titles beyond 1st year curriculum	98	0
# of upper division courses, excluding seminars, with an enrollment:		
Under 25	45	0
25 - 49	37	0
50 - 74	7	0
75 - 99	6	0
100 +	7	0
# of seminars	11	0
# of seminar positions available	110	
# of seminar positions filled	111	0
# of positions available in simulation courses	191	
# of simulation positions filled	172	0
# of positions available in faculty supervised clinical courses	98	
# of fac. sup. clin. positions filled	91	0
# involved in field placements	127	0
# involved in law journals	31	0
# in moot court or trial competitions	92	0
# of credit hours required to graduate	135	

Enrollment & Attrition

	Full-Time							Part-Time							Attrition			
	Men		Women		Minorities		Total	Men		Women		Minorities		Total	Academic	Other	Total	
	#	%	#	%	#	%	#	#	%	#	%	#	%	#	#	#	#	%
1st Year	75	43.9	96	56.1	42	24.6	171	0	0.0	0	0.0	0	0.0	0	0	0	0	0.0
2nd Year	80	49.7	81	50.3	57	35.4	161	0	0.0	0	0.0	0	0.0	0	0	0	0	0.0
3rd Year	98	59.0	68	41.0	80	48.2	166	0	0.0	0	0.0	0	0.0	0	0	0	0	0.0
4th Year								0	0.0	0	0.0	0	0.0	0	0	0	0	0.0
Total	253	50.8	245	49.2	179	35.9	498	0	0.0	0	0.0	0	0.0	0	0	0	0	0.0
JD Degrees Awarded	80	55.9	63	44.1	52	36.4	143	0	0.0	0	0.0	0	0.0	0				

GPA & LSAT Scores

	Full Time	Part Time	Total
# of apps	1,960	0	1,960
# admits	498	0	498
# of matrics	172	0	172
75% GPA	3.77	0.00	
25% GPA	3.38	0.00	
75% LSAT	166	0	
25% LSAT	157	0	

Tuition/Living Expenses

	Resident	Non-resident
Full-Time	$5,050	$12,500
Part-Time	$0	$0

Estimated living expenses for Singles		
Living on campus	Living off campus	Living at home
$10,974	$10,974	$5,727

Financial Aid

	Full-time		Part-time		Total	
	#	%	#	%	#	%
Total # receiving grants	255	51.2	0	0.0	255	51.2
Less than 1/2 tuition	248	49.8	0	0.0	248	49.8
Half to full tuition	4	0.8	0	0.0	4	0.8
Full tuition	3	0.6	0	0.0	3	0.6
More than full tuition	0	0.0	0	0.0	0	0.0
Median Grant Amount	$900		$0			

Refunds

Refunds of Admissions or Seat Deposit prior to commencement of classes? No

Refunds of Pre-paid tuition prior to commencement of classes? Yes

If yes, fully refundable before the start of classes? Yes

Joint Degrees Offered

Educ Ldrshp, Environ Mgmt, Asian LL.M., Economics, Business Adm, Med. Ethics, Philosophy, Intl Studies

Advanced Degrees Offered

LL.M.	Asian & Comparative Law
LL.M.	Law & Marine Affairs
LL.M.	International Environmental Law
LL.M.	Sustainable International Development
LL.M.	Taxation
Ph.D.	Asian & Comparative Law

Career Placement

	Total	%
Employment status known	142	94.0
Employment status unknown	9	6.0
Employed	127	89.4
Pursuing graduate degrees	3	2.1
Unemployed seeking employment	12	8.5
Unemployed not seeking employment	0	0.0
Type of Employment		
# employed in law firms	65	51.2
# employed in business & industry	20	15.7
# employed in government	19	15.0
# employed in public interest	2	1.6
# employed as judicial clerks	18	14.2
# employed in academia	3	2.4
Geographic Location		
# employed in state	94	74.0
# employed in foreign countries	0	0.0
# of states where employed	14	

Bar Passage Rate

Jurisdiction	WA
# from school taking bar for the first time	107
School's pass rate for all first-time takers	86%
State's pass rate for all first-time takers	83%
State's pass rate for all first-time takers from ABA approved law schools	

WAYNE STATE UNIVERSITY

468 Ferry Mall
Detroit, MI 48202
(313)577-3933
http://www.science.wayne.edu/~law

ABA Approved Since 1936

The Basics

Type of School: **PUBLIC**
Application deadline*: **3/15**
Application fee: **$20**
Financial Aid deadline*: **4/23**
Student faculty ratio: **26.2 to 1**

First year can start other than Fall: **No**
Student housing: **No**
--exclusively for law students: **No**
Term: **Semester**

*pr=preferred

Faculty

	Men		Women		Minorities		Total
	#	%	#	%	#	%	
Full-time	15	71	6	29	2	10	21
Other full-time	0	0	0	0	0	0	0
Deans, librarians, & others who teach	1	33	2	67	0	0	3
Part-time	18	78	5	22	1	4	23
Total	34	72	13	28	3	6	47
Deans, librarians, & others who teach < 1/2	1	100	0	0	0	0	1

Library

# of volumes & volume equivalents	541,119	# of professional staff	6
# of titles	219,343	Hours per week with professional staff	69
# of active serial subscriptions	4,631	Hours per week without professional staff	28
Study seating capacity inside the library	506	# of student computer work stations for entire law school	52
Square feet of law library	28,257	# of additional networked connections	0
Square feet of law school (excl. Library)	41,942		

Curriculum

	Full time	Part time
Typical first-year section size	84	59
Is there typically a "small section" of the first year class, other than Legal Writing, taught by full-time faculty?	No	No
If yes, typical size offered last year	N/A	N/A
# of classroom course titles beyond 1st year curriculum	37	20
# of upper division courses, excluding seminars, with an enrollment:		
Under 25	18	10
25 - 49	15	11
50 - 74	4	3
75 - 99	2	2
100 +	8	4
# of seminars	9	3
# of seminar positions available	251	
# of seminar positions filled	109	35
# of positions available in simulation courses	486	
# of simulation positions filled	133	232
# of positions available in faculty supervised clinical courses	0	
# of fac. sup. clin. positions filled	0	0
# involved in field placements	134	12
# involved in law journals	53	11
# in moot court or trial competitions	143	23
# of credit hours required to graduate	86	

Enrollment & Attrition

	Full-Time							Part-Time							Attrition			
	Men		Women		Minorities		Total	Men		Women		Minorities		Total	Academic	Other	Total	
	#	%	#	%	#	%	#	#	%	#	%	#	%	#	#	#	#	%
1st Year	81	54.4	68	45.6	18	12.1	149	31	43.7	40	56.3	16	22.5	71	3	24	27	12
2nd Year	83	50.6	81	49.4	26	15.9	164	24	53.3	21	46.7	10	22.2	45	2	7	9	3.6
3rd Year	105	51.2	100	48.8	33	16.1	205	14	48.3	15	51.7	4	13.8	29	1	1	2	1.0
4th Year								43	61.4	27	38.6	8	11.4	70	1	0	1	1.7
Total	269	51.9	249	48.1	77	14.9	518	112	52.1	103	47.9	38	17.7	215	7	32	39	5.2
JD Degrees Awarded	82	53.6	71	46.4	16	10.5	153	24	60.0	16	40.0	4	10.0	40				

GPA & LSAT Scores

	Full Time	Part Time	Total
# of apps	735	314	1,049
# admits	382	108	490
# of matrics	150	77	227
75% GPA	3.56	3.47	
25% GPA	3.07	2.94	
75% LSAT	158	158	
25% LSAT	152	151	

Tuition/Living Expenses

	Resident	Non-resident
Full-Time	$6,052	$13,080
Part-Time	$4,364	$9,384

Estimated living expenses for Singles		
Living on campus	Living off campus	Living at home
$14,001	$14,001	$8,851

Career Placement

	Total	%
Employment status known	177	88.9
Employment status unknown	22	11.1
Employed	159	89.8
Pursuing graduate degrees	2	1.1
Unemployed seeking employment	2	1.1
Unemployed not seeking employment	14	7.9
Type of Employment		
# employed in law firms	90	56.6
# employed in business & industry	29	18.2
# employed in government	23	14.5
# employed in public interest	6	3.8
# employed as judicial clerks	6	3.8
# employed in academia	5	3.1
Geographic Location		
# employed in state	149	93.7
# employed in foreign countries	0	0.0
# of states where employed	4	

Financial Aid

	Full-time		Part-time		Total	
	#	%	#	%	#	%
Total # receiving grants	370	71.4	0	0.0	370	50.5
Less than 1/2 tuition	370	71.4	0	0.0	370	50.5
Half to full tuition	0	0.0	0	0.0	0	0.0
Full tuition	0	0.0	0	0.0	0	0.0
More than full tuition	0	0.0	0	0.0	0	0.0
Median Grant Amount	$1,500		$0			

Refunds

Refunds of Admissions or Seat Deposit prior to commencement of classes? Yes

100% refund to 05/15/00

Refunds of Pre-paid tuition prior to commencement of classes? No

If yes, fully refundable before the start of classes? No

Joint Degrees Offered

JD/MA Hist., JD/MA Pol.Sc, JD/MBA

Advanced Degrees Offered

LL.M.	General
LL.M.	Corporate and Finance Law
LL.M.	Labor Law
LL.M.	Taxation

Bar Passage Rate

Jurisdiction	MI
# from school taking bar for the first time	193
School's pass rate for all first-time takers	83%
State's pass rate for all first-time takers	70%
State's pass rate for all first-time takers from ABA approved law schools	70%

WEST VIRGINIA UNIVERSITY

P.O. Box 6130
Morgantown, WV 26506-6130
(304)293-3199
gopher://wvnvm.wvnet.edu/11/wc/wvu

ABA Approved Since 1923

The Basics

Type of School: **PUBLIC**
Application deadline*: **2/1**
Application fee: **$45**
Financial Aid deadline*: **3/1**
Student faculty ratio: **14.3 to 1**

First year can start other than Fall: **No**
Student housing: **No**
--exclusively for law students: **No**
Term: **Semester**

*pr=preferred

Faculty

	Men #	Men %	Women #	Women %	Minorities #	Minorities %	Total
Full-time	17	65	9	35	2	8	26
Other full-time	0	0	0	0	0	0	0
Deans, librarians, & others who teach	0	0	2	100	0	0	2
Part-time	12	86	2	14	0	0	14
Total	29	69	13	31	2	5	42
Deans, librarians, & others who teach < 1/2	1	100	0	0	0	0	1

Library

# of volumes & volume equivalents	233,277	# of professional staff	4
# of titles	39,658	Hours per week with professional staff	40
# of active serial subscriptions	2,925	Hours per week without professional staff	56
Study seating capacity inside the library	274	# of student computer work stations for entire law school	53
Square feet of law library	32,346	# of additional networked connections	0
Square feet of law school (excl. Library)	99,620		

Curriculum

	Full time	Part time
Typical first-year section size	72	0
Is there typically a "small section" of the first year class, other than Legal Writing, taught by full-time faculty?	No	No
If yes, typical size offered last year	N/A	N/A
# of classroom course titles beyond 1st year curriculum	55	0
# of upper division courses, excluding seminars, with an enrollment:		
Under 25	31	0
25 - 49	26	0
50 - 74	11	0
75 - 99	3	0
100 +	0	0
# of seminars	13	0
# of seminar positions available	213	
# of seminar positions filled	179	0
# of positions available in simulation courses	345	
# of simulation positions filled	325	0
# of positions available in faculty supervised clinical courses	24	
# of fac. sup. clin. positions filled	24	0
# involved in field placements	0	0
# involved in law journals	37	0
# in moot court or trial competitions	112	0
# of credit hours required to graduate	93	

Enrollment & Attrition

	Full-Time							Part-Time							Attrition			
	Men		Women		Minorities		Total	Men		Women		Minorities		Total	Academic	Other	Total	
	#	%	#	%	#	%	#	#	%	#	%	#	%	#	#	#	#	%
1st Year	68	47.2	76	52.8	6	4.2	144	3	50.0	3	50.0	0	0.0	6	0	6	6	4.2
2nd Year	82	59.4	56	40.6	4	2.9	138	0	0.0	2	100.0	0	0.0	2	2	1	3	2.0
3rd Year	65	47.4	72	52.6	10	7.3	137	3	60.0	2	40.0	0	0.0	5	0	0	0	0.0
4th Year								0	0.0	0	0.0	0	0.0	0	0	0	0	0.0
Total	215	51.3	204	48.7	20	4.8	419	6	46.2	7	53.8	0	0.0	13	2	7	9	2.1
JD Degrees Awarded	71	51.8	66	48.2	15	10.9	137	2	100.0	0	0.0	0	0.0	2				

GPA & LSAT Scores

	Full Time	Part Time	Total
# of apps	539	2	541
# admits	296	2	298
# of matrics	148	0	148
75% GPA	3.63	0.00	
25% GPA	3.09	0.00	
75% LSAT	156	0	
25% LSAT	149	0	

Tuition/Living Expenses

	Resident	Non-resident
Full-Time	$4,288	$11,168
Part-Time	$0	$0

Estimated living expenses for Singles		
Living on campus	Living off campus	Living at home
$7,580	$9,500	$4,680

Career Placement

	Total	%
Employment status known	133	98.5
Employment status unknown	2	1.5
Employed	121	91.0
Pursuing graduate degrees	2	1.5
Unemployed seeking employment	7	5.3
Unemployed not seeking employment	3	2.3
Type of Employment		
# employed in law firms	78	64.5
# employed in business & industry	11	9.1
# employed in government	18	14.9
# employed in public interest	3	2.5
# employed as judicial clerks	6	5.0
# employed in academia	5	4.1
Geographic Location		
# employed in state	96	79.3
# employed in foreign countries	0	0.0
# of states where employed	12	

Financial Aid

	Full-time		Part-time		Total	
	#	%	#	%	#	%
Total # receiving grants	100	23.9	0	0.0	100	23.1
Less than 1/2 tuition	71	17.0	0	0.0	71	16.4
Half to full tuition	4	1.0	0	0.0	4	0.9
Full tuition	16	3.8	0	0.0	16	3.7
More than full tuition	9	2.2	0	0.0	9	2.1
Median Grant Amount	$2,860		$0			

Refunds

Refunds of Admissions or Seat Deposit prior to commencement of classes? Yes

80% refund from 04/01/96 to 06/01/96

Refunds of Pre-paid tuition prior to commencement of classes? Yes

If yes, fully refundable before the start of classes? Yes

Joint Degrees Offered

MPA, MBA

Advanced Degrees Offered

No Advanced Degrees

Bar Passage Rate

Jurisdiction	WV
# from school taking bar for the first time	91
School's pass rate for all first-time takers	91%
State's pass rate for all first-time takers	89%
State's pass rate for all first-time takers from ABA approved law schools	89%

WESTERN NEW ENGLAND COLLEGE

1215 Wilbraham Road
Springfield, MA 01119
(413)782-1412
http://www.law.wnec.edu

ABA Approved Since 1974

The Basics

Type of School: **PRIVATE**
Application deadline*: **rolling**
Application fee: **$35**
Financial Aid deadline*: **4/1**
Student faculty ratio: **20.0 to 1**

First year can start other than Fall: **No**
Student housing: **No**
--exclusively for law students: **No**
Term: **Semester**

*pr=preferred

Faculty

	Men		Women		Minorities		Total
	#	%	#	%	#	%	
Full-time	21	81	5	19	2	8	26
Other full-time	0	0	0	0	0	0	0
Deans, librarians, & others who teach	1	100	0	0	0	0	1
Part-time	9	56	7	44	0	0	16
Total	31	72	12	28	2	5	43
Deans, librarians, & others who teach < 1/2	0	0	0	0	0	0	0

Library

# of volumes & volume equivalents	325,233	# of professional staff	5
# of titles	39,434	Hours per week with professional staff	69
# of active serial subscriptions	4,328	Hours per week without professional staff	34
Study seating capacity inside the library	397	# of student computer work stations for entire law school	48
Square feet of law library	30,151	# of additional networked connections	0
Square feet of law school (excl. Library)	54,627		

Curriculum

	Full time	Part time
Typical first-year section size	80	65
Is there typically a "small section" of the first year class, other than Legal Writing, taught by full-time faculty?	No	No
If yes, typical size offered last year	N/A	N/A
# of classroom course titles beyond 1st year curriculum	53	52
# of upper division courses, excluding seminars, with an enrollment:		
Under 25	20	27
25 - 49	17	18
50 - 74	9	9
75 - 99	9	1
100 +	0	0
# of seminars	2	0
# of seminar positions available	45	
# of seminar positions filled	21	0
# of positions available in simulation courses	487	
# of simulation positions filled	231	176
# of positions available in faculty supervised clinical courses	20	
# of fac. sup. clin. positions filled	19	1
# involved in field placements	120	14
# involved in law journals	24	9
# in moot court or trial competitions	27	5
# of credit hours required to graduate	88	

Enrollment & Attrition

	Full-Time							Part-Time							Attrition			
	Men		Women		Minorities		Total	Men		Women		Minorities		Total	Academic	Other	Total	
	#	%	#	%	#	%	#	#	%	#	%	#	%	#	#	#	#	%
1st Year	73	54.9	60	45.1	14	10.5	133	29	39.7	44	60.3	2	2.7	73	0	5	5	2.2
2nd Year	66	51.2	63	48.8	15	11.6	129	33	55.0	27	45.0	6	10.0	60	11	27	38	17
3rd Year	84	53.2	74	46.8	17	10.8	158	32	52.5	29	47.5	4	6.6	61	1	1	2	1.0
4th Year								35	49.3	36	50.7	5	7.0	71	0	0	0	0.0
Total	223	53.1	197	46.9	46	11.0	420	129	48.7	136	51.3	17	6.4	265	12	33	45	6.1
JD Degrees Awarded	76	50.0	76	50.0	14	9.2	152	33	51.6	31	48.4	3	4.7	64				

GPA & LSAT Scores

	Full Time	Part Time	Total
# of apps	1,181	225	1,406
# admits	725	155	880
# of matrics	134	74	208
75% GPA	3.25	3.27	
25% GPA	2.71	2.69	
75% LSAT	153	153	
25% LSAT	147	146	

Tuition/Living Expenses

	Resident	Non-resident
Full-Time	$15,506	$15,506
Part-Time	$11,592	$11,592

Estimated living expenses for Singles		
Living on campus	Living off campus	Living at home
$7,695	$8,413	$4,455

Financial Aid

	Full-time		Part-time		Total	
	#	%	#	%	#	%
Total # receiving grants	43	10.2	16	6.0	59	8.6
Less than 1/2 tuition	36	8.6	14	5.3	50	7.3
Half to full tuition	4	1.0	1	0.4	5	0.7
Full tuition	3	0.7	1	0.4	4	0.6
More than full tuition	0	0.0	0	0.0	0	0.0
Median Grant Amount	$3,828		$3,828			

Refunds

Refunds of Admissions or Seat Deposit prior to commencement of classes? No

Refunds of Pre-paid tuition prior to commencement of classes? No

If yes, fully refundable before the start of classes? No

Joint Degrees Offered

No Joint Degrees

Advanced Degrees Offered

No Advanced Degrees

Career Placement

	Total	%
Employment status known	207	90.0
Employment status unknown	23	10.0
Employed	174	84.1
Pursuing graduate degrees	5	2.4
Unemployed seeking employment	20	9.7
Unemployed not seeking employment	8	3.9
Type of Employment		
# employed in law firms	72	41.4
# employed in business & industry	40	23.0
# employed in government	38	21.8
# employed in public interest	9	5.2
# employed as judicial clerks	11	6.3
# employed in academia	4	2.3
Geographic Location		
# employed in state	56	32.2
# employed in foreign countries	0	0.0
# of states where employed	21	

Bar Passage Rate

Jurisdiction	MA	CT
# from school taking bar for the first time	98	62
School's pass rate for all first-time takers	77%	91%
State's pass rate for all first-time takers	83%	83%
State's pass rate for all first-time takers from ABA approved law schools	85%	78%

WHITTIER COLLEGE

5353 West Third Street
Los Angeles, CA 90020-4801
(213)938-3621
http://www.whittier.edu

ABA Approved Since 1978

The Basics

Type of School: **PRIVATE**
Application deadline*: **3/15**
Application fee: **$50**
Financial Aid deadline*: **6/1**
Student faculty ratio: **21.1 to 1**

First year can start other than Fall: **Yes**
Student housing: **No**
--exclusively for law students: **No**
Term: **Semester**

***pr=preferred**

Faculty

	Men #	Men %	Women #	Women %	Minorities #	Minorities %	Total
Full-time	16	73	6	27	3	14	22
Other full-time	0	0	3	100	1	33	3
Deans, librarians, & others who teach	0	0	0	0	0	0	0
Part-time	17	71	7	29	1	4	24
Total	33	67	16	33	5	10	49
Deans, librarians, & others who teach < 1/2	3	100	0	0	0	0	3

Library

# of volumes & volume equivalents	283,821	# of professional staff	6
# of titles	100,816	Hours per week with professional staff	85
# of active serial subscriptions	4,915	Hours per week without professional staff	16
Study seating capacity inside the library	315	# of student computer work stations for entire law school	68
Square feet of law library	26,000	# of additional networked connections	0
Square feet of law school (excl. Library)	71,050		

Curriculum

	Full time	Part time
Typical first-year section size	80	80
Is there typically a "small section" of the first year class, other than Legal Writing, taught by full-time faculty?	Yes	Yes
If yes, typical size offered last year	40	40
# of classroom course titles beyond 1st year curriculum	47	27
# of upper division courses, excluding seminars, with an enrollment:		
Under 25	35	20
25 - 49	12	12
50 - 74	7	4
75 - 99	8	0
100 +	1	0
# of seminars	9	0
# of seminar positions available	180	
# of seminar positions filled	109	38
# of positions available in simulation courses	676	
# of simulation positions filled	545	131
# of positions available in faculty supervised clinical courses	0	
# of fac. sup. clin. positions filled	0	0
# involved in field placements	113	31
# involved in law journals	43	13
# in moot court or trial competitions	74	22
# of credit hours required to graduate	87	

Enrollment & Attrition

	Full-Time Men #	Men %	Women #	Women %	Minorities #	Minorities %	Total #	Part-Time Men #	Men %	Women #	Women %	Minorities #	Minorities %	Total #	Attrition Academic #	Other #	Total #	%
1st Year	83	55.7	66	44.3	62	41.6	149	34	48.6	36	51.4	23	32.9	70	28	36	64	29
2nd Year	52	44.1	66	55.9	39	33.1	118	29	58.0	21	42.0	20	40.0	50	8	6	14	6.9
3rd Year	68	48.9	71	51.1	45	32.4	139	28	50.0	28	50.0	18	32.1	56	2	1	3	1.8
4th Year								28	52.8	25	47.2	16	30.2	53	0	0	0	0.0
Total	203	50.0	203	50.0	146	36.0	406	119	52.0	110	48.0	77	33.6	229	38	43	81	12
JD Degrees Awarded	70	60.9	45	39.1	33	28.7	115	28	52.8	25	47.2	9	17.0	53				

GPA & LSAT Scores

	Full Time	Part Time	Total
# of apps	2,140	381	2,521
# admits	1,045	183	1,228
# of matrics	186	70	256
75% GPA	3.16	3.32	
25% GPA	2.65	2.65	
75% LSAT	153	154	
25% LSAT	147	148	

Tuition/Living Expenses

	Resident	Non-resident
Full-Time	$18,934	$18,934
Part-Time	$11,374	$11,374

Estimated living expenses for Singles		
Living on campus	Living off campus	Living at home
N/A	$14,958	N/A

Career Placement

	Total	%
Employment status known	156	89.7
Employment status unknown	18	10.3
Employed	112	71.8
Pursuing graduate degrees	11	7.1
Unemployed seeking employment	17	10.9
Unemployed not seeking employment	16	10.3
Type of Employment		
# employed in law firms	67	59.8
# employed in business & industry	31	27.7
# employed in government	9	8.0
# employed in public interest	2	1.8
# employed as judicial clerks	1	0.9
# employed in academia	2	1.8
Geographic Location		
# employed in state	100	89.3
# employed in foreign countries	1	0.9
# of states where employed	11	

Financial Aid

	Full-time		Part-time		Total	
	#	%	#	%	#	%
Total # receiving grants	146	36.0	60	26.2	206	32.4
Less than 1/2 tuition	131	32.3	55	24.0	186	29.3
Half to full tuition	14	3.5	5	2.2	19	3.0
Full tuition	1	0.3	0	0.0	1	0.2
More than full tuition	0	0.0	0	0.0	0	0.0
Median Grant Amount	$5,000		$3,000			

Refunds

Refunds of Admissions or Seat Deposit prior to commencement of classes? No

Refunds of Pre-paid tuition prior to commencement of classes? Yes

If yes, fully refundable before the start of classes? Yes

Joint Degrees Offered

No Joint Degrees

Advanced Degrees Offered

No Advanced Degrees

Bar Passage Rate

Jurisdiction	CA
# from school taking bar for the first time	78
School's pass rate for all first-time takers	72%
State's pass rate for all first-time takers	73%
State's pass rate for all first-time takers from ABA approved law schools	83%

WIDENER UNIVERSITY

4601 Concord Pike
P.O. Box 7474
Wilmington, DE 19803-0474
(302)477-2100
http://www.widener.edu/law/law.html

ABA Approved Since 1975

The Basics

Type of School: PRIVATE
Application deadline*: 5/15
Application fee: $60
Financial Aid deadline*: 3/31
Student faculty ratio: 23.9 to 1

First year can start other than Fall: No
Student housing: Yes
--exclusively for law students: Yes
Term: Semester

*pr=preferred

Faculty

	Men		Women		Minorities		Total
	#	%	#	%	#	%	
Full-time	22	56	17	44	1	3	39
Other full-time	0	0	8	100	2	25	8
Deans, librarians, & others who teach	5	71	2	29	1	14	7
Part-time	28	80	7	20	4	11	35
Total	55	62	34	38	8	9	89
Deans, librarians, & others who teach < 1/2	1	33	2	67	0	0	3

Library

# of volumes & volume equivalents	385,090	# of professional staff	10
# of titles	81,942	Hours per week with professional staff	77
# of active serial subscriptions	5,634	Hours per week without professional staff	30
Study seating capacity inside the library	653	# of student computer work stations for entire law school	100
Square feet of law library	41,590	# of additional networked connections	0
Square feet of law school (excl. Library)	164,127		

Curriculum

	Full time	Part time
Typical first-year section size	96	78
Is there typically a "small section" of the first year class, other than Legal Writing, taught by full-time faculty?	No	No
If yes, typical size offered last year	N/A	N/A
# of classroom course titles beyond 1st year curriculum	92	93
# of upper division courses, excluding seminars, with an enrollment:		
Under 25	18	64
25 - 49	22	26
50 - 74	22	10
75 - 99	9	2
100 +	4	4
# of seminars	27	21
# of seminar positions available	960	
# of seminar positions filled	357	284
# of positions available in simulation courses	761	
# of simulation positions filled	381	380
# of positions available in faculty supervised clinical courses	79	
# of fac. sup. clin. positions filled	57	22
# involved in field placements	144	52
# involved in law journals	246	48
# in moot court or trial competitions	113	29
# of credit hours required to graduate	87	

Enrollment & Attrition

	Full-Time							Part-Time							Attrition			
	Men		Women		Minorities		Total	Men		Women		Minorities		Total	Academic	Other	Total	
	#	%	#	%	#	%	#	#	%	#	%	#	%	#	#	#	#	%
1st Year	157	54.9	129	45.1	17	5.9	286	76	49.7	77	50.3	8	5.2	153	0	41	41	10
2nd Year	136	52.3	124	47.7	15	5.8	260	66	60.6	43	39.4	11	10.1	109	23	17	40	10
3rd Year	159	58.5	113	41.5	14	5.1	272	58	56.9	44	43.1	13	12.7	102	3	12	15	4.2
4th Year								60	66.7	30	33.3	6	6.7	90	0	4	4	3.5
Total	452	55.3	366	44.7	46	5.6	818	260	57.3	194	42.7	38	8.4	454	26	74	100	7.8
JD Degrees Awarded	140	56.5	108	43.5	8	3.2	248	82	62.6	49	37.4	4	3.1	131				

GPA & LSAT Scores

	Full Time	Part Time	Total
# of apps	1,221	330	1,551
# admits	813	211	1,024
# of matrics	285	155	440
75% GPA	3.23	3.27	
25% GPA	2.75	2.62	
75% LSAT	151	154	
25% LSAT	147	147	

Tuition/Living Expenses

	Resident	Non-resident
Full-Time	$16,900	$16,900
Part-Time	$12,690	$12,690

Estimated living expenses for Singles		
Living on campus	Living off campus	Living at home
$11,170	$11,170	$8,020

Career Placement

	Total	%
Employment status known	386	93.2
Employment status unknown	28	6.8
Employed	319	82.6
Pursuing graduate degrees	8	2.1
Unemployed seeking employment	55	14.3
Unemployed not seeking employment	4	1.0
Type of Employment		
# employed in law firms	136	42.6
# employed in business & industry	84	26.3
# employed in government	29	9.1
# employed in public interest	7	2.2
# employed as judicial clerks	60	18.8
# employed in academia	3	0.9
Geographic Location		
# employed in state	63	19.8
# employed in foreign countries	0	0.0
# of states where employed	16	

Financial Aid

	Full-time		Part-time		Total	
	#	%	#	%	#	%
Total # receiving grants	71	8.7	39	8.6	110	8.6
Less than 1/2 tuition	33	4.0	18	4.0	51	4.0
Half to full tuition	22	2.7	15	3.3	37	2.9
Full tuition	16	2.0	6	1.3	22	1.7
More than full tuition	0	0.0	0	0.0	0	0.0
Median Grant Amount	$8,425		$6,320			

Refunds

Refunds of Admissions or Seat Deposit prior to commencement of classes? No

Refunds of Pre-paid tuition prior to commencement of classes? Yes

If yes, fully refundable before the start of classes? Yes

Joint Degrees Offered

JD/MBA, JD/PsyD

Advanced Degrees Offered

LLM Master of Laws in Corporate Law & Finance
LLM Master of Laws in Health Law

Bar Passage Rate

Jurisdiction	PA	DE
# from school taking bar for the first time	213	62
School's pass rate for all first-time takers	65%	53%
State's pass rate for all first-time takers	73%	
State's pass rate for all first-time takers from ABA approved law schools	73%	

WIDENER UNIVERSITY-HARRISBURG

3800 Vartan Way
P.O. Box 69381
Harrisburg, PA 17106-9381
(717)541-3900
http://www.widener.edu/law/law.html

ABA Approved Since 1989

The Basics

Type of School: **PRIVATE**
Application deadline*: **5/15**
Application fee: **$60**
Financial Aid deadline*: **3/31**
Student faculty ratio: **18.5 to 1**

First year can start other than Fall: **No**
Student housing: **No**
--exclusively for law students: **No**
Term: **Semester**

*pr=preferred

Faculty

	Men #	Men %	Women #	Women %	Minorities #	Minorities %	Total
Full-time	14	64	8	36	1	5	22
Other full-time	0	0	1	100	0	0	1
Deans, librarians, & others who teach	0	0	1	100	0	0	1
Part-time	11	69	5	31	0	0	16
Total	25	63	15	38	1	3	40
Deans, librarians, & others who teach < 1/2	1	100	0	0	0	0	1

Library

# of volumes & volume equivalents	188,663	# of professional staff	5
# of titles	19,114	Hours per week with professional staff	80
# of active serial subscriptions	4,207	Hours per week without professional staff	24
Study seating capacity inside the library	358	# of student computer work stations for entire law school	52
Square feet of law library	20,587	# of additional networked connections	0
Square feet of law school (excl. Library)	69,292		

Curriculum

	Full time	Part time
Typical first-year section size	147	55
Is there typically a "small section" of the first year class, other than Legal Writing, taught by full-time faculty?	No	No
If yes, typical size offered last year	N/A	N/A
# of classroom course titles beyond 1st year curriculum	56	64
# of upper division courses, excluding seminars, with an enrollment:		
Under 25	17	19
25 - 49	12	12
50 - 74	7	5
75 - 99	8	2
100 +	2	0
# of seminars	10	13
# of seminar positions available	460	
# of seminar positions filled	129	183
# of positions available in simulation courses	425	
# of simulation positions filled	277	79
# of positions available in faculty supervised clinical courses	60	
# of fac. sup. clin. positions filled	37	7
# involved in field placements	92	51
# involved in law journals	99	17
# in moot court or trial competitions	68	8
# of credit hours required to graduate	87	

Enrollment & Attrition

	Full-Time Men #	Men %	Women #	Women %	Minorities #	Minorities %	Total #	Part-Time Men #	Men %	Women #	Women %	Minorities #	Minorities %	Total #	Attrition Academic #	Other #	Total #	%
1st Year	63	60.0	42	40.0	6	5.7	105	32	68.1	15	31.9	0	0.0	47	0	19	19	9.6
2nd Year	83	58.9	58	41.1	3	2.1	141	20	60.6	13	39.4	2	6.1	33	12	8	20	9.9
3rd Year	89	62.2	54	37.8	4	2.8	143	27	64.3	15	35.7	3	7.1	42	6	3	9	3.8
4th Year								14	51.9	13	48.1	2	7.4	27	0	2	2	3.7
Total	235	60.4	154	39.6	13	3.3	389	93	62.4	56	37.6	7	4.7	149	18	32	50	7.2
JD Degrees Awarded	110	58.5	78	41.5	6	3.2	188	33	48.5	35	51.5	4	5.9	68				

GPA & LSAT Scores

	Full Time	Part Time	Total
# of apps	346	103	449
# admits	243	67	310
# of matrics	107	48	155
75% GPA	3.25	3.31	
25% GPA	2.64	2.68	
75% LSAT	151	154	
25% LSAT	145	149	

Tuition/Living Expenses

	Resident	Non-resident
Full-Time	$16,900	$16,900
Part-Time	$12,690	$12,690

Estimated living expenses for Singles		
Living on campus	Living off campus	Living at home
N/A	$11,170	$8,020

Career Placement

	Total	%
Employment status known	192	83.8
Employment status unknown	37	16.2
Employed	159	82.8
Pursuing graduate degrees	3	1.6
Unemployed seeking employment	29	15.1
Unemployed not seeking employment	1	0.5
Type of Employment		
# employed in law firms	68	42.8
# employed in business & industry	28	17.6
# employed in government	39	24.5
# employed in public interest	3	1.9
# employed as judicial clerks	17	10.7
# employed in academia	4	2.5
Geographic Location		
# employed in state	115	72.3
# employed in foreign countries	0	0.0
# of states where employed	13	

Financial Aid

	Full-time		Part-time		Total	
	#	%	#	%	#	%
Total # receiving grants	33	8.5	17	11.4	50	9.3
Less than 1/2 tuition	18	4.6	3	2.0	21	3.9
Half to full tuition	8	2.1	12	8.1	20	3.7
Full tuition	7	1.8	2	1.3	9	1.7
More than full tuition	0	0.0	0	0.0	0	0.0
Median Grant Amount	$5,500		$6,320			

Refunds

Refunds of Admissions or Seat Deposit prior to commencement of classes? No

Refunds of Pre-paid tuition prior to commencement of classes? Yes

If yes, fully refundable before the start of classes? Yes

Joint Degrees Offered

No Joint Degrees

Advanced Degrees Offered

LLM Master of Laws in Corporate Law & Finance
LLM Master of Laws in Health Law

Bar Passage Rate

Jurisdiction	PA
# from school taking bar for the first time	144
School's pass rate for all first-time takers	57%
State's pass rate for all first-time takers	73%
State's pass rate for all first-time takers from ABA approved law schools	73%

WILLAMETTE UNIVERSITY

245 Winter St. SE
Salem, OR 97301-3922
(503)370-6402
http://www.willamette.edu

ABA Approved Since 1938

The Basics

Type of School: **PRIVATE**	First year can start other than Fall: **No**
Application deadline*: **4/1**	Student housing: **Yes**
Application fee: **$40**	--exclusively for law students: **No**
Financial Aid deadline*: **2/1**	Term: **Semester**
Student faculty ratio: **19.2 to 1**	

*pr=preferred

Faculty

	Men		Women		Minorities		Total
	#	%	#	%	#	%	
Full-time	15	79	4	21	1	5	19
Other full-time	1	25	3	75	0	0	4
Deans, librarians, & others who teach	2	67	1	33	0	0	3
Part-time	5	83	1	17	0	0	6
Total	23	72	9	28	1	3	32
Deans, librarians, & others who teach < 1/2	2	100	0	0	0	0	2

Library

# of volumes & volume equivalents	266,702	# of professional staff	6
# of titles	37,089	Hours per week with professional staff	79
# of active serial subscriptions	4,264	Hours per week without professional staff	34
Study seating capacity inside the library	398	# of student computer work stations for entire law school	44
Square feet of law library	38,552	# of additional networked connections	16
Square feet of law school (excl. Library)	64,523		

Curriculum

	Full time	Part time
Typical first-year section size	100	0
Is there typically a "small section" of the first year class, other than Legal Writing, taught by full-time faculty?	Yes	No
If yes, typical size offered last year	22	N/A
# of classroom course titles beyond 1st year curriculum	73	0
# of upper division courses, excluding seminars, with an enrollment:		
Under 25	14	0
25 - 49	22	0
50 - 74	12	0
75 - 99	9	0
100 +	2	0
# of seminars	14	0
# of seminar positions available	248	
# of seminar positions filled	196	0
# of positions available in simulation courses	305	
# of simulation positions filled	238	0
# of positions available in faculty supervised clinical courses	32	
# of fac. sup. clin. positions filled	27	0
# involved in field placements	1	0
# involved in law journals	59	0
# in moot court or trial competitions	135	0
# of credit hours required to graduate	88	

Enrollment & Attrition

	Full-Time							Part-Time							Attrition			
	Men		Women		Minorities		Total	Men		Women		Minorities		Total	Academic	Other	Total	
	#	%	#	%	#	%	#	#	%	#	%	#	%	#	#	#	#	%
1st Year	76	55.1	62	44.9	18	13.0	138	0	0.0	0	0.0	0	0.0	0	4	11	15	11
2nd Year	69	53.1	61	46.9	16	12.3	130	0	0.0	0	0.0	0	0.0	0	4	4	8	4.5
3rd Year	108	63.5	62	36.5	17	10.0	170	0	0.0	0	0.0	0	0.0	0	0	0	0	0.0
4th Year								0	0.0	0	0.0	0	0.0	0	0	0	0	0.0
Total	253	57.8	185	42.2	51	11.6	438	0	0.0	0	0.0	0	0.0	0	8	15	23	5.0
JD Degrees Awarded	90	63.8	51	36.2	17	12.1	141	0	0.0	0	0.0	0	0.0	0				

GPA & LSAT Scores

	Full Time	Part Time	Total
# of apps	1,037	0	1,037
# admits	554	0	554
# of matrics	136	0	136
75% GPA	3.44	0.00	
25% GPA	2.84	0.00	
75% LSAT	158	0	
25% LSAT	152	0	

Tuition/Living Expenses

	Resident	Non-resident
Full-Time	$16,350	$16,350
Part-Time	$0	$0

Estimated living expenses for Singles		
Living on campus	Living off campus	Living at home
$10,820	$10,820	$3,640

Career Placement

	Total	%
Employment status known	148	93.7
Employment status unknown	10	6.3
Employed	127	85.8
Pursuing graduate degrees	5	3.4
Unemployed seeking employment	10	6.8
Unemployed not seeking employment	6	4.1
Type of Employment		
# employed in law firms	74	58.3
# employed in business & industry	20	15.7
# employed in government	17	13.4
# employed in public interest	1	0.8
# employed as judicial clerks	14	11.0
# employed in academia	1	0.8
Geographic Location		
# employed in state	84	66.1
# employed in foreign countries	1	0.8
# of states where employed	12	

Financial Aid

	Full-time		Part-time		Total	
	#	%	#	%	#	%
Total # receiving grants	103	23.5	0	0.0	103	23.5
Less than 1/2 tuition	84	19.2	0	0.0	84	19.2
Half to full tuition	17	3.9	0	0.0	17	3.9
Full tuition	2	0.5	0	0.0	2	0.5
More than full tuition	0	0.0	0	0.0	0	0.0
Median Grant Amount	$7,000		$7,000			

Refunds

Refunds of Admissions or Seat Deposit prior to commencement of classes? No

Refunds of Pre-paid tuition prior to commencement of classes? Yes

If yes, fully refundable before the start of classes? Yes

Joint Degrees Offered

JD/M Mgt.

Advanced Degrees Offered

No Advanced Degrees

Bar Passage Rate

Jurisdiction	OR
# from school taking bar for the first time	97
School's pass rate for all first-time takers	91%
State's pass rate for all first-time takers	85%
State's pass rate for all first-time takers from ABA approved law schools	

WILLIAM AND MARY SCHOOL OF LAW

P.O. Box 8795
Williamsburg, VA 23187-8795
(757)221-3800
http://www.wm.edu/law

ABA Approved Since 1932

The Basics

Type of School: **PUBLIC**
Application deadline*: **3/1**
Application fee: **$40**
Financial Aid deadline*: **2/1**
Student faculty ratio: **18.5 to 1**
First year can start other than Fall: **No**
Student housing: **Yes**
--exclusively for law students: **No**
Term: **Semester**

*pr=preferred

Faculty

	Men #	Men %	Women #	Women %	Minorities #	Minorities %	Total
Full-time	17	71	7	29	4	17	24
Other full-time	0	0	0	0	0	0	0
Deans, librarians, & others who teach	3	75	1	25	0	0	4
Part-time	15	68	7	32	3	14	22
Total	35	70	15	30	7	14	50
Deans, librarians, & others who teach < 1/2	1	100	0	0	0	0	1

Library

# of volumes & volume equivalents	331,340	# of professional staff	7
# of titles	57,475	Hours per week with professional staff	64
# of active serial subscriptions	5,146	Hours per week without professional staff	58
Study seating capacity inside the library	420	# of student computer work stations for entire law school	62
Square feet of law library	35,347	# of additional networked connections	0
Square feet of law school (excl. Library)	32,913		

Curriculum

	Full time	Part time
Typical first-year section size	70	0
Is there typically a "small section" of the first year class, other than Legal Writing, taught by full-time faculty?	Yes	No
If yes, typical size offered last year	60	N/A
# of classroom course titles beyond 1st year curriculum	97	0
# of upper division courses, excluding seminars, with an enrollment:		
Under 25	48	0
25 - 49	11	0
50 - 74	12	0
75 - 99	8	0
100 +	2	0
# of seminars	15	0
# of seminar positions available	234	
# of seminar positions filled	207	0
# of positions available in simulation courses	494	
# of simulation positions filled	484	0
# of positions available in faculty supervised clinical courses	20	
# of fac. sup. clin. positions filled	20	0
# involved in field placements	134	0
# involved in law journals	136	0
# in moot court or trial competitions	148	0
# of credit hours required to graduate	90	

Enrollment & Attrition

	Full-Time Men #	Men %	Women #	Women %	Minorities #	Minorities %	Total #	Part-Time Men #	Men %	Women #	Women %	Minorities #	Minorities %	Total #	Attrition Academic #	Other #	Total #	%
1st Year	104	52.5	94	47.5	48	24.2	198	0	0.0	0	0.0	0	0.0	0	0	11	11	6.0
2nd Year	89	51.7	83	48.3	34	19.8	172	0	0.0	0	0.0	0	0.0	0	0	4	4	2.4
3rd Year	94	58.0	68	42.0	28	17.3	162	0	0.0	0	0.0	0	0.0	0	0	1	1	0.6
4th Year								0	0.0	0	0.0	0	0.0	0	0	0	0	0.0
Total	287	53.9	245	46.1	110	20.7	532	0	0.0	0	0.0	0	0.0	0	0	16	16	3.1
JD Degrees Awarded	100	58.5	71	41.5	22	12.9	171	0	0.0	0	0.0	0	0.0	0				

GPA & LSAT Scores

	Full Time	Part Time	Total
# of apps	2,681	0	2,681
# admits	776	0	776
# of matrics	200	0	200
75% GPA	3.54	0.00	
25% GPA	3.02	0.00	
75% LSAT	165	0	
25% LSAT	160	0	

Tuition/Living Expenses

	Resident	Non-resident
Full-Time	$6,674	$17,002
Part-Time	$0	$0

Estimated living expenses for Singles		
Living on campus	Living off campus	Living at home
$10,230	$10,230	$10,230

Career Placement

	Total	%
Employment status known	165	100.0
Employment status unknown	0	0.0
Employed	159	96.4
Pursuing graduate degrees	1	0.6
Unemployed seeking employment	2	1.2
Unemployed not seeking employment	3	1.8
Type of Employment		
# employed in law firms	95	59.8
# employed in business & industry	12	7.5
# employed in government	11	6.9
# employed in public interest	9	5.7
# employed as judicial clerks	32	20.1
# employed in academia	0	0.0
Geographic Location		
# employed in state	87	54.7
# employed in foreign countries	0	0.0
# of states where employed	22	

Financial Aid

	Full-time		Part-time		Total	
	#	%	#	%	#	%
Total # receiving grants	225	42.3	0	0.0	225	42.3
Less than 1/2 tuition	152	28.6	0	0.0	152	28.6
Half to full tuition	73	13.7	0	0.0	73	13.7
Full tuition	0	0.0	0	0.0	0	0.0
More than full tuition	0	0.0	0	0.0	0	0.0
Median Grant Amount	$2,000		$0			

Refunds

Refunds of Admissions or Seat Deposit prior to commencement of classes? No

Refunds of Pre-paid tuition prior to commencement of classes? Yes

If yes, fully refundable before the start of classes? No

Joint Degrees Offered

JD/MPP, JD/MBA, JD/MA

Advanced Degrees Offered

LLM American Legal System

Bar Passage Rate

Jurisdiction	VA
# from school taking bar for the first time	100
School's pass rate for all first-time takers	87%
State's pass rate for all first-time takers	76%
State's pass rate for all first-time takers from ABA approved law schools	77%

WILLIAM MITCHELL COLLEGE OF LAW

875 Summit Avenue
St. Paul, MN 55105-3076
(612)227-9171
http://www.wmitchell.edu

ABA Approved Since 1938

The Basics

Type of School: **PRIVATE**
Application deadline: **4/15**
Application fee: **$35**
Financial Aid deadline: **3/15**
Student faculty ratio: **23.4 to 1**
First year can start other than Fall: **No**
Student housing: **No**
--exclusively for law students: **No**
Term: **Semester**

Faculty

	Men		Women		Minorities		Total
	#	%	#	%	#	%	
Full-time	21	68	10	32	3	10	31
Other full-time	0	0	0	0	0	0	0
Deans, librarians, & others who teach	1	100	0	0	0	0	1
Part-time	38	61	24	39	3	5	62
Total	60	64	34	36	6	6	94
Deans, librarians, & others who teach < 1/2	1	50	1	50	0	0	2

Library

# of volumes & volume equivalents	267,614	# of professional staff	9
# of titles	92,303	Hours per week with professional staff	77
# of active serial subscriptions	4,565	Hours per week without professional staff	29
Study seating capacity inside the library	672	# of student computer work stations for entire law school	59
Square feet of law library	53,000	# of additional networked connections	0
Square feet of law school (excl. Library)	147,000		

Curriculum

	Full time	Part time
Typical first-year section size	79	75
Is there typically a "small section" of the first year class, other than Legal Writing, taught by full-time faculty?	No	No
If yes, typical size offered last year	N/A	N/A
# of classroom course titles beyond 1st year curriculum	51	63
# of upper division courses, excluding seminars, with an enrollment:		
Under 25	34	43
25 - 49	33	35
50 - 74	12	14
75 - 99	6	7
100 +	0	0
# of seminars	12	10
# of seminar positions available	459	
# of seminar positions filled	240	158
# of positions available in simulation courses	790	
# of simulation positions filled	347	409
# of positions available in faculty supervised clinical courses	26	
# of fac. sup. clin. positions filled	23	0
# involved in field placements	189	107
# involved in law journals	58	17
# in moot court or trial competitions	70	30
# of credit hours required to graduate	86	

Enrollment & Attrition

	Full-Time							Part-Time							Attrition			
	Men		Women		Minorities		Total	Men		Women		Minorities		Total	Academic	Other	Total	
	#	%	#	%	#	%	#	#	%	#	%	#	%	#	#	#	#	%
1st Year	94	56.6	72	43.4	17	10.2	166	64	53.3	56	46.7	8	6.7	120	2	14	16	4.7
2nd Year	83	46.9	94	53.1	19	10.7	177	80	57.6	59	42.4	15	10.8	139	3	22	25	7.6
3rd Year	100	52.1	92	47.9	23	12.0	192	71	51.8	66	48.2	15	10.9	137	4	2	6	2.0
4th Year								57	49.6	58	50.4	14	12.2	115	3	0	3	2.9
Total	277	51.8	258	48.2	59	11.0	535	272	53.2	239	46.8	52	10.2	511	12	38	50	4.7
JD Degrees Awarded	88	52.1	81	47.9	22	13.0	169	52	44.1	66	55.9	14	11.9	118				

WILLIAM MITCHELL COLLEGE OF LAW

GPA & LSAT Scores

	Full Time	Part Time	Total
# of apps	N/A	N/A	1,200
# admits	N/A	N/A	799
# of matrics	168	126	294
75% GPA	3.40	3.38	
25% GPA	2.90	2.82	
75% LSAT	158	158	
25% LSAT	150	148	

Tuition/Living Expenses

	Resident	Non-resident
Full-Time	$15,360	$15,360
Part-Time	$11,160	$11,160

Estimated living expenses for Singles		
Living on campus	Living off campus	Living at home
N/A	$11,060	$5,350

Career Placement

	Total	%
Employment status known	274	89.5
Employment status unknown	32	10.5
Employed	254	92.7
Pursuing graduate degrees	1	0.4
Unemployed seeking employment	18	6.6
Unemployed not seeking employment	1	0.4
Type of Employment		
# employed in law firms	107	42.1
# employed in business & industry	64	25.2
# employed in government	34	13.4
# employed in public interest	7	2.8
# employed as judicial clerks	27	10.6
# employed in academia	15	5.9
Geographic Location		
# employed in state	232	91.3
# employed in foreign countries	0	0.0
# of states where employed	11	

Financial Aid

	Full-time		Part-time		Total	
	#	%	#	%	#	%
Total # receiving grants	188	35.1	117	22.9	305	29.2
Less than 1/2 tuition	151	28.2	80	15.7	231	22.1
Half to full tuition	14	2.6	25	4.9	39	3.7
Full tuition	22	4.1	12	2.4	34	3.3
More than full tuition	1	0.2	0	0.0	1	0.1
Median Grant Amount	$3,409		$3,348			

Refunds

Refunds of Admissions or Seat Deposit prior to commencement of classes? No

Refunds of Pre-paid tuition prior to commencement of classes? Yes

If yes, fully refundable before the start of classes? Yes

Joint Degrees Offered

No Joint Degrees

Advanced Degrees Offered

LLM Taxation

Bar Passage Rate

Jurisdiction	MN
# from school taking bar for the first time	257
School's pass rate for all first-time takers	85%
State's pass rate for all first-time takers	90%
State's pass rate for all first-time takers from ABA approved law schools	90%

WISCONSIN, UNIVERSITY OF

975 Bascom Mall
Madison, WI 53706-1399
(608)262-2240
http://www.wisc.edu

ABA Approved Since 1923

The Basics

Type of School: **PUBLIC**
Application deadline*: **2/1**
Application fee: **$38**
Financial Aid deadline*: **3/1**
Student faculty ratio: **20.4 to 1**

First year can start other than Fall: **No**
Student housing: **No**
--exclusively for law students: **No**
Term: **Semester**

*pr=preferred

Faculty

	Men #	Men %	Women #	Women %	Minorities #	Minorities %	Total
Full-time	24	71	10	29	3	9	34
Other full-time	7	64	4	36	1	9	11
Deans, librarians, & others who teach	3	100	0	0	0	0	3
Part-time	33	63	19	37	3	6	52
Total	67	67	33	33	7	7	100
Deans, librarians, & others who teach < 1/2	3	100	0	0	1	33	3

Library

# of volumes & volume equivalents	454,650	# of professional staff	13
# of titles	216,580	Hours per week with professional staff	73
# of active serial subscriptions	4,961	Hours per week without professional staff	34
Study seating capacity inside the library	600	# of student computer work stations for entire law school	60
Square feet of law library	54,741	# of additional networked connections	0
Square feet of law school (excl. Library)	56,310		

Curriculum

	Full time	Part time
Typical first-year section size	66	0
Is there typically a "small section" of the first year class, other than Legal Writing, taught by full-time faculty?	Yes	No
If yes, typical size offered last year	23	N/A
# of classroom course titles beyond 1st year curriculum	202	0
# of upper division courses, excluding seminars, with an enrollment:		
Under 25	138	0
25 - 49	41	0
50 - 74	44	0
75 - 99	13	0
100 +	2	0
# of seminars	36	0
# of seminar positions available	574	
# of seminar positions filled	574	0
# of positions available in simulation courses	504	
# of simulation positions filled	504	0
# of positions available in faculty supervised clinical courses	144	
# of fac. sup. clin. positions filled	144	0
# involved in field placements	224	0
# involved in law journals	172	0
# in moot court or trial competitions	141	0
# of credit hours required to graduate	90	

Enrollment & Attrition

	Full-Time							Part-Time							Attrition			
	Men		Women		Minorities		Total	Men		Women		Minorities		Total	Academic	Other	Total	
	#	%	#	%	#	%	#	#	%	#	%	#	%	#	#	#	#	%
1st Year	143	50.4	141	49.6	80	28.2	284	11	44.0	14	56.0	5	20.0	25	0	14	14	4.6
2nd Year	149	56.7	114	43.3	67	25.5	263	13	52.0	12	48.0	3	12.0	25	0	12	12	3.8
3rd Year	134	55.6	107	44.4	46	19.1	241	14	48.3	15	51.7	3	10.3	29	1	1	2	0.8
4th Year								0	0.0	0	0.0	0	0.0	0	0	0	0	0.0
Total	426	54.1	362	45.9	193	24.5	788	38	48.1	41	51.9	11	13.9	79	1	27	28	3.2
JD Degrees Awarded	147	55.3	119	44.7	41	15.4	266	2	50.0	2	50.0	1	25.0	4				

GPA & LSAT Scores

	Full Time	Part Time	Total
# of apps	1,947	0	1,947
# admits	754	0	754
# of matrics	267	0	267
75% GPA	3.64	0.00	
25% GPA	3.13	0.00	
75% LSAT	161	0	
25% LSAT	153	0	

Tuition/Living Expenses

	Resident	Non-resident
Full-Time	$5,504	$14,261
Part-Time	$4,586	$11,882

Estimated living expenses for Singles		
Living on campus	Living off campus	Living at home
$9,110	$9,110	$5,120

Career Placement

	Total	%
Employment status known	276	96.5
Employment status unknown	10	3.5
Employed	246	89.1
Pursuing graduate degrees	1	0.4
Unemployed seeking employment	26	9.4
Unemployed not seeking employment	3	1.1
Type of Employment		
# employed in law firms	149	60.6
# employed in business & industry	24	9.8
# employed in government	29	11.8
# employed in public interest	11	4.5
# employed as judicial clerks	24	9.8
# employed in academia	2	0.8
Geographic Location		
# employed in state	160	65.0
# employed in foreign countries	5	2.0
# of states where employed	20	

Financial Aid

	Full-time		Part-time		Total	
	#	%	#	%	#	%
Total # receiving grants	94	11.9	0	0.0	94	10.8
Less than 1/2 tuition	3	0.4	0	0.0	3	0.3
Half to full tuition	35	4.4	0	0.0	35	4.0
Full tuition	0	0.0	0	0.0	0	0.0
More than full tuition	56	7.1	0	0.0	56	6.5
Median Grant Amount	$9,072		$0			

Refunds

Refunds of Admissions or Seat Deposit prior to commencement of classes? No

Refunds of Pre-paid tuition prior to commencement of classes? Yes

If yes, fully refundable before the start of classes? Yes

Joint Degrees Offered

Law/Business, Law/Iberio-, Amer Stud, Law/Environ-, mental Stud, Law/Library, Info Scien, Law/Philos, Law/Sociolo, Law/Public, Policy Adm, Law/Educa, Admin, Law/Indust, Relations

Advanced Degrees Offered

LL.M. S.J.D. M.L.I.	Field of research selected by degree candidate with approval by the Graduate Programs Committee and candidate's major professor.

Bar Passage Rate

Jurisdiction	
# from school taking bar for the first time	
School's pass rate for all first-time takers	
State's pass rate for all first-time takers	
State's pass rate for all first-time takers from ABA approved law schools	

WYOMING, UNIVERSITY OF

P.O. Box 3035
Laramie, WY 82071
(307)766-6416
http://www.uwyo.edu/law/law.htm

ABA Approved Since 1923

The Basics

Type of School: PUBLIC
Application deadline*: 4/1
Application fee: $35
Financial Aid deadline*: 2/15
Student faculty ratio: 14.7 to 1
First year can start other than Fall: No
Student housing: Yes
--exclusively for law students: No
Term: Semester
*pr=preferred

Faculty

	Men		Women		Minorities		Total
	#	%	#	%	#	%	
Full-time	7	58	5	42	0	0	12
Other full-time	0	0	0	0	0	0	0
Deans, librarians, & others who teach	1	100	0	0	0	0	1
Part-time	6	86	1	14	0	0	7
Total	14	70	6	30	0	0	20
Deans, librarians, & others who teach < 1/2	1	33	2	67	0	0	3

Library

# of volumes & volume equivalents	198,153	# of professional staff	3
# of titles	20,060	Hours per week with professional staff	62
# of active serial subscriptions	2,504	Hours per week without professional staff	45
Study seating capacity inside the library	248	# of student computer work stations for entire law school	26
Square feet of law library	30,000	# of additional networked connections	2
Square feet of law school (excl. Library)	30,060		

Curriculum

	Full time	Part time
Typical first-year section size	80	0
Is there typically a "small section" of the first year class, other than Legal Writing, taught by full-time faculty?	No	No
If yes, typical size offered last year	N/A	N/A
# of classroom course titles beyond 1st year curriculum	53	0
# of upper division courses, excluding seminars, with an enrollment:		
Under 25	31	0
25 - 49	11	0
50 - 74	8	0
75 - 99	1	0
100 +	0	0
# of seminars	7	0
# of seminar positions available	70	
# of seminar positions filled	51	0
# of positions available in simulation courses	100	
# of simulation positions filled	89	0
# of positions available in faculty supervised clinical courses	55	
# of fac. sup. clin. positions filled	61	0
# involved in field placements	34	0
# involved in law journals	23	0
# in moot court or trial competitions	16	0
# of credit hours required to graduate	88	

Enrollment & Attrition

	Full-Time							Part-Time							Attrition			
	Men		Women		Minorities		Total	Men		Women		Minorities		Total	Academic	Other	Total	
	#	%	#	%	#	%	#	#	%	#	%	#	%	#	#	#	#	%
1st Year	46	59.0	32	41.0	3	3.8	78	0	0.0	0	0.0	0	0.0	0	3	13	16	21
2nd Year	33	52.4	30	47.6	2	3.2	63	0	0.0	0	0.0	0	0.0	0	3	0	3	4.2
3rd Year	40	57.1	30	42.9	8	11.4	70	0	0.0	0	0.0	0	0.0	0	0	0	0	0.0
4th Year								0	0.0	0	0.0	0	0.0	0	0	0	0	0.0
Total	119	56.4	92	43.6	13	6.2	211	0	0.0	0	0.0	0	0.0	0	6	13	19	8.4
JD Degrees Awarded	46	61.3	29	38.7	4	5.3	75	0	0.0	0	0.0	0	0.0	0				

GPA & LSAT Scores

	Full Time	Part Time	Total
# of apps	548	0	548
# admits	257	0	257
# of matrics	78	0	78
75% GPA	3.59	0.00	
25% GPA	3.06	0.00	
75% LSAT	157	0	
25% LSAT	150	0	

Tuition/Living Expenses

	Resident	Non-resident
Full-Time	$3,920	$8,648
Part-Time	$0	$0

Estimated living expenses for Singles		
Living on campus	Living off campus	Living at home
$6,740	$8,500	$4,000

Career Placement

	Total	%
Employment status known	67	97.1
Employment status unknown	2	2.9
Employed	57	85.1
Pursuing graduate degrees	3	4.5
Unemployed seeking employment	6	9.0
Unemployed not seeking employment	1	1.5
Type of Employment		
# employed in law firms	37	64.9
# employed in business & industry	5	8.8
# employed in government	6	10.5
# employed in public interest	4	7.0
# employed as judicial clerks	5	8.8
# employed in academia	0	0.0
Geographic Location		
# employed in state	35	61.4
# employed in foreign countries	0	0.0
# of states where employed	12	

Financial Aid

	Full-time		Part-time		Total	
	#	%	#	%	#	%
Total # receiving grants	54	25.6	0	0.0	54	25.6
Less than 1/2 tuition	41	19.4	0	0.0	41	19.4
Half to full tuition	7	3.3	0	0.0	7	3.3
Full tuition	4	1.9	0	0.0	4	1.9
More than full tuition	2	1.0	0	0.0	2	0.9
Median Grant Amount	$1,600		$0			

Refunds

Refunds of Admissions or Seat Deposit prior to commencement of classes? No

Refunds of Pre-paid tuition prior to commencement of classes? No

If yes, fully refundable before the start of classes? No

Joint Degrees Offered

JD/MBA, JD/MPA

Advanced Degrees Offered

No Advanced Degrees

Bar Passage Rate

Jurisdiction	WY
# from school taking bar for the first time	37
School's pass rate for all first-time takers	62%
State's pass rate for all first-time takers	59%
State's pass rate for all first-time takers from ABA approved law schools	59%

YALE UNIVERSITY

P.O. Box 208215
New Haven, CT 06520-8215
(203)432-1660
http://www.yale.edu/lawweb/lawschool

ABA Approved Since 1923

The Basics

Type of School: **PRIVATE**
Application deadline*: **2/15**
Application fee: **$65**
Financial Aid deadline*: **3/15**
Student faculty ratio: **10.9 to 1**

First year can start other than Fall: **No**
Student housing: **Yes**
--exclusively for law students: **Yes**
Term: **Semester**

*pr=preferred

Faculty

	Men #	Men %	Women #	Women %	Minorities #	Minorities %	Total
Full-time	37	82	8	18	5	11	45
Other full-time	0	0	0	0	0	0	0
Deans, librarians, & others who teach	3	100	0	0	0	0	3
Part-time	16	64	9	36	3	12	25
Total	56	77	17	23	8	11	73
Deans, librarians, & others who teach < 1/2	0	0	0	0	0	0	0

Library

# of volumes & volume equivalents	941,261	# of professional staff	0
# of titles	244,742	Hours per week with professional staff	87
# of active serial subscriptions	9,147	Hours per week without professional staff	81
Study seating capacity inside the library	250	# of student computer work stations for entire law school	73
Square feet of law library	55,186	# of additional networked connections	0
Square feet of law school (excl. Library)	57,506		

Curriculum

	Full time	Part time
Typical first-year section size	85	0
Is there typically a "small section" of the first year class, other than Legal Writing, taught by full-time faculty?	Yes	No
If yes, typical size offered last year	16	N/A
# of classroom course titles beyond 1st year curriculum	129	0
# of upper division courses, excluding seminars, with an enrollment:		
Under 25	30	0
25 - 49	21	0
50 - 74	11	0
75 - 99	6	0
100 +	7	0
# of seminars	54	0
# of seminar positions available	1,080	
# of seminar positions filled	594	0
# of positions available in simulation courses	0	
# of simulation positions filled	0	0
# of positions available in faculty supervised clinical courses	180	
# of fac. sup. clin. positions filled	180	0
# involved in field placements	2	0
# involved in law journals	313	0
# in moot court or trial competitions	65	0
# of credit hours required to graduate	82	

Enrollment & Attrition

	Full-Time							Part-Time							Attrition			
	Men		Women		Minorities		Total	Men		Women		Minorities		Total	Academic	Other	Total	
	#	%	#	%	#	%	#	#	%	#	%	#	%	#	#	#	#	%
1st Year	122	61.6	76	38.4	62	31.3	198	0	0.0	0	0.0	0	0.0	0	1	0	1	0.6
2nd Year	97	55.1	79	44.9	44	25.0	176	0	0.0	0	0.0	0	0.0	0	0	1	1	0.5
3rd Year	113	54.3	95	45.7	50	24.0	208	0	0.0	0	0.0	0	0.0	0	0	0	0	0.0
4th Year								0	0.0	0	0.0	0	0.0	0	0	0	0	0.0
Total	332	57.0	250	43.0	156	26.8	582	0	0.0	0	0.0	0	0.0	0	1	1	2	0.3
JD Degrees Awarded	111	61.0	71	39.0	53	29.1	182	0	0.0	0	0.0	0	0.0	0				

GPA & LSAT Scores

	Full Time	Part Time	Total
# of apps	3,811	0	3,811
# admits	253	0	253
# of matrics	198	0	198
75% GPA	3.94	0.00	
25% GPA	3.73	0.00	
75% LSAT	175	0	
25% LSAT	168	0	

Tuition/Living Expenses

	Resident	Non-resident
Full-Time	$22,692	$22,692
Part-Time	$0	$0

Estimated living expenses for Singles		
Living on campus	Living off campus	Living at home
$10,816	N/A	N/A

Financial Aid

	Full-time		Part-time		Total	
	#	%	#	%	#	%
Total # receiving grants	247	42.4	0	0.0	247	42.4
Less than 1/2 tuition	153	26.3	0	0.0	153	26.3
Half to full tuition	82	14.1	0	0.0	82	14.1
Full tuition	1	0.2	0	0.0	1	0.2
More than full tuition	11	1.9	0	0.0	11	1.9
Median Grant Amount	$8,972		$0			

Refunds

Refunds of Admissions or Seat Deposit prior to commencement of classes? Yes

100% refund to 06/15/97
0% refund from 06/15/97 to / /

Refunds of Pre-paid tuition prior to commencement of classes? Yes

If yes, fully refundable before the start of classes? Yes

100% refund to 09/02/97

Joint Degrees Offered

Ph.D. Hist., Ph.D. Hist., Ph.D. Econ., Ph.D. PolSci, Ph.D. AmStu, M.P.P.M., M.E.S. Fores, MA, Ph.D. PolSci, Ph.D. Sociol, M.A.R., M.D., M.E.S. Fores, M.P.P.M., Economics

Advanced Degrees Offered

LLM
JSD

Career Placement

	Total	%
Employment status known	204	97.6
Employment status unknown	5	2.4
Employed	195	95.6
Pursuing graduate degrees	8	3.9
Unemployed seeking employment	1	0.5
Unemployed not seeking employment	0	0.0
Type of Employment		
# employed in law firms	83	42.6
# employed in business & industry	7	3.6
# employed in government	8	4.1
# employed in public interest	5	2.6
# employed as judicial clerks	88	45.1
# employed in academia	4	2.1
Geographic Location		
# employed in state	8	4.1
# employed in foreign countries	1	0.5
# of states where employed	36	

Bar Passage Rate

Jurisdiction	NY
# from school taking bar for the first time	85
School's pass rate for all first-time takers	97%
State's pass rate for all first-time takers	78%
State's pass rate for all first-time takers from ABA approved law schools	

YESHIVA UNIVERSITY

55 Fifth Avenue
New York, NY 10003
(212)790-0200
http://www.yu.edu/csl/law

ABA Approved Since 1978

The Basics

Type of School: **PRIVATE**
Application deadline*: **4/1**
Application fee: **$60**
Financial Aid deadline*: **4/15**
Student faculty ratio: **21.3 to 1**

First year can start other than Fall: **Yes**
Student housing: **No**
--exclusively for law students: **No**
Term: **Semester**

*pr=preferred

Faculty

	Men #	Men %	Women #	Women %	Minorities #	Minorities %	Total
Full-time	29	76	9	24	2	5	38
Other full-time	0	0	0	0	0	0	0
Deans, librarians, & others who teach	1	50	1	50	0	0	2
Part-time	35	67	17	33	1	2	52
Total	65	71	27	29	3	3	92
Deans, librarians, & others who teach < 1/2	1	100	0	0	0	0	1

Library

# of volumes & volume equivalents	400,499	# of professional staff	6
# of titles	61,368	Hours per week with professional staff	62
# of active serial subscriptions	5,786	Hours per week without professional staff	26
Study seating capacity inside the library	510	# of student computer work stations for entire law school	87
Square feet of law library	37,012	# of additional networked connections	0
Square feet of law school (excl. Library)	74,988		

Curriculum

	Full time	Part time
Typical first-year section size	55	0
Is there typically a "small section" of the first year class, other than Legal Writing, taught by full-time faculty?	No	No
If yes, typical size offered last year	N/A	N/A
# of classroom course titles beyond 1st year curriculum	134	0
# of upper division courses, excluding seminars, with an enrollment:		
Under 25	24	0
25 - 49	31	0
50 - 74	22	0
75 - 99	10	0
100 +	13	0
# of seminars	44	0
# of seminar positions available	880	
# of seminar positions filled	603	0
# of positions available in simulation courses	362	
# of simulation positions filled	344	0
# of positions available in faculty supervised clinical courses	104	
# of fac. sup. clin. positions filled	104	0
# involved in field placements	454	0
# involved in law journals	242	0
# in moot court or trial competitions	40	0
# of credit hours required to graduate	84	

Enrollment & Attrition

	Full-Time							Part-Time							Attrition			
	Men		Women		Minorities		Total	Men		Women		Minorities		Total	Academic	Other	Total	
	#	%	#	%	#	%	#	#	%	#	%	#	%	#	#	#	#	%
1st Year	159	55.2	129	44.8	65	22.6	288	0	0.0	0	0.0	0	0.0	0	0	0	0	0.0
2nd Year	184	52.9	164	47.1	58	16.7	348	0	0.0	0	0.0	0	0.0	0	0	13	13	3.6
3rd Year	179	53.3	157	46.7	31	9.2	336	0	0.0	0	0.0	0	0.0	0	0	0	0	0.0
4th Year								0	0.0	0	0.0	0	0.0	0	0	0	0	0.0
Total	522	53.7	450	46.3	154	15.8	972	0	0.0	0	0.0	0	0.0	0	0	13	13	1.3
JD Degrees Awarded	155	50.8	150	49.2	41	13.4	305	0	0.0	0	0.0	0	0.0	0				

GPA & LSAT Scores

	Full Time	Part Time	Total
# of apps	2,205	0	2,205
# admits	1,062	0	1,062
# of matrics	332	0	332
75% GPA	3.46	0.00	
25% GPA	2.94	0.00	
75% LSAT	159	0	
25% LSAT	152	0	

Tuition/Living Expenses

	Resident	Non-resident
Full-Time	$19,055	$19,055
Part-Time	$0	$0

Estimated living expenses for Singles		
Living on campus	Living off campus	Living at home
N/A	$17,742	$8,067

Financial Aid

	Full-time		Part-time		Total	
	#	%	#	%	#	%
Total # receiving grants	515	53.0	0	0.0	515	53.0
Less than 1/2 tuition	460	47.3	0	0.0	460	47.3
Half to full tuition	54	5.6	0	0.0	54	5.6
Full tuition	1	0.1	0	0.0	1	0.1
More than full tuition	0	0.0	0	0.0	0	0.0
Median Grant Amount	$4,000		$0			

Refunds

Refunds of Admissions or Seat Deposit prior to commencement of classes? Yes

67% refund from 04/01/96 to 05/15/96
33% refund from 05/16/96 to 06/28/96
0% refund from 06/29/96 to / /

Refunds of Pre-paid tuition prior to commencement of classes? Yes

If yes, fully refundable before the start of classes? Yes

Joint Degrees Offered

No Joint Degrees

Advanced Degrees Offered

No Advanced Degrees

Career Placement

	Total	%
Employment status known	222	74.8
Employment status unknown	75	25.3
Employed	199	89.6
Pursuing graduate degrees	2	0.9
Unemployed seeking employment	21	9.5
Unemployed not seeking employment	0	0.0
Type of Employment		
# employed in law firms	114	57.3
# employed in business & industry	32	16.1
# employed in government	22	11.1
# employed in public interest	6	3.0
# employed as judicial clerks	18	9.1
# employed in academia	7	3.5
Geographic Location		
# employed in state	162	81.4
# employed in foreign countries	1	0.5
# of states where employed	0	

Bar Passage Rate

Jurisdiction	NY
# from school taking bar for the first time	248
School's pass rate for all first-time takers	76%
State's pass rate for all first-time takers	78%
State's pass rate for all first-time takers from ABA approved law schools	

Chapter Thirteen

Unapproved Law Schools

Below is a list of non ABA approved law schools as of October 1, 1996. A law school in the United States that is not approved by the ABA has either not applied for approval or does not satisfy the requirements of the ABA Standards for Approval of Law Schools. The list below is not comprehensive; but it is the most current data on record at the Office of the Consultant on Legal Education. You may wish to contact the bar admission authorities in the state(s) in which you intend to practice for more information on whether graduation from a law school that is not approved will qualify you to take the bar examination in that state. Graduation from a state-approved law school which is not ABA approved may qualify a person to take the bar examination in the state in which the school is located, but may not qualify the person for the examination in other states. For your convenience, chapter six contains contact information for bar admission authorities.

ALABAMA

Birmingham School of Law
923 Frank Nelson Building
Birmingham, AL

Miles Law School
P.O. Box 3800
Birmingham, AL 35208

Jones School of Law
Faulkner University
5345 Atlanta Highway
Montgomery, AL 36193-4601

CALIFORNIA

American College of Law
1717 S. State College Blvd.
Suite 100
Anaheim, CA 92806

Cal Northern
School of Law
2525 Dominic Drive, Suite F
Chico, CA 95928

California Pacific
School of Law
1600 Truxtun Avenue, Suite 100
Bakersfield, CA 93301

Central California
College of Law
2135 Fresno Street
Room 317
Fresno, CA 93721

Chapman University
School of Law
1240 South State College Road
Anaheim, CA 92806

Citrus Belt Law School
3775 Elizabeth Street
Riverside, CA 92506-2495

Empire College School of Law
3033 Cleveland Avenue
Suite 102
Santa Rosa, CA 95403

Glendale College of Law
220 North Glendale Avenue
Glendale, CA 91206

Humphreys College of Law
6650 Inglewood Avenue
Stockton, CA 95207

John F. Kennedy University
School of Law
547 Ygnacio Valley Road
Walnut Creek, CA 94596

Lincoln University
The Law School
281 Masonic Ave.
San Francisco, CA 94118

Lincoln Law
School of Sacramento
3140 "J" Street
Sacramento, CA 95816

Lincoln Law
School of San Jose
2160 Lundy Avenue
San Jose, CA 95131-1852

Monterey College of Law
404 West Franklin Street
Monterey, CA 93940

National University
School of Law
8380 Miramar Road
San Diego, CA 92126-4431

New College of California
School of Law
50 Fell Street
San Francisco, CA 94102

Northrop University
School of Law
5800 West Arbor Vitae Street
Inglewood, CA 90306

Pacific Coast University
College of Law
440 Redondo Avenue #203
Long Beach, CA 90814

Peninsula University
College of Law
436 Dell Avenue
Mountain View, CA 94043

People's College of Law
Faculty Curriculum Coordinator
660 South Bonnie Brae Street
Los Angeles, CA 90057

San Francisco Law School
20 Haight Street
San Francisco, CA 94102

San Joaquin College of Law
3385 East Shields Avenue
Fresno, CA 93726

Santa Barbara College of Law
911 Tremonto Road
Santa Barbara, CA 93101

Simon Greenleaf School of Law
3855 E. La Palma Avenue
Anaheim, CA 92801

Southern California College of Law
595 West Lambert Road
Brae, CA 92621

Southern California Institute of Law
Santa Barbara Campus:
1525 State Street, #202
Santa Barbara, CA 93101
Ventura Campus:
877 South Victoria Avenue, #111
Ventura, CA 93003

University of La Verne College of Law
21300 Oxnard Street
Woodland Hills, CA 91367

University of La Verne College of Law
1950 Third Street
La Verne, CA 91750

University of West Los Angeles School of Law
1155 West Arbor Vitae Street
Inglewood, CA 90301-2902

Ventura College of Law
4475 Market Street
Ventura, CA 93001

Western State University College of Law
P.O. Box 4310
1111 N. State College Boulevard
Fullerton, CA 92631

FLORIDA

Florida Coastal School of Law
7555 Beach Blvd.
Jacksonville, FL 32216

University of Orlando School of Law
6441 East Colonial Drive
Orlando, FL 32807

GEORGIA

Atlanta Law School
56 Tenth Street, N.E.
Atlanta, GA 30309

John Marshall Law School
805 Peachtree Street, N.E.
Atlanta, GA 30308

MASSACHUSETTS

Massachusetts School of Law
Woodland Park
500 Federal Street
Andover, MA 01810

Southern New England School of Law
874 Purchase Street
New Bedford, MA 02740-6232

PENNSYLVANIA

St. Matthew First Baptist Church School of Law
634 East Chelten Avenue
Philadelphia, PA 29144

PUERTO RICO

Eugenio Maria De Hostos School of Law
GPO Box 1900
Mayaguez, Puerto Rico 00681

TENNESSEE

Nashville School of Law
2934 Sidco Drive
Nashville, TN 37204

TEXAS

The Reynaldo G. Garza School of Law
905 North Shore Drive
San Benito, TX 78586

Please note that this book contains information concerning those law schools that were approved by the ABA as of October 1, 1996. The approval status of an individual law school could change, however. Therefore, if you would like to confirm whether an individual law school is approved by the ABA at a specific time after October 1, you should contact the ABA directly. Or you can access this information on the Section of Legal Education and Admissions to the Bar's Website. http://www.abanet.org/legaled

Chapter Fourteen

Legal Education Statistics

Fall 1996 Law School Attendance Figures for ABA Approved Law Schools

		Full Time	Part Time	TOTAL
First Year	Total	36,471	6,774	**43,245**
	Women	16,376	3,026	**19,402**
Second Year	Total	35,106	5,333	**40,439**
	Women	15,852	2,226	**18,078**
Third Year	Total	35,887	4,857	**40,744**
	Women	15,768	2,062	**17,830**
Fourth Year	Total	0	4,195	**4,195**
	Women	0	1,813	**1,813**
J.D. Total	Total	107,464	21,159	**128,623**
	Women	47,996	9,127	**57,123**
Post J.D.	Total	2,953	2,279	**5,232**
	Women	1,036	850	**1,886**
Other	Total	634	460	**1,094**
	Women	307	217	**524**
Grand Total	**Total**	**111,051**	**23,898**	**134,949**
	Women	**49,339**	**10,194**	**59,533**

Number of Professional Degrees Conferred in 1996 for ABA Approved Law Schools

		Full Time	Part Time	TOTAL
J.D./LL.B.	Total	35,030	4,890	**39,920**
	Women	15,404	1,962	**17,366**
LL.M.	Total	1,862	768	**2,630**
	Women	633	284	**917**
M.C.L./M.C.J.	Total	170	7	**177**
	Women	56	5	**61**
S.J.D./J.S.D.	Total	33	0	**33**
	Women	9	0	**9**
Other*	Total	302	157	**459**
	Women	98	62	**160**
TOTAL	Total	**37,397**	**5,822**	**43,219**
	Women	**16,200**	**2,313**	**18,513**

*Other professional degrees category includes DCL and JSM degrees.

Number of Teachers in ABA Approved Law Schools, 1996

	Women	Minorities	Total
Full-Time	1,515	713	**5,495**
Part-Time	1,383	434	**4,980**
Deans & Administrators	1,951	491	**3,028**
Librarians	958	212	**1,444**

LEGAL EDUCATION AND BAR ADMISSIONS STATISTICS 1963-1996

Academic Year	*Number of Schools*	*First Year Enrollment*	*First Year Women Enrollment*	*Total J.D. Enrollment*	*Total J.D. Women Enrollment*	*Total Overall* Enrollment*	*Regular LSAT Administrations*	*Saturday Sabbath LSAT Administrations*	*Total LSAT Administrations*	*J.D. or LL.B. Awarded*	*Admission to the Bar*
1963-64	135	20,776	877	46,666	1,739	49,552	37,598	N.A.	37,598	9,638	10,788
1964-65	135**	22,753	986	51,079	2,056	54,265	39,406	N.A.	39,406	10,491	12,023
1965-66	136	24,167	1,064	56,510	2,374	59,744	44,905	N.A.	44,905	11,507	13,109
1966-67	135	24,077	1,059	59,236	2,520	62,556	47,110	N.A.	47,110	13,115	14,644
1967-68	136	24,267	1,179	61,084	2,769	64,406	49,756	N.A.	49,756	14,738	16,007
1968-69	138	23,652	1,742	59,498	3,554	62,779	59,050	N.A.	59,050	16,077	17,764
1969-70	144	29,128	2,103	64,416	4,485	68,386	74,092	N.A.	74,092	16,733	19,123
1970-71	146	34,289	3,542	78,018	6,682	82,041	107,479	N.A.	107,479	17,183	17,922
1971-72	147	36,171	4,326	91,225	8,567	94,468	119,694	N.A.	119,694	17,006	20,485
1972-73	149	35,131	5,508	98,042	11,878	101,707	121,262	N.A.	121,262	22,342	25,086
1973-74	151	37,018	7,464	101,675	16,303	106,102	135,397	N.A.	135,397	27,756	30,879
1974-75	157	38,074	9,006	105,708	21,283	110,713	133,546	N.A.	133,546	28,729	30,707
1975-76	163	39,038	10,472	111,047	26,020	116,991	133,316****	N.A.	133,316****	29,961	34,930
1976-77	163	39,996	11,354	112,401	29,343	117,451	128,135	N.A.	128,135	32,597	35,741
1977-78	163	39,676	11,928	113,080	31,650	118,557	127,760****	N.A.	127,760****	33,640	37,302
1978-79	167	40,479	13,324	116,150	35,775	121,606	115,284****	N.A.	115,284****	33,317	39,068
1979-80	169	40,717	13,490	117,297	37,534	122,860	112,466****	679	113,145	34,590	42,756
1980-81	171	42,296	15,272	119,501	40,834	125,397	107,373****	649	108,022	35,059	41,997
1981-82	172	42,521	15,811	120,879	43,245	127,312	118,565***	726	119,291	35,598	42,382
1982-83	172	42,034	16,136	121,791	45,539	127,828	111,620***	505	112,125	34,846	42,905
1983-84	173	41,159	16,049	121,201	46,361	127,195	104,621	455	105,076	36,389	41,684
1984-85	174	40,747	16,236	119,847	46,897	125,698	95,120****	443	95,563	36,687	42,630
1985-86	175	40,796	16,510	118,700	47,486	124,092	91,397****	451	91,848	36,829	42,450
1986-87	175†	40,195	14,491	117,813	47,920	123,277	100,751	484	101,235	36,121	40,247††
1987-88	175†	41,055	17,506	117,997	48,920	123,198	115,407	581	115,988	35,478	39,918††
1988-89	174	42,860	18,395	120,694	50,932	125,870	136,367	721	137,088	35,701	46,528
1989-90	175	43,826	18,722	124,471	53,113	129,698	138,087	778	138,865	35,520	47,174
1990-91	175	44,104	18,592	127,261	54,097	132,433	151,846****	839	152,685	36,385	43,286††
1991-92	176	44,050	18,773	129,580	55,110	135,157	144,736	831	145,567	38,800	54,577
1992-93	176	42,793	18,325	128,212	54,644	133,783	139,306	748	140,054	39,425	57,117
1993-94	176	43,644	19,059	127,802	55,134	133,339	131,439	589	132,028	40,213	51,152
1994-95	177†††	44,298	19,312	128,989	55,808	134,784	127,905	648	128,553	39,710	57,875
1995-96	178	43,676	19,462	129,318	56,923	135,518	114,121	635	114,756	39,191	56,613
1996-97	179	43,245	19,402	128,623	57,123	134,949	N.A	N.A.	N.A.	39,920	N.A.

NOTES: Enrollment is in American Bar Association-approved schools as of October 1. The LSAT test year begins in June and ends in February of the following year. J.D. or LL.B. degrees are those awarded by approved schools for the academic year ending in the first year stated. 39,920 degrees were awarded in the year beginning with the fall, 1995, term and ending with the summer, 1996 term. Total new admissions to the bar are for the 1995 calendar year and include those admitted by office study, diploma privilege, and examination and study at an unapproved law school. The great bulk of those admitted were graduated from approved schools.

*Total overall enrollment includes post-J.D. and other.

**Stanford enrollment not included.

***These are updated figures for 1982-83 and 1983-84.

****These numbers were updated by LSAC/LSAS in 1993.

†This number includes Oral Roberts University, Coburn School of Law, which terminated its program effective June 1, 1986. However, the Council advised it to retain degree-ranting authority for those former students who completed satisfactorily 30 additional hours in ABA-approved law schools by Sept, 1, 1988.

††Data was not complete for these years, thus figure is lower than prior years.

†††Roger Williams not included.

SURVEY OF MINORITY GROUP STUDENTS ENROLLED IN J.D. PROGRAMS IN APPROVED LAW SCHOOLS*

Minority Classification	No. of Schools Reporting†	Academic Year	1st Year	2nd Year	3rd Year	4th Year	Total
Black American	176/179	1996-97	3,223	3,013	2,991	315	9,542
	175/178	1995-96	3,474	3,161	2,855	289	9,779
	174/177	1994-95	3,600	3,000	2,771	310	9,681
	173/176	1993-94	3,455	2,846	2,573	282	9,156
	173/176	1992-93	3,303	2,603	2,465	267	8,638
	173/176	1991-92	3,169	2,556	2,196	228	8,149
	172/175	1990-91	2,982	2,222	2,023	205	7,432
	172/175	1989-90	2,628	2,128	1,816	219	6,791
	171/174	1988-89	2,463	1,913	1,728	217	6,321
	171/175	1987-88	2,339	1,761	1,690	238	6,028
Mexican American	176/179	1996-97	861	768	751	49	2,429
	175/178	1995-96	896	820	743	36	2,495
	174/177	1994-95	902	739	719	42	2,402
	173/176	1993-94	838	698	639	28	2,203
	173/176	1992-93	807	744	683	24	2,258
	173/176	1991-92	770	644	584	29	2,027
	172/175	1990-91	768	624	527	31	1,950
	172/175	1989-90	640	531	469	23	1,663
	171/174	1988-89	656	510	458	33	1,657
	171/175	1987-88**	610	528	472	34	1,644
Puerto Rican†	176/179	1996-97	206	213	238	29	686
	175/178	1995-96	236	238	214	17	705
	174/177	1994-95	263	244	186	25	718
	173/176	1993-94	275	195	177	17	664
	173/176	1992-93	202	193	177	15	587
	173/176	1991-92	208	177	140	14	539
	172/175	1990-91	183	153	158	12	506
	172/175	1989-90	171	150	156	6	483
	171/174	1988-89	168	156	141	13	478
	171/175	1987-88**	178	134	140	7	459
Other Hispanic-American	176/179	1996-97	1,346	1,167	1,199	88	3,880
	175/178	1995-96	1,304	1,273	1,079	114	3,770
	174/177	1994-95	1,367	1,120	1,071	94	3,652
	173/176	1993-94	1,259	1,124	988	74	3,445
	173/176	1992-93	1,210	966	883	65	3,124
	173/176	1991-92	1,123	938	853	61	2,975
	172/175	1990-91	1,023	798	705	56	2,582
	172/175	1989-90	1,019	783	734	51	2,587
	171/174	1988-89	819	710	610	68	2,207
	171/175	1987-88**	750	623	543	55	1,971
American Indian or Alaskan Native	176/179	1996-97	391	397	310	18	1,116
	175/178	1995-96	436	338	294	17	1,085
	174/177	1994-95	377	283	290	12	962
	173/176	1993-94	336	280	243	14	873
	173/176	1992-93	313	243	206	14	776
	173/176	1991-92	286	219	176	11	692
	172/175	1990-91	224	185	129	16	554
	172/175	1989-90	220	147	143	17	527
	171/174	1988-89	177	165	149	8	499
	171/175	1987-88	189	144	148	11	492

SURVEY OF MINORITY GROUP STUDENTS *(continued)*[*]

Minority Classification	No. of Schools Reporting†	Academic Year	1st Year	2nd Year	3rd Year	4th Year	Total
Asian or Pacific Islander	176/179	1996-97	2,695	2,451	2,380	180	7,706
	175/178	1995-96	2,773	2,572	2,225	149	7,719
	174/177	1994-95	2,740	2,247	2,087	122	7,196
	173/176	1993-94	2,432	2,101	1,789	136	6,458
	173/176	1992-93	2,235	1,873	1,618	97	5,823
	173/176	1991-92	2,019	1,621	1,306	82	5,028
	172/175	1990-91	1,753	1,343	1,134	76	4,306
	172/175	1989-90	1,501	1,151	946	78	3,676
	171/174	1988-89	1,282	954	825	72	3,133
	171/175	1987-88	1,064	804	724	64	2,656
Total Minority	176/179	1996-97	8,722	8,009	7,869	679	25,279
	175/178	1995-96	9,119	8,402	7,411	622	25,554
	174/177	1994-95	9,249	7,633	7,124	605	24,611
	173/176	1993-94	8,595	7,244	6,409	551	22,799
	173/176	1992-93	8,070	6,682	6,032	482	21,266
	173/176	1991-92	7,575	6,155	5,255	425	19,410
	172/175	1990-91	6,933	5,325	4,676	396	17,330
	172/175	1989-90	6,172	4,890	4,264	394	15,720
	171/174	1988-89	5,565	4,408	3,911	411	14,295
	171/175	1987-88	5,130	3,994	3,717	409	13,250

[**]Revised figures 5/89.
†Puerto Rican students enrolled in three ABA-approved law schools in Puerto Rico totaled 1,617 students.

Chapter Fifteen

Selected Policies

(What follows are several Polices as adopted by the Council of the Section of Legal Education and Admissions to the Bar of the American Bar Association. To order a copy of the ABA Standards for Approval of Law Schools and Interpretations call (800) 285-2221. The cost is $12.00 plus shipping and handling.)

Policy 3. Statement of Good Practice on Impartiality and Propriety in the Process of Law School Accreditation

(A) Those who have significant responsibility in the process leading to accreditation of law schools serve a vital and quasi-judicial function in the legal system of the United States. It is important to the fair and effective functioning of the system of law school accreditation and to the maintenance of public and professional respect for that system that those who act in it act impartially and avoid even the appearance of impropriety.

(B) One who has significant responsibility in this system or who has had significant responsibility in this system within a period of two years past, as enumerated in paragraph "D" below should not serve as a consultant to a law school in any matter relating to:

(1) accreditation by the American Bar Association;

(2) membership in the Association of American Law Schools; or

(3) re-evaluation and continuation of American Bar Association accreditation or membership in the Association of American Law Schools.

(C) This restriction applies to service as consultant whether or not that service is for compensation. It does not apply to informal advice which an advisor renders (l) without fee; (2) informally and (3) which he or she discloses fully to the other members of the accreditation or membership body on which he or she serves or has served; nor does it apply to the routine or official advice and assistance which is rendered by members of a site evaluation team or hearing commission, by the Consultant on Legal Education to the American Bar Association, by the Executive Director of the Association of American Law Schools, or by persons acting on behalf of the Consultant or Executive Director, (4) or by a person acting in the normal course of his or her employment.

(D) This restriction applies to:

(1) members of the Accreditation Committee of the Council on Legal Education and Admissions to the Bar of the American Bar Association;

(2) the President, other Officers, members of the Board of Governors, and members of the Council of the Section of Legal Education and Admissions to the Bar of the American Bar Association;

(3) members of the Accreditation and Academic Freedom Committees of the Association of American Law Schools;

(4) the President and members of the Executive Committee of the Association of American Law Schools;

(5) members of the professional staff of the American Bar Association or the Association of American Law Schools, except as provided in paragraph "C" above;

(6) a member of a site evaluation team or hearing commission for either Association accepting appointment as a consultant to a law school that he or she has evaluated or conducted hearings on, in behalf of either Association within two years after the site evaluation or while either Association still has under consideration matters developed by the site evaluation, whichever is longer;

(7) the Executive Director of the Association of American Law Schools or other person acting on behalf of the Association of American Law Schools may not acquiesce in the appointment as consultant on readiness of any person who by this Statement should not accept appointment as a school's consultant.

(E) Service as a consultant for a law school does not disqualify a person from any of the offices or committees in paragraph "D." However, the officer or committee member should excuse himself or herself from participation in discussion, formal or informal, of the affairs of a school which he or she has served as consultant or employee and from taking part in any vote with respect to its status.

(F) A person who has served as a consultant or employee of a law school within two years prior to assuming a significant responsibility in the accreditation process should decline to participate in the determination of the accreditation status of the school with which he or she previously served.

(G) The Consultant on Legal Education to the American Bar Association, Executive Director of the Association of American Law Schools or either of them if they are acting cooperatively shall bring this regulation to the attention of persons who are nominated for or appointed to any of the positions enumerated in paragraph "D" above and to all persons who are holding these positions or who have held them within two years past, at the time the regulation becomes effective.

Adopted by the Council of the Section of Legal Education and Admissions to the Bar—December 10, 1977.

Adopted by the AALS Executive Committee—December 27, 1977.

Policy 4. Pass/Fail Grading

At its August, 1970 meeting the Council of the Section of Legal Education and Admissions to the Bar decided to endorse the following statement issued earlier by the Law School Admission Council on the impact of pass/fail grading by undergraduate colleges upon the law school admission process. This statement has also been endorsed by the Executive Committee of the Association of American Law Schools.

The adoption by an increasing number of colleges and universities of pass/fail or similar grading systems for some or all of their students' work has implications for the law school admissions process. When a student with a transcript bearing such grades seeks to enter law school, law school admissions committees will be deprived of data that have served them well in the past in making the admissions decision. In the belief that college and university faculties and administrations who are considering conversion of a conventional grading system to a pass/fail or some variant system may be interested in the possible effect of such grading systems upon their graduates who seek admission to law school, the Law School Admission Council issues this statement.

The Law School Admission Test (LSAT) was developed more than twenty years ago in response to an expressed need of law schools for additional data upon which to base their admissions decisions. Validity studies conducted over the years demonstrate that the LSAT score contributes significantly to the prediction of an applicant's grades in law school and thus aids in the making of the admissions decision. These studies show that the LSAT score and the undergraduate grade-point average are the two best quantitative predictors, and that when they are used together they are better than either used separately. College grades represent both academic competence and achievement; the LSAT score largely indicates academic competence—the kind relevant to the study of law. The academic achievement of an applicant to law school indicates the extent of his preparation and motivation for the study of law. It is apparent, then, that college grades make a significant contribution to prediction of law school grades that is not supplied by the LSAT score.

Where an applicant for admission to law school submits a transcript in which all or virtually all of his grades are on pass/fail basis, and submits no other indication of his level of achievement in college, the admissions committee can make little specific use of his college work in predicting his law school grades. This means that this prediction must be based on the LSAT score, even though the committee would much prefer not to place sole reliance on the test scores in making this prediction. Even when such a transcript is supplemented by a narrative evaluation of the applicant by several of his teachers and deans, the committee can make only limited use of the college work in predicting performance in law school. Like interviews, these evaluations give the committee some help in making the admissions judgment, but they are largely helpful in deciding which risks to take and which to reject.

Where the applicant for admission to law school submits a transcript containing some conventional grades and some pass/fail grades, the admissions committee can develop a grade-point average for that portion of the student's college work bearing the conventional grades. However, many admissions officers will not feel justified in assigning to that average the conventional weight. They may well assume that the student chose to receive a conventional grade in those courses in which he gauged his probabilities for a premium grade to be good. This indicates that his grade-point average so developed will overstate his academic competence and achievement as compared with the average of a student whose grades are all conventional. Furthermore, the committee may reasonably assume that the applicant did not make the same effort in the courses graded on a pass/fail basis as he did in those graded on the conventional basis. In short, a grade-point average based only upon the limited part of a student's work in which conventional grades were assigned seems to overstate in a compound way the student's general academic ability and achievement. Therefore, it is understandable that many admissions officers are already discounting such a grade-point average, and discounting it more if there is a large proportion of pass/fail grades.

The Council recognizes that the increased use of the pass/fail grading system—or some variant thereof—will mean that law school admissions committees and officers will place an increased reliance upon the LSAT score, a greater reliance than either the Council or law school admissions committee would like. The Council recognizes that there are many educational considerations to be taken into account by the faculty and administration in determining the appropriate grading system for that college or university. The Council, of course, respects the authority and judgment of the college and university faculty and administration in making that decision. The Law School Admission Council offers this statement concerning the effect of pass/fail grades upon the proper evaluation of a college graduate's application for admission to law school only in the hope that it may be useful to college faculties and administrations in determining what grading system to use.

Policy 7. Correspondence Study

The American Bar Association expressly disapproves of correspondence law courses as a means of preparation for bar examination and for practice. Before one pursues a correspondence law course, it is suggested that he first familiarize himself with the rules and regulations of the state in which he intends to practice and

inquire whether correspondence law courses are acceptable under the applicable rules and regulations of the state and any governmental agency with which one expects to secure employment. Correspondence law school graduates may take the bar examinations only in California and even there only under special conditions.

Policy 8. Postponement of Graduation

WHEREAS, most state supreme courts require graduation from an ABA approved law school as a requisite for bar admissions in order to assure the public that persons representing them in legal matters have received a quality legal education, and

WHEREAS, some individuals begin and complete substantially all of their legal education at unapproved law schools, which law schools have been inspected for possible ABA provisional approval but are found not to meet the ABA Standards during the time of such attendance; and these individuals may then delay their formal graduation until after the law school received ABA provisional approval, and

WHEREAS, some law schools receiving ABA provisional approval have permitted students to delay their graduation until such approval was received by the school and have then awarded degrees dated subsequent to receipt of ABA provisional approval to such students,

THEREFORE, the Council of the Section of Legal Education and Admissions to the Bar hereby adopts a policy disapproving this practice, and requests that all provisionally approved law schools, all other schools seeking provisional approval, all law school site team members and all state bar admitting authorities be notified of this policy.

Policy 13. Law School Admission Fees

The American Bar Association Section of Legal Education and Admissions to the Bar condemns the practice of requiring persons seeking admission to a law school to pay a fee, in addition to the regular application fee, to be placed on a list of persons who will be admitted if additional places become available, commonly known as a "waiting list."

Policy 20. Rating of Law Schools

No rating of law schools beyond the simple statement of their accreditation status is attempted or advocated by the official organizations in legal education. Qualities that make one kind of school good for one student may not be as important to another. The American Bar Association and its Section of Legal Education and Admissions to the Bar have issued disclaimers of any law school rating system. Prospective law students should consider a variety of factors in making their choice among schools.

Policy 25. Propriety of Examination by Public Authority before Admission to Practice

A half century ago the American Bar Association adopted standards for legal education, the second of which is as follows:

> "The American Bar Association is of the opinion that graduation from a law school should not confer the right of admission to the bar, and that every candidate should be subject to an examination by public authority to determine his fitness."

The criticism of bar examinations, which is daily becoming more prevalent, makes it most appropriate for the Council of the Section of Legal Education and Admissions to the Bar and the Board of Managers of the National Conference of Bar Examiners to state their opinion on the matter of the so-called Diploma Privilege.
It is the position of the Council and Board that the above-quoted standard, adopted in 1921, is as valid today—perhaps more so with the mobility of law graduates—as it was at the time and that every applicant for admission to the bar should be subject to examination by public authority.

Very great progress has taken place in the caliber of legal education in the fifty years intervening since 1921. In part the improvement in legal education has been the result of experimentation in teaching techniques. Not all such experiments have proved successful. Public authority should not dictate teaching techniques but it should make sure that all applicants have the training necessary to adequately serve the public upon their admission.

Not only are law schools quite properly experimenting in teaching techniques but they are experimenting in curriculum content. Again, public authority should not dictate curriculum content but by examination should determine that the content of the applicant's education is such that upon admission he will be able to adequately serve the public. In one of the jurisdictions where graduates of certain law schools are admitted without examination, the Court found it necessary to a certain extent to dictate the curriculum content of those schools—an unfortunate limitation on the educational freedom of these schools.

Bar examinations themselves serve additional functions. They encourage law graduates to study subjects not taken in law school. They require the applicant to review all he has learned in law school with a result that he is made to realize the interrelation of the various divisions of the law—to view the separate subject courses which he took in law school as a related whole. This the curriculum of most law schools does not achieve. Also, it is the first time many of the applicants will have been examined by persons other than those who taught them, a valuable experience in preparation for appearing before a completely strange judge.

To reiterate, it is the position of the Council and the Board of Managers that there must be examination by public authority. This is not to say that public authority must not be very careful in its examination procedure to make sure that it is fulfilling its responsibilities. It should continually strive to make its methods of examination more effective so that the results will be the nondiscriminatory admission of none not qualified and the exclusion of none qualified, even though this requires the use of innovative examining techniques and constant consideration of the ever changing needs of our society. The necessity to train lawyers to represent all members of society is a continual challenge to teachers of law and legal education. To test this properly the examining authority can perform effectively and satisfactorily only if it makes responsive changes in its techniques.

Policy 26. Period of Time for Completion of Requirements to Obtain J. D. Degree

The normal maximum period for a full-time law student to complete requirements for a J.D. degree is five years. The normal maximum completion time for a part-time law student to complete requirements for a J.D. degree is six years.

Policy 30. Encouragement of Increased Emphasis on Pro-Bono Activities

Law Schools should make law students aware of the special needs of those persons often under-represented in legal matters, including minorities, the poor, elderly and handicapped members of society, facilitate student services to these groups and should instill a sense in their students of the profession's obligation to provide legal services to those who are unable to afford them.

Policy 31. Student Tuition and Fee Refund Policy

It is the policy of the Council that all law schools approved by the American Bar Association have and make publicly available an equitable student tuition and fee refund policy. This policy shall contain a complete statement of all student tuition and fees and a schedule for the equitable refund of student tuition and fees.

Policy 32. Policy on Timely Grading of Law School Examinations

The Council of the Section of Legal Education and Admissions to the Bar reports that as a result of the expressed concern of the Law Student Division concerning timely grading of examinations, the Consultant on Legal Education to the American Bar Association has conducted a survey of grading practices at all law schools approved by the American Bar Association. The Law Student Division proposal and resultant survey has promoted thoughtful discussion among the deans and faculties of ABA approved law schools. The Council urges that all law schools continue adoption and maintenance of timely grading practices of law school examinations. The Council is aware that on occasion, a faculty member may not honor their professional obligation in this regard. The Council urges enforcement by each school of its own adopted policies, and urges completion of the grading and notice provision to the students not later than 30 days following the last examination of the term.

Policy 35. Law School Policy Encouraging Faculty to Engage in Reasonable Post-Examination Review With Students

It is recommended that a law school have a policy encouraging faculty members to engage in reasonable post examination review with students, preferably individual review upon request. Absent good cause, students should also have a right to reasonably review their examination papers. This does not mean that faculty members are obligated to review examinations individually with all students in every course. A reasonable policy may take into account the workload of individual teachers, the number of examinations in the course, the academic needs of the particular students requesting review, and the availability of review in courses throughout the school. Faculty members may choose to carry out such a policy using alternative means, including engaging in individual review of examinations upon student's request, by holding a general review concerning the examination open to all students, or by providing an outline or exemplar of good examination answers. (June, 1990)

Policy 41. Student Complaints

It is the policy of the Council that each law school approved by the American Bar Association should communicate in written form to its students the manner in which it receives and responds to student complaints.

Chapter Sixteen

Public/Private Listings

Below are two lists of all the ABA approved law schools as of October 1, 1996. The first list contains all of the 76 public ABA approved law schools. The second list contains all of the 103 private ABA approved law schools.

PUBLIC

Akron, University of
Alabama, University of
Arizona State University
Arizona, University of
Arkansas-Fayetteville, University of
Arkansas-Little Rock, University of
Baltimore, University of
California-Berkeley, University of
California-Davis, University of
California-Hastings, University of
California-Los Angeles, University of
Cincinnati, University of
City New York—Queens College
Cleveland State University
College of William and Mary
Colorado, University of
Connecticut, University of
District of Columbia School of Law
Florida State University
Florida, University of
George Mason University
Georgia State University
Georgia, University of
Hawaii, University of
Houston, University of
Idaho, University of
Illinois, University of
Indiana University-Bloomington
Indiana University-Indianapolis
Iowa, University of
Kansas, University of
Kentucky, University of
Louisiana State University
Louisville, University of
Maine, University of
Maryland, University of
Memphis State University
Michigan, University of
Minnesota, University of
Mississippi, University of
Missouri-Columbia, University of
Missouri-Kansas City, University of
Montana, University of
Nebraska, University of
New Mexico, University of
North Carolina Central University
North Carolina, University of
North Dakota, University of
Northern Illinois University
Northern Kentucky University
Ohio State University
Oklahoma, University of
Oregon, University of
Pittsburgh, University of
Puerto Rico, University of
Rutgers University-Camden
Rutgers University-Newark
South Carolina, University of
South Dakota, University of
Southern Illinois University
Southern University
State University of New York-Buffalo
Temple University
Tennessee, University of
Texas Southern University
Texas Tech University
Texas, University of
Toledo, University of
Utah, University of
Virginia, University of
Washburn University
Washington, University of
Wayne State University
West Virginia University
Wisconsin, University of
Wyoming, University of

PRIVATE

American University
Baylor University
Boston College
Boston University
Brigham Young University
Brooklyn University
California Western School of Law
Campbell University
Capital University
Case Western University
Catholic University of America
Catholic University of Puerto Rico
Chicago, University of
Columbia University
Cornell University
Creighton University
Dayton, University of
Denver, University of
DePaul University
Detroit College of Law at Michigan State University
Detroit Mercy, University of
Dickinson School of Law
Drake University
Duke University
Duquesne University
Emory University
Fordham University
Franklin Pierce Law Center
George Washington University
Georgetown University
Golden Gate University
Gonzaga University
Hamline University
Harvard University
Hofstra University
Howard University
Illinois Institute of Technology, Chicago-Kent
Inter-American University of Puerto Rico
John Marshall Law School
Lewis and Clark College
Loyola University-Chicago
Loyola University-Los Angeles
Loyola University-New Orleans
Marquette University
Mercer University
Miami, University of
Mississippi College
New England School of Law
New York Law School
New York University
Northeastern University
Northwestern University
Notre Dame, University of
Nova Southeastern University
Ohio Northern University
Oklahoma City University
Pace University
Pacific, University of the
Pennsylvania
Pepperdine University
Quinnipiac College School of Law
Regent University
Richmond, University of
Roger Williams University
Samford University
San Diego, University of
San Francisco, University of
Santa Clara University
Seattle University (formerly Puget Sound)
Seton Hall University
South Texas College of Law
Southern California, University of
Southern Methodist University
Southwestern University
St. John's University
St. Louis University
St. Mary's University
St. Thomas University
Stanford University
Stetson University
Suffolk University
Syracuse University
Texas Wesleyan
Thomas Jefferson
Thomas M. Cooley Law School
Touro College
Tulane University
Tulsa, University of
Union University, Albany Law School
Valparaiso University
Vanderbilt University
Vermont Law School
Villanova University
Wake Forest University
Washington and Lee University
Washington St. Louis
Western New England College
Whittier College
Widener University
Widener University (Harrisburg)
Willamette University
William Mitchell College of Law
Yale University
Yeshiva University

Chapter Seventeen

Law Services

Excerpted, with permission, from* The Official Guide to U.S. Law Schools, *Law School Admission Council, Inc. (1998)

Working with Law Services

Law Services administers the LSAT and serves as a liaison for much of the communication between you and the law schools. You are expected to send your individual law school application **directly to each law school** to which you apply; however, your test scores, transcripts, and other academic information and biographical data are sent to the law schools through the Law School Data Assembly Services (LSDAS).

Comprehensive information about LSAT registration and LSDAS subscription is set forth in complete detail in the *LSAT/LSDAS Registration and Information Book*, published annually. This publication is available at no charge through Law Services or any of 1,500 national distribution sites located on undergraduate campuses (principally prelaw advising offices and career centers) and at law schools. (Law Services operators will provide a list of distribution locations nearest your zip code; call 215-968-1001.)

You need not subscribe to the LSDAS at the same time you register for the LSAT, but doing so will simplify the process. Application deadlines for the law schools to which you apply dictate when you should subscribe to the LSDAS.

Planning Ahead for Law School Deadlines

Most law schools have a variety of application requirements and deadlines that you must meet to be considered for admission. Many of the deadlines are listed in this book. If you are applying to a number of schools, the various deadlines and requirements can be confusing. It probably will be helpful if you set up a detailed calendar that will remind you of when and what you must do to complete an application.

You will also want to be sure you can make an LSAT score available to a law school before its application deadline. In registering for the LSAT, be sure to give yourself enough time to select a convenient testing location and prepare for the actual test.

Below is a chart listing all the scheduled test administrations, including alternate dates for Saturday Sabbath observers, along with corresponding deadlines and fees.

Basic LSAT Date and Deadline Information (1997-1998)

All scheduled administrations of the LSAT, both for regular test takers and test takers who are Saturday Sabbath observers, are listed below along with corresponding regular registration deadlines. Dates shown represent postmark deadlines for mail registrations and receipt deadlines for telephone and online registration. The basic fee for the LSAT is $84 (published test centers only).

For information on deadlines and fees for late registrations and nonpublished test centers (domestic and foreign), partial refunds, and early score reporting by telephone (TelScore), please refer to the current *LSAT/LSDAS Registration and Information Book*, or call Law Services directly at 215-968-1001. You can also find complete registration information on their World Wide Web site at *http://www.lsac.org*.

LSAT Test Dates

■ Regular	Monday, June 16, 1997	Saturday, Oct. 4, 1997	Saturday, Dec. 6, 1997	Saturday, Feb. 7, 1998 Nondisclosed*
■ Saturday Sabbath Observers		Monday, October 1997 Nondisclosed*	Monday, Dec. 8, 1997 Nondisclosed*	Monday, Feb. 7, 1998 Nondisclosed*
■ Score Report mailed (approx.)	July 15, 1997	Nov. 5, 1997	Jan. 8, 1998	March 5, 1998

Regular Registration Deadline (mail, telephone, and online)

■ Domestic	May 16, 1997	Sept. 5, 1997	Nov. 7, 1997	Jan. 9, 1998
■ Foreign	May 9, 1997	Aug. 29, 1997	Oct. 31, 1997	Jan. 2, 1998

*Persons who take a nondisclosed test receive only their scores. They do not receive their test questions, answer key, or individual responses.

Law School Forums Sponsored by LSAC

If you are considering law school -- attend a Law School Forum. Free admission. No preregistration. In one place, you can: talk with representatives of LSAC-member law schools from across the United States; obtain admission materials, catalogs, and financial aid information; view video programs about the law school admission process, legal education and careers, and minority perspectives on legal education; attend informational sessions on the law school admission process, financing a legal education, and issues of importance to minority applicants, and purchase Law Services publications and LSAT® preparation materials. Forum hours are generally from noon to either 6 or 7 P.M. on Fridays and from 10 A.M. to either 3 or 4 P.M. on Saturdays, **depending on the city**. To confirm closing times and learn further details, call (215) 968-1001. Check the LSAC Web site at http://www.lsac.org, or watch for ads in your local media preceding the event. For further information contact: Law School Forums, Law Services, Box 40, Newtown, PA 18940-0040. The locations of the Law School Forums for 1997 are listed below.

Atlanta, Georgia
Friday, September 12-Saturday, September 13
Omni Hotel at CNN Center
100 CNN Center
Atlanta, GA

Boston, Massachusetts
Friday, October 31-Saturday, November 1
Marriott Copley Place
110 Huntington Avenue
Boston, MA

Chicago, Illinois
Friday, October 17-Saturday, October 18
JW Marriott
5150 Westheimer
Houston, TX

Los Angeles, California
Friday, November 14-Saturday, November 15
Wyndham Hotel at LAX
6225 West Century Blvd.
Los Angeles, CA

New York, New York
Friday, September 19-Saturday, September 20
New York, Marriott World Trade Center
Three World Trade Center
New York, NY

Washington, DC
Saturday, July 12; 10 A.M. - 4 P.M.
Renaissance Mayflower Hotel
1127 Connecticut Avenue, S.W.
Washington, DC

Chapter Eighteen
Websites

AMERICAN BAR ASSOCIATION
http://www.abanet.org

AALS

Association of American Law Schools
http://www.aals.org

AALL

American Association of Law Libraries
http://www.aallnet.org

THE SECTION OF LEGAL EDUCATION AND ADMISSIONS TO THE BAR
http://www.abanet.org/legaled

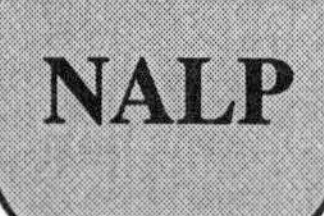

LSAC

Law School Admission Council
http://www.lsac.org

NALP

National Association for Law Placement
http://www.nalp.org

ABA Approved Law Schools
http://www.abanet.org/legaled/approved.html

NOTES:

NOTES: